THE
COOLIE
TRADE

THE COOLIE TRADE

*The Traffic in Chinese Laborers
to Latin America 1847-1874*

ARNOLD J. MEAGHER

To order additional copies of this book, contact:
Xlibris Corporation
1-888-795-4274
www.Xlibris.com
Orders@Xlibris.com

44381

Contents

TABLE OF ILLUSTRATIONS

Page

MAPS

FIGURES

TABLE OF TABLES

A thorough study of the roots of modern human trafficking and Chinese emigration.

Against the backdrop of China's rapid advance to the forefront of the world economy and sharp scrutiny over global trends in human trafficking, Meagher's exhaustive survey of Chinese indentured labor is a richly informative, timely release. His volume, much broader in scope than the Latin America in his subtitle indicates, is a careful examination of cultural, political and socioeconomic factors that contributed to this phenomenon. Meagher argues that the termination of the African slave trade, an urgent need for laborers in the West and a deteriorating Chinese economy conspired to spawn the emigration of more than a quarter million Chinese laborers to Latin America in the span of 28 years. Beginning in 1847, Chinese emigration quickly evolved into a prosperous black market cottage industry that, alongside the illicit opium trade, attracted enterprising, often dubious characters. These overlords relentlessly plundered China's human resources to satisfy a labor vacuum in the West. Scheming brokers often used any means available—false promises, deceit and fraud—to lure prey aboard ships. Victims of kidnapping account for more than a quarter of the human cargo, while appalling prison-like conditions, mutinies and disease resulted in a 12 percent mortality rate during the nine-month voyage. Great Britain and the United States abandoned the coolie trade in the mid 1860s after much public outcry. Trafficking, however, continued to flourish until 1874 aboard other ships sailing for Latin America, often destined for Cuba and Peru, where booming sugar, guano and mining industries demanded a steady flow of fresh workers. This authoritative account is acutely critical of the coolie trade as a means by which the slave trade continued in the West, but suggests it did have its advantages: challenging draconian Chinese taboos that once forbade emigration and introducing Chinese culture to Western society.

The author's fluid, conversational style elevates Meagher's work from the weight that often bogs down other academic texts.
Engaging and topical fare.

—Kirkus Discoveries

DEDICATION

To the many victims of slavery and forced labor,
past and present, across our planet

Abbreviations Used in Footnotes

AHU	Arquivo Histórico Ultramarino, Lisbon
BFO	British Foreign Office, Public Record Office, London
BCO	British Colonial Office, Public Record Office, London
BPP	British Parliamentary Papers
BPP, ASS	British Parliamentary Papers, Area Studies Series
JIA	*Journal of the Indian Archipelago and Eastern Asia*

Author's Note

At the urging of friends, I decided to publish this work, completed in 1975 but languishing ever since in a closet drawer. The manuscript was presented in partial fulfillment of a PhD degree in philosophy at the University of California, Davis. Now, in 2008, as China is expanding its economic and political influence throughout Latin America, the timing may be right for the manuscript to come out of the closet. In recent years, trade between China and Latin America has soared, climbing from $2+ billion in 1990 to over $70 billion today and continuing to climb.

To the researcher and historian, this is primarily a resource document citing (1) the correspondence of consuls and diplomats on the China coast and in Latin America contained in the archives of the British Public Record Office and in the British Parliamentary Papers; (2) the China coast newspapers of the nineteenth century, both English and Portuguese, including the official weekly publications of the Hong Kong and Macau governments; and (3) the official correspondence between Macau and Lisbon contained in Lisbon's Arquivo Histórico Ultramarino.

To the Chinese entrepreneur and diplomat seeking economic opportunities and raw materials throughout Latin America to feed China's rapidly growing economy, this document may be a very useful resource in understanding the economic, cultural, and political impact of the Coolie Trade on both China and Latin America.

To the student of history, this is the detailed story, not found elsewhere, of the coming of over 250,000 Chinese indentured laborers to the Caribbean and South America from 1847 to 1874, placing this movement of mostly male laborers, from one end of the earth to the other, in historical perspective following the abolition of the slave trade and the emancipation of the slaves.

AJM

Acknowledgments

I am particularly indebted to Professor Rollie E. Poppino, whose direction, advice, and encouragement made this study possible. I am also deeply grateful to Professors Kwang-Ching Liu and Arnold J. Buaer for their constructive criticism and valuable suggestions.

I am thankful to the staffs of the archives and libraries of the British Museum and the Public Record Office London; the Arquivo Histórico Ultramarino, Biblioteca Nacional and the Biblioteca da Sociedade de Geografia of Lison; and the libraries of the University of Hong Kong, the Hong Kong Supreme Court, the Chinese University of Hong Kong, and the Biblioteca Nacional de Macau. I am particularly grateful to Luís Gonzaga Gomes, president of the Instituto Luís de Camões of Macau, for his gracious hospitality and useful advice. I am also thankful to the staff of the Interlibrary Loan Service of the University of California, Davis Campus.

A teaching fellowship financed by the U.S. Department of State enabled me to spend a year in Hong Kong and Macau, and financial assistance from the Chancellor's Patent Fund, University of California, Davis, helped me to stop in London and Lisbon en route to and from the China coast.

Finally, I am thankful to Jackie Devlin, my wife, for painstakingly reading the many rough drafts and helping with the organization and literary style.

AJM

INTRODUCTION

The phenomenon of indentured[1] labor, which followed upon the abolition of slavery, spread throughout the Western world in the latter two-thirds of the nineteenth century, appearing in such far-flung places as Mauritius, South Africa, Latin America, Australia, Malaya, and the Fiji Islands.[2] Indentured labor, i.e., labor contracted under penal sanctions, was essentially a compulsory system of labor, which in practice differed little from slavery. Unlike slaves, indentured workers were supposed to receive a monthly wage and their term of service, at least in principle, was for a fixed period of from five to eight years; but these provisions were not always adhered to, and in all other respects, indentured workers were no better off than the slaves they replaced.

The widespread appearance of indentured labor is not adequately accounted for by either of the two major schools of thought in the controversy over the downfall of slavery. If the primary motivations for the abolition of slavery were humanitarian,[3] then why did humanitarians look the other way when slave owners resorted to another form of forced labor in the system of indenture? If, on the other hand, the abolition of slavery was an economic consequence of the rise of industrialism and capitalism, as Eric Williams in his *Capitalism*

---

[1] Indenture was originally a deed or contract between two or more parties written on one piece of parchment or paper and cut in two in a serrated or zigzag line so that when brought together the two edges tallied, showing that they were parts of the same original document. Later, indenture came to denote a legal instrument for binding an apprentice or servant to his master, or a contract by which a person bound himself to service. See *The Oxford English Dictionary*. Vol. V (Oxford: Clarendon Press, 1933), 198-199.

[2] For a survey of indentured labor, see W. Kloosterboer, *Involuntary Labour since the Abolition of Slavery* (Leiden: E. J. Brill, 1960).

[3] See Reginald Coupland, *The British Anti-Slavery Movement*, 2nd ed. (London: Frank Cass, 1964).

and Slavery would have us believe,[4] then why did the same factors that rejected forced African labor so easily accept forced Chinese and Indian labor?

Did the principles of humanitarianism not also extend to the peoples of Asia? Or did some latent racism preclude "Asiatics" (as Chinese and Indians were called) or at least preclude them from being defended with the same vigor as Africans? Or, lulled into a false sense of security and accomplishment, were humanitarians taken in by the trappings of indenture—the written contract, the monthly wage, and the limitation on the period of service? The latter could be an out for the humanitarian interpretation of the abolition movement, but what of the economic determinism of the Williams school? Indenture's camouflage might possibly have fooled the humanitarians, but the same could not be said of the economic forces of determinism. Perhaps the economic factors, like the humanitarian principles, did not have universal validity, but only applied to African slavery?

The question must then be raised that perhaps indentured labor was an economically viable alternative both to slave and wage labor, at least in some areas of the world? And as such, was indenture a conscious hard-nosed compromise between the proponents of slavery and the abolitionists? Else, how to explain the fact that England, which led the fight against slavery, and whose statesmen condemned slavery as the very antithesis of progress, also led the way in sanctioning indentured labor?

The victims of indenture consisted principally of natives of the subcontinent of India, Pacific Islanders, and Chinese. Indian indenture has received extensive treatment from British and Indian scholars, with the most recent work by the British historian Hugh Tinker, *A New System of Slavery: The Export of Indian Labour Overseas, 1830-1920*, presenting an overall study of the entire process of the emigration of indentured Indian laborers to more than a dozen countries.[5] Polynesian indenture has been treated in the general

---

4   Eric E. Williams, *Capitalism and Slavery*, 2nd ed. (New York: Russell and Russell, 1961).

5   Hugh Tinker, *A New System of Slavery: The Export of Indian Labour Overseas, 1830-1920* (London: Oxford University Press, 1974). See also the more specific studies: S. B. Mookherji, *The Indenture System in Mauritius, 1837-1915* (Calcutta: Firma K. L. Mukhopadhyay, 1962); Kernial Singh Sandhu, *Indians in Malaya: Some Aspects of the Immigration and Settlement* (Cambridge: University Press, 1969); John Wesley Coulter, *Fiji: Little India of the Pacific* (Chicago: University of Chicago Press, 1942); I. M. Cumpston, *Indians Overseas in British Territories, 1834-1854* (London: Oxford University Press, 1953).

histories of the islands of the South Pacific, as well as in a number of articles.[6] Chinese indenture has attracted limited attention. After the turn of the century, there was a series of descriptive accounts of Chinese indentured laborers in Hawaii and in the British colonies of South Africa and British Guiana.[7] More recently, scholars have begun to examine Chinese indenture in Latin America. Watt Stewart's pioneer work, *Chinese Bondage in Peru*, was published in 1951,[8] and Marshall K. Powers's unpublished dissertation, "Chinese Coolie Migration to Cuba," was written in 1953.[9] Duvon C. Corbitt's poorly organized *A Study of the Chinese in Cuba, 1847-1947* appeared in 1971,[10] and in the same year; Robert Lee Irick completed his dissertation, "Ch'ing Policy Toward the Coolie Trade, 1847-1878," which is as yet unpublished.[11] Apart from Juan Jiménez Pastrama's study, *Los Chinos en las Luchas por la Liberación Cubana, 1847-1930*,[12] a few articles, and occasional chapters in books concerned with emigration, native Latin American scholars have largely ignored the Chinese in their midst.

---

[6] *Pacific Islands*, 4 vols. (Geographical Handbook Series, Naval Intelligence Division, 1945); Douglas L. Oliver, *The Pacific Islands*, revised ed. (New York: Doubleday and Company, Inc., 1961); Stephen H. Roberts, *Population Problems of the Pacific* (New York: AMS Press, 1969, first printed in 1927); P. J. Stewart, "New Zealand and the Pacific Labor Traffic 1870-1874," *Pacific Historical Review* vol. XXX, no. 1 (February, 1961); Ower W. Parnaby, "The Regulation of Indentured Labour to Figi, 1864-1888," *Journal of the Polynesian Society*, vol. LXV, no. 1 (March 1956).

[7] Katherine Coman, *The History of Contract Labour in the Hawaiian Islands* (New York: Macmillan Company, 1903); Cecil Clementi, *The Chinese in British Guiana* (Guiana: Argosy Company Limited, 1915); Persia Crawford Campbell, *Chinese Coolie Emigration to Countries within the British Empire* (New York: Negro Universities Press, 1969, first printed in 1923).

[8] Watt Stewart, *Chinese Bondage in Peru: A History of the Chinese Coolie in Peru, 1849-1874* (Durham, North Carolina: Duke University Press, 1951).

[9] Marshall K. Powers, "Chinese Coolie Migration to Cuba" (unpublished dissertation, University of Florida, 1953).

[10] Duvon C. Corbitt, *A Study of the Chinese in Cuba, 1847-1947* (Wilmore, Kentucky: Asbury College, 1971).

[11] Robert Lee Irick, "Ch'ing Policy Toward the Coolie Trade, 1847-1878" (unpublished dissertation, Harvard University, 1971).

[12] Juan Jiménez Pastrama, *Los Chinos en las Luchas por la Liberación Cubana, 1847-1930* (Habana: Instituto de Historia, 1963).

It is the purpose of this work to present a comprehensive study of Chinese indentured labor in Latin America. In an attempt to place the coming of over 250,000 Chinese indentured laborers to the Caribbean and South America from 1847 to 1874 in some kind of historical perspective, the following chapters will trace the gradual rise and acceptance of the indentured system of labor in the Western world following the abolition of the slave trade and the emancipation of the slaves. Conditions both in China and in Latin America, which triggered and sustained a flow of Chinese labor for over a quarter of a century, will be examined. The transoceanic passages of the laborers will be chronicled. Finally, the experience of Chinese indentured laborers in the Caribbean and South America will be explored.

This work relies heavily upon the following: 1) the correspondence of consuls and diplomats on the China coast and in Latin America contained in the archives of the British Public Record Office and in the British Parliamentary Papers; 2) the China coast newspapers of the nineteenth century, both English and Portuguese, including the official weekly publications of the Hong Kong and Macau[13] governments; and 3) the official correspondence between Macau and Lisbon contained in Lisbon's Arquivo Historico Ultramarino. Though there are gaps in the historical record—which further research in Cuba, Peru, and the West Indies, as well as in Portuguese and Spanish archives, would help resolve—there is a great deal more information available on the movement of Chinese laborers to Latin America than the contemporary movement of Chinese to California. This is at least partially explained by the fact that the entire process of Chinese immigration to Latin America was in the hands of Westerners who tried to keep records of some kind, while immigration to California was in the hands of the Chinese themselves, who evidently chose not to do so. With the exceptions of Clementi and Campbell, who used the British archives in relation to the British West Indies, none of the above sources has been used by any of the existing works on Chinese immigration to Latin America.

What of Chinese sources? Chinese periodical literature developed in Hong Kong and the treaty ports under Protestant missionary auspices in the second quarter of the nineteenth century. By the 1860s and 1870s, there were major Chinese newspapers in Hong Kong and Shanghai, which carried

---

[13]   This is the current official Portuguese spelling and is used throughout except in quotations and titles that use the older spelling "Macao."

reports on the "coolie-trade."[14] These have yet to be explored by historians. Chinese documentary material dealing with diplomatic questions arising out of emigration has, however, been studied by Irick, and sections of chapter 8 of the present work depend largely upon Irick's study.

Because of the evils associated with the nineteenth-century immigration of Chinese to Latin America, the movement was dubbed the "coolie trade," a euphemism that echoes the "slave trade," and was intended to be no less condemnatory. The term "coolie" would seem to have been of Indian origin and was first used to denote Tamil menial laborers from Madras. In British documents of the 1840s and 1850s, the term is exclusively reserved to designate Indian laborers. Later it came to be predicated of Chinese laborers and was used generally of any unskilled worker.[15]

The reader should be advised of one more historiographical fact. Heretofore, the burden of responsibility for the abuses surrounding the "coolie trade" has been laid at the door of the Portuguese. If our understanding of the movement was confined to published British sources, particularly the Parliamentary Papers, it would be difficult not to do the same thing. But evidence from other sources clearly shows that responsibility for the evils perpetrated on the Chinese, if it is to be allotted, must be more evenly distributed among many Western nations, principally Great Britain, Spain, Peru, Portugal, France, and the United States. This is not to exonerate the Portuguese, but rather, to place responsibility where it properly belongs—in the lap of Western civilization, which was also responsible for the African slave trade. Like the Africans in the slave trade, the Chinese also bear some responsibility for the sufferings of their fellow countrymen.

---

[14] Chu Shih-chia, *Mei-Kuo p'o-hai Hua kung shih-liao* (historical materials on American persecution of Chinese laborers; Peiping, Chung-hua shu-chu, 1958), 73-74; Roswell S. Britton, *The Chinese Periodical Press, 1800-1912* (Shanghai: Kelly and Walsh, Limited, 1933), 16-40.

[15] For a discussion of the origin of the term "coolie," see Irick, "Ch'ing Policy Toward the Coolie Trade, 1847-1878," 2-5; *Notes and Queries on China and Japan*, vol. 1 (June 29, 1867), 77; "Coolies," *Mission Life* vol. IV (September 1867), 19-21.

CHAPTER I

THE INTERCONTINENTAL SEARCH FOR LABORERS

Their fathers destroy Caribs; their sons weep for Caribs and grind up negroes; their grandsons pity negroes, and put Coolies, Chinese, and whatever other unresting race they can lay hands on into the mill.

"The Coolie Trade," *DeBow's Review*, vol. 27 (1859), 299.

The Abolition of the Slave Trade and the Emancipation of Slaves

Plantation agriculture has been an experimental field for the use of a variety of workers: natives, convicts, indentured Europeans, African slaves, free Africans, Pacific Islanders, and Asians. Historically the plantation has specialized in the production of a single commodity for export, such as coffee, sugar, tobacco, cotton, tea, rubber. Because tropical or subtropical regions, where these crops flourished, were thinly populated, or because the local people were deemed unsuitable,[1] the sizeable labor supply demanded by large scale commercial production had to be imported.

Thus, in the Americas, where indigenous labor was scarce, as on the North Atlantic seaboard and in the Caribbean, English and French colonists during the seventeenth and eighteenth centuries recruited their labor from convicts and indentured servants transported from Europe—many of the latter being kidnapped or deceived into embarking for the New World.[2] But the labor supply from Europe was not equal to the demand, and African slaves were

---

[1] It was popular opinion that natives accustomed to a life of leisure amid tropical exuberance were incapable of regular daily toil in mines and plantations.

[2] P. P. Courteney, *Plantation Agriculture* (New York: Frederick A. Praeger, 1965), 21; Franklin W. Knight, *Slave Society in Cuba During the Nineteenth Century* (Madison: University of Wisconsin Press, 1970), 118; Noel Deerr, *The History of Sugar*, 2 vols. (London: Chapman and Hall, 1949), II, 383.

introduced to work in cotton, tobacco, and sugar plantations. In Brazil, the Portuguese were similarly faced with a sparse native population, and they too turned to Africa for their labor needs. In Spanish America, European disease decimated the native population, and various attempts to enslave the indigenous Indian proved to be an inadequate solution to the labor problem. Beginning in the sixteenth century, African slaves partially replaced the Indian in mines and on plantations in Cuba, Mexico, Central America, and along the Spanish Main down to Peru.

Negro slavery in the Americas was almost three centuries old when agitation by humanitarians and Ricardian free traders caused governments to outlaw the slave trade. Denmark was the first country to do so, ending her trade in 1802. England followed in 1807, forbidding any trade in slaves within her dominions. The United States outlawed slaving in 1808, the Netherlands in 1814, France in 1818, Spain in 1820. Portugal forbade trading in slaves north of the equator in 1815 and in 1836 extended the ban to all her possessions. With encouragement from the British, most of the newly independent countries of Latin America inserted a clause in their constitutions banning the slave trade. Hence, by the late 1830s, trading in slaves was formally illegal, though the traffic continued clandestinely for many decades.

Contrary to what was expected, the outlawing of the slave trade had little effect on slavery itself. It was generally believed that planters would be forced to treat their slaves more humanely in order to conserve and prolong their life of service, and that as the lot of the slaves improved, slavery would gradually decline and hopefully die a natural death.[3] But it soon became clear that as with the slave trade, the amelioration of slavery was impracticable, and abolition was the only answer.

England led the way with the Emancipation Act of 1833, which abolished slavery throughout the British Empire as of August 1, 1834. Complete emancipation was preceded by a maximum of six years of apprenticeship, during which time both slave and planter were to adjust to their new circumstances. The British Parliament, however, persuaded the legislatures of the colonies to cut short the term of apprenticeship, and the slaves received their full freedom in August 1838.[4] Other countries followed: France freed its

---

[3]   William Law Mathieson, *British Slave Emancipation, 1838-1849* (New York: Octagon Books, Inc., 1967), 1.

[4]   *Ibid.*, 19.

slaves in 1848, Peru in 1855, Holland and the United States in 1863, Portugal in 1878, Spain in 1885, and Brazil in 1888. But the impetus for emancipation did not come from those directly involved in slavery. Most slaveholders were adamantly opposed to abolition, and when they were confronted with the fact of emancipation, they resorted to other forms of compulsory labor.

The Growth of Sugar Plantations and Demands for Labor

Prior to the nineteenth century, plantations were largely confined to the southern United States and to certain regions of the Caribbean and South America. Sugar, tobacco, and cotton were the principal crops, and their production was almost solely dependent upon African slave labor. As creatures of mercantilism, plantations traditionally were tied to the demand cycle of the mother countries of Europe. In the nineteenth century, with European nations experiencing unprecedented industrial and demographic growth, there was a continually increasing demand for tropical produce, particularly sugar. Plantations, handicapped by the loss of their labor supply, were unable to satiate this growing appetite, and sugar plantations financed by Western capitalists were promoted in such far-flung places as the islands of Mauritius and Réunion in the Indian Ocean, the Fiji Islands, Hawaii, Australia, South Africa, and Malaya.

The labor requirements of these ventures were enormous. The cultivation of sugar called for large numbers of laborers both in the cane fields and in the sugar mills (the ripe cane had to be processed within a few hours of being harvested, an operation that required a highly disciplined workforce[5]), and with the African slave trade outlawed, Indians, Pacific Islanders, and Chinese were recruited to fill the labor vacuum. The system of indentured servitude that was used to exploit these new workers was first developed on the island of Mauritius.

The sugar plantations of the British colony of Mauritius were the first to look beyond Africa for cheap labor on a large scale. Shortly after the British took Mauritius from the French in 1810, it became a penal colony for Indian convicts.[6] These convicts had good reputations as laborers, and consequently, when the system of African slavery was threatened, Mauritian planters sought

---

5   Alan H. Adamson, *Sugar without Slaves: The Political Economy of British Guiana, 1838-1904* (New Haven: Yale University Press, 1972), 6.

6   Mookherji, *The Indenture System in Mauritius*, 14.

to tap the vast reservoir of Indian manpower. Experimental contingents of indentured Indian laborers were introduced into Mauritius in 1830 and 1834, and after the emancipation of the colony's 61,000 slaves in 1835, the importation of Indian labor rapidly increased. Between 1834 and 1839, 25,458 Indians (almost all males) were imported by the sugar planters.[7]

The Indians came under contract to work for five years on the sugar estates. The expenses of transportation to Mauritius and repatriation at the end of their five-year term were to be paid by the employer. Each laborer was to receive five rupees ($2.25), a month, plus food, clothes, and accommodation. Six months' pay, or thirty rupees was advanced to each recruit when he placed his thumb imprint on the contract agreement prior to departure. A change of employer during the period of indenture was not permitted, and wages remained fixed notwithstanding increased prices and profits.[8]

In practice, it was a system of compulsory labor akin to slavery. The Mauritian planter, long accustomed to coercive control over his slaves, overlooked what to him were mere theoretical differences between the contract laborer and the slave. In 1839, India's colonial government, disturbed over reports of abuses of its subjects, prohibited further recruitment. Subsequent investigations revealed that despite strict government legislation enacted in 1837 to police the migration of Indian labor, that recruits were induced to come to Calcutta and other ports of embarkation by misrepresentation and deceit; that kidnapping prevailed to a considerable extent; that prior to departure, laborers were kept in a state of close imprisonment; and that the money advanced to them was a source of fraudulent gain to the agents employed in their recruitment and shipment. Furthermore, the hardships and miseries of the passage to Mauritius were shown to be most serious, with mortality approaching 10 percent.[9]

---

[7]   *Ibid.*, 17; Fred H. Hitchins, *The Colonial Land and Emigration Commission* (Philadelphia: University of Pennsylvania Press, 1931), 235.

[8]   Mookherji, *The Indenture System in Mauritius*, 15; C. Kondapi, *Indians Overseas, 1838-1949* (New Delhi: Oxford University Press, 1951), 8.

[9]   "Report of the Committee appointed by the Supreme Governor of India to inquire into abuses alleged to exist in exporting from Bengal Hill Coolies; together with an Appendix containing the oral and written evidence taken by the Committee and the official documents laid before them." Calcutta, 1939 (BPP, vol. XVI, 1841), 5-6.

Simultaneous investigations conducted in Mauritius demonstrated that Indian laborers were compelled to work as much as fifteen hours a day, that housing was deplorable, that wages were suffered to run up to twelve months in arrears, and that in some instances wages were never paid.[10] Nevertheless, after a three-year moratorium, the pleas of the planters won out over the best interests of the indentured Indians, and emigration was resumed in 1843.[11]

Indentured Indian labor was generally regarded as the "salvation of Mauritius."[12] In 1860, Herman Merivale, permanent undersecretary in the Colonial Office, hailed it as a "novel phenomenon in economic history."[13] He pointed out that with the importation of nearly 150,000 Indian laborers in a span of ten years, the export of the colony almost doubled and that the prosperity of the island was raised "to a pitch far exceeding what it had attained in times of slavers."[14] The solution to the labor problems of those faced with the loss of their slaves had been found.

Sugar planters around the world, stimulated by the success of the experiment in Mauritius, sought to adopt similar systems of indentured labor. Besides the sugar colonies in the Americas, which will be discussed in some detail presently, planters in Réunion, Natal (South Africa), Malaya, Queensland (Australia), and the Fiji Islands turned to India for a supply of labor.

A French merchant, Joseph Argand, brought 130 Indians to the French colony of Réunion in 1830, and a regular traffic was under way in 1835.[15] By 1882, 86,905 Indians had been imported into the colony.[16] Natal commenced importing Indian indentured labor in 1860. When the traffic was stopped in 1866 because of irregularities, the sugar planters discovered that the Indians were indispensable to their industry and clamored for its renewal. It was resumed in 1874 and continued without interruption until it was terminated

[10] Mookherji, *The Indenture System in Mauritius*, 27; E. Lyulph Stanley, "The Treatment of Indian Immigrants in Mauritius," *Forthnightly Review*, vol. XXIII (June 1, 1873), 797.

[11] Kondapi, *Indians Overseas*, 10.

[12] Mookherji, *The Indenture System in Mauritius*, 20.

[13] Herman Merivale, *Lectures on Colonization and Colonies* (London: Oxford University Press, 1928), 345.

[14] *Ibid.*, 346.

[15] Deerr, *The History of Sugar*, II, 388.

[16] Paul Guiral, *L'Immigration Réglementée aux Antilles Francaises et à la Réunion* (Paris: Jouve et Cie, 1911), 130.

by the Indian government in 1911. During the entire period, 152,529 Indian laborers were brought to Natal.[17]

There is some disagreement as to when Indians were first introduced to British Malaya, but a system of indentured Indian labor on Malayan sugar plantations was well established by the late 1850s. The traffic, largely in the hands of speculators, was uncontrolled until 1872. There are no statistics available prior to 1866, and from that year until the abolition of the traffic in 1910, some 122,000 Indians were imported.[18]

The sugar boom even gave rise to an organized labor traffic in natives of the Pacific Islands. In 1837 and 1838, 1,283 Indian contract laborers were engaged as shepherds in New South Wales, Australia.[19] A decade later, two shiploads of Loyalty Islanders were imported for the same purpose.[20] This was considerably closer to home, and when development spread northward into Queensland and sugar and cotton plantations sprang up in the 1860s, Australians recruited natives from the New Hebrides, the Bismarck Archipelago, and the Solomon islands.[21]

About the same time, European planters in the Fiji islands were recruiting laborers from the same sources as well as from the Ellice, Cook, and Tokelau groups.[22] Ships seeking laborers for the sugar plantations on the Peruvian coast were also active in the area and, from 1861 to 1863, carried off between two and three thousand islanders.[23] Some years later, 2,500 natives of the Gilbert and New Hebrides islands were transported to the sugar plantations

[17]   Lilian Charlotte Ann Knowles, *The Economic Development of the British Overseas Empire*, 3 vols. (London: George Routledge and Sons, 1928-1936), III, 26-29; Kondapi, *Indians Overseas*, 21-29.

[18]   Sandhu, *Indians in Malaya*; 76-81; Sinnappah Arasaratnam, *Indians in Malaysia and Singapore* (Bombay: Oxford University Press, 1970, 10-21. Sandhu suggests that the total number of Indian laborers to enter Malaya up to 1910 was close to 250,000.

[19]   Deerr, *The History of Sugar*, II, 392.

[20]   *Pacific Islands*, I, 300.

[21]   *Ibid.*, 301; Guy Hardy Scholefield, *The Pacific: Its Past and Present* (London: John Murray, 1919), 50-52.

[22]   *Pacific Islands*, I, 301; Oliver, *The Pacific Islands*, 125-131; Roberts, *Population Problems of the Pacific*, 207-212.

[23]   Juan de Arona, *La Inmigración en el Perú* (Lima: Imprensa de Universo de Carlos Prince, 1891), 37; *Pacific Islands*, I, 302.

of Hawaii,[24] but in both Peru and Hawaii, the islanders proved to be unsatisfactory.

The recruitment of Pacific Islanders, or Kanakas,[25] rapidly degenerated into slave hunting and slave trading, and came to be known as "blackbirding."[26] Blackbirders or speculators, mostly British, enticed the natives on board their ships with offers of presents and then forced them below and closed the hatches upon them.[27] Some traders were known to have dressed in cassocks and surplices and, posing as missionaries, seduced natives on board their vessels.[28] In retaliation, the islanders killed innocent European traders and missionaries.

The Legislative Council of New Zealand took upon itself the mantle of protector of the islanders and complained to London in 1871:

> For some years past a traffic which can only be characterised as a slave trade, and which is attended with all its evil and iniquitous consequences, has been carried on among islands of the Pacific, by means of which the inhabitants have been taken away for the purpose of supplying labour to the plantations of Queensland and Fiji islands. That as a result of this traffic and the forcible abduction of the natives from their homes, scenes of violence and bloodshed are of frequent occurrence among the islands.[29]

The British Parliament passed the Pacific Islanders Protection Act in 1872, which appointed a high commissioner to police British subjects residing outside British dominions in the Pacific Ocean. Kidnapping of the natives

---

[24] Ralph S. Kuykendall, *The Hawaiian Kingdom*, 3 vols. (Honolulu, University of Hawaii Press, 1967), III, 126-128.

[25] "Kanaka" is the Polynesian word for the human person.

[26] "Blackbird" was a synonym for a slave.

[27] W. T. Wawn, *The South Sea Islanders and the Queensland Labor Trade: A Record of Voyages and Experiences in the Western Pacific from 1875 to 1891* (London: 1893), 8-10.

[28] P. J. Stewart, "New Zealand and the Pacific Labor Traffic, 1870-1874," 53.

[29] *Ibid.*, 51. During the nineteenth century, Europeans introduced disease, firearms, and blackbirding to the Pacific Islands; and as a result, it is estimated that the population of Polynesia and Melanesia declined from 4 million to 1.2 million. See J. H. Holmes, *Australia, New Zealand and the Southwest Pacific* (London: Thomas Nelson and Sons, 1969), 17.

was now a punishable crime, and when native chiefs ceded Fiji to Great Britain in 1874, the high commissioner had a base from which to enforce the law.[30] Gradually, abuses subsided, but the importation of island labor to Queensland continued until 1901.[31] When Fiji became a Crown colony in 1874, it became eligible to receive Indian laborers. From 1879 to 1916, 60,537 Indians came to Fiji, many of them opting to stay after their term of indenture expired.[32]

With the exception of Hawaii and the French colony of Réunion, all of the above territories importing indentured laborers were British colonies, and the planter-dominated local governments bargained for and obtained the approval of the imperial government in London for this new form of compulsory labor, which some were quick to classify as a "new slavery."

Indenture: Britain's Reluctant Compromise

The problem of an adequate labor supply had always been a major concern of colonists and planters in Britain's tropical colonies. Because of the popular myth that the white man could not withstand the enervating rays of the tropical sun,[33] labor in the fields was largely confined to African slaves. With emancipation, the labor problem assumed crisis proportions.

In the densely populated smaller colonies in the West Indies—such as Antigua, St. Kitts, and Barbados—where almost all the land was already preempted, the freed slave had little option but to continue working on the old plantation.[34] But in sparsely populated colonies with large areas of public and Crown lands readily available to buyer or squatter as in British Guiana, Jamaica, Trinidad, and Mauritius, emancipated Negroes, by cultivating their own plots of ground, could dispense with regular work on the plantations. In fact, most emancipated negroes looked upon plantation labor as synonymous

---

30   W. P. Morrell, *Britain in the Pacific Islands* (Oxford: Clarendon Press, 1960), 178-183; Scholefield, *The Pacific: Its Past and Present*, 60-61.

31   Scholefield, *The Pacific: Its Past and Present*, 70.

32   Coulter, *Fiji: Little India of the Pacific*, 17.

33   For an extended discussion of Europe's understanding of the tropics see Philip D. Curtin, *The Image of Africa: British Ideas and Action, 1780-1850* (Madison: University of Wisconsin Press, 1964), 58-87.

34   Mathieson, *British Slave Emancipation, 1838-1849*, 35-57.

with slavery and unworthy of a free man.[35] The behavior of the planters in attempting by various legal maneuvers to force them to work for low wages further alienated them.[36]

The confident expectations of the abolitionists that the bulk of the freed slaves would continue to work as wage earners on the sugar estates were not realized. Various schemes to find a new source of labor met with failure. Immigrants were brought in from Scotland, Ireland, Germany, Madeira, and Malta, but they proved such easy victims to disease that importation of labor from Europe was abandoned.[37] Following the example of Mauritius, John Gladstone, a sugar planter and father of the British Liberal Party statesman James Gladstone, landed two shiploads of Indian laborers in British Guiana in 1838.[38] Reports of inhumane treatment of the Indians on some of the sugar estates brought an outcry from the Anti-Slavery Society, which, together with concern on the part of the Indian government over alleged abuses both in British Guiana and Mauritius, led to suspension of the emigration in 1839.[39] Free Africans were introduced from the smaller and more popular West Indian islands, but they soon went the way of the emancipated slaves.[40] In 1841, the British government authorized the introduction of Africans from the Kroo coast, but the scheme was surrounded with so many safeguards against the revival of the slave trade that the results were disappointing.[41]

By 1842, the plight of the West Indian sugar planters was critical. In most instances, sugar production had diminished by one-third since emancipation.[42] For a time, planters remained solvent because of higher sugar prices, but prices commenced to fall at the beginning of 1841, dropping to 39 shillings a hundredweight in 1842 as compared to 58 shillings in the summer of

---

[35]   Adamson, *Sugar without Slaves*, 34.

[36]   W. P. Morrell, *British Colonial Policy in the Age of Peel and Russell* (Oxford: Clarendon Press, 1930), 150-151.

[37]   Mathieson, *British Slave Emancipation*, 118-119; Deerr, *The History of Sugar*, II, 384-385.

[38]   Kondapi, *Indians Overseas*, 16.

[39]   Edgar L. Erickson, "The Introduction of East Indian Coolies into the British West Indies," *Journal of Modern History*, vol. VI, no. 2 (June 1934), 128-133.

[40]   Persia Crawford Campbell, *Chinese Coolie Emigration to Countries within the British Empire* (New York, Negro Universities Press, 1969, First Published in 1923), 87.

[41]   Morrell, *British Colonial Policy in the Age of Peel and Russell*, 158.

[42]

1840.[43] Many planters went bankrupt and were forced to sell or abandon their plantations.[44] The very fabric of West Indian society seemed threatened.

A parliamentary committee appointed in 1842 to investigate the West Indian situation urged the resumption of indentured emigration from India.[45] Lord Stanley, who became colonial secretary in 1841, was at first unfavorably disposed to the proposal.[46] He was fearful of a popular clamor in England against it, and in any event, he was determined "to prevent the institution of any order approximating to slavery."[47]

But attitudes were changing. In the 1830s, as a logical consequence of political liberal theory, wage labor became Britain's official policy for her colonies.[48] However, the maxims of laissez-faire had no solutions for the many problems encountered in the West Indies, South Africa, and Mauritius in the changeover from slavery to wage labor. Disappointed over the economic failure of emancipation, many government officials in London were one with the planters in believing that for the tropics, some form of forced labor was a necessity, at least in the transition period.[49] Liberal ideals were succumbing to the pressure of special circumstances. Furthermore, threats to the sugar duties, which gave West Indian sugar a privileged position on the English market, swung public sympathy toward the distressed planters. At the same time, the prestige of the abolitionists was undergoing a decline.[50] The climate was favorable for compromise, and the success of the system of indentured Indian immigration to Mauritius pointed the way.

Despite the considered opinion of the Indian government that "no amount of vigilance would prevent the frequent infliction of grievous oppressions and deceits upon large numbers of persons helpless from their poverty and from their utter

---

43   Ibid.

44   Adamson, *Sugar without Slaves*, 160.

45   Erickson, "The Introduction of East Indian Coolies into the British West Indies," 134.

46   Morrell, *British Colonial Policy in the Age of Peel and Russell*, 160.

47   Stanley to Peel, November 27, 1843. Kenneth N. Bell and W. P. Morrell, *Select Documents on British Colonial Policy, 1830-1860* (Oxford: Clarendon Press, 1968), 423; Hitchins, *The Colonial Land and Emigration Commission*, 251.

48   Curtin, *The Image of Africa*, 452. See also J. H. Plumb, *In the Light of History* (London: Allen Lane, Penguin Press, 1972), 111-112.

49   Curtin, *The Image of Africa*, 453-455; Adamson, *Sugar without Slaves*, 50-53.

50   Cumpstan, *Indians Overseas in British Territories*, 177.

ignorance and inexperience,"[51] the British government, in July 1844, sanctioned the resumption of Indian immigration to British colonies under controlled conditions.[52] Some years later, T. W. C. Murdock, chairman of the Colonial Land and Emigration Commissioners, justified the decision in this way:

> If the planters cannot obtain labour, which will enable them to continue sugar cultivation, they will . . . abandon their estates. The land will fall out of cultivation or be appropriated by the creole population. The whites will disappear, and with them civilization, morality and religion.[53]

Thinking such as this guaranteed the continuance of indentured labor in the sugar colonies for the remainder of the century. What had been introduced as a short-term remedy for the distressed sugar industry became a more or less permanent institution.

Now that a workable substitute for slave labor had been found, it seemed to the British government that it had the answer to a particularly vexing problem—the suppression of the African slave trade. As long as the illegal traffic in Africans was economically profitable, it could not be completely suppressed. But if countries, traditionally dependent upon African slavery, were provided with an alternative labor supply, there would be little or no incentive to continue a slave trade that had become expensive and hazardous. The British Foreign Office, which was directly concerned with the suppression of the slave trade, was particularly interested in the possibilities of such a plan.

The first overtures were made to Brazil, the principal importer of African slaves. In 1843, Mr. Ellis, Britain's special ambassador to Brazil to renegotiate the slave treaty of 1826, offered the help of his government in obtaining "60,000 coolies" in return for Brazil's "cooperation in rendering the blockade of the African coasts more effective."[54] The imperial government, with its

---

51 As quoted in Kondapi, *Indians Overseas*, 9.

52 Erickson, "The Introduction of East Indian Coolies into the British West Indies," 135.

53 "Memorial on Immigration into the West Indies," February 18, 1859 (BPP vol. XX, 1859).

54 The offer was revealed by Brazilian prime minister Cansação de Sinimbú in a speech to the Brazilian senate in October 1879 presenting the views of the Brazilian government on Chinese immigration. The speech was printed in the *Rio News*, October 5, 1879.

planter class experiencing no major difficulties in obtaining slaves, rejected the offer.[55]

When France abolished slavery in 1848, the French West Indian colonies of Martinique and Guadeloupe, as well as Réunion in the Indian Ocean, experienced the same difficulties that the British colonies faced after 1834. Accordingly, in the early 1850s, France began to look to British India for laborers, recruitment in her own small possessions in India having proved inadequate. A French request to recruit beyond French territory was turned down, as the court of directors of the British East India Company strongly objected to the idea.[56] The French threatened to seek labor on the west coast of Africa.[57] The British regarded the threat as a bluff, but when it was learned that France had contracted with the established West African firm of Victor Regis to purchase 20,000 indentured Africans for Martinique and Guadeloupe,[58] the British Foreign Office suggested that in return for the abandonment of the African scheme, France could obtain Indian laborers under the same system of control that applied to the British colonies.[59] Because of opposition from the India Office and the Indian government, negotiations dragged on for nearly a decade. Eventually, on the insistence of the Foreign Office, which regarded Indian immigration to French possessions as a "matter of great importance to checking the slave trade,"[60] a Coolie Convention, permitting French colonies to recruit laborers in British India, was signed in Paris on July 1, 1861.[61] A similar concession was granted to the Dutch for Surinam in 1870, as the apprenticeship period of the Surinam Negroes, who were emancipated in 1863, was coming to a close.[62] But a proposal by the Foreign Office to extend the privilege to Cuba met with such hostility from the Indian Government that nothing came of it.[63]

[55] Ibid.

[56] Earl Granville to Count Walewski (French ambassador to Britain), January 3, 1852 (BFO 425/37).

[57] Walewski of Malmesbury, December 13, 1852 (BFO 425/37).

[58] John W. Cell, *British Colonial Administration in the Mid-Nineteenth Century: The Policy Making Process* (New Haven: Yale University Press, 1970), 258.

[59] Hitchins, *The Colonial Land and Emigration Commission*, 265.

[60] Hammond to Clerk, January 15, 1858 (BFO 425/17).

[61] Hitchins, *The Colonial Land and Emigration Commission*, 265.

[62] "Reports Respecting the Condition of Coolies in Surinam" (BPP vol. LXXVIII, 1877); Kondapi, *Indians Overeseas*, 6.

[63] "Mr. Geoghegan's Report on Coolie Emigration from India" (BPP vol. XLVIII, 1874), 56.

Already in the 1850s, it had become apparent that there were not enough Indian laborers to meet the demand. The West Indian colonies had to face severe competition from more popular Mauritius and were unable to recruit a sufficient number of laborers for their needs. For this reason, and because of India's reluctance to allow her subjects to migrate outside the British Empire, and hence beyond British supervision and control, the British government began to look to China as the major source of labor for tropical colonies. British policy on the matter was clearly set forth by Lord John Russell, the British foreign secretary in July 1860:

> No doubt the difficulties of suppressing the Slave Trade arise mainly from the demand which exists in Cuba and similar countries for laborers suited to a hot climate; and if this demand could be lawfully supplied, the incentives to engage in an illegal traffic in African laborers would be greatly diminished and the price of a slave might be enhanced far beyond that of a free laborer. This supply, Her Majesty's government confidently believe, may be obtained from China . . . Her Majesty's government, therefore propose, with a view to the final extinction of the Slave Trade:
>
> 1. A systematic plan of cruizing on the coast of Cuba by the vessels of Great Britain, Spain and the United States;
> 2. Laws of registration and inspection on the Island of Cuba, by which the employment of slaves imported contrary to law might be detected by Spanish authorities;
> 3. A plan of emigration from China regulated by agents of European nations in conjunction with the Chinese authorities.[64]

Proposals 1 and 2 met with stiff opposition. The United States refused to participate in policing Cuba's coastal waters, regarding any such activity as a violation of sovereignty,[65] and Spain was incensed at Britain's "unwarranted" interference in her internal affairs.[66] But no voices were raised against number 3, which remained an integral part of British foreign policy for the duration of the "coolie trade."

---

[64] Russell to Cowley, July 11, 1860 (BPP, ASS, *China*, vol. IV), 241-243.

[65] Trescot to Lyons, September, 1860 (U.S. Congress, Ex. Doc. No. 7, House 36th Cong., 2nd sess.), 446.

[66] Edwards to Russell, August 21, 1860 (*British and Foreign State Papers*, vol. LXVIII), 1052-1053.

The Labor Needs of Cuba, Peru, and Brazil

Though slavery was not abolished in Peru until 1855 and in Cuba and Brazil until the 1880s, planters began complaining of a serious shortage of labor before the middle of the century. British determination to stop the African slave trade, backed by high-powered diplomacy and virtual control of the seas by the British navy, succeeded in diminishing the flow of new slaves across the Atlantic. At the same time, countries such as those mentioned above, stimulated by an infusion of European capital, were experiencing rapid economic development, a situation that put an increasing stress on existing labor resources. The Spanish island of Cuba was perhaps the most severely affected.

Large-scale plantation agriculture did not begin in Cuba until 1789 when the Spanish government first permitted unrestricted importation of African slaves.[67] The island had extensive areas of undeveloped land suitable for sugar, coffee, and tobacco growing. With the help of French planters, who fled Haiti following the revolt of the slaves in 1791, the cultivation of these crops developed rapidly.[68] In 1775, there were 473 sugar plantations on the island; in 1817, there were over 780; and by 1850, the number had exceeded 1,750.[69] Sugar production rose even more dramatically. Exports, which were averaging 1.5 million hundredweight annually in the early 1820s, climbed to 6 million hundredweight in 1851.[70] Tobacco production almost trebled in the same period.[71] Coffee prospered initially, but because of competition with Brazil, production declined after 1835; and following the disastrous

---

[67] Arthur F. Corwin, *Spain and the Abolition of Slavery in Cuba, 1818-1886* (Austin: University of Texas Press, 1967), 13.

[68] There was also an influx of French settlers from Louisiana, who chose exile when the United States purchased the territory from Napoleon. See Franklin W. Knight, *Slave Society in Cuba during the Nineteenth Century* (Madison: University of Wisconsin Press), 12-13.

[69] Alexander Humboldt, *The Island of Cuba*, translated from the Spanish with notes and a preliminary essay by J. S. Thrasher (New York: Negro Universities Press, 1969, first published in 1856), 281-282.

[70] *Ibid.*, 255.

[71] Ibid., 289.

hurricanes of 1844 and 1846, which wiped out many coffee plantations, many planters converted from coffee to sugar.[72]

This unprecedented growth of plantation agriculture relied heavily on imported capital, technology, and labor. African slaves supplied the bulk of the labor force. According to customhouse returns, 225,574 slaves were imported through the port of Havana between 1790 and 1820, and an estimated 56,000 were imported through other ports.[73] Alexander Humboldt's own calculations, which allowed for illicit importations and omissions in the official returns, put the total at 372,449 for the same period.[74] In 1817, Britain succeeded in signing a treaty with Spain, ending the African slave trade, to become effective in May 1820. A second treaty in 1835 was designed to stop the loopholes of the first, whereby slaving continued. But with the connivance of Spanish and Cuban officials, this also was evaded. However, British vigilance was strict enough (between 1824 and 1866, British cruisers stationed in Cuban waters seized 107 slave ships with 26,026 Africans on board[75]) to cause an acute labor shortage. Consequently, between 1830 and 1860, the price of slaves on the Cuban market doubled to an average of $1,000 per head, a price that even the larger planters could scarcely afford.[76] The introduction of labor-saving machinery into the sugar mills was more than offset by the expansion of the sugar industry, which needed more hands than other plantation crops.[77]

In desperation, planters sought to revive the white colonization schemes begun in 1790 following the scare of the Haiti slave revolt.[78] An insurrection of slaves in Matanzas in 1843 prompted planters of the province to petition

---

[72] Hubert S. Aimes, *A History of Slavery in Cuba, 1511 to 1868* (New York: G. P. Putnam's Sons, 1907), 155; Richard H. Dana, *To Cuba and Back: A Vacation Voyage* (Boston: Ticknor and Fields, 1859), 68; Humboldt, *The Island of Cuba*, 284.

[73] Humboldt, *The Island of Cuba*, 218-219.

[74] Ibid., 219.

[75] Knight, *Slave Society in Cuba*, 29.

[76] Juan Pérez de la Riva, "Aspectos Económicos del Tráfico de Cúlies Chinés a Cuba, 1853-1874," *Universidad de la Habana*, vol. CLXXIII (May-June 1965), 96; Knight, *Slave Society in Cuba*, 29.

[77] Aimes, *A History of Slavery in Cuba*, 153-157.

[78] Duvon C. Corbitt, "Immigration in Cuba," *Hispanic American Historical Review*, vol. 22, no. 2 (May 1942), 296.

the government to abolish the slave trade.[79] The lesson of Haiti was again brought to the fore and the Junta de Fomento, a government-sponsored corporation of prominent merchants and planters, recommended the total abolition of the slave trade and the vigorous renewal of white colonization. Pointing out that there were 440,000 whites and 660,000 people of color on the island, the Junta offered prizes of P12,000 (pesos) to the first three planters to establish at least 50 white families on their estates. Half that amount went to planters who settled 25 families, and a prize of P20,000 was offered for the development of a sugar plantation and mill with an exclusively white labor force.[80] In response, various schemes, from the importation of indentured Spaniards and Canary Islanders to the purchase of Yucatan Indians (some of them kidnapped) were attempted.[81] But the overall results were far from encouraging. The Junta de Fomento disclosed in 1846 that all efforts to introduce white laborers produced a total of only 1,073.[82] Meanwhile, slave importation had dwindled to a trickle. From 1823 to 1841, an average of 8,500 slaves arrived annually; but in 1845, the number was a mere 900, and in the following year it, dropped to 500.[83]

In March 1846, the slaving firm of Zulueta and Company proposed introducing 1,000 Chinese under an eight-year contract. Ready to try anything, the Junta de Fomento welcomed the proposal and allocated P100,000 to the scheme.[84] As Marshall K. Powers points out in his dissertation, "Chinese Coolie Migration to Cuba," the adoption of a system of indentured labor, pioneered by the British in Mauritius and in the West Indies, was

---

[79] The petition appears in José Antonio Saco, *Historia de la Esclavitud de la Raza Africana en el Nuevo Mundo y especial de los Países Americo-Hispanos* (Habana: Cultura S. A. 1938), iv, 195-201. See also Augustin Cochin, *The Results of Slavery*, translated by Mary L. Booth (New York: Negro Universities Press, 1969, first published in 1863), 171-173.

[80] Corbitt, "Immigration in Cuba," 300-301.

[81] Ibid., 297-302. Corbitt provides an excellent summary of the many colonization schemes attempted. See also his article, "Los Colonos Yucatecos," *Revista Bimestre Cubana*, vol. 39 (January-February, 1937), 64-99.

[82] Corbitt, "Immigration in Cuba," 301.

[83] Aimes, *A History of Slavery in Cuba*, 158.

[84] Duvon C. Corbitt, *A Study of the Chinese in Cuba, 1847-1947* (Wilmore, Kentucky: Asbury College, 1971), 4.

politically safe.[85] Indenture did not have the stigma of slavery, while it gave to the planters virtually unlimited control over the laborer, at least for a period of years. Under the auspices of white colonization, an initial contingent of 571 male Chinese arrived in Havana in June 1847.[86]

Peru's road to the importation of Chinese laborers was somewhat similar to that of Cuba: an expanding economy coupled with the emancipation of a declining slave population, a futile search for European laborers and only as a last resort turning to China. After Peru's war for independence ended successfully in 1825, the country languished economically for two decades as contentious generals engaged in an internecine struggle for power. Anarchy reigned until 1845, when the able and practical-minded general Ramon Castilla seized the presidency and restored law and order. Almost immediately, the country, which had been tottering on the brink of bankruptcy, experienced an economic upswing. Capitalists began to agitate for internal improvements such as railways, irrigation canals, harbors, and roads.[87] These projects, together with expanding sugar and cotton production and the promising new industry of guano mining, demanded labor.

Guano, the bird droppings, which for untold centuries had been accumulating on the uninhabited islands off the coast of Peru, was proclaimed by European scientists in the 1840s to be rich in nitrogen and hence of considerable commercial value as a fertilizer. Over the ages, millions of pelicans, cormorants, and gannets, attracted to the area by the abundance of fish in the cold Humboldt current, had been nesting and dropping their excrement on the barren offshore islands. Undisturbed by rain, this bird manure formed great mounds more than a hundred feet high.[88] The Incas had used it extensively to fertilize the shallow soil of the high Andes,[89] but exploitation was minimal

---

[85]   Marshall K. Powers, "Chinese Coolie Migration to Cuba," (unpublished dissertation, University of Florida, 1953), 29.

[86]   Corbitt, *A Study of the Chinese in Cuba*, 6.

[87]   Cesar Antonio Ugarte, *Bosquejo de la História Económica de Perú* (Lima: Imprensa Cabieses, 1926), 54-60.

[88]   See Figure 17.

[89]   Garcilaso de la Vega, *Royal Commentaries of the Incas and General History of Peru*, translated by Harold V. Livermore (Austin: University of Texas Press, 1966), Part 1, Book 5, Chapter III, 246-247; Robert E. Coker, "Peru's Wealth-Producing Birds," *National Geographic Magazine*, vol. XXXVII, no. 6 (June 1920), 541.

during the 300 years of Spanish rule.[90] Now rediscovered, hundreds of ships were engaged in carrying it to depleted lands around the world, and laborers had to be found to mine this new source of wealth.

Unlike Cuba, Peru in the 1840s seemed to have a sufficiency of manpower in its native Indian population to meet the nation's needs. Of an estimated population of 1,200,000 in 1826, 673,000 were pure Indians and almost all of them were living as peasants in the sierras.[91] But this rather obvious source of labor was largely ignored. Watt Stewart in his monograph *Chinese Bondage in Peru* observes that Peru's labor system "did not enlist the cooperation of the native laborer," but he makes no attempt to explain why.[92]

Colonial Peru was in many respects a country divided into two separate communities: the coastlands consisting of large plantations where Negro slaves provided most of the labor for their Spanish-descended masters, and the sierra, or highlands, where Indians continued for the most part their ancient way of life either as tenants in a dual system of ownership with their Spanish overlords or as participants in the traditional communal system of land tenure found among most Indian tribes in the Andean plateaus.[93] The mountains that traverse the country from north to south and the lack of roads and an adequate communication system further served to isolate the highlands from the coast.

In colonial times, the Indians were subjected to the mita, a compulsory system of labor, which the Spaniards adopted from the Incas. However, this forced labor was more or less confined to mining in the Andes as the coastal planters looked to Africa for their labor supply. It was generally believed that the Indians, being used to altitudes of between ten thousand and seventeen thousand feet, were incapable of working for long periods at low altitudes. In the high Andes, their lungs and hearts developed to abnormal sizes, which made them prone to tuberculosis and heart disease when they descended to the coast.[94] Following the proclamation of independence, Peru's liberator, San Martin, inspired by the enlightened ideas of the day, abolished the mita,

---

[90]   Robert Cushman Murphy, *Oceanic Birds of South America*, 2 vols. (New York: Macmillan Company, 1936), I, 286-287.

[91]   Robert Marett, *Peru* (New York: Praeger Publishers, 1969), 83.

[92]   Stewart, *Chinese Bondage in Peru*, 3.

[93]   George M. McBride, "Features of the Agrarian System in Peru," *Geographical Review*, vol. XV, (January 1925), 138.

[94]   Brian Fawcett, "How China Came to Peru," *Geographical Magazine*, vol. XXXVI, no. 6 (October 1964), 426.

thus permitting the Indian to further isolate himself and insuring him against recruitment for the coastal plantations.

The number of Negro slaves in Peru in 1821 was given as 41,228.[95] San Martin decreed freedom for all children born of slaves from 1826 onward and granted instant freedom to slaves who enlisted in his army of liberation, and many did so.[96] These steps were very unpopular with the powerful land-owning elite; and in the late 1830s, as the children of slaves began to leave their homes and claim their freedom, the government made an about-face, declaring that free slaves, because they generally led idle and immoral lives, were to remain under the protection of the owners of their parents until the mature age of fifty years.[97] About the same time, the government was seriously considering the resumption of the slave trade, but strenuous British pressure caused the project to be dropped.[98] As very few new slaves had reached Peru since the end of the eighteenth century, the slave population was dwindling rapidly; and when President Ramon Castilla, for reasons of political expediency, abolished slavery altogether in 1855, there were only 17,000 slaves in the country.[99]

The determined efforts of the government in the decades following independence to attract European colonists were totally unsuccessful. José Gregorio Paz Soldán, the Peruvian minister for external affairs expressed in 1846 the nation's disappointment:

> From the first days of our independence we flattered ourselves with the alluring hope that the superabundance of the population of Europe was going to overflow into our shores and cover them with laborers . . . But for twenty-three years we have hoped for them in vain and even now the first is yet to appear.[100]

---

[95] Mario E. Del Rio, *La Inmigración y su Desarrollo en el Perú* (Lima: Sanmarti y Cia, 1929), 38.

[96] Fernando Romero, "The Slave Trade and the Negro in South America," *Hispanic American Historical Review*, vol. XXIV, no. 3 (August 1944), 385; *British and Foreign State Papers* (1839-40), vol. XXVIII), 906-908.

[97] *British and Foreign State Papers* (1839-1840), vol. 28, 906-908.

[98] James Ferguson King, "The Latin American Republics and the Suppression of the Slave Trade," *Hispanic American Historical Review*, vol. XXIV, no. 3 (August 1944), 408.

[99] Rio, *La Inmigración y su Desarrollo en el Perú*, 38.

[100] Arona, *La Inmigración en el Perú*, 82; Ugarte, *Bosquejo de la História Económica del Perú*, 60-61.

Nobody seemed to consider the possibility of enticing the Indian down from the mountains. The Peruvian planters, like their counterparts in Natal who passed over the native Hottentots squatting on their doorsteps and brought in laborers from India,[101] reached to the other side of the Pacific to tap China's seemingly unlimited manpower.

Following the circulation of a questionnaire to the prefects of the departments and to the Agricultural Society to collect data relative to the labor problem, the National Congress in 1849 passed a law granting the sum of P30 for each colonist introduced into the country.[102] But since the planters wanted "hands and not colonists,"[103] the government also granted to Domingo Elías, the spokesman for the planters, the exclusive privilege for a term of four years of importing Chinese laborers into the departments of Lima and La Liberdad.[104] Thus began what Paz Soldán, writing in 1891, called "the only real immigration to Peru."[105]

As with Cuba and Peru, a major problem confronting the Brazilian nation in the nineteenth century was a shortage of labor.[106] Because of Portugal's policy of exclusion, immigration to Brazil throughout the colonial period consisted almost entirely of Portuguese and Africans. An estimate of the total population of Brazil in 1800 gives the figure 3,617,900, made up of 843,000 whites (mostly of Portuguese extraction), 259,400 Indians, 426,000 mulattoes, 159,500 free Negroes, and 1,930,000 African slaves.[107] This small population, relative to the vastness of the country, and its high proportion of blacks to whites (more than two to one) caused the government of the empire to abandon the centuries-old policy of isolation and to promote immigration.

---

[101] W. Kloosterboer, *Involuntary Labor since the Abolition of Slavery*, 22.

[102] Watt Stewart, *Chinese Bondage in Peru*, 13.

[103] Arona, *La Inmigración en el Perú*, 36.

[104] Ugarte, *Busquejo de la Historia Económica del Perú*, 62; Stewart, *Chinese Bondage in Peru*, 13, 17.

[105] Arona (Paz Soldán), *La Inmigración en el Perú*, 39.

[106] Robert Conrad, *The Destruction of Brazilian Slavery, 1850, 1888* (Berkeley: University of California Press, 1972), 30-46; Celso Furtado, *The Economic Growth of Brazil: A Survey from Colonial to Modern Times*, translated by Ricardo W. de Aguiar and Eric Charles Drysdale (Berkeley: University of California Press, 1963), 125-174; Stanley J. Stein, *Vassouras, A Brazilian Coffee Country, 1850-1900* (Cambridge, Massachusetts: Harvard University Press, 1957), 47.

[107] Lawrence Hill, ed., *Brazil* (Berkeley: University of California Press, 1947), 13.

However, during the first half of the nineteenth century, Brazilian planters and others showed little enthusiasm for the many government-sponsored attempts at colonization. They did not share the government's concern for a more diversified agriculture, the settlement of the frontiers, and the "whitening" of the population. Colonization schemes had a failure ratio of more than two to one, and smarting from severe criticism from the planters for spending large sums of money on such projects, the federal government withdrew from actively promoting immigration in 1830. One of the projects that failed was the attempted settlement of several hundred Chinese in the vicinity of Rio de Janeiro in the second decade of the century with the object of introducing tea growing to Brazil.[108] The principal need of the planters was farm hands, and despite Brazil's treaty with Britain in November 1826 making it illegal for Brazilian subjects to participate in the slave trade, enough new slaves were being introduced to meet existing demands.[109] As already related, in 1843 the planters rejected Britain's offer to substitute Asians for African slaves.[110]

The year 1850 marked a turning point in Brazilian attitudes to immigration and colonization. In 1849 and 1850, British cruisers seized and destroyed Brazilian slave ships within Brazil's territorial waters. Humiliated and threatened with a blockade of its ports, the Brazilian government reluctantly acceded to British demands to end the slave trade.[111] By 1852, Brazil had effectively suppressed the traffic in Africans, and the price of slaves on the internal market had doubled.[112]

The declining sugar plantations in the north could not afford slaves at the new inflated prices, and the expanding coffee plantations of the provinces of Rio de Janeiro and São Paulo could not get enough at any price.[113]

---

[108] Carlos Francisco Moura, "Colonos Chineses no Brasil no Reinado de D. João VI," *Boletim do Instituto Luis de Camões*, vol. VII, no. 2 (Summer 1973), 185-191; D. P. Kidder and J. C. Fletcher, *Brazil and the Brazilians* (Boston: Little, Brown and Company, 1867), 418-419.

[109] Lobert Conrad, "The Contraband Slave Trade to Brazil, 1831-1845," *Hispanic American Historical Review*, vol. 44, no. 4 (November 1969), 617-638.

[110] See pages 22-23.

[111] Leslie Bethell, *The Abolition of the Brazilian Slave Trade; Britain, Brazil and the Slave Trade Question, 1807-1869* (Cambridge, England: University Press, 1970), 327-363.

[112] Conrad, *The Destruction of Brazilian Slavery*, 49.

[113] Ibid., 31.

Everywhere there was a shortage of hands, and there was a resurgence of interest in immigration and colonization schemes on the part of the federal and provincial governments, as well as by the private sector.

One possible solution to the labor problem that commanded widespread attention was the introduction of Chinese laborers.[114] Though some Brazilians were adamantly opposed to the introduction of a new race that could only serve to "mongolize" the population,[115] the sugar planters of Bahia in 1855 sent an emissary, a Dr. Fairbanks, to the China coast to recruit laborers.[116] At the same time, the federal government contracted with the Boston firm of Sampson and Tappan to bring 2,000 Chinese laborers to Brazilian shores.[117]

The Reputation of the Chinese as Laborers

Interest in the Chinese as possible substitutes for African slaves was not altogether a new phenomenon. As early as 1792, an anonymous pamphlet published in London recommended that the slaves in the West Indies be replaced by Chinese servants, "the Chinese national character being considered as favorable to the scheme of substitution."[118] The basis for such a recommendation is not given, but in all probability, it rested upon the near universal esteem in which the Chinese were held by British administrators and planters in Southeast Asia.

Sir Thomas Stamford Raffles, the founder of Singapore and one of the leading architects of the British Empire in the East, said of the Chinese, "We

---

[114] José Pedro Xavier Pinheiro, *Importação de Trabalhadores Chins: Memoria Apresentada ao Ministerio da Agricultura, Comercio e Obras Publicas* (Rio de Janeiro: Typographia de João Ignacio da Silva, 1869), 34-38; José Honório Rodrigues, "Brasil e Extremo Oriente," *Politica Externa Independente*, ano I, no. 2 (August 1965), 65-69.

[115] José Honório Rodrigues, *Brazil and Africa* (Berkeley: University of California Press, 1965), 86.

[116] Clarendon to Macedo, August 30, 1855 (BFO 13/336).

[117] *Report of the Committee Appointed by the Government of the "Board of Trade" to take into Consideration the Communication of Messrs. Sampson and Tappan* (Boston: J. H. Eastburn's Press, 1856), 10.

[118] The Pamphlet, *Remarks on the New Sugar Bill and on the National Compacts Respecting the Sugar Trade and the Slave Trade* (London, 1792), was reviewed in *Gentleman's Magazine*, vol. LXII, Part 2 (November 1792), 1023-1024.

find them dispersing themselves abroad and carrying with them a spirit of enterprize and speculation combined with an industry and prudence that makes them flourish and acquire opulence wherever they settle."[119] The Chinese were particularly renowned as cultivators of sugar, migrating as many of them did from the sugar-producing districts of Fukien province in southeast China. The development of the sugar industry in Java, Sumatra, and Penang in the eighteenth and early nineteenth centuries was largely due to their skill and labor.[120] Chinese laborers were imported to work on sugar plantations in India around 1800.[121] When it became evident that England would abolish the African slave trade, it was not surprising to find Englishmen, who were conversant with the success of the Chinese in Southeast Asia, recommending their introduction as substitutes for African slaves.

William Layman, a captain in the Royal Navy who had considerable experience in both the East and West Indies and had made several visits to China, was seemingly the first to propose to the British government that Chinese be recruited as laborers for British colonies. In his proposal, formally presented in 1802 and entitled "Hints for the Cultivation of Trinidad," Layman argues that of all the people in the world, the Chinese were "the best calculated to transform the woody wastes and drowned parts of Trinidad into rich, fertile and productive land."[122] They were "inured to a hot climate, are frugal, illustrious and peaceful, skilled in tropical produce . . . excellent cultivators of sugar."[123] Furthermore, they would cultivate such crops as rice, coconut, and tobacco and thus render the West Indies less dependent on the United States of America—a consideration that was of some interest to Britain at the turn of the century.[124] The Chinese would also serve as a counterbalance to the Negroes in the event of an insurrection while being

---

[119] Lea E. Williams, "Indonesia's Chinese Educate Raffles," *Indonesie*, vol. 9 (1956), 373.

[120] Deerr, *The History of Sugar*, II, 402.

[121] Ibid., 399.

[122] William Layman, "Hints for the Cultivation of Trinidad" (BCO 295/2).

[123] William Layman, *Outline of a Plan for the Better Cultivation, Security and Defence of the British West Indies, Being the Original Suggestion for Providing an Effectual Substitute for the African Slave Trade and Preventing the Dependence of those Colonies on America for Supplies* (London: Black, Parry and Kingsbury, 1807), 22.

[124] Ibid., 84.

forceful examples of civilized and industrious living.[125] Robert Townsend
Farquhar, lieutenant-governor of Penang, was of the same mind as Layman
and suggested that Chinese immigration to the West Indies would generate
commerce between India, China, and South America.[126]

The British government was deeply interested, and secretly arranged
through the British East India Company to bring an experimental group of
200 Chinese to Trinidad in 1806.[127] Though the venture was a conspicuous
failure,[128] the London government deemed the question of Chinese
immigration of sufficient importance to appoint a parliamentary committee
in 1811 to investigate the "practicality and expediency of supplying our
West Indian colonies with free laborers from the East."[129] The committee
recommended the introduction of Chinese laborers but warned of the
difficulty of obtaining women and advised caution lest any systematic attempt
to evade Chinese anti-emigration laws arouse the ire of the Chinese to the
detriment of British commerce.[130]

Nothing came of the committee's recommendation, but British
entrepreneurs, convinced of the superiority of the Chinese as agriculturists,
continued to press for their introduction into the West Indies. In a pamphlet
published in 1836, one Captain Wildey wrote,

> A Chinaman will perform as much labor within the tropics and in a
> given time, as two Europeans and that too without coercion, or the
> least possible constraint and without any apparent effort or fatigue.
> Their habits as a labouring class of people are unexceptionable. They
> are industrious, patient, sober, honest and tranquil . . . Their physical

125 Ibid.

126 Robert Townsend Farquhar, *Suggestions Arising from the Abolition of the African
     Slave Trade for Supplying the Demands of the West Indian Colonies with Agricultural
     Laborers* (London: John Stockdale, 1807), 62.

127 Hobart to Macqueen, April 21, 1803 (BCO 295/14).

128 For a detailed account of the experiment, see B. W. Higman, "The Chinese in
     Trinidad, 1806-1838," *Caribbean Studies*, vol. XII, no. 3 (October 1972), 21-44.

129 "Report from the Select Committee Appointed to Consider the Practicality and
     Expediency of Supplying our West Indian Colonies with Free Laborers from
     the East," (BPP, 1810-1811, 225, II), 409.

130 Ibid.

powers far exceed those of the negro tribes of Africa, of the Javanese, the natives of the Malayan Peninsula, the Hindoo, the Gentoo, or any other caste in India.[131]

Another Englishman, Leonard Wray, who had practical experience as a planter in the West Indies, India, and Southeast Asia, hailed the Chinese as the "best class of emigrants under heaven."[132] In his treatise on sugar cultivation, he wrote,

> Of all laborers who have come under my observation, I know of none who can in any way be compared to the Chinese, for enterprise, energy, sobriety, intelligence, application, physical power, determined perseverance, cheerfulness, and prudent economy combined. I do not advance this on light grounds: on the contrary, I assert it as the result of the most mature consideration, of the most searching observation, during a period of sixteen years' actual practical experience, divided between the West Indies, Bengal, and the settlements in the Strait of Malacca; during which time I have had hundreds (I may say thousands) of Negroes, Hindostanees, Bengallees, Chuliahs, Malays and Chinese working under my management and direction.[133]

There is no evidence that such glowing tributes were challenged or contradicted, at least prior to 1850. The industry of the Chinese was proverbial, and Europeans accepted it as gospel.[134] It was logical then that they would turn to China when their tropical colonies began to cry for laborers.

---

[131]   Captain Wildey, *A Treatise on Chinese Laborers as Compared with Europeans, the Tribes of Africa and the Various Castes of Asiatics with a View to their Introduction into our West Indian Colonies as Free Labourers* (London: T. Hurst, 1836), 17.

[132]   Leonard Wray, *The Practical Sugar Planter: A Complete Account of the Cultivation and Manufacture of the Sugar Cane according to the Latest and Most Improved Methods* (London: Smith, Elder and Company, 1848), 82.

[133]   Ibid., 83-84.

[134]   J. Crawford, "Memorandum Respecting Chinese Emigration into the West Indies," September 1, 1843 (BCO 318/160).

CHAPTER II

RECRUITING LABORERS ON THE CHINA COAST

Any considerable inquiry for coolies, any competition for obtaining them, indeed any demand for a single human being beyond the spontaneous supply of volunteers, will in China lead to abuses. Such are the venality and profligacy of public officers, such the passion for gain among multitudes of the people, that the coolie trade will inevitably be associated with irregularities and cruelties. Let it only be understood that men are wanted and they will be obtained, obtained by collusions, crimpings, frauds, falsehoods, violences, understandings with the mandarins, and the abominations will of course be maximized where authority is most feeble and the demand most active.

Dr. John Bowring, Governor of Hong Kong to the
Earl of Malmesbury, January 5, 1853
(BPP, ASS, *China*, vol. 3), 97.

The Beginnings of Chinese Emigration

The records of Chinese chronicles abound with travel adventures, naval expeditions, and trading exploits that date back to the third and fourth centuries BC, and artifacts discovered throughout Southeast Asia point to the existence of contact with Chinese culture at an even earlier date.[1]

During the Han Dynasty (206 BC to 220 AD), Chinese merchants in search of trade and fortune traversed the South China Sea, penetrated the Indian Archipelago, traded with distant Ceylon and even ventured as far

---

[1] Charles P. Fitzgerald, *The Southern Expansion of the Chinese People: Southern Fields and Southern Ocean* (London: Barrie and Jenkins, 1972), xvi; Victor Purcell, *The Chinese in Southeast Asia* (London: Oxford University Press, 1965), 11.

as Arabia.[2] Chinese wares were known to Imperial Rome. The poet Virgil (70-19 BC) wrote of the "most delicate wool" (silk) of China,[3] and Pliny the Elder in the first century AD complained of the long voyages made solely to obtain this luxurious Chinese product so that Roman ladies could flaunt their charms in public.[4] In the first centuries of the Christian era, Arab, Indian, and Persian traders made their way to China while the Chinese opted to stay at home.[5] By the fourth and fifth centuries, Chinese vessels were again feeling their way along the coasts for foreign lands.[6] In 399, a Buddhist monk from Northern China named Fa-hsien (Fa-hein) visited India, Ceylon, Malaya, and Sumatra; and his account of his experiences suggests that at that time, a regular commerce existed between China and some of the kingdoms of Southeast Asia.[7] The fact that Asian states, such as Vietnam and Cambodia from the Han Dynasty onward were at least nominally under Chinese suzerainty, facilitated overseas commercial intercourse and expedited emigration.

However, despite these early cultural and commercial contacts with the outside world, the first significant overseas migration from China did not take place until the seventh century when fishermen and merchants from the seaboard cities of Fukien and Kwangtung settled in the Pescadores Islands and Formosa.[8] These pioneer settlers, in cooperation with the great trading

---

[2]   Pyau Ling, "Causes of Chinese Emigration," *American Academy of Political and Social Science*, vol. XXXIX, no. 128 (January 1912), 79.

[3]   *Ibid.*, 78.

[4]   H. Rackham, *Pliny's Natural History with an English Translation in Ten Volumes* vol. II (London William Heinemann, 1942), 378-379.

[5]   Purcell, *The Chinese in Southeast Asia*, 12.

[6]   Willem P. Groeneveldt, a nineteenth-century commentator on Chinese penetration into Southeast Asia stated that "[Chinese] have not gained their knowledge of Southeast Asia by bold voyages of discovery: slowly and cautiously they have crept along its shores". See his *Notes on the Malay Archipelago and Malacca: Miscellaneous Papers Relating to the Indian Archipelago* (London: 1887), I, 126-262. Fitzgerald questions this assertion in *The Southern Expansion of the Chinese People*, 8.

[7]   James Legge, *A Record of Buddhist Kingdoms: Being an Account by the Chinese monk Fa-hein of his Travels in India and Ceylon (AD 399-414) in Search of the Buddhist Books of Discipline* (Oxford: The Clarendon Press, 1886).

[8]   Ta Chen, *Chinese Migrations, With Special Reference to Labor Conditions* (Washington: Government Printing Office, 1923), 37.

ports of Canton and Changchow, opened up trading routes to what are now the Philippine Islands, the Malay Peninsula, and the East Indies. With the expansion of trade, small settlements or trading posts of Chinese sprang up all over Southeast Asia, often as ghettoes in the principal towns. This paved the way for subsequent overseas immigration.

In the fifteenth century, the imperial Eunuch Cheng Ho was commissioned by the Ming emperors to explore the "Western Ocean."[9] He made seven voyages, which took him beyond the archipelago to the Gulf of Aden, visiting more than thirty countries. His tales of the fabulous wealth in the strange lands he visited, recounted in popular ballads and folk songs, greatly stimulated overseas trade and migration. In this period also, the power of the Ming emperors was extended to neighboring nations, and the young and adventurous left in large numbers to seek their fortunes in the Philippines, Borneo, Sumatra, Java, the Malay Peninsula, and the East Indies.[10]

When the Portuguese, the Spaniards, and the Dutch found their way to Southeast Asia in the sixteenth century, the Chinese were there to greet them. These strangers, being relatively few in number, soon discovered that the Chinese were indispensable if they were to succeed in exploiting the trading potential of the area. The Chinese were sought after not only as traders and intermediaries with the natives but also as craftsmen and personal servants. The Portuguese explorer Simão d'Andrade visited Canton with a squadron of four ships in August 1519 and carried off a number of Chinese youths, boys and girls, to be used as household servants and slaves.[11]

According to the French traveller Jean Mocquet, who visited Goa in the first decade of the seventeenth century, Chinese servants were in big

---

[9]   Purcell, *The Chinese in Southeast Asia*, 16; Chen, *Chinese Migrations*, 39. There is evidence that the Chinese around the thirteenth century had some knowledge of Australia; see James Colwell, *A Century in the Pacific* (London: C. H. Kelly, 1914), 18.

[10]   Tsen-ming Huang, *The Legal Status of Chinese Abroad* (Taipei, Taiwan: China Cultural Service, 1954), 32.

[11]   C. R. Boxer, "Notes on Chinese Abroad in the Late Ming and Early Manchu Periods Compiled from Contemporary European Sources (1500-1750)," *T'ien Hsia Monthly*, vol. XIX, no. 5 (December 1939), 451; T'ien-tse Chang, *Sino-Portuguese Trade from 1514 to 1644; a Synthesis of Portuguese and Chinese Sources* (Leyden: E. J. Brill, 1934), 86.

demand as they were considered loyal, intelligent, and hardworking.[12] After the Portuguese occupied Macau in 1557, a traffic in Chinese, kidnapped in Canton by native crimps and exported through Macau, persisted for over three centuries despite the efforts of Chinese and Portuguese authorities to suppress the nefarious practice.[13]

The Spaniards also found the Chinese extraordinarily useful, and shortly after they established themselves in the Philippines in 1565, a lively trade developed between Manila and Changchow on the Fukien coast.[14] When the Dutch arrived on the scene and founded Batavia (modern Djakarta) in 1619, Governor Jan Pieterszoon Coen directed that Chinese be kidnapped from the coasts of Fukien and Kwangtung so as to populate the newly acquired Dutch possessions of Java; the Moluccas, or Spice Islands; and Banda.[15] Though persecuted and subjected to periodic massacres at the hands of both the Spaniards and the Dutch, the Chinese population nonetheless steadily increased in the Philippines and the Dutch East Indies in the seventeenth and eighteenth centuries.[16]

---

[12] Jean Mocquet, *Voyages en Afrique, Asia, Indes Orientales et Occidentales* (Paris: Impr. Aux, Frais du Gouvernement, 1830).

[13] Boxer, "Notes on Chinese Abroad . . . ," 457-458; Manuel Teixeira, "The So-called Slave Trade at Macao," *Proceedings of the International Association of Historians of Asia, Second Biennial Conference October 6-9, 1962* (Taipei, Taiwan: 1962), 639.

[14] George Philipps, "Early Spanish Trade with Chin Cheo (Changchow)," *China Review*, vol. XIX (1891), 243; Shao-hsing Chen, "The Migration of Chinese from Fokien to the Philippines under the Spanish Colonization and to Taiwan under the Dutch Colonization: An Analysis of Their Pattern of Development and Their Correspondences," *Proceedings of the International Association of Asia, Second Biennial Conference*, 463; Charles R. Boxer, *The Great Ship from Amacon: Annals of the Macao and the Old Japan Trade, 1555-1640* (Lisbon: Centro De Estudos Historicos Ultramarinos, 1963), 3.

[15] T'ien-tse Chang, "China and the Netherlands East Indies," *China Quarterly*, vol. 3, no. 1 (Winter 1937-38), 48; Charles R. Boxer, *The Dutch Seaborne Empire, 1600-1800* (New York: Knopf, 1965), 235.

[16] In 1639, 1660 and 1763 revolts by the Chinese in the Philippines were followed by massacres. Also oppression of the Chinese at Batavia culminated in their massacre in 1740. See Harley F. MacNair, "The Relation of China to Her Nationals Abroad," *Chinese Social and Political Science Review*, vol. VII, no. 1 (January 1923), 28-29.

The English, who were relative latecomers to Southeast Asia, were interested primarily in India and the China trade, and hence British predominance was not established until the second half of the eighteenth century. The English—as well as the Portuguese, the Spaniards, and the Dutch before them—were keenly aware of the value of the Chinese in any imperial enterprise or undertaking. From as early as 1689, the directors of the British East India Company made vigorous efforts to attract Chinese craftsmen and laborers to Bencoolen, a Company outpost on the west coast of Sumatra.[17] After its occupation by the company in 1786, Penang received "Chinese artisans and husbandmen, recruited by the supercargoes at Canton and sent in the Company's ships."[18] From the founding of the company in 1600, Chinese sailors had been engaged to fill deficiencies in the crews of its vessels. Canton compradores and crimps put the Chinese on board downriver at Lintin away from the eyes of local authorities who might try to enforce imperial prohibitions against emigration.[19] From the beginning of the nineteenth century, the company was chiefly concerned with holding on to its monopolistic trading arrangements at Canton, and hence sought to minimize the possibility of conflict with Chinese officialdom by having sailors and emigrants shipped to Macau and from there to the company's possessions.[20] In this way, Chinese laborers were brought to Borneo,[21] Sumatra,[22]

---

[17]   John Bastin, *The British in West Sumatra, 1685-1826* (Kuala Lampur: University of Malaya Press, 1965), 39; William Marsden, *The History of Sumatra* (Kuala Lampur: Oxford University Press, 1966, first printed in London in 1811), 451; John Bastin, *The Native Policies of Sir Stamford Raffles in Java and Sumatra: An Economic Interpretation* (Oxford: Clarendon Press, 1957), 77.

[18]   Hosea Balboa Morse, *The Chronicles of the East India Company Trade to China, 1635-1834* (Oxford: Clarendon Press, 1926), II, 427.

[19]   Ibid., 428; [BRADDELL], "Notices of Pinang," 148; Staunton to Roberts, December 18, 1802 (BCO, 295/3).

[20]   Roberts to Willesley, May 24, 1804 (G. 34/135, Straits Settlements, India Office Library and Records, London); Morse, *The Chronicles of the East India Company*, III, 203-204, 376; Nicolas Tarling, *British Policy in the Malay Peninsula and Archipelago, 1824-1871* (Kuala Lampur: Oxford University Press, 1969), 9.

[21]   H. R. C. Wright, *East-Indian Economic Problems: The Age of Cornwallis and Raffles* (London: Luzac and Company, 1961), 295.

[22]   Bastin, *The British in West Sumatra, 1685-1825*, 40; Bastin, *The Native Policies of Sir Stamford Raffles*, 119-120.

Banka,[23] Singapore,[24] India,[25] and even to the South Atlantic island of St. Helena.[26] When Napoleon Bonaparte was banished to that island in 1815, its governor, Sir Hudson Lowe, put in an order to the company for an "augmentation of 350 Chinese" to cater to the general's needs.[27]

European colonial expansion not only encouraged and facilitated Chinese dispersion throughout Southeast Asia but through contact with Europeans some Chinese in the course of the seventeenth, eighteenth and early nineteenth centuries traveled as far afield as Europe[28] and the New World.[29] Nevertheless, it was not until the opening of China's ports to foreign trade in the Anglo-Chinese Treaty of 1842 that Chinese immigration expanded to the Western World.

In the second half of the nineteenth century and the first decades of the twentieth century, there occurred what could be called a Chinese diaspora. Chinese nationals as laborers, seamen, and traders went to almost all parts of the globe, and the Chinese saying "Wherever the ocean waves touch there are overseas Chinese"[30] was for the first time a reality. The only places that did not attract the Chinese were the heartland of Africa, the distinctly Mohammedan countries, and Central Europe. This phase of Chinese overseas migration coincided with the great movement of Europeans across the Atlantic to the Americas, but the two movements were manifestly distinct in character.

---

23 Wright, *East-Indian Economic Problems*, 319; Morse, *Chronicles of the East India Company*, III, 203-204.

24 J. Lumsdaine, W. R. Jennings and E. Presgrove, "Report on the Population, etc. of the Town and Suburbs of Fort Marlborough 1819-1820," in John Bastin (ed.), *The Journal of Thomas Ortho Travers, 1813-1820* (Singapore: A. G. Banfield, 1960), 168.

25 MacQueen to Camden, February 10, 1806 (BCO 295/15).

26 Chairman of East India Company to Canning, June 20, 1816 (G. 32/162, Correspondence Relating to General Bonaparte's Removal to St. Helena, India Office Library and Records, London).

27 Morse, *The Chronicles of the East India Company*, III, 116.

28 There were Chinese in Lisbon in 1540. See Boxer, "Notes on the Chinese Abroad . . . ," 542-543.

29 See chapter VI.

30 Tin-yuke Char, "Restrictions on Chinese in English Speaking Countries," *Chinese Social and Political Science Review*, vol. XVI, no. 3 (October 1932), 476.

Nature and Causes of Chinese Emigration

While the vast majority of Europeans who emigrated did so with the intention of settling permanently, and in time adopted the customs, manners, and dress of the country of settlement, the Chinese intended to stay for a limited period only; and hence, as far as possible, they avoided any adaptation to the culture of the host country. Since Europeans set out to establish a new life and a new home, usually the whole family—male and female, young and old—emigrated. With the Chinese, only the young men went overseas.

These differences, which were to generate bitter feelings between the Chinese and European immigrants in the New World, had their foundations in the distinct cultures of the two peoples. Though in both Europe and China the most fundamental factor underlying the entire emigration phenomenon was the extraordinary increase in population far outstripping the productivity of the land, the European could break with his ancestral home, whereas the Chinese could not. The attachment of the average Chinese to his village; his strong kin ties; and his duties to his parents and ancestors, which could not be adequately fulfilled in a foreign country, constituted a formidable obstacle to immigration. The people of China were not only deeply attached to family and lineage, but to them the Middle Kingdom was the center of civilization, and all foreign countries were barbarian nations where there was little to gain and much to lose. Not only would respectable people not wish to emigrate, but even desperate criminals dreaded banishment to distant lands. In this context, to the vast majority of the population, the thought of leaving the Celestial Empire permanently was intolerable. Consequently, apart from some merchants who went overseas to make their fortunes, only the poorest of the poor emigrated, and these were almost exclusively peasants who were faced with the stark alternative: starvation or emigration. But even among the starving and the utterly destitute, emigration was undertaken only as a temporary measure, as few intended to remain abroad. The *China Mail* commenting on the reluctance of the average Chinese to emigrate stated,

> No matter how flattering the future prospect held out, he will not venture
> to leave his own country upon the chance of making his fortune among
> strangers, unless compelled by necessity. When he has reached this state
> of destitution he may be safely regarded as a desperate man to whom

the future is but a little less blank than the present, and who is ready to risk any suffering in order to save himself the pangs of imminent starvation.[31]

Although many aspects of China's demographic growth remain obscure, it is generally accepted that the population trebled in the two hundred years from 1650 to 1850, reaching an estimated 430 million.[32] Keeping pace with this population increase and sustaining it was a continual improvement in the utilization of land and food production. The development of early-ripening rice, from one hundred to thirty days after transplantation, not only introduced a double cropping system, but facilitated the spread of rice cultivation to well-watered hills and marginal areas such as marshy flats that were usually submerged for most of the year.[33] The introduction in the sixteenth century of American food plants such as maize, sweet potatoes, and peanuts, as well as Irish potatoes, enabled the people to cultivate hitherto untouched dry hills and mountain slopes.[34] But by the nineteenth century, this process was reaching its saturation point. Heavy rains washed away the topsoil from the mountain slopes, and rivers silted up, causing floodings in the valleys, which meant diminishing crop returns. Famine stalked the land.[35]

Added to the food crisis and partly resulting from it was increased political unrest. In the decade from 1841 to 1850, not a year passed without a local

---

[31] *China Mail*, November 10, 1871.

[32] Ping-ti Ho, *Studies on the Population of China, 1368-1953* (Cambridge, Massachusetts: Harvard University Press, 1959), xi; J. P. Durand, "The Population Statistics of China, AD 2 to 1953," *Population Studies*, vol. XII, no. 2 (1960), 209-256.

[33] Ho, *Studies on the Population of China*, 173-174.

[34] Ibid., 183-184.

[35] Ibid., 175-183; Dwight H. Perkins in *Agricultural Development in China, 1368-1968* (Chicago: Aldine Publishing Company, 1969), presents a somewhat different picture, taking account of largescale internal migration and reclamation. Mark Elvin argues that a major cause of food shortages was the continuing increase in population coupled with a technological standstill in agriculture. See *The Pattern of China's Past* (Stanford, California: Stanford University Press, 1973), 301; See also Yao Shang-yu, "Floods and Droughts in Chinese History," *Far Eastern Quarterly*, vol. II, no. 4 (August 1943), 357-78.

uprising of some kind.[36] The limited means of sustenance forced people such as the Hakkas—who had migrated earlier from Northern China and settled in the Nan-ling mountain range in Northern Kwantung province, Southern Kiangsi, and Southern Fukien—to commence moving toward the valleys and the coast.[37] This resulted in armed conflicts with the people already settled there. These conflicts reached a climax in the 1850s with a number of bloody clashes between the Hakkas and the Punti, natives of Kiangsi.[38]

Furthermore, the Manchu government was in decline,[39] and war with Britain accelerated the process. Traditionally, the effectiveness of China's imperial government depended heavily on prestige. The defeat of the imperial army in the Opium Wars of 1839-1842 and the subsequent Treaty of Nanking that granted concessions to foreign powers dealt serious blows to the government's image. Many people, particularly the gentry, deeply resented the government's inability to repel foreign aggression.[40] An indemnity of £21 million exacted by Great Britain for its losses in the war brought on a financial crisis. A weak and discredited central government felt powerless to

---

[36] S. Y. Teng, *The Taiping Rebellion and Western Powers: A Comprehensive Study* (Oxford: Clarendon Press, 1971), 29-30.

[37] Ting-yu Hsieh, "Origin and Migration of the Hakkas," *The Chinese Social and Political Science Review*, vol. 13 (1929), 202-227; Jen Yu-wen, *The Taiping Revolutionary Movement* (New Haven: Yale University Press, 1973), 10-11.

[38] Ho, *Studies on the Population of China*, 166; Jen, *The Taiping Revolutionary Movement*, 54; [Edwin Stevens], "Clanship among the Chinese; Feuds between Different Clans near Canton; Substitutes for those who are Guilty of Murder; Republicanism among the Clans," *Chinese Repository*, vol. IV (January 1836), 411-415; R. Lechler, "The Hakka Chinese," *Chinese Recorder*, vol. 9 (September-October 1878), 355.

[39] "Memorial Showing the Daily Increase of Enervation and Degeneracy in the Province of Kwangtung and the Urgent Necessity that exists for Correction and Reform of the Civil Administration and Military Discipline, in order to Maintain the Native Spirit and to Improve the Condition of the People. With this View the Imperial Perusal of the Memorial is Humbly Solicited," *Chinese Repository*, vol. VI (April 1838), 593-605; Franz Michael, *The Taiping Rebellion: History and Documents*, 3 vols. (Seattle: University of Washington Press), I, 16-17; Theodore Hamberg, *The Visions of Hung-Siu-tshuen and the Origin of the Kwangsi Insurrection* (Hong Kong 1854), 3.

[40] John F. Davis, *The History of China* (London, 1844), 168.

cope with insurrections, riots, and roving bands of local militia who took the law into their own hands.[41]

Internal strife assumed unprecedented proportions in the Christian-inspired Taiping Rebellion, which raged from 1851 to 1864 and nearly toppled the Manchu Dynasty. Before it was successfully quelled, 16 provinces were ravaged, 600 cities were sacked and pillaged, and perhaps as many as 20 to 30 million people were killed. Countless millions were left homeless.[42]

Given these economic and political conditions, the surprising thing is that relatively so few Chinese emigrated. In the years 1847-1874, which coincided with one of the worst periods of social upheaval in China's history, approximately 1.5 million out of a population of 430 million left for foreign shores.[43] That was approximately one-third of 1 percent (.35). At the same time, the inhabitants of the British Isles, who (with the possible exception of the Irish) were by no means experiencing problems of the magnitude that were plaguing the Chinese, left their homelands in droves. In the twenty-eight years from 1847-1875, 5,400,755 emigrated. These accounted for approximately 23 percent of the population.[44]

---

[41] Jen, *The Taiping Revolutionary Movement*, 53-54; John F. Davis, *China During the War and Since the Peace*, 2 vols. (London: Longman, Brown, Green, and Longmans, 1852), I, 182-187.

[42] Teng, *The Taiping Rebellion and Western Powers*, 411. Ping-ti Ho suggests that the estimate of 20 to 30 million killed is much too low, see *Studies on the Population of China*, 275.

[43] The figure 1.5 million is perhaps a conservative estimate. During the period in question over 540,000 Chinese emigrated from the port of Hong Kong (table 4) and over 210,000 emigrated from Macau (table 5). Statistics on emigration from Canton, Amoy, Swatow and other points along the China coast to Southeast Asia are unavailable but from what is known about the annual arrivals of Chinese in the Straits settlements, Netherlands Indies, and the Philippine Islands emigration from these ports at least equalled the exodus from Hong Kong and Macau. See Leonard Unger, "The Chinese in Southeast Asia," *The Geographical Review*, vol. XXIV (1944), 201; "The Chinese in Singapore," *JIA*, series 1, vol. 2 (1848), 286.

[44] The percentage estimate is derived from statistics provided by William A. Carrothers, *Emigration from the British Isles, with Special Reference to the Development of Overseas Dominions* (New York: Augustus M. Kelley, 1966), 33, 305-306.

Official Attitude of the Chinese Government

Reinforcing the inbred reluctance of the Chinese to venture abroad was the official attitude of government toward those who sailed beyond the sea. Chinese rulers generally looked upon emigration with disfavor. According to Confucian principles, anyone who would desert his ancestral graves was not only unfilial but a renegade. Hence, rarely did Chinese travelers and overseas merchants have the sympathy and protection of their government. In response to a Spanish letter attempting to justify the massacre of 20,000 to 30,000 Chinese in Manila in 1603, the Emperor Shen-tsung of the Ming Dynasty, while rebuking the Spaniards, stated that he would not take any punitive action as those who had been killed were vile people who had not returned to their country after leaving it for trade.[45] A massacre in Batavia in 1740, where 10,000 Chinese lost their lives at the hands of the Dutch moved Emperor Kao Tsung Shun to say he was "little solicitous for the fate of unworthy subjects who, in the pursuit of lucre, had quitted their country and abandoned the tombs of their ancestors."[46]

Though the Ming Dynasty (1368-1644) was much more open to foreign trade and contact with foreigners than the later Manchu Dynasty (1644-1911), both forbade their subjects to go overseas and obliged merchants to obtain a license before leaving the country.[47] The unlicensed emigrant was liable to severe punishment. The Manchu rulers, believing that emigrants were likely to include political dissidents fleeing to the support of the Ming partisan Koxinga (Cheng Ch'eng-kung), who had established himself on

---

[45]   Harley F. MacNair, "The Relation of China to Her Nationals Abroad," *The Chinese Social and Political Science Review*, vol. 7, no. 1 (January 1923), 23; Purcell, *The Chinese in Southeast Asia*, 514; Edgar Wickberg, *The Chinese in Philippine Life 1850-1898* (New Haven: Yale University Press, 1965), 214.

[46]   MacNair, "The Relation of China to her Nationals Abroad," 30; Purcell, *The Chinese in Southeast Asia*, 407.

[47]   MacNair, "The Relation of China to her Nationals Abroad," 25; C. G. F. Simkin, *The Traditional Trade of Asia* (London: Oxford University Press, 1968), 202; Wu Hung-chu, "China's Attitude Towards Foreign Nations and Nationals Historically Considered," *Chinese Social and Political Science Review*, vol. X, 31-32; John E. Wills Jr., *Pepper, Guns and Porkeys: The Dutch East India Company and China, 1622-1681* (Cambridge, Massachusetts: Harvard University Press, 1974), 4-14.

Formosa, strengthened the prohibition. They attached to the Ta Tsing Leu Lee (Ta-ch'ing lu-li, or the penal code of China) this statement:

> All officers of the government, soldiers and private citizens who clandestinely proceed to sea to trade, or who remove to foreign islands for the purpose of inhabiting and cultivating the same, shall be punished according to the law against communicating with rebels and enemies and consequently suffer death by being beheaded. The governors of cities of the second and third orders shall likewise be beheaded, when found guilty of combining with or artfully conniving at the conduct of such persons.[48]

This law, though too severe to be enforced by a weak government, was not put aside until the Treaty of Peking in 1860 and was not repealed until September 18, 1893.[49]

Even after Koxinga's defeat in 1683, the Manchu emperors remained adamantly opposed to emigration. A decree of the Emperor K'ang Hsi in 1712 declared that those who intended to stay abroad permanently should be returned home with the cooperation of foreign governments and be beheaded.[50] Five years later, he relented and announced that those who emigrated prior to 1717 could return without punishment.[51] His successor, Emperor Yung-cheng, allowed traders who obtained a government license to go abroad for a fixed number of years, but they could not take their families.[52]

Despite these stringent laws, emigrants continued to leave from China's southern ports either in Chinese junks or in foreign boats that came to Canton to trade.[53] Local officials, whose task it was to enforce the law, reaped a rich harvest by collecting large sums from returning emigrants or from

---

[48] Harley F. MacNair, *The Chinese Abroad* (Shanghai: Commercial Press Limited, 1924), 1-2. See also "Minister on Chinese Emigrants Abroad," *China Review*, vol. 21, 138; John W. Foster, *American Diplomacy in the Orient* (Boston, Houghton: Mifflin and Company, 1903), 279.

[49] Chen, *Chinese Migrations*, 18.

[50] Sing-wu Wang, "The Attitude of the Ch'ing Court Toward Chinese Emigration," *Chinese Culture*, vol. IX, no. 4 (December 1968), 62.

[51] Ibid.; William J. Cator, *The Economic Position of the Chinese in the Netherlands Indies* (Chicago: University of Chicago Press, 1936), 26.

[52] Wang, "The Attitude of the Ch'ing Court Toward Chinese Emigration," 63.

[53] Ibid.

their families. The words of one returnee reflect the prevailing climate of recrimination and extortion:

> We are afraid of the so-called inspection of mandarins, the oppression of their sub-officials and the ill treatment of our own clansmen and neighbors. At our return to China, we would be falsely accused as robbers and pirates, as spies of the barbarians (foreigners), as purchasers and abductors of slaves. Many who have savings of long years would be robbed, others would have their homes torn down and would be prohibited from building new ones; still others would be compelled to be responsible for forged documents of debts and liabilities. Alone and helpless we are considered strangers by our own relations. Upon whom shall we rely for help in a country where we are surrounded on all sides by thieves.[54]

One aspect of the emigration prohibition, however, was rigidly enforced by local officials. It would seem that women, whether single or married, were absolutely forbidden to emigrate.[55] This not only guaranteed that the men would return, but it also ensured that they would make regular remittances to their families while overseas. The little evidence that is available indicates that these remittances were substantial. Captain James Low, British superintendent of the Province Wellesley in the Strait of Malacca in the 1830s, stated that when Penang had only 3,000 Chinese, the annual remittances to China amounted to ten thousand Spanish dollars.[56] Another observer, writing in

---

54   H. Gottwaldt, *Die Uberseeische Auswanderung der Chinesen und ihre Einwirkung auf die gelbe und Weisse Rasse* (Bremen, 1903), 7. The translation is taken from Chen, *Chinese Migrations*, 17; see also C. Toogood Downing, *The Fan-Qui in China in 1836-7*, 3 vols. (London: Colburn, 1838), II, 273.

55   Thomas John Newbold, *Political and Statistical Account of the British Settlements in the Straits of Malacca; viz. Pinang, Malacca and Singapore with a History of the Malayan States on the Peninsula of Malacca*, 2 vols. (London: John Murray, 1839), I, 10; Harry S. Parkes, "General Remarks on Chinese Emigration," September, 1852 (BPP, ASS, *China*, vol. III), 39; Samuel Wells Williams, *The Middle Kingdom*, 2 vols. (New York: Charles Scribner's Sons, 1913), I, 279; "Memorial of Hsueh Fu-ch'en, Chinese Minister to Great Britain and France," *North China Herald*, December 15, 1893.

56   Newbold, *Political and Statistical Account of the British Settlement in the Straits of Malacca*, I, 11.

1847, estimated that Chinese in Singapore sent from forty thousand to seventy thousand Spanish dollars annually to their families at home.[57] That a percentage of this money found its way into the pockets of local officials in China is highly probable.

Evidently, a tradition of local officials profiteering from illegal emigration had sprung up along China's southern coast and persisted throughout the seventeenth, eighteenth, and nineteenth centuries. This is not to say that all local officials were corrupt. There were some who sought to enforce the emigration laws, particularly in regard to "coolie emigration" to Latin America, while others tried to halt abuses by having emigration regulated and controlled.[58] Up to 1860, the policy of the Manchu government was clearly to abide by existing laws prohibiting emigration, and it repulsed any attempt to discuss regulated emigration, which foreigners and some local authorities were advocating. When the American minister to China, William Reed, suggested in 1858 that Chinese and foreign officials should get together to abolish the sale of opium and the kidnapping of coolies, the imperial government replied, "The two items on the prohibition of opium and enticing Chinese from the ports are both matters which local officials must handle, nor do they have to wait for these barbarians to ask them."[59]

Somewhat reluctantly, China's government was eventually persuaded to allow its people to emigrate, and an article to this effect was written into the Treaty of Peking in 1860.[60] Subsequently, the Tsungli Yamen (the Committee of the Grand Council in charge of foreign affairs) in cooperation with the ministers of Britain and France drew up a "convention to regulate the engagement of Chinese emigrants by British and French subjects," which was signed in Peking on March 5, 1866.[61] This convention established an emigration system whereby

---

[57] "Annual Remittances by Chinese Emigrants in Singapore to the Families in China," *JIA*, series 1, vol. I (1847), 36.

[58] See chapter VIII.

[59] Earl Swisher, *China's Management of the American Barbarians: A Study of Sino-American Relations, 1841-1861, with Documents* (New Haven: Yale University, Far Eastern Publications, 1951), 453.

[60] William Frederick Mayers, *Treaties between the Empire of China and Foreign Powers* (London: Trubner and Company, 1877), 9.

[61] For a full text of the Convention see Chen, *Chinese Migrations*, 165-167; William Frederick Mayers, *Treaties between the Empire of China and Foreign Powers together with Regulations for the Conduct of Foreign Trade, Conventions, Agreements, Regulations, etc.* (Shanghai: North China Herald Limited, 1906), 32-36; BFO 17/873.

licensed emigration agents at the treaty ports and under the joint supervision of foreign consuls and Chinese authorities could engage voluntary emigrants to go overseas for a period of not more than five years. All other forms of contract emigration were forbidden; and the use of force, fraud, or kidnapping to secure emigrants was declared punishable by death. Though the British and the French governments refused to ratify the convention, its terms were adopted by the Chinese government and promulgated in the seaboard provinces as the law of the land. With this about-face, emigration was no longer the exclusive concern of provincial governors and local officials. It had become an issue of national importance. The Tsungli Yamen commenced taking an active interest in the welfare of the Chinese abroad, which eventually led to the establishment of Chinese legations in foreign countries.[62]

Geographical Origin of Emigrants

The official constraints imposed upon emigration, as well as the strong cultural bias against it, had the effect of limiting emigration to the coastal provinces. The principal centers of emigration were located in the provinces of Fukien and Kwangtung in the south and Shantung and Hopeh (Chihli) in the north. Few Chinese from the Yangtze valley or from the west and southwest went overseas. Seemingly, these people, even in the face of starvation and death, never considered leaving China. Emigration from Shantung and Hopeh went primarily to Siberia, to South Africa in the first decade of the twentieth century, and to France during World War I.[63]

The bulk of emigration, however, came from the two southern provinces of Fukien and Kwangtung. Not only did these provinces possess excellent seaports, but the people were of an independent and adventurous spirit and had a long tradition of overseas trade and contact with foreigners.[64] Prior to the nineteenth century, China's intercourse with Southeast Asia was confined almost exclusively to Kwangtung and southern Fukien. This orientation toward the sea predisposed the people to opt for emigration in periods of crisis and economic distress.

---

[62] For an elaboration of this development see chapter IX.

[63] Chen, *Chinese Migrations*, 128, 143; George E. Payne, *An Experiment in Alien Labor* (Chicago: University of Chicago Press, 1912); George W. Hinman, "The Oriental Dispersion: An Economic and Missionary Problem," *The Chinese Recorder*, vol. LVI (July 1925), 448-449.

[64] Ling, "Causes of Chinese Emigration," 75.

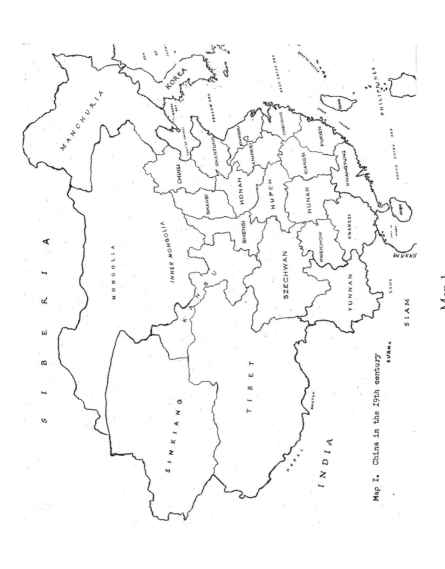

Map 1

China in the nineteenth century

In both Kwangtung and Fukien, the terrain is quite mountainous, particularly along the coast, with the notable exception of the fertile Pearl River Delta around Canton. The entire area was densely populated. According to official figures, the population of Fukien in 1851 was over 20 million, which was an average of 435 persons per square mile. Kwangtung was somewhat better off with a population of 28.4 million and an average of 338 persons to the square mile.[65] These people had no place to go when population pressures, diminishing crop yields, drought, and flooding caused food shortages. High mountains barred access to the interior, which in any event was also densely populated. The sea and the lands beyond it afforded the only avenue of relief. In his assessment of Chinese emigration, Harry S. Parkes, the British commissioner in Canton, wrote in 1852,

> Emigration from this province [Kwangtung] and the adjoining one of Fuhkien [sic] dates from a very early period, and it is these two provinces alone that have sent forth the myriads which have reclaimed the Islands of Formosa and Hainan; introduced industry and various of the most useful arts into the countries of Cochin China, Camboja and Siam; settled many of the islands of the Indian Archipelago and contributed more than any other race to the rise and prosperity of the European settlements in Java, the Philippines and the Malayan Peninsula.[66]

The pattern of Chinese emigration, which developed over the centuries, centered around speech or dialect groups. Those speaking the same dialect tended to go to the same destination overseas, where they would be welcomed and understood by fellow countrymen who spoke the same language. With speech as the distinguishing factor, there were five major emigrant communities in southeast China: Hokkien, Teochiu, Cantonese, Hakka, and Hainanese.[67] Map 2 outlines their principal places of origin.

---

[65] These figures are derived from data appearing in Perkins, *Agricultural Development in China, 1368-1968*, 212, 219.

[66] Harry S. Parkes, "General Remarks on Chinese Emigration," September, 1852 (BPP, ASS, *China*, vol. II), 33-34.

[67] Only the Hokkiens and the Teochius spoke dialects of the same language. See George W. Skinner, *Chinese Society in Thailand: An Analytical History* (New York: Cornell University Press, 1957), 35; Chen, *Emigrant Communities*, 23; Purcell, *The Chinese in Southeast Asia*, 6-7.

Map 2

Map of China showing the principal emigrant areas

Sources: Purcell, *The Chinese in Southeast Asia*, 6-7 (map); Skinner, *Chinese Society in Thailand*, 32-40 (map); Ju-kang T'ien, *The Chinese Structure of Sarawak: A Study of Social Structure* (London, London School of Economics and Political Science, 1950) (map); Yuen Ren Chao, "Languages and Dialects in China," *Geographical Journal*, Vol. CII, No. 2 (August, 1943), 63-66 (map); Ghing Chieh Chang, "The Chinese in Latin America: A Preliminary Geographical Survey with Special Reference to Cuba and Jamaica" (Unpublished dissertation, University of Maryland, 1965), 41-44 (maps); Chen, *Emigrant Communities*, 23; Cator, *The Economic Position of the Chinese in the Netherlands Indies*, 28 (map).

The Hokkiens (the name is simply the pronunciation of "Fukien" in their own dialect[68]) inhabit the hinterland around the port of Amoy; and they went primarily to Thailand, Java, the Philippines, and the Malay Peninsula.[69] George W. Skinner, in his study of the Chinese in Thailand, suggests that since Canton was the only port legally open to foreign traders from the commencement of the Ch'ing Dynasty in 1644, Chinese merchants at Amoy, using their own junks, developed a clandestine trade with Southeast Asia, thus facilitating a movement of Hokkiens into the area. This would seem to be a plausible explanation for the fact that Chinese from Amoy, prior to the opening of the treaty ports in 1842, far outnumbered other dialect groups in Southeast Asia.[70] The Teochius, located in the Han River delta surrounding the port of Swatow in northern Kwangtung, went to Sumatra, Malaya, and Thailand.[71] The Cantonese, as the name suggests, occupied the Pearl River Delta around Canton. They immigrated wherever commercial opportunities were good and were found all over Southeast Asia. Cantonese also formed the vast majority of the Chinese who went to California, Australia, and Latin America.[72] The Hakkas are scattered all over southern China but are particularly numerous in an area that encompasses the southwest corner of Fukien, northern Kwangtung, eastern Kwangsi, and small portions of southern Kiangsi and Hunan. Like the Cantonese, they went to all parts of Southeast Asia, with large numbers settling in Borneo from the middle of the eighteenth century.[73] The Hainanese, inhabitants of the Island of Hainan off the coast of Kwangtung, immigrated principally to Thailand.[74]

Chinese from all five emigrant communities found their way to Latin America in the nineteenth century. Since Macau was the principal embarkation port for Peru and Cuba, and Hong Kong was the principal port for the British West Indies, Cantonese from the areas immediately behind these ports constituted the overwhelming majority of Chinese who went to Latin America from 1847-1875.

---

68   Skinner, *Chinese Society in Thailand*, 37.

69   Fitzgerald, *The Southern Expansion of the Chinese People*, 147.

70   Skinner, *Chinese Society in Thailand*, 40.

71   Fitzgerald, *The Southern Expansion of the Chinese People*, 147.

72   Kil Young Zo, "Chinese Emigration into the United States 1850-1880" (unpublished dissertation, Columbia University, 1971), 55; Chang, "The Chinese in Latin America," 41-43; Arthur Huck, *The Chinese in Australia* (Croydon: Victoria, Lugmans, Green and Company Limited, 1967), 17.

73   Fitzgerald, *The Southern Expansion of the Chinese People*, 147.

74   Skinner, *Chinese Society in Thailand*, 84, 86, 89-90.

However, in the early years of the "coolie trade," about 10,000 Hokkiens departed for Latin America from Amoy, and approximately 25,500 Teochius sailed thither from Swatow.[75] As far as it is known, no emigrant ships left from Amoy for Latin America after 1858 or from Swatow after 1860. Nevertheless, some Hokkiens and Teochius continued to go there, being brought in small groups to Macau whence they were transhipped to Cuba and Peru. Hakkas departed for South America from Amoy and Swatow as well as from Canton, Hong Kong, and Macau, but the total is not known. Undoubtedly, some Hainanese were also shipped from Macau, but the number would seem to be negligible. Approximately 1,200 sailed from Shanghai, with 355 going to French Guiana and the rest to Cuba.[76]

Recruiting Techniques

In the first half of the nineteenth century, when Western capitalists began to invest in tin mining as well as in sugar and spice plantations in Southeast Asia, Chinese merchants and labor contractors in Singapore, Penang, and Malacca sent their agents to China to recruit laborers. At first these agents were often returned emigrants who rounded up relatives and acquaintances from their native villages and clans.[77] As the demand for laborers increased, a class of professional recruiters appeared whose task it was to cajole peasants into emigrating. They received a "capitation fee" of one Spanish dollar per emigrant.[78] Since emigration was illegal, the vocation of professional recruiter, or crimp,[79] as he has been more commonly called, did not attract the better-

---

[75] See table 3.

[76] Ibid.

[77] James C. Jackson, "Chinese Agricultural Pioneering in Singapore and Jahore, 1800-1917," *Journal of the Malayan Branch of the Royal Asiatic Society*, vol. XXXVIII, no. 207 (July 1965), 94; "Report of the Committee Appointed to Consider and Take Evidence upon the Conditions of Chinese Laborers in the Colony," *Proceedings of the Legislative Council of the Straits Settlements*, Paper 22, ccxlii.

[78] "Notes on the Chinese of Pinang," *JIA*, series 1, vol. VIII (1854), 2; Mills, *British Rule in Eastern Asia*, 237-238; Victor Purcell, *The Chinese in Malaya* (London: Oxford University Press, 1948), 59; Barth, *Bitter Strength*, 53.

[79] The origin of the word is unknown, but it was commonly used in the nineteenth century and earlier to denote an "agent" who supplied soldiers and sailors by decoying, drugging, kidnapping or any other illegal means. See *The Encyclopedia Britannica*, 13th ed., 1926.

type citizen. In fact, crimps were generally an unprincipled lot, and abuses sprang up at the very heart of the system.[80] The British resident of Singapore wrote in 1827, "A communication must be made to the Governor of Macao to inform him that no Chinese shall be allowed to land from a Portuguese ship unless accompanied by a certificate that all passengers on such a ship voluntarily embarked on her."[81] Deceit and fraud had already crept into the emigration movement.

When the West first entered the China labor market in 1847, the "capitation fee" jumped to three dollars a head, which was more or less equivalent to a month's wages for the ordinary laborer in Kwangtung and Fukien.[82] This stimulated and expanded the crimping business. However, in the early 1850s, the recruiter's task was a relatively easy one, as thousands of refugees, uprooted by civil strife and fleeing the famine-plagued hinterland, crammed into the coastal cities. The recruiter rounded up many of these unfortunate people, holding out to them the free food and lodging that the emigration depot offered prospective candidates. Many had no idea of where they were going. They did not select any one country above another. The destination of the first ship seeking emigrants determined where they went, as the emigration broker sought to get them off his hands as quickly as possible.[83]

Walter Medhurst, British consul at Amoy, went on board an emigrant vessel at that port in 1848 and found the passengers to be "the most abject, loathsome wretches I ever saw. They were all beggars out of the streets and most of them had a villainous appearance."[84] Since skippers of emigrant vessels were only interested in young and healthy laborers, a medical examination supposedly eliminated the diseased, the aged, and the weak. An eyewitness

---

[80]   Bowring to Malmesbury, January 5, 1853 (BPP, ASS, *China*, vol. III), 99.

[81]   Eunice Thio, "The Singapore Chinese Protectorate: Events and Conditions Leading to Its Establishment, 1823-1873," *Journal of the South Seas Society*, vol. 16 (1960), 59. See also Wong Lin Ken, "The Trade of Singapore with China, 1819-69," *Journal of the Malayan Branch of the Royal Asiatic Society*, vol. 33, part IV (December 1960), 113.

[82]   Bowring to Malbesbury, January 5, 1853 (BPP, ASS, *China*, vol. III), 99.

[83]   *Friend of China*, December 25, 1852.

[84]   BPP, "Report from the Select Committee on Consular Service and Appointments; together with the Proceedings of the Committee and Minutes of Evidence," July 27, 1858, paragraph 1965.

described the scene as prospective emigrants at Amoy awaited the decision of the medical examiner:

> The care with which the poor fellows take to conceal any little physical defect that he thinks will prejudice him in the opinion of the medical man, who really holds in his hands the destiny, life and death of many of these unfortunate creatures . . . men of advanced years pick out their grey hairs and make themselves look as young as possible; boys try to appear [as] men . . . and no one is under 19 or over 33 according to their own account.[85]

These men had reached that stage of destitution in which they were ready to risk any degradation or hardship to save themselves from the pangs of starvation. Emigration afforded them immediate and tangible relief. They were assured of food, clothing, and shelter, as well as a small advance, which could provide their families with the basic necessities of life at least for a while. Most had come to the emigration depot as a last resort, and rejection often meant death.[86]

Local Chinese authorities, charged with enforcing the imperial ban on emigration were on the horns of a dilemma. Charles A. Winchester, British consul at Amoy in the 1850s, explained their predicament:

> The overpopulation of China in years of scarcity occasions great anxiety to the local authorities, and often leads to their disgrace; for any commotions which arise from famine are almost certainly attributed to their neglect or mismanagement. The mandarins know well that emigration relieves the pressure of surplus population on the supplies of food, and deport wild and lawless vagabonds, who are better off out of the country. The mandarins, therefore, dare not put a check on emigration; they see that it is not for the public interest of their districts to do so, not to speak of the pecuniary interest, which some way or another, Chinese officers always contrive to find in the continuance of a forbidden practice.[87]

---

[85] *Friend of China*, December 25, 1852.

[86] *Friend of China*, December 25, 1852, reported that in 1851 25 percent of the population of Amoy died of hunger and disease.

[87] "Note by Charles A. Winchester," August 26, 1852 (BPP, ASS, *China*, vol. III), 20.

Most local officials, at least initially, connived at emigration or looked the other way.[88] The conscientious were afraid to object openly to the breach of the law lest their action provoke a conflict with the Western powers whose merchants were deeply involved in the business and thus bring down on themselves the wrath of their superiors. Hence, emigration and crimping grew apace with the active or tacit approval of local government. William M. Cooper, acting British consul at Swatow, described the process as it developed at that port:

> Bad characters, discarded by their families, are seen by the officials and village elders on their way to the coolie house with a sense of relief and satisfaction, and not seldom is the coolie broker aided in his object of obtaining men by persons of this class and frequently by the relations of the men themselves. Thus the trade is allowed to take root with the concurrence of the heads of the people who not only rid themselves by means of it of a nuisance and a burden but make money by the transaction, and a connection is formed which the broker in his thirst for dollars, becoming gradually hardened and more ruthless is not slow to avail himself of in carrying out with greater boldness evil designs on his victims.[89]

The bad and the unwanted were often rejected as not meeting the required medical standard, and anyway, they were not unlimited in number. As the supply diminished, the "capitation fee" increased from $3 to $7 to $10, to $20, to $35, and in some instances reaching as high as $95[90]-$35

---

88   Martin R. Montgomery, *China: Political Commercial and Social, in an Official Report to Her Majesty's Government*, 2 vols. (London: James Madden, 1847), I, 79; Cooper to Alcock, October 20, 1866, Confidential Print, "Correspondence Respecting Chinese Emigration to British and French Colonies, 1865-1869" (BFO 881/744); Bowring to Malmesbury, August 3, 1852 (BFO 17/192); "Die Ausfuhrung der Chinesen durch Europuer eis Kulis nach Westindien und Sudamerika, und Auswanderung nach Californien und Australien," *Das Ausland*, vol. 30, no. 37 (September 11, 1857), 886.

89   Cooper to Alcock, October 20, 1866, *Confidential Print*, "Correspondence Respecting Chinese Emigration to British and French Colonies, 1865-1869 (BFO 881/744); See also the *Hong Kong Daily Press*, January 1, 1874.

90   Cooper to Alcock, October 20, 1866, *Confidential Print*, "Correspondence Respecting Chinese Emigration to British and French Colonies, 1865-1869," (BFO 881/744); Hillebrand, *Report on the Supply of Labor*, 5; Mayers, *The Treaty Ports of China and Japan*, 228; *Friend of China*, December 1, 1860.

approximated as year's wages for a laborer around Amoy and Swatow.[91] With such instant riches dangling before them, reckless and irresponsible crimps used every stratagem imaginable to obtain laborers. Persuasion gave way to deceit, fraud, and violence.

The principal method employed to allure men to the emigration ports was the promise of employment, or putting them in the way of learning a trade and thus gaining a decent livelihood.[92] In a densely populated country with millions struggling for survival, it is difficult to overestimate the attractiveness of such an offer. What made the bait so effective was that the crimps were usually kinsmen, friends, or acquaintances of the victim, who had no cause to mistrust them.[93]

A favorite pretense among crimps was to enlist men as "braves" (*yung*) or temporary soldiers for the imperial army.[94] Some were engaged as cooks and servants for the British and French troops stationed at Canton.[95] Others were offered odd jobs in warehouses or on ships in the ports of Amoy, Swatow, Canton, and Macau. When they arrived at these places, they were given a hard-luck story about the job not materializing. Being far from home and penniless, they accepted advances in food, clothing, and money, which they were unable to repay; hence, they became pawned to the creditor, who was one of the crimp's agents. The creditor put the squeeze on them for repayment, suggesting that they volunteer to emigrate, obtain the advance money, and pay their debts. At this point, it was often intimated to them that there were ways of escaping from emigration depots.[96] Reduced to desperate straits, many felt they had little option but to accept this way of paying their debts and trusted to their wits to get out of the obligations they undertook.

Another popular means of getting individuals into the clutches of the emigration broker was to offer them money to gamble at one of the licensed establishments of the port cities, where it was prearranged for them to lose, and consequently, they were "morally persuaded" to surrender their persons in payment, as it seems that the law of the land could be so construed that a man's body could be held as security for his debts.[97] Captain Gustave Gerlott,

---

[91] Bowring to Malmesbury, January 5, 1853 (BPP, ASS, *China*, vol. III), 99.

[92] *Overland China Mail*, May 26, 1871.

[93] Ibid.

[94] Mayers to Alcock, November 1, 1866 (BFO 17/873).

[95] *Friend of China*, December 8, 1860.

[96] MacDonnell to Herbert, June 22, 1872 (BFO 17/881).

[97] *North China Herald*, October 10, 1872. See also Edmond Plauchet, "La Traite des Culies a Macao," *Revue des Deux Mondes*, vol. CVI (1 Juillet, 1873), 184.

who was at one time a skipper of a "coolie ship," explained the system from his personal observation:

> Large hulks are moored in the harbors of Shanghai and Canton and fitted as gambling halls on the most extensive scale. Runners circulate through the city to draw the poor and unemployed—mostly of the lowest class. Once on board they watch with wonder at the vast sums exchanging hands. A crimp watches John Chinaman intently and when the proper time has arrived steps up to him with the inquiry: "Why don't you bet?" "I have no money or I would", is the answer. "Oh! That is nothing at all. I will stake you if you pay me back four times if you win. If you lose though you must hire as a coolie and let me get my money back." John is only too glad to take the chance and in a few minutes is in possession for the first time in his life of 5 or 6 dollars in copper cash. He plays and loses.[98]

A rather fruitful source of emigrants were the prisoners taken in clan wars, which raged from time to time, particularly in northern and western Kwangtung. The natives of Kwangtung were known as the Punti, and there was bitter animosity between them and the Hakka people who were relatively latecomers to the area. Though the two tribes lived side by side for centuries, they spoke separate dialects and almost never intermarried. Occasionally, the bitter feelings flared into bloody clashes. In the 1850s, when government forces were weakened by the Taiping Rebellion, the hatred flared up anew, this time taking on the aspect of an all-out war. The prisoners taken in battle, instead of losing their heads, were carried off and sold to crimps. In this way, the adult male population of entire villages found themselves on board emigrant vessels.[99]

---

[98]   *Hong Kong Mercury and Shipping Gazette*, July 16, 1866; See also "A Correct Statement of the Wicked Practice of Decoying and Kidnapping, Respectfully Laid before his Excellency," Enclosure in No. 1, Kennedy to Kimberly, June 7, 1872 (BPP, ASS, *China*, vol. 4), 313-316.

[99]   Mayers, *The Treaty Ports of China and Japan*, 22; Charles Carleton Coffin, *Our New Way Around the World* (London: Sampson, Low, Son and Marston, 1869), 288; John Scarth, *Twelve Years in China: The People, the Rebels, and the Mandarins* (Edinburgh: Thomas Constable and Company, 1860), 52; Hosea B. Morse, *The Trade and Administration of China* (Shanghai: Kelly and Walsh, 1921), 227.

Debt bondage, gambling, deceit, and fraud were the chief tools of the crimping business. To the foreign ship captain or foreign emigration agent, intent on obtaining a full complement of emigrants as quickly as possible, the "capitation fee" was the fastest and simplest means available. When a foreign vessel arrived at one of the embarkation ports, a head crimp or native emigration broker would enter into an agreement with the ship's agent or captain to deliver a set number of emigrants at a fixed price per head by a certain date. Failure to meet the deadline not only meant the loss of the "capitation fee" but also the loss of the considerable outlay in time and money in securing emigrants. The Chinese merchants at Hong Kong, in a statement to the governor of the colony, explained the insidious dynamics of the system:

> Directly he has entered into an agreement, he must not delay for a minute: he must hurry to the four points of the compass and invite laborers. If he is at all pressed for time, he must devise crafty schemes as numerous as trees in a wood. He either makes use of a stupefying drug, or practices deception or forcibly kidnaps. He puts into force every kind of evil device and repeats them without end. He is anxious to complete his number and close his responsibility. For this reason he conceives in his heart a plan for kidnapping. He is driven to it by the force of circumstances.[100]

To assist him in his enterprise and to insure himself against financial ruin, the head crimp usually engaged subordinate crimps under an agreement similar to that entered into with the foreigner. These in turn often engaged others, always of course, at lower rates per head. Thus vagabonds and idlers of all kinds were enlisted as crimps. In some districts, it became generally known that any person who took an emigrant to a certain place was handsomely remunerated. Many, finding themselves in financial straits, succumbed to the temptation to induce an acquaintance, a friend, and even members of their own families to fall into the head crimp's net. In 1859, soldiers of the governor-general of Kwangtung captured a number of native crafts engaged in crimping on the Pearl River in the vicinity of Canton. Of forty-one "emigrants" rescued, twenty-six testified that they were tricked by a kinsman

---

[100] "A Correct Statement of the Wicked Practice of Decoying and Kidnapping, Respectfully laid before his Excellency, Enclosure in No. 1, Kennedy to Kimberly, June 7, 1872 (BPP, ASS, *China*, vol. IV), 314.

or an old acquaintance into accompanying him to where they were sold to crimps.[101] The following depositions tell the story:

> Lih-chih deposes: I am aged 32 from Chieh-yang district. On the 2nd day of the 10th month I met, at Shih-lung, a acquaintance named Seen-a-te, who stated that a younger brother of his was a shopkeeper at Chang-chow, and he persuaded me to go thither to seek employment; I consented and went with him in a boat. On the 4th we reached Chang-chow, where Seen-a-te taking a sampan, put me on board a coolie vessel where I was kept in confinement. Before being sold, I was seized and set at liberty.[102]

> Chin-chang-shin (a kidnapper) states: I am 29 years of age, and belong to Pae-wei village in the district of Polo. My father is dead. My mother Chang-she is 57 years old. She had three sons of whom I am the eldest. I have neither wife nor child. Hitherto I have exercised the trade of pewterer at home. Through losing all my money at gambling, and knowing Tae-as-shin, a coolie broker, at Chang-chow, I, on the 29th of October, kidnapped my cousin Chin-ah-urh, who lived with me, to sell him, in order to get money to spend, by telling him that I had employment for him on board ship; thus getting him of his own accord to accompany me on board a Hwei-chow passage boat going to Canton. On the 31st, off Chang-chow, a small boat came alongside, pulled by Tae-ah-shin and took us two, Chin-ah-urh and myself, to a fishing boat, whence Tae-ah-shin took Chin-ah-urh for fifteen dollars, which he gave me. By chance the neighboring boat had a gambling table in it and there I gambled away all the fifteen dollars.[103]

Kidnapping would seem to have been used by the crimps as a last resort. It became common from the late 1850s onward when competition between rival foreign emigration agencies sent the "capitation fee" soaring to as high

---

[101] "Depositions of 41 Kidnapped Chinese," Inclosure 19 in No. 6, Bowring to Malmesbury, April 15, 1859 (BPP, ASS, *China*, vol. IV), 128-135. See also "Depositions of Kidnapped Coolies brought from Whampoa," Enclosure 26 in No. 13, (Ibid.), 202-233.

[102] Ibid., 134.

[103] Ibid., 136.

as $95 on occasions, and increased awareness and vigilance on the part of the people in general rendered other means unproductive. Kidnapping was not a new phenomenon to Chinese society. The abduction of the wealthy or their children for ransom was a common occurrence, and kidnapping male children for sale in Southeast Asia had been a recurring problem.[104] Even recruiting new members for secret societies often entailed the kidnap and forced initiation of the individual.[105] What was new was that adult males of all classes were being spirited away and sold to foreigners, never to be heard from again. British Consul Alcock reported from Canton in April 1859:

> When no man could leave his own house, even in public thoroughfares and open day, without a danger of being hustled under false pretences of debt or delinquency, and carried off a prisoner in the hands of crimps to be sold to the purveyors of coolies at so much a head and carried off to sea, never again to be heard of; the whole population of the city and adjoining districts were roused to a sense of common peril.[106]

To the man in the street, this was an intolerable situation, and suspected kidnappers were on occasion summarily executed on the spot by an aroused populace.[107] The authorities, moved by the demands of the people, decreed the death penalty for kidnappers.[108]

But kidnapping continued. The money was seemingly worth any risk. Hoe Teik, aged thirty-four years, formerly a hawker of cakes and sweetbreads at Amoy and a habitual opium smoker confessed, when caught, that he kidnapped 154 natives of Amoy during 1860 and received over $5,000. He received as much as $70 for a man after the execution of some kidnappers early in the year. Later, the price dropped to $35. He further confessed that there were altogether eighty kidnappers in the Amoy area. Being unrepentant of his crimes, he was crucified instead of the usual decapitation.[109]

---

[104] *Overland Friend of China*, April 25, 1857.

[105] Gustave Schlegel, *Thian Ti Hwui, The Hung League or Heaven-Earth League: A Secret Society in China and India* (Batavia, Lange and Company, 1866), 57.

[106] Alcock to Bowring, April 12, 1859 (BPP, ASS, *China*, Vol. IV), 105.

[107] Ibid.

[108] Robertson to Alcock, March, 1867 (BFO 17/874).

[109] *Friend of China*, December 1, 1860.

Native crimps like Hoe Teik took their victims to fast boats called lorchas (Western-sailing vessels with Chinese rigging), whence they were shipped in small batches directly to the emigrant vessels or to emigration depots at Macau.[110] Lorchas and sometimes junks, manned mostly by former pirates prowled the waters of the Canton delta and the rivers along the coasts of Fukien and Kwangtung, coaxing villagers to go aboard for "trade" or waylaying and carrying off unwary fishermen or people on the way home from market.[111] The French Emigration Company at Canton bought three Chinese war junks and, retaining the original official insignia, sailed up the rivers displaying a sign: "We engage Men for Meritorious Works."[112] When the Chinese authorities commenced capturing some of these crimping vessels, other means had to be found, and victims were transported in boats used to carry the dead. This worked for a time until officials felt that deaths were occurring much too frequently for their locality. One such boat was boarded and was found to contain an empty coffin and five kidnap victims stowed away under hatches.[113]

Although crimping in all its forms, including kidnapping, was carried on almost exclusively by native Chinese (Macau Portuguese were accused of manning some of the crimping boats[114]), foreigners provided the incentive with the "capitation fee," and ships under foreign flags carried the victims

---

[110] Hunt to Jones, February 22, 1869, *Confidential Print*, "Correspondence Respecting Chinese Emigration to British and French Colonies, 1865-1869," (BFO 881/744); Hillebrand, *Report on the Supply of Labor*, 3.

[111] Robertson to Wade, April 23, 1873 (BFO 17/882); *Hong Kong Mercury and Shipping Gazette*, October 23, 1866; *Hong Kong Daily Press*, August 9, 1865; Arthur Evans Moule, *Half a Century in China: Recollections and Observations* (London: Hodder and Stoughton, 1911), 101.

[112] *Hong Kong Mercury and Shipping Gazette*, June 4, 1866.

[113] *North China Herald*, September 14, 1872; *Hong Kong Times, Daily Advertiser and Shipping Gazette*, August 27, 1873.

[114] Frederick Well Williams, ed., "The Journal of Samuel Wells Williams," *Journal of the North China Branch of the Royal Asiatic Society*, Vol. XLII (1911), 231; *Hong Kong Mercury and Shipping Gazette*, July 16, 1866, October 23, 1866; *Hong Kong Daily Press*, August 9, 1865; Mayers, *The Treaty Ports of China and Japan*, 228; Robertson to Wade, April 23, 1873 (BFO 17/882), Hunt to Jones, February 22, 1869, *Confidential Print*, "Correspondence Respecting Chinese Emigration to British and French Colonies, 1865-1869," (BFO 881/744).

overseas. It was the unanimous conclusion of the consuls of Spain, France, Belgium, United States, and Oldenburg, stationed at Canton, that the payment of the "capitation fee" was the root cause of most of the abuses and evils of contract emigration.[115] That foreigners were ignorant of the abuses perpetrated on their behalf by the crimps is extremely unlikely. However, most foreigners felt that crimps were indispensable. Crimping had become the traditional way of obtaining emigrants along China's southern coast, and without the crimp, it was believed that few emigrants could be obtained.[116] The *Friend of China* philosophized, "If soldiers cannot be induced to enlist without the rhetoric of the recruiting sergeant, neither can we expect such stay at homes as the Chinese to go abroad without the persuasion of the native agent."[117]

The assumption that crimping was the only means of obtaining emigrants was shown to be false by John Gardiner Austin, the British emigration agent in China from 1858-1862. Austin, formerly immigration agent-general of British Guiana, initiated a radical change in the method of collecting emigrants on the China coast. He completely abandoned the "capitation fee" and the system of recruitment by native agents. In their place, he established an emigration house under the joint supervision of British and Chinese authorities. People wishing to immigrate to the British West Indies were required to apply in person, and candidates were free to come and go as they pleased. He posted notices to this effect throughout the countryside. However, he first obtained the cooperation of the Chinese provincial authorities, some of the leading gentry, and the Allied commanders, who were then in occupation of Canton.[118] Governor-general Laou of Kwangtung issued a proclamation making it known to the people that Mr. Austin's scheme had the approval of the provincial government and even sent officials into the villages of the interior to explain

---

[115] Consuls at Canton to the Allied Commanders, February 11, 1860 (BFO 97/102B). See also Antonio Sergio de Sousa a Ministro e Secretario d'Estado dos Negocios da Marinha e Ultramar, Agosto 31, 1868 (AHU, Pasta 25).

[116] *Hong Kong Daily Press*, January 1, 1874.

[117] *The Friend of China*, March 9, 1861.

[118] Cecil Clementi, *The Chinese in British Guiana* (Guiana: Argosy Company, 1915), chapter VI, 74-140; Persia Crawford Campbell, *Chinese Coolie Emigration to Countries within the British Empire* (New York: Negro Universities Press, 1969, first published in 1923), 121-125; Stanley Lane-Poole, *Sir Harry Parkes in China* (London: Methuen and Company, 1901), 193.

the system to the local elders and gentry.[119] Austin also enlisted the help of local missionaries, principally Rev. William Lobscheid and Rev. James Jones, who had many years' experience working with the Chinese in the interior and played key roles in breaking down local prejudices against emigration.[120] During the years 1859-1866, under the system set up by Mr. Austin, 9,987 Chinese under a five-year contract left their homeland for the British West Indies.[121] Though this could scarcely have been accomplished without the active cooperation of local Chinese officials, it successfully demonstrated that native agents were not indispensable. Austin also destroyed another myth about Chinese emigration by successfully introducing family emigration and the emigration of women.

Recruiting Female Emigrants

> So intensely strong and so universal is the sentiment
> that no female with any sense of propriety or
> modesty could consent to quit her native home, that
> it would be impossible to induce any but women of
> low and lost character to emigrate.
>
> Sir John Bowring to Earl of Malmesbury,
> October 1, 1852 (BPP, ASS, *China*, vol. 3), 33.

In traditional Chinese society, the place of woman was in the home, where she was expected to strive to attain the Confucian ideal of "helpful wife and wise mother."[122] In the home, she ruled supreme. She was called

---

[119] For a full text of the Proclamation in English see Parkes to Hammond, November 13, 1859, Inclosure 9 in No. 6 (BPP, ASS, *China*, Vol. IV), 120-121.

[120] Clementi, *The Chinese in British Guiana*, 80-81; William Lobscheid, *Chinese Emigration to the West Indies, A Trip through British Guiana Undertaken for the Purpose of Ascertaining the Condition of the Chinese who have Emigrated under Government Contract with Supplementary Papers Relating to Contract Labor and the Slave Trade* (Demerara, "Royal Gazette," 1866), 2.

[121] Campbell, *Chinese Coolie Emigration*, 130.

[122] Olga Lang, *Chinese Family and Society* (New Haven, Yale University Press, 1946), 42-53; Christopher Lucas, *Women in China* (Hong Kong, Dragonfly Books, 1965), 29.

nei-jen or "inside person,"[123] while her husband attended to business matters and everything outside the home. Woman's principal function in society was to produce male progeny, which was essential if ceremonies honoring ancestors were to be continued.[124] This sacred obligation could only be performed satisfactorily by males. Hence society accorded to motherhood, and particularly to mothers bearing male offspring, a special status of honor.

Stanford Lyman, in his essay "Overseas Chinese in America and Indonesia," argues that "wives were in effect the property of the lineage more than they were the helpmates of their husbands."[125] The role of women was so bound up with the extended family or clan that they seldom left their own village even when their husbands migrated elsewhere.[126] The cultural bias against emigration was seemingly much more stringent on women than on men. Partly because of this, as well as for pecuniary considerations already mentioned, local officials strictly enforced the law prohibiting emigration when it came to women.

It is not surprising then that few females went overseas. Chinese immigrating to Southeast Asia rarely took their families with them. As far as it is known, no Chinese women had come to Singapore up to 1837.[127] In the second decade of the nineteenth century, when over 1,000 Chinese were arriving annually at Batavia, Thomas Stamford Raffles, lieutenant governor of the territory, wrote, "There were no women on Java who came directly from China".[128] Few Chinese women even migrated to Hong Kong. In 1844,

---

[123] Isaac Taylor Headland, *Home Life in China* (London, Methuen and Company Limited, 1914), 92.

[124] Kenneth Scott Latourette, *The Chinese: Their History and Culture* (New York, The Macmillan Company, 1941), 196.

[125] Stanford Lyman, "Overseas Chinese in America and Indonesia," *Pacific Affairs*, Vol. XXXIV, No. 4 (Winter, 1961-62), 386.

[126] "Memorandum Respecting Chinese Emigration to the West Indies," September 1, 1843 (CO 318/160); "General Remarks on Chinese Emigration," September, 1852 (BPP, ASS, *China*, Vol. III), 39; Nai-tsiu Hu, "Internal Chinese Migration," *Agrarian China* (Secretariat of the Institute of Pacific Relations, London, 1939), 256.

[127] Charles B. Buckley, *An Anecdotal History of Old Times in Singapore* (Kuala Lampur, University of Malaya Press, 1965), 320.

[128] Thomas Stamford Raffles, *The History of Java*, 2 vols. (London, Black, Parbury and Allen, 1817), I, 74. See also C. E. Wurtzburg, *Raffles of the Easter Isles* (London, Hodder and Stroughton, 1954), 140.

the Chinese population of the island was 19,000, and of that number, not more than 1,000 were women and children.[129] Records of the Philippine government show 193 Chinese women in the Philippines in 1870 in a Chinese population of 23,000. In 1880, the Chinese male population had jumped to 66,000, but the number of females remained virtually the same at 194, or three females per 1,000 males.[130] As late as 1911, there were only 204 women to every 1,000 men among the Chinese population of Malacca.[131]

This dearth of Chinese women in overseas Chinese communities led to the importation of females from China for purposes of prostitution.[132] This practice would seem to have been carried on under the auspices of Chinese secret societies in Southeast Asia, but so little is known about it that it is difficult to say how extensive or widespread it was. In 1863, a Chinese secret society in Singapore was reported to have requested 500 girls from China, aged thirteen to sixteen years. Their market price in Singapore was from $100 to $400 each.[133] However, given the small number of Chinese women in overseas communities, their involvement in prostitution must have been quite limited.

Western observers, commenting on Chinese society around the middle of the nineteenth century, were seemingly in agreement that female infanticide and the sale of young girls were quite prevalent, at least along China's southern coast.[134] Though mothers were highly esteemed in China, female children were generally regarded as much less valuable than males. The social convention

---

[129] Martin R. Montgomery, *Reports, Minutes and Despatches on the British Position and Prospects in China* (London, Harrison and Company, 1846), 12.

[130] Edgar Wickberg, *The Chinese in Philippine Life, 1850-1898* (New Haven, Yale University Press, 1965), 174.

[131] Kernial Singh Sandhu, "Chinese Colonization of Malacca: A Study of Population Change, 1500 to 1957 AD," *Malayan Journal of Tropical Geography*, Vol. XV, 9.

[132] *Ibid.*; Vaughan, *Manners and Customs of the Chinese in the Straits Settlements*, 9.

[133] L. F. Comber, *Chinese Secret Societies in Malaya: A Survey of the Triad Society from 1800 to 1900* (Singapore, Donald Moore, 1959), 95. See also Wilford Blythe, *The Impact of Chinese Secret Societies in Malaya* (London, Oxford University Press, 1969), 204.

[134] Williams, *The Middle Kingdom*, I, 136, II, 239-241; Charles Gutzlaff, *Journal of Three Voyages along the Coast of China in 1831, 1832 and 1833* (London, Frederick Westley and AH Davis, 1834), 174-175; Scarth, *Twelve Years in China*, 102-103; White to Barkly, June 21, 1851 (BPP, ASS, *China*, Vol. III), 198; MacDonnell to Alcock, August 3, 1869 (BFO 17/877).

of binding women's feet rendered most women incapable of working in the fields or contributing to the family's prosperity.[135] The birth of a girl was held to be a misfortune, particularly in times of economic hardship, and not infrequently, they were allowed to die; or as they grew up, they were given as second wives or concubines for a remuneration. In most instances, this was not a cold-blooded sale, but rather an arrangement whereby parents were relieved of an economic burden, and the girl's future was secure.

This practice led some Westerners to believe that female emigrants could be obtained for a price. James T. White, who was sent by the British government to China in 1851 to investigate the possibility of obtaining Chinese laborers for the British West Indies, advised his superiors that

> Domestic female slavery is universal throughout China and girls are purchased at prices varying from $10 to $60 dollars, or even upwards, according to their age and supposed intelligence . . . poor people will, as a matter of course, sell their girls to families where they will be taken care of . . . If, therefore it be an object to obtain women and families, a bonus must be given for them, and by this means only can the difficulty (of female emigration) be overcome.[136]

White proposed that advances of from twenty to thirty dollars be made to male emigrants on condition that they obtain women and marry them prior

---

[135] Footbinding was almost universal, but the Hakka people, the boat population of the coast, as well as the very poor did not conform to the custom. Lin Yutang, born and educated in China, traces the custom to the T'ang dynasty and suggests that it was a by-product of male chauvinism: "The small feet of Chinese women are not only pleasing in men's eyes but in a strange and subtle way they influence the whole carriage and walking gait of women, throwing the hips backward, somewhat like the modern high-heeled shoes, and effecting an extremely gingerly gait, the body 'shimmering' all over and ready to fall at the slightest touch. Looking at a woman with bound feet walking is like looking at a rope dancer, tantalizing to the highest degree. The bound foot is indeed the highest sophistication of the Chinese sensual imagination." Lin Yutang, *My Country and My People* (New York, John Day, 1935), 167. See also Howard S. Levy, *Chinese Foot-binding: The History of a Curious Erotic Custom* (New York, Walton Rawls, 1966).

[136] White to Barkly, June 21, 1851 (BPP, ASS, *China*, Vol. III), 198.

to their departure for the British colonies.[137] Sir John Bowring, governor of Hong Kong, and Charles A. Winchester, British vice consul at Amoy, warning that such a scheme could only result in the "wholesale purchase and shipment of prostitutes," vehemently rejected the idea.[138] Others saw some merit in the proposal. William Cane, lieutenant-governor of Hong Kong, suggested that since many of these women were sold into prostitution in China as children, they would welcome an opportunity to escape from their bondage and might well become grateful and virtuous wives.[139] The Emigration Commissioners in London agreed with Caine and supported the proposal.[140] The Earl of Clarendon, however, viewed the matter with some alarm, regarding it as establishing a slave market in Chinese women under the official protection of the British government.[141] The plan was consequently dropped, but was revived in modified form some years later.

The first evidence of a traffic in Chinese women to Western nations surfaced as an advertisement in the Cuban newspaper *Diario de la Habana* of June 12, 1847, which read,

> For sale: A Chinese girl with two daughters, one of 12-13 years and the other of 5-6, useful for whatever you may desire. Also one mule.[142]

Sir George Bonham, governor of Hong Kong, reported in 1854 that half a dozen Chinese women returned to that colony from San Francisco and by brandishing large sums of money "induced 30 or 40 other young girls to accompany them back to California."[143]

The Spanish government in Madrid, concerned over the exclusively male character of Chinese immigration to Cuba, issued a royal decree in September, 1855, authorizing Rafael Rodriguez Torices to bring 10,000 Chinese to Cuba

---

[137] White to Barkly, June 19, 1851 (*Ibid.*), 203; White to Emigration Commissioners, December 10, 1853, (*Ibid.*), 327.

[138] Emigration Commissioners to Merivale, July 27, 1853, 321; Bowring to Clarendon, June 5, 1854 (*Ibid.*), 348.

[139] Caine to the Duke of Newcastle, June 5, 1854 (*Ibid.*), 52-53.

[140] Emigration Commissioners to Merivale, May 2, 1854 (*Ibid.*), 335-336.

[141] Newcastle to the Governor's of Jamaica, British Guiana, Trinidad and Mauritius, June 12, 1854 (BFO 881/744).

[142] Powers, "Chinese Coolie Migration to Cuba," 90.

[143] Bonham to Hammond, July 4, 1854 (BPP, ASS, *China*, Vol. III), 341.

with the stipulation that one-sixth must be women.[144] In anticipation of the decree, Antonio Martinez, a Macau-Portuguese, purchased female children at Ningpo and Shanghai in March 1855. He was in the process of shipping 44 of them to Macau in the English merchant vessel *Inglewood*, when the British captain, Richard Burton, and some of the crew came down with fever. The ship put in at Amoy. The stench from the children's cabin was such that some of the sailors, fearing for the lives of the children, reported the situation to the British consul. The children were removed and placed in the charge of the local Chinese authorities. Depositions taken from the crew revealed that the children were purchased at $3 to $8 dollars each, and that Martinez boasted that he would make a profit of $1,600 when they were delivered at Macau. They were supposedly destined for Cuba. All 44 of them were placed in a small cabin on board the *Inglewood* that measured eighteen feet by nine feet, and five feet ten inches between decks. The oldest among them was eight years of age. When removed from the ship, they were in a most filthy state with vermin and ugly sores all over their bodies.[145] The captain of the *Inglewood* was subsequently fined, and Macau authorities convicted two Portuguese of complicity in the horrible affair.[146]

The Hong Kong *Daily Press* reported that a 250-ton bark left Swatow in 1858 with "upwards of 300 China girls" bound for Cuba. The ship put in at the Cape of Good Hope in distress with many of the crew sick and a number of deaths among the passengers.[147] That was the last that was heard of her. As far as it is known, she never arrived in Cuba.

According to the official newspaper of the Portuguese colony of Macau, *O Boletim da Provincia de Macau e Timor*, most emigrant vessels departing for Cuba and Peru from 1871 to 1874 carried an average of half a dozen "menores Chinas," or minors. In three instances, the minors were designated as girls. Two ships bound for Peru in 1871 had two female children each on board, and in the following year, a ship bound for Cuba also had two girls among its passengers. Whether the remaining 274 minors were all boys, it is impossible to say. As far as can be ascertained, these young people were sold in Cuba and

---

[144]   Powers, "Chinese Coolie Migration to Cuba," 131-132.

[145]   For the depositions of the crew see Woodgate to Hammond, March 14, 1855, Inclosures 1-22 (BPP, ASS, *China*, Vol. III), 395-411.

[146]   Guimarães to Bowring, April 3, 1856 (BFO 97/102A).

[147]   Quoted in "The Chinese Coolie Trade," *The Anti-Slavery Reporter*, Vol. VII, No. 6 (June 1, 1859), 143-144.

Peru as domestic servants.[148] That the practice of conveying minors to the Americas existed prior to 1871 is evident from a letter of Captain Gerlott of the Peruvian emigrant vessel *Compañía Marítima del Perú, No. 1*, in which he relates how two small girls he took to Peru in 1865 sold in Callao for $800 each.[149] The price would indicate that something other than domestic work was being planned for them.

The total number of females taken to Cuba and Peru during the period of the "coolie trade" cannot have been very great. Paul Leroy-Beaulieu in his study *De La Colonisation Chez les Peuples Modernes* cites a report of the Spanish senate, dated July 1884, where it was stated that a total of 70,000 Chinese, including 1,000 Chinese women, were brought to Cuba.[150] Since the actual number of Chinese emigrants was double that amount, the accurateness of the figure on women is highly questionable. The Cuban census of 1861 put the total Chinese population of the island at 34,834, of whom 57 were women.[151] The census of 1899 lists 49 Chinese women in a total Chinese population of 14,863.[152] These low figures correspond with a report of British Consul General Crawford in September 1868, which stated that out of a total of 101,597 Chinese imported into Cuba up to that date, only 60 were females.[153] This writer has come across no estimate of the number of Chinese women taken to Peru.

Attempts to import Chinese women into the British West Indies were somewhat more successful. When Chinese immigration to the British colonies resumed in 1859, after a lapse of five years, the Duke of Newcastle strongly urged that at least 10 percent of the emigrants be women.[154] Working closely

---

[148] *O Boletim da Provincia de Macau e Timor*, November 1, 1873. This newspaper was published weekly under various titles: *O Boletim da Provincia de Macao, Timor e Solor; O Boletim do Governo de Macao; O Boletim da Provincia de Macau e Timor*. Hereafter it will be cited simply as *O Boletim*. See also the *Daily Advertiser and Shipping Gazette*, July 17, 1872.

[149] *The Hong Kong Mercury and Shipping Gazette*, July 24, 1866.

[150] Paul Leroy-Beaulieu, *De la Colonisation Chez les Peuples Modernes* (Paris, Librairie Guillaumin et Cie, 1886), 257.

[151] United States War Department, *Report on the Census of Cuba, 1899* (Washington, Government Printing Office, 1900), 71.

[152] *Ibid.*, 220.

[153] Crawford to the Foreign Office, September 5, 1868 (BFO 17/880).

[154] Walpole to Austin, August 15, 1859 (BCO 386/135).

with Chinese officials, local gentry, and Western missionaries, the British emigration agent in China, J. Gardiner Austin, surprised the critics by exceeding the stipulated minimum. In the years from 1859 to 1874, out of a total of 15,054 Chinese emigrants to the British West Indies, 2,500 were women, a handsome 16.61 percent. The following table gives the annual figures on female emigration and where they went:

Table 1
Chinese Female Immigration to British Possessions

Year	Total Chinese Emigration	Females	Percentage of Females
BRITISH GUIANA			
1859	761	0	0
1860	1,966	331	16.80
1861	3,501	405	14.40
1862	2,690	515	19.14
1863	413	104	25.18
1864	515	160	31.07
1865	1,768	418	23.64
1866	789	35	4.39
1874	*388*	*45*	*11.60*
Totals	12,800	2,122	16.58
TRINIDAD			
1862	550	174	31.64
1865	612	182	29.74
1866	*612*	*6*	*.98*
Totals	1,774	362	20.40
BRITISH HONDURAS			
1866	480	16	3.33
Grand Totals	15,054	2,500	16.61

Sources: Clementi, *The Chinese in British Guiana*, Tables, ii, iii; "General Report of Emigration Commissioners," 1861-1866 (BPP, *Emigration*, Vols. XIV, XV and XVI).

The secret to Austin's success lay in the active cooperation of Chinese officials and gentry, who approved of his scheme for voluntary emigration, regarding it as an honest attempt to do away with the evils of crimping.[155] This stamp of approval from local Chinese leaders helped to break down some of the traditions and prejudices against women going overseas, and lifted the fear of official retaliation against family or clan for allowing female members to emigrate. Success in the actual recruitment of women, however, would seem to have been due principally to the efforts of Reverend William Lobscheid, who recruited families from among his converts to Christianity and in at least one instance arranged for an entire Hakka village, which had its crops destroyed in a feud with a neighboring village, to immigrate to British Guiana.[156]

There was at least one other key factor contributing to the British success in recruiting women. According to Thomas Sampson, who became the British emigration agent after Austin returned to England in 1862, clan and village fueds in the 1850s and the early 1860s left large numbers of women destitute widows. These women constituted the primary source from which "wives" were obtained for men who wished to cash in on the $20 gratuity given to emigrants taking their wives with them.[157] The *Friend of China* reported in 1861 that some of these women were tricked into volunteering to go to the West Indies,[158] but flagrant abuses would seem to have been minimal. As the feuds decreased during the 1860s, this major source of female emigrants gradually dried up, and as reflected in tables 1 and 2, it became increasingly difficult to obtain women of any kind.[159]

The Reverend William Lobscheid was also instrumental in obtaining Chinese female emigrants for the Dutch possession of Surinam,[160] and a small number of Chinese women went to the French possession of Martinique.

---

[155]   Parkes to Straubenzee, November 1, 1859 (BPP, ASS, *China*, Vol. IV), 117.

[156]   Clementi, *The Chinese in British Guiana*, 76-82, 100; "Twentieth General Report of Emigration Commissioners, 1860," (BPP, *Emigration*, Vol. XIV), 52; Eitel, *Europe in China: The History of Hong Kong*, 273.

[157]   *The Hong Kong Daily Press*, July 17, 1873; Clementi, *The Chinese in British Guiana*, 78, 191; "Public Notice," Canton, November 5, 1859 (BPP, ASS, *China*, Vol. IV), 125.

[158]   *The Friend of China*, April 13, 1861.

[159]   *Hong Kong Daily Press*, July 17, 1873.

[160]   Hillebrand, *Report on the Supply of Labor*, 14.

Table 2
Chinese Female Immigration to Dutch and French Possessions

SURINAM			
Year	Total Chinese Immigration	Females	Percentage of Females
1865	493	120	24.34
1866	325	203	24.61
1867	291	9	3.09
1868	252	3	1.19
1869	*500*	*11*	*2.20*
Totals	2,361	346	14.65
MARTINIQUE			
1859	426	38	8.92

Sources: *Hong Kong Government Gazette*, Vol. XIII, March 9, 1867; Vol. XIV, March 7, 1868; Vol. XX, March 20, 1869.

A recorded total of 2,952 Chinese women out of a total of 251,809 Chinese emigrants came to the Caribbean and South America from 1849 to 1874. That was a mere 1.17 percent, or approximately 1 female to every 100 males. However, the vast majority, or 2,884, was concentrated in the European colonies, with only 62 known to have gone to Cuba and six to Peru. This enormous disparity between the sexes was not only a major hardship to the Chinese male in Latin America, but the aberrations deriving from it were used by some to depict the Chinese as an immoral people, unsuitable and unworthy of assimilation into Western civilization.

CHAPTER III

THE PORTS OF DEPARTURE

In the Footsteps of the Opium Trade

The opium stations, dotted along China's southern coast, were early adopted as convenient places for the shipment of Chinese emigrants to the western world. Opium had been known and used in China for centuries, mostly as medicine. The habit of mixing it with tobacco and smoking it originated in the Dutch East Indies and was introduced into China around the beginning of the seventeenth century.[1] Alarmed at the reports of the ill effects of the drug, Emperor Yung-cheng issued an edict in 1729 prohibiting its importation.[2] But the people had grown to like it and a contraband trade developed.

Well-armed British and American ships, loaded with opium, anchored a short distance from shore and Chinese fast boats ferried it secretly inland. Proclamations, penalties, and executions failed to stamp out the traffic. By the first decades of the nineteenth century, Indian and Turkish opium more than paid for the tea and silk of China that was so much sought after by the West.[3]

The "receiving ships," as the floating warehouses of opium were called, initially anchored at Whampoa, the outer deep water port of Canton. From time to time, there was some trading at the Portuguese enclave of Macau, but in 1822, Lintin island at the mouth of the Pearl River estuary became the principal

---

[1]   Hsin-pao Chang, *Commissioner Lin and the Opium War* (Cambridge, Mass., Harvard University Press, 1964), 16.

[2]   *Ibid.*, 17.

[3]   Michael Greenberg, *British Trade and the Opening of China, 1800-42* (Cambridge, Cambridge University Press, 1951), 9-14; A. J. Sargent, *Anglo Chinese Commerce and Diplomacy* (Oxford, The Clarendon Press, 1907), 53-57; Charles C. Steele, "American Trade in Opium to China, Prior to 1820," *Pacific Historical Review*, Vol. IX, No. 4 (December 1940), 425-444.

opium depot for the Canton area.[4] Cumsingmoon, a sheltered harbor lying across from Lintin island, became a refuge for opium ships in bad weather or when they were in need of repair.[5] Among some of the other opium depots scattered along China's tattered coastline were Namoa island at the mouth of the Han River adjacent to Swatow; Wusung, the outer port of Shanghai on the Yangtze River; and the British possession of Hong Kong (see map 2).[6]

Through handsome bribes to local officials, a system of connivance and noninterference by Chinese authorities had become the established pattern at these depots. It was natural then that Western merchants interested in developing yet another illegal and lucrative trade on the China coast would gravitate to these sanctuaries.

The initial shipments of Chinese emigrants that sailed from Amoy for Cuba in 1847 were experimental. The voyages were deemed successful. Two years later, 75 emigrants left Cumsingmoon for Peru, and in 1850, over 1,600 followed them. Cumsingmoon was more of an anchorage than a port. It had sprung into existence in the early 1840s when opium ships began to frequent its sheltered harbor. By 1847 it had a population of from 3,000 to 4,000 composed mainly of petty traders, boat people, and pirates.[7] There being no duly constituted authority, irregularities of all kinds flourished.[8] Three of the six ships that departed from there in 1850 with emigrants for Peru experienced mutinies with serious loss of life.[9] This beginning augured ill for the future of Chinese immigration to Latin America. In subsequent years, the traffic in emigrants returned to Amoy and spread to Canton, Swatow, Hong Kong, and Macau. Crime and irregularities accompanied it wherever it went.

The Port of Amoy

Public attention was first drawn to the problems besetting emigration from China to the Western world by a disturbance at Amoy in 1852. Amoy, an

---

[4]   C. Toogood Downing, *The Fan-Qui in China in 1836-7*, 3 vols. (London, Henry Colburn, 1838), III, 167.

[5]   *Ibid.*, I, 50.

[6]   For a full list of opium stations see *The Friend of China*, March 6, 1868.

[7]   "Report from the Select Committee on Commercial Relations with China," (BPP, ASS, *China*, Vol. XXXVIII), 159.

[8]   Bowring to Malmesbury, January 5, 1853 (BPP, ASS, *China*, Vol. III), 97.

[9]   See Table 17.

island about ten miles in diameter, lies in the wide and spacious estuary on the coast of southern Fukien. A narrow channel separates it from the mainland. A few miles inland lay the provincial capital of Chang-chow and beyond that stretched the densely populated black tea and sugar country of the province of Fukien (map 3). Amoy was at this time the principal emigration center for Southeast Asia, and Western ships had been involved in that traffic even prior to the opening of the port to foreign trade by the Treaty of Nanking in 1842. Opium smugglers also frequented the port, and there were said to be over six hundred opium dens on the island.[10]

In the early 1850s, Amoy had a population of about 250,000, and it was estimated that the surrounding neighborhood could easily provide 50,000 emigrants annually.[11] Between 1845 and August of 1852, 5,715 emigrants left the area for places other than Southeast Asia: 2,666 went to Australia, 990 to Havana, 469 to British Guiana, 420 to Peru, 380 to the French island of Bourbon, 380 to Hawaii, and 410 to California.[12] Two British firms—Messrs. Syme, Muir and Company, and Tait and Company—handled most of this traffic. Syme, Muir and Company had erected a large shed next to the customhouse to accommodate emigrants awaiting shipment. This structure and others like it were known as barracoons,[13] a term borrowed from the African slave trade where it connoted an enclosure or barracks for the temporary confinement of slaves. On the China coast, the operation of the barracoons was usually distinct from the shipping end of the emigration business. Emigrants were collected in these buildings by speculators with the help of crimps and were sold to shipping companies or captains of vessels at so much per head, the price varying with the amount of competition.[14] The governor of Hong Kong described the procedure:

---

[10]   Islay Burns, *Memoir of the Reverend William C. Burns, MA, Missionary to China from the English Presbyterian Church* (London, James Nisbet and Company, 1870), 378; Tong, *United States Diplomacy in China 1844-60*, 61; Hunter, *The Fan-kwae at Canton*, 66.

[11]   "Journal of Occurrences," *Chinese Repository* Vol. XVI, No. 4 April, 1847), 208; Burns, *Memoir of the Reverend William C. Burns*, 378.

[12]   Bowring to Malmesbury, Inclosure 3, September 25, 1853 (BPP, ASS, *China*, Vol. III), 19-20.

[13]   The word would seem to be a corruption of the Portuguese *barracão* or the Spanish *barracón*, augmentative of *barraca*, which means a small cabin or hut.

[14]   Mayers to Alcock, November 1, 1866 (BFO 17/873).

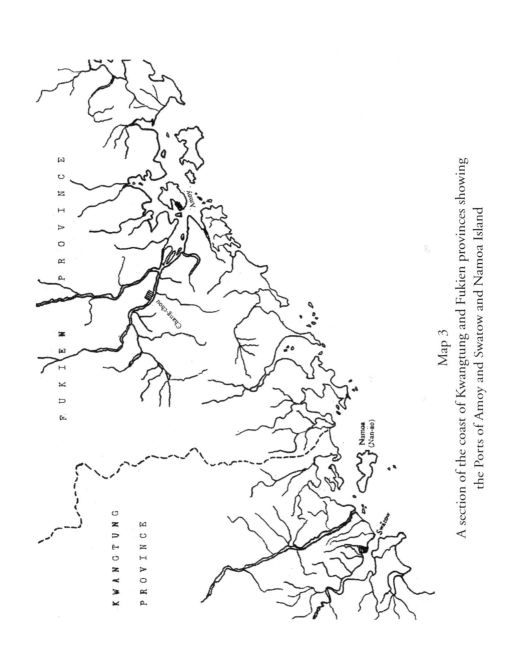

Map 3

A section of the coast of Kwangtung and Fukien provinces showing
the Ports of Amoy and Swatow and Namoa Island

I have myself seen the arrangement for the shipment of coolies at Amoy: hundreds of them gathered together in barracoons, stripped naked, and stamped or painted with the letter C (California), P (Peru), or S (Sandwich Islands), on their breasts, according to the destination for which they were intended.[15]

Figure 1. The Port of Amoy Circa 1870 (Taken from *Le Tour du Monde*, Vol XXIX, 1875,412)

Instead of erecting a shed, Tait and Company, after the manner of the opium trade, used a ship, the *Emigrant*, as a floating depot.[16] This had the advantage of attracting little public attention, and it was much easier to prevent emigrants from escaping once they had signed their contract.

During the 1852 emigration season, the emigration agent for Cuba made it known that he needed 8,000 emigrants.[17] This sudden demand increased the activity of the crimps who perpetrated numerous frauds in rounding up prospective recruits. The local population became alarmed. Placards, a common form of social protest, appeared decrying "pig-dealing," or the selling of people to foreigners.[18] A crimp in the employ of Syme, Muir and

---

[15]   Bowring to Malmesbury, August 3, 1853 (BPP, ASS, *China*, Vol. III), 14.

[16]   Bowring to Malmesbury, February 7, 1853 (BPP, ASS, *China*, Vol. III), 113.

[17]   Borwing to Malmesbury, October 1, 1852 (*Ibid.*), 29, 89; Newcastle to Barkly, January 31, 1853, Sub-enclosure to Enclosure 3 (*Ibid.*), 224.

[18]   According to Samuel Wells Williams the Cantonese called contract-emigrants "Chu-tsai", literally pigs, "after the mode of catching and carrying pigs in

Company was apprehended by the local authorities in November, 1852, and was accused of abducting unwilling emigrants. Francis D. Syme of Syme, Muir and Company and his clerk, William A. Cornabé forcibly "rescued" their employee from the local police station. When the people learned of this, they were aroused to an ugly anger. In the ensuing demonstrations two British subjects were assaulted, one being seriously wounded. To protect British lives and property, a party of marines were despatched from Her Majesty's man-of-war, the *Salamander*, which was lying offshore. The animosity of the people was directed principally against the barracoon and they were intent on destroying it. They stormed the building a number of times pelting the soldiers guarding it with stones, and only dispersed after the soldiers opened fire upon them killing eleven or twelve and wounding between twelve and sixteen.

In a formal investigation of the disturbance that heard evidence from the entire British mercantile community as well as from missionaries and several Chinese witnesses, it was conclusively shown that the hostile actions of the people were due to the abuses surrounding emigration, "which have been the natural result of the recklessness and cupidity of shippers, and the employment of rascally emigration brokers."[19]

In the wake of the disturbance, numerous proclamations appeared throughout the city, setting forth the determination of the people to stamp out abuses. A proclamation issued by the "Inhabitants of the Eighteen Wards," declared that anybody found transacting business with the hongs of Syme, Muir and Company and Tait and Company would be put to death, and that crimps caught deluding innocent people to emigrate would not be handed over to the authorities but would be killed on the spot.[20] In such an atmosphere, local authorities could not risk countenancing continued immigration to the West, particularly the operations of the abovementioned British firms. Furthermore, the abuses of emigration posed a serious threat to legitimate commerce. Dr. John Bowring wrote to the Earl of Malmesbury,

---

baskets," See *The Chinese Commercial Guide* (Hong Kong, A. Shortrede and Company, 1863), 224.

[19] The minutes of the investigation and the depositions taken from those examined are to be found in BPP, ASS, *China*, Vol. III, 49-95.

[20] *Ibid.*, 84. For a proclamation issued by the "Scholars and Merchants of Amoy," see U.S. House, Ex. Doc. No. 105, 34 Cong. Sess. 1.

Nothing could be more fatal to our interests and prospects in China, than that the shipment of emigrants should be connected with breaches of the public tranquility, that it should make foreigners odious to the Chinese people, and interference with that growing disposition to friendly intercourse which was so remarkable at Amoy and its neighborhood, and was producing such an extension of our commercial relations until interrupted by the irregularities which have had their origin in the cupidity of the collectors and shippers of coolies.[21]

Consequently, the barracoon was torn down, and the unfortunate crimp, whose incarceration and rescue triggered the entire episode, was handed over to the Chinese authorities. These actions helped restore a measure of calm. The British Consular Court at Amoy merely fined Francis D. Syme $200 and William A. Cornabé $20 for breach of treaty regulations with China.[22] The *Emigrant*, the floating depot of Tait and Company, and the bulk of the emigration business moved to Namoa (Nanao), an island near the port of Swatow, which had long been a haven for opium traders.[23]

Swatow and Namoa

Though the port of Swatow was not officially opened to foreign trade until 1860,[24] the local authorities, finding opium a rich source of revenue, had long permitted opium vessels to anchor there. Agents of the two great British opium houses, Dent and Company and Jardine, Matheson and Company, had built residences and warehouses on the adjacent island of Namoa.[25] It was reported in 1853 that Tait and Company had erected barracoons on the island and had succeeded in buying over the local mandarins for one tael (6s 8d or $1.50) for every emigrant shipped.[26] William Breck, the U.S. consul at Swatow, estimated in 1861 that 40,000 to 50,000 laborers had been

---

[21] Bowring to Malmesbury, December 20, 1852 (BPP, ASS, *China*, Vol. III), 41.

[22] Backhouse to Bowring, December 18, 1852 (*Ibid.*), 48-49.

[23] Bowring to Malmesbury, February 7, 1853 (*Ibid.*), 113; Breck to Cass, March 6, 1861 (U.S. Dept. of State, Despatches from U.S. Consuls at Swatow, 1860-1881).

[24] Morse, *The Trade and Administration of China*, 278.

[25] Scarth, *Twelve Years in China*, 47; Theodore Walrond (ed.), *Letters and Journals of James, Eighth Earl of Elgin* (London, John Murray, 1872), 226; Burns, *Memoir of the Reverend William C. Burns*, 378; Abend, *Treaty Ports*, 104.

[26] Bowring to Malmesbury, January 18, 1853 (BPP, ASS, *China*, Vol. III), 109.

Table 3

The Ports of Departure of Chinese Emigrants to Latin America, 1847-1874

PORTS	1847	1848	1849	1850	1851	1852	1853	1854	1855	1856	1857	1858	1859	1860	1861	1862	1863	1864	1865	1866	1867	1868	1869	1870	1871	1872	1873	1874	TOTALS
AMOY	652				2,964	616	604	100	600	1,026	1,454					385			1,092	972									11,402
CUMSINGMOON			75	1,665	352	1,350	1,370	325																					5,137
CANTON					254	350				348			972	1,996	1,486	326	930	594								510	388		13,262
SWATOW					702	5,540	1,800	7,320	4,232	4,852		2,101		400															24,953
SHANGHAI												130	355																485
NINGPO									47																				47
HONG KONG					813			310	397	1,019	560		369	1,032	583	1,922			493	825	291	252	500	381					10,934
MACAU						250	558		6,812	7,037	9,053	9,053	4,787	4,878	4,042	2,116	661											2,371	205,626
SINGAPORE									303											512									615
UNKNOWN								895					552	292	683									828					3,050
TOTALS	632		75	1,665																									275,511

Source: Compiled from tables 25-48 in appendix VI.

"seduced, stolen and taken to Havana and the Chincha Islands, not one of whom has ever returned."[27] This would seem to have been an exaggerated guess on Consul Breck's part. As far as it can be ascertained, somewhere between 25,000 and 30,000 emigrants sailed from Swatow for Cuba, Peru, and the British West Indies between 1852 and 1860.[28]

Figure 2. The Port of Swatow circa 1870 (taken from *Le Tour du Monde*, Vol. XXIX, 1875, 411)

Hallett Abend, in his work *Treaty Ports*, states that 8,000 emigrants died on Namoa island of plague and starvation in one year while waiting for emigrant ships.[29] This is not substantiated by any other sources. That abuses abounded there can be little doubt. Between 1855 and 1860, seven mutinies took place on ships that sailed from Swatow.[30] Consul Breck observed that the Swatow people hated foreigners because of the "many wicked practices that had been perpetrated upon them."[31]

---

[27]   Breck to Cass, March 6, 1861 (U.S. Dept. of State, Despatches from U.S. Consuls at Swatow, 1860-1881).

[28]   See Table 3.

[29]   Abend, *Treaty Ports*.

[30]   See Table 17.

[31]   Breck to Cass, March 6, 1861 (U.S. Dept. of State, Despatches from U.S. Consuls at Swatow, 1860-1881).

The notoriety that was seemingly endemic to the emigration traffic posed a serious threat to all trade on the China coast, illegal as well as legal. The opium interests were becoming alarmed at the possible consequences of continual disturbances at their opium stations. The opium trade was illegal not only in Chinese law but in British law as well. Her Majesty's government pledged itself in the Treaty of Nanking that British subjects and ships would not trade other than at ports designated in the treaty. But in regard to the opium trade, the British government had adopted a policy of noninterference. Was emigration to be treated in like manner? The opium houses were decidedly opposed to such a step.[32] Dr. John Bowring, in writing to Malmesbury, the secretary of state for foreign affairs, in 1853, asked the rhetorical question, "Shall we, ought we, to extend the opium indulgence to another species of traffic wholly unprotected by the guarantees which the wealth, position, and the high character of great opium houses offer?"[33] A proposal in December 1853 by James T. White, the British emigration agent, to embark emigrants from Namoa, elicited a sharp remonstrance from the British Foreign Office,[34] and he was instructed to confine his activities to ports legally open to British trade.[35] Under pressure from the opium houses, which exerted considerable influence with the local Chinese authorities, as well as in London, the emigration traffic gradually shifted from the opium stations to the legal ports. The last emigrant ship for Latin America from Cumsingmoon sailed in 1854 and from Namoa in 1860. Immigration to Latin America from Amoy ceased in 1858. Various attempts during the 1860s to revive emigration at these ports were largely unsuccessful. A proclamation by Governor-general Laou in March 1860, sanctioning emigration from Swatow, had no visible effect as far as the traffic to South America was concerned.[36] A few emigrant vessels left Amoy for Latin America in 1862, 1865, and 1866. However, up to the termination of the traffic in 1874, small batches of emigrants continued to leave these ports clandestinely in native boats to rendezvous with emigrant vessels elsewhere.[37]

---

32   White to Walcott, December 26, 1852 (BPP, ASS, *China*, Vol. III), 230.

33   Bowring to Malmesbury, January 5, 1853 (*Ibid.*), 97-100.

34   Addington to Merivale, April 4, 1854 (*Ibid.*), 332-333.

35   Emigration Commissioners to White, February 24, 1854 (*Ibid.*), 331-332.

36   See BFO 97/102B for the full text of the proclamation.

37   Cooper to Alcock, October 20, 1866 (BFO 17/873).

The Port of Hong Kong

Following the disturbances at Amoy and confronted with opposition to emigration at the opium ports from the opium houses and the Foreign Office, the British emigration agent moved his recruiting operation to Hong Kong. By Article III of the Treaty of Nanking, (1842), China ceded permanently the island of Hong Kong to the British.[38] Though the island consisted of twenty-nine square miles of barren rock, it had an enormous deepwater harbor that was well sheltered from all sides. To attract commerce, Sir Henry Pottinger, British superintendent of trade on the China coast, declared Hong Kong a free port without customs or duties of any kind.[39] After an initial outburst of enthusiasm, trade languished, as Chinese officials on the mainland forbade Chinese junks and traders to frequent the new port.[40] For the remainder of the 1840s, Hong Kong survived as the center of the illegal opium trade.[41] It became a haunt for pirates, vagabonds, and thieves—a haven for the "discontented and bad spirits of the Empire," who looked upon British law as a farce when compared with Chinese justice.[42]

Figure 3. The port of Hong Kong circa 1870 (taken from *Le Tour du Monde*, Vol. XXIX, 1875, 353)

---

38 Mayers, *Treaties Between the Empire of China and Foreign Powers*, 1-2.

39 E. J. Eitel, *Europe in China: The History of Hong Kong from the Beginning to the Year 1882* (London: Luzac and Company, 1895), 132.

40 *Ibid.*, 183.

41 G. B. Endacott, *A History of Hong Kong* (London: Oxford University Press, 1958), 73, 130-131; Baruch Boxer, *Ocean Shipping in the Evolution of Hong Kong* (Chicago: University of Chicago Press, 1961), 13.

42 Eitel, *Europe in China: The History of Hong Kong*, 251.

Table 4

Emigration from the Port of Hong Kong, 1854-1880

DESTINATION	1854	1855	1856	1857	1858	1859	1860	1861	1862	1863	1864	1865	1866	1867	1868	1869	1870	1871	1872	1873	1874	1875	1876	1877	1878	1879	1880	TOTALS
U.S.A.	10496	4867	4867	5803	4989	?	?	7754	?	7320	2920	?	2280	2995	5609	?	?	5595	1056	1763	1653	3748	1494	1064	104	9019	7346	177,415+
AUSTRALIA	4341	11091	7602	17728	8967	?	?	2809	?	352	851	?	1148	276	274	?	?	1345	375	40	1242	912	1250	7346	1447	3263	4856	92,209+
SOUTHEAST ASIA	15	794	329				66														1425	1779	2252	2006	2249	2030	3766	186,109
NEW ZEALAND																		2555	178	560	766	478	48	121	345	135	7	5,191
CANADA										137					259								661	265	355	282	435	2,394
Br. GUIANA				1205*	292*		1313*	2297*	1910*			493*																6,808
CUBA			1203*	2126*	1662*																							4,991
PERU																382*	381*											763
SURINAM													825*	291*	252*	501*												1,869
HAWAII												527*	262*									111	1118	1102				3,120
TAHITI											337*	698*																1,035
INDIA											2370*											15						2,385
TOTALS	14357	12563	14466	25967	15910	10217	15183	12840	1421	7809	6607	6,076	6,845	5115	4283	8704												543,097+

* Denotes contract emigration

Sources: *Hong Kong Government Gazette*, 1854-1882; Bowring to Molesworth, October 6, 1855 (BPP, ASS, *China*, Vol. IV), 38-39; Robinson to Newcastle, July 3, 1860 (BFO 97/102B); *O Boletim*, August 31, 1861.

At the end of the 1840s, a fortunate combination of events brought prosperity to the island. In 1848, the British navy destroyed two pirate fleets that had virtually controlled China's southern coastline, exacting payments from all trading and fishing junks.[43] In 1850, as a result of the Taiping Rebellion, Chinese emigrants and capital, seeking a safe refuge from the clutches of marauders, commenced to flow to Hong Kong.[44] The discovery of gold in California and Australia gave rise to a thriving business in emigration.

In these early days of growth and prosperity, no records were kept, and hence there is no exact tally on emigration from the port. U.S. consul Henry Arthur Jr. reported that 7,785 emigrants sailed from there for San Francisco in 1851.[45] The same year, the *William Watson*, flying the British flag set sail with emigrants for Peru, and in 1853, emigration commenced to the British West Indies and to Australia. Table 5 shows the number of emigrants that passed through the port of Hong Kong from 1854 to 1880 as reported by the harbormaster in the colony's official newspaper, the *Hong Kong Government Gazette*. A breakdown of the figures for the years 1859-60, 1862, 1865, and 1868-69 is not given, and those for 1854 are for the first six months of the year only. The vast majority of the more than 543,097 emigrants that departed from Hong Kong in this twenty-six-year period did so under the credit-ticket system. They went principally to the United States, Australia, New Zealand, Canada, and Southeast Asia. Approximately, 18,842, or 3.5 percent, left the port under the contract system.

As elsewhere on the China coast, emigration at Hong Kong was fraught with irregularities. The Chinese Passengers Act, passed by the British Parliament in 1855 to counteract abuses, made it incumbent on all British ships, carrying passengers from Chinese ports, to undergo inspection by a British emigration officer.[46] This official was to ascertain that all passengers were emigrating of their own free will and that each ship was properly equipped and ventilated for the voyage. But the provisions of the act were not strictly enforced.[47] In 1856, two British ships, *Duke of Portland* and *John Calvin*, which sailed from Hong Kong with emigrants for Havana, reported

---

[43] *Ibid.*, 270.

[44] *Ibid.*, 259.

[45] Arthur to Webster, March 29, 1852 (U.S. Department of State, Dispatches from United States Consuls in Hong Kong, 1844-1906).

[46] For the full text of the Act see BFO 97/101, 849-858.

[47] Bowring to Labouchere, July 26, 1856 (BPP, ASS, *China*, Vol. IV), 56-57.

a mortality of over 40 percent for the voyage.[48] An investigation revealed that both ships evaded the law. The emigrants on the *Duke of Portland* mutinied, and the *John Calvin* put out to sea although only 81 of its 298 passengers declared themselves willing to emigrate before the Hong Kong emigration officer.[49] The following year, secret barracoons housing unwilling emigrants were discovered on the island.[50]

The Hong Kong government, under considerable pressure from London, enacted a number of progressively restrictive ordinances to eliminate abuses. Emigration brokers were licensed and bonded.[51] No Chinese passengers could legally embark on an emigration vessel without first obtaining a permit from the emigration officer.[52] All houses for the reception of intending emigrants had to be licensed and operated according to rules specified by the government.[53] No ship could lawfully proceed to sea with Chinese emigrants without a license from the governor of the colony.[54] Chinese contract emigration departing from Hong Kong could only proceed to British colonies.[55]

But there were serious doubts about the efficacy of these measures. The colony's gambling houses were accused of supplying the neighboring port of Macau with contract laborers for Cuba and Peru.[56] Kidnappings were common occurrences.[57] In 1867, Chief Justice John Smale called upon Sir Richard Graves MacDonnell, the governor of Hong Kong, to prohibit all contract emigration as it was impossible to regulate it satisfactorily.[58] The governor responded that outlawing contract emigration would be an injustice to those who wished to emigrate as well as to British West Indian planters, who sorely needed laborers.[59]

---

[48] Labouchere to Bowring, June 29, 1857 (*Ibid.*), 75-76.

[49] *Ibid.*

[50] Eitel, *Europe in China: The History of Hong Kong*, 344.

[51] *Hong Kong Government Gazette*, October 24, 1857.

[52] *Ibid.*, June 22, 1867.

[53] *Ibid.*, July 17, 1869.

[54] *Ibid.*, September 25, 1869.

[55] British Foreign Office to the Governor of Hong Kong, December 14, 1869 (BFO 17/877).

[56] *The Daily Press* (Hong Kong), April 3, 1872.

[57] Eitel, *Europe in China: The History of Hong Kong*, 501; *Hong Kong Daily Press*, May 27, 1873.

[58] BPP, ASS, *China*, Vol. XV (1868-69), 9.

[59] *Ibid.*, 11-13.

There was another reason for allowing the emigration to continue, which the governor did not mention. It would seem that a considerable amount of Hong Kong money was tied up in the traffic. R. Rowett, a member of Hong Kong's legislative council, charged that even some of London's commercial houses and banks were financially very much involved in contract emigration on the China coast.[60] During the 1860s and early 1870s, while Hong Kong newspapers thundered against the abuses of emigration at Macau, Hong Kong merchants quietly reaped rich profits from outfitting and provisioning almost all foreign ships engaged in emigration from China. When Sir A. E. Kennedy, on assuming the office of Governor of Hong Kong in 1872, officially acknowledged to the London government that "Macau coolie ships are almost invariably fitted in the port of Hong Kong,"[61] a shocked colonial secretary called for new legislation.[62] As soon as the Queen's confirmation of the "Chinese Emigrant Ship Ordinance, 1873" was received in the colony in August of that year, seven emigrant vessels, being outfitted in the harbor for the Macau emigration trade, were ordered to leave.[63] But the new British ordinance came too late to have any direct effect on the Macau traffic, as the Portuguese government decided to terminate all emigration from Macau early in 1874.

The island of Hong Kong was not particularly well suited to contract emigration. Emigrants had to be obtained from the mainland, and the well-organized Chinese-controlled immigration to California and Australia did not welcome competition from agents recruiting for Latin America. Furthermore, British public opinion, kept informed by the Anti-Slavery Society of the atrocities connected with Chinese immigration to South America and the Caribbean, looked upon all contract emigration on the China coast with suspicion and pressured the London government to close Hong Kong to the traffic. To British officials in China, however, the solution to the problems of contract emigration lay in persuading the Chinese government to legalize and regulate emigration, thus controlling the operations of crimps, who were regarded as the chief perpetrators of abuses.[64] An opportunity to test this belief presented itself at Canton in 1859.

---

[60]   Eitel, *Europe in China: The History of Hong Kong*, 500.

[61]   Kennedy to Kimberley, October 19, 1872 (BPP, ASS, *China*, Vol. IV), 317-318.

[62]   Kimberley to Kennedy, December 17, 1872 (*Ibid.*), 318-319.

[63]   Kennedy to Kimberley, August 29, 1873 (*Ibid.*), 365-366.

[64]   Bonham to Hammond, July 4, 1854 (*Ibid.*, Vol. III), 338-341; Alcock to Bowring, April 12, 1859 (*Ibid.*, Vol. IV), 111.

Canton and Whampoa

The port city of Canton, situated eighty miles inland at the head of the Pearl River Delta, was for centuries China's principal point of contact with the Western world. Canton was the first Chinese port regularly visited by Western traders. The Arabs came there in the seventh century. The Portuguese arrived in the sixteenth century, followed by the Spaniards, the Dutch, and the English. Whampoa, twelve miles downstream from Canton, served as a deepwater anchorage for large vessels.

From 1760, all the foreign commerce of China was by imperial decree limited to the port of Canton.[65] Foreigners were restricted to dealing with a select group of Chinese merchants (cohong), who were directly answerable to the government in Peking. This monopolistic system, together with the controversy surrounding the opium trade, led to increasing friction that erupted into open conflict between China and Great Britain in what came to be known as the Opium War, 1839-1842. The Treaty of Nanking, signed on August 29, 1842, brought peace and replaced the closed cohong system with five ports at which foreigners could live and trade.

Canton was a traditional center of emigration as well as of trade. Prior to the 1840s, most Cantonese emigrants went to Southeast Asia, many of them going by way of Macau. In 1848, ten emigrants departed from Canton for California, and these were followed by about 900 others in 1849.[66] A regular flow of emigrants to the Americas ensued, with some going to Peru, but the vast majority went to California. British consul Adam W. Elmslie, in response to an inquiry from the British Foreign Office in 1852, stated that the local Cantonese authorities did not interfere in any way whatsoever with emigration, that placards were distributed throughout the countryside notifying the people of the departure of emigrant vessels, and that recruitment was carried on openly.[67] Toward the end of the decade, however, the mood changed. Competition among crimps, in particular among those supplying receiving ships anchored at Whampoa, led to a multiplication of abuses, until it was deemed unsafe for a native to walk the streets of Canton even in broad daylight.[68] Governor-

---

[65] John King Fairbanks, *Trade and Diplomacy on the China Coast: The Opening of the Treaty Ports, 1842-1854* (Stanford, Stanford University Press, 1964), 51.

[66] Elmslie to Bowring, August 25, 1852 (BPP, ASS, *China*, Vol. III), 17.

[67] *Ibid.*

[68] Alcock to Bowring, April 12, 1859 (*Ibid.*, Vol. IV), 105.

general Laou, the highest-ranking Chinese official residing in Canton, claimed that the many schemes of kidnappers were the "offspring of the receiving ship system."[69] In 1859, there were at least six receiving ships anchored at Whampoa: the *Pioneer, Governor Morton*, and *Messenger* flying the U.S. flag, the *Westward Ho* with Peruvian registration, the *Fanny Kirchner* under the flag of the German state of Oldenburg, and the *Sooloo* flying the Dutch colors.[70] These ships served as feeders for the barracoons at Macau. Small boats, plying their recruiting trade among the maze of streams and canals in the neighborhood of Canton (see figure 7), supplied the receiving ships with emigrants. The system was particularly effective from the recruiter's standpoint. When a batch of emigrants was delivered to a receiving ship, anyone who insisted that he was unwilling to emigrate was handed back to the crimp, who so terrified him by refinements of torture that when he was presented to another receiving ship, he gladly chose deportation rather than incur the risk of falling into the crimp's hands again.[71]

Outraged by the growing number of kidnappings, the people commenced to administer their own merciless brand of instant justice. Several crimps caught in the act of coercing a victim, or merely suspected of doing so, were lynched or beaten to death by mobs.[72] In April 1859, the Chinese mercantile community appealed to the foreign consuls at Canton to take some action to stop the kidnappings.[73] The following day, the Allied commanders, who had been in occupation of Canton since January 1858, and fearing for the safety of the foreign community, issued a proclamation warning the people against crimps and strictly prohibiting kidnapping.[74] But as prohibition alone could hardly suffice to stop the evil, the Allied commanders brought pressure to bear on the provincial authorities to legalize and regulate emigration.[75] On April 9, Peh-kwei, governor of the Province of Kwangtung, following the lead of two district magistrates, solemnly proclaimed that kidnapping would be punished by death, that a reward of $40 would be paid for the arrest and

---

[69]   Laou to Perry, November, 1859 (BFO 881/894).
[70]   Hale to Winchester, December 9, 1859 (BFO 881/894).
[71]   Mayers to Parkes, January 6, 1859 (BFO 881/894).
[72]   Alcock to Bowring, April 12, 1859 (BFO 881/894); Bruce to Russell, January 22, 1860 (BPP, ASS, *China*, Vol. IV), 172.
[73]   For the text of the petition see Bowring to Malmesbury, April 15, 1859, Inclosure 2 (*Ibid.*), 106-107.
[74]   For the text of the proclamation see *Ibid.*, Inclosure 4, 108.
[75]   Bruce to Malmesbury, May 3, 1859 (*Ibid.*), 112.

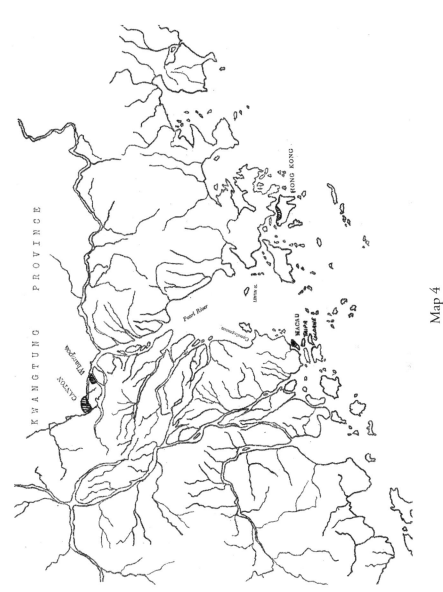

Map 4

The Pearl River Delta, Kwangtung Province

conviction of every kidnapper, but that those compelled by poverty to seek a livelihood overseas could lawfully do so.[76] This was in many respects a revolutionary pronouncement. By authorizing voluntary emigration, Governor Peh-kwei acted in direct opposition to the laws of the empire. The British minister at Shanghai, Frederick W. A. Bruce, wrote to the Foreign Office:

> It is a novel and important fact in Chinese administration to see a high officer and his magistrates setting aside a traditional maxim, which the circumstances of the population renders no longer applicable and admitting virtually that laws must be subservient to the exigencies of social change and progress.[77]

Though Governor Peh-kwei died shortly after his historic proclamation, his successor, Governor-general Laou, working closely with the Chinese and foreign communities sanctioned a system of voluntary emigration that attempted to do away with crimping. A set of regulations governing the establishment of licensed emigration houses and depots were promulgated.[78] Consequently, British, French, and Spanish emigration agents set up recruiting centers in the city of Canton.[79] As outlined in chapter II, the British venture was well organized and was relatively successful. The French and Spanish depots, however, experienced difficulties in obtaining recruits. Some of their agents were directly associated with the irregularities at Whampoa, which made the people and the authorities suspicious of their stated intentions to comply fully with the new regulations.[80] Under the new system, the French ship *Gallilee* took 426 Cantonese to the French colony of Martinique in 1859 and two ships, one American and the other Chilean, left for Cuba with 647 passengers in 1860. Four more vessels departed for Cuba in 1861 with approximately 1,500 emigrants, and in the 1865-1866 emigration season, nine ships sailed for Cuba with a total of 2,716.

---

[76]   For the texts of the proclamations of Peh-kwei and the magistrates see *Ibid.*, 109-110. See also P. Darby de Thiersant, *L'Emigration Chinois* (Paris, Paul Dupont, 1872), 3-4.

[77]   Bruce to Malmesbury, May 3, 1859 (*Ibid.*), 112.

[78]   Parkes to Hammond, November 13, 1859, Inclosure 12 (*Ibid.*), 122-123; C. B. Fisher, *Personal Narrative of Three Years Service in China* (London, Richard Bentley, 1863), 323-328.

[79]   Fisher, *Personal Narrative of Three Years Service in China*, 323.

[80]   Allied Commissioners to Perry, March 10, 1860 (BPP, ASS, *China*, Vol. IV), 235-236.

The British depot closed down in 1866 when the London government refused to ratify a new code of regulations drawn up by British, French, and Chinese representatives in the Emigration Convention of March of that year.[81] Thereafter, the only recorded sailings of contract emigration from Canton were the Spanish ship *Salvadora* that took 510 emigrants to Cuba in 1872 and the British vessel *Corona* that shipped 288 to British Guiana in 1873.

At the time that the new regulations for voluntary emigration were announced in November 1859, Governor-general Laou dispatched a force of war junks to the Whampoa anchorage to put a stop to the abuses there.[82] A number of unwilling emigrants were rescued and thirty-six crimps were arrested. Subsequently, eighteen of these crimps were publicly beheaded at Canton "as a warning to the people."[83] A Chinese cruiser was then stationed at Whampoa as a deterrent to further abuses.[84] These actions merely slowed down the activities of the crimps. The policing of the innumerable streams and channels of the delta, where fishermen and crimps could not be differentiated, was almost an impossible task. As long as shipments of emigrants continued without adequate supervision at Macau and to a lesser extent at Hong Kong, crimps were prepared to run the risk of losing their heads in return for substantial profits.

Shanghai, Wusung, and Ningpo

In sanctioning voluntary emigration from Canton in October 1859, Governor-general Laou acted contrary to orders from Peking. In July of that year, following disturbances at Shanghai and Ningpo, Ho Kuei-ch'ing, imperial commissioner for foreign affairs, reiterated China's traditional prohibition against emigration.[85] This was the first time that the Peking government had taken official cognizance of the "coolie trade" as a matter of national concern.[86]

---

[81] Clementi, *The Chinese in British Guiana*, 206-207.

[82] Laou to Allied Commissioners, November 8, 1859 (BPP, ASS, *China*, Vol. IV), 127-128.

[83] Proclamation by Governor-General Laou, Inclosure 6 in No. 7 (*Ibid.*), 148.

[84] Parkes to Bruce, November 26, 1859 (Ibid.), 149.

[85] Bruce to Russell, December 5, 1859 (BFO 881/894).

[86] Irick, "Ch'ing Policy Toward the Coolie Trade, 1847-1878," 463-464.

Shanghai and Ningpo were two of the five ports opened to foreign trade in 1842. Shanghai was then a small walled city lying fourteen miles above the mouth of the Whangpu River, a tributary to the Yangtze. Because of its ideal position at the gateway to the great Yangtze valley, it had been for years a port of some significance, but after it was opened to foreign trade, it quickly became a major commercial metropolis.[87] By the 1870s, it was handling over 60 percent of the total foreign trade of China. Wusung, situated at the juncture of the Whangpu and the Yangtze rivers, was Shanghai's outer port, and from the early 1840s, it was an outlet for opium for the Shanghai area.[88]

The port of Ningpo, in the northeastern corner of Chekiang province, was an ancient seat of learning and a center of Buddhism. The proximity of the superior port of Shanghai hindered its commercial development. However, from the early 1840s, it too had its opium station on the island of Chusan that lay at the entrance to the harbor.[89]

The people of these northern port cities, and of northern China in general, were not at all disposed to emigrate.[90] In 1849, 200 emigrants were persuaded to sail on the *Amazon*, a British vessel, for California, and in 1851, 20 or 30 departed for Australia.[91] There is no evidence of any further emigration until the abortive attempt in 1855 to ship to Cuba some 47 female children from the vicinity of Shanghai and Ningpo.[92] This incident brought forth condemnatory proclamations from the governor-general of Fukien and Chekiang,[93] as well as from the Taotai of Ningpo.[94]

In 1856, the French vessel *Caffarette* sailed from Wusung with emigrants for Cuba.[95] The same year, a Peruvian vessel, the *Antonio Terry*, left Wusung for Callao supposedly in ballast,[96] but in all probability, there was a full compliment of emigrants on board. Due to the vigilance of the local Chinese

---

[87] Fairbanks, *Trade and Diplomacy on the China Coast*, 155.

[88] Fairbanks, *Trade and Diplomacy on the China Coast*, 135, 229.

[89] Ibid., 135.

[90] Hague to Bowring, September 14, 1852 (BPP, ASS, *China*, Vol. III), 26-27; *North China Herald*, January 7, 1860 (Supplement).

[91] Alcock to Bowring, September 1, 1852 (BPP, ASS, *China*, Vol. III), 26-28.

[92] The incident is discussed in Chapter II.

[93] *The Friend of China*, July 11, 1855.

[94] "A Special Prohibitory Proclamation," April, 1855 (BFO 97/101).

[95] *The North China Herald*, August 9, 1856.

[96] *North China Herald*, August 2, 1856.

authorities, who were adamantly opposed to emigration, emigrant ships, by some subterfuge, either were declared as leaving the port in "ballast," or were merely taking passengers to some other Chinese port, to which there could be little objection.[97] The foreign communities and foreign consuls at Shanghai and Ningpo were equally determined to prevent abuses such as had taken place at Amoy and were reportedly at this time a daily occurrence at Swatow. When Andrew Connolly, a British merchant, collected 160 Chinese laborers in the French settlement of Shanghai for shipment overseas, Her Majesty's consul, D. B. Robertson, denounced him to the Taotai.[98] William Reed, the United States minister to China, attempted to prevent an American ship, the *Wandering Jew*, from sailing with emigrants for Cuba in January 1858. Over the objections of Chinese officials, the U.S. vice consul at Shanghai, William Knapp Jr., stating that the ship was merely transporting Chinese passengers from Wusung to Amoy, gave the ship her sailing papers. Knapp was relieved of his post, and his successor, Albert L. Freeman, determined to discover whether or not the passengers had embarked voluntarily, made a personal visit to the vessel. An examination revealed that of the 236 Chinese on board, 117 claimed that they were there against their will. Many of them stated that a crimp in the employ of Mr. Connolly had deceived them. These men were released.[99] The *Wandering Jew* sailed with the others to Amoy where she filled out her cargo with 231 more before setting out for Cuba.[100]

Further incidents led to a serious threat to the foreign community in July and August of 1859. In April of that year, two French vessels, the *Admiral Baudin* and the *Indien*, departed from Shanghai in "ballast" but actually were carrying emigrants to the French colonies of Martinique and Guadaloupe.[101] In July, Chinese passengers on another French ship, the *Gertrude*, chartered to Spanish agents, attempted to escape as the ship lay at anchor at Wusung. The crew opened fire upon them, and about 40 were killed or drowned.[102] At the appearance of many bodies in the river,

---

[97] Robertson to Bowring, July 26, 1856 (BFO 97/102A).

[98] Robertson to Bowring, March 5, 1856 (BFO 97/102A).

[99] "Report from the Committee on Commerce," April 16, 1860 (U.S. House Report, No. 443, 1 sess. 36 Cong.), 20-22.

[100] Felix Erenchún, *Anales de la Isla de Cuba: Diccionario Administrativo, Económico, Estadístico y Legislativo*, 4 vols. (Habana, Imprenta la Habanera, 1858), II (1856), 1332.

[101] *North China Herald*, April 9, and 30, 1859.

[102] Ibid., August 6, 1859.

the people became alarmed, and a crowd of about 5,000, armed with clubs and knives attacked two British sailors, mistaking them for kidnappers. They killed one and seriously wounded the other. When Horatio N. Lay, inspector general of the Chinese Maritime Customs and a missionary, the Reverend John Hobson, attempted to interfere, the mob turned its fury upon them. Lay was stabbed several times, and Hobson was badly beaten.[103] Eventually, the Chinese authorities succeeded in dispersing the people and restoring order.

The riot took place on July 29. The following day, Siamese visitors to Shanghai were attacked by a mob, and one was pushed into a pool and drowned.[104] This could hardly have been a case of mistaken identity. The incident can only be explained by the fact that in December 1857, a Siamese vessel, the *Bangkok Mark*, while at anchor at Shanghai, was discovered to have on board 42 kidnapped children ranging in age from eight to seventeen years. They had been sold to the captain for $2 to $6 each and were destined for Siam (modern Thailand).[105]

Placards appeared in Shanghai and Wusung, condemning foreigners and associating kidnapping with missionary endeavors. The following sample, dated July 30, reflects the thinking and mood of the aroused populace:

> The Intendant and Magistrates have issued notifications at Shanghai to the effect that foreigners with hearts of wolves are in the habit of coming to the towns and villages, where, acting in concert with natives professing their doctrine, they make a show of hiring people to assist them, their real purpose being to entrap men to their perdition. Hateful and detestable beings! Of a truth all natives professing their doctrine are devils, are demons. Now, lest the simple people in their greed of gain be beguiled in this way, let the people of the towns and villages with joint effort and united heart set upon and kill every foreigner that is associated with natives professing his doctrine in the teaching of religion; that the deceiving of man may be put a stop to.[106]

---

[103] Smith to Cass, September 3, 1859 (U. S. Department of State, Despatches from U.S. Consuls in Shanghai, 1847-1906).

[104] Irick, "Ch'ing Policy Toward the Coolie Trade, 1847-1878," 81.

[105] *North China Herald*, December 26, 1857.

[106] *North China Herald*, August 27, 1859.

In subsequent weeks, there was a number of attacks on missionaries and churches, and two foreign sailors were beaten to death.[107] Riots also broke out at Ningpo, and foreigners were assaulted.[108]

Meanwhile, the French minister to China, A. de Bourboulon ordered the *Gertrude* to submit to an inspection by Chinese officials, and all of the 157 passengers found on board, most of them from Ningpo, were released to their homes.[109] A crimping boat, with 34 kidnapped Chinese, intercepted by the river police was chopped up and publicly displayed together with the heads of four crimps, natives of Ningpo.[110] This pacified the people somewhat, and gradually the tension subsided.

An imperial edict of August 22, 1859, called for swift punishment of kidnappers and the leaders of the mob attacks on foreigners.[111] Representatives of foreign governments and foreign consuls at Shanghai and Ningpo pledged themselves to do all in their power to prevent their subjects from hiring Chinese to go abroad.[112] No further contract emigration from the area, at least for the remainder of the nineteenth century, is recorded.

In one port after another, contract emigration showed itself to be disruptive of the peace. The opposition of foreign commercial communities on the China coast to its presence in their midst, as well as the growing vigilance of local Chinese authorities, gradually pushed the traffic to Macau, where it was concentrated for most of the 1860s and the early 1870s.

The Port of Macau

The settlement of Macao is a monument of Chinese toleration and of Portuguese tenacity . . . It said as much for the tact of the Portuguese as for the forbearance of the Chinese authorities that such an isolated

---

107 Ibid.; Irick, "Ch'ing Policy Toward the Coolie Trade, 1847-1878," 83; Smith to Cass, September 3, 1859 (U.S. Dept. of State, Despatches from U.S. Consuls in Shanghai, 1847-1906).

108 Bruce to Russell, December 2, 1859 (BFO 17/315).

109 Bruce to Russell, August 15, 1859 (BFO 17/315); *North China Herald*, August 26, 1859.

110 Irick, "Ch'ing Policy Toward the Coolie Trade, 1847-1878," 85; *North China Herald*, August 27, 1859.

111 Irick, "Ch'ing Policy Toward the Coolie Trade, 1847-1878," 84.

112 Ibid., 88, 91.

position as that of Macao should have been held without force . . . on terms of mutual amity for nearly four hundred years.

Alexander Michie, *The Englishman in China*
(London, William Blackwood and Sons, 1900), 287, 290.

Figure 4. The port of Macau circa 1870 (taken from *Le Tour du Monde*, Vol. XXIX, 1875, 405)

Macau is the oldest European outpost in the Far East. The Portuguese arrived on the China coast in 1513, and after three decades of attempts to establish an enclave on Chinese soil, they finally settled on the peninsula of Macau with the blessing of the local Chinese authorities.[113] The concession was seemingly a reward for Portuguese help in extirpating pirates who were a constant menace to commerce and were even then bold enough to lay siege to Canton.[114] Situated at the mouth of the Pearl River estuary, sixty-

---

[113] Luis Gonzaga Gomes, *Páginas da História de Macau* (Macau, Notícias de Macau, 1966), 1, 37.

[114] "Historical Landmarks of Macao," *The Chinese Recorder*, Vol. XVIII, No. 5 (May 1877), 178; Michie, *The Englishmen in China*, 289-290.

five miles from Canton and possessing a large sheltered harbor, the two-and-a-half-mile-long-by-one-mile-wide peninsula was ideal as yet another link in the chain of Portuguese trading stations, which extended from Africa to Japan. Nor were the local Chinese authorities ill-pleased to have so effective a counterpoise to pirates strategically placed at the entrance to the Pearl River.[115]

After 1557, when the Portuguese were first permitted to build warehouses at Macau,[116] the port developed rapidly, virtually controlling all foreign commerce with the great emporium of Canton. During the eighteenth and early nineteenth centuries, the English and Dutch East India companies maintained establishments at Macau.[117] The entire foreign mercantile community, forbidden to reside at Canton except during the trading season or to bring their wives and families there, made the Macau peninsula its home. For nearly three hundred years, Macau served as the gateway to the Chinese Empire, and through it glimpses of Chinese life and culture filtered to the outside world.

From the Chinese standpoint, Macau was an ideal location for the sometimes-unruly barbarians. There they could be effectively quarantined and controlled. The merchants did not complain too strenuously as Macau, wafted by cool breezes, was by far the most comfortable spot on the south China coast during the hot summer months. With its pleasant climate and quaint mixture of Oriental and European cultures, Macau was to many a weary European merchant the "gem of the Orient earth and ocean sea," as Sir John Bowring poetically classified it.[118] To this day, well served by fast hydrofoil craft, it remains a favored resort of tourists and businessmen and their families escaping for a restful weekend from overcrowded Hong Kong, some forty miles away across the estuary.

In allowing the Portuguese to establish themselves at Macau, the Chinese did not thereby forfeit their sovereignty over the peninsula. A ground rent of 550 taels ($750) was paid annually to the magistrate of the district of Heung-shan, and though the Portuguese set up their own

---

[115] Michie, *The Englishman in China*, 290.

[116] Carlos Francisco Moura, *Macau e o Comércio Português com a China e o Japão nos Séculos XVI e XVII* (Macau, Imprensa Nacional, 1973), 9-10.

[117] Michie, *The Englishman in China*, 191.

[118] "Historical Landmarks of Macao," *The Chinese Recorder*, Vol. XVIII, No. 5 (May 1887), 175.

local government, the peninsula was administered jointly by Chinese and Portuguese officials.[119] This arrangement persisted for almost three centuries.

When Western nations commenced signing treaties with China in the 1840s, Portugal sought to clarify and consolidate its hold on Macau, but the Chinese were reluctant to negotiate. In 1849, the Portuguese governor of Macau, João Maria Ferreira do Amaral, expelled the Chinese customs officials, stopped payment of the ground rent, and refused to acknowledge Chinese overlordship.[120] But it was not until 1887, through persistent diplomacy on the part of the Portuguese, that the Chinese government ceded the peninsula to Portugal in perpetuity, together with the islands of Taipa and Coloane (map 4).[121]

After Macau lost the opium trade in 1822, the colony experienced a rapid decline.[122] During the 1830s and 1840s, when piracy was rampant in the China sea, well-armed lorchas, based at Macau and manned by Macaese, enjoyed a monopoly of the lucrative business of providing protection to merchant and fishing vessels all along the China coast.[123] Renowned for their fearless courage, the Macaese were at times recruited by Chinese admirals to do battle with pirate fleets.[124] Given permission to enter Chinese waters in pursuit of their prey, they became well acquainted with the many ports, inlets, bays, and rivers up and down the coast.[125] The system worked well for a while until the lorchas betrayed their trust by adopting methods of extortion and

---

[119] "Historical Landmarks of Macao," *The Chinese Recorder*, Vol. XVIII, No. 7 (July 1887), 273; Michie, *The Englishman in China*, 290; Fairbanks, *Trade and Diplomacy on the China Coast*, 47.

[120] J. D. Thomson, "Historical Landmarks of Macao," *The Chinese Recorder*, Vol. XIX, No. 10 (October, 1888), 451-452.

[121] Godfrey E. P. Hertslet, *Treaties, etc., Between Great Britain and China and between China and Foreign Powers* (London, Harrison and Sons, 1908), I, 422-423.

[122] "Historical Landmarks of Macao," *The Chinese Recorder*, Vol. XVIII, No. 11 (November, 1887), 427.

[123] Gomes, *Páginas da História de Macau*, 223-232; Montalto de Jesus, *Historic Macao* (Hong Kong, C. A. Kelly and Walsh Limited, 1902), 319.

[124] *The Friend of China*, February 5, 1851.

[125] Gomes, *Páginas da História de Macau*, 232.

plunder that rivaled those of the pirates.[126] The protectors turned oppressors and, having lost the support and respect of their clientele, were finally routed at Ningpo in 1851. There, native junks came to terms with a pirate fleet, and together they massacred the Macaese.[127]

The founding of Hong Kong and the opening of the treaty ports in 1842 were near-fatal blows to Macau's faltering economy. British and American traders abandoned Macau for the incomparably superior harbor of Hong Kong: the Macau harbor was silting up, and large vessels had to anchor three to four miles from shore.[128] By midcentury, the colony was reduced to near destitution.[129] P. G. Mesnier, private secretary to the governor of Macau, summed up its predicament: "Macao sank, and in her hopeless insignificance and misery was tempted by the Coolie Trade."[130]

Macau had many advantages as an emigration port. It had served as an outlet for Chinese emigrants for centuries,[131] and in recent decades, an increasing number had departed from there for Southeast Asia.[132] The opium trade and the convoy system gave the Macaese a working relationship with Chinese officials and the local population all along the coast, and provided them with an unparalleled understanding of China's navigable rivers and coastal waters. After 1851, the lorchas lying unemployed in the harbor were ready for use as passenger boats to supply emigrant ships, and empty warehouses could easily be converted into emigration depots. It was almost as if the colony had intentionally prepared

---

[126] MacGowan, "Piracies, Riots and Lynch Law at Ningpo," *Shanghai Almanac for 1853 and Miscellany* (Shanghai, Herald Office, 1853); Michie, *The Englishman in China*, 302; Gomes, *Páginas de História de Macau*, 233-234.

[127] Cooke, *China and Lower Bengal*, 131.

[128] Marquis de Moges, *Recollections of Baron Gros's Embassy to China and Japan in 1857-58* (London, Richard Griffin and Company, 1860), 91.

[129] *The Friend of China*, March 13, 1847.

[130] P. G. Mesnier, "A Reply to 'Macao and its Slave Trace,'", *The China Review*, Vol. II, No. 2 (1873), 119.

[131] See Chapter II.

[132] Andrew Ljungstedt, *An Historical Sketch of the Portuguese Settlements in China and of the Roman Catholic Church and Mission in China* (Boston, James Monroe and Company, 1836), 129.

itself to cope with the exodus of refugees from the Taiping Rebellion that commenced in the 1850s.

Yet emigration from Macau to the Americas developed slowly. Shippers preferred the ports of Amoy, Swatow, Cumsingmoon, and Canton because they were closer to the sources of supply. When it became progressively more difficult to operate from these ports, immigration to California and Australia was confined to Hong Kong, and the traffic to Latin America shifted to Macau. Two Frenchmen, Guillon and Durand, were the first to organize contract emigration from the Portuguese colony.[133] Under their auspices, the British ships *Mariner* and *Coromandel* sailed for Peru with 813 Chinese laborers in 1851.[134] The following year, a Portuguese ship, the *Sophia*, departed for Cuba with 250 emigrants,[135] and the *Ohio*, registered in Boston, sailed with passengers for California.[136] For the next four years, an average of five to six passenger ships sailed annually for Latin America with only one emigrant vessel sailing for California[137] and another for Australia.[138] In 1857, there was a marked increase in the traffic with the departure of 13 ships carrying over 8,000 passengers, all of them destined for Cuba. From that point on, with the exception of the years 1861 and 1862, Macau handled the bulk of Chinese contract immigration to Latin America. When the traffic came to an end in March 1874, over 210,000 Chinese had passed through Macau to South America and the Caribbean.[139] That accounted for approximately 75 percent of Chinese emigrants to the area in the years 1847 to 1874.

The Chinese population of Macau, like that of Hong Kong, experienced a rapid growth during the 1850s and early 1860s. In 1849, before the traffic in laborers to the West had commenced, there resided in the colony

---

[133]   "Relatorio da Emigração Chineza em Macao," *O Boletim* (August 10, 1861). See also Manuel de Castro Sampaio, *Os Chins de Macao* (Hong Kong, Typographia de Noranha e Filhos, 1867), 136.

[134]   *The Friend of China*, January 1, 1851.

[135]   "Relatorio da Emigração Chineza em Macao," *O Boletim*, August 10, 1861.

[136]   "Consular Return of U.S. ships at Macau from January 1, 1852 to July 1, 1852 Inclusive," (U.S. Dept. of State, Despatches from U.S. Consuls in Macao, 1849-1869).

[137]   "U.S. Vessels Arriving and Departing at Macao, January 1, 1852 to June 30, 1853," (U.S. Dept. of State, Despatches from U.S. Consuls in Macao 1849-1869).

[138]   *O Boletim*, August 31, 1861.

[139]   See Table 5.

Table 5

Emigration from the Port of Macau, 1851 to 1874

DESTINATION	1851	1852	1853	1854	1855	1856	1857	1858	1859	1860	1861	1862	1863	1864	1865	1866	1867	1868	1869	1870	1871	1872	1873	1874	TOTALS
CUBA		250	1,837	500	681	2,253	7,256	8,957	7,695	5,773	2,840	752	2,922	4,355	5,027	6,348	11,298	4,835	4,301	1,064	5,705	4,242	7,012	2,371	122,454
PERU	813		200	58		450		300	321	2,098	564	1,459	3,758	6,358	4,677	6,810	5,248	3,711	4,835	2,543	10,814	6,613	5,826		81,552
BR. GUIANA								300	460																760
SURINAM								500																	500
COSTA RICA																						685			685
SOUTHEAST ASIA							150	22	493	246		325	339	325		865		288	259	228	458	158			3,833
MOZAMBIQUE							30																		30
CALIFORNIA		one ship	one ship																						?
AUSTRALIA						240																			240
TOTALS	813	250+	2,037+	558	681	2,943	7,438	9,779	8,969	8,119	3,404	2,536	6,999	10,712	9,742	9,494	16,546	12,494	9,395	3,635	16,977	11,698	12,838	2,371	210,054+

Sources: *O Boletim*, 1851–1874; "Consular Returns of U.S. Ships at Macao from January 1, 1852 to July 1, 1852 inclusive" (U.S. Department of State, Despatches from U.S. Consuls in Macao, 1849–1869); "U.S. Vessels Arriving and Departing from Macao, January 1, 1853 to June 30, 1853" (Ibid.); Robertson to Alcock, March 21, 1867 (BFO 17/874).

4,587 people designated as "Christians" (including 490 African slaves) and 25,000 Chinese.[140] In the following decades, the number of Westerners remained virtually unchanged, but by 1867, the Chinese population had risen to 71,842. Of this number, 15,590 lived on 2,471 boats in the harbor, and approximately two-thirds of them were considered to be natives of Macau. Of the 56,252 Chinese residing on the peninsula, only 5,723 were actually born there: 48,617 came from Canton and its environs; 1,797 were natives of the province of Fukien; 63 migrated from the provision of Kuangsi; 39 came from Shanghai, and 13 came from Hong Kong.[141]

Many of the newcomers were pirates and other fugitives from justice.[142] Most of them were destitute, and the languishing Macau economy could not possibly provide them with a decent livelihood. The expanding emigration business afforded the only opportunity to make a living, and many of them joined its ranks. When emigration from Macau was terminated in 1874, some 20,000 to 30,000 Chinese lost their jobs.[143] Almost all of them were employed as crimps.

As elsewhere, abuse in emigration from Macau appeared early. The Macau government responded with humanitarian and restrictive legislation that acted as a temporary check on the more flagrant abuses, but it ultimately failed to eliminate the evils of the system. An ordinance enacted by Governor Isidoro Francisco Guimarães in September 1853 provided for sanitary accommodation for the emigrants on shore as well as on board ship and commanded that those rejected because of ill health or old age be returned to their homes, the emigration brokers paying all expenses.[144] To counteract the shipping of unwilling emigrants, it was decreed in November 1855 that all emigration contracts be registered and that emigrants be inspected prior to embarkation by the procurator and again by the harbormaster on board ship.[145] In June of the following year, it was further legislated that all *corretores*,

---

[140] João de Andrade Corvo, *Relatorio e Documentos sobre a Abolição da Emigração de Chinas Contratados em Macau Apresentado as Cortes na Sessão Legislativa de 1874* (Lisboa, Imprensa Nacional, 1874), 72.

[141] Ibid, 73.

[142] Mesnier, "A Reply to 'Macao and Its Slave Trade,'" 122.

[143] Robertson to Tenderdon, March 7, 1874 (BFO 17/885); Kennedy to Kimberley, December 31, 1873 (BFO 17/885).

[144] *O Boletim*, October 27, 1855.

[145] Ibid., November 10, 1855.

or emigration brokers, be licensed, bonded for $200, and subject to forfeiture of their bond and license as well as imprisonment for coercing the unwilling into going overseas.[146]

John Bowring, the governor of Hong Kong, advised the Foreign Office in London, that Governor Guimarães of Macau admitted to him privately that notwithstanding stringent legislation, he found it all but impossible to eradicate existing abuses.[147] By this time, it was apparent that the root cause of most of the abuses lay with the employment of crimps.[148] It was also apparent that without crimps, emigrants could not be obtained. Hence legislation concentrated on controlling the activities of crimps and limiting their opportunities for fraud and deception.

In 1860, Governor Guimarães issued further regulations. The new legislation was patterned on the emigration system approved the previous year by the local Chinese authorities and the Allied commanders at Canton. The post of superintendent of emigration was created, with a fixed salary paid by the government so that it would be completely independent of vested interests. Emigrants were not to be kept under restraint at any time but must be allowed to come and go as they pleased, and barracoons must be open daily between 8:00 a.m. and 4:00 p.m. to all who wished to enter them.[149]

The Macau barracoons had been accused by the Chinese mercantile community at Canton of being virtual prisons.[150] When British consul Charles A. Winchester, who was highly critical of emigration abuses at Amoy and Canton, inspected one of these establishments in 1855, he found it to be "exceedingly well arranged and worthy of imitation. I found 480 stout men and boys well lodged and well clothed and looking clean and comfortable and the arrangement of the place was in every way satisfactory."[151] Four years later, a visit by British consul O. Cleverly revealed that the barracoons

---

[146] Ibid., June 7, 1856.

[147] Bowring to Clarendon, June 27, 1856 (FO 97/102A).

[148] Corvo, *Relatorio e Documentos*, 10; Antonio Joaquim Bastos Jr., *O Futuro de Macau ou as Vantagens que hão de Resultar da Admissão d'Uma Delegação de Alfandega Chineza em Macau* (Macau, Typographia Mercantil, 1873), 8.

[149] *O Boletim*, May 5, 1860.

[150] "Petition of the Chinese Mercantile Community at Canton," April 16, 1859 (BPP, ASS, *China*, Vol. IV), 106-107.

[151] Winchester to Bowring, July 22, 1855 (BFO 97/1023).

were under heavy guard, but that in "every other respect the conditions were excellent."[152]

Seemingly, competition among emigration brokers and crimps brought about the change from open to closed and guarded barracoons. Prospective emigrants, after entering into a contract with one broker, would disappear only, to present themselves at another barracoon, hoping thereby to obtain another round of food, clothing, lodging, and advance money. Or emigrants about to be shipped would claim to have been coerced or kidnapped and upon release would repeat their act elsewhere.[153] To defend themselves against such practices, barracoons did indeed take on the appearance of prisons, closely guarding emigrants who had signed contracts. Even after the 1860 decree that commanded barracoons to be open to all who wished to come and go, the presence of sentries armed with heavy clubs at open doors indicated something less than full compliance with the law.[154]

Continued abuses brought a growing chorus of protests from newspapers on the China coast as well as from Chinese and foreign officials, and some prominent members of the Portuguese community at Macau began to take a hard look at what the emigration traffic was doing to the colony. The Emigration Convention drawn up between China, Britain, and France in 1866 limited emigration to the treaty ports and prohibited emigrants from going to any country not having diplomatic relations with China.[155] This made emigration from Macau illegal, at least as far as the Chinese government was concerned. Lest there be any doubt, Price Kung, in a letter to Rutherford Alcock, the British commissioner in China, stated that emigration from Macau was prohibited by the treaty and requested that British merchant ships be prevented from taking any part in the Macau traffic.[156]

Throughout the 1860s, the Macau government made several attempts to come to some agreement with China on the subject of emigration but was rebuffed.[157] The Macau authorities maintained that the worst abuses were perpetrated outside their jurisdiction by the Chinese themselves all along the

---

[152] Cleverly to Winchester, December 24, 1859 (BFO 97/102B).

[153] *O Boletim*, May 29, 1871; Corvo, *Relatorio e Documentos*.

[154] W. A. P. Martin, *A Cycle of Cathay or China, South and North* (Edinburgh, Oliphant, Anderson and Ferrier, 1896), 32.

[155] See Article 22 of the Emigration Convention in Appendix 2.

[156] Kung to Alcock, March 15, 1866 (BFO 17/873).

[157] Corvo, *Relatorio e Documentos*, 26-29, 30-33.

China coast, and that China's refusal to cooperate was one of the principal causes of the perpetuation of the irregularities. It was pointed out that many of the 15,138 Chinese handed over to local Chinese authorities from 1868 to 1872 by the superintendent of emigration at Macau, because they were unwilling to emigrate, ended up back in the barracoons.[158] *O Oriente*, a Macau newspaper, accused Chinese officials of being in league with crimps.[159]

Revisions in Macau's emigration laws in 1868,[160] 1871,[161] 1872,[162] and 1873[163] attempted to emulate the provisions of the Emigration Convention of 1866. These and other measures were meant to demonstrate to the Chinese authorities in Peking that the Macau government disapproved of the abuses of subjects of a friendly nation.[164] In November 1868, when the Portuguese consul at Lima reported that 48 Chinese laborers on a hacienda on the Peruvian coast were branded on the cheek like slaves, Governor Horta suspended emigration from Macau to Peru.[165] The Portuguese government in Lisbon complained to the Spanish government about the treatment of Chinese in Cuba.[166] When Antonio Sergio de Sousa took over the governorship of Macau in 1870, he personally examined many emigrants and released large numbers of them to their homes.[167] In 1873, Governor Januario decreed that all contracts entered into with Chinese emigrants at Macau contain the stipulation that they be provided with a return passage to China and that the length of the contract be reduced from eight to six years.[168]

These actions may have demonstrated a measure of good will, but they failed to stop abuses. In April 1873, Governor Januario, admitted that his government was totally powerless to eliminate fraud and deception from the

---

[158] Ibid., 72.

[159] *O Oriente*, June 27, 1872.

[160] *O Boletim*, August 24, 1868.

[161] Ibid., May 29, 1871.

[162] Ibid., June 1, 1872.

[163] Ibid., January 25, 1873, July 19, 1873.

[164] Horta a Ministro e Secretario d'Estado dos Negocios da Marinha e Ultramar, Novembro 25, 1868 (AHU, Pasta 25, Macao, 1868).

[165] Horta a Consul do Perú, Novembro 18, 1868 (AHU, Pasta 25, Macao, 1868); *O Boletim*, November 23, 1868.

[166] *Gazeta de Macau e Timor*, October 15, 1872.

[167] Smale to Foster, August 17, 1870 (BFO 17/878).

[168] *O Boletim*, January 25, 1873, July 19, 1873.

emigration traffic.[169] It was maintained that the crimps so brainwashed the emigrants into doing and saying as they dictated, so as to deceive the hated foreigner, that even three separate examinations before emigration officials were unable to detect all the victims of coercion.[170]

But the crimps could not have been so successful without the collusion of Macau officials. *O Echo do Povo*, a Portuguese-language newspaper based in Hong Kong, had hammered away at the abuses of emigration at Macau throughout the 1860s, blaming the Macau authorities as much as the crimps.[171] But it was not until 1872 that some elements in Macau itself began to voice their opposition to the traffic. The newspaper *Gazeta de Macau e Timor* called for a reassessment of the emigration trade, suggesting that its continuance might be doing the colony more harm than good. Its editors argued,

> If a colony lives at the expense of this social phenomenon (emigration), transitory by its very nature, and neglects opportunities to pursue the more stable commercial adventures and to deploy its energies in the development of resources which could endure indefinitely, the time will certainly come when the colony will be abandoned to impotence and misery.[172]

A growing body of opinion, both in government and among the people, regarded the emigration traffic as an evil that had corrupted the morals of the colony and alienated it from more legitimate sources of prosperity. P. G. Mesnier summed up the thinking of many Macaese when he wrote in the *China Review* in the fall of 1873, "This trade is not a hen that lays golden eggs; it is a minotaur that makes an Augean stable of Macau."[173] João de Andrade

---

[169] Corvo, *Relatorio e Documentos*, 47.

[170] Sousa a Ministro e Secretario d'Estado, Agosto 31, 1868 (AHU, Pasta 25, Macao, 1868); Januario a Ministro e Secretario d'Estado, Junho 20, 1872 (Ibid., Pasta 27, Macao, 1872); MacDonnell to Hubert, June 22, 1872 (BFO 17/881).

[171] As outlined by Jeffrey L. Grossman in a seminar paper entitled "The Portuguese View of the Chinese Contract Labor Trade: 1851-1874" (Harvard University, May, 1972), the *O Echo do Povo* carried on a continuous debate on Macau emigration throughout the 1860s with the *Ta-Ssi Yang-Kuo*, a Macau newspaper which defended the traffic.

[172] *Gazeta de Macau e Timor*, October 15, 1872.

[173] Mesnier, "A Reply to 'Macao and Its Slave Trade,'" 125.

Corvo, minister and secretary of state for overseas affairs, in his report to the Cortes in Lisbon on Macau emigration, explained that the real interests of the colony were sacrificed to an illusory prosperity, which sapped the energy of the population and discredited the Portuguese name.[174] He pointed out that the commerce of Macau had been stationary in recent years and that the rising cost of supervising the emigration process offset the growth in government revenues from the increased traffic.[175] Besides, the relations with China were becoming less and less cordial and might come to open hostility if the traffic was not abandoned.[176]

Bowing to pressure from all sides[177] the Portuguese government in Lisbon directed Governor Januario to terminate emigration from Macau.[178] A decree published in the colony's official newspaper on December 27, 1873, proclaimed an end to Chinese contract emigration as of March 27, 1874.[179] The announcement was received by the Macaese with mixed feelings. By a stroke of a pen, a business that poured $200,000 annually into the colony's coffers was wiped out and 20,000 to 30,000 people were thrown out of work.[180] Nevertheless, to the credit of Macau, the majority of the voting population of the colony sanctioned the painful surgery by selecting, in a bitterly contested election on March 1, 1874, an anti-emigration candidate to represent them in the Cortes in Lisbon over his opponent, who was put forward by the pro-emigration faction.[181]

The last ship with Chinese contract laborers to Latin America sailed from Macau on March 27, 1874, the day before the decree banning emigration became effective.[182] A traffic that commenced at the port of Amoy in 1847; that flourished at the ports of Cumsingmoon, Amoy, Swatow, Hong Kong, and Canton for brief periods; that was unsuccessful in its attempt to become established at Shanghai and Ningpo; and that for the final decade of its twenty-eight-year history was concentrated at Macau was at an end.

---

[174] Corvo, *Relatorio e Documentos*, 71.

[175] Ibid., 82-83.

[176] Ibid., 71.

[177] See Chapter VIII for an analysis of the various pressures involved.

[178] Corvo, *Relatorio e Documentos*, 85.

[179] *O Boletim*, December 27, 1873.

[180] Mesnier, "A Reply to 'Macao and Its Slave Trade,'" 125.

[181] *Gazeta de Macau e Timor*, March 3, 1874.

[182] *O Boletim*, March 28, 1874.

Thereafter, various attempts by Spain and Peru to revive the traffic proved futile, and though some Chinese did immigrate to Latin America in the last quarter of the nineteenth century, they did so as free agents. However, not all of the more than 275,000 Chinese who embarked for Latin America under the auspices of the "coolie trade" were destined to set foot on American soil, as the voyage took a heavy toll.

CHAPTER IV

THE VOYAGE TO THE NEW WORLD

The Coolie Ship

There's a ship gliding gracefully over the wave
Away for a foreign shore,
She is freighted with many a dusky slave
Some three or four hundred or more;
But the ship without and the ship within
Oh! What a contrast of beauty and sin.

The sky above wears its fairest blue
And the waters are bounding bright,
The wind whistles forth like a cheery tune
To some revelling gay delight;
But gaze on the stiffling hold below
Oh! What a picture of human woe.

The fever is raging, the death damp lies
On many a dusky brow,
But no one friend of their youth to smooth
The pillow of sickness now;
Stowed closely away by measurement true
In steaming bunks of six feet by two.

Daily some victim is hurriedly launched
To his rest in the deep green sea,
While the frantic shouts of his comrades plead
O death! Make me likewise free;
Misery chanting her loudest song
Why should we longer each life prolong.

Anonymous
Printed in the *Friend of China*
September 6, 1856

Immigration to Southeast Asia

B efore judgment can be passed on the process of transporting Chinese laborers to Latin America, a close examination must be made of the entire system, its antecedents, its inception and development, as well as the details of the voyage itself. Since before 1860 the traffic was for the most part unregulated, much of what took place went unrecorded. It was not until the late 1850s that the two principal emigration ports of Hong Kong and Macau commenced keeping regular records of emigrant ships. No official records of emigration were kept at any of the other ports during the entire period. Hence, there are gaps in the story, but sufficient information exists to enable one to make an informed judgment.

Prior to 1842, Chinese emigration was largely confined to Southeast Asia and was conveyed there almost exclusively in Chinese junks.[1] These vessels date back to the second century BC.[2] Built of wood and of varying sizes, displacing anywhere from twenty to nine hundred tons, they sailed out and home again with each change of monsoon. At least from the sixteenth century, following the arrival of Europeans to Southeast Asia, Chinese junks, in an extension southward of coastal commerce, carried a steady stream of traders, artisans, and laborers to Indochina, Siam, Malaya, Sumatra, Java, Borneo, and the Philippines. Leaving China at the commencement of the northeast monsoon in December or January, they sailed down the China sea before strong fair winds, hugging the coastline or hopping from island to island, reaching their destination in ten to forty days.

After Sir Stamford Raffles founded Singapore in 1819, it became the principal port of call for Chinese traders and the arrival of the junks was one of the most important events in the commercial life of the island and was anxiously awaited each year, particularly by the Chinese community. The junks usually brought a wide variety of Chinese goods: earthenware, dried fruits and

---

[1] Portuguese ships brought Chinese emigrants from Macau to Penang and Singapore in the first decades of the nineteenth century. See Wilfred Blythe, *The Impact of Chinese Secret Societies in Malaya* (London, Oxford University Press, 1969), 167.

[2] For detailed descriptions and illustrations of junks see G. R. C. Worcester, *The Junks and Sampans of the Yangtze*, 2 vols. (Shanghai, The Marine Customs, 1947-48); also Ivon A. Donnelly, *Chinese Junks and other Native Crafts* (Shanghai, Kelly and Walsh, 1924).

vegetables, silks, medicine, and tobacco specially cured for the Chinese palate.[3] But by far the most valuable commodities were the emigrants, who were avidly sought after by the gold and tin mines and the spice and sugar plantations.

The system by which the emigration business was conducted varied little over the years. In 1805, it was reported that emigrants who could not afford to pay their passage "pawned their persons to the owners or captains of the junks for a passage and victuals," and that this kind of an arrangement had grown into a regular system of trade involving 10 to 12,000 men annually.[4] A more detailed description of the system was recorded in 1855:

> The passenger (called "Sinkay") not having money to pay for his passage enters into an agreement with the master of the junk to bind himself apprentice to someone at the port of arrival for one year, without wages, only receiving food, clothing and a small sum for barbers expenses, tobacco and other little luxuries; the balance of consideration for the labor of the year is to be handed over to the master of the junk, as payment for the passage money. The Sinkays are kept on board the junks, as security for the passage money, till taken by an employer who in consideration of obtaining his services for one year at a low rate pays part of a year's wages in advance, with which advance the Sinkay clears himself with the junk master.[5]

That was the operation in principle, but since the demand for laborers was great, there came into existence a credit-ticket system whereby professional recruiters and emigration brokers in China, working in conjunction with their counterparts in Southeast Asia, advanced the emigrants the expenses of the voyage and guaranteed them employment at their destination. Since this was essentially a speculative venture on the part of the brokers, the arrangement often entailed selling the new arrival to the highest bidder on the docks of Singapore, Penang, and Malacca. The scene has been described by J. D. Vaughan, superintendent of police at Penang during the 1840s:

> The anchor is scarcely cast when the resident Chinese flock on board to buy sinkes as they term it. The charterer gets for a master workman,

---

3   Lin Ken Wong, "The Trade of Singapore with China," *Journal of the Malayan Branch of the Royal Asiatic Society*, Vol. XXXIII, part 4 (December, 1960), 111.

4   [Thomas Braddell] "Notices of Pinang (sic)," *JIA*, Series I, Vol. VI (1852), 167.

5   "Notes on the Chinese in the Straits," *JIA*, Series 1, Vol. IX, (1855), 114.

either tailor, goldsmith or carpenter, 10 to 15 dollars, for a cooly 6 to 10 dollars, for a sickly man 3 to 4 or less.[6]

There being no regulations of any kind, the more a skipper or a broker could cram onto his junk, the greater was his profit. There are accounts of junks carrying as many as 1,200 to 1,600 emigrants.[7] These were undoubtedly special passenger junks, whereas the majority of the emigrants seemingly made the voyage in regular trading junks as additional cargo. Charles Gutzlaff described the conditions:

> The junks which transport them in great numbers remind one of an African slaver. The deck is filled with them, and there the poor wretches are exposed to the inclemency of the weather and without any shelter, for the cargo fills the junk below. Their food consists of dry rice and an allowance of water; but when the passages are very long there is often a want of both and many of them actually starve to death.[8]

An inquiry into the loss of life on two junks that arrived in Singapore revealed that one lost 250 out of 600 on the passage while the other lost 200 out of 400.[9] Evidently, it was better speculation for a junk to commence with 600 and lose 250 than to start with 300 or less, which was probably much closer to its capacity.

---

[6]   [J. D. Vaughan], "Notes on the Chinese of Pinang (sic)," *JIA* series 1, Vol. VIII (1854), 2.

[7]   "A narrative of the loss of a Chinese vessel, bound to Batavia with 1600 persons on board, of whom 198 were saved by the English ship *Indiana*, commanded by Lieutenant Pearl of the Royal Navy," *Chinese Repository*, Vol. VI, No. 3 (July, 1837), 149-153; also John Crawford, *Journal of an Embassy from the Governor-General of India to the Courts of Siam and Cochin-China*, 2nd ed., 2 vols. (London, Henry Colburn and Richard Bentley, 1830), II, 162.

[8]   *Journal of Three Voyages along the Coast of China in 1831, 1832 and 1833, with Notices of Siam, Corea and the Loochoo islands, to which is Prefixed an Introductory Essay on Policy, Religion, etc. of China by the Rev. W. Ellis*, 3d ed. (London, Thomas Ward and Company, 1840), 146.

[9]   John Cameron, *Our Tropical Possessions in Malayan India: Being a Descriptive Account of Singapore, Penang, Province Wellesley and Malacca; Their People, Products, Commerce and Government* (London, Smith, Elder and Company, 1865), 43.

Estimating the magnitude of this traffic is rather difficult, for nobody kept a record of the comings and goings of the junks. That it was considerable can be deduced from the steady growth of the Chinese population throughout Southeast Asia as indicated in table 6. George Windsor Earl, voyaging through the Indian Archipelago in the early 1830s, reported that from 5,000 to 8,000 Chinese arrived annually at Singapore.[10] J. D. Vaughan estimated that from 2,000 to 3,000 landed each year at Penang,[11] and in 1851, it was reckoned that from 2,500 to 3,000 arrived yearly at Malacca.[12] Siah U Chin, who immigrated to Singapore from Swatow in 1823 and made a fortune in gambier[13] stated that in the 1846-47 season, 10,475 Chinese arrived at that port in 108 junks and 11 square-rigged vessels. About one-eighth of these remained in Singapore while the rest were transshipped to other parts of the archipelago.[14]

Chinese immigration to Southeast Asia in the first half of the nineteenth century was a growing and lucrative business. And as might be expected, following the Opium War (1839-1841) and the subsequent opening of the treaty ports of China to foreign commerce, British, French, Spanish, German, and American ships began to encroach upon the traditional junk monopoly of the passenger trade. A British visitor to Amoy in 1846 reported that during that year, five "European or American vessels" left that port with Chinese passengers for the Straits of Malacca.[15] Junks, with their flat bottoms, were excellent coast and river crafts, but they could not compete on the open seas with the much faster square-rigged vessels, brigs, barks, and schooners of the West. Though the junks gradually lost out, the control of emigration remained in the hands of Chinese merchants and brokers who now chartered Western vessels to ply their trade.

---

[10] *The Eastern Seas or Voyages and Adventures in the Indian Archipelago in 1832-33-34* (London, William H. Allen and Company, 1837), 367. See also David Abeel, *Journal of a Residence in China and the Neighboring Countries from 1830 to 1833* (London, James Nisbit and Company, 1835), xv.

[11] "Notes on the Chinese at Pinang," *JIA*, Series I, Vol. VIII (1854), 2.

[12] H. Croockewit, "The Tin Mines of Malacca," *JIA*, Series I, Vol. VIII (1854), 123.

[13] A plant extract used in dyeing and tanning and produced from the leaves of the uncaria gambir. The extract is known in pharmacy as catechu.

[14] "The Chinese in Singapore," *JIA*, Series I, Vol. II, (1848), 283.

[15] George Smith, *A Narrative of an Exploratory Visit to each of the Consular Cities of China and to the Islands of Hong Kong and Chuson in the Years of 1844, 1845 and 1846* (London, Seeley, Burnside and Seeley, 1857), 482.

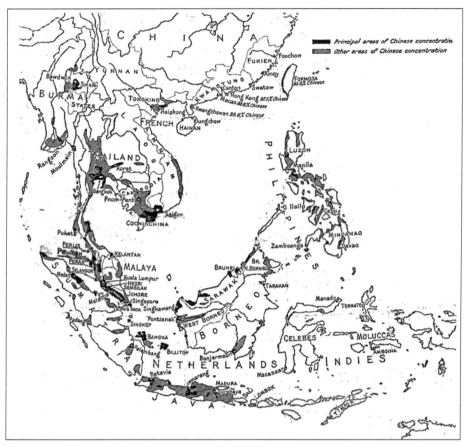

Map 5 Showing areas of Chinese concentration in Southeast Asia
(adapted from *Geographical Review*, Vol. XXXIV, April, 1944, 198)

Table 6

Growth of the Chinese Population in Southeast Asia from 1820 to 1860

	Singapore		Penang		Malacca	
Year	Chinese	% of total pop.	Chinese	% of total pop.	Chinese	% of total pop
1820	3,000★	60%	7,900	22%	1,000	5%
1830	6,600	39%	9,000	26%	4,800	16%
1840	17,200	43%	9,700	24%	6,900	15%
1850	28,000	47%	15,500	36%	10,600	17%
1860	50,000	61%	28,000	47%	10,000	15%

★Note: the figures are approximations and rounded to the nearest hundred.
Source: Adapted from Lennox A. Mills, *British Malaya, 1824-1867*
(London, Oxford University Press, 1966), 217-218.

Immigration Expands Westward

With the involvement of Western shipping in Chinese immigration to Southeast Asia, it was a comparatively easy step to expand the movement beyond the Nanyang (literally Southern Ocean, a Chinese term for Southeast Asia as a whole) to North and South America and Australia. In what is regarded by some as the beginning of the coolie trade, the French bark *Joseph and Claire* left Amoy in 1845 with 180 indentured Chinese laborers for the sugar plantations of Mauritius.[16] Chinese had gone to Mauritius as contract laborers prior to this date, but not directly from the China coast.[17] Two years later, the *Oquendo*, a Spanish brig, and the *Duke of Argyle*, a British vessel, set sail for Cuba with 220 and 412 indentured emigrants, respectively. In 1848, the British-owned *Nimrod* conveyed 120 Chinese to Sydney, Australia; and the Danish ship *Frederek William* took 75 to Peru in 1849. The same year, some 200 emigrants sailed from Shanghai for California on the *Amazon*, a British vessel. The movement westward had begun. In subsequent years, Chinese laborers under contract for three, five, and eight years departed the coasts of China for Hawaii, California, Australia, Mauritius, Bombay, Tahiti, Borneo, Labuan, Java, Manila, and Louisiana, as well as for Latin America. There are no complete statistics on this exodus of contract labor, but table 7 gives a partial listing of Chinese contract laborers to countries other than Latin America.

The long-established pattern of immigration to Southeast Asia served as the model for the expansion of the movement to the West and facilitated its commencement. However, there were some differences. While the average Chinese emigrant was willing to trust his fellow countrymen and take his chances on making his fortune in Southeast Asia, he was extremely reluctant to go further afield particularly when the invitation to do so came from a barbarian. The Chinese emigrant was no reckless adventurer, and if he did consent to explore new horizons, it was only with the security of written contracts that guaranteed to him a fixed wage for a set period of time after which he could return to his homeland. It was under such conditions that earlier experiments in Chinese labor to Trinidad, to Brazil, and Mauritius

---

[16]   Martin R. Montgomery, *China*, 2 vols. (London, James Madden, 1847) Vol. I, 79. A second French ship left Amoy in 1846 with 200 men for Mauritius, see Winchester to Bowring, August 26, 1854 (BPP, ASS, *China*, Vol. III), 19.

[17]   In 1843 five ships sailed from the British colony of Singapore with 582 Chinese for Mauritius. See Table 7.

had taken place.[18] Now again in the late 1840s, when new efforts were being made to tap China's immense labor resources, the written contract seems to have played a key role.

Chinese emigrants throughout the nineteenth century were variously classified as "contract" or "indentured," "credit-ticket" or "free" laborers. The "contract" or "indentured" laborer bound himself to service in a written agreement for a specified number of years on specified terms. The "credit-ticket" or "free" emigrant agreed, usually verbally, to work for whoever extended the credit for his passage until his debt was paid. In neither case was the emigrant truly free, and once in the clutches of his employer or creditor, he often found himself reduced to virtual slavery for an indefinite period, if not for life. A small minority of emigrants paid their own passage money or had it paid for them by relatives or friends. These were the free emigrants, but the vast majority were too poor to pay and hence were at the mercy of unscrupulous brokers and merchants.

According to Harry Parkes, the British interpreter at the Canton consulate in the early 1850s, the greater numbers of the emigrants to Southeast Asia proceeded thither under some form of contractual agreement for a stated number of years at a fixed rate of pay or a share in the profits of the plantation or business.[19] However, the written contract seems to have been almost universally employed at the commencement of immigration to the Western world Despite the fact that Californians strongly objected to the introduction of laborers under any kind of bondage, it is known that at least some ships bound for California carried indentured laborers. The United States ship *Oneca*, which left Hong Kong in December 1851 for San Francisco, was reported by the *Friend of China* to have 275 passengers "engaged for a term of years."[20] The investigation into the disastrous mutiny aboard the *Robert Browne* revealed that the ship was bound for San Francisco with emigrants under a written contract for five years' service.[21] Robert Irick suggests that the *Robert Browne* was secretly bound for South America.[22]

---

[18]   See Chapters I and VI.

[19]   BPP, ASS, *China*, Vol. III, 37-38.

[20]   *Friend of China*, June 11, 1851.

[21]   Ibid., May 12, 1852.

[22]   Irick, "The Ch'ing Policy Towards the Coolie Trade, 1847-1878," 499-500, Footnote 65.

Table 7

Indentured Chinese Emigrants to Places other than Latin America in the Nineteenth Century*

Year	Australia	Bombay	Borneo	California	Hawaii	Java	Labuan	Manila	Mauritius	Réunion	Tahiti
1843									582		
1845										180	
1846										200	
1848	269										
1849	150							500			
1850	406										
1851	1,871			275	192				234		
1852	977			410	101						
1853	407			300							
1854	914				206						
1856	200										
1858	337										
1864		2,370									337
1865			62		527						698
1866					260	436	164				
1870							70				

*Note: This table only includes those emigrants known to have been indentured, and since the fact of indenture was often concealed or simply not mentioned, the table is by no means complete.

Source: Adapted from table 49 in appendix VI.

The existing evidence does not support such a contention. It is possible that the surviving members of the crew who testified that the ship was destined for California were deceived as were the passengers. But the fact that the Hong Kong newspapers of the day registered no surprise that a ship bound for San Francisco should be carrying contract laborers indicated that this was the norm rather than the exception.

The editor of the *Alta*, a California newspaper, claimed in 1855 that a large percentage of Chinese in California were contract laborers.[23] This is supported by a dispatch of February 1849 from John W. Davis, the United States commissioner to China, who described Chinese immigration to California in these terms:

> A new species of enterprise is springing up between this country and the West Coast of the United States. A large number of Chinese coolies (laborers) and mechanics are being hired for a term of years at low wages to be shipped to California, and then to be rehired to labor at their various vocations to the stipulations of a written contract between parties.[24]

Even twenty-two years later, in 1871, the United States consul in Hong Kong, David H. Bailey, after four months of intensive investigation of Chinese emigration at that port, concluded thus:

> Emigration from China to all parts of the world is an organized business or trade, in which men of large capital and Hongs of great wealth engage as a regular traffic, by which men are bought and sold for so much per head, precisely as a piece of merchandise is handled at its market value . . . The coolie of China is bought by the rich trader, to serve his purchaser at low wages, for a series of years in a foreign country, under contract, for the faithful performance of which, in many instances, he gives a mortgage on his wife and children; with a stipulation that at the end of his term of service he is to be brought back to China by his purchaser. This contract is sold by the dealer, through his agents in the United States and elsewhere at a large advance and is a source of great

---

23   Gunther Barth, *Bitter Strength: A History of the Chinese in the United States, 1850-1870* (Cambridge, Massachusetts, Harvard University Press, 1964), 57.

24   Davis to Clayton, February 22, 1849, U.S. Dept. of State, *Diplomatic Despatches*, Vol. V.

profit to capitalists who have the means to buy and sell large numbers of men. This contract, in the United States, is no doubt null and void, but nevertheless the coolie will comply strictly with all its terms, a copy of which in Chinese characters is always in his possession; and this he will do because his purchaser holds his household lares in the land to which he always hopes and expects to return in pledge for the faithful performance of his bonds.[25]

If this then was the credit-ticket system, how did it materially differ from the trade in contract laborers to Latin America? Excluding the treatment that Chinese laborers received in North and South America, two major factors set the trades apart. In 1852, a number of Chinese returned to Hong Kong from San Francisco with modest fortunes in gold.[26] This was incentive enough to attract large numbers of poverty-stricken people and eliminated the need for any strong-arm methods of persuasion. Secondly, Chinese merchants in Hong Kong and in San Francisco quickly gained control of the movement and, by the subtle manipulation of family and ancestral ties, regulated and controlled the life and work of the emigrants at all times and in all places. Hence immigration to California was outwardly quite different from the "coolie trade," its indentured nature being largely invisible—so much so that Dr. Bowring could inform the British Foreign Office in January 1852 that "Chinese immigration to California is now almost wholly confined to independent emigrants who pay their own passage money and are in a condition to look to their own arrangements."[27]

It would seem that much the same happened in respect to Chinese immigration to Australia, only that there, the transition from contract labor to the credit-ticket system was slower in coming. The reason being that gold was not discovered in Victoria until 1853, and the control of emigration was not in the hands of the Chinese until later in the decade.[28]

---

[25] Bailey to Davis, April 25, 1871, Hong Kong, U.S. Dept. of State, Despatches of United States Consuls in Hong Kong, 1844-1906.

[26] Bowring to Malmesbury, May 17, 1852 (BPP, ASS, *China*, Vol. III), 2. See also Léon Rousset, "Les Chinois Hors de Chez Eux," *Le Correspondent*, Vol. CXII (10 Juillet, 1888), 100-102.

[27] Bowring to Malmesbury, January 5, 1853 (Ibid.).

[28] BPP, *Emigration*, Vol. XII, "Fifteenth General Report of the Colonial Land and Emigration Commissioners, 1855," 36-37.

The inference here is that Chinese emigration could best be promoted by the Chinese themselves. In the immigration to California and Australia, the written contract entered into with Western capitalists served as a primer to start the movement, and gold and Chinese know-how quickly expanded the trickle into a stream, the problem eventually being how to stop it. In Latin America and elsewhere, where there was no gold rush, and where Chinese emigration remained in Western hands, getting the movement to flow was an ongoing problem. In these circumstances, the labor contract and the art of persuasion, often pushed to extremes, were deemed a necessity if laborers were to be obtained.

Windfall Profits

The call of the "Gold Mountains," the name given by the Chinese to the California Ranges and the gold fields of Victoria and New South Wales, brought a rush of emigrants to the seaports along China's southern coastline. Western capitalists were ready to pay inflated prices for laborers, and Chinese in their thousands were persuaded to leave their homeland. This was a unique windfall to Western shipping. The opening of the treaty ports to foreign commerce in 1842 had glutted the China sea with flags of almost all nations. Now even old hulks and vessels in all stages of unseaworthiness were pressed into service.[29] Many ships with poor or nonexistent ventilation were entirely unsuitable for passengers, but reckless and irresponsible skippers ignored any such considerations and took every shortcut to increase their earnings.

The bigger and better-equipped ships, mostly belonging to British and American companies, were snatched up for the trade in passengers to California, which was at its height in 1853, while the agents for Cuba, Peru, and British Guiana had to be content with anything that could stay afloat.[30] The consequences were not surprising. Four of the seven ships that sailed for South America in 1850 suffered mutinies, and on three that reached their destination, 251 emigrants of the 920 that embarked, or 27 percent, died at sea. Besides the inadequate facilities of the vessels, there was the added liability of the character of the emigrants themselves. The editor of the *Friend of China*

---

[29]   W. F. Mayers and N. B. Dennys, *The Treaty Ports of China and Japan* (London, Trubner and Company, 1857), 67; *Overland Register and Price Current*, June 7, 1854; White to Rogers, March 10, 1853 (BPP, ASS, *China*, Vol. III), 250.

[30]   Mayers and Dennys, *The Treaty Ports of China and Japan*, 67. See also *Overland Register and Price Current*, June 6, 1854. Rousset, "Les Chinois Hors de Chez Eux," 97-98.

urged shipmasters at the opening of the emigration season in 1853 to think long and hard before they engaged in the traffic in laborers to South America:

> The candidates for emigration will be the scum of the empire, or kidnapped men who retaliate on the ship that takes them; friends of kidnapped men who have committed suicide in the guano pits; jail birds who have escaped; rebels who know the use of arms and who have witnessed every atrocity and act of barbarous torture; Triads from the Straits that carry the kris and know something of navigation; wretches with manacle marks on their legs, whose necks the lumbering forms of a British court of justice have saved and to whom European blood will be nectar. A precious witches cauldron! Bubble! Bubble! Bubble! We say beware![31]

As events were to prove, the warning was timely, but few took heed, for the profits of the trade far outweighed the risks. The same newspaper estimated that a vessel taking 300 emigrants to Peru in 1852 could clear $86,000 after all expenses were paid.[32] Earlier it reported that the British ship *Coromandel* sold its cargo of 350 emigrants at Callao for $407 each, which, allowing $100 per head for expenses, meant a profit of over $300 per emigrant to importer Don D. Elias.[33] James J. O'Kelly, correspondent for the *New York Herald*, who visited a ship that brought 900 Chinese to Havana in 1873, reported that the cargo, which cost $40,000 in China, was worth $450,000 to the importers.[34] Even by conservative estimates, the profit was at least five times that which could be realized from a similar voyage to San Francisco. The average fare per passenger from China to California was $50, which amounted to $15,000 for a cargo of 300 emigrants.[35] The big money in the California trade was realized by the Chinese brokers who advanced the passage money to their countrymen and in return controlled their labor in the New World. In the traffic to Latin America, the shipowners themselves or the companies that chartered the ships, by selling the labor of the emigrant for the contract period, reaped immediate and vast returns on their investment. The following tables, pieced together from the accounts of contemporary observers, provide a breakdown of the transactions:

---

[31]   *Friend of China*, November 23, 1853.

[32]   Ibid., September 25, 1852.

[33]   Ibid., March 24, 1852.

[34]   *The Mambi-Land, or Adventures of a Herald Correspondent in Cuba* (London, Sampson, Low, Marston and Company, 1874), 66.

[35]   Barth, *Bitter Strength*, 68.

Table 8
Income Statement on Shipment of 300 Chinese
Emigrants to Cuba

Revenues

Sale of 270 labor contracts at Havana from $125-$500 each,
$33,750-$135,000 (allowing for 10% mortality at sea)

Expenses

To crimp or kidnapper	$3-$45
Brokerage fee	$4-$8
Advance to emigrant	$8-$12
Clothing for passage	$5-$12
Provisions for voyage	$12-$15
Commission to agent in China	$5
Consular fee	$5
Freight per passenger	$50-$75
Cost per emigrant	$92-$177
Total outlay for 300 emigrants	$27,600-$53,100
Net profit	$6,150-$81,900

Sources: Hong Kong Mercury and Shipping Gazette, December 3, 1866; Mayers
and Dennys, *The Treaty Ports of China and Japan*, 228; "Emigration and
the Coolie Trade in China," *Westminster Review*, Vol. M., No. 1 (July,
1873), 90; *Hong Kong Daily Press*, April 5, 1871.

Table 9
Income Statement on Shipment of 300 Chinese
Emigrants to Peru

Revenues

Sale of 270 labor contracts at Callao from $300-$450 each . . . .
$81,000-$121,500 (allowing for 10% mortality at sea)
Government bounty of $30 per emigrant .... $8,100[*]

Expenses

Charter of vessel for 9 months at $1,025 per month	$9,225
Outfitting vessel at $8 per passenger	$2,400
Outlay on each emigrant to day of departure-$70	$21,000
Provisions for voyage at $15 per emigrant	$4,500
Wages of captain and crew	$8,000
Outlay for 300 emigrants	$45,125
Net profit	$43,975-$84,475

★Note: This bounty ceased permanently with the Peruvian government's
prohibition of Chinese immigration in March 1856.

Sources: The *Friend of China*, September 25, 1852; Stewart, *Chinese Bondage in Peru*, 80, 82; Mayers and Dennys, *Treaty Ports of China and Japan*, 228; Mr. Robertson, June 9, 1866 (BFO 17/873), 119; William Hillebrand, *Report on the Supply of Labor, etc., to the Honorable Board of Immigration of the Hawaiian Islands* (Honolulu, Government Press, 1867), 5.

These tabulations do not include the fees at the port of destination and the expenses incurred in disposing of the emigrants. Nor do they include the bribes or hush money exacted by local Chinese authorities at the port of embarkation, which no doubt varied considerably, but could be taken to be at least equivalent to the regular consular fee of five dollars per emigrant. Notwithstanding these extra expenses, that the profit of the trade compared favorably with those of the slave trade can be seen from the income statement on a shipment of five hundred slaves from Angola to Brazil in 1845 drawn up by Edmund Gabriel, Acting British Commissioner to Loanda:

Table 10

Income Statement on Shipment of 500 Slaves from Angola to Brazil in 1845

Revenues

Sale of 450 slaves at £60 each, £ 27,000 (allowing for 10% mortality at sea)

Expenses

Purchase of 500 slaves at £ 3.10 each .... £ 1,750

Freight to Brazil at £ 17.10 each 8,500

Provisions 600

Expenses of landing 500

Preparing slaves for sale 350

Total outlay .... £ 11,700

Net Profit .... £ 15,300 (or $68,000)★

★Note: The rate of exchange taken here is four shillings and sixpence to the dollar.

Source: Gabriel to Aberdeen, December 31, 1845 (BFO 881/316).

The freight of tea from China to the Americas in the early 1850s averaged $19 per ton, or $9,500 for a cargo of five hundred tons.[36] Hence, a ship trading in Chinese emigrants to Cuba or Peru netted a profit of from five to ten times that of a ship trading in tea.

These enormous profits attracted ships of all sizes and types carrying the flags of nineteen nations. Initially, British, French, and Peruvian flags predominated. British bottoms carried the bulk of the emigrants from 1852 to 1854 after United States clippers invaded the China tea trade in 1851 and sent British shipping scrambling for employment.[37] In 1855, the British Parliament under pressure from the Anti-Slavery lobby and in response to repeated appeals from British consuls on the China Coast passed the "Chinese Passengers Act," whereby British ships, before proceeding to sea with Chinese passengers, had to obtain the certificate of an emigration officer that the vessel was seaworthy, properly ventilated, and provisioned and capable in every respect of carrying its passengers safely to their destination. It was decided to appoint emigration officers only at Hong Kong, and all ships had to proceed thither for their papers and examination. The penalty for noncompliance was forfeiture of the ship together with all its appurtenances. The *Merchantile Marine Magazine and Nautical Record* denounced the act as "inquisitorial" and "destructive of the Chinese passenger trade" and lamented, "The annals of Parliamentary enactments would be searched in vain to discover any instance of statutory interference so stringent and so arbitrary, but also openly provoked."[38] It was generally felt that the Parliamentary

---

[36] "Report of Consul Roberton on the Trade of the Port of Canton for the year 1854," (BPP, ASS, *China*, Vol. VI), 17.

[37] British navigation laws were so protective as to give the ship-building industry little incentive to make improvements. The laws were repealed in 1849, but the change came too late to ward off American competition. However, by the middle of the 1850s British ships were challenging their American counterparts: see Basil Lubbock, *The Clipper Ships* (Glasgow, James Brown and Son, 1914), 58. Also White to Barkly, July 19, 1851 (BPP, ASS, *China*, Vol. III), 203.

[38] "The Chinese Passengers Act," *The Mercantile Marine and Nautical Record*, Vol. XXI, No. 22 (October, 1855), 387.

restrictions were the inevitable result of the failure of the shipowners and their agents to correct abuses in the trade. Prior to the passage of the act, mutinies had occurred on seven British vessels carrying emigrants to South America.[39]

Though the act was inadequate to regulate the traffic and, furthermore, was not enforced by British officials in China until the end of the decade, notice had been served on British shipping, and larger American vessels began to replace the smaller British ships. The first ship on record flying the United States flag to participate in this trade was the *Ohio*, which took 300 Chinese laborers from Cumsingmoon to Peru in 1852. The following year, the *Minna* took a shipment of emigrants to Peru from Canton. The *Sea Witch* and the *Boy* entered the trade in 1854, and in 1855, thirteen vessels with Chinese emigrants for South America sailed under the United States flag. A slowdown in Chinese immigration to California, as well as increased competition in the tea trade from the British, who were fast catching up with American technology, caused many of the famous tea clippers built by such celebrated craftsmen as Donald McKay of Boston and J. Abraham of Baltimore to enter the "coolie trade." Household names—at least along the eastern seaboard of the United States—such as *Westward Ho, Winged Racer, Bald Eagle, Flora Temple, Nightingale, Challenge*, and all ships that had set records and brought glory to the American shipping industry in the tea races from China to the London market in the early 1850s were now reduced to the ignominy of what some regarded as trafficking in slavery.[40]

---

[39]   See list of mutinies, Table 17.

[40]   Basil Lubbock, *Coolie Ships and Oil Sailors,* 36; Arthur H. Clark, *The Clipper Ship Era: An Epitome of Famous American and British Clipper Ships, Their Owners, Builders, Commanders and Crews, 1843-1869* (London, G. P. Pubnam's Sons, 1911), 196-197.

Figure 5. The clipper ship Nightingale. Built for the China tea trade, the Nightingale was bought and sailed by the notorious slave captain Francis Bowen of Salem. Of 1066 tons, she entered the "Coolie Trade" in 1856. (From Clipper Ship Prints by N. Currier and Currier and Ives, New York, Antique Bulletin Publishing Company 1930, 43)

American diplomats in China tried to stop this growing involvement of United States ships. Warning that the involvement of the American flag might be a possible source of friction between the United States and China, they claimed that the contract for service under which the Chinese laborer was shipped was in violation of the act of Congress prohibiting the slave trade.[41] One United States firm, Messrs. Sampson and Tappan of Boston, owners of the clipper ships *Westward Ho* and *Winged Racer*, after communicating with Dr. Peter Parker, the American commissioner in China, cancelled their contract with the Brazilian government to ship 2,000 Chinese laborers to Rio de Janeiro and withdrew from the trade. The contract with Brazil was signed in 1855, and only one shipload had been delivered when it was terminated the following year.[42]

---

[41]   Eldon Griffin, *Clippers and Consuls; American Consular and Commercial Relations with Eastern Asia, 1845-1860* (Wilmington, Delaware, Scholarly Resources Inc. 1972), 194-199.

[42]   José Pedro Xavier Pinheiro, *Importação de Trabalhadores Chins: Memoria Apresentada ao* Ministerio *da Agricultura, Commercio e Obras Publicas* (Rio

Other United States firms, however, persisted in the trade with an average of eight ships participating annually from 1856 to 1861. These firms challenged the claim that the traffic was prohibited by United States laws, and their position received support from J. S. Black, the attorney general of the United States, who, in a letter to Lewis Cass, the secretary of state, in 1859, expressed the opinion that the trade in Chinese emigrants did not come under the provisions of any existing United States laws and suggested that Congress alone could remedy the evil.[43] As in the case with Great Britain, it took several mutinies on board United States ships and an aroused public opinion to move Congress to act. In February 1862, a law was passed prohibiting all United States citizens and the American flag from participating in any manner whatsoever in the traffic in Chinese emigrants to Latin America. The penalty for its violation was forfeiture of the vessel together with a fine of up to $2,000 and a year in prison. The last ship flying the United States flag carrying emigrants to South America sailed for Peru from Macau on January 26, 1862.[44]

Some American clippers were bought by Peruvians, Portuguese, and Italians and, with changed names and flags, continued what they had been doing. The *White Falcon* and the *Climax* became the *Napoleon Canevaro* and the *Antonio Terry* under the Peruvian flag; the *Telegraph* became the *Galileo*, flying the Italian colors; and the *Twilight* became *Dom Pedro I* under the Portuguese flag.[45] These flags, together with the French and Spanish colors, carried the bulk of the trade until its cessation in 1874.[46] The flag of San Salvador made a dramatic appearance in 1863, flying over what were formerly Peruvian vessels. This persisted until 1871, and thereafter, the ships reverted to carrying their former colors. Some of these ships were first transferred

---

de Janeiro, Typographia de João Ignacio da Silva, 1869), 147-149; *Report of the Committee Appointed by the Government of the "Board of Trade" to take into consideration the Communication of Messers. Sampson and Tappan, dated April 24, 1856* (Boston, J. H. Eastburn's Press, 1856), 12-19; *Boston Board of Trade 1857: Third Annual Report* (Boston, George C. Rand and Avery, 1857), 15-18.

[43]   Black to Cass, March 11, 1859 (U.S. Congress, House Report No. 443, I sess. 36 Cong.), 23.

[44]   See Table 36 in Appendix VI.

[45]   Lubbock, *Coolie Ships and Oil Sailors*, 38.

[46]   See Table 11 for the national registration of ships carrying Chinese emigrants to Cuba.

to the Italian flag in 1867, which coincided with the outbreak of civil war in Peru. The owners may have adopted this measure in an effort to avoid entanglement in internal Peruvian politics, which would seem to indicate that the controlling interests lay outside the country, perhaps in New York or London. That the flying of a particular flag did not always reveal the nationality of the ships' true owners was underscored by Rutherford Alcock, the British commissioner in China, in a letter to Lord Stanley at the Foreign Office, which stated, "British ships undergo a simulated sale at Hong Kong, carry coolies to South America under another flag, then by another simulated sale the ship reverts to the original owners."[47]

Of the 742 ships, of which there is some record that left the coasts of China with Chinese laborers for Latin America, 130 sailed under the French flag; 115 under that of Peru; 102 under the British flag; 80 under Spanish colors; 62 under the United States flag; 43 under Italian registration; 37 each under the Portuguese and Salvadorian flags; 28 under the Dutch flag; 15 each under the Russian and German colors, eight under Chilean registration; 6 under the Austrian flag; 4 each under the Norwegian and Belgian flags; 3 under Danish colors; 1 each under the Mexican, Colombian, Ecuadorian, and Swiss flags; and forty-nine whose flags are unknown.

The vast majority of these ships were sailing vessels, brigs, barks, and schooners; and in the early days of the trade, they were rather small, averaging around five hundred tons. From the middle of the 1850s onward, when the tea clippers entered the trade, many vessels were from a thousand to fifteen hundred tons. Some, like the *Bald Eagle* and the *Nightingale* of the United States, were veterans of the African slave trade.[48] A dozen or so were specially built for the traffic in New York, San Francisco, and Marseilles.[49] But most were regular cargo ships that carried coal or guano or some other commodity to the China coast and were there outfitted to carry passengers on the homeward voyage.

Two of the ships built at Marseilles, the *Francis I* and the *Charles Martel*, had auxiliary steam power, which was used only during calms or storms when sails were ineffective or hazardous.[50] These first appeared in 1857. Although

---

47   Alcock to Stanley, November 26, 1866 (BFO 17/873). See also Crawford to Granville, September 3, 1873 (BFO 881/2598).

48   Lubbock, *Coolie Ships and Oil Sailors*, 19, 49.

49   *Hong Kong Mercury and Shipping Gazette*, July 16, 1855; *The Friend of China*, May 23, 1857.

50   *The Friend of China*, May 23, 1857.

British and American steamers were being used on regular runs on the China coast between Hong Kong, Canton and Macau as early as 1844, steamships were slow to undertake the ocean voyages.[51]

Table 11

National Registration of Ships that Transported Chinese Emigrants to Cuba from 1847-Sept. 1, 1873, and Mortality on the Voyage

Flag	Vessels	Tonnage	Embarked	Landed	Died at Sea	Percentage of deaths
French	104	64,664	38,540	33,795	4,745	12.31
Spanish	78	47,604	31.356	28,685	3,271	10.43
British	35	27,815	13,697	11,457	2,240	16.31
American	34	40,576	18,206	16,419	1,787	9.80
Portuguese	21	15,847	8,228	7,266	962	11.70
Dutch	19	14,906	8,133	7,132	981	12.09
Russian	12	9,857	5,471	5,093	378	6.90
German	8	4,207	2,176	1,932	244	11.21
Peruvian	6	4,979	2,609	1,999	610	23.38
Italian	5	5,586	2,832	2,505	327	11.20
Norwegian	5	2,296	1,366	1,104	262	19.18
Salvadorian	4	4,145	2,031	1,943	88	4.33
Chilean	4	1,702	926	743	183	19.76
Belgian	3	2,482	1,199	1,182	17	1.42
Austrian	3	1,377	936	864	72	7.70
Danish	1	1,021	470	291	179	38.00
Totals	342	249,065	138,156	121,810	16,346	11.83

Source: compiled by John V. Crawford, British Consul General at Havana, See BFO 881/2598.

Seemingly, obtaining the proper grade of coal in Asia and en route was initially a problem.[52] The first full steamers to take Chinese passengers to

---

[51]   C. A. Gibson-Hill, "The Steamers Employed in Asian Waters, 1819-1839," *Journal of the Malayan Branch of the Royal Asiatic Society*, Vol. XXVII (May, 1854), 120.

[52]   Edward K. Haviland, *American Steam Navigation in China 1845-1878* (Salem, Mass., The American Neptune Incorporated, 1956-1958), 3.

South America were the *Cleopatra*, *Scotia*, and *Mauritius* in 1858. All three were converted sailing vessels, and as far as it can be ascertained, only made one run each.[53] The *Cataluña*, a 1,300-ton Spanish steamer, made the trip annually from 1866 to 1871, and in 1872, there were six steamers in the trade. At about the same time, steamers were taking over from sailing vessels in the passenger trades from China to California, Australia, and Southeast Asia, as well as from Europe to North America.

The length of the voyage varied considerably depending upon the season of the year, calms, storms, and stopovers at various points en route to replenish supplies and, if necessary, to repair damages. The longest voyage on record was made by the French vessel *Carmelina*, 1,285 tons, which left Macau with 653 emigrants on November 7, 1867, and arrived at Havana on September 12, 1868, 214 days later. In 1852, the British ship *Lord Elgin*, on a voyage from Amoy to British Guiana with 154 emigrants, took 177 days. But these were the exceptions. The official computation as to the duration of various voyages from Hong Kong determined in 1853 was 100 days to California, 120 days to Peru, and 147 days to the West Indies.[54] These calculations served as a guide to ships in determining the amount of provisions to take on board. Though some vessels took longer than these liberal estimates, the average trip to Peru lasted about 110 days and to the West Indies about 120 days. Steamers bettered these averages by about ten to twenty days.[55]

Ocean Routes

Most passenger vessels, adhering to the centuries-old tradition of the junks, departed the China coast during the northeasterly monsoon, which commenced in the middle of September and lasted until the coming of the southerly winds around the beginning of May. These latter added to the length and hazards of the outward voyages and regulations in Canton, Hong Kong, and Macau from 1860 onward forbade passenger vessels to set sail between May 1 and September 15.[56] This rule was more or less faithfully adhered to by the smaller vessels but was widely ignored by the larger clipper ships and particularly by steamers. Map 6 shows the various routes frequented by "coolie ships." Vessels bound for Peru

---

[53]   *Overland Friend of China*, May 5, 1858.

[54]   Proclamation of the Governor of Hong Kong, December 28, 1853 (BPP, ASS, *China*, Vol. IX), 23.

[55]   See Tables 25-48 in Appendix VI.

[56]   Parkes to Hammond, May 21, 1860 (BFO 97/102B).

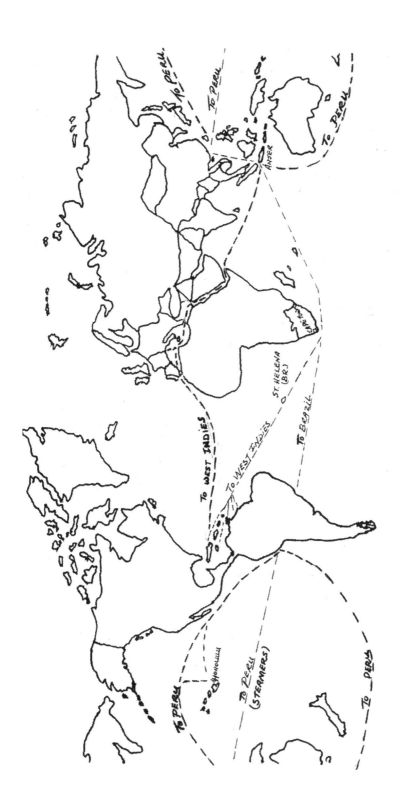

Map 6

Showing routes of "coolie ships" to the Caribbean and South America

had a choice of three routes. Some sailed northward to Japan and picked up the prevailing westerly winds above latitude 30, stopping sometimes at Honolulu for replenishment of supplies.[57] Others made their way down through the reef-strewn China sea, through the Straits of Sunda, then south of Australia and New Zealand, and across the Pacific to Callao.[58] Only steamers dared to go into the teeth of the southeast trades and cut directly across the Pacific from the China coast to Callao. But even for steamers, this was hazardous, for besides contrary winds, the entire voyage was through the tropics, which caused acute problems of hygiene and control of disease.

Ships bound for Cuba and the West Indies invariably sailed down the China sea, stopping for water and supplies at Anjer on the coast of Batavia, then across the whole expanse of the Indian Ocean to the Cape of Good Hope and up the Atlantic on the homeward stretch, touching at the island of St. Helena if supplies were running short. After the Suez Canal opened in 1869, some ships went by way of the Mediterranean, which reduced considerably the length of the voyage.[59]

In an era when the seas were still largely uncharted and Lloyds of London were reporting over 3,000 missing ships annually,[60] the Chinese passenger traffic to South America experienced surprisingly few shipwrecks. In the twenty-eight-year history of the trade, only seven ships were reported lost at sea. According to the British Emigration Commissioners, in the twenty-one years from 1852 to 1872, fifty-nine passenger vessels dispatched from the United Kingdom suffered shipwreck.[61] Skippers in the Chinese passenger trade to South America were evidently excellent sailors and perhaps only in this respect might they be proud of their record.

---

[57] Hillebrand, *Report on the Supply of Labor to the Honorable Board of Immigration of the Hawaiian Islands*, 7.

[58] See the map of winds and ocean routes in M.F. Maury, *Explanations and Sailing Directions to Accompany the Winds and Current Charts* (Philadelphia, E.C. and J. Biddle, 1855, Seventh edition), Plate XVIII.

[59] Juan Perez de la Riva, "Aspectas Económicos del Tráfico de Culies Chinos (sic) a Cuba, 1853-1874," *Universidad de la Havana*, Vol. CLXXIII (May-June, 1965), 101.

[60] Between 1846 and 1850 Lloyds listed 12,041 sailing vessels and 322 steamers as lost at sea. See *The Boston Board of Trade; Second Annual Report* (Boston, Moore and Crosley, 1856), 78-79.

[61] "Thirty Third General Report of the Emigration Commissioners (BPP, *Emigration*, Vol. XVIII), 81-83. See also William Shaw Lindsay, *The History of Merchant Shipping and Ancient Commerce*, 4 vols. (London, Sampson, Low, Marston, Low, and Searle, 1874-76), II, 324.

Outfitting a Coolie Ship

A few ships were specially built for the trade in Chinese passengers to Latin America,[62] but most were cargo vessels that were outfitted and adopted for passengers at Hong Kong.[63] The remodeling operation is described by Don Aldus, a world traveler and adventurer who made the voyage on a coolie ship from Macau to Havana sometime in the 1860s:

> The bunks for the emigrants consist of two rows of shelves running the whole length of the ship both sides, as well as down the center. These shelves are six feet wide with an eight inch footboard secured to the outside to prevent them slipping off. After the shelves and footboards are completed the next operation is to measure and number each bedspace, allowing to each man a [space] . . . of from twenty to twenty-four inches, the latter being the legal allowance, but it would appear they are not over particular in this matter as they seldom exceed twenty one inches. There is no kind of division between the sleepers- in short each shelf simply represented one hundred and fifty in a bed.[64]

Two other eyewitness accounts of the conversion process from cargo to passenger vessel are in essential agreement with the above description, which would seem to indicate that this arrangement of space per passenger was the norm, at least during the 1860s and 1870s.[65]

That this was similar to the method of stowing slaves for the middle passage can be seen from figure 6. However, Chinese immigrants to South America were not so tightly packed together in the bunks that they had to lie in each other's lap like a "row of spoons" as happened on some slave ships.[66]

---

[62] See page 162.

[63] Kennedy to Kimberley, October 19, 1872 (BPP, ASS, *China*, Vol. IV), 317; See also G.B. Endacott, *A History of Hong Kong* (London, Oxford University Press, 1968), 127-130.

[64] Don Aldus, *Coolie Traffic and Kidnapping* (London, McCorquodale and Company, 1876), 31.

[65] E. Holden, "A Chapter on the Coolie Trade," *Harper's Magazine*, Vol. XXIX, No. 169 (June, 1864), 3; Steere to Bailey [Inclosure 3] (U.S. Dept. of State, *Foreign Relations*, 1873, vol. I), 207-208.

[66] Brantz Mayer, *Captain Canot, or Twenty Years of an African Slaver* (London, George Routledge and Company, 1855), 70.

The twenty-one inches allowed each passenger at least enabled him to lie on his back, though the close proximity of one's neighbors without any dividing partition no doubt caused much friction on the long voyage, as well as facilitated the spread of disease.

At the outset of the trade, competition among ships took the form of overcrowding. British vessels generally ignored the regulations imposed by the British Parliament, which established the minimum amount of space allotted to each passenger and ruled that no British ship could carry a greater number of passengers than one for every two tons of registry. Governor Bonham of Hong Kong admitted in 1854 that the provisions of the Passengers Act passed by Parliament in 1852 could not be "strictly adhered to," as any attempt to enforce them would only drive shipping to other Chinese ports to the detriment of the colony of Hong Kong.[67]

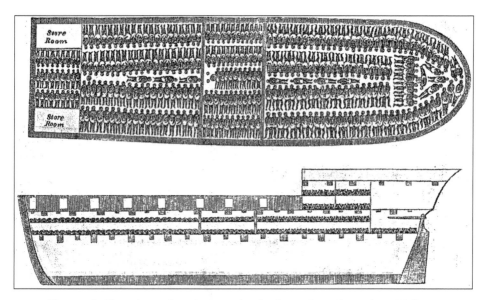

Figure 6. Drawings showing method of stowing slaves in 1786 on the ship *Brookes* of Liverpool. [From Thomas Clarkson's *The History of the Rise, Progress and Accomplishment of the Abolition of the Slave Trade*, 2 vols. (London, Longman, Hurst, Rees and Orme, 1808), I, Face page 111.].

---

[67]   Bonham to Newcastle, January 6, 1854 (BPP, ASS, *China*, Vol. IV), 22.

Under pressure from shipowners, Parliament relented somewhat and, in 1853, amended the Passengers Act to state that "twelve instead of fifteen 'superficial feet' to be sufficient space for natives of Asia and Africa who may be conveyed from Hong Kong through the tropics."[68] In 1860, both Spain[69] and the port of Macau[70] adopted the British rule, limiting emigrant vessels to one passenger for every two tons, and in 1868, Peru[71] passed a similar legislation. However, overcrowding continued throughout, with ships averaging approximately one passenger to every one and a half tons' registry.[72]

While passengers occupied the between-deck, the holds were filled with water casks and provisions. Commodities such as beef and pork, often imported live from Europe and America, were put on board at Hong Kong; and articles of Chinese produce, tea, fish, and rice were loaded together with the passengers at Macau, Swatow, Amoy, and Cumsingmoon. Cooking galleys were erected on the upper deck, with enormous boilers that looked like "smelting pots," each one capable of cooking enough rice for fifty passengers. There were also smaller pots for cooking eggs, fish, beef, and vegetables.[73]

Over each hatchway were placed crossed bars of stout iron arched in the center with a small opening at the top so as to control or easily prohibit the egress of passengers from below.[74] The hatches leading to the provisions in the hold were encircled with iron bars that were securely fastened to both decks so as to prevent stealing by the passengers, and also served as impregnable cages in which armed guards could take up a position in the between-deck in the event of mutiny and demand the restoration of order.[75] A short distance in front of the captain's cabin, a barricade eight to ten feet high stretched from rail to rail on the upper deck and was firmly bolted down so as to withstand the combined force of any number of men. "Sixteen-pound" canons peered through

---

[68]   Newcastle to Bonham, September 9, 1853 (Ibid.), 21.

[69]   "Rules for the Introduction of Chinese Laborers into the Island of Cuba," (*British and Foreign State Papers*, Consular Reports, 1860, Vol. XLVII), 1040.

[70]   *O Boletim*, October 13, 1860.

[71]   Stewart, *Chinese Bondage in Peru*, 63.

[72]   This is apparent from Tables 25-48 in Appendix VI.

[73]   Aldus, *Coolie Traffic and Kidnapping*, 45.

[74]   Holden, "A Chapter on the Chinese Coolie Trade," 3.

[75]   Aldus, *Coolie Traffic and Kidnapping*, 48.

portholes in the barricade, while others stood atop the poop deck overlooking the structure and threatening instant death to any would-be troublemaker. This fortress provided sleeping quarters for the crew and was so arranged that from behind it a small band of armed men could command the entire deck. To Don Aldus, a vessel so outfitted looked like a "floating menagerie for wild beasts."[76]

These precautions, modeled after those undertaken on board convict ships,[77] were deemed essential, not only as a safeguard against mutinous attacks, but as a deterrent to them. The erection of protective barricades and iron cages was a common practice on vessels transporting passengers between Canton, Hong Kong, and Macau. George Wingrove Cooke, the *Times* correspondent to China, observed in 1857 that:

> The passage boats to Macau are little armouries to protect themselves against piracy. In the *Fei Ma,* the Chinese passengers are put down in the hold twelve feet deep and the ladder is taken away. A sailor keeps guard over them with a drawn cutlass. One of the Yankee ships has an iron cage on deck into which the Chinese passengers are invited to walk and are then locked up. The Peninsular and Oriental boat has a better but more costly precaution; she carries no Chinese passengers.[78]

In the 1840s and 1850s, fear of piracy was universal in the China Seas. No ship was safe, and it was common knowledge that pirates, with a view to plunder, volunteered as emigrants for South America.[79] However, it was simpler for ships carrying large numbers of Chinese passengers to build protective cages for the crew than to put everybody on board behind bars. After 1862, when a Hong Kong ordinance prohibited the erection of barricades and gratings, the fittings were carried out to sea and then erected.[80]

---

[76] Ibid., 46. For a description of similar structures on board the British ships *Glentanner* and *Lord Elgin* see Barkly to Parkington, January 23, 1853, (BPP, ASS, *China,* Vol. III), 137; also A.D. Blue, "Piracy on the China Coast," *Journal of the Hong Kong Branch of the Royal Asiatic Society,* Vol. V (1965), 78.

[77] Charles Bateson, *The Convict Ships 1787-1868* (Glasgow, Brown, Son and Ferguson Limited, 1959), 59-61.

[78] George Wingrove Cooke, *China and Lower Bengal: Being the Times Correspondent in the Years 1857-58* (London, Routledge, Warne and Routledge, 1861), 67.

[79] William Speer, *The Oldest and the Newest Empire: China and the United States* (Hartford, Connecticut, S.S. Scranton and Company, 1870), 483.

[80] Kennedy to Kimberly, October 19, 1872 (BPP, ASS, *China,* Vol. IV), 317.

The final preparation for the voyage consisted of ensuring some ventilation between decks. The more conscientious skippers had two or three planks lifted at given distances on the main deck along the whole length of the ship. Watertight coverings, elevated eight inches from the deck, were placed over these openings, with iron bars running through them so as to prevent passengers from escaping. Ventilators were mounted at strategic openings, and two large pipes were positioned at either end of the ship to draw off the foul air from below.[81] These measures, together with the hatches and portholes (if any) provided a modicum of fresh air to passengers. In the early days of the trade, such necessities as fresh air were often overlooked or neglected.[82] The hatches were apparently the only means of getting air to the between deck. In December 1851, the *Futtah Salaam*, a British ship, left Hong Kong with 234 emigrants for Mauritius. During a three-day storm at sea, the emigrants were put below, and the hatches were fastened down, but before the storm had subsided, all were found dead.[83] A similar catastrophe befell the United States ship *Waverly* bound from Swatow to Peru in 1855. Following an attempted mutiny, its 450 passengers were forced below, and the hatches were closed. When they were opened fourteen to fifteen hours later, 257 had died of suffocation.[84]

Embarkation

The preparations complete, the ship sailed to the port or receiving vessel, where the emigrants were waiting or were in the process of being collected. The embarkation procedure took anywhere from a few days to several weeks. Emigrant vessels usually anchored at some distance from shore so as to discourage passengers from trying to escape by swimming or being picked up by one of the countless crafts that infested the waters along China's coastline. Hence passengers were ferried to the ship in sampans[85] and were unceremoniously loaded on board. Those who refused to climb the gangway

---

[81] Aldus, *Coolie Traffic and Kidnapping*, 36.

[82] See the report of Dr. E.A. Manget, Acting Health Officer in British Guiana (BPP, ASS, *China*, Vol. III), 138.

[83] *The Friend of China*, April 7, 1852.

[84] Bowring to Clarendon, November 15, 1855 (BFO 97/101).

[85] The name given to all boats on the China coast too small to be classified as junks. See Arthur de Carle Sowerby, "The Junks, Sampans, and Inland Waterways of China," *The China Journal of Science and Arts*, Vol. X, No. 5 (May 1929), 245.

ladder were "hoisted up by rope like any other bale of merchandise."[86] Most were naked to the waist, wearing only loose trousers and broad-rimmed straw hats and carrying a small box containing shaving equipment, chopsticks, a toothbrush, and a piece of bone used to scrape the tongue (a habit that was religiously observed). A small purse or pouch strung around the waist and a piece of muslin worn around the neck that served as a towel completed the list of their personal belongings.[87]

Figure 7. "Coolies Embarking" (From *Harpers New Monthly Magazine*, Vol. XXIX, June 1864)

Once on board, they were mustered in rows on the upper deck for naked inspection, which had a twofold purpose: to ensure that they were healthy

---

[86] Aldus, *Coolie Traffic and Kidnapping*, 42.
[87] Holden, "A Chapter on the Coolie Trade," 5.

and free from contagious disease and to see that no weapons or opium were hidden on their persons. Their belongings were also searched, the contents of boxes and bags being emptied out on deck and minutely examined.[88] This done, they were conducted to their allotted places on the bunks below, where they were to spend most of the voyage.

As long as land was in sight, some would repent of their decision to emigrate and attempt to escape by jumping overboard. Others grew despondent and became sick or, believing that they would be eaten by barbarians or thrown into the sea as bait for fish or that their blood would be used to make opium, chose suicide rather than undergo such an ignominious end.[89] Some harkened to the whispered invitation of pirates to join in an attempt to take control of the ship. Professional gamblers made their way on board, cheated their fellow countrymen of their advance money, and then tried to make good their escape.[90] Weeping parents and relatives, some real and some feigned, approached the ships to look for a missing father or son among the emigrants. Some skippers assisted such people in their search, while others bluntly refused their requests and fired upon them when they refused to go away.[91] With embarking full of such unpleasant problems, understandably, skippers and crews were uneasy until they weighed anchor. This usually took place after the emigrants were bedded down for the night, so as to obviate the anguish they would naturally feel as they gazed at the receding shore.

Discipline on Board

From the moment the passengers came on board, the ships were under a military discipline. Rules and regulations were posted in prominent places

---

88 Aldus, *Coolie Traffic and Kidnapping*, 43.

89 Scary tales such as those mentioned were prevalent along China's southern coastline, some even appearing as placards to warn would-be emigrants of their horrible fate. See the translation of a placard posted in Canton in October, 1855 (BFO 97/102A).

90 Peddar to Alcock, May 28, 1869 (BFO 17/887); *The Friend of China*, March 2, 1861; "The Immigration Convention of 1866," *China Review*, Vol. I (July 1872), 69.

91 So wrote the third officer of the British ship *Catherine Glen* in a letter of June 30, 1859. See the *Anti-Slavery Reporter*, Vol. VII, No. 10 (October 1859), 224.

in Chinese and in one or other of the European languages, and punishment for their violation was often brutal and harsh. One such set of rules was as follows:

1. Every coolie to bathe at least once a day, weather and health permitting.
2. Clothes to be washed once a week, viz., Saturday.
3. No spitting allowed upon either deck, save into the spittoons provided for that purpose.

Crimes punishable with the lash

Perjury	1/2 dozen
Theft	1 dozen
Illegal gambling	1 dozen
Fighting	1/2 dozen
Depositing filth between decks	1/2 dozen
Smoking below	1 dozen

NB. Any coolie or coolies discovered conspiring to mutiny, shall, when found guilty, be punished with the cats not exceeding four dozens and afterwards be handcuffed and chained to the ringbolts of the deck during the master's pleasure.[92]

Floggings were daily occurrences on these vessels. In the eighteenth and early nineteenth centuries, the cat-o-nine tails was regarded as an indispensable instrument of discipline and was regularly used in the navies and armies of the world, as well as in penal institutions. In the context of the day, the punishments listed above seem rather humane, but too often, captains, fearful for the safety of their ships, meted out excessive punishment at the mere rumor of a mutiny or uprising. Chinese in Cuba testified before the commission sent by the government of China to investigate the condition of Chinese laborers on that island that on the voyage, a few were selected indiscriminately daily and flogged as a means of intimidating all others.[93]

---

[92] Aldus, *Coolie Traffic and Kidnapping*, 51-52.

[93] *Chinese Emigration: The Cuba Commission* (Shanghai, Imperial Maritime Customs Press, 1876), 13.

"Preserving the Peace"

Figure 8. Preserving the peace on board the US ship **Norway** on voyage from Macau to Havana in 1858 (From *Harpers New Monthly Magazine*, Vol. XXIX, June 1864)

Occupying the hours between meals was a perennial problem that challenged the ingenuity of skippers and crews. Much of the time was spent in gambling with dominoes and cards, which usually gave rise to quarreling and fighting. When not so engaged, passengers strummed on one-string violins or created a vast assortment of noises on six-foot-long clarinets without keys, cymbals, gongs, drums, and trumpets.[94] Some emigrants brought their own musical instruments, but normally, they were part of the ship's standard equipment.[95] Occasionally, some kind of rudimentary theatricals were attempted to everybody's enjoyment.[96] Enlightened captains organized reading classes, which were very popular, as most were eager to learn or better their skill.[97] On one ship, the announcement of prizes of tobacco and silver

---

[94] Holden, "A Chapter on the Coolie Trade," 5.
[95] See Table 12.
[96] Holden, "A Chapter on the Coolie Trade," 5.
[97] Aldus, *Coolie Traffic and Kidnapping*, 209.

dollars for the best piece of wickerwork had almost everybody on board weaving objects of all shapes and sizes from empty provision baskets.[98] Had such enterprising techniques been more widely used, there might have been less need of the lash to discourage mischief.

Table 12

Invoice of Stores shipped for the use of Chinese Emigrants on the *Lord Elgin* on the voyage from Amoy to Demerara in 1852

350 bamboo pillows	50 tubs of cabbage
350 sleeping mats	5 peculs of garlic
100 razors	10 peculs of salt
10 choppers	2 tubs of vinegar
500 rice bowls	2 peculs of tea
250 tea cups	10 dried fish
100 rice ladles	20 peculs of salt fish
200 brooms	12 peculs of tea oil
250 combs	20 peculs of potatoes
4 baskets of soup peculs	50 large plates
50 baskets	50 cutties of sulphur
50 mess rids	160 white waistcoats
6 bottles of mustard	160 yellow trousers
12 rice measures	160 black trousers
6 gongs	160 black jackets
14 guitars	160 yellow jackets
12 flutes	320 sheets
2 bundles of playing cards	295 pairs of shoes
50 catties of tobacco	200 wooden shoes
10 iron puns	22 tubs of salt beef
100 bricks for cooking places	33 peculs, cooking places
90 jars surd peculs	8 large water tubs
15 peculs of biscuits	500 bales of chop sticks
10 peculs of sugar	

Source: BPP, ASS, *China*, Vol. III, 144.

---

[98]   Aldus, *Coolie Traffic and Kidnapping*, 156.

Disease

But overshadowing all disciplinary problems and casting a gloom over the entire voyage was the ever-present threat of death—not only death by violence, which will be examined in the following chapter, but death through despair and disease. Messrs. Torices, Ferran, and Dupieris, one of the principal importers of Chinese labor at Havana, issued a pamphlet of instructions to the captains and medical officers of ships that transported Chinese emigrants. Therein particular attention was drawn to the following list of diseases to which Chinese emigrants were said to be highly susceptible: "dyspepsia, scurvy, diarrhea, dysentery, anasarca or dropsy of the skin, gastric fevers, worms, ulcers, ophthalmia, anemia, nostalgia or homesickness, nervous inflammation of the brain, delirium of opium smokers, the itch and scurf."[99] The Portuguese consuls at Callao and Havana, commencing in 1856, made regular reports to the governor of Macau on the mortality in emigrant ships that embarked from that port, and they listed dysentery, scurvy, dropsy, fever, and opium withdrawal as the most frequent causes of death.[100]

Though from the mid-1850s onward, emigrant ships were supposed to be equipped with a hospital and abundant medical supplies, as well as a qualified doctor of medicine to attend to the needs of the passengers, in many cases, hospitals did not exist, medical supplies were inadequate, and the only doctors that could be obtained were native Chinese, who were unacquainted with Western medicine, and who more often than not were the type that used their position to extort money from the sick in return for their favors or for opium.[101]

---

[99] *The Friend of China*, December 29, 1860.
[100] See *O Boletim* for the years 1865 through 1873.
[101] BFO 97/1028; Aldus, *Coolie Traffic and Kidnapping*, 218.

Figure 9. The Clippers ship *Challenge*. The *Challenge* was built in 1951 and made a record voyage of 108 days from New York to San Francisco the same year. She entered the "Coolie Trade" in 1857. (From F.J. Peters, (comp.) Clipper Ship Prints by N. Currier and Currier and Ives, New York, Antique Bulletin Publishing company, 1930, 70).

As a matter of policy, all vessels carried a supply of opium, which was intended to be given to users in diminishing doses so as to wean them from the habit.[102] However, on at least one ship, a special place was set apart on deck for opium smoking, where ten lamps were kept burning and to which emigrants resorted daily, twenty at a time, to partake of the drug.[103] One might conclude from this that the majority of the emigrants were opium smokers,[104] but it could also mean that opium was being used to keep passengers in a lethargic state, and hence more easily controlled.

---

[102] Berkly to Pakington, January 24, 1853 (BPP, ASS, *China*, Vol. III), 137; See also the report of Thomas H. Somerville, medical doctor on board the American ship *Kitty Simpson* (Ibid.), 448-449.

[103] See the "Statement of Chin-a-Sin before the Hong Kong Police Magistrate," May 17, 1871 (BPP, ASS, *China*, Vol. IV), 272-273.

[104] The doctor on board the *Kitty Simpson* stated that "in his judgment two thirds of the coolies on board had at some period in their lives been addicted to the use of opium," March 18, 1858 (Ibid., Vol. III), 448.

Suicides by jumping overboard were frequent occurrences. Captain Wilson, a native of the Island of St. Kitts in the Caribbean, who spent several years in the trade between China and Peru during the 1850s, related how some skippers dealt with this problem:

> The men will sometimes make a fearful yell and leap into the open sea. I have been quite astonished to see how foolishly some of the American captains would act on such occasions. They allow their sentries to fire and sink them. I can't see what they can gain from that, as when they have killed them they are a dead loss. I always put salt in the gun, which stings them. Then I lower the boats and pick them up.[105]

Other emigrants simply lay down and died of despair. The pamphlet of instructions mentioned above refers to this malady as "nostalgia or homesickness" and offered the following remedy:

> Nostalgia, strictly speaking is not a disease, but is a proximate and powerful cause thereof . . . The proper means for relieving this entirely mental affection must be drawn from the same sources as the evil itself; we should therefore endeavour to occupy his mind and all our endeavours should tend in that direction in order to cure him. We must endeavour to awaken his ambition: the Chinese have a natural propensity that way; it will therefore be easy to succeed. You must make him understand that he is coming to a country in which he will gain money, where he may exercise economy by means of which he will be enabled to return after the expiration of his contract; that he will take back with him some money and knowledge that he may turn to profit when he is back with his family that he need never again leave. The interpreter must tell him these things without having the appearance of telling them to him merely for the purpose of curing him of his affection; it must be a conversation that will interest the homesick man and there is no doubt that the thoughts that will occupy his mind and the part that he will have taken in conversation, will

---

[105] "The Coolie Traffic," *Anti-Slavery Reporter*, Vol. VI, No. 4, (April, 1858), 84. According to one commentator American captains had the reputation of being the most cruel in their treatment of the emigrants. See Ed. Du Hailly, "Les Chinois Hors de Chez Eux," *Revue des Deux Mondes*, Vol. LXVI (15 Novembre, 1866), 451.

have their effect on breaking the vicious thread of ideas which occupied his mind and kept him in a state of inaction, or at least of oppression. As soon as you shall have succeeded in distracting him a little, you should make him take some exercise and oblige him to take some nourishment.[106]

This psychological prescription, which would do justice to a modern-day psychiatrist, reveals a depth of compassion and understanding that one does not expect to find in such a traffic of human life. It was perhaps inevitable that the misdeeds and cruelties of some captains and crews were accepted as the norm. However, it would seem that most captains were genuinely concerned with the well-being of their passengers, if only to have them reach their destination alive. It was to the interest of the captains to be so concerned, for they received a bonus of up to five dollars per head on emigrants landed live and in good health. Marshall Powers stated, without revealing his source, that captains were paid a fixed sum for their cargo dead or alive,[107] which, if true, would have encouraged excesses of cruelty and deprivations of all kinds. Not only would such an arrangement be quite contrary to the commercial nature of the trade, but there seems to be no evidence to substantiate such an assertion. The only instance this writer has unearthed that in any way approaches Powers's contention was the case of the British ship *Lady Montague* in which her skipper, Captain Smith, reportedly received $60 per day for the voyage to Callao. Consequently, he took the longest route possible, sailing around Australia with resulting heavy loss of life.[108] All other evidence indicates that ships were not remunerated for passengers lost at sea and that captains and medical doctors received their per capita bonus only on emigrants delivered in reasonably healthy condition.[109] In fact, the *Friend of China* reported that skippers and doctors were penalized by having their bonuses cut by up to 50 percent if mortality exceeded 5 percent.[110]

---

[106] As quoted in *The Friend of China*, December 29, 1860.

[107] Powers, "Chinese Coolie Migration to Cuba," 88.

[108] William Lobscheid, *Chinese Emigration to the West Indies; A Trip Through British Guiana Undertaken for the Purpose of Ascertaining the Condition of the Chinese who have Emigrated under Government Contract with Supplementary Papers Relating to Contract Labor and the Slave Trade* (Demerara, "Royal Gazette" 1866), xii.

[109] "Testimony of the doctor on board the Norwegian ship *Norma*", (BFO, 97/102B); *Hong Kong Mercury and Shipping Gazette*, October 31, 1866; *South Pacific Times*, June 1, 1872.

[110] *The Friend of China*, January 5, 1861.

Water was considered to be the primary cause of dysentery and scurvy.[111] It was exceedingly difficult to obtain wholesome water in Chinese ports, and fresh water obtained at Anjer, Cape Hope, or St. Helena, though perhaps sufficiently pure, incurred the risk of an outbreak of the dreaded diseases.[112] Consequently, captains sought to equip their ships with water tanks large enough to last the entire voyage. Understandably, water was usually rationed, with each passenger being allotted from one gallon to as little as one pint per day depending upon the ship and its circumstances.[113] Some ships did not resort to rationing, but to conserve their supply and eliminate wastage, water caskets were so arranged on deck that passengers could drink from them at will through reeds inserted into them.[114] One skipper attributed the absence of scurvy on his ship to his treatment of the water twice weekly with six gallons of port wine and one gallon of "anti-scorbutic medicine," which reportedly the emigrants drank with "great avidity and enjoyment."[115] In the late 1850s, the newly launched French steamer *François I* boasted of having a condensing machine to convert steam into fresh water at the rate of seventy-five gallons daily, which was in no way adequate to the ship's needs but could help in emergency situations.[116]

The food also was a perennial problem. With the exception of rice, other foods such as fish, meat, and vegetables were often excessively salted and quickly became putrid, causing diarrhea and scurvy.[117] Some sought to get around this by taking on fresh vegetables and live pigs and sheep at their stops on route.[118] Moreover, many of the emigrants had led a life of privations and of precarious subsistence and passing from near starvation to a full allowance of food frequently produced dysentery, which, in their feeble condition, they could seldom fight off successfully. Dr. Thomas Gwynne of the British ship *Edwin Fox*, Dr. E. B. Pellew of the British ship *Tasmania*, and Dr. Thomas

---

[111] Ibid., August 16, 1856; BFO 97/102B.

[112] Aldus, *Coolie Traffic and Kidnapping*, 140. See also Crawford to Clarendon, Havana, November 26, 1856 (BPP, ASS, *China*, Vol. III), 420.

[113] See the Proclamation of the Governor of Hong Kong, December 28, 1853 (BPP, ASS, *China*, Vol. IV), 23; *Chinese Emigration: The Cuba Commission*, 12.

[114] John Scrath, *Twelve Years in China* (Edinburgh, Thomas Constable and Company, 1860), 259.

[115] Aldus, *Coolie Traffic and Kidnapping*, 325.

[116] *The Friend of China*, June 10, 1857.

[117] Crawford to Malmesbury, Havana, May 2, 1858 (BPP, ASS, *China*, Vol. III), 447.

[118] White to Emigration Commissioners, December 10, 1853 (BFO 881/744).

Somerville of the American ship *Kitty Simpson*—all of whom accompanied Chinese emigrants to Havana in 1858—concurred in the opinion that the considerable mortality on the voyage was directly attributable to the debilitated condition of the emigrants prior to embarkation, which rendered them not only prone to disease but also unable to contend with it when attacked.[119] Dr. Somerville testified that of the 430 emigrants who embarked on board the *Kitty Simpson*, only 50 were in moderately good health. Of the others, he said,

> The remainder are feeble, sickly, emaciated wretches, whom hardship, disease and hunger had reduced to the lowest ebb of vitality. From the legs and arms of many of them almost all trace of muscular substance had disappeared, and the bones seemed covered only by the dusky shrivelled skin that hung about them in loose folds, while their sallow complexions, sunken eyes, short coughs, etc., afforded ample evidence of the irreparable mischief their constitutions had sustained.[120]

Among men so circumstanced, it was little wonder that disease was rife and that many of them succumbed to the rigors of the voyage.

Mortality at Sea

The last rite for the dead, as described by an eyewitness, was simple and perfunctory:

> the corpse is laid out on the coarse bed rug provided them for sleeping under, after which every article of clothing is brought and placed beside it; it is then rolled up in a piece of old canvas, which is sewn by the sail maker. This done, it is next taken on the forecastle deck and launched into the sea feet first, and if the deceased had any friends during life, they are to be found standing (after having placed a few coins in his winding sheet), ready to toss a few more after him as he drops into the deep, declaring they would be of some service to him when he awakened.[121]

---

[119] See the reports made to the British Consul General at Havana, March 18 and April 30, 1858 (BPP, ASS, *China*, Vol. III), 448-449.

[120] Ibid.

[121] Aldus, *Coolie Traffic and Kidnapping*, 133.

Table 13
Number of Chinese Imported into Cuba Annually
from 1847-Sept. 1, 1873 and Mortality on the Voyage

Year	Vessels	Tonnage	Embarked	Landed	Died at Sea	Percentages of deaths
1847	2	979	612	571	41	6.69
1853	15	8,349	5,150	4,307	843	16.36
1854	4	2,375	1,750	1,711	39	2.22
1855	6	6,544	3,130	2,985	145	4.63
1856	15	10,677	6,152	4,970	1,182	19.21
1857	28	18.940	10,101	8,547	1,554	15.38
1858	33	32,842	16,411	13,384	3,027	18.44
1859	16	13,828	8,539	7,207	1,332	15.59
1853-59	117	93,555	51,233	43,111	8,122	15,85
1860	17	15,104	7,227	6,219	1,008	13.94
1861	16	15,919	7,212	6,922	290	4.02
1862	1	759	400	344	56	14.00
1863	3	2,007	1,045	951	94	8.99
1864	7	5,513	2,664	2,132	532	19.96
1865	20	12,769	6,810	6,403	407	5.97
1866	43	24,187	14,169	13,043	1,126	7.94
1867	42	26,449	15,661	14,414	1,247	7.96
1868	21	15,265	8,400	7,668	732	8.71
1869	19	13,692	7,340	5,865	1,475	20.09
1860-69	189	131,734	70,928	63,961	6,967	9.82
1870	3	2,305	1,312	1,249	63	4.80
1871	5	2,820	1,827	1,649	178	9.74
1872	20	12,886	8,914	8,148	766	8.59
1873	6	4,786	3,330	3,121	209	6.27
1870-73	34	22,797	15,383	14,167	1,216	7.90
1847-73	342	249,065	138,156	121,810	16,305	11.83

Source: compiled by John V. Crawford, British Consul General at Havana, see BFO 881/2598.

Table 14

Mortality on Board Vessels Carrying Chinese Emigrants to Peru
from 1860 to 1874

Year	Vessels	Tonnage	Embarked	Landed	Died at Sea	Percentages of deaths
1860			2,007	1,413	594	29.59
1861			1,860	1,440	420	22.58
1862			1,716	1,003	713	41.55
1863			2,301	1,628	673	29.24
1864			7,010	6,410	600	8.55
1865	11	8,217	4,779	3,394	1,385	28.98
1866	6	4,026	1,971	1,895	76	3.85
1867	3	3,205	1,542	1,490	52	3.37
1868	5	3,864	2,141	1,945	196	9.15
1869	9	8.031	4,166	4.061	105	2.52
1860-69			29,493	24,679	4,814	16.32
1870	27	23,081	12,383	11,151	1,232	9.94
1871	24	18,485	10,549	9,977	572	5.42
1872	29	23,830	13,256	11,999	1,257	9.48
1873	9	9,184	5,063	4,478	585	11.55
1874	4	4,644	2,371	2,339	32	1.34
1870-74	93	79,224	43,622	39,944	3,678	8.43
1860-74			73,116	64,324	8,492	11.61

Sources: Figures for 1860 to 1864 inclusive are from Thomas J. Hutchinson, *Two Years in Peru with Exploration of its Antiquities*, 2 vols. (London, 1873), I, 246. From 1865 to 1874 figures are from *O Boletim* for the years 1865-74. This table only includes voyages for which statistics are available. Hence the annual totals are incomplete.

Table 15

Number of Chinese Imported into the British West Indies Annually
from 1852 to 1873 and Mortality on the Voyage

Year	Vessels	Tonnage	Embarked	Landed	Died at Sea	Percentages of deaths
1852	5	3,361	1,510	1,330	180	11.88
1853	1	674	314	305	9	2.55
1854	1	724	310	267★	43	13.87
1858	1	545	300	249	51	17.00
1859	2	2,060	830	819	11	1.32
1852-59	10	7,464	3,264	2,970	294	9.00
1860	6	4,768	1,925	1,898	28	1.45
1861	11	10,051	3,780	3,632	154	4.07
1862	6	6,593	2,628	2,469	157	5.97
1863	2	2,162	930	905	30	3.22
1864	2	1,287	594	582	14	2.35
1865	7	5,312	2,398	2,297	110	4.57
1866	3	2,905	1,278	789	170	13.30
1860-66	37	33,078	13,533	12,572	663	4.67
1873	1	1,200	388	388	1	.25
1852-73	48	41,742	17,185	15,903	958	5.57

★An additional 205 Chinese landed in Jamaica from Panama in 1854.

Sources: "The Annual Report of the British Emigration Commission," from 1852
to 1873, (BPP, *Emigration*, Vols. IX-XVIII); Clementi, *The Chinese in
British Guiana*, Tables, ii, iii.

The death toll from disease of all kinds came to approximately 26,000. Another 3,000 to 4,000 died in mutinies. In all, about 12 percent of the emigrants who set out from China for Latin America between 1847 and 1874 died at sea. In 342 voyages to Cuba deaths amounted to 11.83 percent,[122] as compared to one-tenth of 1 percent on 15,057 voyages conveying emigrants from the British Isles during the same period.[123] Statistics on the voyages to Peru are incomplete, but those that are available show that from 1860 to 1874, 11.61 percent died on the voyage.[124] The overall mortality on Chinese emigrant vessels to the British West Indies was considerably lower at 5.57 percent.[125] Mortality declined somewhat after regulatory measures were enacted in the late 1850s and early 1860s as the following figures indicate:

Table 16

Mortality on Emigrant Ships from China to Latin America 1847-1874
(in percent of deaths from all causes)

Years	To Cuba	To Peru	To British West Indies
1847-1849	6.69	0	—
1850-1859	15.85	unkown	9.00
1860-1869	9.82	16.32	4.67
1870-1874	7.90	8.43	.25

Some have attempted to place the blame for the heavy loss of life on the fact that a great deal of the migration was in the hands of private speculators.[126] This would appear to be a major factor, for the movement of Chinese to the British West Indies, which was controlled and operated by the

---

[122]   See Table 13.

[123]   "Thirty Third General Report of the Emigration Commissioners", (BPP, *Emigration*, Vol. XVIII), 83.

[124]   See Table 14.

[125]   See Table 15. For a breakdown of this figure for Guyana, Trinidad and Jamaica see Table 22.

[126]   *New York Daily Times*, July 31, 1860.

British government, had only about half the casualties that the movements to Cuba and Peru experienced. Yet it could be pointed out that in the less hazardous voyage from Calcutta to the West Indies, the government controlled migration of contract Indian laborers suffered an equally high mortality rate of 13.38 percent for the years 1856 through 1859.[127] Hence, it would seem that the enormous death rate can be attributed to no single cause but to a combination of factors such as ill-equipped ships; lack of government supervision; overcrowding; the semi-involuntary nature of the migration; lack of proper food, water, and medical care; and above all, the weakened physical state of the emigrants themselves, which was aggravated by the conditions on board the vessels.

---

[127] "Mr. Geoghegan's Report on Coolie Emigration from India," (BPP, Vol. XLVII, 1874), 71.

CHAPTER V

MUTINIES—GAMBLES FOR LIBERTY AND PLUNDER

At 11 a.m. the coolie cooks came off and refused to cook any longer (unless they were paid every month) . . . I promised I would do all I could . . . but that would not satisfy them and all the coolies came aft for the intention to kill me . . . I killed about four or five and drove all below between decks. In the afternoon at 3 p.m. I was obliged to get water on deck. I went down and found that they had broke [sic] the lock on the cistern hatch and had got hold of some of the provisions. There was one of them which was very impudent and I killed him . . .

> Written by Captain French in the log of the U.S. ship *Waverly* bound from Swatow to Callao with 450 emigrants in 1855 ["The Coolie Trade," *De Bow's Review*, Vol. XXIII (July, 1857), 33]

Mutinies Condemned

A tally of contemporary accounts in newspapers, in consular reports, and magazine articles reveals that mutinies occurred on at least 68 vessels carrying Chinese contract laborers to the Western world. Table 17 lists the ships reported to have experienced mutinies in the period from 1847 to 1874. The table attempts to present all the available information on each incident, but little is known about some mutinies, and furthermore, one suspects that many attempted mutinies went unrecorded. The United States vessel *Robert Browne* experienced a mutiny en route from Amoy to San Francisco in 1852.[1] Emigrants on the *Spartan*, a British ship, bound for Sydney, Australia, in

---

[1] *The Friend of China*, April 28, 1852; "De Chinezen in de Verstroijing," *Vadorlandsche Letter-Oefeningen*, Vol. II (1859), 156.

1853, rose upon the crew,[2] and in 1861, the *Ville d'Agen*, flying the French flag and destined for Pondicherry, India, had to put back into Hong Kong because the passengers revolted.[3] The remaining 65 mutinies took place on vessels bound for Cuba, Peru, and British Guiana.

Newspapers (chiefly in the United States and Great Britain) that had been outspoken in opposing the African slave trade and African slavery, looked upon these mutinies as the spontaneous uprisings of outraged passengers, kidnapped from their homeland and subjected to harsh and cruel treatment at the hands of captains and crews.[4] In a characteristic response, the *Commercial Advertiser*, a Honolulu newspaper editorialized thus:

> If every ship engaged in this business were blown out of the water it would be a good thing for humanity. All the atrocities of the African slave trade and the horrors of the Middle Passage may be found in these coolie ships.[5]

The British Court of Hong Kong went beyond condemnation and exonerated a confessed mutineer. In a celebrated case, Judge Smale, chief justice of the colony of Hong Kong, refused to hand over to the Chinese authorities Kwok-Asing, accused of being the ringleader of the mutiny on board the French vessel *Nouvelle Penelope* and the murderer of her captain. In his judgment, Justice Smale, indicated that he regarded the *Nouvelle Penelope* as a slaver, and hence the killing of the captain was justifiable homicide. He summed up his ruling in the following statement: "A man under unlawful restraint of his personal liberty at sea, as well as on shore, has the right to take life to free himself from such constraint."[6] In effect, the ruling placed moral responsibility for the mutinies on the emigrant vessels, their captains, owners, and charterers.

---

2   Bowring to Malmesbury, February 7, 1853 (BPP, ASS, *China*, Vol. III), 113; *Overland Register and Price Current*, February 11, 1853; *The Friend of China*, February 3, 1853; Alfred Jacobs, "Les Chinois Hors de la Chine," *Revue des Deux Mondes*, Vol. XVII (1 Novembre, 1858), 124-125.

3   "Macao and its Slave Trade," *China Review*, Vol. II, No. 1 (July, 1873), 18.

4   *New York Times*, October 10, 1870, January 16, 1871, July 2, 1871; July 2, 1871; *London Times*, April 21, 1860.

5   As quoted in BPP Vol. XLVII (1871), 9-10.

6   *The Daily Press* (Hong Kong), January 24, 1871, April 1, 1871. The judge's decision was appealed to the Privy Council and was revoked as not based on

Table 17

Ships Carrying Chinese Emigrants on which Mutinies Occurred, 1847-1874

TABLE 17

Ships Carrying Chinese Emigrants on which Mutinies Occurred, 1847-1874

YEAR	NAME OF SHIP	FLAG	CAPTAIN	Tonnage	REMARKS
1850	Lady Montague	British	J.R. Smith	763	Emigrants told destination Calif.at Callao they mutinied,foiled.
"	Albert	French	Jean Paine	292	20 days at sea emigrants mutinied,killed capt.3 crew,plundered ship.
"	Chili	French	J.Verniol	576	Four days at sea emigrants mutinied,leaders flogged,put in irons.
1851	Victory	British	W.L.Wullens	579	At sea emigrants mutinied,killed capt.3 crew,plundered ship.
1852	Beatrice		Edwards	576	Ship put into Singapore leaky,emigrants mutinied and escaped.
"	Robert Browne	American	Bryson	605	8 days out,emigrants mutinied,killed capt.6 crew,landed near Formosa
"	Gertrude	British	Campbell	550	Mutiny put down,ship's carpenter and 5 emigrants killed.
"	Panama	British	Fisler	549	Many mutinies in China sea.16 ringleaders put ashore at Singapore.
"	Samuel Boddington	British	J.W.Hurst	669	Plot to take ship discovered,6 jumped overboard,ringleaders in irons.
"	Lady Amherst	British	Reid	446	Mutiny,capt. killed,ringleaders put ashore at Singapore.
1853	Rosa Elias	Portuguese	G. Wheatley	233	Mutiny over water shortage,captain killed,ship put into Singapore.
"	Adamastor	Portuguese		400	Emigrants mutinied and deserted ship at Singapore.
"	Spartan	British	Marshall	364	2nd mate,15 emigrants killed in mutiny, 11 others later hanged.
1855	Samuel Enderby	British		395	Nearing Java emigrants attacked crew, mutiny foiled.
"	Waverly	American	F.O.Wellman		Ship put into Manila,emigrants mutinied,hatches closed,251 suffocated.
"	Winged Racer	American	Goram	1,203	At anchor at Swatow emigrants mutinied, 60 flogged.
"	Bald Eagle	American	P. Bowen		Emigrants set ship afire,hatches battened down,some suffocated.
1856	Banca	Dutch	Hymena	490	At anchor at Macao mutiny set ship afire, revolt foiled.
"	Resploneo	Portuguese	Fernandes		Sixth day at sea mutiny,crew took to boats,emigrants went ashore.
"	Duke of Portland	British	G.N.Seymour		At anchor at Hong Kong emigrants mutinied,revolt foiled.
1857	Challenge	American	Kenney	1,600	A few days from Swatow emigrants mutinied. Revolt put down.
"	Francis I (St.)	British			Two mutinies put down by heavily armed crew.
"	Guinare		Wardrop	1,002	Emigrants set ship afire,13 killed, 18 ringleaders executed.
"	Port de Bordeaux	French			One day at sea emigrants set ship afire, capt. gave up charter.
"	Kate Hooper	American	Jackson	1,507	Near Gaspar Straits emigrants set ship afire,5 killed,revolt foiled.
"	Fernandez			413	Emigrants set ship afire, 13 killed, mutiny foiled.
"	Carmen	Peruvian	L.Casogli		Emigrants set ship afire,crew took to boats,ship sunk, all perished.
"	Henrietta Maria	Dutch	Bakker		Mutiny near Cochin China,crew fled ship,ship found with only 100.
1858	Anais	French	Carignao	632	Near Hong Kong emigrants revolted,killed capt.officers,put ashore.
"	Bella Carmen	Peruvian			Emigrants revolted,killed 9 of crew, plundered ship.
1859	Flora Temple	American	Johnson	1,722	Emigrants mutinied,ship struck a reef and sank,only crew escaped.
"	Norvy	American	H.B.Major	2,434	Three days from Macao emigrants set ship afire, revolt foiled.
1860	Stepbound	American	S.B.Hussey	1,524	Mutiny near Anjer, revolt foiled.
"	Sebastopol			956	Mutiny,put down.
"	Greyhound	Chilean		294	Near Canton emigrants mutinied,1 killed,9 jumped overboard, foiled.
"	Lou	Peruvian			Near Macao emigrants mutinied,some jumped overboard,revolt foiled.

	Ship	Captain	Embarked	Landed	No.	No.	No.	No.	Remarks
"	Messenger		1,201	433		?	?	90	Emigrants mutinied in China sea, upwards of 100 shot.
1861	Encarnacion		690	289		2	?	99	Mutiny foiled.
"	Leonidas				I	I	?		Near Macao emigrants mutinied, most of crew wounded, revolt foiled.
"	Ville d'Agen	Wood			I	I	?		Emigrants mutinied, ship put into Hong Kong in distress.
1865	Pride of the Ganges	Fourson	301			12	?		Capt. and purser killed in mutiny, emigrants landed ship on Hainan.
"	LaVille de St.Lo		260	160		4	?		Mutiny, 12 emigrants killed, ship put into Saigon.
"	Caroline		360			4	?		Emigrants mutinied, 4 killed, revolt foiled.
1866	Emmanuel	L.de Condroy	358	160		?	?		Mutiny put down.
"	La Flora		510			?	?		Mutiny foiled.
"	Louis					?	?		Mutiny attempt failed, ship put back to Canton.
"	Napoleon Canevaro	R. Demaro	1,215	662		662	662		Emigrants set ship afire, crew took to boats, explosion, all killed.
"	Eugene et Adele	A. Girard	853	446	I	35	?		Mutiny, capt. killed and 35 emigrants, revolt foiled.
"	Jeddo	J. West	480			3	141	164	Emigrants set ship afire, capt. ran ship ashore, 144 died in fire.
"	Hong Kong		260			I	?		Emigrants mutinied, many died, rest landed on China coast.
1867	Bangkok	E. Chappot	400	233		2	4	229	Mutiny put down.
"	Orixa	Giraud	937	554		?	1541		Mutiny foiled.
1868	Lucy	D. Dedier	615	360		2	33	327	Mutiny put down.
"	Esperanza	E. Boju	397	300		2	21	573	Emigrants mutinied, ship put in at Anjer.
"	Theresa	S. Bollo	1,091	293	16	?	?		Near New Zealand emigrants mutinied, killed 16 crew, ship back to Macao.
"	Providenza	A. Mattine	660	792		?	?		Mutiny.
"	Cavalti				all	?	?	69	Ship put in at Hakodote, Japan with capt. and 42 emigrants, mutiny.
1869	Temaris	F. Ramee	545	500	I	?	251	69	Emigrants mutinied, killed capt.
"	Callao	L.Lavarillo	1,528	652		?	31	822	Mutiny put down.
1870	NouvellePenalope		490	510	I 9	?	?		Emigrants killed capt. and 9 of crew, ship wrecked near Macao.
"	Uncovah	J. Rossiano	988	537		124	?		Emigrants set ship afire, 124 died, others rescued.
"	Frederic	Niceise	381			16	?		Near Batavia emigrants set ship afire, crew and 365 rescued.
"	Hankow					436	436		Emigrants set ship afire, crew and 112 escaped.
"	Nelly	A. Poilhouth	895	548		436	436	410	Mutiny put down.
"	L'Olivier	A. Aucan	393	233		2	24		Emigrants mutinied, ship stranded near Sumatra.
1871	Don Juan	G. Garvay	1,203	565		607	607		Emigrants set ship afire, crew and only 58 emigrants escaped.
1872	Jacques Seurin	A. Heq	450	300		2	63	237	Near Macao emigrants mutinied, some killed, revolt foiled.
"	Petchoy	J.Parvjo	1,021	1107		2	74	923	Three mutinies and attempt to burn ship, all foiled.
Totals	68				13 II 23 6 3 4 2 2 2 2 1 1				

* Denotes ship continued on its voyage, but number of passengers unknown.

- Denotes ship did not continue its voyage.

Sources: B.F.O. IX/8091 B.P.P., A.S.S. China, Vol.IV, 286–287; The China Mail; The Friend of China; The Daily Press; Overland Register and Price Current; Overland Friend of China; North China Herald; Hong Kong Mercury and Shipping Gazette; The Hong Kong Shipping List; B.F.O. 17/881; B.F.O. 17/873; B.F.O. 17/806; B.F.O. 91/1011; B.F.O. 91/1011; B.F.O. 681/744; The Anti-Slavery Reporter; R.A.Johnson, "Coolie Labour and Coolie Immigration"Cornhill Magazine, Vol.XXI, No.91(July, 1867); 74–83; "The Coolie Trade", De Bows Review, Vol.XXIII (July, 1857), 30–55; E. Holden, "A Chapter on the Coolie Trade", Harper's New Monthly Magazine, Vol.XXX, No.166(June, 1864), I–II; "Piracy in the China Seas", Nautical Magazine and Naval Chronicle, Vol.XXI (April, 1852), 220–229; "Danger of Shipping Coolies", Nautical Magazine and Naval Chronicle, Vol.XXVI(May, 1857), 275; "Macao and its Slave Trade", China Review, Vol.II, 80, I(July, 1873), 9–20; Montalto de Jesus, Historic Macao, 330–341; Thiersant, L'Emigration Chinois, 141 Latbook, Coolie Ships and Oil Sailers, 26–51; U.S.Congress, House, Ex. Doc. No.105, I Sess., 34 Cong., 71–151; U.S.Congress, House, Ex. Doc. No.16, 2 Sess. 37 Cong., 2–55.

A Hong Kong daily newspaper warned that this was to give dissatisfied emigrants and pirates a license to kill and that no ship would be safe in the China sea.[7] Under attack and not having any precedent for his bold decision, Judge Smale petitioned the United States Embassy in Japan for information on the case of the bark *Cayalti*, which drifted into Hakadote harbor in November 1868, flying the United States flag and with only her captain and 100 Chinese emigrants on board. The rest of the crew and an undetermined number of passengers had been killed in a bloody revolt.[8] He was indeed gratified to learn that the United States Department of State ruled that the suspected mutineers were guilty of no crime and had adopted the language of the Supreme Court of the United States in its historic decision concerning the slaver *Amistad* to assert their innocence.

In 1839, the *Amistad* set out from Cuba with 54 black males for the slave market of the Southern United States. Through the cunning and leadership of a young man named Cinque, the slaves picked the locks on their chains, armed themselves with machetes, and killed the captain but spared the lives of the other two members of the crew on condition that they would steer the ship back to Africa.[9] Some weeks later, the ship was captured by the United States brig *Washington* off Long Island, New York, and in the ensuing legal battle that became a cause célèbre between the North and South, the Supreme Court ruled thus:

> We may lament the dreadful acts by which they asserted their liberty and took possession of the *Amistad* and endeavoured to regain their native country, but they cannot be deemed pirates or robbers in the sense of the law of nations.[10]

---

sufficient evidence. See James W. Norton Kyshe, *The History of the Laws and Courts of Hong Kong*, 2 vols. (London and Hong Kong, 1898), II, 186-187.

[7]   *The Daily Press* (Hong Kong), April 25, 1871.

[8]   Apparently this was a Peruvian vessel that had assumed the United States flag to safeguard itself from belligerent capture in the war between Peru and Spain. See the letter of Seward to Valkenburg, February 19, 1869, printed in the *China Mail*, December 15, 1871.

[9]   For a description of the mutiny and subsequent events see Addison B. C. Whipple, *Tall Ships and Great Captains: A Narrative of Famous Sailing Ships Through the Ages and the Courageous Men who Sailed them, Fought or Raced them across the Sea* (New York, Harper and Brothers, 1951), 146-159.

[10] Richard Peters, *Reports of Cases Argued and Adjusted in the Supreme Court of the United States, January term 1841* (Philadelphia, Thomas, Cowperthwait and Company, 1841), Vol. XV, 593-594.

Independently, Judge Smale had used similar reasoning to arrive at the same conclusion with regard to the mutiny of the *Nouvelle Penelope*.[11]

Sailors and Mutineers

During the twenty-eight years of the Chinese "coolie trade" to South America and the West Indies, 1847-1874, about one voyage in every eleven experienced a mutiny, and casualties were not limited to passengers. Over 4,000 emigrants, 12 captains, and a minimum of 200 sailors lost their lives in these revolts on the high seas. Understandably, some crews, when they learned that their ship was assigned to the "coolie trade," refused to go to sea.[12] Even the notorious American slave captain Francis Bowen, known as the Prince of Slavers, found the trade in Chinese laborers to the Chincha Islands in the late 1850s too dangerous and returned to slaving.[13] However, most vessels seemed to have little difficulty in obtaining a full crew.

The ordinary seaman aboard these emigrant ships averaged $15 a month as compared with between $8 and $12 a month for his counterpart in the tea trade.[14] Skilled laborers, such as carpenters, made from $35 to $40 a month, and a captain's monthly salary was on the order of $100.[15] But

---

[11] The impact of the *Nouvelle Penelope* case on world opinion is discussed in Chapter VIII.

[12] Backhouse to Bowring, February 3, 1853 (BPP, ASS, *China*, Vol. III), 113; White to Walcott, February 23, 1853, (Ibid.), 245; *Overland Register and Price Current*, October 29, 1852.

[13] Lubbock, *Coolie Ships and Oil Sailors*, 49.

[14] The Daily Press (Hong Kong), May 23, 1871; DeLong to Fish (Inclosure 3), November 6, 1872 (U.S. Congress, House, Ex. Doc. No. 1, 1 Sess. 43 Cong.), 559; Griffin, *Clippers and Consuls*, 29; Samuel E. Morison, *The Maritime History of Massachusetts, 1783-1860* (Boston, Houghton, Mifflin Company, 1921), 353; Essom M. Gale, "Far Eastern Trade Routes and Cargoes: A New England Ship Captain's Letters, 1850-1856," *Proceedings of the Pacific Coast Branch of the American Historical Association*, 1930, 121.

[15] Memorandum from Cecil C. Smith, February 3, 1873 (BPP, ASS, *China*, Vol. IV), 327; W.M. Robinet to Captain Henry Edwards, Cumsingmoon, January 16, 1851 (Heard Papers, Baker Library Harvard University, Boston).

over and above their salaries, captains, and sometimes officers, received a commission of up to $5 per head on all emigrants landed alive and in good health at Havana and Callao.[16] Furthermore, in keeping with the practice of the times, they were able to ship goods from China on their own account, which they sold to the Chinese in the New World at exorbitant prices, netting up to $1,000 on a single voyage.[17] These handsome remunerations attracted sailors of all nationalities. The crew of the American vessel *Staghound* was typical of most ships in the trade, consisting of nineteen Englishmen, eight Americans, six Frenchmen, four Germans, two Norwegians, one Dane, one Belgian, and one Dutchman.[18]

Most merchant vessels at the middle of the nineteenth century were manned by what Samuel E. Morison in *The Maritime History of Massachusetts* calls an "international proletariat of the sea"[19]—an assortment of vagrants, adventurers, and drunks—the misfits and castaways of society, many of them fleeing from justice in their native lands. Such men had very little in common, but when thrown together in a "coolie ship," they were as one in their dislike for the Chinese, whom they regarded as less than human.[20] Any show of insubordination or arrogance was summarily and brutally dealt with. Offenders were flogged and tied to the ringbolts or the hatch gratings by their queues for days on end, and disturbances in the between-deck brought a volley of gunfire aimed at random through the iron grills of the hatches.[21] Mr. O. Jackson, the engineer of the *Fatchoy*, a Spanish ship taking emigrants from Macau to Havana in 1873, related how, following an attempted mutiny,

---

[16]   *Hong Kong Mercury and Shipping Gazette*, October 31, 1866.

[17]   Memorandum from Cecil C. Smith, February 3, 1873 (BPP, ASS, *China*, Vol. IV), 327.

[18]   Anthon to Cass, April 30, 1860 (U.S. Congress, House, Ex. Doc. No. 16, 2 Sess. 37 Cong.), 10.

[19]   Morison, *The Maritime History of Massachusetts, 1783-1860*, 353.

[20]   Aldus, *Coolie Traffic and Kidnapping*, 120.

[21]   Holden, "A Chapter on the Coolie Trade," 7. See Figures 10 and 11. See also the statement of Henry Foss, seaman on the *Don Juan* (U.S. Dept. of State, Despatches from U.S. Consuls in Hong Kong, May, 1871).

Figure 10. "Tied to the hatches". (From *Harpers New Monthly Magazine*, Vol. XXIX, June 1864)

130 or more were put in irons. The next morning the Spanish captain had them brought up; some bags of rice were placed on the deck and the prisoners were laid across the bags, faces down, stripped to the skin and unmercifully flogged by two men keeping time with their whips, the blood flowing at every blow, when in a short time the deck was covered with blood. As each Chinaman was flogged he was washed with salt and water and sent below.[22]

The Chinese emigrants, for their part, looked upon Westerners as uncivilized barbarians and deeply resented their overlordship. The emigrant ship represented a microcosm of the clash of two proud civilizations, each regarding the other as inferior and each determined to demonstrate its superiority whenever possible. Other factors aggravated this potentially explosive situation.

---

[22] "The Portuguese China Coolie Slave-Trade to Cuba," *Anti-Slavery Reporter*, Vol. XVIII, No. 5 (April, 1873), 146-147.

Figure 11. "Firing Down the Hatch". (From *Harpers New Monthly Magazine* Vol. XXIX, June 1864)

Under the conditions and procedures of recruitment that prevailed along the China coast, there is little doubt that some passengers on board almost every emigrant vessel bound for South America were kidnapped or otherwise forced or tricked into going abroad against their will. Captain Seymour, who put down a mutiny on his ship, *Duke of Portland*, in 1856, stated that about one-third of the 332 Chinese passengers on board had been kidnapped.[23] Chun Apew, a petty trader from Canton, who volunteered to immigrate to Peru after he lost everything he owned gambling, testified at the trial of Kwok-Asing that about 100 of the 310 emigrants on the *Nouvelle Penelope* complained that they were on board against their will. All others were willing to go.[24]

But besides voluntary and involuntary emigrants, most vessels contained a third category that fell somewhere between the two. These were men who,

---

[23]   Clarendon to Bowring (Sub-Inclosure to Inclosure No. 9), October 18, 1856 (BPP, ASS, *China*, Vol. III), 424.

[24]   Bailey to Davis (Inclosure 1), April 7, 1871 (U.S. Dept. of State, *Foreign Relations*, 1871), 203-204.

though not willing to emigrate, were induced to do so by ready cash, hoping that by some chance such as success at gambling, they would be able to purchase their way out or provide a substitute, or in some way escape the fulfillment of their contract. The evidence of the surviving passengers of the *Don Juan* shows that they were persuaded by an $8 advance to make false statements about their willingness to emigrate with the understanding that by some subterfuge, they would escape before the ship weighed anchor.[25] Hence one could venture to say that anywhere from one-third to two-thirds of the passengers on any given ship were, to say the least, disillusioned and discontented with their lot.

In these circumstances, it is easy to see how unfair treatment or cruelty on the part of the ship's crew could readily spark a revolt. And it would seem that initially, the majority of mutinies were spontaneous uprisings seeking to escape from involuntary bondage or protesting real or imagined grievances. At the outset, ships did not have interpreters, and problems arising from difficulties of communication between passengers and crew tended to escalate into a confrontation.[26] However, it is also easy to see how such a situation could easily be exploited, and some were quick to take advantage of the opportunity.

The limited evidence as supplied by official investigations of the mutinies and accounts in the press, suggest that from the middle 1850s onward, mutineers in most instances were the tools of a small number of men who had their eyes on plunder. In the sixteen cases of mutiny in which some kind of official or unofficial *post mortem* took place, emigrants complained of being badly treated in six instances.[27] On two occasions, they explicitly stated they had no complaints whatsoever against the captain or crew,[28] and in thirteen cases, there was evidence that some, with prior planning, volunteered as emigrants so as to exploit the grievances and prejudices of the passengers, arouse them to mutiny, and plunder the ship.[29]

---

[25] Whitfield to Kimberly (Inclosures 2-5 in No. 1), May 24, 1871 (BPP, ASS, *China*, Vol. IV), 268-273.

[26] Barkly to Pakington, January 24, 1853 (Ibid., Vol. III), 137.

[27] *The Friend of China*, April 28, 1852, June 1, 1853; *Overland Register and Price Current*, September 28, 1850, February 11, 1853.

[28] *The Friend of China*, August 6, 1856, November 10, 1860.

[29] *The Friend of China*, March 10, 1852, July 2, 1853, April 1, 1857, March 2, 1861; Holden, "A Chapter on the Coolie Trade," 6; "The Danger of Shipping,"

The leaders of the mutinies would seem to have been for the most part pirates and ex-pirates. In the 1840s, the British Navy embarked upon a campaign to exterminate piracy in the China sea,[30] and with British warships bearing down upon them, many pirates abandoned their junks and turned to plundering emigrant vessels as a challenging, exciting, and rewarding alternative. In answer to an inquiry from the U.S. Department of State in 1854, James Keenan, U.S. consul at Hong Kong, estimated that there were 100,000 pirates in Chinese waters.[31] Justice Smale sidestepped the fact that Kwok-Asing confessed that the mutiny on the *Nouvelle Penelope* was the third incident of this kind in which he was involved.[32] It was a common practice for successful mutineers to reenlist as emigrants to try their luck again. Over 70 passengers from the *Nouvelle Penelope* were arrested in the barracoons at Macau as they waited to board other vessels.[33]

Statements made by emigrants from the *Don Juan* were quite explicit in detailing the manner in which they were decoyed or kidnapped, but the same witnesses were extremely vague or reluctant to provide information on the origin of the fire that consumed the ship together with most of its passengers. They had nothing whatsoever to say about the mutiny, which, according to the unanimous testimony of the crew, took place prior to the fire.[34] This led the *Daily Press* of Hong Kong to speculate that the unwillingness of the survivors to communicate all that they knew was perhaps a conspiracy of silence.[35] There were hints that pirates in league with compradores, emigration

---

Nautical Magazine and Naval Chronicle, Vol. XXI (May 1853), 275; C. A. Montalto de Jesus, *Historic Macao* (Hong Kong, Kelly and Wash Limited, 1902), 336; *Overland Register and Price Current*, October 29, 1852, July 22, 1858; *The Daily Press* (Hong Kong), May 29, 1871, June 10, 1873.

[30] Grace Estelle Fox, *British Admirals and Chinese Pirates, 1832-1869* (London, K. Paul, Trench, Trubner and Company Ltd., 1940).

[31] Memorandum from James Keenan, August 9, 1854 (U.S. Dept. of State, Despatches from U.S. Consuls, 1854).

[32] Robertson to Wade, November 19, 1870 (FO 17/878); Henri Cordier, *Histoire des Relationes de la Chine* (Paris, Ancienne Librarie Germer Baillirre e C[ie], 1907), 511.

[33] Antonio Sergio de Souza a Ministro e Secretario d'Estado dos Negocios da Marinha e Ultramar, November 10, 1870 (AHU, Macau, Pasta 27, 1870).

[34] Whitfield to Kimberly (Inclosures 2-8 in No. 1), May 24, 1871 (BPP, ASS, China, Vol. IV), 268-278; *Overland China Mail*, May 26, 1871.

[35] *The Daily Press*, May 29, 1871.

brokers, and crimps planned the mutiny, and that perhaps some secret society had master-minded this and other mutinies.

In 1861, the *Friend of China* went so far as to accuse "high authorities" in the Canton government with connivance in the revolts on board the ships *Sebastopol, Greyhound,* and *Leonidas.* The paper alleged that the revolts were part of a plan to discredit and eventually stop "coolie emigration."[36] No solid evidence was brought forward to substantiate this, although it was known that such influential Chinese organizations as the Tungwa Hospital Committee of Hong Kong and the Benevolent Society of Canton actively befriended mutineers.[37]

Immigration to Latin America, controlled by Westerners, was in competition with the Chinese-controlled movements to Southeast Asia, California, and Australia. There were no reported instances of mutiny in these migrations after they came under the control of the Chinese. The mutinies on the *Robert Browne* and the *Spartan* took place prior to Chinese interests taking over the movements, and at least in the case of the former, the voyage was a private speculative venture on the part of the captain, who happened to own the vessel he commanded.[38] Whether or not mutineers received official encouragement or were connected with secret societies, it is impossible to say. But this much is clear: their exploits were largely planned operations, and they succeeded in discrediting the "coolie trade," which served the vested interests of some groups along China's southern coast.

The Mutinies

Almost all mutinies occurred within a few days' sail from the China coast or as the emigrants sighted land nearing the Gaspar or Sunda Straits prior to entering the Indian Ocean. At a propitious moment, when the crew was preoccupied, bands of emigrants would hurl themselves upon the guards and try by sheer force of numbers to take control of the ship. If they succeeded, as they did in at least thirteen occasions, they compelled the surviving members of the crew to sail the ship back to China or to some nearby island, or they themselves did so, and there ran the ship ashore, plundered it, and escaped.

---

[36]   *The Friend of China*, March 2, 1861.

[37]   *The Daily Press*, (Hong Kong), May 23, 1871.

[38]   *The Friend of China*, May 12, 1852.

Figure 12. "A Mutinous Passenger" (From *Harpers New Monthly Magazine*, Vol. XXIX June, 1864)

If, on the other hand, they were beaten back and forced below and the hatches bolted upon them, they made every effort to set fire to the ship, making a pyre of their bedding, belongings, and wood torn from the bunks.[39]

---

[39] Testimony of Captain Wood regarding the mutiny on board the U.S. vessel *Leonidas* (U.S. Congress, House, Ex. Doc. No. 16, 2 Sess. 37 Cong.), 28; "The Coolie Trade," *DeBow's Review*, Vol. XXIII (July, 1857), 34-35.

E. Holden, who was a passenger on the *Norway*, which shipped 1,038 Chinese laborers to Cuba in 1859, gives us an eyewitness account:

> The foiled wretches, maddened at defeat in the very outset, rushed with furious yells from one hatch to another, swinging lighted firebrands or striving to wrench away the iron bars that covered them, or hurling bolts and clubs at every face that peered down at them from above. The red glare of the flames lit up the sky, reflecting grimly against the swelling sails, and in spite of a constant stream of water from the pumps seemed scarcely to diminish.[40]

Setting the ship afire was a typical pirate tactic. It was a desperate gamble to throw the crew into confusion and to force them to abandon the ship. On occasions, the strategy paid off; but at other times, it ended in catastrophe, as the terrified crew took to the boats, leaving the hatches securely fastened, and the passengers trapped in the between-deck suffocated or burned to death.

Figure 13. "Writing Demands with Blood of a Fallen Comrade". (From *Harpers New Monthly Magazine*, Vol. XXIX, June, 1864)

---

[40] Holden, "A Chapter on the Coolie Trade," 7. See Figure 12.

The worst recorded disaster was that of the United States clipper *Flora Temple*, which sailed from Macau for Havana on October 3, 1859. A few days' distance from shore, the emigrants mutinied and set fire to the ship. Volleys from the crew's muskets forced them below, and the hatches were battened down. In the confusion, the ship struck a reef and sank. The crew took to the boats, but all 850 passengers perished.[41] In 1866, the crew of the Italian vessel *Napoleon Canevaro*, two days out from Macau, discovered a plot to seize the ship. When the emigrants were forced below, they set a fire in the between-deck; and when the flames reached 8,000 packets of firecrackers in the hold, a mighty explosion ripped the vessel apart, killing all 662 passengers. The captain and crew moments before escaped in the boats.[42] A similar tragedy befell the Peruvian ship *Don Juan* (formerly *Dolores Ugarte*) within two days of her sailing from Macau in May, 1871. Following a disturbance among the 665 emigrants, a fire broke out in a storeroom. Water hoses put down between the gratings of the padlocked hatches were rejected by the passengers, and the nozzles were pushed out portholes so that the water spouted uselessly into the sea. The fire rapidly got beyond control, and the ship burned to the water's edge. Only the crew and some 58 emigrants who happened to be on the upper deck escaped the holocaust.[43]

These are some of the more catastrophic failures. In less dramatic instances, when mutineers failed to obtain their objectives, they sometimes resorted to bargaining, threatening to burn the ship if their demands were not complied with. In one instance, they wrote their demands with the blood of a fallen comrade, which read,

> Three hundred coolies to be allowed on deck at one time. They shall navigate the ship and take her to Siam, where a certain number may

---

[41]   Lubbock, *Coolie Ships and Oil Sailors*, 40; Ward to Cass, February 24, 1860 (U.S. Congress, House, Ex. Doc. No. 88, 1 Sess. 36 Cong.), 31.

[42]   *Hong Kong Times, Daily Advertiser and Shipping Gazette*, September 8, 1874; R.A. Johnson, "Coolie Labor and Coolie Immigration," *Cornhill Magazine*, Vol. XVI, No. 91 (July, 1867), 75.

[43]   Meade to Hammond (and Inclosures), July 25, 1871 (BPP, ASS, *China*, Vol. IV), 267-280; *The Daily Press* (Hong Kong), May 9, 1871, May 22, 1871, M. Léon Couturat, "L'Émigration Chinoise," *Bulletin de la Societé Royale de Géographie D'Anvers*, Vol. V (1880), 474.

leave her, after which she shall be allowed to proceed on her course. No signals of any kind shall be made to attract attention of other vessels.[44]

But once the crew got the upper hand, mutineers had little option but to surrender their leaders for punishment or burn the ship beneath themselves. Ringleaders were usually flogged and tied to the ringbolts, where they remained sometimes for the rest of the voyage, or they were put ashore somewhere en route.[45] The *Straits Times*, a Singapore newspaper, bitterly complained in 1857 that the island was becoming a dumping ground for mutineers and pirates.[46]

Not much is known about successful mutinies. Captured vessels were run ashore and plundered. The few fortunate crew members who survived to tell their story, told of the mutineers gambling and fighting among themselves, with many being killed or thrown overboard.[47] Two emigrants on the captured Peruvian bark *Rosa Elias*, who angered their leaders by taking a watch from one of the crew and hiding it for themselves, were hacked to pieces and thrown into the sea.[48] It is difficult to imagine disillusioned or even kidnapped emigrants turning into ruthless killers even of their own countrymen.

Although the French flag suffered the largest number of mutinies, there is no evidence to indicate that conditions on board vessels of any one nationality were significantly better or worse than conditions on others, and hence less or more prone to mutiny. In fact, relative to the number of vessels involved under each flag, mutinies were rather evenly distributed, as table 18 illustrates. But it should be noted that the British flag, which was at this time committed to policing the oceans of the world in an effort to suppress the African slave trade, fared no better than the flags of less crusading nations.

---

[44]   Holden, "A Chapter on the Coolie Trade," 9. See Figure 13.

[45]   "Danger of Shipping Coolies," *Nautical Magazine and Naval Chronicle*, Vol. XXI (May, 1853), 275; *The Friend of China*, November 10, 1852; *Overland Register and Price Current*, January 28, 1853, November 27, 1853.

[46]   *The Friend of China*, April 1, 1857.

[47]   "Piracy in the China Seas," *Nautical Magazine and Naval Chronicle*, Vol. XXI (April, 1852), 222.

[48]   *The Friend of China*, June 1, 1853.

Table 18

Percentage of Mutinies to Number of Voyages under Various
Flags Carrying Chinese Emigrants to Latin America from 1847-1874

Flag	Number of Voyages	Number of Mutinies	Percentage
French	141	23	16.31
Peruvian	119	6	5.04
British	105	13	12.38
Spanish	91	3	3.29
American	64	11	17.18
Italian	44	4	9.09
Portuguese	38	2	5.26
Dutch	32	2	6.25
Salvadorian	32	2	6.25
Chilean	12	1	8.33
Belgian	5	1	20.00
German	17	none	
Russian	14	"	
Austrian	5	"	
Norwegian	3	"	
Danish	3	"	
Swedish	1	"	
Mexican	1	"	
Colombian	1	"	
Ecuadorian	1	"	
Unknown	7	"	
Totals	736	68	9.23

Source: Compiled from table 17 and tables 25-48 in appendix VI.

Better than one of every eight British ships in the "coolie trade" experienced
a mutiny. This was a shade below French and Yankee ships, which had the
highest percentage, with a ratio of one mutiny to every six voyages.

However, as is evident from table 19, ships departing from the Chinese
ports of Cumsingmoon, Amoy, Canton, and Swatow, where there was little

or no supervision over emigration, had a much higher incidence of mutiny than those departing from the British and Portuguese colonies of Hong Kong and Macau, where some measure of control was enforced.

Table 19

Percentages of Mutinies to Number of Vessels Departing from Ports to Latin America with Chinese Emigrants from 1847-1874

Port of Departure	Number of Voyages	Number of Mutinies	Percentage
Macau	501	35	6.98
Swatow	64	7	10.93
Canton (Whampoa)	59	9	15.25
Hong Kong	38	3	7.89
Amoy	36	7	19.44
Cumsingmoon	18	6	33.33
Shanghai	3	none	
Singapore	3	"	
Nigpo	1	"	
Batavia	1	"	
Unknown	12	1	8.33
Totals	736	68	9.23

Source: Compiled from table 17 and tables 25-48 in appendix VI.

Marshall K. Powers, in his dissertation, claims that the conditions on the voyages were much more brutal in the 1860s after the two "humanitarian nations," Great Britain and the United States, withdrew from the trade.[49] But if mutinies are taken as a measure of brutality, then the reverse is true, for in proportion to the number of vessels employed in the trade, there were almost twice as many mutinies in the 1850s as in the 1860s. And furthermore, there was a significant drop in the death rate from the early 1860s onward.[50] In the later years, shipmasters took greater precautions to prevent mutinies, but

---

[49]   Powers, "Chinese Coolie Migration to Cuba," 183.

[50]   See Table 16.

uprisings and instances of high mortality received wider publicity in all their gory details, and this may have led Powers to his conclusion.

To a world press that did not discriminate between spontaneous and premeditated revolts, the mutinies and awful tragedies that followed upon them were convincing proof that Chinese immigration to Latin America was nothing less than a new slave trade. And with world attention focused on the evils of the traffic, Western governments, as well as the imperial government of China, were under considerable pressure to do something to stop this abominable commerce in human life.

CHAPTER VI

CHINESE INDENTURED LABORERS IN LATIN AMERICA (I)

La cuestión de los asiáticos, ó chinos, no es otra sino la cuestión de brazos.

Mariano Torrente, *Bosquejo Económico Político de la Isla de Cuba*
(Madrid, Imprenta de D. Manuel Pita, 1852), 402

No hay donde al chino no lo halles,
Desde el ensaque del huano,
Hasta el cultivo en los valles;
Desde el servicio de mano,
Hasta el barrido de calles.

Aún de la plebe es sirviente,
Y no hay servicio ¿lo oís?
Que él no abarque diligente.
¿Y la gente del país?
¡Està pensando en ser gente!

Juan de Arona (Paz Soldán), *La Inmigración en el Perú*
(Lima, Imprenta del Universo de Carlos Prince, 1891), 40

Early Contacts between China and the New World

The arrival of the first Manila galleon, the *San Pablo*, at Acapulco in June, 1565, could be said to mark the beginning of Sino-American relations. The *San Pablo* was one of a fleet of five ships, under the command of Miguel Lopez de Legaspi, that sailed from New Spain in November 1564, charged with the task of taking possession of the Philippines, establishing contact with China, and discovering a trade route across the Pacific.[1] Though

---

[1] William Lytle Schurz, *The Manila Galleon* (New York, E.P. Dutton and Company, 1959), 22-24.

the Spaniards did not succeed in trading directly with the Celestial Empire,[2] Chinese traders flocked to Manila, where at the beginning of the seventeenth century, there were more than 20,000 Chinese.[3] It was from this port that the famous Manila galleons brought their precious cargoes of silks, porcelain, and spices across the Pacific to Acapulco and the New World. The long, perilous voyage was an annual event that persisted for two and a half centuries, the final crossing taking place in 1815.[4]

To the peoples of America, the galleons were the China ships; and together with the merchandise of the East, the Spaniards brought along with them Chinese as servants and galley slaves.[5] Alexander Humboldt suggests that as a result of the frequent communication between Acapulco and Manila, many Asiatics, both Chinese and Malays, settled in the New World.[6] He himself encountered Chinese in Cuba who had come on one of the galleons.[7] The ecclesiastical records of the seventeenth century of the diocese of Michoacán, Mexico, list several Chinese households as paying tithes of the rice they had cultivated.[8] Part of the native population of Acapulco consisted of a mixture of Indians and Orientals that was generally known as "Chinese."[9] Mexico City also had a Chinese colony in the first half of the seventeenth century. In 1635, the town council heard a complaint from the barber's guild to the effect that the Chinese barbers of the city were refusing to employ local apprentices. The council ruled that the number of Chinese barbershops be limited to twelve

---

[2]   In 1598 the Spaniards obtained from China a trading site called *El Pinal* or "The Pine Grove", probably on the island of Hong Kong, but the violent opposition of the Portuguese caused them to abandon it. See Schurz, *The Manila Galleon*, 66.

[3]   George Philipps, "Early Spanish Trade with Chin Cheo (Changchow)," *China Review*, Vol. XIX (1891), 244.

[4]   Schurz, *The Manila Galleons*, 15.

[5]   Homer H. Dubs and Robert S. Smith, "Chinese in Mexico City in 1635," *Far Eastern Quarterly*, Vol. I, No. 4 (August, 1942), 387-389.

[6]   Alexander Humboldt, *Political Essay on the Kingdom of New Spain*, translated from the French by John Black, 2 vols. (London, Longman, Hurst, Rees, Orme and Brown, 1811), I, 130.

[7]   E. Chang Rodriguez, "Chinese Labor Migration into Latin America in the Nineteenth Century," *Revista de Historia de México*, No. 46 (December, 1958), 377.

[8]   *El Obispado de Michoacán en el Siglo XVIII* (Morelia, Michoacán, Fímax Publicistas, 1973), 118, 130-131.

[9]   Schurz, *The Manila Galleons*, 374.

and that these be outside the city-center.[10] Nothing is known of Chinese in other pursuits at this time in Mexico City, but it can be reasonably presumed that if they owned over a dozen barbershops, they were also in other service-oriented businesses.

Following upon a *cédula* of 1601, that attempted to prohibit the employment of native Indians in the woolen textile mills (*obrajes*) of Peru, Chinese were recruited from the Philippines to take their place.[11] There were also Chinese reported in Minas Gerais, Brazil, in the first half of the eighteenth century, in all probability brought there by some enterprising Portuguese trader from Malacca or Macau.[12] But what would seem to be the first planned settlement of Chinese in the New World was a group of about 70 Chinese artisans brought to the northwest coast of America by merchants of the British East India Company in 1789 in the hope of setting up a permanent trading post at Nootka Sound on the west coast of Vancouver Island, British Columbia.[13] According to John Meares, a lieutenant in the Royal Navy and the leader of the expedition, the settlement was to supply the Chinese market at Canton with furs and ginseng,[14] which could be easily and cheaply obtained from the local Indians.[15]

The 70 Chinese artisans complained that they were led to believe that they were going to Bengal. But the plan was to furnish them with Polynesian wives, and thus they could settle Nootka Sound.[16] However, the plan failed to

---

[10]   Dubs, "Chinese in Mexico City in 1635," 387-89.

[11]   C. H. Haring, *The Spanish Empire in America* (New York: Harcourt, Brace and World, Inc., 1947), 60, footnote 55.

[12]   C.R. Boxer, *The Golden Age of Brazil, 1695-1750* (Berkeley, University of California Press, 1969), 175; João Rodrigues de Brito, *A Economia Brasileira: No Alvorecer do Século XIX* (Salvador, Brasil, Livraria Progresso, 194-), 94.

[13]   Hubert Howe Bancroft, *History of the Northwest* Coast, 2 vols. (San Francisco, A. L. Bancroft and Company, 1884), I, 210-211.

[14]   Ginseng, found in China and North America, is an herb with an aromatic root used medicinally by the Chinese.

[15]   John Meares, *Voyages Made in the Years 1788 and 1789 from China to the Northwest Coast of America* (London, Logographic Press, 1790), 2; "Mr. Meares' Memorial," April 30, 1790 (BPP, Vol. LXXXVI, 1790). For a summary of the various expeditions made by Meares and others to Nootka Sound see Vincent T. Harlow, *The Founding of the Second British Empire, 1763-1793*, 2 vols. (London, Longmans, Green and Company Ltd., 1964), II, 419-450.

[16]   Bancroft, *History of the Northwest* Coast, I, 211, footnote 13.

materialize, as the Spanish warship *Princessa*, commanded by Don Estevan José Martínez, seized the British vessels carrying the prospective settlers shortly after they arrived at Nootka Sound.[17] The Spaniards regarded British plans to establish a settlement on Vancouver Island as a violation of Spanish sovereignty. By virtue of prior discovery, Spain claimed the northwest coast of America as part of her domain.[18] The captured vessels were sent to Fort Blas in New Spain.[19] But it is not clear what happened to the Chinese. Meares states that Martínez compelled them to enter into the service of Spain and put them to work in the mines, which the British had opened on Vancouver Island,[20] but Bancroft found no evidence to support this in Spanish documents.[21]

Some seventeen years elapsed before the British East India Company sponsored a second attempt to establish a settlement of Chinese in the Americas—this time in Trinidad. At the turn of the century, the British government became somewhat enamored of the prospect of introducing Chinese into its possessions in the West Indies. It was felt that Chinese would not only serve to offset the possibility of insurrection by the Negroes, but would promote commerce and trade between the West and East Indies and thus counteract the growing trade of the United States of America across the Pacific.[22] Trinidad was chosen to try out the idea. The vision of the Port of Spain becoming a depot for goods from the East, from which they could be dispensed throughout South America, won over the cooperation of the East India Company.[23]

At the suggestion of Her Majesty's government, the company entrusted the undertaking to Kenneth Macqueen, who had many years experience working with the Chinese in Southeast Asia.[24] On the advice of Lieutenant-Governor Farquhar of Penang, the Chinese were obtained by means of "the

---

[17] Ibid.; Harlow, *The Founding of the Second British Empire*, II, 441-442.

[18] Bancroft, *History of the Northwest Coast*, I, 227.

[19] Ibid., 222.

[20] "Mr. Meares' Memorial."

[21] Bancroft, *History of the Northwest Coast*, I, 211, footnote 13.

[22] "Letter to His Majesty's Ministery to the Court of Directors of the East India Company," April 20, 1803 (BCO 295/14); "Extracts from the Minutes of a meeting held at Government House," October 15, 1806 (BCO 295/14).

[23] Barlow, Udney and Lumsden to the Governor of Trinidad (BCO 295/14).

[24] Hobart to Macqueen, April 21, 1803 (BCO 295/14).

usual mode, which has been practiced with such success throughout the British and Dutch settlements in the Eastern Archipelago,"[25] and Antonio da (sic) Campos, a Portuguese merchant of Macau, brought 141 Chinese to Penang in January 1806.[26] Six Chinese from Penang were persuaded to join the group and under the leadership of Macqueen the party sailed for Calcutta. Another 53 men were recruited from the Chinese colony in Calcutta, and a total of 200 Chinese proceeded to Trinidad on the ship *Fortitude*, which also had a cargo of merchandise valued at 102,000 rupees.[27]

Though the governor of Trinidad was forewarned of the coming of the Chinese months in advance, when the *Fortitude* docked at the Port of Spain in October 1806, little or no preparation had been made to receive the new settlers.[28] During the first year, dislike of plantation labor and the absence of Chinese women caused much discontent, and when the *Fortitude* sailed for China in July 1807, 61 disillusioned Chinese were on board.[29] Within the next few years, most of the others also returned home. By 1825, there were only 12 Chinese on the island.[30]

To compound the failure of the undertaking, the *Fortitude* together with its cargo of tea and piece goods were seized by the Royal Navy as being in violation of the Navigation Acts. They were later sold at public auction with the proceeds divided between the local commander of the Royal Navy and the King.[31] The owner of both the ship and the merchandise, the East India Company, received nothing.[32] This totally undermined the prospects for trade, and the experiment with Chinese colonists was abandoned.

Among the first planned immigrant settlements sponsored by a Latin

---

[25] Farquhar to the Select Committee of Supercargoes at Canton, April 15, 1805 (BCO 295/13).

[26] Barlow, Udney and Lumsden to the Governor of Trinidad, April 14, 1806 (BCO 295/14). Antonio da Campos received 25 Spanish dollars for each of the 141 Chinese. See "Farquhar's Promisory Note to Captain da Campos," (BCO 295/13).

[27] "Extracts from the Minutes of a Meeting held at Government House," October 15, 1806 (BCO 295/14); Macqueen to Camden, September 15, 1806 (BCO 295/15); Barlow, Udney and Lumsden to the Governor of Trinidad, April 14, 1806 (BCO 295/14).

[28] Higman, "The Chinese in Trinidad," 28-29.

[29] Ibid., 33.

[30] Ibid., 34.

[31] Hislop to Windham, February 17, 1807 (BCO 295/16).

[32] Higman, "The Chinese in Trinidad," 43.

American government was a group of Chinese imported by the Prince Regent Dom João of Brazil to the vicinity of Rio de Janeiro between 1810 and 1820. The first to recommend the introduction of Chinese to Brazil would seem to have been João Rodrigues de Brito, the chief magistrate of the captaincy of Bahia. Rodrigues was acquainted with the reputation of the Chinese in British possessions in Southeast Asia, and, in an address to the Bahian senate in 1807, recommended the importation of Chinese and East Indian laborers as a possible solution to Bahia's labor problems.[33]

Two years later, the matter of Chinese immigration was again brought to the attention of Brazilians, but this time, the recommendation came from a rather unexpected quarter. When the Portuguese colony of Macau learned of the flight of Portugal's Royal Court to Rio de Janeiro, it quickly dispatched the frigate *Ullysses* with assurances of loyalty, fifty boxes of gifts from China and Japan, and an offer to supply the court with all the Chinese laborers and artisans that it would need to "create a new capital."[34] The chief magistrate of Macau, Miguel de Arriaga Brum de Silveira, was primarily interested in the development of trade with Brazil but recognized that Chinese immigration might provide the excuse, if not the basis, for the establishment of a regular commerce between the two Portuguese colonies.[35] He stressed the industriousness of the Chinese, their contribution to the development of British possessions in Southeast Asia, and suggested that they could introduce and cultivate products from the East unknown in Brazil.[36]

The *Ullysses* left Macau on March 19, 1809, with a crew of eighty-nine and three official representatives from the Macau government, and arrived at Rio de Janeiro eight months later on November 25.[37] The Royal Court must have been favorably impressed, as the restrictions on commerce with the Orient were revoked,[38] and Chinese immigration was given Royal

---

33   João Rodrigues de Brito, *A Economia Brasileira*, 94-95.

34   Miguel de Arriaga Brum de Silveira a Real Pessoa de V.A.R., 6 de Março de 1809 (AHU, Macau, 1809, Maço 29).

35   Ibid. The plan was set forth in an anonymous paper entitled "Providencias Lembradas para o Augmento e Prosperidade de Macao" (AHU, Macau, 1810, Maço 30).

36   Miguel de Arriaga Brum de Silveira a Real Pessoa de V.A.R., 6 de Março de 1809 (AHU, Macau, 1809, Maço 29); Miguel de Arriaga Brum de Silveira a V. Ex. 26 Agosto de 1812 (AHU, Macau, 1812-13, Maço 33).

37   AHU, Macau, 1809, Maço 29.

38   Carlos Francisco Moura, "Relacões entre Macau e o Brasil no Início do Século XIX, segundo as 'Memórias para Servir à História do Reino do Brasil,' do Padre Pererreca," *Boletim do Instituto Luís de Camoẽs*, vol. VII, no. 3 (Autumn 1973), 263.

approval.[39] The Count of Linhares, the Portuguese foreign minister at Rio de Janeiro, boasted of bringing 2 million Chinese to Brazil.[40]

A lively trade sprung up between Macau and the Brazilian ports of Bahia (Salvador) and Rio de Janeiro. Besides Chinese artisans and laborers, ships from Macau brought silks, spices, various kinds of teas, and Chinese pottery,[41] items that were much sought after in the new cosmopolitan atmosphere, which the Royal Court had bestowed on Rio de Janeiro. On the return voyages, the vessels carried from Brazil an assortment of wines, cheese, butter, iron bars, canvas, and *patacas* (Brazilian silver coins).[42]

It is not clear when precisely the first Chinese settlers arrived in Brazil from Macau, or how many actually came. In the correspondence of Miguel de Arriaga Brum de Silveira, it is stated that 140 Chinese laborers sailed on the ships *Maria* and *Luz*, which departed for Brazil in 1813, and 10 Chinese carpenters went on the *Ullysses* the following year.[43] This would seem to be but a partial listing. One source estimated that a total of between 400 and 500 arrived at Rio de Janeiro.[44] Whether or not any Chinese settled in Bahia or other parts of Brazil, it is not known.

The Chinese are remembered best for their work in the Rio de Janiero Botanical Garden. There they cultivated tea and such Eastern spices as cinnamon, nutmeg, clove, allspice, and camphor.[45] The gardens were a pet project of Prince Regent Dom João (who was crowned King João VI of the United Kingdom of Portugal and Brazil in 1816), and they were widely admired for their Oriental spices and fruits.[46] In 1813, there arrived from Macau on the

---

[39]   Miguel de Arriaga Brum de Silveira a V. Ex.ᵃ, 26 Agosto de 1812 (AHU, Macau, 1812-13, Maço 33).

[40]   W. L. von Eschwege, *Pluto Brasiliensis*, 2 vols. (São Paulo: Companhia Editora Nacional, 1944), II, 452.

[41]   AHU, Macau, 1813-14, Maço 34; 1815-16, Maço 35; 1816-17, Maço 36; 1817, Maço 37.

[42]   Ibid.

[43]   Miguel de Arriaga Brum de Silveira a V. Ex.ᵃ, Macau, 30 Dezembro, de 1813 (AHU, Macau, 1813-14, Maço 34).

[44]   Eschwege, *Pluto Brasiliensis*, II, 452.

[45]   C. S. Stewart, *A Visit to the South Seas in the United States Ship Vincennes during the Years 1829 and 1830, including Notices of Brazil, Peru, Manilla, the Cape of Good Hope and St. Helena*, 2 vols. (New York, John P. Haven, 1833), I, 93-94. See Figure 14.

[46]   Maria Graham, *Journal of a Voyage to Brazil and Residence There during Part of the Years 1821, 1822, 1823* (London, Longman, Hurst, Rees, Orme, Brown, Green and J. Murray, 1824), 163, 287; Carl Seidler, *Dez Anos no Brasil* [Titulo do Original: *ZEHN JAHRE in Brasilien, Wahrend de Regierung Don Pedro's und nach*

ship *Luz* two boxes of tea plants and a box each of litchi, bamboo, longan, and orange plants.[47] With the expertise of the Chinese, Dom João thought that tea cultivation on a large scale could be introduced to Brazil, but his son, Dom Pedro, whom he left behind as regent when he returned to Portugal in 1821, felt it more advantageous to sell coffee and buy tea, a move that the British heartily approved of since they were contemplating growing tea commercially in India.[48]

Figure 14. Chinese Cultivating Tea in the Botanical Gardens, Rio de Janeiro, (Taken from Maurice Rugendas, *Voyage Pittoresque dans le Bresil,* Paris, Engelmann & Cie., 1835)

---

dessen Entthronung.--Mit besconderer Hinsicht auf das Schicksal der Auslandischen Truppen und der deutchen Colonisten, Quedlinburg und Leipzig, Druck und Verlag von Gottfr. Basse, 1835], Tradução e Notas do General Bertoldo Klinger (São Paulo, Livraria Martins, 1835), 56-57; Conde de Suzannet, *O Brasil em 1845: Semelhanças e Differenças Apos um Século,* Tradução de Márcia de Moura Castro (Rio de Janeiro, Livraria Editōra da Casa do Estudante do Brasil, 1954), 60.

[47]   AHU, Macau, 1813-14, Maço 34.

[48]   Graham, *Journal of a Voyage to Brazil,* 287; Seidler, *Dez Anos no Brasil,* 57.

The decision to discontinue tea cultivation, together with problems arising from the absence of Chinese women, brought an end to Chinese immigration. The cultivators of tea and Oriental spices became street vendors and cooks.[49] The experiment was a failure, and apart from a small group of Chinese from the Philippines taken to Cuba in 1830 as domestic servants,[50] there was a lapse of about thirty years before the next venture in Chinese immigration to Latin America, which launched the "coolie trade."

Chinese Laborers in Cuba

Response to the initial group of 571 Chinese laborers landed at Havana in June 1847 was mixed. Upon their arrival, the Chinese were placed in a barracoon, which was used to house runaway slaves. There they were divided into lots of ten.[51] Planters who had subscribed for them in advance were then permitted to choose from among the various lots. Some took as many as five lots, others only one. A railroad company took two lots, and the governor of the island, Leopoldo O'Donnell, took two Chinese, who, in all probability were destined for domestic service.[52] All had to pay 170 pesos per head for the Chinese or, more specifically, for each of the eight-year contracts, which the laborers had signed with an agent of Zulueta and Company prior to leaving China.[53]

Early in 1848, because of reports of rebellious and unsatisfactory behavior of the Chinese, the Junta de Fomento (Development Council), which had sponsored the experiment, solicited statements from the planters on the conduct of their new field hands. Some planters complained that the Chinese were almost unmanageable. They showed little disposition to work, resisted discipline, quarreled among themselves, and served as a bad example to the Negro slaves.[54] But the report of planter Francisco Diago, which warmly praised the performance of the Chinese, was more typical. Diago wrote that he was highly satisfied with the Chinese "in all the tasks to which our slave population

---

[49]   João Mauricio Rugendas, *Viagem Pitoresca Através do Brasil*, Tradução de Sérgio Milliet (São Paulo, Livraria Martins Editora S.A., 4ª Edição, 1949), 156.

[50]   Chin Chieh Chang, "The Chinese in Latin America" (unpublished dissertation, University of Maryland, 1956), 9.

[51]   Corbitt, *A Study of the Chinese in Cuba*, 7.

[52]   Ibid.

[53]   Ibid.

[54]   Ibid., 8-10. See also Pastrama, *Los Chinos en las Luchas por la Liberación Cubana*, 35-36.

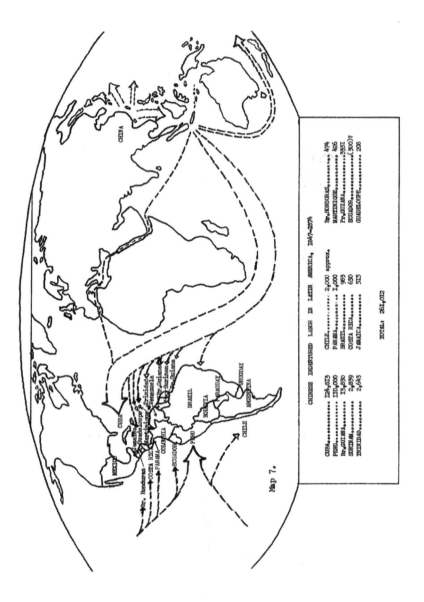

Map 7

Chinese indentured labor in Latin America, 1847-1874

are accustomed from light chores of domestic service in the city to the most fatiguing tasks demanded by our sugar mills."[55] He went on to suggest that unfavorable reports from some estates were perhaps due to a lack of sensitivity to the Chinese character and misunderstandings arising from the mutual ignorance of planters and Chinese of each other's language and culture.[56] Felix Erenchún was in substantial agreement with Diago when he wrote in 1856,

> When the (Chinese) colonists were first introduced they encountered the inconveniences common to all such experiments; these men, possessed of an advanced civilization, which, though different from our own, could not be treated like the bozales from Africa. Homicides, rebellions and uprisings were frequent on some plantations, while more tactful and prudent planters obtained better results. Many of the problems arose from lack of interpreters. At present, although there are still many who doubt the advantage of this type of colonist, the original difficulties occur less frequently, which is due in large measure to the existence of competent interpreters.[57]

Satisfied that the majority of the planters were favorable to the continuation of Chinese immigration and citing Leonard Wray's praise of the Chinese from *The Practical Sugar Planter*, the Junta de Fomento on December 10, 1851, unanimously resolved that "the immigration of Asiatic colonists, contracted in China, was not only advantageous but indispensable, and merited the special protection of the Junta, and the government."[58] The government had originally intended to limit Chinese immigration to the Junta de Fomento, but now the junta decided to entrust the recruitment and transportation of

---

[55] Cited in Mariano Torrente, *Bosquejo Económico Político de la Isla de Cuba* (Madrid, Imprenta de D. Manuel Pita, 1852), 40. See also Antonio L. Valverde, "La Trata de Chinos en la Isla de Cuba," *Reforma Social*, Vol. I (July, 1914), 486; Antonio L. Valverde, *Colonización y Inmigración en Cuba* (Habana, Academia de la Historia, 1923), 53-54.

[56] Torrente, *Bosquejo Económico Político de la Isla de Cuba*, 413.

[57] Erenchún, *Anales de la Isla de Cuba*, II (1856), 778.

[58] Antonio L. Valverde, *Estudios Jurídicos e Históricos* (Habana, Imp. "Avisador Commercial," 1918), 30-31.

Chinese immigrants to private concerns, which in effect threw the traffic open to speculation and commercial exploitation.

The junta's decision to step aside in favor of private enterprise triggered a rush of applications for permission to engage in transporting Chinese immigrants to Cuba.[59] Most of those applying and their financial backers were veterans of the African slave trade.[60] The commercial houses of Manuel B. Pareda and Villoldo Waldrop and Company were the first to apply. Wealthy planters like Domingo Aldama, J. M. Morales, and Drake and Brothers petitioned for permission to import Chinese for themselves and their friends. Other planters formed companies such as *Empresa de Colonización* (*Colonizadora*), *La Alianza*, *La Compañía de Hacendados*, which assumed all risks and directly controlled the entire operation, from the recruitment of laborers in China to their sale to the planters in Cuba.[61] These powerful companies had their own agents and barracoons on the China coast, and in the 1860s, after both Great Britain and the United States of America prohibited vessels flying their flags from participating in the traffic, the companies purchased their own ships, some of which were steamers.[62]

The rush to populate the island with Chinese was not without opposition. Most Cuban men of letters were opposed to any large-scale introduction of "Asiatics," as the Chinese were commonly known in Cuba. Urbano Feijoo Sotomayor, writing in 1853, stated that from his own personal experience, he found the Chinese to be "proud, arrogant, disposed to insurrection, having no qualms about murder, reluctant to work though skillful, without morality or shame."[63] He argued that it would be highly imprudent to introduce on a grand scale another race with a different language, religion, and culture to a country that was "already confused because of the heterogeneity of its people."[64] José Antonio Saco, eminent Cuban humanitarian and protagonist for the abolition

---

[59] Valverde, "La Trata de Chinos en la Isla de Cuba," 487.

[60] Ibid.; Pérez de la Riva, "Aspectos Económicos del Tráfico de Cúlies Chinos a Cuba, 1853-1874," 96.

[61] Pérez de la Riva, "Aspectos Económicos del Tráfico de Cúlies Chinos á Cuba," 99-101.

[62] Ibid.

[63] Urbano Feijoo Sotomayor, *Isla de Cuba: Inmigración de Trabajadores Españoles* (Habana, Imprenta de J. M. Eleizegui, 1853), 52.

[64] Ibid., 53.

of slavery, felt that because the Chinese were so totally different, any attempt to assimilate them into the Cuban way of life was doomed to failure.[65] Even the Spanish government expressed reservations about the wisdom of introducing into Cuba an intelligent and progressive race that did not profess the Catholic religion and that might be a bad influence on the Negro population.[66] But such philosophical and political considerations gave way before the more immediate needs of the planters for laborers and the greed of Spanish and Cuban speculators for the profits that such a traffic would bring. However, the Madrid government attempted to maintain some control over the situation. The *Real Orden* of September 16, 1852, which granted permission to Manuel B. Pareda and Villoldo Waldrop and Company to bring a maximum of 6,000 Chinese colonists to the island, stipulated that each and every endeavor to introduce Chinese to Cuba had to receive royal approval.[67]

Figure 15. Chinese harvesting Sugarcane in Cuba, (Taken from *Le Tour du Monde,* Vol. II, 1860, 350)

---

[65]   José Antonio Saco, *Colección Póstuma de Papeles Científicos, Históricos, Políticos y de Otros Ramos sobre la Isla de Cuba* (Habana, 1881), 144-145; José Antonio Saco, "Los Chinos en Cuba," *La America* [Madrid], Vol. VIII, No. 3 (February 12, 1864), 1.

[66]   Erenchún, *Anales de la Isla de Cuba* (1856), 780.

[67]   Ibid., 779.

That approval was easily obtained is evidenced by the number of Chinese that were introduced. Estimates of the total number of Chinese imported into Cuba from 1847 to 1874 range from 114,232 to 250,000. The first figure is the result of a tabulation of arrivals made by Duvon C. Corbitt from the shipping column of the Havana newspaper *Diario de la Marina*. Corbitt states that a few issues of the paper were missing, and in one or two instances, the number of passengers on vessels was not reported.[68] Hence his figure falls a little short of the actual total. Francisco Abella, who spent several years on the China coast as an agent for companies importing Chinese to Cuba, reported that 140,084 Chinese left their homeland for Havana and that 124,205 arrived there.[69] This approximates the totals given by John V. Crawford, British consul general at Havana, which can be found in table 13, and which corresponds closely to the figures reported by Felix Erenchún for 1847 to 1859.[70] Unfortunately, Crawford's tabulations are also incomplete, since they do not include those arriving subsequent to September 1, 1873. The most complete tabulation is given by Juan Pérez de la Riva in an article entitled "Demografía de los Culíes Chinos en Cuba (1853-74)."[71] He obtained the statistics, which are reproduced in table 20, from the Cuban government publication *Boletín de Colonización*. His figures are in substantial agreement with those of Crawford and Erenchún and hence can be accepted as reasonably accurate. However, Pérez de la Riva claims that thousands of Chinese from California were smuggled into Cuba in the decade from 1865 to 1875, coming by way of Mexico and New Orleans. He suggests that this illegal and

---

[68]   Corbitt, *A Study of the Chinese in Cuba*, 24.

[69]   Francisco Abella, *Projecto de Emigración Libre China Dirigido a los Sres. Hacendados de la Isla de Cuba* (Habana, Imprenta y Librería "El Iris," 1874), cited in Corbitt, *A Study of the Chinese in Cuba*, 24.

[70]   "Number of the Chinese Imported into Cuba Yearly since 1847," John V. Crawford, September 1, 1873 (BFO 881/2598); Erenchún, *Anales de la Isla de Cuba*, II (1856), 1329-1333.

[71]   Juan Pérez de la Riva, "Demografía del los Culíes Chinos en Cuba (1853-74)," *Revista de la Biblioteca Nacional "José Martí"*, Vol. LVII, No. 4, (1966), 3-31. An editorial note acknowledges that the article is an extract from an unpublished work by the same author entitled "Los Culíes en Cuba, 1847-1880. Contribución al Estudio de la Emigración Contratada en el Caribe."

Table 20

Chinese Emigration into Cuba, 1847-1874, and Mortality on the Voyage

Year	Embarked	Landed	Died at sea	Percentage of deaths
1847	612	571	41	6.7
1853	5,150	4,307	843	16.3
1854	1,750	1,711	39	2.2
1855	3,130	2,985	145	4.6
1856	6,152	4,968	1,084	19.3
1857	10,116	8,547	1,575	15.5
1858	16,414	13,385	3,019	18.4
1859	8,549	7,204	1,345	15.7
1860	7,204	6,193	1,011	14.03
1861	7,252	6,973	279	3.8
1862	356	344	12	3.3
1863	1,045	952	93	8.8
1864	2,664	2,153	511	19.1
1865	6,794	6,400	394	5.7
1866	13,368	12,391	977	7.3
1867	15,616	14,263	1,353	8.6
1868	8,100	7,368	732	9.03
1869	6,720	5,660	1,060	15.7
1870	1,312	1,227	85	6.4
1871	1,577	1,448	89	5.6
1872	8,915	8,160	755	8.4
1873	5,856	5,093	(763)	13.02
1874	2,863	2,490	(373)	13.02
Totals	141,391	124,813	16,576	11.72

Source: Adapted from the table given in Pérez de la Riva, "Demografía de los Culíes Chinos en Cuba (1853-1874)," 6.

unrecorded immigration could boost the total to 150,000.[72] The round figure
of 250,000 put forward by Antonio Chuffat Latour, a Cuban of Chinese
descent, must be discounted as a wild guess.[73]

Since the Chinese were brought to Cuba to replace the dwindling
Negro slave population on the plantations, the question of their status
naturally arises. Were they free laborers or slaves? How did the Cubans
treat them? An examination of the legislation governing their entry and
stay on the island reveals that the law, which in some respects attempted
to protect them from the arbitrary excesses of planters and local
administrators accustomed to slave labor, made it extremely difficult for
them to escape the "temporary bondage" to which their initial contract
committed them.[74]

Conflicts between the planters and the initial group of Chinese that arrived
in 1847 occasioned the *Reglamento* of April 10, 1849, which in itself was
an unfavorable commentary on the attitude of Cuba's colonial government
toward its contract laborers. This piece of colonial legislation counseled the
planter to appoint an overseer for every ten Chinese so as "to guide, watch over,
and assist the laborers in their work."[75] To help the overseer in his task, he was
empowered to administer twenty to thirty lashes for acts of disobedience, and
should a laborer persist in his disobedient path, the overseer could shackle his
ankles with irons and condemn him to sleeping in the stocks for up to two
months.[76] This so blatantly reduced the contract laborer to virtual slavery that
the Spanish government in Madrid, when it granted permission in 1852 for

---

[72] Pérez de la Riva, "Demografía de los Culíes Chinos en Cuba (1853-74)," 4-5.

[73] Antonio Chuffat Latour, *Apunte Histórico de los Chinos en Cuba* (Havana,
      Molina y Ciá, 1927), 12, cited by Corbitt, *A Study of the Chinese in Cuba*,
      24. The United States War Department in its *Report of the Census of Cuba,
      1899* (Washington, Government Printing Office, 1900), 71, estimated that
      between 1853 and 1873 132,435 Chinese were shipped from China to Cuba
      with a mortality of 13 per cent, which meant that 115,219 landed in Cuba.

[74] See Appendix I for legislation of the Spanish and Cuban governments regarding
      Chinese immigrants.

[75] José Maria Zamora y Coronado, *Biblioteca de legislación Ultramarina*,
      7 vols. (Madrid, Imprenta de Algeria y Charlain, 1844-1849), Primer
      Suplemento, 49. See also Jímenez Pastrama, *Los Chinos en la Liberación
      Cubana*, 39-40.

[76] See Articles XI and XII of *Reglamento* of 1849 in Appendix I.

the continuation of Chinese immigration, demanded that the *Reglamento* of 1849 be revised or new legislation be drawn up that would be protective of the Chinese laborer's rights as well as spell out his obligations.[77]

The new regulations contained in the Royal Decree of March 22, 1854, drastically limited the power of the planter to punish erring contract laborers, and conferred upon the laborer whose contract had been completed all the rights enjoyed by other aliens. He could take out a letter of domicile and, after five years, become a citizen. He could set himself up in business or form with his fellow countrymen a group of independent workmen and accept whatever employment best suited their interests. He could form a family with one of the Chinese women that every importer of Chinese laborers was required to bring to Cuba and so become a permanent and productive member of society.[78]

However, the subsequent decree of July 7, 1860, which abrogated all previous legislation pertaining to Chinese immigration, reflected a radical change of heart toward the Chinese as colonists, at least on the part of the government in Madrid. Aware of the strife surrounding the Chinese in California, and fearful that the introduction of large numbers of Chinese to Cuba on a permanent basis would be detrimental to the best interests of the island, the Spanish government decreed that all Chinese brought to Cuba after February 5, 1861, on the completion of their eight-year contract, had to re-indenture themselves or else leave the island within two months. If they failed to do either one, they would be compelled to earn enough money on public works to pay the passage to the destination of their choice.[79] The requirement that a certain percentage of Chinese immigrants be female was dropped, and although Articles 31 to 68 spelled out in minute detail the reciprocal rights and obligations of laborers and masters, the provisions beneficial to the laborers were overshadowed by the fact that as long as the laborer remained in Cuba, he was condemned by law to a life of indenture.

---

[77] Erenchún, *Anales de la Isla de Cuba* (1856), 779; Guillermo Tejeiro, *Historia Illustrada de la Colonia China en Cuba* (Havana, 1947). The pages of this book are not numbered, but see section entitled, "Origen de la Colonia."

[78] See Articles III to LV of Decree of 1854 in Appendix I. See also "Memorandum concerning legislation of Spanish and Colonial Governments regarding Chinese Immigrants," (BFO 17/888).

[79] See Articles 7 and 18 of the Decree of 1860 in Appendix I.

The planters were elated with the new legislation. It enabled them to retain an already acclimated force of laborers without expending new capital in their acquisition.[80] But the Chinese, faced with choosing between a life of forced labor and expulsion from the country, were deprived of any worthwhile recompense for their years of bondage. Only by the most rigid self-denial or luck at gambling could a laborer save sufficiently during his eight years of indenture for the expenses of his return trip to China. But if on the completion of his contract he was allowed to use his natural shrewdness and business acumen with the knowledge he had acquired of the language and the habits of the people, he would do reasonably well.[81] But this was now closed to him. With all incentives to continue in an eight-year contract thus removed, many Chinese fled from their masters and conspired to evade the law.[82]

The Royal Decree of 1860 remained the basic code governing Chinese who entered Cuba under contract. All subsequent legislation merely attempted to enforce its provisions.[83] But as far as it is known, no Chinese were ever expelled from the island. Throughout the entire period of the "coolie trade," only 140, a mere fraction of 1 percent of all those who entered Cuba, were reported to have returned to China, and these seemingly left voluntarily, paying their own passage.[84] Cuba needed laborers, and the colonial government was in no way anxious to deport the Chinese. Rather, it conspired with the planters to persuade and, when necessary, to force those who completed their contract to re-indenture.[85] Chinese not under contract and who had no letter of domicile to prove that they arrived in Cuba prior to February 15, 1861 (the effective date of the 1860 decree), were rounded up as vagabonds, assigned to public works, and later resold to the planters.[86]

Runaway and fugitive Chinese from the plantations were a constant problem. When the Ten Years' War broke out in 1868, the insurgents promised

---

[80]   "Asiatics," translation of an article from the Cuban newspaper *El Diario de la Marina* of October 20, 1871 (U.S. Dept. of State, *Foreign Relations*, 1871), 223.

[81]   "Memorandum concerning legislation of Spanish and Colonial Governments regarding Chinese Immigrants" (BFO 17/888).

[82]   "Asiatics," 223.

[83]   "Memorandum concerning legislation of Spanish and Colonial Governments regarding Chinese Immigrants" (BFO 17/888).

[84]   *Hong Kong Government Gazette*, March 7, 1868, March 20, 1869.

[85]   Powers, "Chinese Coolie Migration to Cuba," 157-158.

[86]   "Memorandum concerning Legislation of Spanish and Colonial Governments Regarding Chinese Immigrants" (BFO 17/888).

freedom to the Chinese as well as to the slaves, and many of them joined the ranks of the rebels.[87] The situation became so serious that in 1870, the Cuban authorities complained to the home government that Chinese immigration impeded the pacification of the island and urged that it be promptly stopped and that all Chinese not engaged in agriculture and without letters of domicile be immediately deported.[88] When the Madrid government complied with the request, Cuban police set about inspecting the papers of the 7,000 Chinese residents of Havana and arrested 1,500 of them before the colonial government suspended the operation, explaining that progress in the war rendered such steps unnecessary.[89]

But if the law seemed oppressive, it grossly understated the actual suffering of the Chinese contract laborer in Cuba. The plantations in the provinces were far removed from the seat of Spanish authority in Havana and were virtually self-governing. Havana was far removed from Spain, and the colonial government traditionally made no effort to enforce decrees, which emanated from the Spanish Court at Madrid and which were not to its liking. In these circumstances it is not surprising that the provisions of the law, which sought to protect the Chinese laborer from personal abuse and injustices, were ignored or violated with impunity.

The most damaging indictment of the treatment of the Chinese in Cuba is provided by the Chinese laborers themselves. In 1874, the Chinese government sent a commission to Cuba to investigate reports of mistreatment of its nationals. Ch'en Lanpin, who headed the Chinese Educational Mission in the United States, was placed in charge of the investigation; and A. Macpherson, British commissioner of customs at Hankow, and A. Huber, French commissioner of customs at Tientsin, were appointed to accompany him. The three-man commission, over a period of almost two months, visited plantations, depots, jails, and hospitals, personally interviewing Chinese laborers, using a questionnaire drawn up by the Tsungli Yamen. They took 1,176 depositions and received 85 petitions supported by 1,665 signatures. In their report, they summarized their findings in these words:

---

[87] Powers, "Chinese Coolie Migration to Cuba," 151-156; Corbitt, *A Study of the Chinese in Cuba*, 21; Jiménez Pastrama, *Los Chinos en la Liberación* Cubana, 69-81.

[88] "Memorandum concerning Legislation of Spanish and Colonial Governments regarding Chinese Immigrants" (BFO 17/888).

[89] "Asiatics," 225.

The depositions and petitions show . . . that on arrival at Havana
they were sold into slavery—a small proportion being disposed of to
families and shops, whilst the large majority became the property of
sugar planters; that the cruelty displayed even towards those of the
former class is great, and that it assumes in the case of those of the latter,
proportions that are unendurable. The labor, too, on the plantations
is shown to be excessively severe, and the food to be insufficient; the
hours of labor are too long, and the chastisements by rods, whips,
chains, stocks, etc., etc., productive of suffering and injury. During
the past years a large number have been killed by blows, have died
from the effects of wounds and have hanged themselves, cut their
throats, poisoned themselves with opium, and thrown themselves
into wells and sugar caldrons. It was also possible to verify by personal
inspection wounds inflicted upon others, the fractured and maimed
limbs, blindness, the heads full of sores, the teeth struck out, the ears
mutilated, and the skin and flesh lacerated, proofs of cruelty to the
eyes of all.[90]

Sections of the Spanish press representing the interests of Cuban
planters angrily denounced the commission as hostile to Spanish rule in
Cuba and hence incapable of conducting an objective investigation.[91] The
commission's failure to solicit the views of planters and Cuban officials,
so as to get both sides of the story, would seem to support such a charge.
Among the 1,176 depositions, the commissioners found only two, which
stated that the laborer was treated fairly.[92] One of the questions presented
by the Chinese government for the guidance of the commissioners asked,
"Some employers are cruel by nature and harsh to the employed; others
are kindly and treat coolies well. What remarkable cases illustrate each
side?"[93] Although the commission visited the plantation Las Cañas on
the invitation of its owner, Señor Juan Poey, renowned for his benign and

---

90   *Chinese Emigration: The Cuba Commission*, 3. The report of the Commission
      may also be found in BFO 233/50 and 233/66.
91   Layard to Granville, Madrid, February 10, 1874 (BFO 17/885); Layard to Earl
      of Derby, Madrid, October 13, 1874 (BFO 881/12594).
92   *Chinese Emigration: The Cuba Commission*, 27.
93   Ibid., 36.

humanitarian treatment of both Chinese and Negro laborers,[94] its response to the question was totally negative, dismissing employers who treated their workers kindly with the statement "When a master treats a servant well . . . there is nothing in his action which can result in any record of instances of it being preserved."[95] This would seem to indicate that the commission interpreted its inquiry to be more of a forum for complaints than an attempt to weigh the evidence. If this be true, it would explain the completely derogatory and condemnatory tone of the report. It would not of course invalidate its findings, but rather underline the fact that they do not represent the entire picture.

The basic conclusion of the report that indentured Chinese laborers in Cuba were treated as slaves cannot be seriously questioned, as this is supported by the accounts of numerous observers both Cuban and foreign.[96] Even the governor of the island, Francisco Serrano y Domínguez, admitted that notwithstanding the law, Chinese indenture was a "temporary slavery."[97] But it must be pointed out that the Commission's report reflects the condition of the Chinese in 1874, when abuses were perhaps at a peak. The influx of African slaves had ceased since 1865. The Ten Years' War was in progress, and in the turmoil, both Chinese and Negroes were fleeing from the plantations. Sugar production had never been higher and was continuing to rise. There was a severe shortage of labor, and planters were using every available means, including force, to retain their workers.[98]

Although there is evidence of the ill-treatment of Chinese from their

---

[94]   "Report from Havana," February 6, 1871 (BFO 541/18).

[95]   *Chinese Emigration: The Cuba Commission*, 36.

[96]   James J. O'Kelly, *The Mambi-Land, or Adventures of a Herald Correspondent in Cuba* (London, Sampson, Low, Marston and Company, 1874), 60; Saco, "Los Chinos en Cuba," *La America*, Vol. VIII, No. 5 (March 12, 1864), 3; Manuel Villanueva, "La Emigración de Colonos Chinos," *Revista Contemporanea* [Madrid], Vol. VII (February 15, 1877), 342; John S. C. Abbott, *South and North, or Impressions Received during a Trip to Cuba and the South* (New York, Negro Universities Press, 1969, originally published in 1860), 48; "The Coolie Traffic," *Anti-Slavery Reporter*, Vol. IV, No. 5 (May 1, 1856), 113; Crawford to Granville, September 3, 1873 (BFO 881/2598).

[97]   Carlos Sedáno y Cruzat, *Cuba Desde 1850 á 1873* (Madrid, Imprenta Nacional, 1873), 263. Serrano y Domínguez was Governor from 1859 to 1862.

[98]   Dunlop to Earl of Derby, Havana, July 8, 1874 (BFO 17/885); Dunlop to Earl of Derby, Havana, September 1, 1874 (BFO 17/886).

introduction to the island in 1847, John V. Crawford, British consul general at Havana, reported to his government in 1860,

> With regard to the treatment of Chinese laborers on this island I have taken a good deal of pains to inform myself, and the result of my observations and inquiries has been that they are exceedingly justly dealt with; that they are well treated and seldom if ever have cause for complaint.[99]

A few years earlier, a similar statement attesting to the good treatment of the Chinese in Cuba was made by the consul general of Portugal.[100] One suspects that these statements reflected the treatment of the Chinese in Havana rather than on the plantations throughout the country. By 1871, Consul Crawford had a totally different opinion and advised his government that "the Chinese under contract here on the plantations are with perhaps a very few exceptions, treated very much as slaves.[101] And in 1873, he left no room for any doubt whatsoever when he wrote to the Foreign Office,

> The Chinese coolie is treated here precisely as a slave. He is beaten, ironed and often cruelly punished, frequently driven to suicide or crime; he can be sold or transferred like any other chattel, and at the expiring of his contract instead of receiving his liberty or release from bondage he must either leave the island, declare himself a Spanish subject or suffer himself to be dealt with as an "*emancipado*," and hired out on contract after contract until he dies.[102]

As was often the case in societies dependent upon African slaves,[103] the exploitation of the Chinese in Cuba would seem to have been cruelest when

---

[99]   Crawford to _____, Havana, March 24, 1860. The letter was printed in the *Friend of China*, December 29, 1860.

[100] "Chinese Coolie Trade of Havana," *Merchants' Magazine*, Vol. XXXVII, No. 4 (October, 1857), 518; *The Friend of China*, May 16, 1857.

[101] Crawford to Granville, Havana, November 3, 1871 (BFO 541/18).

[102] Crawford to Granville, Havana, September 3, 1873 (BFO 881/2598).

[103] Sidney W. Mintz, "Review of *Slavery* by Stanley M. Elkins," *American Anthropologist*, Vol. LXIII (1961), 579-585. See also Michael Banton, *Race Relations* (New York, Basic Books, Inc., 1967), 113-114.

agricultural exploitation was at its highest and the demand for labor was greatest.[104]

Some of the details of the sufferings of Chinese laborers in Cuba are graphically recorded in the commission's report, as well as in accounts of foreign visitors and consular officials. Shortly after the Junta de Fomento handed over Chinese immigration to private enterprise in 1853, Chinese laborers were sold in the open market in Havana to the highest bidder, much in the same way as Negro slaves were sold.[105] Upon the arrival of the emigrant vessel from China at Havana, where all immigrants had to be cleared, the ship was put in quarantine and inspected for disease. The sick were sent to hospital and the rest to barracoons, where they awaited the purchase of their contract by their future employers.[106] The Chinese themselves relate what happened:

> On landing, four or five foreigners on horseback, armed with whips led us like a herd of cattle to the barracoon to be sold.
>
> At Havana, after a detention at the quarantine station, our queues were cut, and we awaited in the man-market the inspection of a buyer and the settlement of a price.
>
> When offered for sale at the men-market we were divided into three classes, first, second and third, and were forced to remove all our clothes so that our person might be examined and the price fixed. This covered us with shame.[107]

Their testimony is corroborated by Richard H. Dana, who was in Havana in 1859 and visited the Chinese "men-market":

> Yesterday I drove out to the Cerro to see the coolie jail or market where the imported coolies are kept for sale. It is a well known place and open to all

---

[104]   This traditional view of Africal slavery is challenged by Robert William Fogel and Stanley L. Engerman in their controversial work *Time on the Cross: The Economics of American Negro Slavery* (Boston, Little, Brown, 1974), 109-157.

[105]   Pérez de la Riva, "Aspectos Económicos del Tráfico de Cúlies Chinos a Cuba," 110; Corbitt, *A Study of the Chinese in Cuba*, 25.

[106]   Pérez de la Riva, "Aspectos Económicos del Tráfico de Cúlies Chinos a Cuba," 109.

[107]   *Chinese Emigration: The Cuba Commission*, 17-18.

visitors. The building has a fair looking front and through this I enter, past two porters, into an open yard in the rear where, on the gravel ground, are squatting a double line of coolies, with heads shaved except a tuft on the crown, dressed in loose Chinese garments of yellow and blue. The dealer who is a calm, shrewd, heartless looking man speaking English as well as if it were his native tongue, comes out with me, calls to the coolies, and they all stand up in a double line facing inward, and we pass through them, preceded by a driver armed with the usual badge of the plantation driver, the short limber whip. The dealer does not hesitate to tell me the terms on which the contracts are made, as the trade is not illegal.[108]

Before leaving China, each immigrant signed a contract committing himself to work for eight years at whatever tasks assigned to him in return for four dollars a month, plus food, shelter, clothing, and medical care. The contracts, written in Chinese and in Spanish (samples of which can be found in appendix V), varied little over the years. They were drawn up in legal form and signed by the importer, the laborer, and a foreign consul at the port of departure in China. Their basic function would seem to have been to set the traffic in indentured laborers apart from the slave traffic, which was illegal. Technically, what was auctioned at Havana was the piece of paper containing the laborer's contract. But Cubans never talked of hiring Chinese; rather, they spoke openly of "buying coolies,"[109] and the contract, as a legal document, merely served to facilitate the transfer of control or ownership of the laborer from importer to employer and from one employer to another.

The Chinese were universally acknowledged to be more intelligent and skillful than the Negro slaves.[110] They made excellent mechanics and not only manned the more complex machinery of the sugar mills and factories, but were employed as firemen and breakmen on railroads.[111] They also excelled as

---

[108] Richard H. Dana, *To Cuba and Back: A Vacation Voyage* (Boston, Ticknor and Fields, 1859), 103-104.

[109] Antonio Gallenga, *The Pearl of the Antilles* (London, Chapman and Hall, 1873), 88.

[110] Dana, *To Cuba and Back*, 44; Julia Ward Howe, *A Trip to Cuba* (Boston, Tricknor and Fields, 1860), 219; "Life in Cuba," *Harper's Magazine*, Vol. XLIII, No. 255 (August, 1871), 363.

[111] Robert Russell, *North America: Its Agriculture and Climate* (Edinburgh, Adam and Charles Black, 1857), 194; Dana, *To Cuba and Back*, 46; R.W. Gibbes, *Cuba for Invalids* (New York, W.A. Townsend and Company, 1860), 91.

cooks and domestic servants[112] and were reputed to turn out the best hand-rolled cigars in Havana.[113]

Yet despite their expertise, one Negro slave was worth two Chinese laborers on the open market. The price that a planter paid for an eight-year contract of a Chinese laborer fluctuated between $170 and $500.[114] The governor of Cuba, count of Valmaseda (Blas Villate y de la Hera), calculated that the 109,092 Chinese who landed at Havana between June 1847 and October 1871 were sold for the mean price of $340 per head.[115] The price of Negro slaves during the same period ranged from $375 to over $1,000.[116] In the 1850s, an able-bodied African slave, hired out to a plantation, cost the planter $20 a month,[117] whereas the Chinese laborer only cost the planter around $11 monthly.[118] At first glance, the Chinese would seem to have been by far the cheapest source of labor available to Cuban employers, but there were hidden costs and risks in hiring Chinese, which help explain the disparity.

First of all, the Negro slave had some assets, which the Chinese laborer lacked. Though the Chinese were acknowledged to be superior to the Negro indoors, the Negro was considered to be superior in the fields, as he was more robust and could better withstand the heat of the tropical sun.[119] The Negro was

---

[112] Maturin M. Ballou, *Due South, or Cuba, Past and Present* (Boston, Houghton, Mifflin and Company, 1898), 273; Samuel Hazard, *Cuba with Pen and Pencil* (Hartford, Hartford Publishing Company, 1871), 273.

[113] Ballou, *Due South, or Cuba, Past and Present*, 54; Hazard, *Cuba with Pen and Pencil*, 150; "Life in Cuba," *Harper's Magazine*, 359.

[114] Corbitt, *A Study of the Chinese in Cuba*, 25.

[115] Pérez de la Riva, "Aspectos Económicos del Tráfico de Cúlies Chinos a Cuba," 107.

[116] Aimes, *A History of Slavery in Cuba*, Appendix I, 257-268; Knight, *Slave Society in Cuba*, 29.

[117] Russell, *North America*, 215.

[118] The eight-year contract of a Chinese laborer cost the planter an average of $340, plus $292 for food for eight years at 10 cents per day, plus $48 for clothes, plus $384 wages at $4 a month. This amounted to a total expenditure of $1064 for a Chinese laborer for eight years or approximately $11 a month. This was exclusive of medical expenses or interest on the planter's capital outlay. See Hincks to Cardwell, March 6, 1866 (BFO 17/873).

[119] Eliza Moore Ripley, *From Flag to Flag: A Woman's Adventures and Experiences in the South during the War in Mexico and in Cuba* (New York, D. Appleton and Company, 1889), 177; Henry A. Murray, *Roads of the Slave and the Free, or*

generally docile and could be disciplined with little fear of retaliation. He was the planter's property for life, and from generations of experience, the planter knew how to exploit him. He was, therefore, a reasonably secure investment. Furthermore, the Negro slave was a scarce resource and getting scarcer, which tended to keep his market price at a premium. An investment in Chinese labor, on the other hand, was much less secure. The planter purchased the labor of the Chinese only for a limited time, and although he regularly obtained, more often than not by unjust means, a renewal or extension of the eight-year contract, he had to bribe local officials for their cooperation.[120] Besides, the Chinese were unpredictable and difficult to manage. They demanded separate quarters from the Negroes, resisted discipline, rebelled frequently with significant loss of life, or they took their own lives—all of which meant considerable financial loss to the planter by disrupting the daily routine of the plantation, as well as losing some of his laborers and the investment they represented.

According to one source, 70 percent of all Chinese contract laborers arriving in Cuba were employed on the plantations; 20 percent were apprenticed to a trade as tailors, smiths, shoemakers, saddlers, hatmakers, cigar and cigarette makers; and 10 percent were employed as cooks, coachmen, gardeners, waiters, hotel, and house servants.[121] These estimates were made in 1866, but the higher figure of 90 percent employed on plantations suggested by the report of the Cuba Commission would seem to be more accurate at least for the later years of the traffic.[122]

Plantation labor was by far the most grueling work. During the sugar season, laborers had to work from eighteen to twenty hours a day, sometimes getting only a few hours' sleep.[123] Since most plantations were run by managers for absentee owners,[124] production figures were what mattered most, and laborers were often literally worked to death. According to the Cuba Commission:

    Cuba, the United States and Canada (2 vols., London, John W. Parker and Son, 1855), I, 310.

[120] Corbitt, *A Study of the Chinese in Cuba*, 72.

[121] "Letter from Havana," *Hong Kong Mercury and Shipping Gazette*, October 31, 1866.

[122] *Chinese Emigration: The Cuba Commission*, 18.

[123] Russell, *North America*, 225. See Figure 15.

[124] Dana, *To Cuba and Back*, 55.

On all plantations the owners have established prisons, to which stocks and various instruments of torture are attached, and the administrator and overseers constantly and at will make use of hounds, knives, bludgeons, and whips, so that the Chinese are in constant terror of death.[125]

Rather than endure the sufferings heaped upon them, many Chinese, in the belief that their spirit would be transported back to China, committed suicide.[126] As a suicide-prevention measure, one planter, who was losing two Chinese laborers a day, resorted to burning the bodies of suicide victims in the presence of their assembled countrymen. A new pyre was then readied to await the next unfortunate victim.[127] Epidemics of suicide were such common occurrences that plantation owners were forced to make concessions to their Chinese laborers. On some plantations, the Chinese could not be whipped except by their own countrymen,[128] they were given separate quarters from the Negroes,[129] and at times were allowed to do "piece work."[130]

Some have estimated that 70 to 75 percent of the Chinese laborers in Cuba died before the completion of their eight years of indenture.[131] This seems an incredibly high death rate, particularly since most of the Chinese who entered Cuba were in the prime of life. According to the calculations of the Cuba Commission, there were 68,825 Chinese in Cuba in 1874.[132]

---

[125] *Chinese Emigration: The Cuba Commission*, 25.

[126] Ripley, *From Flag to Flag*, 178; Howe, *A Trip to Cuba*, 219; Valverde, *Estudios Jurídicos e Historicos*, 34; "Sugar Making in Cuba," *Harper's Magazine*, Vol. XXX (March, 1865), 446; Pérez de la Riva, "Demografía de los Culies Chinos en Cuba (1853-74)," 13-16; Frederick W. Seward, *Reminiscences of a War-Time Statesman and Diplomat, 1839-1915* (New York, G.P. Putnam's Sons, 1916), 335.

[127] Henry B. Auchincloss, "The Chinese in Cuba," *Merchant's Magazine*, Vol. LII (March, 1865), 189.

[128] Bunch to Hammond, April 24, 1866 (BFO 17/873).

[129] "Sugar Making in Cuba," 444.

[130] Gallenga, *The Pearl of the Antilles*, 128; Auchincloss, "The Chinese in Cuba," 186; "Letter from Havana," *Hong Kong Mercury and Shipping Gazette*, October 31, 1866.

[131] O'Kelly, *The Mambi-Land*, 66; Ballou, *Due South, or Cuba, Past and Present*, 272; Gonzalo de Quesada, *The Chinese and Cuban Independence* (Leipzig, Breitkopf and Hartel, 1925), 46, cited in Corbitt, *A Study of the Chinese in Cuba*, 80; Gonzalo de Quesada, *Los Chinos y La Revolución Cubana* (Havana, Ucar, García y Cía, 1946), 17.

[132] *Chinese Emigration: The Cuba Commission*, 80.

Subtracting this number from the total of 125,634 that entered the island from 1847 to 1874, as well as deducting the 140 known to have returned to China, leaves us with 56,669 deaths, or a mortality of 45 percent over a period of twenty-seven years. This is considerably lower than 70 to 75 percent over a period of eight years and would seem to be closer to the truth.

Figure 16. Chinese fruit stand in Havana, circa 1870 (Taken from "Life in Cuba", *Harpers New Monthly Magazine*, Vol. XLIII, August 1871, 355)

The Chinese, who were fortunate enough to survive their years of indenture and obtain their freedom, turned their backs on the plantations and gravitated toward the cities. They became artisans, cooks, shopkeepers, gardeners, and peddlers.[133] Market gardening was a favorite attraction, and in a short time, it was controlled by the Chinese.[134] In 1858, two Chinese opened a fruit store and a café in Havana, thus laying the foundations of

---

[133] Corbitt, *A Study of the Chinese in Cuba*, 89; *Chinese Emigration: The Cuba Commission*, 52. See Figure

[134] Corbitt, *A Study of the Chinese in Cuba*, 89; William J. Clark, *Commercial Cuba: A Book for Businessmen* (New York, Charles Scribner's Sons, 1898), 17.

what was to become the city's "Chinatown."[135] Due to the absence of Chinese women, relatively few married. The Cuba Commission, in its inquiries, found two Chinese married to Chinese women, two married to white women, and a half a dozen or so married to mulattoes and Negresses.[136]

James J. O'Kelly, in his visit to Cuba in 1873, observed that the free Chinese were "treated as were the Jews of the Middle Ages," and were subject to harassment and extortion at the hands of the police.[137] The Royal Decree of 1860 designated the governor of the island the protector of all Chinese immigrants,[138] but there is no evidence that this responsibility was ever taken seriously. The consul general of Portugal attempted to act as the protector of the Chinese who embarked from Macau, but with little success.[139] In 1872, some influential Chinese in Havana persuaded the colonial government to appoint a foreign resident in that city to act as the representative of the Chinese and to mediate complaints. But after a short four months, the government discarded the arrangement. A year later, on instructions from Madrid, an inspector of Chinese immigration was appointed, whose task it was to investigate the treatment of the Chinese and to enforce existing laws.[140] However, effective protection to the Chinese community was not forthcoming until the appointment of Liu Sheng-pu as Chinese consul general in Havana in 1878, following the signing of an immigration convention between China and Spain in November 1877.[141]

Chinese Laborers in the Andean Countries

The vast majority of Chinese contract laborers transported to the west coast of South America in the nineteenth century were concentrated on the narrow coastal plains of Peru. A relatively small number were brought to Chile, and a few found their way to Guayaquil, Ecuador.

---

[135] Corbitt, *A Study of the Chinese in Cuba*, 89.

[136] *Chinese Emigration: The Cuba Commission*, 85.

[137] O'Kelly, *The Mambi-Land*, 66.

[138] See Article XXXI of the Royal Decree of 1860 in Appendix I.

[139] "Memorandum Concerning Legislation of Spanish and Colonial Government Regarding Chinese Immigrants" (BFO 17/888), 209.

[140] Ibid.

[141] Wu Paak-shing, "China and Cuba: A Study in Diplomatic History," *China Quarterly*, Vol. III (Autumn 1938), 396.

The history of their introduction to Peru falls into two separate periods: from 1849 to 1856, the year the Peruvian government intervened to stop the trade, and from 1861, when the ban was lifted, to 1874. During a quarter of a century, Peru received approximately 110,000 Chinese laborers.[142] Of this number, several thousands were employed in the offshore guano islands, between 5,000 and 10,000 helped build railroads into the Andes, but close to 80,000 or between 70 and 75 percent were assigned to the sugar and cotton plantations along the coast.[143]

The presence of Chinese laborers in Peru was first brought to the attention of the rest of the world by reports of their cruel exploitation on the guano-producing Chincha Islands. From 1840 to 1880, Peru's export economy was based on the rich guano deposits on its offshore islands.[144] In the peak years during the 1860s, as much as 400,000 tons of this manure, valued at $24 million was shipped annually to the farms of Europe, North America, and Asia.[145] The Chincha Islands, Peru's three principal guano islands, lying one hundred miles south of Callao and about twelve miles offshore in the Bay of Pisco, became a focus of entrepreneurial exploitation, greed, and corruption. Merchant vessels of many nations, but principally British and American, flocked to the Peruvian coast to partake of the carrying trade. According to one eyewitness, as many as 200 ships lay at anchor at one time off the Chincha Islands, awaiting their turn to be loaded.[146] Hutchinson stated that

---

[142]   There is some uncertainty as to the number of Chinese who came to Peru. Stewart in *Chinese Bondage in Peru*, 74, puts the total at around 90,000. But the official bulletin of the Macau government, together with newspapers on the China coast and consular despatches, list 115,179 laborers as having set out from China for Peru, plus 36 emigrant vessels for which the number of passengers is not given. If each of these vessels carried an average of 350 (a conservative estimate) the total number of Chinese laborers that left China for Peru was 127,779. Fifteen vessels, carrying 6,506 laborers, were lost at sea or returned to China. Then deducting a further ten percent for mortality on the voyage leaves us with 109,146 arriving in Peru from 1847 to 1874. See Tables 25-48 in Appendix VI.

[143]   Stewart, *Chinese Bondage in Peru*, 89; Levin, *The Export Economies*, 88.

[144]   Levin, *The Export Economies*, 27; Heraclio Bonilla, *Guano y Burguesía en el Peru* (Lima, Instituto de Estudios Peruanos, 1974), 138.

[145]   Levin, *The Export Economies*, 31.

[146]   "The Guano Islands," *Chambers Journal*, Vol. XXV, No. 367 (January 12, 1861), 17.

433 vessels, with a combined tonnage of 348,554, took guano from the Chincha Islands in 1860.[147]

To cope with its new booming industry, Peru had to import not only capital and entrepreneurship, but also labor.[148] During the 1840s, most of the labor for the guano fields was supplied by convicts and army deserters through the cooperation of the Peruvian government. Supplementing this penal labor was a small number of black slaves and Peruvian and Chilean peons.[149] But these sources were limited, and the expansion of the industry demanded an expanded labor force.

In December 1849, one month after Domingo Elías persuaded the Peruvian Congress to grant to him and to his partner, Juan Rodríguez, the exclusive privilege of importing Chinese laborers to Peru, he signed a six-year contract with the Peruvian government to be the sole extractor and loader of guano on the Chincha Islands.[150] J. J. Von Tschudi, who traveled throughout Peru in the 1830s and early 1840s, characterized Elías as "the richest and most speculative cultivator on the whole coast."[151] Through contacts with British entrepreneurs, Elías was undoubtedly aware of the excellent reputation of the Chinese as laborers in Southeast Asia and of their availability on the China coast. The passage of the new Peruvian emigration law in November 1849, engineered by Elías, was dubbed by its opponents as the "Chinese Law," since it was intended to facilitate the introduction of Chinese "colonists."[152] Prior to the passage of the law, Elías and Rodríguez had already set the wheels in motion to import Chinese labor, and in October 1849, the first shipment of 75 laborers arrived from the China coast in the Danish vessel *Frederek William*.[153] Elías needed laborers for his new undertaking in the guano industry, and consequently, most of

---

[147] Hutchinson, *Two Years in Peru*, I, 109.

[148] Levin, *The Export Economies*, 14, 40.

[149] Ibid., 86.

[150] Ibid., 87.

[151] J.J. Von Tschudi, *Travels in Peru, on the Coast, in the Sierra, across the Cordilleras and the Andes, into the Primeval Forests*, translated from the German by Thomasina Ross (New York, A.S. Barnes and Company, 1854), 164-165.

[152] Stewart, *Chinese Bondage in Peru*, 13.

[153] Levin, *The Export Economies*, 87; Deerr, *The History of Sugar*, II, 404.

the newcomers and hundreds, which came after them, were shipped to the Chincha Islands.[154]

It is not known exactly how many Chinese were employed in the guano industry on Peru's offshore islands, but it would seem that they constituted the bulk of the workforce.[155] In 1853, the Chincha Islands reportedly had 600 Chinese, 50 black slaves, and 200 Peruvian and Chilean laborers.[156] George Washington Peck, who visited the islands in 1854, stated that there were about 300 Chinese employed on the middle island and from 700 to 800 on the north island.[157] Hutchinson found 500 Chinese on the Guanape Islands in 1871 in the employ of the Guano Loading Company.[158] Hence, as many as 1,000 to 1,500 Chinese laborers may have been extracting guano at a given time. Since due to death and illness, replacements were frequent—it was claimed that the average working life of the Chinese guano laborer was but a short three years[159]—the total number of Chinese employed on the guano islands from 1849 to the end of the export trade in the late 1870s may have been close to 10,000.

According to eyewitness accounts, the life of the Chinese laborer on the guano islands was one of the most abject slavery, at least during the 1850s and 1860s. The climatic conditions of the islands alone made human habitation and labor a real hardship. A tropical sun beats down on them virtually the entire year. The humidity is high, and there is no fresh water and a complete lack of rain. Hence there is no vegetation of any kind. Besides birds and sea lions, the only other living things are parasitic insects and their natural enemies—spiders, scorpions, lizards, and bats.[160] All food and drinking water must be brought from the mainland. The Chinese, however, supplemented their food allowance

---

[154]   Levin, *The Export Economies*, 87.

[155]   Stewart, *Chinese Bondage in Peru*, 96.

[156]   Levin, *The Export Economies*, 88.

[157]   George Washington Peck, *Melbourne and the Chincha Islands, with Sketches of Lima and a Voyage Round the World* (New York, Charles Scribner, 1854), 170, 206.

[158]   Hutchinson, *Two Years in Peru*, II, 130.

[159]   "The Chincha Islands," *Nautical Magazine and Naval Chronicle*, Vol. XXV (April, 1856), 182.

[160]   Coker, "Peru's Wealth-Producing Birds," 537, 559-560.

by killing some of the birds and preserving the meat by drying it in the sun.[161]

Figure 17. Chinese Laborers Digging Guano on the Middle Chincha Island. Photograph by Captain Spence Merriman Murphy, "The Peruvian Guano Islands Seventy Years Ago," Natural History, Vol. XXVII, 1927, 422

---

[161] Robert E. Coker, "Habits and Economic Relations of the Guano Birds of Peru," *Proceedings of the United States National Museum*, Vol. LVI, No. 2298 (1920), 509.

The housing on the islands consisted of hastily built low bamboo huts with flat roofs of matted cane.[162] On the northernmost Chincha island, where the principal station was located, there was a poorly equipped hospital and a gaily decorated gambling house, where the laborers lost most of their meager earnings. There were no other recreational facilities. At one end of the island, literally an acre of guano was set apart as a cemetery for seamen and laborers.[163]

Besides the dismal environment, the labor exacted of the Chinese was extremely punishing. The guano, baked in the hot sun, formed over the centuries into a hard claylike loam. When excavated by pick and shovel, it usually disintegrated to become "like ashes."[164] Each laborer had to dig a minimum of five tons of guano daily,[165] seven days a week, and cart it in wheelbarrows for a distance of one hundred yards to a quarter of a mile to wooden chutes that carried it to boxcars at a lower level.[166] The boxcars then transported it on rails to the cliffs above the anchorages, where they were capsized and their contents shot down long canvas hoses into boats waiting below, or sometimes directly into the holds of the ships.[167] A. J. Duffield, an Englishman who visited the guano islands in the early 1870s to investigate the state of the guano industry for British holders of Peruvian bonds, wrote,

---

[162] "Letter from the Chincha Islands," *The Friend of China*, supplement, March 28, 1855; "The Guano Islands," 17.

[163] "The Guano Islands," 18; "Letter from the Chincha Islands."

[164] "The Guano Islands," 17; Levin, *The Export Economies*, 31.

[165] Peck, *Melbourne and the Chincha Islands*, 208; "Chinese Immigration and the Guano Trade," *Anti-Slavery Reporter*, Vol. III, No. 2 (February 1, 1855), 40; "Letter from the Chincha Islands." Levin States that each laborer had to dig four tons daily, but this would seem to be true only of later years, when the pressure of public opinion succeeded in lightening the work load. See *The Export Economies*, 31. See Figure 17.

[166] "Letter from the Chincha Islands;" Levin, *The Export Economies*, 31. See Figure 18.

[167] Because the Chincha Islands rise abruptly from the sea, some large ships, notwithstanding the swell of the sea, were able to load directly at the chutes. See Robert Cushman Murphy, "The Peruvian Guano Islands of Seventy Years Ago," *Natural History*, Vol. XXVIII, No. 5 (September-October, 1927), 445; William H. Rowe, *The Maritime History of Maine: Three Centuries of Shipbuilding and Seafaring* (New York, W.W. Norton and Company, 1948), 222. See Figure 19.

No hell has ever been conceived by the Hebrew, the Irish, the Italian, or even the Scotch mind for appeasing the anger and satisfying the vengeance of their awful gods, that can be equalled to the fierceness of its heat, the horror of its stink, and the damnation of those compelled to labor there, to a deposit of Peruvian guano when being shovelled into ships.[168]

Should a laborer fail to fulfill his daily quota, he was flogged by Negro overseers with "raw hide whips, some five feet long," and then compelled to complete his allotted task.[169] A visitor to the Chincha Islands in 1853 made this report:

The Chinese work almost naked under a tropical sun where it never rains. They are slender figures and do not look strong. Negro drivers—the most ugly looking blacks I ever saw—are stationed among them with heavy thongs which I have seem them use. The poor coolies have no hope of reward, no days of rest. The smoke of their torment goes up on Sundays as well as on weekdays. It blows away in a yellow cloud miles to leeward, and I never saw it without thinking what a hell on earth these islands must be. That I don't exaggerate in this account, anyone who has been here will readily bear witness. The fact that some of the Chinese almost every week commit suicide to escape their fate shows the true state of their case. Kossuth told me that more than sixty had killed themselves during the year he has been stationed here, chiefly by throwing themselves from the cliffs.[170]

In June 1854, nine British shipmasters, who had witnessed the treatment of the Chinese on the Chincha Islands, memorialized the British Privy Council of Trade, detailing the cruelties meted out to these unfortunate men and requesting that the British government do something about it, since most of them were transported to the islands in British ships.[171] The British

---

[168] Alexander J. Duffield, *Peru in the Guano Age* (London, Richard Bentley and Son, 1877), 77-78.

[169] "Chinese Immigration and the Guano Trade," 40.

[170] "Letter from the Chincha Islands." Kossuth, a Hungarian refugee, was the principal overseer on the middle island, and had the reputation of treating the Chinese with great severity; see Went to Sullivan, September 21, 1854 (BFO 61/148); Peck, *Melbourne and the Chincha Islands*, 208.

[171] "Memorial to the Right Honorable Lords of the Privy Council of Trade," June 27, 1854 (BPP, ASS, *China*, Vol. III), 343-345.

Foreign Office, through Her Majesty's chargé d'affaires at Lima, protested the alleged atrocities to the Peruvian government,[172] and John Bowring, the superintendent of British trade in China, issued a proclamation prohibiting British ships from transporting Chinese laborers to the Chincha Islands.[173] These measures moved the Peruvian government to direct Carlos Lagomarcino, the governor of the Chincha Islands, to conduct an investigation.[174]

An official government report on conditions on the Chincha Islands of the previous year, 1853, told of frequent whippings and that hardly a day went by without an attempted suicide.[175] Subsequent laws were enacted to remedy these abuses.[176] Lagormarcino found that conditions on the islands had improved,[177] but the government ordered that all ill-treatment cease forthwith, that the Chinese laborers be supplied with good and ample provisions and that their monthly wage be doubled from $4 to $8.[178] The British firm of William Gibbs and Company succeeded Domingo Elías in the extraction and loading of guano; and Kossuth, the chief overseer, with a reputation for cruelty, was dismissed.[179]

Satisfied that the condition of the Chinese had been ameliorated, the superintendent of British trade in China withdrew the ban on British vessels carrying Chinese to the Chincha Islands.[180] But the cruel treatment of the Chinese on Peru's guano islands did not cease. Subsequent reports tell of the Chinese being constantly overworked and of guards being placed around the islands to prevent them from escaping from their unhappy fate through suicide.[181]

---

[172] Clarendon to Sullivan, July 15, 1854 (Ibid.), 346.

[173] *Hong Kong Government Gazette*, September 16, 1854.

[174] Sanchez to Sullivan, December 12, 1854 (BPP, ASS, *China*, Vol. III), 383-384.

[175] *Informes Sobre la Existencia de Huano en las Islas de Chincha Presentados por la Comision Nombrada por el Gobierno Peruano* (Lima, 1854), 4, 5, 11, cited in Levin, *The Export Economies*, 88.

[176] Stewart, *Chinese Bondage in Peru*, 21.

[177] Lagormarcino to Sanchez, June 22, 1854 (BPP, ASS, *China*, Vol. III), 384-385.

[178] "Peruvian Government Decree," September 15, 1854 (BFO 61/148). Sullivan to Clarendon, September 11, 1854 (BFP 61/147).

[179] Sullivan to Clarendon, September 11, 1854 (BFO 61/147).

[180] Bowring to Clarendon, February 3, 1855 (BPP, ASS, *China*, Vol. III), 391.

[181] "The Guano Islands," 17-18; Fitz-Roy Cole, *The Peruvians at Home* (London, 1877), 199, cited by Stewart, *Chinese Bondage in Peru*, 96-97. Williamson to the Secretary of State, September 20, 1870 (U.S. Dept. of State, Consular Despatches, Callao 6), cited in Stewart, *Chinese Bondage in Peru*, 97-98.

The abuses against the Chinese on the guano islands and the sharp criticism that they engendered, together with opposition to the continued introduction of Chinese from Peru's laboring class,[182] led the Peruvian government in March 1856 to abrogate the Chinese Law and prohibit the further immigration of Asiatics.[183] In taking this action, the government candidly acknowledged that the traffic in Chinese laborers had degenerated "into a kind of Negro slave trade."[184] Though the Chinese provided much-needed labor for the exploiters of guano, as well as for the *hacendados*, the cost in human suffering and the consequent blight on the national honor of Peru far outweighed the benefits. But the needs of the all-powerful landowners were still not met, and special licenses to import a limited number of Chinese laborers were granted for special cases.[185] Thus the door was left ajar to be reopened whenever the pressures became too great for a weak government.

Early in 1861, the evident approach of civil war in the United States and the resulting disruption of its cotton trade caused a stampede among Peruvian planters to convert their lands to cotton.[186] This provided the added pressure to force the government to reconsider its ban on Chinese contract labor. In March, the Peruvian Congress, overruling a veto by President Ramón Castilla, recinded its prohibition.[187] The new law merely made the traffic in Chinese laborers legal again, as during the previous year, 1,413 Chinese arrived at the port of Callao.[188]

During the 1850s, most of the Chinese coming to Peru were assigned not to the guano fields but to the plantations of the coastal departments of Lima and La Liberdad.[189] After the traffic was officially resumed in 1861, and until its end in 1874, Peruvian agriculture continued to absorb most of the new arrivals.[190] Unfortunately, relatively little is known about the Chinese on Peruvian plantations

---

[182] Ugarte, *Bosquejo de la História Económica del Perú*, 63.

[183] Sewart, *Chinese Bondage in Peru*, 21, 23.

[184] Ibid., 22.

[185] Ibid., 23; Chang Rodriguez, "Chinese Labor Migration into Latin America in the Nineteenth Century," 388-389.

[186] Ephraim George Squier, *Peru: Incidents of Travel and Exploration in the Land of the Incas* (London, Macmillan and Company, 1877), 219-220.

[187] For the full text of the new law see Stewart, *Chinese Bondage in Peru*, 26-27.

[188] Hutchinson, *Two Years in Peru*, I, 246.

[189] Stewart, *Chinese Bondage in Peru*, 20, 84.

[190] Ibid., 89; *Millones, Minorías Ethnicas en el Perú*, 73.

in the nineteenth century. Unlike the guano industry with its international market that attracted the attention of foreign diplomats and visitors, Peru's sugar and cotton plantations did not arouse the same public interest, hence the full story of the Chinese laborer on Peru's coastal plantations must await further research.[191]

The reception of the Chinese laborers at Callao, the port of entry to Peru, was similar to that at Havana. Emigrant vessels were quarantined and inspected by the health authorities to verify their freedom from contagious diseases.[192] The contracts of the laborers were then auctioned off to the highest bidder, with prospective buyers making what one commentator called a shameful examination, humiliating to the Chinese as well as to those who witnessed it.[193] A correspondent of a Lima newspaper, the *South Pacific Times*, described the selection process:

> It seems to be the correct thing to squeeze the coolie's biceps, give him a pinch or two in the region of the ribs, and then twist him around like a top so as to get a good glance at his physique generally. There is often a look of bewilderment on the Chinamen's face whilst undergoing this process—that is to say as far as his Mongolian features are capable of expressing such emotion. But it is not always so, for there are some smart perky coolies who are only too anxious to show off their points—especially if some companion has just been selected and told to stand to one side.[194]

The price paid per laborer ranged from $300 in the early 1850s[195] to a high of $500[196] with the average price for the duration of the trade being close to $400.[197] At the outset, the contracts were for five years with a wage of $4 per

---

[191] Scholars are currently examining records and papers from some of the coastal plantations which have recently come into government hands and are housed at the Centro de Documentación Agraria, Lima. Humberto Rodríguez P. is the director of the center.

[192] Stewart, *Chinese Bondage in Peru*, 77.

[193] Felix Cipriano C. Zegarra, *La Condición Jurídica de los Estranjeros en el Perú* (Santiago, Imprenta de la Liberdad, 1872), 127-128.

[194] "Trefoil," *South Pacific Times*, May 27, 1873, as cited in Stewart, *Chinese Bondage in Peru*, 81.

[195] *The Friend of China*, September 25, 1852.

[196] Juan de Arona (Paz Soldán), *La Inmigración en el Perú* (Lima, Imprenta del Universo de Carlos Prince, 1891), 43.

[197] Stewart, *Chinese Bondage in Peru*, 82; Trevitt to Seward, October 1, 1861 (U.S. Congress, House, Ex. Doc. No. 16, 37 Cong. 2 Sess.), 36-37; Steere to Bailey,

month and the employer providing food, housing, and medical care.[198] But the period of indenture was soon extended to eight years, and the employer also provided the laborer with clothing, which made it similar to the Cuban contract.[199] Lack of information makes it impossible to assess the total cost to the Peruvian employer of Chinese contract labor and how it compared with the cost of free labor. Juan de Arona estimated that an eight-year contract costing the employer $500, plus wages of $4 a month and upkeep, about equaled the daily wage of a free unskilled worker, which was 60¢. But he points out that free laborers were scarce, and that an employer with indentured labor always had workers when he needed them, a consideration that Peruvian planters deemed essential to their economic well-being.[200]

Peru's sugar and cotton plantations were confined to the valleys along the coast from the departments of Lambayeque in the north to Arequipa in the south, and it would seem that almost all of them employed Chinese contract labor. In 1871, the *Callao and Lima Gazette* noted that the lands along the coast "are, at present cultivated by Chinese,"[201] which would indicate that at least at that time, most of the laborers were Chinese. Hutchinson, in his visit to the Cañete valley in the southern section of the Department of Lima, observed that Henry Swayne employed over 1,500 Chinese on his four estates of more than ten thousand acres.[202] An American visitor to Peru stated that the larger plantations had as many as 1,000 Chinese laborers each.[203] However, it must be noted that the Peruvian planter was concerned with what could be called the "balance of power." Fully aware that the Chinese, being without families, had no ties to bind them to the plantation, the planter sought to

---

Inclosure 3 in Bailey to Davis, September 12, 1873 (U.S. Dept. of State, *Foreign Relations*, 1873, Vol. I), 208.

[198] Stewart, *Chinese Bondage in Peru*, 19.

[199] Millones, *Minorías Ethnicas en el Perú*, 76.

[200] Arona, *La Inmigración en el Perú*, 43; Stewart, citing the Peruvian newspaper *La Patria* of October 14, 1873, states that the cost of free labor was 1.50 soles per day, which is more than double Arona's figure. See *Chinese in Bondage in Peru*, 105-106.

[201] *Callao and Lima Gazette*, August 15, 1871, as cited in Stewart, *Chinese Bondage in Peru*, 85.

[202] Hutchinson, *Two Years in Peru*, I, 137.

[203] Steere to Bailey, Inclosure 3 in Bailey to Davis, September 12, 1873 (U.S. Dept. of State, *Foreign Relations*, 1873, Vol. I), 207. See also "Wretched Condition

employ Negroes, Indians, and mestizos, who, because of their racial prejudice and animosity to the Chinese, could be counted on to side with the owner in case of a disturbance or an insurrection.[204]

Since the Peruvian planter, like his counterpart in Cuba, was largely a law unto himself, at least on his own estate, the treatment of plantation labor no doubt varied significantly in accordance with the character and disposition of the owner or manager, which partially explains the wide difference of opinion on the treatment of Chinese labor. Clements R. Markham, who visited numerous sugar and cotton plantations along the Peruvian coast, wrote in 1874 that "the landed proprietors of the coast and the sierra of Peru, are as a class, most kindly and considerate employers of labour."[205] Hutchinson states that the treatment of the Chinese on the Swayne estates in the Cañete valley was "exceptionally good."[206] Yet others pointed out that almost every plantation had a private prison and that the Chinese were treated no better than slaves, with many of them dying prematurely from unsanitary conditions; inadequate food and accommodations; excessive work; and the liberal use of whips, irons, and a variety of other means of discipline and torture.[207]

Richard Gibbs, the United States minister at Lima, made this report to his government in 1876:

> I have devoted some attention to the status of the Chinese in this country, having previously visited some of the large sugar estates and noticed the manner in which they were treated and also having gathered information from trustworthy persons who testified to their treatment at various places in the republic. I have come to the conclusion that they were treated as

---

of Chinese Coolies in Peru," *Anti-Slavery Reporter*, Vol. XIX, No. 2 (April 1, 1874), 41.

[204] Cole, *The Peruvians at Home*, 142, cited in Stewart, *Chinese Bondage in Peru*, 101.

[205] Clements R. Markham, "From China to Peru: The Emigration Question," *The Geographical Magazine*, Vol. I (December 1, 1874), 367.

[206] Hutchinson, *Two Years in Peru*, I, 173. See also *Missão do Visconde de San Januario nas Republicas da America do Sul, 1878 e 1879* (Lisboa, Imprensa Nacional, 1880), 276.

[207] "The Chinese Coolies in Peru," *Anti-Slavery Reporter*, Vol. XVIII, No. 7 (October 1, 1873), 198-200; "Mr. Markham's Happy Coolies," Ibid., Vol. XIX, No. 8 (September 1, 1875), 183-185; "The Chinese in Peru," *Mission Life*, Vol. V (March 1, 1868), 249-251; Stewart, *Chinese Bondage in Peru*, 115.

slaves were in former times in the United States, and as I have seen slaves and Chinese used in Cuba during many years of residence there. On some plantations they received every attention due to their position and wants; on others, treatment of the most barbarous kind, worse than brutes.[208]

Other commentators were more specific about some of the abuses. J. B. Steere, in the employ of the University of Michigan in the field of natural history, while on a scientific mission to Peru in the late 1860s and early 1870s, personally observed that:

Those who oversee them [Chinese] at their work often carry heavy whips, which they use in hurrying the slow and indolent. The stocks and irons are frequently used in their punishment and I saw at one estate between thirty and forty come up from their work heavily ironed, and holding up their chains with one hand to keep them from galling their ankles, while they carried their spades, with which they had been at work with the other. The owner of the estate told us that they had attempted to run away . . . . Crimes committed by the coolies are generally punished by their owner, as they are too valuable to pass their time in the public prisons. This is even the case with murder, the penalty for this crime, when the victim is also a coolie, being that the murderer shall work out the term of service of his victim, added to his own.[209]

Two Lima newspapers, *El Comercio* and *La Patria*, accused planters of using every possible pretext to extend unjustly, even at times doubling, the eight-year indenture of the Chinese laborer. Sundays and holidays that the laborer had not worked, as well as the days that he had been sick, were added to his term of service.[210] But what may well have been the most effective means used to keep the Chinese laborer on the plantation long after his term of indenture had expired, was the judicious sale of opium by the plantation store. Many of the Chinese laborers had used opium in China. It has been

---

[208] Gibbs to Fish, November 13, 1876 (U.S. Dept. of State, *Foreign Relations*, 1877), 435.

[209] Steere to Bailey, Inclosure 3 in Bailey to Davis, 208.

[210] *The South Pacific Times*, June 17, 1873; Stewart, *Chinese Bondage in Peru*, 116-117.

noted in Chapter IV that they were at times plied with it on the passage to the New World and some of them may well have been addicted to the drug. Since the laborer was seldom allowed to leave the plantation, he was forced to buy opium at the plantation store, which could charge him any price, or at least a price sufficiently high to keep him constantly in debt, with the consequent obligation to continue working to pay it off. The sale of opium could also have been used to recoup some of the capital outlay in money wages. This is but an hypothesis in search of evidence. To the writer's knowledge only one commentator has stated that the plantation store sold opium.[211] But a Lima correspondent of a Cologne newspaper reported in 1876 that opium valued at 440,000 German marks (approximately $110,000) was imported into Peru in 1870 and by 1874 the annual amount had quadrupled.[212] The quantity of opium indicated that there were at least 50,000 heavy smokers of the drug in Peru.[213] Hopefully the current research by scholars into the records and papers of some of the coastal plantations will shed some light on the question of opium as an instrument of exploitation.

Felix Cipriano C. Zegarra, an outspoken critic of Chinese contract labor, summed up the condition of the Chinese on the plantations:

> (They are) condemned to a ceaseless and unremitting toil, without a ray of hope that their condition will ever be better . . . they do not live, rather they vegetate and at last die like brutes beneath the scourge of their driver or the burden which was too heavy to bear. We only remember the Chinese when, weary of being weary, and vexed with vexation, he arms himself with the dagger of desperation, wounds the air with a cry of rebellion and covers our fields with desolation and blood.[214]

It was not uncommon for the Chinese to rise in rebellion. In the late 1860s and early 1870s, as insurrections among them became more frequent and bloody clashes with Peruvians increased, the general populace became

---

[211] Cole, *The Peruvians at Home*, 197, cited in Stewart, *Chinese Bondage in Peru*, 100.

[212] Friedrich Ratzel, *Die Chinesische Auswanderung ein Beitrag zur Cultur-und Handels Geographie* (Breslau, J. U. Ferns Berlag, 1876), 247.

[213] Ibid., Stewart states that the sale or use of opium was not at that time illegal in Peru, *Chinese Bondage in Peru*, 127.

[214] Zegarra, *La Condición Jurídica de los Estranjeros en el Perú*, 130-131, as translated by Duffield, *Peru in the Guano Age*, 45-46.

fearful for its safety. Steere observed that "every one goes armed and every farm house is a little armory."[215] Stafford Jermingham, the British minister at Lima, reported to his government in 1869 that two Chinese in northern Peru, who were accused of killing a family of seven and an overseer, in separate instances, were burned alive by the people.[216] Anti-Chinese feelings became so intense that a resolution was introduced into Congress in 1870 to prohibit the further importation of Chinese and to expel those already in the country, but it was defeated.[217]

Though commentators differed as to the general condition of the Chinese on the plantations, there seemed to be general agreement that the Chinese employed by Henry Meiggs to build railroads into the Andes, were treated with consideration and humanity. In the administration of President José Balta (1868-1872), the Peruvian government decided to convert guano profits into railroads.[218] Meiggs, an American entrepreneur, who had built the Chilean line from Valparaiso to Santiago in less than the contract time, arrived in Peru in 1868.[219] He contracted with the government to build over 1,000 miles of railroad and employed over 5,000 Chinese, as well as Bolivians and Chileans.[220] Steere observed that the Chinese on Meiggs's railroads "appeared robust and contented,"[221] and Hutchinson declared that they were the only "fat Chinamen in Peru," and that the Chinese would have little to complain about if they were similarly treated everywhere else in the country.[222]

The considerable number of Chinese employed as house servants and in the factories of the Lima-Callao region also seem to have been treated reasonably well.[223] Although some went directly to these occupations upon

---

[215] Steere to Bailey, Inclosure 3 in Bailey to Davis, 208.

[216] Jermingham to Clarendon, March 9, 1869 (BFO 17/877).

[217] Hovey to Fish, September 14, 1870 (U.S. Dept. of State, *Foreign Relations*, 1870), 510.

[218] Bonilla, *Guano y Burguesía en el Perú*, 60.

[219] Watt Stewart, *Henry Meiggs, Yankee Pizarro* (Durham, North Carolina, Duke University Press, 1946), 44; Brian Fawcett, "How China Came to Peru," *The Geographical Magazine*, Vol. XXXVII, No. 6 (October, 1964), 430.

[220] Levin, *The Export Economies*, 101; Stewart, *Henry Meiggs, Yankee Pizarro*, 162-164.

[221] Steere to Bailey, Inclosure 3 in Bailey to Davis, 208.

[222] Hutchinson, *Two Years in Peru*, II, 65-66.

[223] Stewart, *Chinese Bondage in Peru*, 89.

landing at Callao, most were men who managed to survive their term of
indenture on the plantations and in the guano islands.[224] Some became grocers,
tailors, butchers, shoemakers, and bakers and opened their own stores and
restaurants in the vicinity of the major markets in the larger cities.[225]

While under indenture, the Chinese laborer had little or no opportunity
to meet women, and homosexuality was allegedly common.[226] But according
to Ambassador Gibbs, when they became tradesmen or proprietors of small
businesses, they intermarried with "the lower class whites, mestizos and
Cholas" (a mixture of Indian and white), and were "looked upon as quite a
catch, for they made good husbands, industrious, domestic and fond of their
children, while the Cholo (Indian) husband is lazy, indolent, often a drunkard
and brutal to his wife."[227]

A number of Chinese businessmen and merchants in Peru became
moderately wealthy and wielded considerable influence in the Chinese
community.[228] They were accused of fomenting insurrection among their
indentured brothers.[229] That they were concerned with the plight of their
countrymen and sought to help them is evident from the memorials that
they addressed to the Chinese government setting forth the grievances of the
laborers and pleading for help and protection.

In December 1868, Alvin P. Hovey, the United States minister at Lima,
received a complaint from Chinese societies in Peru, which he forwarded to
J. Ross Browne, the American minister in Peking, who in turn presented
it to the Chinese government.[230] In response, Prince Kung requested that
the United States minister in Peru examine into the truth of the allegations

---

[224] Ibid., 87-88; Markham, "From China to Peru: The Emigration Question," 369.

[225] Gibbs to Fish, November 13, 1876 (U.S. Dept. of State, *Foreign Relations*, 1877), 435.

[226] Stewart, *Chinese Bondage in Peru*, 103.

[227] Gibbs to Fish, November 13, 1876 (U.S. Dept. of State, *Foreign Relations*, 1877),
435. See also Stewart, *Chinese Bondage in Peru*, 129.

[228] Stewart, *Chinese Bondage in Peru*, 128-129. Some of the more successful Chinese
never served as indentured laborers, but arrived from Hong Kong and San
Francisco with sufficient means to establish themselves in business. See "The
Chinese Coolies in Peru," *Anti-Slavery Reporter*, Vol. XVIII, No. 7 (October 1,
1873), 198, 200.

[229] Stewart, *Chinese Bondage in Peru*, 128.

[230] Ibid., 129, 139. For the text of the memorial see "Petition of Chinese in Peru,"
December, 1868 (BFO 17/877).

and assist the Chinese in any way he could.[231] In January 1871, a second memorial, signed by the Fukien and Swatow Guild, the Kwangtung Guild, and the Tung Sheng Club, all of Lima, was relayed by the same route as the first to the Chinese government.[232] This petition specifically requested that the Emperor of China send an envoy to Peru to investigate the condition of the Chinese or that the minister of the United States in Lima be commissioned to act as their protector.[233] The emperor advised that the laborers form a commission to present their grievances in detail to the imperial court in Peking.[234]

Peru's reputation for its treatment of Chinese laborers was not an enviable one. Because of acknowledged abuses against the Chinese in the guano industry, the government felt constrained to prohibit Chinese immigration in 1856. In 1868, an alleged branding of 48 Chinese laborers with a red-hot iron on one of the coastal plantations received international publicity,[235] and the governor of Macau temporarily suspended Chinese immigration to Peru.[236] The memorials to Peking from the Chinese societies in Peru resulted in renewed pressure by the Chinese government to stop emigration from Macau altogether,[237] and the governor of Macau, in September 1871, again threatened to suspend immigration to Peru.[238] However, a Consular Convention between Peru and Portugal, signed on February 24, 1872, which guaranteed improved conditions for the Chinese laborer on Peruvian

---

[231] Kung to Williams, July 17, 1871 (U.S. Dept. of State, *Foreign Relations*, 1871), 151.

[232] Wu Paak-shing, "China and Peru: A Study in Diplomatic History," *China Quarterly*, Vol. V, No. 2 (Spring, 1940), 279.

[233] Ibid.; William to Prince Kung, June 8, 1871 (U.S. Dept. of State, *Foreign Relations*, 1871), 150-151.

[234] *El Comercio*, January 17, 1872, as cited in Stewart, *Chinese Bondage in Peru*, 142.

[235] Velarde a Sousa, Agosto 2, 1868 (AHU, Macau, 1868, Pasta 25); Robertson to Hammond, November 28, 1868 (BFO 17/876); Stewart, *Chinese Bondage in Peru*, 148-150.

[236] *O Boletim*, November 23, 1868. The Portuguese Consul at Lima, Narciso Velarde, subsequently reported that the story was untrue and the ban was lifted on May 12, 1869. See *O Boletim*, May 17, 1869; Sousa to MacDonnell, May 12, 1869 (BFO 17/877).

[237] Kung to Williams, July 17, 1871 (U.S. Dept. of State, *Foreign Relations*, 1871), 151.

[238] Secretario do Governo de Macau a Senhor Castro, September 25, 1871 (AHU, Macau, 1871, Pasta 27).

plantations,[239] satisfied the Macau authorities, and the traffic continued uninterrupted.

Ever since Macau suspended immigration to Peru in 1868, there was a growing apprehension among Peruvian planters that the traffic in Chinese laborers would be terminated.[240] Opposition to the traffic was increasing within Peru as well as abroad. The British and American governments had let it be known that they opposed the traffic, and the Chinese government was commencing to take positive steps to curtail the contract emigration of its subjects. In 1870, the Peruvian government was seriously considering sending a mission to China to negotiate a treaty that would guarantee (on the pattern of the Burlingame Treaty) Chinese laborers for its plantations.[241] But due to internal political problems, the question was set aside,[242] and it was not until a Peruvian vessel carrying Chinese laborers from the China coast provoked an international incident that the mission finally materialized.

The *Maria Luz*, under the command of Captain Ricardo Herrera, sailed from Macau on May 28, 1872, with 238 Chinese laborers on board, bound for Peru.[243] Bad weather compelled the ship to put into the Japanese port of Yokohama on July 10, 1872.[244] On the night of July 13, one of the Chinese laborers jumped overboard and was picked up by the British ship *Iron Duke*.[245] The laborer complained that he and some of his countrymen on the *Maria Luz* had been unjustly flogged and placed in irons. He was handed over to the Japanese authorities, who, on learning that others had escaped from the Peruvian vessel with similar complaints of mistreatment, conducted an investigation.[246] The end result was that Captain Herrera was charged with mistreating his passengers, and since the offenses were committed in

---

[239] For the text of the Convention see *Negocios Externos: Relatorio e Documentos Apresentados as Cortes na Sessão Legislativa de 1872 pelo Ministro e Secretario d'Estado dos Negocios Estrangeiros* (Lisboa, Imprensa Nacional, 1872), II, 67-88. See also Stewart, *Chinese Bondage in Peru*, 151.

[240] Stewart, *Chinese Bondage in Peru*, 149.

[241] Ibid., 143.

[242] Ibid., 160.

[243] *O Boletim*, January 11, 1873.

[244] Stewart, *Chinese in Bondage in Peru*, 152.

[245] Markham, "From China to Peru: The Emigration Question," 368.

[246] Stewart, *Chinese Bondage in Peru*, 153-154; Watson to Soyeshima Tane-omi, August 3, 1872 (U.S. Dept. of State, *Foreign Relations*, 1873), I, 529-530.

Japanese waters, he was tried in a Japanese court and sentenced to receive one hundred lashes. But because of the long detention (six weeks) and other inconveniences suffered, he was let off with a severe reprimand.[247] The Chinese passengers were handed over to a representative of the Chinese government to be returned to China.[248]

The Peruvian government regarded the entire episode as an affront to its national honor, and President Manuel Pardo dispatched Aurelio García y García, a captain in the Peruvian Navy, as envoy extraordinary and minister plenipotentiary to the governments of China and Japan, with the task of obtaining reparation for the *Maria Luz* "outrage," and at the same time establishing treaty relations with the two countries.[249]

García y García arrived at Yokohama in February 1873, and after some discussions, both sides agreed to submit the question of reparation to the emperor of Russia for arbitration.[250] A treaty of friendship and commerce was then drawn up and signed on August 21, 1873, with Peru receiving all the privileges of the most favored nation, including freedom of migration from one country to the other.[251] This was the first treaty between a Latin American country and an Oriental nation.

The Peruvian envoy then proceeded to China to try for another first. But the Chinese government was not at all disposed to receive the Peruvian delegation or to conclude a treaty with a country that had barbarously abused Chinese subjects.[252] But through the good offices of the British and American ministers at Peking, García y García was eventually received by the governor-general of Chih-li, Li Hung Chang, at Tientsin in October 1874.[253] But the Chinese authorities made it clear that no treaty could

---

[247] Stewart, *Chinese Bondage in Peru*, 156; DeLong to Fish, September 3, 1872 (U.S. Dept. of State, *Foreign Relations*, 1873), I, 524-525.

[248] Stewart, *Chinese Bondage in Peru*, 156.

[249] Ibid., 161.

[250] For the text of the agreement see "Protocol" June 25, 1873 (U.S. Dept. of State, *Foreign Relations*, 1873), I, 618. The Tsar handed down a decision in favor of Japan on May 29, 1875. For the text of the decision see *North China Herald*, September 11, 1875.

[251] For the text of the treaty see DeLong to Fish, September 2, 1873, Inclosure (U.S. Dept. of State, *Foreign Relations*, 1873), I, 629-630.

[252] Stewart, *Chinese Bondage in Peru*, 176-177.

[253] Ibid., 179-180.

be entered into unless all the Chinese in Peru were first returned to China.[254] After two months of discussions centering around the treatment of Chinese laborers in Peru, García y García was received by Prince Kung in Peking, where he was told that the Chinese government would be happy to enter into treaty relations with Peru.[255] Li Hung Chang was named to conduct the negotiations, and García y García, after spending the winter in Peking, returned to Tientsin in May 1874.[256] A treaty of friendship, commerce, and navigation, as well as a special agreement on emigration, was signed on June 26, 1874.[257]

In the special agreement on emigration, it was decided that the Chinese government should send a commission to Peru "to institute a thorough investigation into the condition of Chinese immigrants in all parts of Peru."[258] Chinese immigrants were placed on a footing of equality with subjects of the most favored nation residing in the country, and the Peruvian government agreed to "repatriate gratuitously" those Chinese who wished to return home upon the completion of their contract. The treaty adopted the principle of free and voluntary emigration set forth in Article V of the Burlingame Treaty and repudiated involuntary or contract emigration. Diplomatic and consular officials were to be exchanged between the two countries, and the Peruvian government would appoint Chinese interpreters to the large centers of Chinese immigration in Peru. The treaty was ratified on August 7, 1875.[259]

Because of Portugal's action in closing Macau to emigration, the traffic in Chinese laborers had come to a halt in March 1874. Peruvian planters, hungry for laborers, hailed the treaty with China as guaranteeing the continuance of

---

[254] Ibid.; Wu, "China and Peru: A Study in Diplomatic History," 281.

[255] Stewart, *Chinese Bondage in Peru*, 190-191.

[256] Ibid., 193.

[257] For the text of the treaty and special agreement see Appendix IV. A Spanish as well as an English version are contained in BFO 17/866.

[258] In 1874 during the treaty negotiations, Li Hung Chang, asked Yung Wing, who was then with the Chinese Educational Mission in the United States, to conduct an investigation of Chinese labor in Peru. Yung Wing arrived in Peru in September 1874, and accompanied by two Americans visited several plantations. His report showed that the Chinese laborers were suffering "great outrages". The Chinese government never did send an official investigating commission to Peru. See Stewart, *Chinese Bondage in Peru*, 200-203.

[259] Wu, "China and Peru, A Study in Diplomatic History," 283.

Chinese immigration, albeit under different conditions.[260] The Peruvian Congress provided an annual subsidy of $160,000 to transport free Chinese emigrants to the country, and contracted with the American firm of Olyphant and Company to run a line of steamers between China and Peru, making twenty-eight trips a year and carrying not less than 500 Chinese laborers on each trip.[261] But due to Peru's bad reputation on the China coast, Olyphant and Company failed in two attempts in 1878 to recruit a single emigrant in Hong Kong or Canton.[262]

Peruvian planters then turned their attention to California, where anti-Chinese riots had left many Chinese unemployed. A small party of 23 Chinese were persuaded to come to Peru before the War of the Pacific (1879-1884) interrupted the movement.[263] But the fact that even the California Chinese were mistreated on the plantations[264] indicates that some Peruvian planters were incapable of seeing labor other than as a commodity to be exploited. This partly explains Peru's failure in the second half of the nineteenth century to attract voluntary labor, European or Oriental.

With such an extensive movement of Chinese to Peru, it might be expected that other Andean countries would also avail themselves of this seemingly abundant source of labor. But there is no evidence to indicate that the labor needs of Ecuador, Bolivia, or Chile throughout the nineteenth century exceeded local resources. In fact, it has been pointed out that Chile, with a much more developed economy than that of either Ecuador or Bolivia, had a surplus of labor and exported upward of 25,000 laborers to Peru between 1868 and 1872 to help Henry Meiggs build his railroads.[265]

---

[260] Stewart, *Chinese Bondage in Peru*, 206.

[261] Haviland, *American Steam Navigation in China, 1848-1878*, 88.

[262] Wu, "China and Peru: A Study of Diplomatic History," 284; Wade to Kennedy, February 22, 1876 (BFO 17/889); "Revival of Chinese Coolie Traffic to Peru," *Anti-Slavery Reporter*, Vol. XXI, No. 4 (October, 1878), 89-90.

[263] Stewart, *Chinese Bondage in Peru*, 214-217; St. John to Marquis of Salisbury, August 27, 1878 (BFO 17/890); Gibbs to Evarts, September 10, 1877 (U.S. Dept. of State, *Foreign Relations*, 1878-79), 716-717; *South Pacific Times*, September 8, 1877, February 9, 1878.

[264] St. John to Marquis of Salisbury, November 26, 1878 (BFO 17/890).

[265] Arnold J. Bauer, "Chilean Rural Labor in the Nineteenth Century," *American Historical Review*, Vol. LXXVI, No. 4 (October, 1871), 1077, 1079; Watt Stewart, "El Trabajador Chileno y los Ferrocarriles del Perú," *Revista Chilena de Historia y Geografía*, Vol. LXXXV, No. 93 (Julio-Diciembre 1938), 128-171.

The only evidence of Chinese in Ecuador in our time period is contained in a petition from Chinese at Guayaquil to Mr. Wing, the United States minister in Quito.[266] The petition, written in late 1872 or early 1873, requested the protection of the United States government against ill-treatment. However, no indication was given of how many Chinese were involved or how they came to be at Guayaquil or what they were doing there. In 1851, a ship flying the Ecuadorian flag, the *Rosarita*, sailed from Canton with an undetermined number of passengers bound for somewhere in South America.[267] While the *Rosarita* quite possibly brought its passengers to Ecuador, the authors of the petition were more probably Chinese who had fled the plantations of northern Peru and escaped into Ecuador, only to find themselves in a similar predicament of exploitation and ill-treatment at the hands of the Ecuadorians.

Similarly, little is known about the Chinese who went to Chile, principally to the mines and nitrate fields of the northern sections of the country. A few Chilean landowners and proprietors of mines in Central Chile would seem to have experimented with Chinese labor around the middle of the nineteenth century. The Chilean historian Benjamin Vicuña Mackenna records seeing in the early 1850s ten Chinese on a hacienda near Quillota, about twenty-five miles northeast of Valparaiso.[268] He also states that at about the same time, a party of nearly 100 Chinese were brought to work the copper mines of La Higuera, a small town near the coast twenty-eight miles north of La Serena, but they proved unsuitable to the task.[269]

Marcelo Segall, in his essay "Esclavitud y Tráfico Culíes en Chile," suggests that the merchant vessels that transported copper and silver from Chile to China in the 1850s brought back laborers as well as tea and silk.[270] The *China Mail* (Hong Kong), in listing the arrivals and departures of foreign ships on the China coast, gives us the following information on merchant shipping between China and Chile:

---

[266] Fish to Low, May 14, 1873, No. 132 (U.S. National Archives, Records of the Dept. of State, Diplomatic Instructions, China).

[267] *Overland Friend of China*, June 23, 1851.

[268] Benjamin Vicuña MacKenna, *Páginas de mi Diario Durante Tres Años de Viajes, 1853, 1854, 1855* (Santiago de Chile, Impr. del Ferrocaril, 1856), 38.

[269] Benjamin Vicuña MacKenna, *El Libro del Cobre y del Carbón de Piedra en Chile* (Santiago de Chile, Imprenta Cervantes, 1883), 185; Elsa Kam-ching Zambrano, *Historia de la Colectividad China en Chile* (Santiago de Chile, Universidad de Chile, 1966), 28; Baron Etienne Hulot, "Les Chinois Partout (Question de L'Immigration Chinoise)," *Revue du Monde Latin* [Paris], (September-October, 1888), 19-20.

[270] Marcelo Segall, "Esclavitud y Tráfico Culíes en Chile," *Journal of Inter-American Studies*, Vol. X, No. 1 (January 1968), 120.

Table 21

Merchant Shipping between China and Chile, 1848-1856

Date	Vessel	Flag	From	Arriving at:
		Arrivals at Chinese Ports		
July 26, 1849	Chile	French	Valparaiso	Canton
January 11, 1852	Apollo	British	Valparaiso	Hong Kong
January 24, 1852	Katherine Sharer	British	Valparaiso	Shanghai
March 23, 1852	Napoleon	Hamburg	Valparaiso	Shanghai
March 1, 1855	Faust	Hamburg	Valparaiso	Hong Kong
		Departures from Chinese Ports		
June 27, 1848	Antonio	British	Canton	Valparaiso
May 2, 1848	Congress	American	Canton	Chile
Sept. 6, 1852	American Packet	Norwegian	Canton	Valparaiso
Dec. 29, 1852	Go Ahead	Chilean	Canton	Valparaiso
April 17, 1853	Eothen	British	Hong Kong	Valparaiso
April 27, 1853	Minna	American	Canton	Valparaiso
August 5, 1854	Faust	Hamburg	Hong Kong	Valparaiso
August 29, 1855	La Ventura	Chilean	Hong Kong	Valparaiso
March 4, 1856	Spray	American	Hong Kong	Valparaiso
March 30, 1856	Greta	American	Hong Kong	Valparaiso
May 20, 1856	Banner	British	Hong Kong	Valparaiso

Source: *China Mail*, 1848-1856. The listing would seem to be incomplete.

While it is highly probable that these ships did bring some Chinese immigrants to Chile, the number would not seem to have been significant. The Chilean census of 1865 lists only seven Chinese residing in the province of Valparaiso and only one in Santiago province.[271] The same census lists seven Chinese living in Coquimbo province and twenty-four in Atacama.[272]

Most of the Chinese brought to Chile by Chilean merchants would seem to have been concentrated in the Bolivian and Peruvian provinces of Antofagasta and Tarapacá. These provinces became part of Chile after the War of the Pacific, but their guano and nitrate fields were exploited almost

---

[271] Kam-ching Zambrano, *Historia de la Colectividad China en Chile*, 33.

[272] Ibid., 31.

exclusively by Chilean capitalists from the middle 1860s.[273] It is difficult to estimate how many Chinese were employed in the nitrate industry. One source states that there were over 4,000 workers employed in the guano trade at Pabellón de Pica, near Iquique, the majority of whom were Chinese.[274] The only other figures available are those of the Chilean census of 1885, which gives 540 Chinese residing in Tarapacá, 88 in Antofagasta, 23 in Atacama, 22 in Coquimbo, 121 in Valparaiso, and 55 in Santiago.[275] No doubt some of these returned with the victorious Chilean army from Peru in 1884. In the War of the Pacific, the Chinese laborer in Peru looked upon the Chilean soldiers as liberators, and they joined the Chilean army in their hundreds as soldiers and auxiliaries, in its march northward to Lima.[276] Colonel Lynch incorporated into his brigade not less than 800 Chinese in the Cañete valley alone.[277] But if we are to believe the Chilean general census, there were less than 1,000 Chinese in all Chile in 1885, which was but a fraction of 1 percent of Chilean labor.

[273] Jay Kinsbruner, *Chile: A Historical Interpretation* (New York, Harper and Row, 1973), 107.

[274] Juan Brüggen, "Geología de las Guaneras en Chile," *Revista Chilena de Historia y Geografía*, Vol. LXXXV, No. 93 (Julio-Diciembre, 1938), 189.

[275] Kam-ching Zambrano, *Historia de la Colectividad China en Chile*, 23, 24, 31, 33.

[276] Segall, "Esclavitud y Tráfico Culíes en Chile," 126-128.

[277] Benjamin Vicuña MacKenna, *Historia de la Campaña de Lima, 1880-1881* (Santiago de Chile, Rafael Jover, 1881), 812-813.

CHAPTER VII

CHINESE INDENTURED LABORERS IN LATIN AMERICA (II)

The law [of British Guiana] is not only defective and inefficient for the protection of the immigrants, it is severe in its provisions for their control and subjection, and it is administered in respect to them harshly, unequally and oppressively. Joseph Beaumont (Chief Justice of British Guiana, 1863-68), *The New Slavery: An Account of the Indian and Chinese Immigrants in British Guiana* (London, W. Rudgway, 1871), 23

There is no fusion possible between those races—Mongolian and Dravidian—with our race. Henrique Augusto Milet, *Auxilio à Lavoura e Crédito Real* (Recife, 1876), 35.[1]

The Chinese in British, Dutch, and French Colonies

While Cuba and Peru found a partial solution to their labor needs in Chinese emigration, the European colonies of England, Holland, and France, consequent upon the cessation of African slave trade and the emancipation of the slaves, looked to India, which became their principal source of imported labor. It was only when the planters became disenchanted with Indian emigration that the colonies turned to the labor market on the China coast. Since the traffic in Indian laborers, upon the insistence of India and the British Colonial Office, was sponsored and controlled by the government, Chinese emigration was, for the most part, similarly conducted. This exhibited a commendable concern for the welfare of the laborer and was an attempt to avoid the evils inherent in an emigration movement operated by private speculators.

---

[1] As cited in Peter L. Eisenberg, *The Sugar Industry in Pernambuco: Modernization without Change, 1840-1910* (Berkeley, University of California Press, 1974), 204.

In the decade following the discontinuance of the apprenticeship system in 1838, the British colonies of Guiana, Trinidad, and Jamaica imported 22,196 indentured Indians from Calcutta and Madras.[2] But because of the preference of Indian laborers for Mauritius, the West Indies were never able to obtain all the laborers that they needed, and those who did come were of inferior quality.[3] When the British government launched its free-trade policy in 1846,[4] which threatened to destroy the sugar industry in the West Indies, many sugar planters were forced into bankruptcy; and, in 1848, faced with an economic depression, the colonies temporarily suspended Indian emigration.[5] At midcentury, when economic conditions began to improve, the colonies were again interested in importing labor, but the planters, disillusioned with the type of laborers that they had received from India in the past, showed a keen interest in experimenting with Chinese emigration.[6] After much deliberation, the British government, early in 1850, gave its consent but made it clear that any such emigration would have to be conducted under government auspices.[7] Consequently, the Court of Policy of British Guiana, the governing body in the colony, appropriated £50,000 in 1851 for Chinese emigration,[8] and Henry Barkly, the governor of the colony, proclaimed a bounty of $100 for every Chinese emigrant introduced into British Guiana, in the fervent hope that "they will form a middle class better capable of standing the climate than the natives of Madeira, more energetic than the East Indian, and less fierce and barbarous than the emigrants from the Kroo coast of Africa."[9]

In 1851, James T. White, the emigration agent for British Guiana in Calcutta, was sent to China to assess the feasibility of Chinese emigration. He was favorably impressed with what he saw and reported that the Chinese would

---

[2] Erickson, "The Introduction of East Indian Coolies into the British West Indies," 130, 138.

[3] Ibid., 138-139.

[4] The British Sugar Act of 1846 equalized duties on foreign and colonial sugar entering Great Britain.

[5] Erickson, "The Introduction of East Indian Coolies into the British West Indies," 139.

[6] Campbell, *Chinese Coolie Emigration*, 93, 99.

[7] Ibid., 99.

[8] Clementi, *The Chinese in British Guiana*, 27.

[9] Barkly to Grey, August 26, 1851 (BPP, ASS, *China*, Vol. III), 127.

"constitute useful laborers and good colonists in the West Indies."[10] In 1852, the British government, having decided on the expenditure of public money to promote Chinese emigration, appointed White as its emigration agent on the China coast with the task of supervising immigration to the West Indies.[11]

Meanwhile, at the urging of impatient planters, Governor Barkly, in late 1851, sanctioned the private venture of George Booker, a British Guiana planter, who dispatched the *Lord Elgin* to the China coast for laborers.[12] Messrs. Hyde, Hodge and Company, a British shipping firm, tempted by the bounty of $100 per emigrant, also arranged to send two ships with Chinese emigrants to British Guiana.[13] When White, who had gone to London in 1852, returned to the China coast, the *Lord Elgin* and the *Glentanner* of Messrs. Hyde, Hodge and Company had already set sail with Chinese laborers; and a third vessel, the *Samuel Boddington*, also belonging to Messrs. Hyde, Hodge and Company, was about to leave.[14]

The three vessels arrived at Georgetown, British Guiana, in 1853 with a total of 647 Chinese laborers, but 164 or over 20 percent had died on the voyage.[15] The high mortality convinced Governor Barkly, that no further shipments should be entrusted to private enterprise, and the bounty on Chinese immigrants was withdrawn.[16] Further emigration could only be conducted under strict government control.

In late 1852 and early 1853, James T. White dispatched three ships with 1,022 Chinese to meet the requests of planters in Trinidad,[17] and in 1854, he sent one ship to Jamaica with 310 laborers,[18] although Sir John Pakington, the governor of the colony, requested 2,000.[19] At this time, shipping on the China coast was extremely scarce as most vessels were snatched up at exorbitant

---

[10] White made a series of reports: White to Barkly, June 21, 1851 (Ibid.), 196-199; White to Barkly, July 19, 1851 (Ibid.), 202-206; White to Barkly, July 23, 1851 (Ibid.), 208-209; White to Barkly, August 21, 1851 (Ibid.), 210-213.

[11] Walcott to White, October 23, 1852 (Ibid.), 217-218.

[12] Clementi, *The Chinese in British Guiana*, 26.

[13] Ibid., 27.

[14] Ibid., 31, 33.

[15] Colonial Land and Emigration Commissioners to Merivale, July 27, 1853 (BPP, ASS, *China*, Vol. III), 319.

[16] Clementi, *The Chinese in British Guiana*, 36.

[17] White to Walcott, January 27, 1853 (BPP, ASS, *China*, Vol. III), 236-237.

[18] White to Walcott, April 7, 1854 (BPP, 1854-1855, Vol. XVII), 148-149.

[19] White to Walcott, February 23, 1853 (BPP, ASS, *China*, Vol. III), 245-247.

rates to transport Chinese to California, Australia, Cuba and Peru. With a ceiling expenditure of $100 for every emigrant landed in the West Indies, White could not compete for shipping and thus the first phase of Chinese immigration to the West Indies came to an abrupt end.[20]

Planters in British Guiana and Trinidad were generally quite pleased with their Chinese laborers,[21] but despite their desire to continue with the Chinese experiment, immigration was not revived until 1859. A lingering obstacle to Chinese immigration, at least as far as the British government was concerned, was its exclusively male character. In 1854, the duke of Newcastle, commenting on the lack of female Chinese emigrants stated that "Her Majesty's government cannot again incur the reproach of forming over again in the West Indies and Mauritius such male communities as were formed in the earlier part of this century in Australia."[22]

In 1856 and again in 1857, the Combined Court of British Guiana earnestly petitioned Her Majesty's government to permit the resumption of Chinese immigration on the understanding that a fixed proportion of the immigrants would be females.[23] The London government finally relented, and as an interim measure, while a system of government-controlled emigration was being established, granted permission to proprietors in British Guiana and Trinidad to introduce immigrants from China at their own expense.[24] Thomas Gerard, who was acquainted with the realities of the China coast, was sent to China with instructions to obtain for British Guiana and Trinidad 2,990 Chinese laborers, half of whom should be women if that was possible.[25] He succeeded in sending two ships with 761 emigrants, all of them males. They arrived in British Guiana in March and May 1859. When the Colonial Office learned that they had actually been obtained from the barracoons at Macau, Gerard was quickly recalled.[26]

Meanwhile, a government emigration scheme was being organized by J. Gardiner Austin, formerly Immigration Agent General of British Guiana. Austin was appointed British emigration agent in China for the West Indies in 1859, and had the good fortune of enlisting the cooperation of Chinese officials as well as

---

[20]   White to Rogers, March 10, 1853 (Ibid.), 249.

[21]   See the reports of various planters in Ibid., 189-193, 267-271.

[22]   Newcastle to the Governors of Jamaica, British Guiana, Trinidad and Mauritius, June 12, 1854 (Ibid.), 337-338.

[23]   Clementi, *The Chinese in British Guiana*, 31, 53-54.

[24]   Stanley to Wodehouse, April 1, 1858 (BPP, ASS, *China*, Vol. III), 440-441.

[25]   Clementi, *The Chinese in British Guiana*, 61.

[26]   Ibid., 71-73.

western missionaries in establishing a system of voluntary and family emigration.[27] All Chinese wishing to emigrate were invited to apply in person at emigration houses in Canton, Amoy, and Swatow, all of which were jointly supervised by a British agent and a Chinese official.[28] The system proved to be signally successful. From 1859 to 1866, 14,666 Chinese were transported to the West Indies, 2,455 of them women. Of this number 12,412 went to British Guiana, 1,774 went to Trinidad, and one vessel with 480 emigrants went to British Honduras.[29]

The signing of the Emigration Convention in Peking in 1866 brought a halt to Chinese immigration to the British West Indies. Article VIII of the Convention granted to every immigrant the right to a return passage home at the end of his term of indenture.[30] Planters in the British colonies regarded this added expense as too costly and petitioned the British government for a revision of the Convention.[31] Both the British and French governments sought to renegotiate the matter with the Chinese government. Negotiations dragged on, and for seven years, the British emigration agency was maintained at Canton at an annual cost to the colonies of £1,600 without sending them a single emigrant.[32] In 1871, Trinidad gave up on receiving any more Chinese.[33] British Guiana persevered only to obtain one shipload of 388 laborers in 1874, whereupon it too abandoned Chinese contract emigration.[34]

The British colonies in the West Indies were by no means dependent on Chinese labor, for as table 22 shows, they were receiving throughout our period a steady flow of laborers mostly from India. However, West Indian planters regarded the Chinese as "by far the most intelligent, the most industrious and the most self-reliant of all the emigrants who came to the colonies."[35] It would seem that the Chinese were a kind of luxury that the colonies indulged in whenever they had some extra capital at hand. It cost an average of $50 to

---

[27] Ibid., 76, 86.

[28] Campbell, *Chinese Coolie Emigration*, 121-122, 130.

[29] Clementi, *The Chinese in British Guiana*, Tables ii, iii; "General Report of Emigration Commissioners," 1861-1866 (BPP, *Emigration*, Vols. XIV, XV, XVI).

[30] See Appendix II.

[31] Clementi, *The Chinese in British Guiana*, 208.

[32] Ibid., 207.

[33] Ibid., 223.

[34] Ibid., 240-241.

[35] Longden to Carnavan, October 31, 1874 (BFO 17/886).

Table 22

Immigration to the British West Indies, 1847-1874★

British Guiana			
	Chinese	Indians	Others	Total
1847-1849	—	7,022	6,424	13,446
1850-1859	1,348	18,278	13,704	33,333
1860-1869	12,094	39,278	12,126	63,442
1870-1874	388	23,156	1,936★★	25,480
Totals	13,830	87,678	34,190	145,701
Jamaica			
1847-1847	—	2,438	3,091	5,529
1850-1859	515	—	2,065	2,580
1960-1869	—	7,663	1,848	9,511
1870-1872★★	—	3,786	—	3,786
Totals	515	13,887	6,904	21,406
Trinidad			
1847-1849	—	2,711	3,135	5,846
1850-1859	988	12,037	1,009	14,034
1860-1869	1,655	20,661	1,629	23,945
1870-1872★★★	—	7,007	—	7,007
Totals	2,643	42,416	5,773	50,832

★   The figures are for arrivals in the British West Indies, exclusive of deaths on the voyage.

★★   Figures for 1873 and 1874 are missing.

★★★   Figures for Jamaica and Trinidad for 1873 and 1874 are unavailable.

Source: BPP, *Emigration*, Vol. XI (1850), Appendix No. 30; Vol. XIII, Appendix No. 23; Vol. XVIII, Appendix No. 11; Vols. XIV, XV and XVI. Clementi, *The Chinese in British Guiana*, Tables ii, iii; Tinker, *A New System of Slavery*, table 7:1.

introduce a laborer from India,[36] while it cost more than double that amount to bring a laborer from the China coast.[37] This cost differential together with the periodic availability of capital probably explains the erratic fluctuation in the demand for Chinese laborers, which varied from as many as 3,500 for all the British colonies in the West Indies in the 1861-62 season to only 840 the following season, a demand fluctuation that created logistical problems for the emigration agent in China.[38]

There is even evidence to indicate that the colonies did not need Indian laborers, or at least to the extent that they were introduced. In 1854, while Jamaica was importing 1,596 Indians and 515 Chinese, large numbers of Jamaica Negroes were going to Panama to work on constructing a railroad across the isthmus.[39] West Indian planters reluctantly accepted the emancipation of their slaves, and instead of improving working conditions in order to retain them, they drove them away with low wages, irregular payments or none at all, and fraudulent exactions leading to litigations that invariably went against the laborers.[40] In Jamaica, planters resorted to charging rent, often excessive, for the cottages on their estates in proportion to the amount of plantation labor performed by their occupants.[41] Such oppressive measures compelled the Negroes to fall back on their own resources and to become small freeholders or squatters. The labor "shortage" that resulted was largely of the planters' own making. Their habits as slaveholders rendered them almost incapable of managing free wage labor, and their cries of a deficiency of "continuous labour" could be translated as a cry for servile labor in some

---

[36]   Morrell, *British Colonial Policy in the Mid-Victorian Age*, 456.

[37]   In the early 1850s the cost of Chinese emigration to British Guiana was $110 per person, in the early 1860s it was $125 and in 1866 it was $139. See Clementi, *The Chinese in British Guiana*, 137.

[38]   Ibid., 174.

[39]   Ronald V. Sires, "Sir Henry Barkly and the Labor Problem in Jamaica, 1853-1856," *Journal of Negro History*, Vol. XXV, No. 2 (April, 1940), 228.

[40]   Hall Pringle, *The Fall of the Sugar Planters of Jamaica with Remarks on their Agricultural Management and on the Labour Question in that Island* (London, Trubner and Company, 1869), 24-25; William G. Sewell, *The Ordeal of Free Labor in the British West Indies* (New York, Harper and Brothers, 1861), 109-113; Morrell, *British Colonial Policy in the Age of Peel and Russell*, 150-152; "Coolie Immigration," *Anti-Slavery Reporter*, Vol. XVI, No. 1 (January 1, 1868), 15-18.

[41]   Pringle, *The Fall of the Sugar Planters of Jamaica*, 24.

form or another. Governor Barkly, of British Guiana explained the planters'
position:

> The disadvantages under which most of the British colonies labour in this
> competition (with slave-grown sugar) do not arise . . . from the dearness
> of Free Labour . . . they are attributable almost entirely to the great
> difficulty of commanding continuous labour, which always constituted
> a crying evil in countries where there exists a great deal of waste land and
> a very small population.
>
> Immigration is the readiest palliative for this evil, but immigration
> without contracts would require to be almost infinite in extent to produce
> any permanent effect upon the supply of labour in British Guiana.[42]

The planters were all too ready to impute to the imperial government
responsibility for their plight, and conciliatory government officials in London
were gradually won over to the notion of contract or indentured labor,
financed in part by public funds.[43] That was a major victory for the planter,
and piecemeal, through increasingly restrictive legislation, he regained the
command of labor, which he had lost through emancipation.[44]

On arrival in the British West Indies, the Chinese laborers were placed
in the charge of a government immigration agent, who assigned them to the
sugar estates, thus avoiding anything in the nature of the public auction of
Havana or Callao. The legislation governing their introduction and indenture
varied little from colony to colony and was rather restrictive, if not oppressive.
Each laborer was required to complete an industrial residence of five years,
and heavy penalties in fines and imprisonment were levied on laborers who
were not under contract, who absented themselves from work, or deserted

---

[42]   Barkly to Grey, October 30, 1849 (BCO 111/269).

[43]   About half the cost of Asiatic immigration to the British West Indies was paid
       from public revenues. Staple items such as fish and flour were taxed, and thus the
       laboring population was compelled to subsidize the introduction of immigrants to
       compete with them in the labor market. Later, an export tax was levied on sugar,
       rum, coffee and dyewoods to help defray the cost of immigration. See Adamson,
       Sugar without Slaves, 106-109; "Immigration into the West Indies," *Anti-Slavery
       Reporter*, Vol. VIII, No. 1 (January 2, 1860), 19-23; "Local Testimony Concerning
       Coolie Immigration to Jamaica," Ibid., Vol. XX, No. 3 (May 15, 1876), 68-69;
       "Cost of Coolie Immigration," Ibid., Vol. XI, No. 7 (July 1, 1863), 165-166.

[44]   Adamson, *Sugar without Slaves*, 109-116.

their employer. The laborer's freedom of movement was severely limited, and planters used the courts habitually to enforce discipline.[45]

The 515 Chinese introduced into Jamaica in 1854—310 directly from China and 205 from Panama[46]—were unhappy with the treatment they received on the estates, and most of them drifted into Spanish Town and Kingston. After releasing some of them from their contracts, the government attempted to settle them on lands on the outskirts of Kingston, but this also failed.[47] Following this none-too-happy experience, the planters opted to be content with Indian labor, and no more Chinese were requested. The census of 1891 revealed that there were 481 Chinese on the island, most of them moderately successful as dealers in provisions or small storekeepers.[48]

Relatively little is known about the 2,643 Chinese who came to Trinidad between 1853 and 1866.[49] Of the 988 who landed at the Port of Spain in the first half of 1853, 107, or over 10 percent, died by the end of the year; and the immigration agent advised that, though the Chinese were the best laborers hitherto imported, it would be advisable not to introduce more until those already in the colony acquired some knowledge of the language and customs of the people, as communication was a serious problem.[50] The next shipments did not arrive until the 1860s. However, the Chinese seemingly attracted little attention until the 1920s, when they were hailed by one writer as among the most progressive elements in Trinidad society, with many of them successful doctors, lawyers, dentists, bankers, and prominent businessmen.[51]

---

[45] The basic law of Trinidad governing Chinese immigration is contained in Ordinance No. 3, March 22, 1853 (BPP, ASS, *China*, Vol. III), 311-314. Chinese immigrants in British Guiana were subject to the provisions of Ordinance No. 7 of 1854 (BPP, *Emigration*, Vol. XII, Appendix No. 60), 171-189. A summary of Jamaica legislation pertaining to Chinese immigration is contained in Sires, "Sir Henry Barkly and the Labor Problem in Jamaica, 1853-1856," 219-220.

[46] See Table 28 in Appendix VI.

[47] Sires, "Sir Henry Barkly and the Labor Problem in Jamaica, 1853-1856," 227-228.

[48] Robert T. Hill, *Cuba and Porto Rico with Other Islands of the West Indies* (New York, The Century Company, 1899), 226; W.M. Cousins, "Chinese in the Caribbean," *The Living Age*, Vol. 332, No. 4297 (January 1, 1927), 16-21.

[49] See Table 22.

[50] Mitchell to the Emigration Commissioners, November 28, 1853 (BPP, *Emigration*, Vol. XII, 1854), 259-262.

[51] Arthur A. Young, "The Progressive Chinese in Trinidad," *The China Weekly Review*, Vol. L, No. 3 (December 21, 1929), 114.

The 474 Chinese who arrived in British Honduras in 1865—brought there no doubt through the influence of the governor of the colony, J. Gardiner Austin, who had been the British emigration agent on the China coast from 1859 to 1862[52]—were allotted to the estates of the British Honduras Company and were put to work felling timber. But by 1869, only 211 were left in the colony, 155 absconded and sought refuge among the Santa Cruz Indians, and 108 had died.[53]

More has been written about the Chinese in British Guiana than in any of the other British colonies in the West Indies. Outstripping her sister colonies in sugar production as well as in size, British Guiana imported the greatest number of both Indian and Chinese laborers.[54] Large numbers usually attracted attention, and the Anti-Slavery Society and the Aborigines Protection Society kept a vigilant eye on the colony's system of indentured labor. Though reports of physical abuse of indentured laborers were infrequent, planters were accused of unfair and unjust practices whereby the indenture period of their workers was arbitrarily extended, sometimes indefinitely. In 1869, G. W. DesVoeux, administrator of the island colony of St. Lucia, who had spent five years as a stipendiary magistrate in British Guiana, wrote to Earl Granville at the Colonial Office, outlining the abuses in the indenture system of British Guiana, the principal complaint being that the stipendiary magistrates (who were totally dependent on the planters for their jobs) actively connived with the planters in abusing the colony's labor laws. He warned that there was "widespread discontent and disaffection throughout the immigrant population both Indian and Chinese (and especially among the latter . . .)," and urged that something be done before the matter got out of hand.[55] The Colonial Office appointed a commission of inquiry, which conducted an investigation into

---

[52]   Clementi, *The Chinese in British Guiana*, 102, 125.

[53]   "Twenty-Seventh General Report of the Emigration Commissioners," 1867 (BPP, *Emigration*, Vol. XVII), 28-29; "Twenty-Ninth General Report of the Emigration Commissioners," 1869 (Ibid.), 26.

[54]   See Table 22.

[55]   Des Voeux to Granville, December 25, 1869 (BPP, Vol. XX, 1871), 487-500. Joseph Beaumont, who was Chief Justice of British Guiana from 1863 to 1868 and sacrificed his position in trying to remedy the judicial system and its bias against the indentured laborer, was in essential agreement with Des Voeux regarding the role of the stipendiary magistrates in abusing the law. See his pamphlet, *The New Slavery: An Account of the Indian and Chinese Immigrants in British Guiana* (London: W. Ridgway, 1871), 77.

all indentured labor, both Indian and Chinese, visiting fifty-four plantations, and filed its report in February 1871.[56]

The report was somewhat ambiguous. In its general conclusions, it exonerated the system of indentured labor in British Guiana from the charges brought against it, but then proceeded to list a variety of serious abuses. While it stated that Des Voeux's allegations against the stipendiary magistrates could not be generally substantiated, it admitted that the laborers were rarely able to obtain justice in the courts.[57] The commissioners acknowledged that the law, in respect to the laborers, was administered harshly. Prison sentences were too long, and fines were exorbitantly high.[58] The inquiry also revealed that the decision of Chief Justice Beaumont in 1867, which ruled that laborers could not be prosecuted for the nonperformance of "tasks," was ignored by the magistrates of the lower courts, who continued to hand down convictions for this offense.[59] The law demanded that the indentured laborer complete "5 tasks" a week. But as Beaumont pointed out, the nature of the "task" was "neither agreed upon, or defined by law or practice." In most instances, the "task" was determined by the overseer, who could arbitrarily declare any work as unsatisfactory and withhold wages.[60] In fact, unjust deductions from wages were one of the most frequent complaints of the indentured laborer.[61] In commenting on the administration of law in regard to the laborers, the commissioners were of the opinion that a "harsh system of law had been kept up not so much for use as that condoning of offenses under it might be bartered against re-indenture."[62] With a long list of offenses hanging over each individual laborer, plus a seductively large bounty of $50 for re-indenture,[63] there was little or no alternative for the vast majority upon the

---

[56] The Complete report with appendices is printed in BPP, Vol. XX, 1871, 483-899.

[57] "Report of the Commissioners Appointed to Enquire into the Treatment of Immigrants in British Guiana," (hereafter referred to as "The British Guiana Commission"), 515-516, 587-590.

[58] Ibid., 605-606.

[59] Ibid., 510-511.

[60] Beaumont, The New Slavery, 77; "The British Guiana Commission," 559.

[61] Edward Jenkins, The Coolie: His Rights and Wrongs (New York, George Routledge and Sons, 1871), 278.

[62] "The British Guiana Commission," 558.

[63] Ibid., 608.

completion of their five-year term but to sign a contract for another five years of servitude.

The commission also uncovered evidence to suggest that indentured labor helped planters to depress the wages of free labor in the colony—a major complaint of the critics of the indenture system.[64] Legislation guaranteed indentured labor the same wage rate as nonindentured workers. This would seem to have been an attempt in good faith to protect the wage level of the indentured worker. But the growth of indentured labor in the 1850s and 1860s had the effect of depressing the wages of free labor thereby also lowering the wages of indentured labor, since they were both tied to one another by statute.[65] Chief Justice Beaumont recounts how one planter, while desirous of hiring a number of free laborers who wished to reside on his estate, was obliged to refuse because he would run the risk of having to raise the wages of his indentured workers.[66] The commission heard testimony to the effect that while wages were high in 1850, they fell throughout the following decade and remained stationary in the 1860s. The commissioners agreed that wages in 1870 were much lower than in 1850.[67]

Though the Commission concluded that the system of indenture was "justifiable,"[68] its investigation produced ample evidence to show that the condition of indentured labor on the plantations was far from satisfactory. Two woodcuts by a Chinese artist cleverly depict how the plantation laborer viewed his situation. The interpretations of the woodcuts given in figures 18 and 19 are those of Chief Justice Beaumont, who reproduced the carvings on the cover and back of his pamphlet, *The New Slavery*, and, together with the woodcuts, constitute an incisive commentary on plantation life in British Guiana in the third quarter of the nineteenth century.

The commission found that the Chinese in British Guiana—unlike their countrymen in Southeast Asia, and even in Trinidad and Jamaica—remained for the most part on the plantations. In 1870, there were 5,210 indentured Chinese (most of them serving their second term of indenture) and 1,159

---

[64] "Coolie Immigration," *Anti-Slavery Reporter*, Vol. XVI, No. 1 (January 1, 1868), 15-18; "Coolie Immigration," Ibid., Vol. XXV, No. 9 (November, 1877), 29; "Immigration into the West Indies," Ibid., Vol. VIII, No. 1 (January 2, 1860), 22.

[65] Adamson, *Sugar without Slaves*, 326.

[66] Beaumont, *The New Slavery*, 79.

[67] "The British Guiana Commission," 683-684.

[68] Ibid., 558.

unindentured Chinese on the estates.[69] This was rather out of character. But plantation labor would seem to have been the only livelihood open to them. The more than 18,000 Portuguese from the Madeira islands who came to the colony between 1845 and 1851 quickly deserted the plantations to become hawkers, small businessmen, and storekeepers. Within a few years, they had a virtual monopoly of the retail trade of the colony.[70] Thus the Chinese were excluded from their traditional avenue of advancement. Furthermore, the sale of private land was extremely rare, and Crown land could only be purchased in blocks of not less than one hundred acres, which put it beyond the reach of the Chinese laborer.[71]

Confined as they were to the plantations, it is not surprising to find that there was a steady emigration of Chinese from British Guiana to neighboring colonies in the last decades of the nineteenth century.[72] Although 2,072 Chinese women entered British Guiana from 1860 to 1874, and some Chinese men married Creole women, the Chinese population declined drastically. According to the 1911 census, there were only 2,622 Chinese left in the colony.[73]

Although the Chinese were ostensibly introduced into British Guiana as "colonists," there was but one feeble attempt to settle them on the land. At the expiration of the indenture of a group of Chinese families who had arrived in 1860 and were mostly converts to Christianity, Governor Hincks gave them Crown land on the west bank of the Demerara river to form an agricultural settlement. Named Hopetown, because of a visit to the new settlement of British Admiral Sir James Hope, the more than 170 Chinese who settled there in 1865 prospered for a while, raising garden produce and burning charcoal for the Georgetown market thirty miles away. But by the turn of the century, the more enterprising Chinese had moved to the city, and the settlement languished.[74]

---

[69]   Ibid., 516.

[70]   Ibid., 525, 578.

[71]   Ibid., 578.

[72]   Clementi, *The Chinese in British Guiana*, 328-331.

[73]   Ibid., 326; Morton H. Fried, "Some Observations on the Chinese in British Guiana," *Social and Economic Studies*, Vol. V, No. 1 (March, 1956), 58.

[74]   "The British Guiana Commission," 671; Clementi, *The Chinese in British Guiana*, 284-317; W. T. Veness, "A Chinese Church in British Guiana," *Mission Life*, Vol. V, No. 2, New Series (1874), 520-523.

Figure 18. The plantation manager's house as seen through the eyes of a Chinese indentured laborer.

Interpretation: On each side of the yard are seen gangs of bound immigrants—Indians on one side, Chinese on the other, presenting various types of each class. In front of each gang appears a representative figure, undergoing at the hands of his driver the operation of having his heart's blood drawn into vessels supported by the manager's boys. In the foreground is seen a pliant coolie in charge of the manager's cattle; on the other a recalcitrant Chinese undergoing necessary discipline at the hands of the constable or driver. The attorney of the absentee proprietor has come to inspect the estate and may be seen seated with much repose and dignity enjoying the cool breeze at the windward corner of the gallery and imbibing in company with the manager—his horse meanwhile awaiting the great man, very much at its ease in the background, where the smoking kitchen affords a further pleasing prospect. Within the house through the open windows, are to be seen the manager's wife and children, fat and well liking; while at the further end of the gallery the overseers are seated with their books, overhauling the pay-list and arranging the stoppages. The butler is seen carrying up the steps what is possibly meant for one of the vessels already filled by the driver's agency below. To the mind's eye of the great man are present (as shown on the label issuing from his cranium) the dignified planter and his placid lady at home in England; while to the mind's eye of the representative Chinese are present (indicated in like manner) his aged parents at home in China—the mother painfully striving to decry her lost son, the father imploring him to return. (From Beaumont, *The New Slavery*)

Figure 19. The plantation hospital as seen through the eyes of a Chinese indentured laborer.

Interpretation: The hospital; this is represented as when visited by the estates' doctor. He has just arrived, and having left his impatient horse (a characteristic beast) in the care of a Chinese at the foot of the hospital stairs, has seated himself in an airy spot at their head, where his patients are marshalled for inspection. On his right stands his lieutenant, the comfortable sick nurse, behind whom may be seen within her chamber, his wife, regaling herself—possibly on bread and honey, but not impossibly (having regard to the dietary table at her husband's hand) on hospital stores and medical comforts. As the diet table hangs on one side, there hangs on the other a wretched Chinaman who has sought so to end his troubles; while another Chinese, a ragged rascal whom the doctor has discharged from hospital, is propelled down the stairs with some vigour of foot and stick by the manager or overseer. Within the main ward are shown three bedded patients, the two farther ones in distressed action, while the nearest has just shut up the story of his days, and passed beyond the tender mercies of the estate, even though at the mortal instant a chicken has been brought to his bedside. In the inner ward are seen two patients placed in the stocks, no doubt for greater facility of treatment. Beneath the hospital is a large pot, in charge of a blowsy black woman. The contents may be fowl soup, but as to that the lively fowls at all events indicate no concern or foreboding. The nurse's pigs are represented in fine condition, while outside their sty appear several convalescents, or chronic cases who having come, prodigals, to this far country would gladly fill their bellies with the husks which the swine reject. They are, however, at present more usefully occupied and (in their hospital shirts and with bandaged limbs) are engaged in hospital economy. One carries upstairs the nauseous bucket. Others are seen hoeing the ground. One poor wretch has given in and thrown down his hoe, and is being condoled or expostulated with by a coolie woman while he crouches over his inefficient leg, helpless from anasarca or intolerable from erysipelatous sores. (From Beaumont, *The New Slavery*)

The lot of the Chinese in the Dutch colony of Surinam would seem to have been somewhat similar to that of the Chinese in British Guiana, as the sugar planters of Surinam were mostly British and modeled their plantations after those of their countrymen to the south.[75] When the planters of British Guiana began to import Chinese laborers in the 1850s, their counterparts in Surinam brought an initial group of 18 Chinese from Java in 1853, followed by 500 from the China coast in 1858.[76] In 1863, the act abolishing slavery in Surinam prescribed a ten-year apprenticeship for all slaves. But their reluctance to perform their allotted tasks moved the government of the colony to promote emigration. Laborers were sought from the Madeira islands, Barbados, and China.[77]

With the help of the Reverend William Lobscheid and the inducement of a monthly wage of $7, plus food, clothes, and lodging, as well as a free return passage at the end of the five years of indenture,[78] the Surinam Immigration Company introduced 2,221 Chinese laborers during the 1860s (see table 23). In the early 1870s, with the end of the apprenticeship system approaching, a renewed attempt was made to obtain Chinese workers, but the British colony of Hong Kong, which supplied Chinese laborers to Surinam in the 1860s, refused to make any exception to the 1869 law restricting contract immigration to British colonies.[79] A hundred Chinese arrived from Java in 1873.[80] Surinam then turned to India, which supplied the colony with laborers during the 1870s by virtue of an emigration convention between the British and Dutch governments in 1870.[81]

---

[75]   Loxdale to Murdock, January 24, 1870 (BFO 17/878).

[76]   J.F. Snelleman, "Chineesche Immigranten in Suriname," *De West-Indische Gids*, Vol. II (1920), 225.

[77]   "Reports Respecting the Condition of Coolies in Surinam" (BPP, Vol. LXXVIII, 1877, Slave Report No. 3), 8.

[78]   MacDonnell to the Duke of Buckingham, August 31, 1868 (BFO 17/876); "Report of Harbor Master Thomsett," Hong Kong, May 10, 1865 (BFO 17/876).

[79]   Meade to the Foreign Office, January 31, 1872 (BFO 17/880).

[80]   Snelleman, "Chineesche Immigranten in Suriname," 226.

[81]   This convention signed at the Hague on September 8, 1870 gave the Netherlands the same privileges and restrictions on recruiting laborers in India as laid down for British colonies. See "Reports Respecting the Condition of Coolies in Surinam."

Table 23

Chinese Immigration to Surinam

Year	Vessel	Flag	Port of Departure	Embarked	Died at Sea	Landed
1853			Java	18?	?	18
1858	Twee Gerusters	Dutch	Macau	243	?	243?
1858	Minister Pahud	Dutch	Macau	257	?	257?
1865	Tricolor	British	Hong Kong	493	?	493?
1866	Whirlwind	British	Hong Kong	409	5	404
1866	Golden Horn	British	Hong Kong	416	13	403
1867	Veritas	British	Hong Kong	291	27	516
1868	Marie Therese	French	Hong Kong	252		
1869	Veritas	British	Hong Kong	202	95	405
1869	Ferdinand Bruum	German	Hong Kong	298		
1873			Java	100?	?	100
Totals:				2,979?	140?	2,839?

Sources: Snelleman, "Chineesche Immigranten in Suriname," 225-226; "Number of Chinese Emigrants who left Hong Kong to Serve under Contracts from 1856 to 1870, inclusive" (BFO 17/889); *Hong Kong Government Gazette* Vol. XIII (March 9, 1867); Vol. XIV (March 7, 1868); Vol. XX (March 20, 1869).

The only available information about the treatment of the Chinese in Surinam is the fact that 464 Chinese were still under indenture on January 1, 1875,[82] six months after the indenture of the last arrivals from China should have expired. This would seem to indicate that Surinam was no exception to the pattern of unjust exploitation of Chinese contract labor.

Like the Dutch, the French also entered into an agreement with the British government to obtain laborers from India for their West Indian colonies of French Guiana, Martinique, and Guadaloupe.[83] Hence Indians constituted

---

[82] "Reports Respecting the Condition of Coolies in Surinam," 9.

[83] "Coolie Emigration to French Colonies" *Saturday Review* Vol. XII, No. 299 (July 20, 1861), 58.

the bulk of the foreign labor force introduced into the French colonies in the third quarter of the nineteenth century, but there was also a sprinkling of Chinese as the following table illustrates.

Table 24
Chinese Immigration to the French West Indies

Year	Vessel	Flag	Port of Depature	Embarked	Died at Sea	Landed
Martinique★						
1959	Galilee	French	Canton	426	?	426?
Guadeloupe						
1859			Shanghai	?	?	208
French Guiana						
1859	Admiral Baudin		Shanghai	355	24	331

★ Gurial states that 1,000 Chinese came to Martinique from 1857 to 1862. See
L'immigration Réglementée aux Antilles Francaises et à la Réunion, 130, also Paul
Chemin Dupontes, *Les Petites Antilles* (Paris: Librairie Orientale e Americanine,
1909), 202.

Sources: Guiral, *L'immigration Réglementée aux Antilles Francaises et à la Réunion*,
86; BFO 97/102B.

Apart from passing references to the presence of Chinese in the French West Indies, nothing would seem to have been written about them.

Chinese Indentured Laborers in Brazil

The Chinese who came to Brazil in the second half of the nineteenth century were relatively few in number and consequently made little or no impact on Brazilian society. Though Chinese emigration was statistically insignificant, the attempts to promote it and the debates that these attempts engendered not only throw some light on the condition of labor, but also provide some insights into the social attitudes of various sectors of Brazilian society.[84]

In the 1850s and 1860s, there were three attempts to bring Chinese laborers to Brazil. The first successful attempt was a private venture by a Rio de Janeiro merchant, Manoel de Almeida Cardosa, who had earlier transported 3,000 Portuguese to Brazil.[85] His first consignment of 303 Chinese arrived at Rio de Janeiro on February 9, 1855, on the United States bark *Elisa Anna*. Recruited in the British colony of Singapore rather than on the China coast, the Chinese would only commit themselves to a two-year contract, at the end of which they were to receive a free return passage to Singapore. Since they were British subjects, the British legation in Rio de Janeiro insisted that the terms of the contract be strictly followed. Because of the shortness of the period of indenture and the financial burden of paying for the return passage, the venture was a financial failure, and Cardosa temporarily abandoned Chinese immigration.[86]

But the Brazilian government had become deeply interested in the Chinese as substitutes for African slaves and, in the same year, signed a contract with Messrs. Sampson and Tappan of Boston for the introduction of 2,000 Chinese within a period of eighteen months, agreeing to pay £20 per immigrant.[87]

---

[84] For a discussion of the various aspects of the debates see Robert Conrad, "Falta de Braços: The Chinese Coolie Controversy in the Brazilian Empire," unpublished paper, University of Illinois at Chicago Circle, 1973; Rodrigues, "Brasil e Extremo Oriente," 65-71; Emilia Viotta de Costa, *De Senzala à Colónia* (São Paulo, Difusão Europeia do Libro, 1966), 140-144; Salvador de Mendonça, *Imigração Chineza: Serie de Artigos Publicados no "Cruzeiro" em Resposta do "Rio News"* (Rio de Janeiro, Typographia a Vapor no "Cruzeiro," 1881); Eisenberg, *The Sugar Industry in Pernambuco*, 204.

[85] I have been unable to discover the outcome of Dr. Fairbanks' recruiting efforts on the China coast in behalf of the sugar planters of Bahia (See Chapter I). As far as it is known the mission was a complete failure.

[86] Pinheiro, *Importação de Trabalhadores Chins*, 34-38; M. Charles Reybaud, *Le Brésil* (Paris, Guillaumin et Cie, 1856), 215-217; Fernando L.B. Basto, *Sintese da Historia da Imigração no Brasil* (Rio de Janeiro, 1970), 57.

[87] *United States Consular Reports*, 1889, Vol. III, 216. At first, the British government through its legation in London and with the help of J. Forster, a member of the British Parliament, attempted to arrange for the introduction of 6,000 Chinese to Brazil. But when this plan failed to materialize a contract was signed with Messrs. Sampson and Tappan. See Pinheiro, *Importação de Trabalhadores Chins*, 44-45.

The contract further stipulated that the laborers be experienced in cultivating sugarcane with 50 to 100 experienced in growing tea. In virtue of this contract, the United States vessel *Sarah* arrived at Rio de Janeiro from Canton in March 1856 with 368 Chinese laborers.[88] Shortly thereafter, Messrs. Sampson and Tappan, under pressure from Peter Parker, the United States commissioner in China, asked to be released from their contract, and no more came.[89]

Planters who employed the Chinese from the *Sarah* complained of their insubordination and refusal to work. The Chinese complained about the poor quality of the food and of attempts to pay them less than their contracts stipulated. On a number of plantations, the situation became so unmanageable that the planters returned the Chinese to the custody of the government depot whence they received them and would have nothing more to do with them.[90] This convinced an already skeptical public of the unsuitability of the Chinese for plantation work. The idea of importing Chinese labor never did have much popular support among Brazilians. Indeed, for some, the very idea of Chinese immigration was "abominable."[91] The arrival of the *Elisa Anna* in 1855 moved one pamphleteer to denounce the Chinese as "worse than the Negro," characterizing them as given to "frightening abberations," "infanticides by conviction," and "thieves by nature."[92] The anti-Chinese feeling was so strong that when Cardosa landed 312 Chinese from Singapore in October 1866 in his own ship *Soberana*, neither planters nor industrialists would employ them. The fact that this time the contracts were for a term of five years seemed to make no difference. Three months elapsed before Cardosa finally persuaded a contractor of public works to take them off his hands.[93]

Notwithstanding public sentiments and past failures, the question of Chinese immigration was again raised toward the close of the 1860s. José Pedro Xavier Pinheiro, one of the principal proponents of Chinese immigration, argued, with

---

[88]   Pinheiro, *Importação de Trabalhadores Chins*, 49.

[89]   *Report of the Committee Appointed by the Government of the "Board of Trade" to take into Consideration the Communication of Messrs. Sampson and Tappan*, 19.

[90]   Pinheiro, *Importação de Trabalhadores Chins*, 51-55.

[91]   Costa, *De Senzala à Colônia*, 140; Jermingham to Clarendon, April 12, 1856 (BFO 97/102A).

[92]   "Breves considerações sôbre Colonização por A. du Calpe," Rio de Janeiro, 1855, in *Memorias* (Arquivo Nacional), Vol. XVI, as cited in Costa, *De Senzala à Colônia*, 140.

[93]   Pinheiro, *Importação de Trabalhadores Chins*, 60-61.

some justification, that the bad experiences Brazil had with Chinese labor were due to failure to recruit the proper type of immigrant and a lack of understanding on the part of Brazilians of the Chinese mentality and character. The experience of other countries revealed that the Chinese were exceptionally good workers, and if properly handled, they could be, in Pinheiro's opinion, Brazil's best hope for solving the labor problems.[94] To assuage the fears of those who believed that the Chinese would "Mongolize" the nation, Pinheiro emphasized that the Chinese were not coming to convert Brazilians to their faith, or to intermarry with them, or to compete with them educationally, but merely to work for modest wages for a short period of time and then return to China.[95]

As the movement for the abolition of slavery began to gather momentum in the late 1860s, it became increasingly clear to the planter that he could not rely on European immigration to replace his slaves, as most Europeans desired only to work their own land.[96] Though most planters, like most Brazilians of the period, were instinctively opposed to Chinese immigration, many of them began to look to Chinese labor as the only viable alternative to bankruptcy and ruin.[97] During 1869 and 1870, various reports and memoranda emanating from the Ministry of Agriculture presented Chinese immigration as the ideal solution for the labor crisis of the coffee and sugar plantations.[98] It was not surprising then when a government decree of July 9, 1870, authorized two Rio de Janeiro merchants, Manoel José de Costa Lima Viana and João Antonio de Miranda e Silva, to import Chinese contract labor.[99]

The decree spelled out the limited role that the Chinese immigrant was to have in Brazilian society. According to Article VI (which reflected a similar provision of the Spanish Royal Decree of 1860),[100] the Chinese, upon completion of their term of indenture, were obliged to re-indenture themselves or leave Brazil within two months at their own expense.[101] The Chinese were

---

[94]   Ibid., 10-15, 55-76.

[95]   Ibid., 21.

[96]   C.F. Van Delden Laërne, *Brazil and Java: Report on Coffee-Culture* (London, W.H. Allen and Company, 1885), 141.

[97]   Quintino Bocayuva, *A Crise na Lavoura* (Rio de Janeiro, 1869), 23, 30, cited in Costa, *De Senzala à Colônia*, 140-141.

[98]   Costa, *De Senzala à Colônia*, 143.

[99]   Ibid., 143.

[100] See Chapter VI.

[101] *Colecção das Leis do Imperio do Brasil de 1870* (Rio de Janeiro, 1870), II, 384.

thus excluded from becoming Brazilian citizens and were virtually condemned to perpetual indenture on the plantations. This government action was no doubt a response to the popular fears of "mongolization," but it also gave substance to the repeated warnings of abolitionists that the introduction of Chinese labor would mean the continuation of slavery in a new form.[102] Like the slave, the Chinese immigrant would be wedded to the plantation, and his life and labor would be under the complete control of the planter. Legally, the Chinese laborer was not a slave, but in practice, he would serve the same function at least temporarily. It was unmistakably clear that neither the government nor the planter desired to import the Chinese as colonists but only as indentured laborers—"*instrumentos de trabalho.*" Brazil's foreign minister, Antonio Moreira de Barros, was quite explicit: "Formerly as a planter, and today as minister, I never considered the introduction of Chinese as an aspect of colonization, but only as one of the means to accomplish the transition of labor."[103]

However, the efforts of the Rio de Janeiro merchants and the company they formed to import Chinese contract laborers failed to accomplish anything.[104] In the early 1870s, it was becoming increasingly difficult to obtain emigrant laborers in China. The Chinese government had begun to enforce its prohibition against contract emigration, and by early 1874, the foreign enclaves of Hong Kong and Macau had severely restricted or completely proscribed such emigration. Hence the efforts of the Brazilians were totally frustrated.

As a last resort, the Brazilian government undertook to negotiate a treaty with China in the hope of removing all obstacles to emigration. The fact that both Peru and Spain had failed to obtain Chinese laborers by means of a treaty did not discourage Prime Minister Cansanção de Sinimbú, who was a firm

---

[102] Conrad, "Falta de Braços: The Chinese Coolie Controversy in the Brazilian Empire," 10-11.

[103] Cited in Laërne, *Brazil and Java*, 145.

[104] Laërne, *Brazil and Java*, 145, states that the company succeeded in bringing over 1,000 Chinese to Brazil in 1874, but another source states that the efforts of the company were a complete failure, see *United States Consular Reports*, Vol. III (1889), 216. The silence of China coast newspapers and all other sources known to the writer on any such shipment of Chinese to Brazil in 1874 would seem to favor the latter conclusion. Furthermore Laërne was apparently unaware of earlier shipments of Chinese to Brazil, which could account for him attributing some success to the efforts of the Rio de Janeiro merchants in 1874.

believer in a Chinese solution to Brazil's labor problems.[105] In 1879, Sinimbú had the government publish a report by Salvador de Mendonça, Brazilian consul general at New York, lauding the Chinese as the world's best manual laborers. Entitled *Trabalhadores Asiaticos*, the report was meant to acquaint Brazilians with the history and culture of China so as to prepare them to deal with Chinese labor more intelligently and effectively than in the past.[106] In an address to the Brazilian Senate on October 1, 1879, Sinimbú staunchly defended Chinese labor, stating that "Chinese immigration to this country is a necessity and without it planting on a large scale will find itself very much embarrassed."[107] Sinimbú also obtained the support of Brazil's Agricultural Congress of 1879. Though individual planters, such as Eduardo Pereira de Abreu, roundly condemned the Chinese as a race that was "corrupt by nature," and "physically and morally depraved by opium," and hence could only see their introduction to Brazil as a "calamity," the majority of planters expressed a willingness to import Chinese, but only as a temporary measure during the difficult period of transition from slavery to wage labor.[108]

But the abolitionists were opposed to all plans for Chinese immigration and vehemently attacked the government's policy. Joaquim Nabuco, leading the opposition, told Brazil's Chamber of Deputies on September 3, 1879, that the Chinese were unsuitable for Brazil for a number of reasons:

> Ethnologically, because they would stir up racial conflict and degrade the existing population; economically, because they would not solve the labor problem; morally, because they would introduce into our society that leprosy of vices which infest all cities where the Chinese establish themselves; finally, politically, because instead of bringing about the liberation of labor, they would only prolong the present sad state of things . . . and insure the continuation of slavery.[109]

---

[105] Conrad, "Falta de Braços: The Chinese Coolie Controversy in the Brazilian Empire," 5.

[106] Salvador de Mendonça, *Trabalhadores Asiaticos* (New York, Typographia do "Novo Mundo", 1879).

[107] *Rio News*, October 5, 1879, cited in *Anti-Slavery Reporter*, Vol. XXI, No. 11 (December, 1879), 273-274.

[108] Congresso Agrícola, *Coleção de Documentos* (Rio de Janeiro, 1878), cited in Costa, *De Senzala à Colônia*, 141-142.

[109] Joaquim Nabuco, "Imigração Chinesa" (Discurso de 3 de Setembro de 1879)," in *Obras Completas*, Vol. XI (São Paulo, Instituto Progresso Editorial S.A. 1949), 60.

The Anglo-Brazilian press also declared its firm opposition. The *Rio News* launched a direct attack on Sinimbú's statement that Chinese labor was essential to the existing system of large proprietors. The paper argued,

> If the great landowners cannot sustain themselves without slavery or without government support, then let them fall! If they are too indolent, too weak, to keep up their establishments without servile labour, then they deserve to fall, and with their fall will come the regeneration of Brazil . . . . there is no country where the same class (agricultural proprietors) has had a more complete control of the Government and better opportunities to strengthen itself by legislation than in Brazil. And yet, we are informed today, by the chief of the Imperial Cabinet, who is himself a large landholder, "that we ought to seek resources for the planters", and that without Chinese servile labour they will become "very much embarrassed." Then let them become "embarrassed" and let them suffer the consequences . . . . Moreover if the Government's influence is to be employed in this matter, instead of introducing a retroactive, servile class, let it use all just means to break up these estates and to give substantial encouragement to the European immigrant and the small proprietor.[110]

This went to the heart of the matter, but a government dominated by planters was not about to heed such advice. Despite widespread opposition and the visions of the "yellow peril," invoked by Nabuco, the positivist Miguel Lemos[111] and others, the Brazilian government sent Eduardo Callado as envoy extraordinary and minister plenipotentiary to China to establish treaty relations and arrange for the transportation of Chinese laborers. Callado arrived at Tientsin in 1881 and was cordially received by Li Hung-chang. With the Treaty of 1874 between China and Peru as a basis for negotiation, a treaty of friendship, commerce, and navigation was signed at Tientsin on October 3, 1881.[112] However, the treaty contained no provisions for the

---

[110] *Rio News*, October 15, 1879, as cited in the *Anti-Slavery Reporter*, Vol. XXI, 11 (December, 1879), 275-276.

[111] Miguel Lemos, *Imigração Chinesa Mensagem do Centro Positivista Brasileiro a S. Ex. O Embaixador do Celeste Imperio junto aos Governos de França e Ingleterra* (Rio de Janeiro, 1881), cited in Rodrigues, "Brasil e Extremo Oriente," 68-69.

[112] Wu Paak-shing, "China's Diplomatic Relations with Brazil," *China Quarterly*, Vol. V, No. 4 (Winter, 1940), 859-860.

emigration of Chinese laborers. It merely provided that Chinese and Brazilian nationals were free to travel, reside, and engage in commerce in each other's country.[113]

This was a severe blow to the proponents of Chinese immigration. But Brazilian planters were not to give up easily. In 1883, a group of planters and merchants from Rio de Janeiro formed the Companhia Comércio e Imigração Chineza to negotiate with the Chinese firm of China Merchants' Steam Navigation Company to bring to Brazil over 21,000 Chinese laborers within a period of three years.[114] Tong King-sing, the managing director of the Chinese firm, arrived in Brazil in October 1883 to formally agree to the undertaking. En route to Brazil, he stopped off in London, where a deputation from the Anti-Slavery Society warned him of the "extreme danger of the Chinese becoming mere slaves in the coffee plantations of Brazil," and obtained from him the promise not to enter into a contract for the supply of forced labor.[115] His visit to Brazil seemed to be going well as he inspected plantations and took orders for five-year contracts.[116] But according to his report to the Anti-Slavery Society, when he learned that the large subsidy of $100,000 that was to be paid to his company by the Brazilian government was in fact to be paid by the planters, he became alarmed. He asked the planters how they planned to recoup such an expenditure, and when they replied "out of the labour of the coolies," he abruptly returned to China via London.[117] The Companhia Comércio e Imigração Chineza was dissolved shortly thereafter, and there was no further Chinese immigration to Brazil until following the dissolution of the empire.

The attempts to bring Chinese to Brazil and the debate surrounding them revealed that a nation that prided itself on racial tolerance possessed

---

[113] The Treaty is printed in the *British and Foreign State Papers*, Vol. LXXII (1880-1881), 560-565.

[114] Conrad, "Falta de Braços: The Chinese Coolie Controversy in the Brazilian Empire," 6; "Scheme for Introducing Indentured Chinese Coolies to Brazil," *Anti-Slavery Reporter*, Vol. III, No. 1, Series 4 (May, 1883), 132-133.

[115] "Scheme for Introducing Indentured Chinese Coolies into Brazil," *Anti-Slavery Reporter*, Vol. III, No. 4, Series 4 (September, 1883), 222-223.

[116] Conrad, "Falta de Braços: The Chinese Coolie Controversy in the Brazilian Empire," 7.

[117] "Proposed Scheme for Introducing Chinese into Brazil," *Anti-Slavery Reporter*, Vol. III, No. 7, Series 4 (December, 1883), 300-301; Laërne, *Brazil and Java*, 149.

rather strong racist attitudes in regard to the Chinese. Brazilians of the empire looked upon the Chinese as inferior and sought to exclude them from participation in Brazilian society. Though the Chinese were regarded as more intelligent and more industrious than the Negro, to the Brazilian mind, servility was their proper status, hence they were aptly suited to plantation labor.

Chinese Indentured Laborers in Other Latin American Countries

Attempts were also made in the third quarter of the nineteenth century to introduce Chinese contract laborers to Panama, Costa Rica, Mexico, Venezuela, and El Salvador; but as far as it is known, only the first three had some results for their efforts. That these countries, particularly Mexico and San Salvador,[118] which possessed an abundance of cheap native labor, should seek to import Chinese workers reflects the low estimation which governments and some sectors of society had of the native manual laborer and their high esteem for the Chinese.

It was Emperor Maximilian who first authorized the introduction of Chinese to Mexico. In December 1865, he granted permission to the Portuguese Manuel B. da Cunha Reis to bring "Asiatics" as colonists to his estates in Veracruz.[119] A few years later, the Lower California Company, with a grant from the Mexican government to colonize Baja, California, and parts of the state of Sonora, sought to bring over 10,000 Chinese colonists.[120] There was some effort made to recruit laborers in China as Hubert H. Bancroft in his work, *The New Pacific*, relates how the following advertisement was in circulation on the China coast in 1870:

> China colony for Mexico. All get rich there, have land. Make first year $400: next year $1,000. Have quick more money than mandarins. Plenty good rice and vegetables cheap. Nice ship, no sickness, plenty of room. Clang Wo.[121]

---

[118] Williams to Seward, September 22, 1868 (U.S. Dept. of State, *Foreign Affairs, 1868*, Part II), 929-930.

[119] Scarlett to Foreign Office, December 15, 1865 (BFO 17/873).

[120] Wiekes to Browne, June 7, 1868 (U.S. Dept. of State, *Diplomatic Correspondence, 1868*, Part I), 528-529.

[121] Hubert H. Bancroft, *The New Pacific* (New York: Bancroft Company, 1900), 594.

There is no record of any Chinese arriving at this time either at Veracruz or Sonora and Baja, California.

In 1884, the Companía Mexicana de Navegación del Pacífico entered into a contract with the Mexican government to establish regular steamer service between Hong Kong and Mexico with the stated purpose of fostering emigration and trade.[122] Chinese contract laborers were to be used to build a railroad across the Isthmus of Tehuantepec as well as to develop large tracts of land on the Pacific coast.[123] The Mexican government sanctioned the scheme and agreed to pay the laborers' passage from China.[124] The Chinese ambassador in Washington advised his government against sanctioning such a scheme,[125] and the Tsungli Yamen made it clear that the Chinese government was opposed to any such emigration, but in view of the fact that a ship had already been chartered and loaded with emigrants at Hong Kong, it would consent to the departure of the vessel, but would approve of no further shipments.[126] However, the governor of Hong Kong, on the assumption that the rights of Chinese laborers could not be adequately protected in Mexico, refused to allow the ship to sail, and the scheme fell through.[127]

Around 1890, some Chinese laborers from other Chinese ports were brought to the Tehuantepec Isthmus,[128] but it was not until Mexico and China signed a Treaty of Amity and Commerce in 1893 that a steady flow of Chinese began to arrive in the northwestern section of Mexico, principally the states of Sonora and Baja, California. By 1910, it was estimated that there were between 20,000 and 40,000 Chinese scattered throughout the country. The story of their persecution during the Revolution of 1910 and subsequent expulsion from the country is told by Charles C. Cumberland in an article entitled "The Senora Chinese and the Mexican Revolution."[129]

---

[122] Schneider to Derby, October, 1884 (BFO 50/451).

[123] St. John to Granville, October 25, 1884 (BFO 50/451).

[124] Ibid.

[125] Parkes to Granville, November 11, 1884 (BFO 50/451).

[126] Tsungli Yamen to Parkes, November 24, 1884 (BFO 50/451).

[127] Foreign Office to Schneider, October 21, 1884 (BFO 50/451).

[128] Victor C. Dahl, "Alien Labor on the Gulf Coast of Mexico, 1880-1900," *The Americas* Vol. XVII (1960-61), 31.

[129] Charles C. Cumberland, "The Sonora Chinese and the Mexican Revolution," *Hispanic American Historical Review*, Vol. XL, No. 2 (May, 1960), 191-211.

In 1855, the Venezuelan government signed a contract with a merchant, Antonio L. Guzman, giving him the exclusive right for a period of four years to bring Chinese laborers into the country. As part of the contract, the government agreed to pay Guzman a bounty of $25 per laborer. The Chinese were to be employed mainly in agriculture under eight-year contracts, but as far as it is known, the plan never materialized.[130] The government of San Salvador also gave its sanction to Chinese immigration. In August 1868, it granted to Don Poncio Darnaculleta, a native of Spain, the exclusive privilege of introducing 1,000 Chinese within four years, but again there is no record of any having come.[131]

A thousand Chinese were brought to Panama in 1854 to help build the Panama railway. They had scarcely been in the country a month when the entire body became affected with a "melancholic suicidal tendency," and scores of them took their own lives.[132] Wang-te-Chang, a Chinese interpreter who interviewed the survivors, stated that the men became ill because of the intermittent heat and rain and that though sick, they were flogged and forced to work by overseers of the American company. Many died of disease, and many committed suicide. Only 205 out of the original 1,000 survived, and they sailed for the plantations of Jamaica in November 1854.[133]

The government of Costa Rica sought to promote Chinese immigration in 1866 by agreeing to pay native contractors $15 for every Chinese contract laborer brought into the country. The United States minister in San José strongly protested the scheme, and seemingly, none came.[134] However, a German company succeeded in introducing 650 Chinese in 1873. About

---

[130] "Landverhuizing de Chinezen," Tijdschrift voor Neerlandsche Indie," Batavia (1856), 110-113.

[131] Williams to Seward, September 22, 1868, Inclosure (U.S. Dept. of State, *Foreign Affairs*, 1868, Part II), 930.

[132] F.N. Otis, *Illustrated History of the Panama Railroad* (New York, Harper and Brothers, 1862), 35-36; Ira E. Bennett, *History of the Panama Canal* (Washington, D.C., Historical Publishing Company, 1915), 90; Tracy Robinson, *Panama: A Personal Record of Forty-six Years, 1861-1907* (New York, Star and Herald Company, 1907), 15; "Chinese Emigration," *Chambers Journal*, Vol. XXXVI, No. 392 (July 6, 1861), 11.

[133] "Copy of Journal of the Chinese Interpreter, Wang-te-Chang, Reporting State of Chinese Immigrants at Panama," (BPP, *Emigration*, Vol. XII, 1855), 149-152.

[134] Menyers to Foreign Office, February 24, 1873 (BFO 17/882).

500 were employed by the Railway Company, and the remainder went to coffee plantations.[135] In 1874, a correspondent of the *Panama Star and Herald* reported an unfortunate incident involving the Chinese workers on the railway company. Seemingly, the Chinese in one of the camps of Messrs. Myers, Douglas and Company, contractors for a large section of the railroad, refused to go to work in a dense fog, and the French overseer began lashing them with his horsewhip and invited some native peons to assist him in subduing them. This led to a major disturbance, and the contractor petitioned the authorities for troops to quell the rebellion. A force of 35 soldiers were dispatched to the camp. On the way, they had too much to drink, and arriving at the camp after midnight, they entered the huts of the sleeping Chinese and began shooting the defenseless men. They killed five and wounded nine others before someone ordered them to stop firing. The captain of the troops was subsequently court-martialled.[136]

The forgoing incident was yet another illustration of the barbarous treatment meted out to the Chinese at the hands of their employers throughout Latin America. In country after country, exploitation and oppression was their lot. Though written contracts spelled out the mutual obligations of employer and worker, the rights of the Chinese and their pleas for justice were generally ignored by societies that were only concerned with extracting from them the maximum amount of work.

---

[135] "Cold-Blooded Murder of Chinese Coolies," *Anti-Slavery Reporter*, Vol. XIX, No. 2 (April 1, 1874), 41-42.

CHAPTER VIII

WORLD OPINION AND THE TERMINATION OF THE "COOLIE TRADE"

Public opinion is stronger than the legislature and nearly as strong as the Ten Commandments.
—Charles Dudley Warner, *My Summer in a Garden* (1870)

It is certainly time that civilized governments expostulate with the authorities of these petty states who derive an income from a traffic in flesh and blood which is even more abominable than the African slave trade, inasmuch as it covers up cruelty in the garb of philanthrophy.
—Editorial, *New York Times* (October 10, 1870)

The "Coolie Trade" Condemned

In the decade from 1850 to 1859, newspapers along the China coast from Hong Kong to Shanghai carried stories of thirty-three mutinies on vessels transporting Chinese emigrants to foreign countries.[1] These stories, often detailing the bloody battles between passengers and crew from the eyewitness accounts of survivors, caused the immigration to be regarded as a "new slavery." The European and American press relayed the news of these tragic happenings to the Western world, and as the nature of this new immigration movement was unfolded in consular reports and public inquiries into the tragedies at sea, editors, as well as people in and out of government, clamored for an end to what some called "the slave trade of the nineteenth century."[2]

The *New York Daily Times* and the *Times* of London simultaneously—on April 21, 1860—called for immediate and energetic action to suppress the

---

[1] See table 17 for list of mutinies.
[2] See the *New York Times*, July 1, 1866.

traffic in Chinese laborers. The former, in an editorial entitled "The American Coolie Trade," directed its appeal to Congress:

> American merchants and shipmasters have been gradually drawn into the most atrocious practices in connection with the coolie trade on the coasts of the Chinese empire. The traditional horrors of the African middle passage have been reenacted, are indeed continually reenacting, under the American flag in Chinese ports and on the Indian seas . . . It is a question of national honor as well as of common humanity.

The previous Monday, April 16, Mr. Elliot of Massachusetts laid a report on the coolie trade before the House of Representatives with the following resolution: "Resolved that the Committee on Commerce be directed to inquire into the expediency of prohibiting by law all American vessels from engaging in the coolie trade or from transporting apprentices so called to the West Indies or other parts of the world."[3] The editorial urged the swift passage of the proposed law and recommended that the United States naval forces in the China sea should be empowered to enforce it if necessary. The *Times* of London suggested that the Earl of Elgin, Her Majesty's high commissioner and plenipotentiary in China, ought to have been instructed "to make suppression of this infamous commerce one of the imperative objects of his mission,"[4] and chastised the humanitarians:

> Where is the Anti-Slavery society and why are its energies so torpid? . . . The atrocities of the Middle Passage which called into action the Wilberforces and the Clarksons of the last generation were not so full proved and were certainly not more harrowing in their circumstances, than are the iniquities perpetrated upon those wretched Chinese who are decoyed from their homes and their families and trepanned on board slavers lying ready for their reception in the Canton River and in the creeks and harbors on the China coast and who are scourged, tortured, bound and manacled, and are carried in their floating penthouse from the East to the West, to linger in a wasting slavery never to return.

---

[3]   *New York Daily Times*, April 17, 1860.

[4]   Lord Elgin was sent to China in 1857 to secure a revision of existing treaties, and to open the Yantse River by negotiation or by force. See W. C. Costin, *Great Britain and China, 1833-1860* (Oxford, Clarendon Press, 1968), Chap. VI.

This was somewhat unfair to the Anti-Slavery Society, for though grown tired and sluggish from success in its long fight to suppress the African slave trade, it had, throughout the 1850s, denounced the abuses of Chinese emigration in the *Anti-Slavery Reporter*, documenting its accusations; and in July of 1859, it had memorialized the Duke of Newcastle, the colonial secretary, requesting the British government to take corrective action.[5]

Nor was the Anti-Slavery Society the first to denounce the traffic and to call for reform. As early as March 1851, the *Friend of China*, published in Hong Kong, issued the warning: "the cause of humanity demands some attention to the circumstances attendant on the transport of coolies from China to the West Coast of South America." The following March, after disclosing abuses that, in the paper's opinion, were directly responsible for several mutinies on board emigrant vessels, it concluded thus: "We think we are justified in designating this Coolee [sic] engagement as synonymous with slavery."[6]

Dr. John Bowring, the superintendent of British trade on the China coast, complained to the Foreign Office in August 1852: "Such horrors, miseries and atrocities of all sorts, such frightful mortality, such acts of piracy and murder have been associated with the transfer of coolies to foreign regions that common humanity forbids the looking with indifference on what is taking place."[7] The Chinese authorities of Kwangtung Province issued a string of proclamations in late 1852, in 1856, and in 1859, decreeing death to the "swindling vagabonds who inveigle the lawful subjects of the Emperor to be slaves of a foreign country."[8] And Karl Marx, then pursuing his studies in the British Museum, heard the distant cry of the oppressed and wrote in his column of April 10, 1857, in the *New York Daily Tribune*, "How silent is the press of England upon the outrageous violations of the treaty daily practiced by foreigners living in China under British protection . . . . we hear nothing of the wrong inflicted 'even unto death' upon misguided and bonded emigrants sold to worse than slavery on the coast of Peru and into Cuban bondage."[9]

---

[5]   See the *Anti-Slavery Reporter*, Vol. III, No. 2 (Feb. 1855), 39-41; Vol. IV, No. 5 (May, 1856), 113.

[6]   *The Friend of China*, March 24, 1852. See also *Overland Friend of China*, March 30, 1852.

[7]   Bowring to Malmesbury, August 3, 1852 (BPP, ASS, *China*, Vol. III), 13-14.

[8]   See the *China Mail*, January 13, 1853; January 24, 1856.

[9]   See also Dona Torr, *Marx on China, 1853-1860: Articles from the New York Daily Tribune* (London, Lawrence and Wishart, 1951), 39.

The international outcry of outraged public opinion, while failing to stop the traffic in Chinese laborers, forced the interested parties and their governments to take corrective action. The government of Macau enacted legislation in 1853, 1855, and in 1856 to eliminate abuses.[10] The British government, concluding that regulation was an absolute necessity, commanded British ships carrying Chinese emigrants to put into Hong Kong for inspection.[11] Dr. Peter Parker, the minister plenipotentiary of the United States in China, publicly denounced the "coolie trade" in January 1856.[12] The president of the Republic of Peru, in the "general interest of humanity and of Peruvian commerce," issued decrees in 1853 and 1854 designed to ameliorate abuses in Chinese immigration, and in March 1856, he prohibited it entirely.[13] The Spanish government issued royal decrees in 1854 and 1860, setting forth minute instructions for the introduction of Chinese to Cuba.[14] Besides governmental action, the various shipping companies drew up their own regulations with detailed instructions for captains and crews. Some even solicited testimony from Chinese in South America as to their satisfaction with their contract and gave these statements wide publicity up and down the China coast.[15]

These actions, declarations of good intent, and propaganda calmed the storms of protest at least temporarily; and Chinese immigration to Latin America, having made some adjustments, settled into a routine that continued for another fifteen years. Nonetheless, rightly or wrongly, the movement had come to be characterized as another slave trade; and from time to time, enough irregularities came to light, and enough tragedies occurred to retain this judgment in the popular mind.

---

[10] *O Boletim*, November 10, 1855; June 7, 1856. See also Manuel de Castro Sampaio, *Os Chins de Macau* (Hong Kong, Typographia de Noronha e Filhos, 1867), 136-139.

[11] This legislation, known as the "Chinese Passenger Act" was passed by Parliament in 1855. For the full text of the Act see *British and Foreign State Papers*, Consular Reports, 1855, 631-636.

[12] Edward V. Gulick, *Peter Parker and the Opening of China* (Cambridge, Massachusetts, Harvard University Press, 1973), 184.

[13] Stewart, *Chinese Bondage in Peru*, 21-22; *The Friend of China*, May 14, 1856; "Coolie Trade" (U.S. Congress, House, Report No. 443, 1 Sess., 36 Cong.), 12.

[14] For a full text of the decree see Appendix I.

[15] *The Friend of China*, July 4, 1857.

The Attitude of Western Governments

Chinese immigration to the West was contemporaneous with a vast movement of Europeans to the Americas that was considered beneficial both to the sending and receiving nations. Europe was being relieved of its excess population, and the New World needed people to open up and develop its territories. In this ideal situation, the laissez-faire doctrine that emigration was a natural right of the individual in which governments should not interfere was accepted without question. So in the Western world at the middle of the nineteenth century, individuals and families were making their own choices about where to live and were moving across continents and oceans.

To Western governments and to Westerners in general, Chinese emigration was part of the same phenomenon. The Chinese too had the right to emigrate to better their condition in life, and that the Chinese government should prohibit its people from emigrating, particularly when the country was overpopulated and under a constant threat of famine, was considered oppressive and uncivilized. Hence, Western governments were sympathetic to and supportive of emigration from China, and while making some gestures toward curbing abuses, they sought to pressure the Chinese government into sanctioning the emigration of its citizens.

The policy of the British government was typical. Fully aware of the opposition of the Chinese government to its subjects going overseas and of the abuses connected with clandestine emigration,[16] the British government felt nonetheless that the emigration of Chinese under contract, when properly conducted, could be very beneficial both to the emigrants themselves and to the countries to which they immigrated.[17] This attitude, which was more or less adopted by other Western nations, with the exception of the United States of America, was dictated by three major considerations: (1) a belief that man possessed an inherent right to emigrate, (2) a determined public opinion in Great Britain against all forms of slavery and servitude,[18] and (3)

---

[16]   Malmesbury to Bowring, July 21, 1852 (BPP, ASS, *China*, Vol. III), 13.

[17]   Russell to Cowley, July 11, 1860 (Ibid., Vol. IV), 242-243. See also Costin, *Great Britain and China*, 175-176.

[18]   Traditional slave-holding societies such as Spain, Portugal, Brazil and Peru, did not have to contend with strong anti-slavery sentiments within their own domain and were therefore not overly concerned with the possibility of the Chinese becoming substitute slaves. The more liberal minded were merely concerned with preventing cruel and inhuman treatment of the Chinese, as well as of the slaves.

a persistent demand for cheap labor in the absence of slaves, particularly in the sugar colonies. Indentured Chinese labor resulted from an attempt to reconcile the last two considerations.[19]

Initially, the Chinese law prohibiting emigration posed a problem as the British government was bound by treaty to uphold the laws of the Chinese Empire. So when Lord Stanley, England's colonial secretary, sanctioned the introduction of Chinese laborers to the West Indies in 1843, he stipulated that for "political causes," the embarkation of Chinese be limited to British possessions in Southeast Asia.[20] However, when Spain and Peru commenced recruiting laborers on the China coast in the late 1840s, Britain followed their lead by sending an official government agent to China to supervise the recruitment of laborers for the British West Indies. The Foreign Office justified this apparent violation of treaty obligations by arguing that since emigration from China was openly taking place, the British government was not obliged to recognize a law that the Chinese government did not enforce.[21]

The British agent James T. White, who had been recruiting laborers in India for the West Indies, was therefore directed to recruit laborers on the coast of China until the Chinese decided to enforce their own laws, whereupon his operations were to be confined to Hong Kong, where Her Majesty's government felt it had the strict right to conduct emigration.[22] In a circular to British consuls on the China coast, John Bowring, British superintendent of trade in China, spelled out British strategy:

> Should the Chinese object or offer impediments to the emigration of Chinese subjects to British colonies, you are required to act in strict conformity with Treaty and not directly or indirectly to aid or abet the shipment of Chinese emigrants to the colonies of Great Britain. But if Chinese subjects, of their own free will, should prefer to risk the penalty attached to the transgression of the law, and to embark without the aid of the Consul or of the Government Agent, for any place within Her Majesty's domains, you are not bound to prevent or even to be ostensibly

---

[19]   See Chapter I.
[20]   Hope to Malcolm, September 4, 1843 (BPP, Vol. 35, 1844), 556.
[21]   Foreign Office to Bowring, October 20, 1852 (BFO 17/186).
[22]   Ibid.

cognizant of such acts; for it is the duty of the Chinese government to enforce its own laws.[23]

White's recruiting efforts were not very successful.[24] Chinese emigration continued to be plagued with irregularities, and the British government became convinced that only through the cooperation of the Chinese authorities could abuses be eliminated.[25] When the Allied Forces of Britain and France occupied Canton in 1858, the local Chinese authorities were persuaded to cooperate in regulating emigration.[26] But, while the provincial government of Kwangtung province was legalizing emigration, Imperial Commissioner Ho, reflecting the sentiments of the imperial court at Peking, was reiterating the old absolute prohibition against Chinese subjects going overseas.[27] The British government had instructed Lord Elgin, whom it had entrusted with the military expedition against Peking in 1860, to press for imperial approval of emigration.[28] Fearful that the Kwangtung authorities might take their cue from Peking and withdraw their cooperation,[29] Elgin, with the concurrence of Baron Gros,[30] the commander of the French army, succeeded in inserting into the Convention of Peace between England and China, signed at Peking on October 24, 1860, the following article:

> As soon as the ratifications of the Treaty of one thousand eight hundred and fifty-eight shall have been exchanged, His Imperial Majesty, the Emperor of China, will, by decree, command the high authorities of every province to proclaim throughout their jurisdiction, that Chinese, in choosing to take service in British Colonies or other ports beyond the sea, are at perfect liberty to enter into engagements with British subjects for that purpose, and to ship themselves and their families on board any

---

23 Bowring to Her Majesty's Consuls in China, December 16, 1852 (BPP, ASS, *China*, Vol. III), 43.

24 Clementi, *The Chinese in British Guiana*, 43.

25 Russell to Cowley, July 11, 1860 (BPP, ASS, *China*, Vol. IV), 242-243.

26 See Chapter III.

27 Bruce to Russell, February 26, 1860 (BFO 881/894).

28 Clarendon to Elgin, April 20, 1857 (BPP, ASS, *China*, Vol. XXXIII), 425.

29 Bruce to Russell, February 26, 1860 (BFO 881/894).

30 Elgin to Russell, October 25, 1860 (BFO 17/331); Elgin to Gross, October 20, 1860 (BFO 881/933).

British vessels at the open ports of China; also that the high authorities aforesaid shall, in concert with Her Britanic Majesty's Representative in China, frame such regulations for the protection of Chinese emigrating as above as the circumstances of the different open ports may demand.[31]

A similar article was inserted into the Convention of Peace between China and France, signed on October 25, 1860.[32]

Chinese and British representatives made an abortive attempt to draw up emigration regulations in the summer of 1861.[33] There the matter rested until 1865 when the Tsungli Yamen, moved by reports of continued kidnapping along China's southern coast,[34] instructed the governor-general of Kwangtung, where emigration was being legally conducted since 1859, to draw up rules governing the emigration of laborers. He promptly complied, and with a few modifications his proposals were embodied in twenty-two articles of a "Convention to Regulate the Engagement of Chinese Emigrants by British and French subjects."[35] The convention was signed on March 5, 1866, by Prince Kung on behalf of China, and by Sir Rutherford Alcock and Henry de Bellonnet, the British and French ministers at Peking.

It would seem that the West had finally obtained a long-sought-after objective—the legalization of Chinese emigration. But the British and French governments were unhappy with some provisions of the convention and refused to ratify it. The British West India Committee strongly objected to Article VIII, Section 2, which guaranteed the emigrant a free return passage to China at the end of his indenture. The committee argued that the financial burden of providing a free return passage rendered the cost of Chinese labor unacceptably high, as well as possibly stirring up discontent among the Chinese already in the West Indies.[36] French merchants involved in the transportation of Chinese laborers to Cuba and Peru protested no less strongly to the French government the limitation of indenture to a

---

[31] Mayers, *Treaties Between the Empire of China and Foreign Powers*, 9 (see Article V).

[32] Ibid., 74 (see Article IX).

[33] Clementi, *The Chinese in British Guiana*, 203.

[34] Campbell, *Chinese Coolie Emigration*, 140.

[35] Clementi, *The Chinese in British Guiana*, 204-206. The full text of the Convention may be found in Appendix II.

[36] Campbell, *Chinese Coolie Emigration*, 141-142.

maximum of five years instead of the normal eight-year term, a change that would undoubtedly hurt their carrying trade.[37] After a protracted correspondence between London and Paris,[38] the two governments finally agreed on the modifications that they would demand of Peking,[39] and called upon all Western nations with interests in China for diplomatic support.[40] Bismarck instructed the Prussian envoy in China to back the Anglo-French position.[41] The Dutch and Portuguese governments advised their representatives to do likewise.[42] The Spanish representative was directed to withhold approval of any changes in the convention until the Spanish government sanctioned them.[43] The United States bluntly stated that its sympathies lay with China, and made it clear that it would gladly cooperate with any measure to eliminate the traffic in Chinese contract laborers altogether.[44]

The Chinese government successfully resisted all pressure to accede to any alterations. Prince Kung explained that in the long interval between the signing of the convention in Peking in March 1866 and the request for its revision in April 1868, the emperor had approved the regulations, and they had been promulgated throughout China as the law of the land, and hence could not be changed.[45] Rutherford Alcock, who had urged the ratification of the convention, advised the Foreign Office that any change in the convention would be looked upon by the Chinese as compromising the dignity of the emperor and that the Tsungli Yamen was not strong enough to withstand the loss of prestige in the eyes of other bodies of state

---

[37]   Ibid., 143.

[38]   Murdoch to Rogers, December 22, 1870 (BFO 17/879).

[39]   The two governments agreed to accept the limited five year contract but refused to pay the back passage. See Campbell, *Chinese Coolie Emigration*, 144-145.

[40]   Stanley to Alcock, December 6, 1867 (BFO 17/875).

[41]   Ibid.

[42]   Campbell, *Chinese Coolie Emigration*, 145.

[43]   Ibid.

[44]   Ford to Stanley, January 20, 1868, cited in Ibid. The reactions of Russia, Denmark, Norway, and Sweden are not recorded, though the continued use of their flags in the carrying trade would indicate that they were not opposed or were indifferent to the Anglo-French position.

[45]   Kung to Alcock, March 13, 1869 (BFO 17/877).

should the Allies insist upon modifications.[46] The matter was therefore quietly dropped.

Of the Western nations, the United States was alone in its opposition to the emigration of Chinese contract laborers. Other Western governments passed laws and regulations to stamp out abuses, but the United States Congress, in February 1862, prohibited American citizens and American ships from any participation whatsoever in the traffic.[47] Throughout the 1850s, while British representatives in China generally counseled the control of Chinese emigration through legislation,[48] American diplomats for the most part urged its complete prohibition.[49]

Humphrey Marshall was the first United States commissioner to China to take notice of the "coolie trade." He arrived in China in January 1853 and immediately requested detailed information on emigration from United States consuls on the China coast.[50] Being a Southerner, he regarded the importation of Chinese laborers into the Caribbean as a possible threat to the interests of Southern planters. He even speculated on the possibility of the British using the Chinese to colonize the Amazon Basin.[51] He therefore advised Washington to prohibit American vessels from carrying Chinese to Latin America.[52]

Peter Parker, who became United States commissioner to China in 1855, offered Washington the same advice as Marshall, but for humanitarian, rather than economic or political reasons. As chargé to the American Legation at Canton, Parker came in direct contact in the early 1850s with the cruelties and deceptions of contract emigration and quickly became a crusader for its

---

[46] Alcock to the Foreign Office, June 8, 1868 (BFO 17/875); see also Murdock to Rogers, December 22, 1870 (BFO 17/879).

[47] See Appendix III for the full text of the Act of Congress.

[48] After 1870 British representatives in China began to urge the British government to abandon contract emigration in favor of completely voluntary emigration. See Wade to Granville, July 26, 1873 (BFO 17/883).

[49] Griffin, *Clippers and Consuls*, 194-199.

[50] Marshall to Everett, March 8, 1853 (U.S. Congress, House, Ex. Doc. 105, 1 Sess., 34 Cong.), 175-178.

[51] Ibid., 176.

[52] Ibid., 177; see also Te-kong Tong, *United States Diplomacy in China, 1844-1860* (Seattle, University of Washington Press, 1964), 118.

abolition.[53] While in Washington in the spring of 1855, he was advised by the secretary of state to denounce the "coolie trade" at "an opportune time."[54] On his return to China, his first official act was to issue in January 1856 a Public Notification, calling upon all Americans on the China coast to desist from contract emigration, classifying it as an "irregular and immoral traffic" that was disruptive of commerce and was jeopardizing Sino-American relations. He warned those who dared to persist in the trade that they would forfeit the protection of the United States government and be liable to heavy penalties, and he instructed United States consuls at the various Chinese ports to give copies of the Notification to the local Chinese authorities.[55]

Parker's public denunciation bore some fruit. It encouraged Chinese officials to condemn the traffic[56] and caused the shipping firm of Sampson and Tappan of Boston to cancel their contract with the Brazilian government to transport Chinese laborers to Rio de Janeiro.[57] But many Americans continued in the traffic, claiming that neither Parker nor any other American official had the legal authority to stop them.[58] Although hampered by the absence of effective legislation, Parker tried in every way to arouse public opinion against the trade and continued to lobby against it when he returned to Washington in 1857.[59]

William B. Reed, Parker's successor, also drew the attention of the United States government to the iniquities of contract emigration. Reed, like Parker, was confronted with tragedies on United States vessels carrying Chinese contract laborers and informed Washington that "as a matter of humanity and policy, I deem it my duty to condemn this traffic, and to beg the early attention of government to its repression, so far at least as it is conducted in American vessels."[60]

---

[53]   Gulick, *Peter Parker and the Opening of China*, 173-174.

[54]   Parker to Sampson and Tappan, September 8, 1856 (U.S. Congress, House, Report No. 443, 1 Sess., 36 Cong.), 7.

[55]   See Appendix III for the full text of the "Notification."

[56]   Pek-kwei, the Governor of the Province of Kwangtung issued a proclamation denouncing the kidnapping of 'emigrants' in April, 1856, see Chapter III.

[57]   Pinheiro, *Importação de Trabalhadores Chins*, 147-149; *Boston Board of Trade 1857: Third Annual Report*, 15-18.

[58]   See Chapter III.

[59]   Gulick, *Peter Parker and the Opening of China*, 184, 199.

[60]   "Coolie Trade: Report," April 16, 1860 (U.S. Congress, House, Report No. 443, I Sess., 36 Cong.), 16.

He urged the seizure of American ships engaged in the trade and ordered United States consuls to do everything in their power to arrest it, setting forth the opinion that the contract for labor under which the Chinese emigrant was shipped was in violation of the laws of the United States.[61] However, he had some doubts about his interpretation of the law, for in a letter to the State Department of April 10, 1858, he earnestly expressed the hope that Congress would act to "give the representatives of the United States here some surer weapons of prevention than notifications and protests."[62]

American officials in China were in a rather delicate position. They had become the chief protagonists for the abolition of the "coolie trade" when at the same time, American vessels had become major carriers in the trade. In 1859, United States Attorney General, J. S. Black, informed Secretary of State Lewis Cass that, contrary to the contention of Commissioner Reed, existing United States laws could not be applied to the "coolie trade," and that only Congress could provide legislation to put a stop to American involvement in the traffic.[63] Although Congress had been informed of the abuses in Chinese emigration since 1855 and was aware of the repeated pleas of American representatives in China for legislation, it did not act until February 1862.[64]

Though Congress outlawed the "coolie trade," this did not preclude America's own self-interest in Chinese laborers. During the 1860s, laborers were urgently needed to complete the Pacific railroad, and the Burlingame Treaty with China in 1868 was essentially an emigration treaty guaranteeing a continuing flow of Chinese laborers to American shores.[65] Article V of the treaty stipulated that

> The United States of America and the Emperor of China, cordially recognise the inherent and inalienable right of man to change his home and ellegiance (sic), and also the mutual advantage of the free migration and emigration of their citizens and subjects respectively from one country to the other for the purpose of curiosity, of trade, or as permanent residents.[66]

---

[61] Ibid., 23.

[62] Ibid., 24.

[63] Black to Cass, March 11, 1859 (Ibid.), 23.

[64] U.S. Congress, *The Congressional Globe*, Vol. XXXII:I (1861-1862), 350, 555, 581, 849, 911.

[65] Dennett, *Americans in Eastern Asia*, 539.

[66] Mayers, *Treaties Between the Empire of China and Foreign Powers*, 94.

In the 1880s, the United States government would reverse itself and renege on its commitment of an open door to Chinese emigrants. Meanwhile, it welcomed free and voluntary emigration and vehemently opposed contract emigration in any form.

A Series of Atrocities

The decision of the United States Congress to prohibit Americans from participating in the "coolie trade" did not immediately affect the flow of Chinese contract laborers to the New World. No other country followed the United States' lead, and the American share of the carrying trade merely passed to other hands. Nonetheless, the ruling constituted a major step in the battle to end the traffic. Its greatest contribution would seem to have been in the realm of public opinion. As the battle to eliminate the African slave trade had shown, an aroused public opinion was a most effective weapon in combating an evil that was spread across continents and involved many nations, defying efficacious legal control or policing. The American government appeared to understand this, and in January 1867, both Houses of Congress unanimously passed a resolution that voiced in measured tones the moral indignation of the American people:

> Whereas the traffic in laborers, transported from China and other eastern countries, known as the coolie trade, is odious to the people of the United States, as inhuman and immoral; and whereas it is abhorrent to the spirit of modern international law and policy, which have substantially extirpated the African slave trade, to permit the establishment in its place of a mode of enslaving men differing from the former in little else than the employment of fraud instead of force to make its victims captive, be it therefore resolved, that it is the duty of this government to give effect to the moral sentiment of the nation, through all its agencies, for the purpose of preventing the further introduction of coolies into this hemisphere, or the adjacent islands.[67]

The moral force of public denouncements diminish rapidly unless stoked by action, and in this regard, the "coolie trade" was its own worst enemy as from the late 1860s onward, one atrocity after another shocked and shaped world opinion.

---

[67]   U.S. Congress, Senate, Ex. Doc. 80, II Sess., 40 Cong., 5.

In 1866, a cargo of fireworks in the hold of the Italian emigrant vessel *Napoleon Canevaro* exploded when the Chinese passengers, two days out from Macau, mutinied and set fire to the ship. All of the 662 emigrants on board were killed, the crew having escaped in the ship's boats.[68] The following year, Chinese pirates seized a party of Annamite officials and their entourage carrying gifts of tribute to the emperor of China. They were taken to Macau where they were placed in barracoons and subjected to torture to force them to enter contracts to go as laborers to Peru. Their presence and plight were accidentally discovered by some Jesuit priests at Macau, who succeeded in freeing them, and they were returned to Annam by way of Hong Kong. However, the Jesuits, in exposing the Annamite scandal incurred the wrath of emigration brokers and were subsequently expelled from the colony—an action that caused some Macaese to have second thoughts about the legitimacy of the emigration traffic.[69]

In 1868, the *Cayalti*, a Peruvian vessel flying the United States flag, drifted into the Japanese harbor of Hakadote with her decks and cabins stained with blood. An unknown number of Chinese emigrants and all the crew except the skipper had died in a bloody mutiny.[70] In another incident, mutinous emigrants set fire to the Salvadorian vessel *Uncovah* off the coast of Sumatra en route to Peru in 1870. An estimated 124 passengers died in the flames. Others were rescued by a passing ship.[71]

Also in 1870, there occurred a mutiny on board the French vessel *Nouvelle Penelope*, the sequel to which, perhaps more than any other event, brought the entire traffic in Chinese laborers under public scrutiny. On October 1, the *Nouvelle Penelope* left Macau with 310 Chinese laborers for Callao. Three days out from port, the passengers mutinied, killing the captain and all of the crew except five, who were spared so as to help navigate the ship back to China, where the emigrants went ashore. The spared members of the crew succeeded

---

[68] See Chapter V.

[69] Bernardino de Sena Fernandes, *Um Appello ao Publico Imparcial* (Macau, Impressa na Typographia Popular, 1869), 24-25; Montalto de Jesus, *Historic Macao*, 334-335; Mesnier, "A Reply to 'Macao and Its Slave Trade'," 120; *O Echo do Povo* (Hong Kong), May 14, 1867; McDonnell to the Duke of Buckingham, July 24, 1867 (BFO 17/874); Smale to Foster, August 17, 1870 (BFO 17/878).

[70] See the letter of Seward to Valkenburg, February 19, 1869, printed in the *China Mail*, December 15, 1871; also "Macao and Its Slave Trade," *China Review*, Vol. 2, No. 1 (July, 1873), 18.

[71] "Macao and Its Slave Trade," 18.

in reaching Canton, where they reported what happened. The French consul, M. Darby, on learning of the tragedy, demanded swift punishment for the mutineers. More than 70 of the passengers of the *Nouvelle Penelope* were apprehended in Macau attempting to embark on other emigrant vessels. Interrogations revealed that 50 of the 310 emigrants on board took an active part in the mutiny, and of these, 31 were adjudged to have participated in the slaying of the crew.[72] The Chinese authorities, after a summary trial at Canton, beheaded 15 of the accused in that city and another 15 in Macau as a lesson to all would-be mutineers.[73] However, the supposed leader of the mutiny, Kwok-Asing, escaped to Hong Kong, where he sought asylum, but Chinese officials demanded his extradition. After a sensational hearing before the Supreme Court of the colony, in which all the frightful horrors of the "coolie trade" were revealed, Chief Justice Smale ruled that the *Nouvelle Penelope* was engaged in a slave trade, and that in such circumstances, mutiny was justified. He therefore refused extradition and ordered the accused released.[74] Although the judge's decision was subsequently revoked by the Privy Council,[75] the evidence produced at the trial shocked public sensitivity.

Because of these frightful tragedies[76] and other highly published incidents such as the case of the *Maria Luz*, discussed in chapter VI, criticism of the "coolie trade" in the early 1870s became loud and bitter, with the Portuguese colony of Macau receiving almost all of the blame. Following the trial of Kwok-Asing the *New York Times* editorialized thus:

> It is high time that a traffic embodying all the worst features of the African slave trade was put a stop to. The contemptible little Portuguese colony which maintains its existence upon the profits derived from the accursed system has long been the disgrace of civilization in the Far East of Asia.[77]

---

[72]   A detailed account of the tragedy and subsequent events is given in José da Silva, *As Fadas de Julho ou A Revolta Fantasiada* (Macao, Typographia de J. da Silva, 1871), VII-XV. See also Robertson to Wade, November 17, 1870 (BPP, ASS, *China*, Vol. IV), 253-255.

[73]   *The Daily Press* (Hong Kong), February 10, 1871.

[74]   The full text of the judges decision was published in *The Daily Press* (Hong Kong), April 5, 1871. It is also contained in the U.S. Dept. of State, *Foreign Relations* (1871), 195-207.

[75]   Norton Kyshe, *The History of the Laws and Courts of Hong Kong*, II, 186-187.

[76]   Those given are but a partial listing. See Table 17 for other tragedies.

[77]   *New York Times*, January 16, 1871.

Sir C. Wingfield called the attention of the British House of Commons and of the British Public to the "iniquitous Chinese coolie trade" on May 23, 1873. In a lengthy speech that was intended "to shame the Government which is the author of the iniquities I shall expose," Wingfield outlined the character of the traffic in Chinese laborers referring to many of the atrocities mentioned above and urged his government to use every legitimate means to bring the traffic to an end.[78] On a number of occasions, Her Majesty's government remonstrated with the Portuguese government in Lisbon on the question of abuses in emigration from Macau, and each time some attempt was made to eliminate them, but to little avail.[79]

The most persistent public criticism of the "coolie trade" came from the China coast newspapers *China Mail, Daily Press,* and *Friend of China* and the Portuguese newspaper *O Echo do Povo,* all of which were published in Hong Kong, and the *North China Herald,* published in Shanghai. These papers, though sometimes with excessive zeal, and not always from altruistic motives,[80] kept the world informed of the true nature of Chinese contract emigration and helped create an atmosphere in which governments most directly involved in the traffic were morally impelled to take some decisive action.

The Final Resolution[81]

Prior to the 1860s, the Chinese government turned a deaf ear to the many promptings both from its own officials and from Western diplomats to intervene in the traffic in laborers on its southern shores. In 1860, with British and French armies occupying Peking, Emperor Hsien Feng hastily signed a peace convention that guaranteed to Chinese citizens the freedom to emigrate. Subsequently, Prince Kung advised officials of the maritime provinces of this

---

[78] *Hansard's Parliamentary Debates,* Vol. CCXVI (1873), 375-395. The full text of the speech is printed in the *Anti-Slavery Reporter,* Vol. XVIII, No. 16 (July 1, 1873), 165-1753.

[79] Murray to the Marquis de Sá, May 27, 1869 (BPP, ASS, *China,* Vol. IV), 252; Murray to the Marquis d'Avila, February 15, 1871 (Ibid.), 258; Doria to the Marquis d'Avila, August 8, 1871 (Ibid.), 279-280.

[80] There was a bitter commercial rivalry between Hong Kong and Macau.

[81] China's role in bringing an end to the "coolie trade" is discussed at some length in Irick, "Ch'ing Policy Toward the Coolie Trade, 1847-1878," and much of what follows is dependent on this work.

change in imperial policy and instructed them to arrange for emigration on the basis of the regulations then in force in Canton.[82]

But the continued occurrence of kidnappings by crimps to supply emigrant vessels moved the Tsungli Yamen to negotiate the Emigration Convention of 1866,[83] which sought to stop the illegal traffic by putting emigration under more direct official control. The provisions of the convention not only sought to eliminate abuses in the recruitment of emigrants, but also sought to protect them during their stay aboard,[84] and to this end, the Chinese government indicated its intention to send Chinese officials from time to time to investigate the working conditions of its laborers in other countries.[85]

The greatest problem confronting the Chinese government in its attempt to regulate emigration was what to do about the growing traffic in laborers at the Portuguese-controlled enclave of Macau. Back in October 1861, after the Allied forces had withdrawn from Canton, local Chinese officials, under instructions from the Tsungli Yamen, limited the recruitment of emigrants to agents of treaty powers.[86] This excluded Cuba and Peru, the two largest importers of Chinese laborers, who then turned to Macau as the only major source of contract laborers open to them. In an addendum to the Emigration Convention of 1866, it was stipulated that emigration was restricted to the treaty ports,[87] and in correspondence with British and American representatives in China, Prince Kung made it clear that his government, by limiting emigration to the treaty ports, intended to prohibit emigration from Macau, where there were no Chinese officials to guarantee adherence to the convention.[88] This was the first official indication of China's determination to do something about the flow of emigrants from the Portuguese colony.

The question of direct Chinese intervention in Macau was a ticklish one. Portugal claimed sovereignty over the peninsula, and unilateral action by the Chinese government could trigger a war, something China could ill afford, particularly since it was not at all clear how the other Western powers

---

[82]   Irick, "Ch'ing Policy Toward the Coolie Trade, 1847-1878," 182.

[83]   Ibid., 187.

[84]   See Articles VIII, IX, X, XXI and XXII of the Convention in Appendix II.

[85]   Irick, "Ch'ing Policy Toward the Coolie Trade, 1847-1878," 192.

[86]   Ibid., 184.

[87]   See the regulations following Article XXII of the Emigration Convention in Appendix II.

[88]   Kung to Alcock, March 15, 1866 (BFO 17/873).

would react.[89] Hence official interference with the Macau traffic was limited to preventing Chinese subjects from going there. Crimps caught recruiting laborers for Macau were summarily beheaded,[90] and the viceroy at Canton in October 1866 dispatched war junks to police the Pearl River estuary warning that any craft found with Portuguese crimps on board would be captured, the boat destroyed, and the crew put to death.[91]

But these measures failed to halt the flow of Chinese emigrants through Macau. Somewhat more effective was the directive from the Tsungli Yamen in 1869, placing the three-dollar processing fee per emigrant paid by recruiters in the custom's bank. This money, which formerly went to local customs officials, would henceforth be given as rewards for the apprehension of crimps.[92] Also in 1869, the Tsungli Yamen, on receiving a petition from the Chinese in Peru complaining of ill-treatment and being informed of many instances of mutinies on board emigrant vessels that departed from Macau, sent a note to the foreign ministers in Peking. The note pointed out that emigration from Macau was in violation of the convention of 1866 and asked the cooperation of the foreign ministers in prohibiting their merchants at that port from participating in the clandestine traffic.[93] Most nations indicated their willingness to cooperate, but France and Britain, still trying to persuade China to change the regulations of the 1866 convention, were noncommittal.[94]

But growing public criticism in the early 1870s of the traffic in Chinese laborers created a climate favorable to a stronger stand by the Chinese government. In August 1871, the viceroy of Kwangtung and Kwangsi, in a letter to the Governor of Macau that complained of the ill-treatment of the Chinese in Peru and the tragedies at sea, appealed to him to stop emigration from his jurisdiction "as a proof of the good relations that exists between our two countries."[95] The Macau governor, Antonio Sergio de Sousa, responded

---

89   Robertson to Tenterdon, March 9, 1874 (BFO 17/885).

90   Irick, "Ch'ing Policy Toward the Coolie Trade, 1847-1878," 237.

91   *Hong Kong Mercury and Shipping Gazette*, October 23, 1866; Robertson to Alcock, March, 1867 (BFO 17/874).

92   Irick, "Ch'ing Policy Toward the Coolie Trade, 1847-1878," 292-293.

93   Ibid., 290-291; Le Gendre to Fish, Inclosure, July 23, 1869 (U.S. Congress, Senate, Ex. Doc. No. 116, 41 Cong., 2 Sess.), 2-3.

94   Irick, "Ch'ing Policy Toward the Coolie Trade, 1847-1878," 291-292.

95   Viceroy of Kwangtung and Kwangsi to the Governor of Macau, August 22, 1871 (AHU, Macao, 1871, Pasta 27).

that he had suspended immigration to Peru pending an investigation of the charges, and that the awful tragedies at sea were beyond his control.[96] The following year, Jui-lin, governor-general of Kwangtung, took more decisive action. Having received a stern rebuke from the Tsungli Yamen, which was occasioned by a memorial to that body from Frederick F. Low, the American minister to China, accusing local officials in South China of complicity in the emigration traffic at Macau, Jui-lin stepped up the river patrol and ordered an inspection of the daily steamers that ran between Canton and Macau.[97] Crimps, regarding the Canton delta as hazardous, moved their recruiting operation to the Chinese mainland west of Macau. Jui-lin dispatched war junks to the area and apprehended three ships with 60 kidnapped Chinese, under the command of Portuguese, who confessed that they were employed by Macau barracoons.[98] Armed with this evidence, Jui-lin sent a dispatch to the governor of Macau, demanding the immediate closing of the barracoons.[99] Subsequently, Jui-lin issued a proclamation warning the people against kidnapping and naming the Portuguese as the chief culprits.[100]

In August 1873, Sir A. E. Kennedy, the governor of Hong Kong, on orders from London, expelled from Hong Kong waters seven coolie ships being outfitted for the Macau traffic.[101] The vessels then proceeded upriver to Whampoa, but Jui-lin, encouraged by Sir B. Robertson, the British consul at Canton, ordered them to leave that port at once.[102] The port of Macau was not equipped to outfit ships for long ocean voyages. Anyway there was no need for these vessels, as Chinese warships had placed a virtual blockade on all the entrances to Macau harbor and were inspecting all vessels entering the colony.[103] The *North China*

---

[96]   Antonio Sergio de Sousa to the Viceroy of Kwangtung and Kwangsi, September 25, 1871 (Ibid.).

[97]   Irick, "Ch'ing Policy Toward the Coolie Trade, 1847-1878," 303; *North China Herald*, September 21, 1872.

[98]   Irick, "Ch'ing Policy Toward the Coolie Trade, 1847-1878," 305; Robertson to Wade, April 23, 1873 (BFO 17/882).

[99]   Irick, "Ch'ing Policy Toward the Coolie Trade, 1847-1878," 306; Robertson to Wade, April 23, 1873 (BFO 17/882).

[100] "Proclamation against Kidnapping," August 6, 1873 (BFO 881/2445).

[101] Kennedy to Kimberley, August 29, 1873 (BPP, ASS, *China*, Vol. IV), 365-366.

[102] "Notice to Masters of Coolie Vessels," September 6, 1873 (Ibid.), 368; Viceroy of Kwangtung to Robertson, September 13, 1873 (Ibid.).

[103] *Hong Kong Times, Daily Advertiser and Shipping Gazette*, September 11, 1873.

Daily News reported on September 4, 1873, that most of the barracoons in Macau had closed down and that "business in coolies is most distressing."[104]

All through 1872 and 1873, pressure on the Macau government to stop the "coolie trade" had been mounting. The British government, on a number of occasions, appealed directly to Lisbon to end the traffic.[105] The Chinese had shown an increased militancy, and, by September 1873, had successfully blockaded Macau harbor. The Macaese themselves, through one of the colony's newspapers, the *Gazeta de Macau e Timor*, had voiced their opposition to the traffic, and João de Andrade Corvo, the Portuguese secretary of state for foreign affairs, advised the cortes in Lisbon that the emigration trade was detrimental to the true development of the colony and that it should be abandoned before it brought about an open conflict with China.[106] After all, why should the Portuguese name suffer the ridicule of world opinion in order to satisfy the labor needs of Cuba and Peru?[107] Portugal herself had no need of Chinese emigrants.

The net result of these pressures, both from within and without the Portuguese world, was that on instructions from Lisbon, Governor Januario of Macau announced on December 27, 1873, that Chinese contract emigration from that port would end three months from that date, on March 27, 1874.[108]

There were some doubts, even on the part of the Portuguese, whether or not the decision could be enforced. There was the enormous problem of what to do with the 20,000 to 30,000 Chinese residents of Macau, who were connected with the traffic, and who were now unemployed.[109] On January 28, 1874, Governor Januario, in an attempt to solve this problem, announced that free emigration would be permitted from the colony and that the barracoons would be reopened as inns or hotels to accommodate Chinese passengers.[110]

---

[104] *North China Daily News*, September 4, 1873, as quoted in BPP, ASS, *China*, Vol. IV, 374.

[105] Murdoch to Herbert, November 2, 1871 (BPP, ASS, *China*, Vol. IV), 291-293; Granville to Murray, February 27, 1873 (Ibid.), 302.

[106] For an elaboration of these developments see Chapter III.

[107] *Gazeta de Macau e Timor*, December 30, 1873.

[108] *O Boletim*, December 27, 1873.

[109] Robertson to Wade, April 23, 1873 (BFO 17/882); *Hong Kong Times, Daily Advertiser and Shipping Gazette*, December 27, 1873.

[110] *O Boletim*, January 31, 1874; Robertson to Tenderden, August 1, 1874, Inclosure I (BPP, ASS, *China*, Vol. IV), 399-403.

Jui-lin quickly informed Januario that if emigration was resumed in any form, he would send gunboats and troops to Macau to bring those engaged in it back to Canton for punishment.[111] Januario replied that he had been deceived by the emigration brokers and that he was rescinding the decree and that no emigration would take place.[112] Januario subsequently conferred with Jui-lin in Canton, and it was agreed and officially proclaimed that the unemployed Chinese in Macau could return to the mainland without fear of punishment provided they resolved to turn their backs for good on their former livelihood.[113]

As a sign of reconciliation and Chinese acceptance of the good intentions of the Portuguese, Chinese officials arrived in Macau in August 1874 and presented three gold medals, inscribed with the Chinese character *Chiang* (meaning "praise"), to Governor Januario and two other Portuguese officials, in recognition of their efforts in stopping the "coolie trade."[114]

---

[111] Robertson to Wade, May 20, 1874 (BPP, ASS, *China*, Vol. IV), 391-393; *Hong Kong Daily Press*, June 21, 1875.

[112] Robertson to Wade, May 20, 1874 (BPP, ASS, *China*, Vol. IV), 393; *Hong Kong Daily Press*, June 21, 1875.

[113] "Proclamation with Regard to the Prohibition of Chinese Emigration from Macau," March, 1874 (BPP, ASS, *China*, Vol. IV), 385.

[114] *North China Herald*, August 15, 1874.

CHAPTER IX

THE "COOLIE TRADE" —AN ASSESSMENT

This [Chinese indenture] is not a question of more or less of this or that safeguard, of an occasional defect here or excess there. But it is that of a monstrous rotten system, rooted in slavery, grown in its stale soil, emulating its worst abuses, and only the more dangerous because it presents itself under false colours, whereas slavery bore the brand of infamy upon its forehead.

—Beaumont, *The New Slavery*, 4

[Chinese emigration is] a new slavery disguised under the cloak of work contracts.

—*Diário de Pernambuco*, March 16, 1880[1]

Chinese "coolie" migration to Latin America was not a natural process. It was initiated and sustained, not by the spontaneous action of free agents, but rather by the persuasion, deceit, and coercion of emigration brokers and recruiters in the employ of Western entrepreneurs and Western capital. The voyage to the Americas was a prolonged battle for survival with the elements, with disease, with ruthless crews, and scheming fellow passengers that took the lives of approximately one emigrant in every eight. In the New World, Chinese indentured laborers, like the Negro slaves they replaced, were exploited, oppressed, and kept in varying degrees of dehumanizing bondage.

All the foregoing cannot be reasonably denied. Were the Chinese laborers then in effect slaves? Was the indenture system that victimized them the old slavery in a new guise? Or was it analogous to serfdom in that it represented an intermediate state or condition somewhere between slavery and freedom? Many contemporary observers and commentators unequivocally condemned the system of Chinese indenture as a "new slavery." That was the considered

---

[1] As cited in Eisenberg, *The Sugar Industry in Pernambuco*, 204.

judgment of John V. Crawford, the British consul general at Havana,[2] of the
Cuba Commission,[3] of Richard Gibbs, the United States minister at Lima,[4] of
the Peruvian historian Felix Cipriano C. Zegarra,[5] of the Brazilian statesman
Joaquim Nabuco,[6] and of Joseph Beaumont, the chief justice of British Guiana
from 1863 to 1868.[7] It was also the near-unanimous verdict of the British
and American press: *London Times*,[8] *Anti-Slavery Reporter*,[9] *Pall Mall Gazette*
(London),[10] *New York Times*,[11] *South Pacific Times* (Lima),[12] *Rio News* (Rio
de Janeiro),[13] and *Diário de Pernambuco*.[14] The *Pall Mall Gazette* epitomized
the prevailing sentiment:

> This traffic [Chinese contract-emigration] in human flesh is slavery in
> every stage of its progress from its inception at Macao . . . along the
> southern coast of China, throughout the passage in tropic seas and at the
> ports of delivery on the Pacific coast where it meets its fatal term.[15]

Apart from the planters and the entrepreneurs who directly profited from
Chinese emigration, the traffic had few defenders. Clements R. Markham, the
British geographer and historian, writing for the *Geographical Magazine* in 1874,

---

2   Crawford to Granville, September 3, 1873 (BFO 881/2598).
3   *Chinese Emigration: The Cuba Commission*, 3.
4   Gibbs to Fish, November 13, 1876 (U.S. Dept. of State, *Foreign Relations*, 1877), 435.
5   Zegarra, *La Condición Jurídica de los Estranjeros en el Perú*, 130-131.
6   Nabuco, "Imigração Chinesa," 60, 67.
7   Beaumont, *The New Slavery*.
8   *London Times*, April 21, 1860.
9   *Anti-Slavery Reporter*, Vol. III, No. 2 (February, 1855), 39-41; Vol. IV, No. 5
    (May, 1856), 113.
10 *Pall Mall Gazette*, cited in the *Hong Kong Times, Daily Advertiser and Shipping
    Gazette*, July 8, 1873.
11 *New York Times*, April 21, 1860; July 31, 1860; February 20, 1868; January 16,
    1871; June 11, 1873.
12 *South Pacific Times*, July 6, 1872.
13 *Rio News*, August 15, 1881, as cited in the *Anti-Slavery Reporter*, Vol. I, No. 9,
    Series 4 (September, 1811), 161.
14 *Diário de Pernambuco*, March 16, 1880.
15 *Pall Mall Gazette*, as cited in the *Hong Kong Times, Daily Advertiser and Shipping
    Gazette*, July 8, 1893.

defended the treatment of Chinese indentured laborers in Peru, claiming that the evils of the system were "grossly exaggerated."[16] Chinese indentured labor in Cuba found an apologist in none other than José Antonio Saco, an ardent opponent of slavery. Saco argued that in Cuban law, the Chinese indentured laborer was a *persona* as opposed to a slave who was legally a *cosa*. In "classic" or chattel slavery, the slave was the property of his master, and like any other piece of property, his master's power over him was, in principle, unlimited. The slave's person and services were wholly at his master's disposal; he could not mate with a partner of his choice, ownership in his person was alienable, and his condition was hereditary. Saco pointed out that the relationship between the Chinese indentured laborer and his employer was determined by a written contract, which set forth the mutual obligations of worker and master. The master was entitled to fixed services only for which he had to pay the laborer an established wage. At the expiration of the contract, the laborer was free to re-indenture himself or to refuse to do so. The Chinese laborer, even while under indenture, could legally marry, could possess property, and could take his master to court to seek redress of grievances. Hence Saco concluded that there was a fundamental difference between the Chinese laborer and the slave.[17]

The legal status of the Chinese indentured laborer throughout Latin America was similar to his status in Cuba. The law obliged the indentured laborer to provide limited services for a limited number of years in return for wages, food, clothing, and shelter. Whereas the slave owner could do with his slave whatever he was not specifically forbidden to do by law, the master of an indentured laborer could require from his worker only such services as the law prescribed. The commission of inquiry into the condition of indentured labor in British Guiana spelled out the distinction between slavery and indenture in this way: "The indentured system differs from slavery principally in this respect—that of his proper civil rights those which are left to the slave, if any, are the exception, while in the case of the indentured laborer the exceptions are those of which he is deprived."[18]

Saco conceded that the lot of the Chinese indentured laborer was a temporary bondage and likened his status to that of the slave of Imperial Rome, whom Saco considered to have been half slave and half free.[19] But Saco seems to have been primarily concerned with the abstract legal status of the indentured

---

[16] Markham, "From China to Peru," 368.

[17] José Antonio Saco, "Los Chinos en Cuba," *La America* (Madrid), Vol. VIII, No. 5 (March 12, 1864), 3.

[18] "The British Guiana Commission," 546.

[19] Saco, "Los Chinos en Cuba," 3.

laborer rather than with his actual condition. In Cuba as well as in Peru, Brazil, and the European colonies of the Caribbean, where slavery was an essential part of the social structure, all workers, whether slave or free, particularly on the plantations, tended to be treated as slaves. Wherever the indentured laborer's legal rights were ignored or cast aside, as was frequently the case, the line of demarcation between indenture and slavery became blurred. But the Chinese laborer deeply resented any and all encroachments on his contractual rights, and because of the different expectations of employer and worker, the relationship between the two was generally oppressive and violence-prone. And it is precisely this condition, in which the Chinese laborer so often found himself, that was roundly condemned as "slavery" by contemporary observers.

Perhaps a distinction must be drawn between the abstract legal system of indenture, as embodied in government decrees and particularly in the written contract of indenture, and the actual day-to-day life of the indentured worker. On the abstract legal level, it would be extremely difficult to refute Saco's assertion that Chinese indenture in Cuba, or for that matter elsewhere in Latin America, was something other than slavery. H. J. Nieboer, in his classic work *Slavery as an Industrial System*, defines slavery as "the fact that one man is the property or possession of another beyond the limits of the family proper."[20] Nowhere in Latin America during the nineteenth century was the indentured laborer legally the property of his employer, though the employer often acted on that assumption. But even in such cases, the servitude was not necessarily perpetual, nor was it inheritable. Hence it would seem to be closer to the truth to conclude that the condition of Chinese indentured labor in Latin America can only be properly described as falling somewhere in the grey area between slavery and freedom. The same must be said of the recruiting process on the China coast, which was a mixture of free choice and coercion, as well as of the voyage, where emigrants, though not chained to one another or to the decks, as in the African slave trade (except in limited instances), were often treated as prisoners and confined in the between-decks. However, the indenture system, as described in the foregoing chapters, would fall under the expanded definition of slavery adopted by the United Nations in the

[20]   H.J. Neiboer, *Slavery as an Industrial System*, 2d rev. ed. (New York, Burt Franklin, 1910), 30. For an analysis of some of the difficulties in formulating a satisfactory definition of slavery see David Brion Davis, *The Problem of Slavery in Western Culture* (Ithaca, New York, Cornell University Press, 1966), 31-35.

Supplementary Convention on Slavery at Geneva in 1956, which included serfdom as a practice analogous to slavery though it has been traditionally regarded as an intermediate state.[21]

But more important than the categorization of Chinese indenture is the question of its impact on Latin America. At this point, not enough is known about the Chinese in the various countries of the Caribbean and South America to warrant precise generalizations; nonetheless, a few tentative observations can be made. The first thing that can be said with some measure of confidence is that Chinese indentured labor was an economically feasible system of labor exploitation that meant the difference between prosperity and ruin for a large number of planters in Cuba and Peru and, to a lesser extent, in the British West Indies. Without the Chinese, plantation agriculture, especially sugar cultivation, would have languished, if not collapsed; and the guano industry and railroad construction would have been seriously curtailed. Chinese labor can also be credited with the prolongation of the plantation system, particularly in Cuba and Peru. With the suppression of the African slave trade and the consequent decline in the supply of Negro slaves, plantations would have been unable to continue operating along traditional lines. The advent of the Chinese not only postponed what seemed to be an inevitable crisis for plantation agriculture but facilitated its expansion. Furthermore, Chinese labor was an interim measure that both slowed down the process of change from slavery to wage labor and at the same time made the transition less than catastrophic for the slaveholder.

The main contribution of the Chinese, at least in the short run (which is all that is under consideration here), was an economic one. Their involvement in other spheres was minimal. With the exceptions of limited participation by some Chinese in the Ten Years' War in Cuba and in the War of the Pacific their indentured condition excluded them from the political process. Though some Latin Americans regarded the Chinese as an indigestible element in society, even by the end of the "coolie trade," there were signs that the process of cultural assimilation had begun. A small number of Chinese had married Creole women and some had become converts to Christianity.[22] Some adopted

---

[21] C.W.W. Greenidge, *Slavery* (London, George Allen and Unwin Limited, 1948), 23-24.

[22] Gibbs to Fish, November 13, 1876 (U.S. Dept. of State, *Foreign Relations*, 1877), 435-436.

Western names and Western dress.[23] The fact that the Chinese were almost all
males and that they were cut off from virtually all communication with their
homeland no doubt accelerated acculturation. The contentions of some that
the extraordinary industry of the Chinese, once they gained their freedom,
exerted a beneficial influence on the traditionally easygoing native workers,[24]
belong to the long-run effects and are beyond the scope of this study.

But the impact that the "coolie trade" had on China overshadowed whatever
significance it had in the New World. The traffic in indentured laborers
revolutionized the attitude of the Chinese government toward emigration. The
problems arising out of the illegal recruitment of emigrants on China's southern
coast compelled the government in Peking to break with centuries of tradition
and to allow its subjects to emigrate. Not only was the "coolie trade" instrumental
in forcing China to abandon her closed-door policy and officially sanction
emigration, but it aroused her to take an active interest in her subjects abroad.
As evidence accumulated that Chinese laborers were being cruelly exploited and
mistreated in Cuba and Peru, the Tsungli Yamen, supported by foreign diplomats
in Peking, strongly urged the sending of envoys to foreign countries for the
protection of overseas Chinese. The reports of the commissions of inquiry sent to
Cuba and Peru convinced the Throne of the need for some such protection, and
the treaties signed between China and Spain, Peru, and Brazil in the 1870s and
1880s had that specific end in view. Irick argues rather convincingly that concern
for overseas Chinese was a major factor in the decision of the Chinese government
to station permanent envoys abroad.[25] Hence the cries of her sons in faraway lands
helped to draw China out of her isolationism and promoted diplomatic contact
with a new area of the globe—the South American continent.

Perhaps equally important for an understanding of the implications
of the "coolie trade" in Chinese history are the following questions: What
was the relationship between the "coolie trade" and the rise of anti-foreign
feelings in China around the middle of the nineteenth century? And what
were the political, social, and economic consequences of the traffic in the
emigrating communities of South China? Only when these and the long-
run consequences of the "coolie trade" are fully explored will it be possible
to make a balanced assessment of its historical significance.

---

[23]   This was particularly true of the Chinese who participated in the Ten Years
       War in Cuba, see Jiménez Pastrama, *Los Chinos en las Luchas por la Liberación
       Cubana*, 70-82.

[24]   Fawcett, "How China Came to Peru," 434; Stewart, *Chinese Bondage in Peru*, 231.

[25]   Irick, "Ch'ing Policy Toward the Coolie Trade, 1847-1878," 320-372, 436-453.

LEGISLATION OF THE GOVERNMENTS OF SPAIN AND CUBA PERTAINING TO CHINESE IMMIGRATION

1. Regulation for the Treatment of Asiatic and Indian Colonists.*

Havana, April 10, 1849.

H is Excellency the Governor and Captain-General has ordered to be published, in 3 consecutive numbers of the official Gazette of this city, for general information, the following regulations for the management and treatment of the Asiatic and Indian colonists of this island.

The introduction into this island of Asiatic colonists, and of the natives proceeding from countries which in other times formed part of the Spanish dominion, were considered useful by the Royal Junta de Fomento (Board for promotion of Agriculture), to afford labour for agriculture, and the Government could not do less than authorize this experiment, as well as all those that lead to the benefit of production and prosperity.

But the planters very soon commenced to find difficulties in the manner of treating and managing the Asiatic race, as now they understood that they formed a new and unknown constituency in the country, thus they were without rules to give them direction by the side of others subject to very special dispositions. It is probable that the same may happen with the indigenous who have commenced to be imported; and to afford a remedy for this evil, I have judged indispensable the adoption of rules, which at the same time that they protect the rights of the colonists, secure also subordination and

---

*   This translation is taken from *British and Foreign State Papers*, vol. xxxviii, 1849-1850, 305-308. A Spanish version of the Regulations can be found in Zamora y Coronado, *Biblioteca de Legislación Ultramarina*, Primer Suplemento, 49-50.

discipline, without which they might injure instead of producing benefit to agriculture. For this it is indispensable to fix properly their obligations, to determine those of the consignees or persons to whom they are delivered, making them understand the limits of domestic punishment, to prevent excesses by private power, and to mark the term from which will begin the intervention of public authority.

And on this point it is to be remembered, from its having been shown by experience already, that without this kind of correction, applied domestically, the proper direction of labour will be altogether impossible, and indiscipline inevitable, and that certainly they will not make the situation of such colonists worse, with respect to that which they occupied in the countries whence they came. Under such principles, and responding to the continual complaints and petitions of those who, for want of rules to refer to in this kind of enterprise, have found themselves embarrassed in the management and treatment of these colonists, and with the reserve to put all in the knowledge of Her Majesty, I have ordered, having also in consideration the tenor of the Law 10, tit. 16, lib. 2, of the "Recopilación de Indias," that from this day shall be observed the following rules, publishing and circulating them to those whom it may concern, for their due fulfilment:

Asiatic Colonists

Art. I.   Those who have charge of Asiatic colonists shall proceed to teach them the dogmas of the Roman Catholic Apostolic Religion, and if they show a wish to embrace it, shall make the corresponding communication to the respective curate or priest, that there should be open to them the way to lead them to the bosom of the Church.

II.   They shall be made to understand the obedience and respect due to the authorities and the superiors on whom they immediately depend.

III.   The Asiatics may, according to their contract, be employed, in the customary hours, in any kind of work on the estates, or out of them.

IV.   There shall be advanced to them 4 dollars a month, besides the aliment of 8 ounces of salt meat or salt fish daily, and one pound and a-half of plantains, sweet potatoes or any other vegetables, and 2 changes of clothes yearly, a blanket, and a woolen shirt.

V.   During their sicknesses they shall be attended on account of their consignees, and if the sickness exceeds 15 days they will not be entitled to the monthly salary of 4 dollars.

VI.   Nor will they be entitled wholly, during the month or months posterior to their running away from the house or estate where they are hired, and the expenses of their capture and restitution shall be deducted from their salary.

In order that this may be affected without any resistance or difficulties, the Lieutenant-Governor, or the Captain of the Partido respectively, will make them understand and obey this just deduction, the effect of their bad conduct.

VII.   These obligations between master and Asiatic will last all the time stipulated in the contracts.

VIII.   On Sundays and full holidays, and during the hours of rest on the other days, the colonists will be permitted to employ themselves on the estate, in manufacturers and other occupations that may conduce to their personal benefit.

IX.   There shall also be permitted them on holidays, and on the same estate, lawful diversions which will serve them for rest and amusement, at the same time that it fortifies them for their work.

X.   Ten Asiatics on the same estate require the direction of a white mayoral, who will take care of and watch them, and attend with them at their work.

XI.   The colonist disobeying the voice of the superior, whether it be refusing to work, or any other obligation, may be corrected with 12 lashes; if he persists, with 18 more, and if even thus he should not enter on his course of duty, he may be put in irons, and made to sleep in the stocks.

If after 2 months have passed (the only time that the correction shall continue), he should not give proof of amendment, in this case the whole shall be brought to the knowledge of the local authority, in order that it may come to that of the superior of the island.

XII.   If 2 or more should refuse to work, notwithstanding the orders or persuasions, there shall be given to them the punishment of 25 lashes, putting them in irons, and they shall also sleep in the stocks for 2 months.

XIII.   If the resistance should be of a number, giving suspicions of a rising to the mayoral or those charged with them, he will inform the local authority, that he presenting himself on the estate, there should be effected the punishment referred to in the anterior Article, or what else that may be necessary, if the disobedience should require other kind of treatment.

XIV.   The colonist that runs away, besides being subject to Article VI, shall be placed in irons for 2 months; for 4 in case of repeating it, and for 6 in the second, and during the punishment he shall also have to sleep in the stocks.

XV.   He who shall harbour the runaway shall pay 4 rials daily to the master of the colonist, and further the expenses of his restitution to the estate. The capture shall be on account of the colonist, and never more than the amount of half of the ordinary (payment of a slave).

XVI.   When it is not known who may be the person having charge of the runaway, he shall be sent to the deposit of that department where the capturer shall be paid; and the expenses occasioned until the consignee appears, or that he be delivered to another, by whom shall be paid the said expenses.

    This delivery shall only take place when the first consignee does not appear at the deposit within 2 months after there has been published in the papers the individual marks of the colonist deposited.

XVII.   The punishment referred to in Articles XI and XII (which may be inflicted by the mayroals alone) should not be executed in the presence of the negroes; and none of those imposed in these regulations may be augmented, although they may be diminished, and graduated according to the fault that has been committed.

XVIII.   If the owner, or person in charge of the estate, should fail to the colonists in that which he is by contract obliged to give them, or should punish them cruelly, or does not understand properly to manage or direct them, the Governor or Lieutenant-Governor of that jurisdiction shall take notice of it, adopting the proper measures against those who are blameable, and giving account of them, with the justification, to the Government and Captain-General.

XIX.   In case the colonists commit faults which amount to crimes, they shall be proceeded against according to the laws, as in other common and ordinary cases.

Indian Colonists

XX.   That which has been ordered in the preceeding Articles, should also be understood with regard to the Indians proceeding from countries which formerly belonged to Spain, with the following differences:

1st.   hat with regard to them the catechising spoken of in the first Article is unnecessary, as they are already Catholics.

2nd.   That for this reason they should attend to preserve in them the adhesion to religious practices, to which they are naturally inclined, fulfiling thus what is ordered on the subject by the laws, and Government, and police regulations.

3rd.   That the obligations and conditions between the Indian and the person to whom he is consigned, last and be fulfilled respectively for the term of his contract.

General Dispositions

XXI.   The colonists, whether they be Asiatics or Indians, who are destined for any kind of work that is not field labour, shall be subject the same as their consignees or persons in charge, to all the dispositions of these regulations, whether they applied to domestic service or any other.

Until the colonists of both classes terminate the contracts which bind them to their consignees, they shall not be able to obtain passport, licence, or pass, unless it should be requested by the said consignee or person in charge, in the same terms which the instructions direct respecting the granting of such documents to the persons of colour not free.

2. Royal Decree, approving the Regulations for the Importation and Management of Colonists in the Island of Cuba.*

Madrid, March 22, 1854.

Having considered the report of the President of my Council of Ministers, and, in accordance with the opinion of the same Council I hereby approve the following Regulations for the importation and management of colonists in the Island of Cuba.

---

*   This translation is taken from *British and Foreign State Papers*, Vol. XLV, 1854-1855, 1092-1103. A Spanish version of the decree can be found in D. Joaquín Rodríguez San Pedro, *Legislación Ultramarina*, 16 vols. (Madrid, Imprentade los Señores Viota, 1865-1869), II, 431-437.

Chap. I—*Of the Importation of Colonists*

Art. I. Private persons, who wish to introduce on their account into the Island of Cuba, Spanish, Chinese, or Yucatan colonists, shall be able to do so from this day, and for the space of 2 years, subjecting themselves to the conditions established in these regulations.

II. The importer of the said colonists must previously obtain permission from the Government, and must for that purpose present a certificate or document, showing that the vessel in which they are to be conveyed is fit for the voyage. If the vessel should be in a foreign port, this certificate or document shall be issued by the Spanish Consul there, and if in a Spanish port by the proper naval authority.

III. Neither of the said permissions shall be conceded unless the person in whose favour it is issued obliges himself to import the number of women which the Government may determine, on taking into consideration the number of the men who are to be imported in each expedition, their nationality, and other circumstances. No tonnage duties shall be paid by the importers for women.

IV. The Government, on conceding the permission of which the previous Articles treat, may exact from the importers any other conditions which it may think fit with regard to the number, nationality, and other circumstances of the colonists who are to be imported.

V. The contracts between the importers and the colonists shall be written in the language of the latter, and shall be *viséd* by Her Majesty's Consul if made abroad, or by the Governor of the province if made in Spanish territory.

VI. These contracts must set forth the following particulars:

1. The age, sex, and place of birth of the colonist.
2. The time for which his contract is to be in force.
3. The wages, and the kind, quantity, and quality of the food and clothing which he is to receive.
4. The obligation to afford him medical assistance during illness.
5. Whether the wages are to be stopped when the colonist falls ill from any cause not connected with his work, or independent of the will of the master.
6. The number of hours during which the colonist obliges himself to work each day, it being declared whether the master is to have the power of increasing that number on some days, provided this

increase shall be compensated by a proportionate diminution on other days.

7. The obligation of the colonist to indemnify the master for the hours of labour lost to him by the colonist's fault.

8. The obligation of the same colonist to subject himself to the discipline of the estate, workshop, or establishment in which he may have to labour.

9. A clause drawn up in these terms: "I, N. N., assent to the rate of wages above stipulated, although I know that what the free labourers and slaves of the Island of Cuba get is much greater, because I consider this difference to be compensated by the other advantages which my master has to afford to me, as stated in this contract."

10. The signature of the colonist, if he can write, and that of the contractor.

VII.   The colonist shall receive, and keep in his possession, a copy of the contract signed by the contractor.

VIII.   If the colonists should be Spaniards, and under age, they shall not be permitted to contract with the importers without the consent of their parents or guardians. If they should be foreigners, and under 14 years of age, the person on whom they depend must be a party to the contract.

IX.   The importers of colonists shall not embark in any vessel more than one person for each ton of measurement on a voyage from the ports of the Peninsula; one person for each ton and a half on voyages made from the ports of China; and in the like proportion for the shorter voyage from Yucatan.

X.   The importers shall also be bound:

1. To provide the vessels with water and wholesome food fully sufficient for the number of persons conveyed, and for the length of the voyage.

2. To adopt the necessary precautions in order to maintain in the said vessels the cleanliness and ventilation indispensable for the health of the passengers.

3. To carry a physician and medicine-chest on board, when the number of persons embarked is above 100.

4. To subject themselves on their arrival at any port of Cuba, to the sanatory and police regulations in force there.

XI.   In order to insure the observance of these regulations the colonists
             must only be imported at the port of Havana, except in case of
             shipwreck or other inevitable accident, which may render the
             arrival and landing at some other port a matter of necessity.

XII.   Within 24 hours after the arrival of the vessel, or after its admission
             to free pratique, the importer shall present a list of the colonists
             embarked by him, accompanied by their contracts, and by a
             return showing the number of those who may have died during
             the passage, and the causes of their death. The Governor Captain-
             General, after seeing these documents, and after taking all the
             steps which he may deem necessary to prevent fraud, will permit
             the disembarkation.

XIII.   The importers of colonists may transfer them to other employers, or
             to planters or individuals, on such terms as they may think fit; the
             latter always obliging themselves to fulfil the contracts entered into
             with the said colonists, and to conform to these regulations. The
             persons receiving such conditions, and if on a transfer of colonists
             the terms of the original contract should be altered without the
             consent of the colonists, such transfer shall be null and void.

XIV.   Both the importers and receivers of colonists shall give an account
             to the Government of the number of the latter transferred or
             received within 24 hours after the conclusion of the contract,
             stating the number, sex, and age of said colonists, the vessel in
             which they arrived, the conditions of the contract made with
             them, the nature of the labour in which they are to be employed,
             and the place where they are going to reside.

             The Government will then deliver to the receiver the contracts
             received from the importer relative to the ceded colonists, after
             entering their contents in the books which shall be kept for that
             purpose in the office of the Political Secretary.

XV.   The residence of the colonists may not be transferred from one
             part of the island to another without a previous intimation to the
             Government.

Chap. II—*Of the Reciprocal Obligations and Rights of the Colonists and their Masters*

XVI.   The Governor Captain-General of the Island of Cuba shall be
             the official protector of the colonists, and shall execute this trust

in the districts through his delegates, the respective Governors or Lieutenant-Governors, who in their turn shall be assisted therein, and without necessity of previous delegation, by the District Captains. These functionaries shall proceed in every case under the direction and orders of the Governors and Lieutenant-Governors.

XVII. In legal matters, and when the masters of the colonists do not appear for them, the Syndics of the Corporations, or their substitutes in the Municipal Juntas, shall be the defenders of the colonists in the inferior Courts, and in the superior Courts, Her Majesty's Fiscal Officers.

XVIII. The delegated protectors shall attend to the proper treatment of the colonists and the fulfilment of their contracts; they shall propose to the official protector the measures which they consider requisite for their welfare and encouragement; and shall settle equitably, and without form of law, the questions which may arise between the colonists and their masters.

If these questions should involve any point of law, the protector shall decide them summarily, taking *vivâ voce* evidence, and hearing the opinion of an assessor.

If the subject should be of greater legal importance, it shall be decided by the proper authority and according to the established forms of law.

XIX. It is understood that the colonists, in signing or accepting their contracts with the importers, renounce the exercise of all civil rights which may be incompatible with the fulfilment of the obligations which they incur, unless some right is treated of which is expressly declared by these regulations.

XX. The colonists may contract marriage with the consent of their masters.

If a colonist, who is of age, should wish to marry, and his master should oppose it, he may redeem himself from his master under the conditions prescribed in Article XXVIII, or he may seek another master, who may receive him with the same conditions.

XXI. The colonists shall exercise over their children all the rights of paternal power, and over their wives all the rights of marital power, in as far as those rights are compatible with the legal condition of the said children and wives.

XXII. The children of the colonists shall follow the condition of their mothers all the time that the contract of the latter lasts, if born during the same; but on completing 18 years of age, they shall be entirely free, although their mothers should continue under contract.

The children under age whom the women have at the time of hiring, shall follow the condition which the women may stipulate with the contractors. If nothing should be stipulated, they shall be entirely free, but they shall have a right to be fed, lodged, and clothed, by the masters of their mothers, under the conditions established for those under 12 years old.

XXIII.   The children of the colonists, born under the power of the masters of their mothers, shall have the same right while they follow the condition of the latter, but with the obligation to render, in the meantime, to the said masters the services of which they are capable, according to their age.

XXIV.   The married colonists may not be transferred to any person who does not, at the same time, take both husband and wife and their children, under 12 years of age. The masters may not oblige the husbands to live habitually separated from their wives, nor the latter from their children under 12 years of age.

XXV.   The colonists may acquire property, and dispose of what may belong to them by valid title, provided the contracts which they may make do not involve any express or tacit conditions, the fulfilment of which may be incompatible with their contracts with the masters.

XXVI.   The colonists may also take legal proceedings against their masters, being represented in the manner prescribed in Article XVIII, and against other persons, being represented by their own masters, if the latter should be willing to undertake their defence.

If the master should decline to do so, or if in a suit between him and a third party the master's interest should be opposed to that of his colonists, the latter must be represented by the Syndic in the inferior Courts, and by Her Majesty's Fiscal in the superior.

XXVII.   The colonists who may have made contracts when under 20 years of age, shall have the right of rescinding them when they attain 25 years of age. Those who may have made contracts when above 20 years old, shall have the same right after 6 years' contract. The masters shall likewise have the power to rescind them at the same periods at which the colonists have this right. The colonist shall in no case be able to make use of the right recognized in this Article, unless he indemnifies his master, either by labour or in some other mode, for what he may owe him.

XXVIII.   Every colonist shall be able to redeem himself at any time from the power of his master, provided he pays him in cash:

1. The amount which he may have paid for his acquisition.
2. That which the same colonist may owe him as compensation for labour, or on any other account.
3. The increased value which, in the judgment of men of skill, the services of the colonist may have acquired since he entered the master's employment.
4. The amount of the loss which the master may incur from the difficulty of replacing the colonist by another.

    The colonist shall not be able to make use of this right in time of "zaffra," or during any other of the pressing employments permitted on holidays.

XXIX.   If any master shall treat a colonist harshly, or shall fail to fulfil his engagements toward him, the colonist may apply to the delegated protector, and if the latter, on hearing both parties, should be convinced of the justice of the complaint, he will allow the contract to be annulled.

    This annulment may be granted, without compensation to the master for what he may have given for the acquisition of the colonist, and without barring any civil or criminal action on the part of either party.

XXX.   In the days and hours of rest, the colonists may work on their own account within the establishment or estate where they reside; and if they should wish to work out of it, they must previously obtain the permission of the master.

    In the same days and hours they may also indulge in such harmless amusements as may not disturb the discipline of the establishment or estate.

XXXI.   The colonists shall freely dispose of the produce of their property and of their work done in the days and hours of rest, but they shall not be allowed to establish any retail trade against the will of their master.

XXXII.   Whenever the colonist wishes to sell his furniture or moveables, he shall inform his master, who shall be preferred *pro tanto* to any other purchaser.

XXXIII.   When the master concedes to his colonist any lot of land for cultivation during the days and hours of rest, the colonist shall acquire the entire produce unless his master may have stipulated otherwise with him.

XXXIV.   The colonists shall not be able to leave the estate or establishment in which they serve without the written permission of their master or his delegate, and any colonists found unprovided with such a permit shall be apprehended by the authorities, and taken home at the master's expense.

XXXV.   When it may have been stipulated in the contracts that the colonists shall have any particular kind of food, or clothes of a particular make or sort, if circumstances should prevent the master from providing the same, the kind, quality, or make, of either may be altered, but not the quantity.

If the colonists should not be content with this change they shall apply to their protector, who will settle the matter fairly between the parties, with due regard to the essential right of the colonists.

XXXVI.   Whatever stipulations may have been made in the contracts as to medical assistants for the colonists, it shall comprise, not only the attendance of the practitioner, but also such medicines and food as the physicians may prescribe during illness and convalescence.

XXXVII.   The colonists shall work for their masters, on every day that is not a holiday, during the number of hours agreed upon in the contract.

It is understood that days which are not holidays, for the purposes of this Article, are all those on which the precept of the church does not prohibit labour, and those which, not withstanding the festival celebrated thereon, shall be authorized by the ecclesiastical authority as working days.

XXXVIII.   Notwithstanding any stipulation to the contrary, the masters shall have no right to exact from their colonists more than 12 hours' daily labour on an average.

XXXIX.   If a contract shall contain a stipulation as to the right of the master to arrange in the manner most advantageous for his interests the hours of labour agreed upon with the colonist, as prescribed in No. 6 of Article VI, that right shall be understood as limited, so that the colonist can never be obliged to work more than 15 hours in one day, and so that he shall always have at least 6 consecutive hours of rest by night or by day.

If the said right should not have been stipulated in the contract, the master shall not have power to exact from the colonist more hours of work in each day than those agreed upon.

XL. The colonist must render to his master all lawful services that he may require, unless it shall have been agreed in the contract that the colonist is to be employed exclusively in certain labours.

In such case the colonist may resist being employed in labours different from those stipulated.

The master may let out to a third person the services of his colonist, for employment in such work as is stipulated in the contract, and to which no condition of the contract is opposed.

XLI. When the colonist is ill or convalescent, he shall not be obliged to work until the medical man declares that he may do so without danger to his health.

XLII. The masters shall pay their colonists the stipulated wages in the form and manner agreed upon in the contract.

XLIII. The colonists shall receive the whole of their wages while they are ill or convalescent from illness contracted in consequence of labour, or from any cause dependent on the will of the master. If the illness should proceed from other causes, the colonist will not have the same right unless it may have been stipulated in the contract.

XLIV. The colonist who, according to his contract, is entitled to receive his wages during illness, arising from whatever cause, shall have no right to demand his wages if his illness arises from any wilful act of his own.

XLV. For all the purposes of the 2 previous Articles and of Article XXXVI, the diseases of the colonist shall be reported upon by the medical men of the estate or establishment in which the colonists are employed, and in default of them, by 2 physicians named by the master.

If the colonist should demur to their opinion, he may apply to the delegated protector, in order that, by his direction, the colonist may be re-examined by 2 practitioners; one to be named by him, and another by the master, by whose decision both parties shall abide without further appeal. If the physicians named by the master and the colonist disagree, the delegated protector shall name a third, whose decision shall be final.

XLVI. The colonists shall compensate their masters for the days and hours during which they may have neglected to work through their own fault, and for that purpose their engagement shall be extended for the necessary time. The colonist shall not receive any wages for the days of labour lost by his fault, unless the contrary be expressly stipulated in the contract.

The regulations of this Article shall hold good without barring the other penalties which the colonist may incur by the offence in question.

XLVII.   In fulfilment of the regulations contained in the first paragraph of the previous Article, the owners or superintendents of the estates or establishments in which the colonists work shall keep books containing an account of the daily labour of the colonists, and of the payments made to them, so that the account of what is owed by or due to any one, may be made out at any time, and in the former case it may be known for what period the respective contracts ought to be prolonged.

XLVIII.   At the end of each month the account corresponding to the labour and payment of each colonist shall be closed, and he shall be informed of the result, in order that if he have any remark to make he may do so at once, or may apply to the protector if he should not concur in the master's statement of the account.

XLIX.   The clause which, with reference to Article VI, paragraph 8, every contract ought to contain, as to the colonist subjecting himself to the discipline of the estate or establishment in which he has to work, and any other stipulation which obliges him to obey his master's orders, shall be always understood with the proviso that the rules or orders prescribed to the colonist shall not be contrary to other conditions of the same contract, nor to the tenor of these regulations.

L.   When any colonist deserts from the estate or establishment in which he is serving, the master shall inform the local authority, in order that the necessary steps may be taken for his pursuit.

The master shall pay at once the expenses occasioned by his capture and restitution, but shall have a right to indemnify himself for them by deducting from the fugitive colonist half the wages due to him.

LI.   If a master should have in his service non-Catholic colonists, he shall provide for their instruction in the doctrines and morality of the true religion, but without employing other means for this purpose than persuasion and conviction; and if any one shall express a wish to conform to the Catholic faith, the master shall inform the parish priest.

LII.   When a colonist shall suffer in his person or interests a wrong or injury not amounting to a crime, from a free man, or from a colonist of another ownership, the master shall take cognizance of the fact, and if he think the complaint just, shall demand from the offender or his master, by friendly or extra-judicial means, the reparation due; and if these means be not sufficient, he shall seek redress before the competent authority, or state the fact to the Syndic, in order that he may do so. If the complaint of the colonist should be thought unfounded, he shall be informed accordingly, and advised to abandon his complaint; but if the colonist should refuse to do so, he may apply to the Syndic to make the proper claim. When the complaint is directed against another colonist belonging to the same master, the latter, or his delegate, shall decide the question in the manner that he thinks just. Either of the parties may appeal against this decision to the protector or his delegate, who shall take cognizance of the matter in the form prescribed in Article XVIII.

LIII. The importers of colonists, and the masters who may fail to comply with any of the obligations or formalities prescribed in this and the previous chapter, shall incur a fine proportionate to the gravity of the case, which shall be imposed summarily without prejudice to the penal or civil responsibility to which they may be subject, and which the authority will have to exact from them in the proper form.

LIV.   The colonists shall not be entitled to claim, at any time, from their master, the Government, or the importers, the payment of the expenses of their return voyage to their country, unless their contracts contain an express stipulation to that effect.

LV.   On the expiration of the contract, the colonists shall have all the rights that belong to them respectively, according to their origin as Spaniards or foreigners, without any difference between them and those who may never have been colonists.

Chap. III—*Of the Disciplinary Jurisdiction of the Masters*

LVI.   The masters shall exercise a disciplinary jurisdiction over their colonists, and in virtue of it shall be able to impose the following punishments:

1. Confinement from 1 to 10 days.
2. Stoppage of wages during that time. The first of these punishments may be inflicted without the second, but the latter may never be applied without the former.

LVII.   Whenever the master inflicts on his colonists either of the penalties mentioned in the previous Article, he shall give information within the next 24 hours to the proper protector, in order that he may investigate, if he think proper, the offence committed, and may alter the sentence of the master if it should appear unjust.

          Any master omitting to give the said notice within the time specified shall be subject to a summary fine of 25 to 100 dollars.

LVIII.   The colonists may, in every case, complain to the protector of any wrong done them by their masters, whether by punishing them without cause, by imposing penalties which are not within their competence, or by otherwise improperly treating them.

          If the protector find the master guilty of any offence, he shall denounce him to the proper tribunal; and if the offence shall be only a slight one, he shall himself impose a fine not exceeding 100 dollars.

LIX.   In order to ensure the fulfilment of the regulations of the 2 preceeding Articles, the protectors shall have the power to visit, when they think proper, the estates or establishments where there are colonists, either personally or by means of other functionaries, and to examine the colonists as they may think fit.

LX.   The delegates of the master in the estate or establishment in which the colonists work, may also exercise disciplinary jurisdiction, but under the pecuniary responsibility of the same master, and without prejudice to the penal responsibility which they may incur.

LXI.   The following offences shall be punished as above (disciplinarmente):

1. Insubordination to the master, to the superintendent, or to any other delegate of the master.
2. Refusal to work or want of punctuality in any particular piece of work.
3. Injuries which do not oblige the party injured to suspend work.
4. Desertion.
5. Drunkenness.
6. Infraction of the rules of discipline established by the master.

7. Offences against good manners not constituting crimes, which cannot be prosecuted unless at the instance of the parties; or which, constituting a crime of this kind, are not prosecuted by the party offended.
8. Any other act done with malice, and from which injury or damage accrues to a third person, and which nevertheless does not constitute an offence subject to legal prosecution.

LXII. The disciplinary jurisdiction shall be exercised by the masters, without prejudice to the right of injured parties to require that the offending colonist shall be punished by the tribunals if there be just cause.

LXIII. The ordinary tribunals, to which the colonists shall present themselves, represented in the form prescribed in Article XXVI, shall have cognizance in all cases of penal or civil responsibility in which the masters are not competent judges according to the regulation in Article LXI.

LXIV. When the punishments pointed out in Article LVI are not sufficient to prevent the colonists from repeating the same or committing other offences, the master shall apply to the protector, who, if the act constitutes an offence according to the laws, shall decide that the guilty colonist may be punished by them; and if not, by additional disciplinary punishment.

LXV. If the colonists of an estate should mutiny, or resist by force and collectively the orders of their superiors, the master may also employ force to bring them to order; and he shall give immediate information to the delegated protector, in order that if the gravity of the case require it, he may take measures for having the guilty colonists punished at once, in the presence of the other colonists.

LXVI. The regulations hitherto in force relative to Chinese and Yucatan colonists are hereby abrogated.

General Regulation

The Governor Captain-General of the island shall take the proper measures in order that every year, by the month of January, lists of the colonists may be made out or corrected; the lists shall state their names, sex, ages, country, whether they are married or single, their trades, the period of their contract, and the name, profession, and domicile of their respective masters.

The same authority shall send to the Presidency of the Council of Ministers an annual abstract of the said registers, stating the number of colonists of each nation, classified by sexes; by ages up to 15 years, from 15 to 50, and from that age upward; by condition, as unmarried, married, or widowers; by occupations, whether agricultural, industrial, or domestic; by the districts in which they reside; and by the time of duration of their contracts, according as they may be under 5 years, from 5 to 10 years, from 10 to 15 years, and from 15 years upward.

Given at the Palace, March 22, 1854.
Signed by the Royal Hand.

The President of the Council of Ministers.

LUIS JOSÉ SARTORIUS.

3.   Royal Decree.*

Ministry for War and the Colonies
Madrid, June 6, 1860.

Wishing to afford the agriculture of the island of Cuba the labourers necessary for preventing any decrease of prosperity, and considering that the introduction of Chinese labourers is a measure attended with less inconvenience than any of the attempts hitherto made in that province, in conformity with what is proposed by the Minister for War and the Colonies, and in agreement with the opinion of the Council of Ministers, and after hearing that of the Council of State, I give my approval to the following regulations for the introduction and discipline of the Chinese labourers in the said island.

Rules for the introduction of Chinese Labourers into the Island of Cuba.

CHAP. I.—Respecting the introduction of the Labourers

ART. I.   The introduction of Chinese labourers into the island of Cuba, is
              authorized in conformity with the orders of the present regulations.

---

*   This translation is taken from *British and Foreign State Papers*, Vol. XLVIII,
     1038-1052. A Spanish version of the decree can be found in Rodriguez San
     Pedro, *Legislación Ultramarina*, II, 439-447.

II. Every importer of Chinese must have a consignee in the island of Cuba, who must be a known landed proprietor, either resident in the same, or a merchant established there. Societies with shares cannot hold this agency: those which by their statutes have the legal right of devoting themselves to this undertaking, will be obliged, notwithstanding, to name a consignee with the above-mentioned qualities, even although the Havana may be the place of residence of the said companies.

III. The consignee mentioned in the preceding Articles, is directly responsible for any failure in carrying out the orders of the present regulations, as far as concerns the undertaking which he represents, but without affecting the responsibility belonging to the captain and officers of the ship.

IV. The authorized consignee in every Immigration Company must inform the Governor Captain-General of the island of Cuba, of the name, size, roll, and captain of every ship freighted for importation, and of the approximate number of Chinese which it is proposed to carry in her. The Governor Captain-General will immediately publish these declarations in the "Havana Gazette," and will communicate them by the first mail to my Government.

V. The intervention and authorization of the Spanish Consul in China, or of his agents or delegates according to the place of the contract or the embarkation, are requisites absolutely indispensable for enabling the Chinese to be received on the island of Cuba. The Consul and his agents are directly responsible for the said embarkations and contracts being arranged according to what is prescribed in these regulations.

VI. Every contract must contain the following particulars:

1stly. The age, sex, and place of origin of the Chinaman contracted for.

2ndly. The time that the contract has to last.

3rdly. The salary, and the kind, quantity, and quality of the nourishment and clothing he is to receive.

4thly. The obligation to give him medical assistance during illness.

5thly. Whether the salary ceases when the labourer falls ill from some cause, not emanating from his labour, or independent of the will of the master.

6thly. The number of hours during which the Chinaman engages to work every day, stating whether the master has the power of increasing them some days, provided he compensates for this increase by the analogous diminution on others.

7thly.   The engagement of the hired labourer to indemnify the master for the hours of work lost through his own fault.

8thly.   The engagement of the labourer himself to subject himself to the discipline of the estate, workship, or establishment to which he is destined.

9thly.   A clause drawn up in these terms, "I, N. N., agree to the stipulated salary, although I know, and am fully aware that that which the free day labourers and the slaves earn on the island of Cuba is much larger, because I consider that this difference is compensated for by the other advantages which my master affords me, which are those that this contract provides."

10thly. The signatures of the Contracting Parties, or that of two witnesses in default of that of the labourer.

VII.   It is an essential condition and must be an express clause in every contract with Chinese, besides those prescribed in the former Article, that the time of his engagement being completed, he cannot remain in the island of Cuba as a labourer without having made another contract of the same kind, as apprentice or workman under the responsibility of a master, or as being engaged in agriculture, or as a domestic servant guaranteed by his master, in every other case he will have to leave the island at his own expense, being obliged to do so 3 months after the termination of the contract.

VIII. Four copies shall be made of the contracts with the Chinese, and the Consular Interpreter shall make 3 copies in translation. The Consul or his agent shall legalize the 4 copies, he shall give one back to the representative of the company, and he shall transmit the 3 remaining, each with its respective translation, one to my Government, and two to the Governor Captain-General of the island of Cuba, who will keep one copy with its translation, and will give the other to the Chinaman, in order that he may keep it in his power as soon as his introduction has been declared legal.

IX.   The person who transmits the Chinese must make a list in quadruple of those embarked on each ship, stating their sex, age, and other personal features, which he will sign and deliver to the Spanish Consul or his agent, who shall legalize the 4 copies, and will return one to the person that sent them, he will keep one, and will transmit the other two directly to my Government, and the Governor Captain-General of the island of Cuba respectively.

X.   Should the labourers be minors, the importers will not be able to make contracts with them without the consent of the person on whom they depend.

XI.   The importers of labourers will not embark on each ship more than one person for every two tons, it being understood that this space or room must be calculated on the whole space that remains for lodging after the stowal of the cargo.

XII.   The importers will also be bound:

> 1stly.   To provide the ships with an amount of water and healthy food, proportioned to the number of persons they carry, and the distance they have to travel over.
>
> 2ndly.   To adopt the necessary precautions in order to preserve in the said ships the cleanliness and ventilation indispensable for the health of the passengers.
>
> 3rdly.   To take a physician and medicine chest on board, when the number of persons embarked exceeds 40.
>
> 4thly.   To subject themselves on their arrival at any port in the island to the sanitary and police regulations in force there.

XIII.   In order to insure the observation of this rule, the labourers cannot be introduced at any port but that of the Havana, except in case of shipwreck or any inevitable accident which may render their arrival and landing at another port imperative.

XIV.   The Spanish Consul in China will give my Government and the Governor Captain-General of the island of Cuba detailed information directly and by the shortest route of every ship which, with this destination, leaves those ports carrying Chinese.

XV.   Within 24 hours after the anchoring of every ship importing Chinese, her agent will make or will be forced to make a deposit in the Spanish bank in the Havana of 50 dollars for every one of the Chinese embarked, without prejudice to what is established in Article III as a general rule. In default of the Company, that sum remains directly and specially destined to the speedy carrying out of the sanitary measures which the state of the Chinese may require; to their immediate and suitable accommodation and assistance in the case of the company not affording them these; to the pecuniary reparations which may be due to the Chinese for acts that may have happened during the embarkation, or the passage, or at their arrival, and after covering these expenses, to the payment of the fines incurred by the company.

This deposit, or the remainder of it, shall be returned to the company as soon as these preceeding responsibilities have been declared wholly or partially satisfied.

XVI. When, from the first examination of the ship's papers, it results that the mortality of the Chinese during the passage has exceeded 6 percent a special inquiry shall be instituted as to the reason, and, according to the result of this inquiry, the Governor Captain-General shall impose a corresponding fine, after having heard the Higher Board of Health and that of Public Works, or he will pass it on to the tribunals in order to bring on a trial, if he prosecutes.

XVII. Within 24 hours after the arrival of a ship, or on admission to free pratique, the consignee shall present a list of the labourers on board, mentioning those who may have died during the passage, and the causes which led to their death. The Governor Captain-General, in view of the document presented, and after making the inquiries he may think necessary for avoiding all fraud, will allow the landing to take place.

XVIII. Two months after the termination of the contract, the Chinaman must either renew it, taking service as an apprentice or workman of some known master, or being employed in agriculture, or as a servant, or he must have left the island as is prescribed by Article VII, and so successively in proportion as they fulfil their engagements, in case of his not doing this he will be employed as a workman on public works, but only for such time that, after covering his personal expenses, enough may remain over to place him on board ship, with the destination of his own choice, or in failure of that, one chosen by the Governor Captain-General.

XIX. The repetition of serious abuses on the part of the company, or the manifest insolvency of the consignee, or of his representative, will cause the loss of the authorization to continue carrying on this traffic. In the case of insolvency, the Governor Captain-General will direct the company to name another acceptable consignee within the term of two months, and if this is not effected, the notices of freights made by the same will be rejected, and the shipments which arrive will be considered as sent without the formalities required by these regulations.

XX.   In the fault of a consignation or of a previous declaration of the freight of a ship, and the probable number of Chinese which it is intended to embark in her, the non-intervention of the Spanish Consul or his agents in the contract and embarkation of the Chinese, and in the fitting out of the ship, and the sentence of the tribunals in serious cases which demand the formalities of a trial, will bring about the loss of all the rights of the company over the Chinese.

XXI.   In the case of the previous Article, the Governor Captain-General will dispose of the landing and lodging of the Chinese at the expense of the consignee, and will leave them at liberty to make contracts as artisans, labourers, or servants, adopting those measures which will most effectually protect them against the disadvantages of their position.

XXII.   If, at the expiration of two months after the landing, the Chinese shall not have succeeded in obtaining the situations of which the previous Article treats, or shall have at any time manifested the wish not to hire themselves out in the island, the Governor Captain-General shall extract from the company the sum necessary for the re-exportation of all of them, and shall dispose of it freely with the greatest possible guarantees, consulting the wishes of the Chinese as far as he is able.

XXIII.   The introducers of Chinese labourers will be able to give them up to other speculators, or to proprietors and private people, with the conditions they think advisable, provided the latter bind themselves to fulfil the contracts entered into with the said labourers, and subject themselves to the prescriptions of these regulations.

Those who give up the Chinese will have a similar power under the same conditions. Any cessions which may be made, changing the conditions of the primitive contracts, will be invalid.

XXIV.   As well as those who import, as those who make over, will inform the Governor Captain-General of the number of labourers they receive or make over within the 24 hours following the conclusion of the contract, stating their number, sex, and age, the name of the ship in which they arrived, and the spot where they are going to reside.

XXV.   Note will be taken in the books kept in the political office of the cessions which are made of Chinese labourers.

XXVI.   The residence of the labourers cannot be changed from one spot in the island to another without previously informing the Government.

XXVII.   The ships arriving with Chinese women on board will be exempt from the payment of tonnage dues for the space which these may occupy.

XXVIII.   The company or its consignee, when failing in the fulfillment of the orders of these regulations, which are not comprised in the foregoing rules, will be punished by the Governor Captain-General, attention being paid to the royal agreement, by fines of 1,000 to 5,000 dollars, and if they do not pay attention to the security and good treatment of the Chinese, by fines of from 2,000 to 10,000 dollars in this latter case.

XXIX.   The fines of which the foregoing Article treats, and the resolutions which the Governor Captain-General may adopt by applying these regulations to individual cases can be appealed against legally before my Government.

XXX.   Without affecting the cases stated in these regulations and in all those in which the Governor Captain-General imposes the fines established, this authority will forward the proceeding to my fiscal in that tribunal, in order that if he thinks it his duty, he may give the necessary instructions to the Promoter Fiscal, in order that he may demand, in the name of the Chinese, for bringing on the actions against the undertaking.

CHAP. II—Of the obligations and rights which the Workmen and their Masters owe each other reciprocally.

XXXI.   The Governor Captain-General of Cuba shall be the natural protector of the Chinese workmen, and shall perform this charge in the district by means of his delegates, the Governors or Lieutenant-Governors respectively, who in their turn shall be assisted, without the necessity of a previous demand by the chiefs of districts. These functionaries shall in all cases act under the orders and guidance of the Governors or Lieutenant-Governors.

XXXII.   In default of their masters, the labourers shall be defended in their law affairs in the first instance by the "Promotores Fiscales" of the principal municipalities, and in the second by the Fiscal of my Royal Pretorial Court.

XXXIII. The protectors named shall see that the labourers are well treated, and that the contracts are fulfilled; they shall propose to the native protector the means they may think necessary for their happiness and prosperity, and shall solve at once, and without judicial forms, the questions which may arise between the labourers and their masters. If these questions should involve any point of right, the protector shall solve them by a verbal judgment, hearing both parties *in voce*, and with the advice of an assessor.

If the affair was of more importance, it should be decided by the proper persons in conformity with the laws, and according to the precedents established in similar matters.

XXXIV. It is understood that on signing and accepting their contracts, the labourers renounce the exercise of all civil rights which may be incompatible with the fulfilment of the obligations that they have contracted, except it is question of some right expressly mentioned in these regulations.

XXXV. The labourers may marry with the consent of their employers.

If an adult labourer intends to marry, and his master should refuse, he may liberate himself from his rule under the conditions prescribed by Article XLII, or look out for another master, who will hire him on the same terms.

XXXVI. The workmen shall exercise all the authority over their children they would in their native land, and marital authority over their wives, as far as one and the other are compatible, with the legal condition of the said children and wives.

XXXVII. The children of the labourers shall follow the conditions of their mothers as long as the contract of the latter shall last, if they are born during its accomplishment, but at 18 years of age, they shall be perfectly free, even if their mother's contract continues.

The children under age which the women may have at the time of hiring themselves shall follow the conditions, which the mother may have stipulated for. If nothing should have been stipulated, they shall be perfectly free; but they shall have a right to be fed, housed, and clothed by the masters of the mothers, under the conditions established for the latter, until they have accomplished their 12th year.

XXXVIII. The same right shall be enjoyed by the children of the workmen, under the orders of the masters of their mothers, as long as they follow the condition of the latter; but with the obligation to perform such services for the masters as their age will admit of.

XXXIX. The married labourers cannot be ceded to any person who does not take both parties, as also any children which they may have under 12 years of age. The masters also cannot oblige the husbands to live constantly separated from the wives, nor the latter from the children under 12 years of age.

XL. The labourers can acquire property, and dispose of that which they possess by onerous or lucrative right, with the understanding that the contracts which they may make, shall not involve any expressed or tacit condition, the accomplishment of which shall be incompatible with the conditions of their contract with their masters.

LXI. The labourers represented as stated in Article XXXII, can appear in justice against their masters, and against strangers, represented by their masters, if the latter choose to take their defence upon themselves.

When the master shall decline this charge, or when in a lawsuit with a third, he should have interests opposed to those of his labourer, the latter must also be represented, in the first instance by the Promoter Fiscal of the principal municipality, and in the second by the Fiscal of my Royal Court.

XLII. Labourers who shall have made contracts when under 21 years of age, shall have a right to annul them when 25 years old.

Those who shall have made contracts being upward of 25 years old, shall have an equal right after the 6 years of contract.

The masters shall also have the power of annulling them at the same periods as the labourers.

In no case can the labourer make use of the right granted him by this Article, until after having indemnified his master by his labour, or otherwise for what he owed him.

XLIII. The labourer can at any time ransom himself from the authority of his master, by paying him in cash:

1stly. The amount he shall have paid for hiring him.
2ndly. The sum the labourer himself may owe him for work, or for any other reason.

3rdly. The greater value the services of the labourer estimated at by experienced men, since his being hands of the master.

4thly. The amount of damages the master may suffer owing the difficulty of replacing the labourer by another.

The labourer cannot make use of this right, in the time of "Zafra," or other peremptory work permitted on feast days.

XLIV. When a master shall have treated his labourer with severity, or shall have been wanting in the obligations contracted with him, the labourer can complain to the delegated protector, and the latter can annul the contract, if on hearing both parties he is convinced of the justice of the complaint. The revision in this case shall be granted without the master being indemnified for what he may have paid for the hiring of the labourer, and without hindrance to the civil or criminal action which may be brought by one or the other party.

XLV. During the days and hours of rest, the labourers may work on their own account in the establishment or country-house where they reside, and if they wished to work out of them, they must previously obtain the permission of the master.

On the same days and hours they may also enjoy honest amusements, which do not interfere with the discipline of the establishment or farm.

XLVI. The labourers shall dispose freely of the produce of their property, and of their labour on the days and hours of rest, but they can establish no retail traffic without the permission of the master.

XLVII. Whenever the labourer wishes to dispose of his own goods, furniture, or movable property, he shall inform his master of it, and he shall give him the preference over any other purchaser.

XLVIII. When the master shall have granted any piece of ground to his labourer, for him to cultivate during the days and hours of rest, the latter shall acquire all the produce of it, unless his master shall have agreed otherwise with him.

XLIX. The labourers cannot go out of the farm or establishment in which they serve, without a written permission from the master of his delegate.

Those found without this document shall be apprehended by the authorities, and reconducted at the master's expense to the place from which they came.

hen it shall have been agreed on in the contracts, to give the labourers any particular kind of food, or clothes of any particular form or quality, and circumstances shall have arisen to prevent the master providing himself with one or the other; the kind, quality, or form of either may be altered, but not the quantity.

If the labourers do not agree to this alteration, they shall address themselves to their protector, who shall decide on the complaint, conciliating as much as possible the interests of the two parties, but in all cases forming a resolution, which shall satisfy the essential rights of the labourers.

LI. In whatever terms medical assistance may have been stipulated for, in favour of the labourers, the said assistance shall comprise, not only the attendance of the doctor, but also the medicines and food prescribed by the latter during the illness and convalescence of the labourers.

LII. The labourers shall work for their masters, on working days, the number of hours agreed in the contracts.

By working days it is understood for the performance of this Article, all those on which the precepts of the Church do not prohibit working, and which notwithstanding the feast celebrated on them, are expressly authorized as working days by the ecclesiastical authority.

LIII. In no case, and notwithstanding any stipulation to the contrary, can the masters exact more than at the rate of 12 hours daily work from their labourers.

LIV. When the right of the master to distribute the number of hours agreed upon with the labourer, in the best manner for his interests, shall have been stated in the contract according to what is stated in No. 6 of Article VI, it shall be understood that the said right is limited, so that the labourer can never be obliged to work more than 15 hours in one day, and that he shall have at least 6 consecutive hours of rest either by night or day.

If the said right should not have been stipulated for in the contract, the master shall not be able to exact more hours of work daily than those agreed upon.

LV. The labourer shall perform for his master all the lawful services which he may require, unless it should have been agreed upon in the contract, what services he was to perform, to the exclusion of all others.

    In this case the labourer can refuse to do other service, than that agreed upon.

    A master can also let out the services of the labourers to a third person, whenever the said labourers are of the number of those stipulated in the contract, or when no clause of the said contract opposes it.

LVI.   When the labourer shall be unwell or convalescent, he shall not be obliged to work, until the doctor states that he can return to his duty, without endangering his health.

LVII.   The masters shall pay the stipulated salary to their labourers, in the form and under the conditions of the contract.

LVIII.   The labourers shall receive their full salary while sick or convalescent from maladies contracted in consequence of, or by any cause dependent on, the will of the master.

    If the malady proceeded from other causes, the workman shall not have such a right, if he shall not have stipulated for it in the contract.

LIX.   The labourer who according to his contract is to draw a salary during his maladies, proceeding from any causes, shall not be able to exact it however when the malady is occasioned by his own acts executed with malice.

LX.   For the performance of what is stated in the two preceding Articles, and in Article LI, the maladies of the workmen shall be examined by the professional men of the farm or establishment in which they work, and in default by two doctors named by the master. If the labourer does not agree with their opinion, he can address himself to the delegated protector, in order that by his instructions he may be re-examined by two doctors, one named by the labourer and the other by the master, to whose decision both parties must submit, without further appeal. If the doctors named by the master and the workman disagree between themselves, a third shall be named by the delegated protector, whose opinion shall be decisive.

LXI.   The labourers shall indemnify their masters for the days and hours which they may have lost by their own fault by prolonging their contract the necessary time.

    The workman shall enjoy no salary for the days lost through his fault, except the contrary should have been expressly stipulated in the contract.

What is stated in this Article, shall be in force without being an obstacle to the other punishments, which the labourer shall incur by the fault in question.

LXII. For the execution of what is ordained in the first paragraph of the preceding Article, the owners or persons in charge of farms or establishments, where there are Chinese labourers shall keep account-books, showing the amount of work done by them daily, and the sum paid to them, so that the amount which one of them owed or was to receive could be shown at once, and in the former case show for how long the respective contracts were to be prolonged.

LXIII. The account of work and payments of each labourer, shall be made up at the end of each month, and he shall be made aware of the result in order that if he had any observation to make, he might do so at once, or apply to the protector in case of his not agreeing to the decision of the master.

LXIV. The clause which in conformity with Article VI, paragraph 8, all contracts ought to contain, obliging the labourer to submit to the discipline of the arm or establishment in which he has to work, and any other which shall oblige him to obey the orders of his master, shall always be interpreted subject to the exception, that the rules and orders given to the labourer, shall not be contrary to other conditions of the same contract, nor to what is stated in these regulations.

LXV. When a labourer shall escape from the farm or establishment in which he serves, his master shall inform the local authorities in order that proper search shall be made for him.

The master shall at once pay the expenses attendant on his capture and restitution, but he shall have the right to indemnify himself by retaining half the salary coming to the fugitive.

LXVI. The master shall take means to teach the labourers the dogmas and the morality of the true religion, but without employing other means for that purpose than persuasion and conviction; and if any one expressed a desire to become converted to the Catholic faith, he shall acquaint the respective parish priest of it, in order that the proper steps may be taken.

LXVII. When a labourer shall receive an injury or offence, which does not constitute a transgression of the law, on his person or to his interests, from a free man or from a labourer of another master, the master shall take information on the subject; and if he thinks the complaint to be well founded, he shall demand reparation from the offender or his master, by friendly and extra-judicial means; and if these means were not sufficient to obtain it, he shall demand reparation before the competent authorities, or shall inform the "Promotor Fiscal" of the facts, in order that he may demand it. If he does not think the complaint founded he shall tell the workman so, exhorting him to desist from his purpose; but if the workman does not agree with his decision, he can apply to the "Promotor Fiscal," to make the proper demand.

When the complaint shall be directed against another labourer belonging to the same master, the latter or his representative shall decide the question, as they think right. Either of the two parties can reclaim against this decision to the protector or his delegate who shall make themselves acquainted with the affair in the form prescribed by Article XXXIII.

LXVIII.   The introducers of labourers, and the masters who shall fail in any of the obligations or formalities laid down in this, and in the preceding chapter shall incur a fine in proportion to the gravity of the offence, which shall be imposed upon them by the Government, without its being any hindrance to the penal or civil responsibility to which they may be subject, and which must be exacted from them by the authorities in the proper manner.

CHAP. III—Respecting the Disciplinary Jurisdiction of the Masters.

LXIX.   The masters shall exercise over their labourers disciplinary jurisdiction, and in virtue of this right, they shall be able to punish them in the following manners:

1st.   Arrest of from one to ten days.
2nd.   Suspension of wages during the same time.
The first of these punishments may be inflicted without the second, but the latter never without the former.

LXX.   Whenever the master shall inflict upon his labourer either of the punishments mentioned in the foregoing Article, he shall give notice of the same within the 24 hours following to the protector, in order that he may judge for himself, if he should think it necessary, of the fault committed, and alter the sentence of the master, should it appear unjust to him.

The master who shall fail to give the said notice within the time prescribed, shall be punished by the competent authority by a fine of from 25 to 100 dollars.

LXXI.   The labourers can always complain to the protector of any injury done to them by their masters, whether of being punished without reason; imposing tasks on them which are beyond their powers, or any other fault in his treatment of them.

If the protector shall find the master guilty of any crime, he shall denounce him to the competent tribunal, and if only of a slight fault, he shall himself impose on him a fine which shall not exceed 100 dollars.

LXXII.   To insure the fulfilment of what is stated in the two last Articles, the protectors shall be able, either themselves or by delegates, to visit, when they think proper, the estates or establishments where labourers are employed, and so collect what information they may deem advisable.

LXXIII. The delegates of the master on the estate or establishment can exercise disciplinary jurisdiction, but under the pecuniary responsibility of the master himself, while they do not cease to be responsible for the penalties they may incur.

LXXIV.   The following faults shall be punished according to discipline:

1st.   Want of subordination to the masters, to the heads of the industrial establishments, or to any other delegate of the master.

2nd.   Refusing to work, or want of punctuality in fulfilling the tasks given to the labourers.

3rd.   Injuries committed which do not produce wounds, which prevent the injured party from working.

4th.   Flight.

5th.   Drunkenness.

6th.   The infraction of the rules of discipline laid down by the master.

7th.   Any offence against decency, as long as it does not consist of one of those crimes which can only be prosecuted at the request of a prosecutor, or that when it did consist of such an offence, the injured party does not complain of him.

8th.   Any other malicious act, and any which may be construed into injuring or aggrieving a third party, and which does not constitute, notwithstanding, a crime which may be officially proceeded against according to law.

LXXV.   The disciplinary jurisdiction shall be exercised by the masters, without prejudice to the right of a third injured party to exact that the offending labourer shall be punished by the tribunals, if there was motive for it.

LXXVI.   In all cases of penal or civil responsibility, in which the masters are not competent judges, the ordinary tribunals shall take cognizance of it, to which the labourers shall present themselves, represented in the manner prescribed in these regulations.

LXXVII.   When the punishments mentioned in Article LXIX shall not be sufficient to prevent the repetition, by the labourer, of the same or other faults, the master will have recourse to the protector, who shall determine, if the act constitutes a crime in the eyes of the law, that the offender shall be punished in accordance to the law, or in a contrary case, by the augmentation of disciplinary punishments.

LXXVIII.   In a case where the labourers on an estate shall rise and resist by force and collectively the orders of the superiors, the master shall also be permitted to use force to bring them into subjection, giving immediate notice to the protector of the district, in order that he, should the gravity of the case require it, shall order that the offenders shall be punished in the presence of the other labourers.

CHAP. IV.—General Arrangements

LXXIX.   All renunciation which may be made of the arrangements in these regulations established in favour of the Chinese, shall be null.

LXXX.   The Governor Captain-General of the island shall adopt the necessary measures, so that in the month of January in every year, the masters shall draw up, a correct return of the labourers, showing in these returns their name, sex, age, condition, the work on which they were employed during the time of their contract; and the name, profession, and habitation of the respective masters.

The same authorities shall send to the Colonial Minister an annual return of the said masters in which shall be stated the number of labourers, classed by sex, by age up to 15 years, from 15 to 50, and from 50 upwards; by condition, of bachelor, married, or widower; by occupations, according as they may be engaged in agricultural, industrial, or domestic occupations; by the districts in which they reside; and by the time of the duration of their contracts, according as there may, from less than 5 years, from 5 to 10 years, from 10 to 15 years, and from 15 years upwards.

LXXXI. The Government reserves the right to suspend or prohibit at any time the introduction of Chinese labourers in the island of Cuba.

The resolution which they have adopted in this sense, shall be published in the Gazette of Madrid and in that of Havana, and from the date of its insertion in the latter, will begin the term within which the expeditions will be still permitted: this term shall not be less than 8 months, and the vessels arriving afterwards shall be considered as in Article XX.

All companies who may engage in this traffic, will understand that, by the act of engaging in it, they acknowledge that the suspension or prohibition of the traffic does not entitle them to any sort of indemnification.

LXXXII. The Royal Decree of March 22, 1854, and all other previous regulations respecting this matter are hereby annulled.

Given at the Palace this 6th day of June, 1860.

Signed by the Royal Hand.
Leopold O'Donnell, Minister of War and Colonies.

CONVENTION TO REGULATE THE ENGAGEMENT OF CHINESE EMIGRANTS BY BRITISH AND FRENCH SUBJECTS

The government of his Majesty the Emperor of China, having requested that, in accordance with the terms of conventions signed at Peking the 24th and 25th of October, 1860, a set of regulations should be framed to secure to Chinese emigrants those safeguards which are required for their moral and physical well-being, the following, after due discussion and deliberation of the Yamen of foreign affairs, have been adopted by the undersigned, and will henceforth be in force:

REGULATIONS

ARTICLE I

Any person desiring to open an emigrant agency in any port in China must make an application in writing to that effect to his consul, enclosing at the same time a copy of the rules which he proposes to observe in his establishment, a copy of the contract which he offers to emigrants, together with the necessary proofs that he has complied with all the conditions imposed by the laws of his country regulating emigration.

ARTICLE II

The consul, after having assured himself of the solvency and respectability of the applicant, and having examined and approved the copies of the rules and contracts, shall communicate them to the Chinese authorities, and shall request them to issue the license necessary for opening an emigration agency.

The license, together with the rules and contracts as approved by the Chinese authorities, will be registered at the consulate.

ARTICLE III

No license to open an emigration agency shall be withdrawn except upon sufficient grounds, and then only with the sanction of the consul. In such a case the emigration agent shall have no claim to compensation for the closing of his establishment and the suspension of his operations.

ARTICLE IV

No modification of the rules and contracts, when once approved by the consul and by the Chinese authorities, shall be made without their express consent. And in order that no emigrant may be ignorant of them, the said rules and contracts shall in all cases be posted up on the door of the emigration agency and in the quarters of the emigrants.

The emigration agents shall be allowed to circulate and make generally known in the towns and villages of the province copies of these rules and contracts, which must in all cases bear the seals of the Chinese authorities and of the consulate.

ARTICLE V

Every emigration agent shall be held responsible, under the laws of his country, for the due execution of the clauses of the contract signed by him until its expiration.

ARTICLE VI

Every Chinese applied to by the emigration agent to find him emigrants shall be provided with a special license from the Chinese authorities, and he alone will be responsible for any act done by him in the above capacity, that may be, whether intentionally or unintentionally, in contravention to the laws of the empire.

ARTICLE VII

Every Chinese wishing to emigrate under an engagement shall cause his name to be entered in a register kept for that purpose, in the presence of the emigration agent and of an inspector deputed by the Chinese government. He will then be at liberty to return to his home, or to remain in the emigration depot, to await the departure of the ship which is to carry him to his destination.

ARTICLE VIII

The contracts shall specify:

1st. The place of destination and the length of the engagement.
2d. The right of the emigrant to be conveyed back to his own country, and the sum that shall be paid at the expiration of his contract to cover the expense of his voyage home and that of his family, should they accompany him.
3d. The number of working days in the year and the length of each day's work.
4th. The wages, rations, clothing and other advantages promised to the emigrant.
5th. Gratuitous medical attendance.
6th. The sum which the emigrant agrees to set aside out of his monthly wages for the benefit of persons to be named by him, should he desire to appropriate any sum to such a purpose.
7th. Copy of the 8th, 9th, 10th, 14th and 22d articles of these regulations.

Any clause which shall purport to render invalid any of the provisions of this regulation is null and void.

ARTICLE IX

The term of each emigrant's engagement shall not exceed five years; at the expiration of which the sum stipulated in the contract shall be paid for him, to cover the expense of his return to his country. In the event of his obtaining permission to remain without an engagement in the colony, this sum will be placed in his own hands.

It shall always be at the option of the emigrant to enter into a second engagement of five years, for which he shall be paid a premium equivalent to one-half the cost of his return to China. In such a case, the sum destined to cover the expense of his return home shall not be paid until the expiration of his second engagement.

Every emigrant who may become invalided and incapable of working, shall be allowed, without waiting for the expiration of his contract, to claim before the legal courts of the colony or territory where he may be, payment on his behalf of the sum destined to cover the expense of his return to China.

ARTICLE X

The emigrant shall in no case be forced to work more than six days out of seven, nor more than nine hours and a half in the day.

The emigrant shall be free to arrange with his employer the conditions of work by the piece or job, and of all extra labor undertaken during days and hours set apart for rest.

The obligation, on holidays, to attend to cattle, or to do such service as the necessities of daily life may demand, shall not be considered as labor.

ARTICLE XI

No engagement to emigrate, entered into by any Chinese subject under twenty years of age, will be valid, unless he produce a certificate from the proper Chinese authorities, stating that he has been authorized to contract such engagement by his parents, or in default of his parents, by the magistrate of the port at which he is to embark.

ARTICLE XII

After four days, but not less, from the date of the entry of the emigrant's name on the register of the agency, the officer deputed by the Chinese government being present, the contract shall be read to the emigrant, and he shall be asked whether he agrees to it, and having answered in the affirmative, he shall then and there append his signature thereto.

ARTICLE XIII

The contract once signed, the emigrant is at the disposal of the agent, and must not absent himself from the depot without the permission of the agent.

Before embarking, every emigrant shall be called before the officer deputed by the Chinese authorities, to ratify his contract, which shall be registered at the consulate.

Twenty-four hours before the sailing of the ship the emigrants shall be mustered on board before the consul and the inspector of customs, or their deputies, and the list shall be finally closed for signature and registration by the consul and the inspector.

Any individual refusing to proceed after this muster shall be bound to pay the expenses of his maintenance in the emigration depot, at the rate of one hundred cash (one-tenth of a tael) per diem. In default of payment he shall be handed over to the Chinese magistrate to be punished according to the laws.

ARTICLE XIV

Any sum handed over to the emigrant before his departure shall only be regarded in the light of a premium upon his engagement. All advances upon his future wages are formally forbidden, except in the case of their being appropriated to the use of his family; and the consul will take especial pains to provide against their being employed in any other way. Such advances shall not exceed six months' wages, and shall be covered by a stoppage of one dollar per month, until the entire debt shall have been paid.

It is absolutely forbidden, whether on the voyage or during the emigrant's stay in the colony or territory in which he may be employed, to make any advances to him in money or kind, payable after the expiration of his engagement. Any agreement of this nature shall be null and void, and shall give the creditor no power to oppose the return of the emigrant to his country at the time fixed by the contract.

ARTICLE XV

The emigrant, during his stay in the depot, shall be bound to conform to the regulations adopted for its internal economy by the consul and the Chinese authorities.

ARTICLE XVI

Any emigrant who may be riotous, or guilty of any misconduct shall be immediately locked up, until the arrival of the officers deputed by the Chinese authorities, to whom he will be handed over to be punished in conformity with the laws of the empire; the officers of the agency being in no case authorized to take the law into their own hands, and inflict any punishment.

ARTICLE XVII

The deputies of the consul and of the Chinese authorities shall at all times be empowered to demand admittance to the agency, and to summon the emigrants before them for the purpose of interrogation.

They will be present at the signing of the contracts and at the embarcation of the coolies.

They will see to the maintenance of order, to the healthiness and cleanliness of the rooms destined to receive the emigrants, to the separation of families and women, and to the arrangements on board the transport ships.

They may at any time demand that experts or medical officers shall be called in, in order to verify any defects which they may have remarked; they may suspend the embarcation of emigrants in ships, the arrangements on board of which may seem to them defective, and they may reject coolies afflicted with contagious diseases.

ARTICLE XVIII

The emigration agent shall be bound to pay into the Custom Bank the sum of three dollars for every male adult entered on the list of coolies embarked, to meet the expenses of inspection.

ARTICLE XIX

Any emigrant claimed by the Chinese government as an offender against the law shall be handed over to the authorities without opposition, through the consul; and in such case the whole sum expended for the maintenance of the emigrant in the agency, or on board ship, shall be repaid immediately to the emigration agent, at the rate of one hundred cash (one-tenth of a tael) per diem.

The sum of the premium advance, clothes, &c., entered in the agency register against such emigrant, shall in like manner be repaid by the Chinese government.

ARTICLE XX

The emigration agent shall not be at liberty to embark emigrants on board any ship which shall not have satisfied the consul that in respect of its internal economy, stores and sanitary arrangements, all the conditions required by the laws of the country to which the said ship may belong are fulfilled.

Should the Chinese authorities, upon the report of the officers deputed by them, conceive it their duty to protest against the embarcation of a body of emigrants in a ship approved by the consul, it shall be in the power of the customs to suspend the granting of the ship's port clearance until further information shall have been obtained, and until the final decision of the legation of the country to which the suspected ship belongs shall have been pronounced.

ARTICLE XXI

On arrival of the ship at her destination, the duplicate of the list of emigrants shall be presented by the captain to be *viséd* by his consul and by the local authorities.

In the margin, and opposite to the name of each emigrant, note shall be made of deaths, births, and diseases during the voyage, and of the destination assigned to each emigrant in the colony or territory in which he is to be employed.

This document shall be sent by the emigration agent to the consul at the port at which the emigrants embarked, and by him delivered to the Chinese authorities.

ARTICLE XXII

In the distribution of the emigrants as laborers the husband shall not be separated from his wife, nor shall parents be separated from their children, being under fifteen years of age.

No laborer shall be bound to change his employer without his consent, except in the event of the factory or plantation upon which he is employed changing hands.

His Imperial Highness the Prince of Kung has further declared, in the name of the government of his Majesty, the Emperor of China:

1st. That the Chinese government throws no obstacle in the way of free emigration; that is to say, to the departure of Chinese subjects, embarking of their own free will and at their own expense, for foreign countries; but that all attempts to bring Chinese under an engagement to emigrate, otherwise than as the present regulations provide, are formally forbidden, and will be prosecuted with the extreme rigor of the law.

2d. That a law of the empire punishes by death those who by fraud or by force may kidnap Chinese subjects for the purpose of sending them abroad against their will.

3d.   That whereas the operations of emigration agents, with a view to the supply of coolie labor abroad, are authorized at all the open ports, when conducted in conformity with these regulations, and under the joint supervision of the consuls and the Chinese authorities, it follows that where this joint supervision cannot be exercised, such operations are formally forbidden.

These declarations are here placed on record, in order that they may have the same force and validity as the regulations contained in the twenty-two articles foregoing.

Done and signed at Peking in triplicate, the 5th of March, 1866.

RUTHERFORD ALCOCK.
Seal and signature of PRINCE KUNG.
HENRY DE BELLONNET.

APPENDIX III

AMERICAN ACTIONS AGAINST THE "COOLIE TRADE"

1. Public Notification of 1856*

The undersigned, commissioner and minister plenipotentiary of the United States of America to China, in accordance with the instructions of his government in relation to the so called coolie trade, 'publicly to discountenance the same on his arrival in China,' issues this public notification to all whom it may concern:

Whereas the history of the traffic in Chinese coolies, as carried on in vessels of the United States and under other flags during the past few years, is replete with illegalities, immoralities, and revolting and inhuman atrocities, strongly resembling those of the African slave trade in former years, some of them exceeding the horrors of the 'middle passage,' women and children having been bought for the purpose, and others not merely seduced under false pretences, ignorant of their destination, but some forcibly abducted and violently borne to countries unknown to them, never to return; and not only by the ancient statutes of the Chinese empire; the imperial government has prohibited the same, threatening with death the "brokers, hardened miscreants, who impose upon the people and seduce them to their destruction'; and

Whereas the correspondence of the imperial government with this legation has evinced its strong disapproval of the traffic, describing it in terms which place it upon a level with the slave trade itself; and admitting the trade proper, *per se*, it has been carried on in *localities where foreign trade* is not permitted by *any treaties*, and is therefore illegal; and the foreign name has been rendered odious by this traffic, hundreds and thousands of lives having been inhumanly sacrificed, not, perhaps, intentionally, but nevertheless they have been sacrificed, and in some instances in a manner than which nothing

---

*　Source: U.S. Congress, House Report No. 443, 1st Sess., 36th Cong., 6-7.

more revolting can be conceived, whilst others who have survived have scarcely been more fortunate; and

Whereas the amicable relations of the two governments are being jeopardized, and honorable and lawful commerce imperiled, and even the lives of those engaged in the inhuman pursuit have been exposed to the vengeance of those whose relations and friends have been bought, kidnapped, or grossly deceived in the progress of the coolie trade:

The undersigned therefore calls upon all citizens of the United States to desist from this irregular and immoral traffic, and makes known to all whom it may concern the high disapprobation thereof of the government of the United States, and forewarns all who may hereafter engage therein that they will not only forfeit the protection of their government while so doing, in whatever consequences they may be involved, but furthermore render themselves liable to the heavy penalties to which the traffic, if as hitherto in some instances conducted, may expose them.

This notification respects the 'coolie trade,' in contradistinction to the voluntary emigration of Chinese adventurers; between these there exists a wide difference.

Regulations for the business of furnishing Chinese labor to countries that may desire the same, and for affording facilities to Chinese voluntarily disposed to render such service, in providing outfit and passage and means, and freedom to return at their option, may be a subject for future treaty stipulation, or government arrangement on the part of the western natives and China. The United States consuls will be instructed to convey copies of this notification to the proper Chinese authorities at the five ports.

Given under my hand and seal of office this 10th day of January, 1856.

PETER PARKER

2. An Act to prohibit the "Coolie Trade" by American Citizens in American Vessels*

Sec. 1. *Be it enacted by the Senate and House of Representatives of the United States of America in Congress assembled*, That no citizen or citizens of the United States, or foreigner coming into or residing within the same, shall, for

---

*   *U.S. Statues at Large*, Vol. XII (1861-1862), 340-341.

himself or for any other person whatsoever, either as master, factor, owner, or otherwise, build, equip, load, or otherwise prepare, any ship or vessel, or any steamship or steam-vessel, registered, enrolled, or licensed, in the United States, or any port within the same, for the purpose of procuring from China, or from any port or place therein, or from any other port or place the inhabitants or subjects of China known as "coolies," to be transported to any foreign country, port, or place whatever, to be disposed of, or sold, or transferred, for any term of years or for any time whatever, as servants or apprentices, or to be held to service or labor. And if any ship or vessel, steamship, or steam-vessel, belonging in whole or in part to citizens of the United States, and registered, enrolled, or otherwise licensed as aforesaid, shall be employed for the said purposes, or in the "coolie trade," so called or shall be caused to procure or carry from China or elsewhere, as aforesaid, any subjects of the Government of China for the purpose of transporting or disposing of them as aforesaid, every such ship or vessel, steamship, or steam-vessel, her tackle, apparel, furniture, and other appurtenances, shall be forfeited to the United States, and shall be liable to be seized, prosecuted, and condemned in any of the circuit courts, or district courts of the United States for the district where the said ship or vessel, steamship, or steam-vessel may be found, seized, or carried.

Sec. 2. *And be it further enacted*, That every person who shall so build, fit out, equip, load, or otherwise prepare, or who shall send to sea, or navigate, as owner, master, factor, agent, or otherwise, any ship or vessel, steamship, or steam-vessel, belonging in whole or in part to citizens of the United States, or registered, enrolled, or licensed within the same, or at any port thereof, knowing or intending that the same shall be employed in that trade or business aforesaid, contrary to the true intent and meaning of this act, or in anywise aiding or abetting therein, shall be severally liable to be indicted therefor, and, on conviction thereof, shall be liable to a fine not exceeding two thousand dollars and be imprisoned not exceeding one year.

Sec. 3. *And be it further enacted*, That if any citizen or citizens of the United States shall, contrary to the true intent and meaning of this act, take on board of any vessel, or receive or transport any such persons as are above described in this act, for the purpose of disposing of them as aforesaid, he or they shall be liable to be indicted therefor, and, on conviction thereof, shall be liable to a fine not exceeding two thousand dollars and be imprisoned not exceeding one year.

Sec. 4. *And be it further enacted*, That nothing in this act hereinbefore contained shall be deemed or construed to apply to or affect any free and voluntary emigration of any Chinese subject, or to any vessel carrying such person as passenger on board the same: *Provided, however*, That a permit or certificate shall be prepared and signed by the consul or consular agent of the United States residing at the port from which such vessel may take her departure, containing the name of such person, and setting forth the fact of his voluntary emigration from such port or place, which certificate shall be given until such consul or consular agent shall be first personally satisfied by evidence produced of the truth of the facts therein contained.

Sec. 5. *And be it further enacted*, That all the provisions of the act of Congress approved February twenty-second, eighteen hundred and forty-seven, entitled "An act to regulate the carriage of passengers in merchant vessels," and all the provisions of the act of Congress approved March third, eighteen hundred and forty-nine, entitled "An act to extend the provisions of all laws now in force relating to the carriage of passengers in merchant vessels and the regulation thereof," shall be extended and shall apply to all vessels owned in whole or in part by citizens of the United States, and registered, enrolled, or licensed within the United States, propelled by wind or by steam, and to all masters thereof, carrying passengers or intending to carry passengers from any foreign port or place without the United States to any other foreign port or place without the United States; and that all penalties and forfeitures provided for in said act shall apply to vessels and masters last aforesaid.

Sec. 6. *And be it further enacted*, That the President of the United States shall be, and he is hereby, authorized and empowered, in such way and at such time as he shall judge proper to the end that the provisions of this act may be enforced according to the true intent and meaning thereof, to direct and order the vessels of the United States, and the masters and commanders thereof, to examine all vessels navigated or owned in whole or in part by citizens of the United States, and registered, enrolled, or licensed under the laws of the United States, wherever they may be, whenever, in the judgment of such master or commanding officer thereof, reasonable cause shall exist to believe that such vessel has on board, in violation of the provisions of this act, any subjects of China known as "coolies," for the purpose of transportation; and upon sufficient proof that such vessel is employed in violation of the provisions of this act, to cause such vessel to be carried, with her officers and crew, into any port or district within the United States, and delivered to the marshal of such district, to be held and disposed of according to the provisions of this act.

Sec. 7. *And be it further enacted*, That this act shall take effect from and after six months from the day of its passage.

APPROVED, February 19, 1862.

CONVENTION AND TREATY BETWEEN THE REPUBLIC OF PERU AND THE EMPEROR OF CHINA*

Signed, in the Spanish, English, and Chinese Languages, at Tientsin, 26th June, 1874.
Ratifications exchanged at Tientsin, 7th August, 1875.

CONVENTION
SPECIAL AGREEMENT BETWEEN PERU AND CHINA

The undersigned, Aurelio García y García, Post-Captain in the Peruvian Navy, Envoy Extraordinary and Minister Plenipotentiary of the Republic of Peru for the Empires of China and Japan; and Li, Minister Plenipotentiary of His Majesty the Emperor of China Imperial Commissioner, Grand Guardian of the Heir Apparent, Grand Secretary, a President of the Board of War, Governor-General of the Province of Chihli, and invested with the dignity of the second order of nobility;

Have concluded the following Special Agreement:—

Inasmuch as, at present, Chinese are known to be residing in great numbers within the territory of Peru, and in view of the representations that have been made to the effect that some of these are suffering grievances, now then the respective Plenipotentiaries, being desirous of establishing amicable relations between the two countries, agree, on the one hand, that a Treaty of Friendship, Commerce, and Mutual Intercourse shall be concluded, and on the other, that with the view of establishing a thorough friendly understanding, the Chinese Governments shall send a Commission to Peru.

---

* Source: Mayers, *Treaties Between the Empire of China and Foreign Powers*, 1992-197.

The said Commission shall institute a thorough investigation into the condition of Chinese immigrants in all parts of Peru, to whom they shall make known the subjects in view by means of public notifications.

The Government of Peru, on their side, will give the fullest possible assistance to the Commission in the fulfilment of its duties, and will treat it with all due courtesy.

On the arrival of the Commission in Peru, the Peruvian Government will order all local or provincial authorities to give to the Commission all the assistance in their power, for the performance of its duties.

In case it should be ascertained that Chinese immigrants whose contracts have not expired, be their numbers what they may, are actually suffering ill-treatment, it is now agreed that the Commission shall communicate the particulars concerning them to the local authorities. In case the employers of such Chinese immigrants decline to acknowledge the ill-treatment, the local authorities shall then send the complaints in question before the tribunals for judicial inquiry and decision.

If the immigrants in any case be dissatisfied with the decision of the primary Judge, it shall be open to the aggrieved parties forthwith to appeal to the higher Courts of Justice of Peru, for further investigation.

The Chinese immigrants will be placed on a footing of equality as regards legal procedure with that enjoyed by the subjects of the most favoured nation residing in Peru.

From the date of the ratification of this special agreement by the Peruvian Government, the said Government will compel the employers of Chinese immigrants whose contracts have expired, and in which it may have been stipulated that they shall be sent back to China, to provide them with passage back to their native country, if they be desirous of returning to China.

In the case of Chinese immigrants in whose contracts no stipulation is made for the return passage on the expiry of the contracts, and provided that the immigrants shall express a wish to return to China, but shall be without the means of providing their own passage, the Peruvian Government will cause them to be repatriated gratuitously, in the ships which leave Peru for China.

The present agreement is written and signed in six copies, viz., two in Spanish, two in Chinese, and two in English. All these versions have the same meaning and intention.

The present Agreement shall be ratified by His Excellency the President of the Republic of Peru, after being approved by the Peruvian Congress, and by

His Majesty the Emperor of China; and the ratifications shall be exchanged at Shanghai or Tientsin.

In token whereof the respective Plenipotentiaries have signed and sealed this Agreement.

Done at Tientsin, this twenty-sixth day of the month of June in the year of our Lord one thousand eight hundred and seventy-four, corresponding to the Chinese date thirteenth day of the fifth moon of the thirteenth year of Tung-Chi.

(Signed)   AURELIO GARCÍA y GARCÍA
(Signed)   LI HUNG-CHANG

================================

TREATY

His Excellency the President of the Republic of Peru and His Majesty the Emperor of China, being sincerely desirous to establish friendly relations between the two countries, have resolved to confirm the same by a Treaty of Friendship, Commerce, and Navigation with the view of laying the foundations of mutual intercourse; and for that purpose, have named as their Plenipotentiaries, that is to say:

His Excellency the President of Peru, Don Aurelio García y García, a Post-Captain in the Peruvian Navy, Envoy Extraordinary and Minister Plenipotentiary of that Republic for the Empires of China and Japan; and His Majesty the Emperor of China, Li, Minister Plenipotentiary, Imperial Commissioner, Grand Guardian of the Heir Apparent, Grand Secretary, a President of the Board of War, Governor-General of the Province of Chih-li, and invested with the dignity of the second order of nobility;

Who, after having examined and exchanged their respective full powers, have together agreed upon the following Treaty for the benefit and protection of the merchants and people of the two countries:—

Art. I.—There shall be peace and friendship between the Republic of Peru and His Majesty the Emperor of China. Their respective citizens and subjects shall reciprocally enjoy in the territories of the high contracting parties full and perfect protection to their persons and property.

Art. II—In order to facilitate friendly intercourse in future, His Excellency the President of Peru may, if he see fit, appoint a Diplomatic Agent to the Court of Peking, and His Majesty the Emperor of China may, in like manner, if he see fit, appoint a Diplomatic Agent to the Government of Peru.

His Majesty the Emperor of China hereby agrees that the Diplomatic Agent so appointed by the Government of Peru, may, with his family and the persons of his suite, permanently reside at Peking, or may visit it occasionally, at the option of the Peruvian Government.

In like manner, the Diplomatic Agent of China may, with his family and the persons of his suite, permanently reside at Lima, or may visit it occasionally, at the option of the Chinese Government.

Art. III—The Diplomatic Agent of each of the contracting parties shall, at their respective residences, enjoy all privileges and immunities accorded to them by international usages.

Art. IV—The Government of Peru may appoint a Consul-General, and for such open ports or cities of China, where it may be considered most expedient for the interest of Peruvian commerce, Consuls, Vice-Consuls, or Consular Agents. These officers shall be treated with due respect by the Chinese authorities, and enjoy the same privileges and immunities as the Consular officers of the most favoured nation.

His Majesty the Emperor of China may appoint a Consul-General, Consuls, Vice-Consuls, or Consular Agents at any port or town of Peru where Consular Officers of any other power are admitted to reside. All of these officers shall enjoy the same rights and privileges as those of the most favoured nation in Peru.

It is further agreed that the appointment of the said Consular Officers shall not be made in merchants residing in the locality.

Art. V—Peruvian citizens are at liberty to travel for the pleasure, or for purposes of trade, in all parts of China, under express condition of being provided with passports written in Spanish and Chinese, issued in due form by the Consuls of Peru and *viséd* by the Chinese authorities. These passports, if demanded, must be produced for examination in the localities passed through. If the passport be not irregular, the bearer will be allowed to proceed, and no opposition shall be offered to his hiring persons, or hiring vessels or carts for the carriage of his baggage or merchandise, and the said merchandise shall be conveyed in accordance with the General Regulations of foreign trade.

If the traveller be without a passport, he shall be handed over to the nearest Consul in order to enable him to procure one. The above provision will in like manner be applicable to cases of a Peruvian citizen committing any offence against the law of China. But he shall in no case be subjected by the Chinese authorities to any kind of ill-treatment or insult.

The citizens of Peru may go on excursions from the open ports or cities to a distance not exceeding 100 *li*, and for a period not exceeding five days, without being provided with a passport.

The above provisions do not apply to the crews of ships, who, when on shore, shall be subject to the disciplinary regulations drawn up by the Consul and the local authorities.

Chinese subjects shall have the liberty to travel at their pleasure throughout the territory of Peru, as long as they behave peaceably, and commit no offence against the laws and regulations of the country.

Art. VI—The Republic of Peru and the Empire of China cordially recognize the inherent and inalienable right of man to change his home. Their citizens and subjects respectively may consequently go freely from the one country to the other for the purpose of curiosity, trade, labour, or as permanent residents. The high contracting parties therefore agree that the citizens and subjects of both countries shall only emigrate with their free and voluntary consent; and join in reprobating any other than an entirely voluntary emigration for the said purpose, and every act of violence or fraud that may be employed in Macao or the ports of China to carry away Chinese subjects. The contracting parties likewise pledge themselves to punish severely, according to their laws, their respective citizens and subjects who may violate the present stipulations, and also to proceed judicially against their respective ships that may be employed in such unlawful operations, imposing the fines which for such cases are established by their laws.

Art. VII—It is further agreed, that for the better understanding and more efficient protection of the Chinese subjects who reside in Peru, the Peruvian Government will appoint official interpreters of the Chinese language in the prefecture of the departments of Peru where the great centres of Chinese immigration exist.

Art. VIII—The merchant ships belonging to Peruvian citizens shall be permitted to frequent all the ports of China open to foreign trade, and to proceed to and fro at pleasure with their merchandise, enjoying the same rights and privileges as those of the most favoured nation.

In like manner the merchant ships belonging to Chinese subjects, may visit all the ports of Peru open to foreign commerce and trade in them, enjoying the same rights and privileges which in Peru are granted to the citizens or subjects of the most favoured nation.

Art. IX—Peruvian citizens shall pay at the ports of China open to foreign trade on all the goods imported or exported by them, the duties enumerated in the tariff which is now in force for the regulation of foreign commerce; but they can, in no case, be called to pay higher or other duties than those required now or in future of the citizens or subjects of the most favoured nation.

No other or higher duties shall be imposed in the ports of Peru on all goods imported or exported by Chinese subjects, than those which are or may be imposed in Peru on the commerce of the most favoured nation.

Art. X—The ship of war of each country respectively shall be at liberty to visit all the ports within the territories of the other, to which the ships of war of other nations are or may be permitted to come. They shall enjoy every facility, and meet no obstacle in purchasing provisions, coals, procuring water, and making necessary repairs. Such ships shall not be liable to the payment of duties of any kind.

Art. XI—Any Peruvian vessels, being from extraordinary causes compelled to seek a place of refuge, shall be permitted to enter any Chinese port whatever, without being subject to the payment of tonnage dues or duties on the goods, if only landed for the purpose of making the necessary repairs of the vessel, and remaining under the supervision of the Superintendent of Customs.

Should any such vessel be wrecked or stranded, the Chinese authorities shall immediately adopt measures for rescuing the crew, and for securing the vessel and cargo. The crew thus saved, shall receive friendly treatment, and, if necessary, shall be furnished with the means of conveyance to the nearest Consular station.

If any Chinese vessels be wrecked or compelled by stress of weather to seek a place of refuge in thecoasts of Peru, the local maritime authorities shall render to them every assistance in their power; the goods and merchandise saved from the wreck shall not be subject to duties, unless cleared for consumption; and the ships shall enjoy the same liberties which in equal cases are granted in Peru to the ships of other nations.

Art. XII—Peruvian citizens in China having reason to complain of a Chinese shall proceed at once to their Consular Officer and state to him their grievance. The Consul will inquire into the case, and do his utmost to arrange it amicably.

In like manner, if a Chinese have reason to complain of a Peruvian citizen in China, the Consular Officer shall listen to his complaint, and endeavour to come to a friendly arrangement.

Should the Consular Officer not succeed in making such an arrangement, then he shall request the assistance of the competent Chinese Officer, that they may together decide the matter according to the principles of equity.

Art. XIII—Chinese subjects guilty of a criminal action towards a Peruvian citizen in China shall be arrested and punished by the Chinese laws.

Peruvian citizens in China, who may commit any crime against a Chinese subject, shall be arrested and punished according to the laws of Peru, by the Peruvian Consular Officer.

Art. XIV—All questions in regard to rights, whether of property or person, arising between Peruvian citizens in China, shall be subject to the jurisdiction of the Peruvian authorities. Disputes between citizens of Peru and those of other foreign nations shall be decided in China according to the treaties existing between Peru and those foreign nations. In all cases, however, of Chinese subjects being concerned in the matter, the Chinese authorities may interfere in the proceeding according to Articles XII and XIII of the Treaty.

Art. XV—Chinese subjects in Peru shall have free and open access to the Courts of Justice of Peru for the prosecution and defence of their just rights; they shall enjoy in this respect the same rights and privileges as native citizens, and shall also be treated in every way like the citizens and subjects of other countries resident in Peru.

Art. XVI—The contracting parties agree, that the Government, public officers, and citizens of the Republic of Peru, shall fully and equally participate in all privileges, rights, immunities, jurisdictions, and advantages that may have been, or may be hereafter granted by His Majesty the Emperor of China, to the Government, public officers, citizens, or subjects of any other nation.

In like manner, the Government, public officers, and subjects of the Empire of China, shall enjoy in Peru all the rights, privileges, immunities, and advantages of every kind which in Peru are enjoyed by the Government, public officers, citizens, or subjects of the most favoured nation.

Art. XVII—In order to prevent for the future any discussion, and considering that the English language, among all foreign languages, is the most generally known in China, this Treaty is written in the Spanish, Chinese, and English languages, and signed in nine copies, three in each language. All these versions have the same sense and signification, but whenever the interpretation on the Spanish and Chinese versions may differ, then reference shall be made to the English text.

Art. XVIII—If in future the high contracting parties desire a modification of any stipulation contained in this Treaty, they shall be at liberty, after the lapse of ten years, dated from the day of the exchange of the ratifications of this Treaty, to open negotiations to that effect. Six months before the expiration of the ten years, either of the contracting parties may officially notify to the other that modifications of the Treaty are desired, and in what these consist. If no such notification is made, the Treaty remains in force for another ten years.

Art. XIX—The present Treaty shall be ratified by His Excellency the President of Peru after being approved by the Peruvian Congress, and by His Majesty the Emperor of China; and the ratifications shall be exchanged at Shanghai or Tientsin as soon as possible. In token whereof, the respective Plenipotentiaries have signed and sealed this Treaty.

Done at Tientsin, this twenty-sixth day of the month of June in the year of our Lord one thousand eight hundred and seventy-four, corresponding to the Chinese date the thirteenth day of the fifth moon of the thirteenth year of Tung-Chi.

(Signed)   AURELIO GARCÍA y GARCÍA
(Signed)   LI HUNG-CHANG.

SAMPLES OF CONTRACTS
OF INDENTURE

1. Contract of Indenture between Cow-hoy, native of China and J. Sevilla, agent for Don Domingo Elías of Peru.*

No. 286
Name: Cow-hoy
Age: 15 years
Profession:
Province: Nam-hoy.

Articles of Agreement made, entered into, and concluded at Cumsingmoon, China, this thirty-fifth day of January in the year of our Lord one thousand eight hundred and fifty-two. Between J. Sevilla, as agent for Don Domingo Elías, of the one part and Cow-hoy, native of the province of Nam-hoy of the other part.

Witness: that in the present agreement for the considerations hereinafter contained, the said Cow-hoy doth hereby promise and agree to proceed on board the vessel called the "Sussanah", whereof J. Lukey is master, now lying in the port of Cumsingmoon, and ready to proceed on a voyage to Arica and Isley and that he will then enter into service as cultivator, farmer, labourer, shepherd, workman or general servant for the period of six years from the commencement of such service; and that the said Cow-hoy will during the continuance of such period, till the soil, clear ground, herd cattle, drive carts, do garden or other such work as he may be required, and make himself generally useful. And that he will work, if required, to the best of his knowledge and ability as a mechanic or tradesman.

---

*   Source: BFO 61/134.

That the said Cow-hoy further binds himself, not only to the observance of this contract with Don Domingo Elías but also to the person or persons whom the said Don Domingo Elías, his attorney or agent shall provide or procure as master or employer.

That during the period aforesaid of six years, he the said Cow-hoy shall work neither for himself nor for any other but for the person or persons who shall be procured for him as master or employed, without his or their permission in writing, and that he shall not absent himself from his or their employment without leave.

That the said Cow-hoy further promises, covenants and agrees with and to the said Don Domingo Elías, his executors, administrators and assigns and to any person or persons to whom this contract may be made over, that a sum of one dollar monthly shall be deducted from the wages to be received by him for such services, for the repayment of the sum of the dollars which he the said Cow-hoy acknowledges to have received on account of his salary from the agent of the said Domingo Elias.

And these presents further witness as the agent, signing this document for Don Domingo Elías, and I hereby bind myself in his name that as soon as possible after the arrival of the above named vessel at her destination, Señor Elías shall provide for Cow-hoy, a master or employer who shall pay him the sum of three dollars per month and shall provide him with good lodgings and a sufficient quantity of wholesome food, and shall in all sickness not arising from misconduct provide him with medical attendance and medicines.

And it is also further agreed that the said Cow-hoy shall have one hour for each of his two daily meals, and that the period for work in each day shall be the usual period for working hours according to the custom of the place in which he may be located.

And it is further agreed that in all cases of sickness of the said Cow-hoy, arising from whatever cause soever, shall be considered as lost time to the master or employer and shall not be calculated in the said period of six years.

And it is further agreed that the said Cow-hoy shall be allowed three days in every year for the performance of his religious duties.

And it is furthermore agreed and declared by and between the said Don Domingo Elías and the said Cow-hoy that the said period of six years shall commence from the day of entering on such service as aforesaid, and that the ward month herein expressed, shall be and be taken to mean one calendar month and that the ward year shall be and be taken to mean twelve of such months.

And for the due fulfillment of requirements of this contract we declare that we hold ourselves bound by all its clauses and have hereunto affixed our signatures in presence of a witness.

Signature of Witness: For Don Domingo Elias
Richard Pollard   his agent, J. Sevilla

                                             Signature of Cow-hoy

2.   Chinese Laborer's Contract of Indenture for Cuba.*

I, a native of, in China, aged, acknowledge that I have agreed with Messrs. Vargas and Co., to that which is set forth in the following Articles:—

1.   I am engaged from the present moment to embark for Havana, in the Island of Cuba, on board such vessel as shall be appointed by the said firm.

2.   I am likewise engaged, and subject for a period of eight years, to work in the said island under the orders of Messrs Forrices, Ferran, and Dupiernis, or of any other persons to whom they may transfer this contract, for which transfer they are authorized by myself, in all descriptions of work that are customary there, in the country, the towns, or wherever they may place me, whether it be in private houses, establishments of any description of manufacture or art, or in sugar mills, tobacco plantations, coffee estates, cattle farms, stud-pastures, farms, and whatever appertains to urban or rural occupations, of whatever kind they may be.

3.   The eight years' engagement which I have contracted in the terms expressed in the preceeding Article shall commence to count from the day on which I shall be allotted to a master, after my arrival at the port of Havana, provided I arrive in good health, and from the eighth day after I leave the hospital or infirmary, if I arrive in ill-health, or incapable of performing labour at the time of my landing.

4.   The hours during which I am to labour will depend upon the description of work in which I shall be employed, and upon the application required by the said work, to be left at the discretion of the master to whom I

---

*   Source: BFO 881/894.

shall be assigned, provided always that my consecutive hours of repose are allowed me every twenty-four hours, beside the time required for dinner and breakfast, conformably with the hours observed in these matters by the other hired labourers in the island.

5. In addition to the hours of repose on working days, I cannot be compelled on Sundays to execute more labour than that which, of necessity, must be performed on such days, according to the kind of task in which I may be employed.

6. I likewise subject myself to the order and discipline observed in the establishment, workshop, estate, or private house where I shall be placed, and submit myself to the system of punishment which in those places is adopted for lack of application and industry, for disobedience of the master's or of his representative's orders, and for all faults not grave enough to require the intervention of the law.

7. For no reason, and under no pretext, can I, during the eight years for which I am bound in this contract, refuse my services to the master who will take me, nor escape, nor attempt to do so, for any cause whatever, nor in virtue of any indemnifications.

8. With regard to the contingency of sickness, I agree and stipulate that if my illness exceed one week in duration, my wages shall be suspended, and shall not again begin to be due until my recovery, or, in other words, until my health allows me to employ myself again in the service of my master.

Messrs. Vargas and Co., in the name of the Company referred to (whom they represent), agree for their part with me:—

1. That from the day when the eight years of my engagement commence to count, my wages, at 4 dollars per month, shall also begin.

2. That I shall be provided with daily rations of 8 oz. of salt meat, 2 1/2 lbs. of yams, and other wholesome and nutritious food.

3. That, during illness, I shall be provided in the infirmary with such assistance as my complaints require, with the comforts, medicines, and treatment called for by my complaint, and requisite for my preservation, for however long a time it may be.

4. That I shall be supplied with two changes of clothing, a woollen shirt, and a blanket every year.

5. The said firm are answerable for my passage to Havana, and my maintenance on board ship.

6. The said firm will advance me the sum of 8 dollars in gold or silver for my outfit for the voyage I am about to undertake.

7. They will likewise supply me with three changes of clothing, a coverlid, and other necessities, which amounting to 4 dollars, make, with the sum specified in the preceeding clause, a total of 12 dollars, which I will repay in Havana to the order of the said firm, by means of a monthly deduction of one dollar from my pay, by the party to whom this contract will be transferred. It is understood that on no other account can any deduction be made from my wages. I acknowledge that I have received in cash and clothing, as stated in the last clause, the sum of 12 dollars therein mentioned, which I will repay at Havana as agreed in the said clause.

I acknowledge likewise that I agree to the stipulated salary, although I am aware that the wages earned by other free labourers and the slaves in the Island of Cuba are much higher, as I consider the difference compensated by the other advantages which are to be allowed me by my employer, and which appear in this agreement.

And in testimony that we will mutually accomplish the conditions which are stated in this document, we, the two contracting parties, sign two copies of the same tenour and effect.

Dated at, 18

Signed:

3. Chinese Laborer's Contract of Indenture for British Guiana.*

Ship, No.

AGREEMENT between, native of China, and Theophilus Sampson, Esq., acting as Agent for the Government of the Colony of British Guiana in the West Indies. Whereas the said T. Sampson has opened an Emigration Office at Canton for obtaining coolies for the Colony of British Guiana, I the said agree to go on board ship, and to go to British Guiana, and there work on the terms set forth below.

---

* Source: BFO 17/886.

1. I agree to work in British Guiana as I may be directed by the Government Emigration Agent, or for any person to whom he may transfer this contract.

2. The period of service is five years, commencing from the day I begin to work; or if on my arrival I be too ill to work, then it shall commence eight days after my recovery.

3. I agree to do any kind of work that I may be lawfully directed to do, whether in town or country, in fields, in factories, in private houses, &c.

4. I shall not be required to work on Sundays, unless I be employed as a domestic servant or to take care of cattle; in such case, and in all cases in which it is the local custom to do so, I must work on Sunday. In all other cases my time during Sunday shall be entirely at my own disposal.

5. A day consists of twenty-four hours, and I may not be required to work more than nine and a-half hours in one day. If I work more than nine and a-half hours one day, I may work an equal length of time less on another, or if not, then my employer shall compensate me.

6. At the end of the five years' service my master will give me 50 dollars in lieu of a return passage to China. If at the expiration of the term of the contract I do not wish to return to China, and if the Authorities of the place still permit me to reside in Guiana, in that case my master shall give me the 50 dollars stipulated in the contract for my own use; and if I wish to enter into another agreement for five years, half of the above sum (namely, 25 dollars) will be given to me by my master as a bonus, and at the end of the second five years the original sum of 50 dollars will be paid me in lieu of a return passage to China.

7. If after arrival I become incurably ill, so as to be unable to work, my master shall at once pay me the 50 dollars to assist me to return to China. If my master does not do so, I may petition the Authorities, who shall on their part recover the money for me.

8. Wherever I may work, or in whatever family I may be employed, I must obey the lawful regulations there in force. On the other hand, should I at any time feel agrieved at the conduct of my master towards me, all reasonable facility shall be afforded me for laying my complaint before the proper officers of the Colony.

9. When the contract shall have been signed and I have embarked, I cannot again return to the shore. If urgent business requires me to do so, I must first obtain the consent of the said Theophilus Sampson, and then I may do so.

10. It is distinctly agreed that this contract binds the coolie to go as a labourer to no other place than to British Guiana.

11. During the five years beginning on the day agreed on in this contract the wages shall be four Spanish dollars a month, or the equivalent in gold, for which my master shall be responsible. The wages shall be paid every month, and shall not be allowed to fall into arrear.

12. Every day food will be issued as follows:—8 oz. salt meat and 2 1/2 lb. of other articles, all of which shall be good and wholesome.

13. In case of illness, medical attendance and medicines and proper food will be provided free of expense till recovery. No matter what such medical expenses may amount to, the master may make no deduction on account of them from the coolie's wages.

14. Each year there will be given to me one suit of clothes and one blanket.

15. Passage to British Guiana will be provided by the said Theophilus Sampson.

16. The said Theophilus Sampson will provide to the emigrant the sum of dollars, or the equivalent in gold, for the use of his family. This sum shall be repaid by the emigrant in British Guiana to the holder of the contract by deductions from his wages at the rate of 1 dollar a month till it all be repaid, but no further deductions from wages may be made. No debt that may be incurred by the coolie during the voyage or in British Guiana may be construed into a lien on his services, or availed of to prolong the period of service specified in this contract.

17. On embarkation, three suits of clothes and everything necessary for the voyage will be provided for the emigrant free of expense to him. The clothes and articles thus provided to be considered a free gift. The coolie is to enjoy their use, and is not to be called upon to return them.

18. While he is working in British Guiana he shall enjoy the protection of the laws of the place. On his return, however, to China, this protection will be abrogated.

19. I, the said coolie, now agree that my wages shall be 4 dollars a month, and I declare my willingness, before my departure, to go to British Guiana. It is therefore understood that hereafter, if I hear or ascertain that the labourers in British Guiana receive more wages than myself, I must still be satisfied with the wages and other compensating advantages secured to me by this contract.

All the foregoing clauses were clearly understood and were read and explained before the contract was signed. Both parties being willing and fully understanding the terms cannot hereafter complain that they were in ignorance thereof. This contract is signed in English and a Chinese translation is annexed, as a proof, each party holding a copy.

Tung Che year moon day, 187.

This done in duplicate, each of the parties aforesaid retaining one copy, at Canton, on the day of, in the year of our Lord 187, in the presence of the Undersigned, who declares that this contract has been signed willingly, and with full knowledge of its contents, by the emigrant labourer named herein.

Emigrant

Signed

Emigration Officer

3A. Chinese Version of the Preceding Contract of Indenture to British Guiana

立合同人在中國　　縣村入氏　　歲現因英屬所派理事官三順來廣京省城設立公所招人前往英屬西印度之崑阿那地方俑工情

一　工人愿承招須遵理事官三順所定日期上船以便兩路搭前往英屬崑阿那地方聽此當面議定合同各規條開列於後

二　工人在崑阿那地方情願遵據英屬所派管理中國人之口事宜辦理中國人之命俑工

三　承工期限以五年為滿自到崑阿那地方作工之日起凡倘到崑阿那身上染病不能作工須俟全愈後八天計起

四　每日作工須有二十四熟鐘時候東人命工人作工以九晷半鐘為度又作工或停工或辦己事

五　工人作過九晷半鐘之限次日作少抵扣倘至不抵扣東人另補

六　情願遵照禮拜日准工人休息之工不論城內城外或在村落田庄耕種牧畜或在機器房製造機器或在家內使喚均皆從命毫無違抗

七　承工期限以五年為滿倘第二次地滿東人預給帮路費銀五十員附船送回中國

八　工作五年限滿日該中國人欲回中國其東人即給與路費銀五十員以便帮附搭便仍送回中華如限滿該工人不欲回中國該處准其留住本地自行使用若該工人自願復行承工即將原約所定五十員給其一半銀二十五員聽其自

九　工作五年限滿日中國人即給與路費銀五十員以便帮附搭便仍送回中華如限滿該工人不欲同中國該處官巡准其

十　到崑阿那役身中染病不能作工不用至五年期滿東人即先給銀五十員附送回中國如果東人不給五十員同官許中國人到官控告該處

十一　用至崑阿那役身中染病不能作工不用至五年期滿東人即先給銀五十員同官許中國人到官控告該處

十二　官巡倘為銀欠付給

十三　工人到崑阿那之後不論在何處作工并不論在某家內充當用人悉皆遵照該處家所定規矩而行不得恣玩惟不論何時該工人意體東人待伊

十四　工人應知來此趁官告訴

十五　工人如該官理事官三順翠然後可以上岸自定立合同落船之後不能復行上岸過有要事必須先知理事官三順翠准然後可以上岸

十六　凡五年之期按照以上作工日期起計每日給工人食肉英科兩計中國六兩并米英科四大員或伸金錢或仲金錢東人按月工銀四大員或麥或茶英科四兩計中國三十兩所給食物概係東人自理每月所得工銀較多不能效尤多索惟有遵照合同所定工銀并

十七　自定立合同之後工人留住英屬印度之崑阿那地方若工人往別地方作工致與原約不符

十八　將該工人工銀扣除至該工人在船或到崑阿那途次應用物件與衣物即承給工人工銀每月在工銀內扣同一元以扣清為度除此別項俱不能任

十九　理事官三順在公所先給洋銀與該工人留作襄家之資俟到崑阿那作工每月在工銀內扣同一元以扣清為度除此別項俱不能任

廿　該工人順在公所先給洋銀將該工人工銀扣至該工人到船開行之時理事官三順當給衣服三套并途次應用物件與衣物即承給工人工銀不取同

廿一　每年東人給工人衣服一套并襪一張

廿二　工人有病東人當出便從醫生與其冶病藥貲及醫病飲食之物一切不用工人自理概係東人辦給不論所用錢銀多少概不扣除

同　治　　　年　　　　月　　　　日
理事官三順應在崑阿那地方准其前往如該工人在中國既曾定每月所得工銀四員係情願方行前往前往明復經詳細涌悼彼此均已明悉將來彼此俱照合同內前後開載各條欵而行不能推
各等徒恐處殺分自守以上各欵登記均在合同之內註明復經詳細涌悼彼此均已明悉將來彼此俱照合同內前後開載各條欵而行不能推
誠恐口無憑立此英字合同結繕譯漢文合同互相一紙為據

立合同人　　的筆

4. Chinese Laborer's Contract of Indenture for Martinique.*

THE Undersigned, native of, in China, aged years, has agreed with MM. Gastel, Malavois, and Assier, to the following:—

1. I engage myself, from the present time, to embark for Martinique, in any ship the persons aforesaid shall indicate.
2. I engage myself equally for a space of eight years to labour in the aforesaid Colony, under the orders of MM. Gastel, Malavois, and Assier, or of the persons to whom they shall transfer this present contract, to do which I authorize them, obliging myself to perform all kinds of labour in that country, both in the country and town; nor shall it matter where they call upon me, whether in particular houses, or establishments of whatever kind, of industry or art, or in plantations, farms, or in general; it is indifferent what sort of work it is, either in country or town.
3. The eight years for which I engage myself in the preceding Article shall be reckoned from the eighth day after my arrival at the said port of Martinique, if I arrive in good health, and in the event of my being ill on my arrival and incapable of work, eight days after I have left the hospital or infirmary.

These eight consecutive years will be composed of ninety-six months, each month composed of twenty-six days of complete and effective labour. The wages will not be due until after twenty-six days of labour.

4. The hours during which I am to labour will depend on the nature of the work given me to perform, and the care which it is necessary to bestow on it, always according to myself each day the time for repose, and for dinner and breakfast, according to the custom already followed with European labourers in the said country.
5. Apart from the hours of repose no one shall be able to make me work on Sundays but according to the established customs applied to Europeans.
6. I submit myself to the order and discipline which is observed in the establishment, workshop, farm, or dwelling-house to which I

---

*   Source: BFO 881/894.

am appointed, on the condition, well understood, that all cause of complaint that I shall have are to be referred to the legal authorities.

7. I engage myself to submit, for each day's absence without legitimate reason, independently of the loss of salary for that day, to a fine of a second day's salary, under the title of interest for damage.

8. In case of illness, exceeding eight days' duration, it is agreed that my salary shall be suspended, and that it shall not commence again until my recovery.

9. On Sundays and fêtes I may employ my time in working for myself in a plot of ground that shall be allotted me, and which I may cultivate if, at the same time, I am not engaged in domestic service; and in that case, because the labours are much lighter, I shall have no claim to these advantages, but I shall be granted clothing and shoes over and above those promised to cultivators.

10. If it happens that my services shall no longer be needed, the present contract may be annulled, with my previous consent, and I shall be free to return to my country or go where I please; but in that case an indemnity shall be granted me, the amount of which shall be decided by the authorities of the country.

11. My wife and my eldest daughter shall be employed in the same establishment to which I shall be allotted, and shall gain, without prejudice to my own salary, a sum of two and a-half piastres per month; and it shall be the same with my sons under 14 years of age, after which age they shall gain the same sum as myself under all the conditions.

12. MM. Gastel, Malavois, and Assier shall have the right to endorse this present contract in favour of any one, always, at the same time, adhering to that which is contained in the said contract.

MM. Gastel, Malavois, and Assier hold themselves obliged on their part towards me:—

1. To pay me a salary of 4 piastres per month, in the currency of the Colony, from the day on which the eight years of my engagement commence.

2. To furnish me each day with 8 oz. of salt fish, or other healthy food, and 2 1/2 lbs. of roots and other nutritious provisions.

3. To have given to me in the infirmary all the cares, remedies, and assistance of a doctor, as long as my sufferings or preservation require them.

4. To give me every year two complete suits of clothing, a flannel shirt, and a coverlid.

5. To furnish, gratis, my passage to Martinique and my nourishment on board.

6. To advance me the sum of 8 piastres in silver or gold for the wants of the voyage I am about to undertake.

7. To furnish three suits of clothing, coverlid, and other necessaries, the value of which is 5 piastres, which, with the 8 piastres of the preceding article, make a sum of 13 piastres, which I engage to repay at Martinique to the order of MM. Gastel, Malavois, and Assier, by means of 1 piastre per month kept back from my salary by the person to whom this contract shall be transferred. It remains well understood that reimbursements are to be executed for no other reason whatever.

I acknowledge to have received in money and effects, in fulfillment of the above clause, the sum of 13 piastres, which I engage to repay at Martinique according to the form established in the preceding Article.

In faith of which we will mutually accomplish all that is related in the document, of which we sign two copies of the same tenour, and having but one effect between us two.

Canton, 1860.

(Signed)   P. DE GASTET, MALAVOIS ET ASSIER.

5. Chinese Laborer's Contract of Indenture for Louisiana, U.S.A.*

AGREEMENT made the _____
day of _____ A.D. 1870, being the _____
day of the _____ Chinese month in the _____
year of the Emperor Tung-chi, between _____ a native of
China, and JOHN WILLIAMS of New Orleans, Louisiana, U.S.A., through
is duly authorised agent and attorney in fact, FRANK M. WILLIAMS.
Witnesseth as follows:—

The said _____ on his part hereby promises and agrees,
to emigrate to the State of Louisiana, U.S.A., to labor for the above-named

---

* Source: BFO 17/878.

JOHN WILLIAMS, his heirs, executors, administrators, or assigns, under the following conditions, and for the considerations hereinafter named.

I.—The said _____ agrees to work on Plantations, or do any other kind of labor that may be assigned to him by his employer, for the period of Five Years, beginning at the time he commences to work; for which he is to be paid by him at the rate of fifty (50) cents per day, United States Currency. One half payable at the end of each month, the balance at the termination of this contract.

II.—He is to be furnished by his employer with comfortable quarters, and rations of (50 lbs.) fifty pounds of Rice, and (15 lbs.) fifteen pounds of Pork per month, or an equivalent in money.

III.—His passage and advance to the U.S.A. amounting to ($100) one hundred dollars to be returned to his employer at the rate of $2 per month.

IV.—In case of sickness he is to be furnished with necessary medicines without charge.

V.—He agrees to work from day-break till dark, with an intermission of one hour each for breakfast and dinner, except for the summer months, when he can take two hours for dinner, provided he is at work by sunrise, and provided further he take his breakfast before going out, and during the Sugar-making, to stand watch at night, as usual on Sugar Plantations, but he is to be paid by his employers fifty (50) cents extra in currency for each night watch, but no labor is to be required of him on Sundays, except when necessary to secure the crop, feeding the stock, and protecting the Plantation generally.

VI.—He promises to render strict obedience to his Employer, and submit himself to the regulations of the Plantation, and in all things to conduct himself as a good and faithful servant.

VII.—When he has worked Five Years, of three hundred and twelve (312) days each (less ten days for holidays), as he has agreed to do, and shall have performed his duties as a servant faithfully and diligently, obeying all orders strictly, his employer hereby obligates himself to send him back to China at his the said JOHN WILLIAMS' own expense, or in lieu thereof the said JOHN WILLIAMS or his assignee or successor will pay him the sum of ($75) seventy-five dollars. It is understood and agreed that in calculating the period of service, a year is to be composed of three hundred and twelve (312) days full labor, during the hours already mentioned, less ten days holidays as aforesaid.

VIII.—He hereby agrees to serve the said JOHN WILLIAMS or such associates as the said JOHN WILLIAMS may appoint within the term of Five Years under this contract.

IN WITNESS whereof he subscribes his name to this Contract, in duplicate, made in Chinese and English.

Done at the City of _____ the _____

WITNESS:—

_____

5A. Chinese Version of the Preceding Contract of Indenture to Louisiana, U.S.A.

花 旗 請 工 合 同

立明合約人大合眾國眾主貴威廉士代理人法冷威廉士今所僱中國人　姓　名　　工人願到英國內魯依西亞拿

地方與貴威廉士或承允人作工

照以後所定條欵開列

一　姓　名　　工人情願往該處做作種地蓮眾主所命之工夫今議五年爲期其期內之工夫以初到之日起計每日發給

二　英國通用之先士五十個每月底先支工銀一半共餘一半要俟五年期滿然後一總支足

三　所有路費一百貳拾係眾家貴威廉先出到後日將工銀扣回每月扣銀二員

四　工人有病醫藥係眾家所出

五　工人每日從天曉時起身用早飯一點鐘午飯一點鐘之久惟夏天午飯之時係放工兩點鐘之久至做群常規要晚夜看守糖

六　搶另每夜給加工錢五十先士禮拜不用做工或過危險水火之炎及簽牲口不在例內

七　工人意願順從眾主命外務須遵守該處常蓮盤力做工

八　五年期滿實祿年只做工三百叁十二日又另放假十日倘勘工無過眷眾主或承充代辦人定必送工人回中國所有船費皆

眾主所出或折銀七十五員　每年做工實三百叁十二日又上所云每日之工上照云一年之中放假十天

慈所僱工之人凖貴威廉在五年期內亦可任意轉变此合同與同事者

慈特簽名此合同內以爲據証立此合約二張各執一張寫明中英字樣

見証人

在　　城立

英　一千八百七十年　月　日

唐　己巳年八月　日

*　Source: B.F.O. 17/878.

Appendix VI

TABLES 25-49

The following tables listing the ships that transported Chinese indentured laborers to Latin America from 1847 to 1874 have been compiled from the sources given below. In instances where two or more sources gave conflicting data, particularly with regard to the number of passengers on board vessels and the number of deaths on the voyage, the writer selected the data from what appeared to be the most reliable source. As might be expected in a trade involving ships and personnel of many nations, the names of captains and vessels are often misspelled, and they are given here as they appeared in the sources. In the writer's judgment the tables list not less than 95 percent of the vessels involved in the traffic, though the reader will observe that little is known about some voyages.

Sources: *O Boletim*; *Hong Kong Government Gazette*; the *Friend of China*; *Overland Friend of China*; *China Mail*; *Hong Kong Daily Press*; *Overland Register and Price Current*; *Hong Kong Mercury and Shipping Gazette*; *Hong Kong Shipping List and Commercial Intelligencer*; *North China Herald*; *North China Herald and Supreme Court and Consular Gazette*; BBP, ASS, *China*, Vols. III, IV; BPP, *Emigration*, Vols. XI-XVIII; BFO 17/873; BFO 17/744; BFO 17/881; BFO 17/886; BFO 17/877; BFO 17/889; BFO 97/101; BFO 881/1738; U.S. Congress, House, Ex. Doc. 105, I Sess., 34 Cong.; U.S. Congress, House, Ex. Doc. 88, Report 443, I Sess., 36 Cong.; U.S. Congress, House, Ex. Doc. 16, II Sess., 37 Cong.; U.S. Congress, Senate, Ex. Doc. 99, I Sess., 34 Cong.; Corbitt, *A Study of the Chinese in Cuba, 1847-1947*; Hutchinson, *Two Years in Peru*; Stewart, *Chinese Bondage in Peru*; Clementi, *The Chinese in British Guiana*; Erenchún, *Anales de la Isla de Cuba*; Lubbock, *Coolie Ships and Oil Sailors*; Millones, *Minorias Etnicas*; Pinheiro, *Importação de Trabalhadores Chins*; Chemin Dupontès, *Les Petites Antilles*; Guiral, *L'Immigration Reglémentée aux Antilles Françaises et à la Réunion*; Tejeiro, *Historia Illustrada de la Colonia China*; Mantalto de Jesus, *Historic Macau*; Thiersant, *L'Emigration Chinois*; Johnson, "Coolie Labor and Coolie Immigration;" Holden, "A Chapter on the Coolie Trade;" Auchincloss, "The Chinese in Cuba;" Valverde, "La Trata de los Chinos en la Isla de Cuba;" Snelleman, "Chineesche Immigranten in Suriname;" "Landverhuizing der Chinezen;" *De Bow's Review*; *The Anti-Slavery Reporter*.

Table 25

List of Ships Transporting Chinese Laborers to Latin America, 1847-1851

YEAR	NAME OF SHIP	FLAG						CAPTAIN	TONNAGE	PORT OF DEPARTURE					DATE OF DEPARTURE	DATE OF ARRIVAL	DAYS ON VOYAGE	DEATHS ON VOYAGE	DESTINATION			REMARKS
		BRITISH	FRENCH	PERUVIAN	SPANISH	DANISH	ECUADORIAN			AMOY	CANTON	HONG KONG	CUMSINGMOON	MACAU					CUBA	PERU	S. AMERICA	
1847	OQUENDO	x							350	220					Jan14?Jn.3?		151	14	206			
"	DUKE OF ARGYLE				x				629	412					Mar10?Jn.12?		147	38	374			10 washed overboard
1849	FREDERIK WILLIAM					x		PAULSEN	470				75		Jn.7?	Ag.?o,1549	149			75		
1850	ROTHEN	x						J.B.SMITH	763		*		440		Fe.?50			109		*		Mutiny
"	LADY MONTAGUE	x	x					JEAN PAINE	292				245		Fe.?50					243		Mutiny, returned China
"	ALBERT		x					J. VERMIOL	376				300		Nv.7?50							Mutiny, returned China
"	CHILI			x				J. WHITE	446				300		Un13?50			48		252		
"	EMPRESSA		x					LAS CASAS	200				180		Oc14?50			4				
"	COROMANDEL	x							663					*	Mr.8?50					*		Ship condemned at Manila
1851	MARINER	x						HARLAND	685					409	Je21?51			9		400		
"	WILLIAM WATSON	x										*								*		
"	COROMANDEL	x	x					BROWN	663					404	Fe21?51			4		400		
"	VICTORY	x						W.L.MULLINS	579				352		De.5?51							Mutiny, all escaped
"	LINDA			x							*				Ap26?51					*		
"	ROSARITO			x							*									*		
"	MARIA		x								*										*	
"	ORIXA		x				x													*	*	96 took coolies from Manuelita at Manila

1. Asterisk denotes port of departure and destination of vessels where the number of passengers is not known.
2. Dash denotes the destination of vessels that did not complete the voyage.

Table 26

List of Ships Transporting Chinese Laborers to Latin America, 1852

YEAR	NAME OF SHIP	FLAG					CAPTAIN	TONNAGE	PORT OF DEPARTURE						DATE OF DEPARTURE	DATE OF ARRIVAL	DAYS ON VOYAGE	DEATHS ON VOYAGE	DESTINATION				REMARKS
		BRITISH	AMERICAN	PERUVIAN	DUTCH	PORTUGUESE			AMOY	CANTON	HONG KONG	CUMSINGMOON	MACAU	SWATOW					CUBA	PERU	Br. GUIANA	TRINIDAD	
1852	MICHNO	x					GONZALES	230															25 sold at Arica.
"	SUSANNAH	x					Lobey	504				5			Ap10'52	Fe.2'52		6		209			
"	EMPRESA			x			WHITE	446				420			Jy12'52			77		845			
"	BEATRICE	x					EDWARDS	276				300			Fe.21'52								Shipwreck, all deserted
"	GERTRUDE						CAMPBELL	605	550						Oc12'52	Mr14'53	15	198	198				Mutiny
"	PANAMA							522	249						Se24'52	Mr14'53	123	226	226				Mutiny
"	BRITISH SOVEREIGN	x					Harris	450	221						Ac18'52				*				
"	LORD ELGIN	x					A.C. M'CLELLAND	251	156						Jy25'52	Se17'52	70				86		½ of coolies escaped
"	GLENTANNER	x						615	305						Se.1'52	c12'52	45				462		
"	SAMUEL BODDINGTON	x					J.W.HURST	669	352						No25'52	Mr.4'53	98	52			300		Mutiny
"	FLENHEIM	x						808	452						Oc25'52	Mr10'53	100	225	225				
"	LADY AMHURST	x					REID	446	275						De.3'52	Mr8'53	25	50					Mutiny
"	INCHINNAN	x		x			ENIS	565						255	No. '52	Mr.20'53	25	53					
"	SIR T. GRESHAM		x					594						347	De. '52	My11'53	108	27	300	228			
"	OHIO		x				RAUFACH	378		254	*				No24'52		72		228	*			
"	SICILE	x						550							Do.4'52							251	
"	CLARENDON			x			G. HILTON						255		De29'52	Ap25'53	114	3		*			
"	CAPRICE			x						*					Fe22'52					*			
"	CARMEN					x				*					Se.4'52					*			
"	SOPHIA					x	ROSARIO	280					250		De. '52	Ap17'53	127	17	233	*			
"	TAGUE				x				404														
"	AUSTRALIA	x					J. NOBLE	1,176					445		De15'52	Mr.4'53	79	13			432		

Table 27

List of Ships Transporting Chinese Laborers to Latin America, 1853

YEAR	NAME OF SHIP	FLAG							CAPTAIN	TONNAGE	PORT OF DEPARTURE						DATE OF DEPARTURE	DATE OF ARRIVAL	DAYS ON VOYAGE	DEATHS ON VOYAGE	DESTINATION				REMARKS
		BRITISH	AMERICAN	PERUVIAN	SPANISH	PORTUGUESE	GERMAN	MEXICAN			AMOY	CANTON	HONG KONG	CUMSINGMOON	MACAU	SWATOW					CUBA	PERU	Br. GUIANA	TRINIDAD	
1853	ROSA ELIAS			x					G. WHEATLEY	253							Mch6'53			96					Mutiny
"	EMPRESA			x					WHITE	446				425	200		My24'53					329			Fever on board
"	ELEANOR LANCASTER	x								400						410	Oc4'53								Mutiny
"	ADAMASTOR					x				400															
"	Columbus		x						HOLDON	476 366	366					390	Ja1'53	My22'53	135	26	350				
"	BELLA GALLERA									800					361		Fe5'53	hn27'53	156	9	381				
"	San ANDRES									460							Fe5'53	hn30'53	146	25	358				
"	NEPAUL	x							NEIL	1,006				420		500	Mr4'53			8		452			
"	ELIZA MORRISON	x							McCULLOCH	797				325			f12'53			16		404			
"	ISABEL QUINTINA			x					BRAZLEY	514							s26'53			9	516				
"	JACUE								LAZANIGA	257							Se11'53			2	198				
"	SIR T.GRESHAM	x								960				200		490	Fe'53	Se1'53	155	50	*				
"	MEDINA	x							SANDFORD	674				200		490	Mr11'53	hn28'53	108	9	380		505		
"	LADY FLORA HASTINGS	x							W. WILD	554				350		314	fa'53	Mn28'53	128	2	348				
"	J.D.URQUELA									500		*									340				
"	SANTA LUCIA				x					295				396				fy12'53	126	56	*				
"	VICTORIA		x							446 250		*													
"	MIRNA	x								366				300			Ae30'53	Se152	56	194					
"	SAPPHO	x					x										My2'53	135	51	249		*			
"	NOVO VIAJANTE					x																*			
"	ROSITA	x										*										*			
"	STATESMAN	x								446					800		Ap24'53	My17'53	121	1 295		*			
"	Helena						x																		
"	Menzies	x								265	350														Fever, put into Hongkong
"	EMIGRANT	x																							

Table 28

List of Ships Transporting Chinese Laborers to Latin America, 1854

YEAR	NAME OF SHIP	BRITISH	AMERICAN	PERUVIAN	SPANISH	DUTCH	CAPTAIN	TONNAGE	AMOY	CANTON	HONG KONG	CUMSINGMOON	MACAU	SWATOW	SHANGHAI	PARANA	DATE OF DEPARTURE	DATE OF ARRIVAL	DAYS ON VOYAGE	DEATHS ON VOYAGE	CUBA	PERU	JAMAICA	PANAMA	REMARKS
1854	ISABEL QUINTINA	x					BRADLEY	574				325					Fe20'54			47					
"	AMAZON	x		x			VINCENT	340									Fe20'54			2		278 / 248			Shipwreck, 10 escaped.
"	GROUINEZA			x			PERRY	700						250			Mr. '54					248 -			
"	SANTIAGO			x			Luciano Rossi	300						500			Jl10'54			250		*			
"	SEAWITCH		x					907					96									*		*	
"	BELLA VASCONGADA				x			251					*				Ja28'54					*		*	
"	ROY	x					A.C.MORSE			*							No25'54	Ag23'54							
"	ROXBURG CASTLE							1,121 604									Mr.'54	Jy4'54	29	21	575				
"	MICENO			x				290									Ap15'54	Ag15'54	117	19	408				
"	COMERCIAL					x		797							500		Jy20'54			8	396	*			Sailed from Macau
"	ENCARNACION			x				500					400							45					
"	EPSON		x											550			Ju27'54	No23'54	117	11	599				
"	EMIGRANTE			x				755															267		
"	CORNWALL	x						580			510						Fe9'54								275 left China.
"	O.I.COMPAGNIE							787									Mr9'54					*			460 left China.
"	LA VENTURA			x				349								195	Ja12'54	No1'54				*	195		140 left China.
"	Vampire	x														10		No15'54					10		
"	THERESA JANE	x																							

Table 29

List of Ships Transporting Chinese Laborers to Latin America, 1855

YEAR	NAME OF SHIP	FLAG						CAPTAIN	TONNAGE	PORT OF DEPARTURE							DATE OF DEPARTURE	DATE OF ARRIVAL	DAYS ON VOYAGE	DEATHS ON VOYAGE	DESTINATION			REMARKS
		BRITISH	AMERICAN	PERUVIAN	SPANISH	GERMAN	CHILEAN			AMOY	CANTON	HONG KONG	MACAU	SWATOW	SINGAPORE	NINGPO					CUBA	PERU	BRAZIL	
1855	AMELIA			X					598					500			Ja. '55			199	808			
"	BELLA GALLEGA				X				1,120					803			Ja.'55	Mb6'55	110	7	796			
"	ROYAL CASTLE	X												*			Ja.'55					*		
"	CARPENTARIA	X							1,460					704			Ja.'55	My3'55	97	27	677			
"	MARTIN LUTHER	X							1,241					596			De.'55	Ju5'55	19	19	577			
"	ZEELAND	X							1,287			400					No.'55							
"	SAMUEL RUSSELL		X						395			397					Jo24'55	Mr4'55	101	4	195			Mutiny.
"	SWORDFISH		X					OSGOOD	1,024				290				Ja27'55	Ap27'55	80	22	375			
"	HOUND		X					AMOS PECK	715				*				Ap25'55	My22'55	108	2	228			
"	FREDERICKSHAM												*				No22'55							
"	SANTIAGO								500					*			Ap6'55					*		
"	GRIMENESA				X				346				251				De25'55					*		
"	PAQUITA												*									*		
"	WINGED RACER		X					GORHAM	1,767				700				De10'55	Mr2'55	105	5	246			Mutiny.
"	SEA WITCH		X					W. LANG	907,600					550			Ja. '55	My6'55	93	154,450		*		Hit reef near Havana.
"	GOLDEN EAGLE	X							1,120									My6'55	104	66	484			
"	SKY LARK		X					S.B.DOW	1,205					525			Se8'55			61	525			
"	BALD EAGLE		X					F.BOWEN	1,702					744			Ap6'55					*		Mutiny.
"	CATALINA		X											250			Se28'55					*		
"	CLARITA		X					E.J.HUNTER	356								Se2.'55					*		
"	DALMATIA		X						689		*						Se10'55					*		
"	FLORIDA		X								*						Se25'55					*		
"	JOHANA CAESAR				X						*						Se27'55	Ja19'56	82			*	966	Mutiny.
"	SARAH		X													*								
"	WAVERLY		X					P.O.WELLMAN	769				450				Oo.'55			12	*	*		
"	WESTWARD HO		X					J.O.McCULLIM	1,122				565				Oc21'55					*		
"	INDIAMAN		X					J.O.McCULLIM 1,165															*		
"	INGLEWOOD	X						BURTON								*								Cargo of natives taken off said he knew.
"	ELISA ANNA			X					470					577			Fe9'55	Fe24'56	116	14	363			
"	AUSTRALIA						X		500					250							*	503		
"	?																							

Table 30

List of Ships Transporting Chinese Laborers to Latin America, 1856

YEAR	NAME OF SHIP	FLAG								CAPTAIN	TONNAGE	PORT OF DEPARTURE						DATE OF DEPARTURE	DATE OF ARRIVAL	DAYS ON VOYAGE	DEATHS ON VOYAGE	DESTINATION		REMARKS
		BRITISH	AMERICAN	FRENCH	PERUVIAN	SPANISH	PORTUGUESE	DUTCH	GERMAN			AMOY	CANTON	HONG KONG	MACAU	SWATOW	SHANGHAI					CUBA	PERU	
1856	CORA				x					VINCENT	1,297	600							Fe24'56		208	292			Mutiny.
"	BANCA							x		FONANA	490				250			De10'56	Ar20'57	116				Mutiny, all escaped.
"	RESOLUÇÃO						x	x		FERNANDES	585				450			De12'56	Ap26'57	173	275			
"	JOHANNA							x		JURGLANSE	551			297	305			De12'56	Ap22'56	155	122			
"	JOHN CALVIN	x								THORNEIL	551							Jal1'56	Je20'56	134	195			
"	DUKE OF PORTLAND	x								G.W.SEYMOUR	455			532				Jy19'56	De28'56	124	6	185		
"	HENRY KILLER	x								EARLY	987				500			De5'56	Ap14'57	132	277	455		
"	KATHERINE GLEN					x				S.JUAN	705				450			De18'56	De2'56	228		320		
"	EMIGRANTE																	My23'56				*		
"	THEREZA TERRIE																							
"	DINA	x						x		HAAN	683				319			Ja14'56	Jy26'56	205	10	305		
"	JOHANNA MARIA				x			x		SEISSING	483				299			No1'56	Fe26'57	117	12	287		
"	DOGGERSBANK							x		ACHENBACK	667				382		*	No28'56	Ar51'57	111	9	377		
"	CAFFARELLO				x					DUROIX	478											*		
"	ELLEN OLIVER	x								EMERSON	667				291			My10'56	De2'56	198	63	228		
"	ANTONIA TERRY					x					1,100							My14'56				*		
"	WALHAOEK	x									1,065				610				Ju '56	167	46	564		
"	Tell	x									286							My25'56						
"	HOPE	x								DREYAR	609		*		504			Fe '56	No14'56	92	92	492		
"	TERESITA					x					495		390					Fe5'56	Je5'56	120	65	325		
"	MICENO				x					MAZARES	250							Se8'56				*		
"	FLORIDA		x							NICHOLSON	669	*	548					De '56	Ap3'57	114	7	341		
"	JOSÉ UGARTE				x						569											*		
"	BELLONA						x				962				586			My13'56	De22'56	262	159	367		
"	SAMUEL WILLETS		x								1,400		*									*		
"	CONDOR					x					398		*					My25'56				*		
"	VRIENDSHAP							x		BULS	800				400			Ap7'57	Ap7'57	104	50	359		
"	NIGHTINGALE		x								1,086				610				Jy '56	108	46	564		
"	WAR HAWK		x							L.B.STIMMONS	1,067	*			500			Ja '56	Ag6'56		60	440		
"	GOLDEN EAGLE	x																Ja25'56				*		
"	JOHANNA CAESAR								x		505							Je29'56						
"	MARIA NATIVIDAD											*										*		

Table 31

List of Ships Transporting Chinese Laborers to Latin America, 1857

YEAR	NAME OF SHIP	FLAG							CAPTAIN	TONNAGE	PORT OF DEPARTURE				DATE OF DEPARTURE	DATE OF ARRIVAL	DAYS ON VOYAGE	DEATHS ON VOYAGE	DESTINATION		REMARKS
		BRITISH	AMERICAN	FRENCH	PERUVIAN	SPANISH	DUTCH	GERMAN			AMOY	HONG KONG	MACAU	SWATOW					CUBA	PERU	
1857	JOSEPH SHEPHERD	x							R. BARBER	630	511				Ja11'57	Ma24'57	108	12	299		Sailed from Hong Kong.
"	COLD STREAM	x							G. TICKELL	796				220	Mr14'57	Je19'57	123	18	202		
"	TUSKINA		x						S.K. CUSHMAN	449		249			Mr29'57	Au4'57	170	77	172		Left from H.K., mutiny
"	GULNARE	x							J. WARDROP	1,002			396		Mr31'57	Au27'57	158	68	268		Via Hong Kong.
"	ROBERT SMALL	x							J.W.R.DRAKE	655		284			Ap12'57	Au22'57	157	11	223		Via Hong Kong.
"	EDWIN FOX	x							J. FERGUSON	892		305			No8'57	Mr20'58	102	40	265		Via Hong Kong.
"	EARL OF BELINGTON	x							J. LAUGHTON	1,274		499			De2'57	Ap3'58	102	129	369		Mutiny, put back to imes
"	PORT DE BORDEAUX			x								550			Ja13'57				—		
"	SUCCESS			x					MONNERET	415		570			Ja24'57		128	25	345		
"	CHRISTEA				x					343		300			Ja24'57	No20'57	147	8	196		
"	S.IGNICES			x						650		570			My6'57	No7'57	202	29	155		
"	FRANCIS I(St.)[1]				x										Ap14'57	No25'57	113	58	849		Mutiny.
"	KATE HOOPER			x					CLAGLADEL	1,600		550			De15'57	Ap12'58	120	38	612		
"	CHARLES HAMEIE(AS)[2]	x							JACKSON	1,507		820			De17'57	Mr9'58	128	154	676		Mutiny.
"	FERNANDEZ			x					HERAULT	413		650			Ap5'57	Se13'57	157	19	351		Mutiny, ship sunk.
"	CARMEN				x				L. CARUGLI	960		591		200	Mr57		200			—	
"	VILLE DE DIEPPE			x					BARKER			300			Mr25'57	Ja15'57	117	81	550		Mutiny.
"	HENRIETTA MARIA			x					CARIGNAC	632		352	*		Ja.'57				—		Mutiny.
"	ANAIS			x						610					Ja28'57						
"	MARIA NATIVIDAD			x						590				250	Fe8'57	Jn14'57	124	9	343		
"	FELIX						x			578	334				My23'57	Oc10'57	14	256		
"	GISSOURS						x								My9'57				*		
"	Helene			x						385					Se13'57	Ja6'57	12	296		
"	AFRICAINE		x						KENNEY	2,006			915		Fe10'57		295	620		
"	CHALLENGE			x					ARTUZA	554			350		De25'57	Ap22'58	111	92	298		
"	JULIAN DE UNZUETA			x						496			355		De20'57	Mo6'58	125	11	359		
"	St.JEAN	x							ADMIRAL	763	376				Ap20'58	Oc10'00	276		
"	KIEFF SIMPSON	x							BROWN	696		430			No28'57	My19'58	110	93	337		
"	DREAM			x					A. WILSON	1,106		503			No15'57	Fe24'58	97	65	436		
"	TICONDEROGA			x					BOYLE	1,679		850			No 1'57	Mr19'58	110	34	616		
"	ORISA			x											De1'57						

1. St., here and throughout these tables denotes a steamer.   2. AS denotes an auxiliary - steamer.

Table 31 (cont.)

| YEAR | NAME OF SHIP | FLAG | | | | | | | | | CAPTAIN | TONNAGE | PORT OF DEPARTURE | | | | DATE OF DEPARTURE | DATE OF ARRIVAL | DAYS ON VOYAGE | DEATHS ON VOYAGE | DESTINATION | | REMARKS |
		BRITISH	AMERICAN	FRENCH	PERUVIAN	SPANISH	DUTCH	GERMAN	CHILEAN			AMOY	HONG KONG	MACAO	SWATOW					CUBA	PERU	
1857	ADMIRAL DUDMAN		x								669				409		Se19d57	150	52	349		
"	WAVERLY						x				749	372					Jn18d57	106	12	356		
"	ARCHITECT				x						500				258		Jn11d57	84	6	296		
"	MARIA						x				426				222		Oc12d57	175	43	172		
"	ALIANZA								x		250				240		Dc26d57	208	80	135		

Table 32

List of Ships Transporting Chinese Laborers to Latin America, 1858

YEAR	NAME OF SHIP	FLAG	CAPTAIN	TONNAGE	PORT OF DEPARTURE (AMOY/MACAU/SWATOW/SHANGHAI)	DATE OF DEPARTURE	DATE OF ARRIVAL	DAYS ON VOYAGE	DEATHS ON VOYAGE	DESTINATION	REMARKS
1858	THREE CRUISERS	Dutch	KENDRAMP	710	Macau 245	Ja6l58					
"	MINISTER PAHUD	Dutch	KLEVIT	777	Macau 257	Ja6l58					
"	SCIADO	Dutch	WENDER	655	Macau 400	Ja22l58	My12l58	108	2	CUBA 398	
"	DON JULIAN	German	CORTEN	533	Macau 400	Ja22l58	My12l58	100	48	CUBA 530	
"	FLORA TEMPLE	American	McCOLE	1,722	Macau 900	Fe19l58	My12l58	78	29	CUBA 855	
"	KEPLER		HASSELHOFF	567	Macau 370					CUBA 292	
"	SWALLOW	American	TUCKER	1,480	Macau 650	Mr15l58	My14l58	105	6	CUBA 644	
"	EVA JOHANA	Dutch	ROCHOWE	1,015	Macau 604	Mr17l58	My26l58	131	92	CUBA 512	
"	BELLA VASCONGADA	Spanish	VOYESTA	640	Macau 385	Mr19l58	My9l58	152	36	CUBA 346	
"	Pieter C. Hoogt	Dutch	KOENS	997	Macau 570	Mr21l58	Mr26l58	151	202	CUBA 366	
"	ADMIRAL V.K.KER	Dutch	KORINGH	1,145	Macau 610	Mr2l58	Je26l58	149	128	CUBA 480	
"	MAURITIUS (St.)	British	D.CRUX SHAW	2,134	Macau 741	My3l58	Je15l58	119	92	CUBA 625	Via Hong Kong.
"	SCOTIA (St.)	British	J. BELL	1,021	Macau 554	Jl2l58	Oc2l58	92	123	CUBA 457	Via Hong Kong.
"	GIUSEPPE ROUCA	Italian	LAVANGA	730	Macau 300	Jn28l58					
"	MARIA ELIZABETH	Dutch	JOREKER	825	Macau 510	Oc20l58	Fe6l58	108	27	CUBA 485	
"	FRANCIS I (St.)	French	GLOSMADHE	1,580	Macau 999	No4l58	Fe1l59	88	154	CUBA 835	Via Hong Kong.
"	ROYAL GEORGE	British	ROBB	585	Macau 300	De8l58	Mr20l59	111	51	CUBA 440	
"	MALABAR	French	LABBE	896	Macau 570	De14l58	Ap11l59	105	50	CUBA 266	
"	TASMANIA	British	J. NEURSE	1,190	Amoy 366	La20l58	An2l59	91	108	CUBA 415	
"	MARY WHITBRIDGE	American	R.CHESEBROUGH	978	Swatow 500						
"	WANDERING JEW	American	G.H.CARLETON	1,139	Amoy 139 / Macau 350	My15l58	Au23l58	95	91	CUBA 225	130 from Shanghai.
"	TRAVANCORE	British	BROWN	594	Macau 266	Jn26l58			31	BR. GUIANA 249	
"	ALAVESA	Spanish		500	Macau 360	Jy2l58	Au5l58	35	209		
"	DIANA	Chilean	O'SULLIVAN	166	Swatow 113	Jy12l58	Au5l58	135	74		
"	FREIA	Danish		1,002	Swatow 470	Jy14l58			291		
"	NORMA	Norwegian		420	Swatow 276				137		
"	WESTWARD HO	Peruvian		1,120	Macau 200	Mr12l58	Jy10l58	114	89	CUBA 611	
"	CLEOPATRA (St.)	British		1,079	Macau 862	My21l58	Oc22l58	44	362	PERU *	
"	CARBON	American		299	Swatow *	My3l58					
"	COMPETITOR	American		871	Swatow 582		Je5l58	98	57	CUBA 225	

Table 33

List of Ships Transporting Chinese Laborers to Latin America, 1859

YEAR	NAME OF SHIP	FLAG	CAPTAIN	TONNAGE	PORT OF DEPARTURE				DATE OF DEPARTURE	DATE OF ARRIVAL	DAYS ON VOYAGE	DEATHS ON VOYAGE	DESTINATION				REMARKS
					CANTON	HONG KONG	MACAU	SHANGHAI					CUBA	PERU	Br. GUIANA	MARTINIQUE	
1859	SUCCESS	French	J.MONNEROT	390			575		1e6'59	Mr27'59	124	89	284				
"	MARIA DE NATIVIDAD	French					921		Ja12'59					*			
"	ALEXANDER RALLI	British	H.ARUE	505			920		1a16'59	My27'59	114	32	396				
"	GENERAL WYNDHAM	American	T.TEXAS	678			461		Fe15'59	My13'59	87	11			460		Via Hong Kong.
"	EMIGRANTE	Spanish	I.B.HARRISON	1,082			610		Fe22'59	Jy20'59	123	32	375				
"	LIVE YANKEE	American	J.F.DeS.JUAN	720		500			Mr4'59	Jn2*'59	87	13	787				
"	CEDER		E.A.TONSHIX	1,501			569		Mr15*'59	Jn2*'59	106	34	308				
"	BELLONA	German	L.ROHLFS	599		500			Mr15*'59	My27'59	100	73	427				
"	DAGUERRE	Dutch	T.O.KLUIN	994			555		Mr11*'59	Ag18*'59	128	31	305				
"	FORMOSA	French	J.L.DEPENOER	566			465		Apl'59	Ag18*'59	138	65	400				
"	PROMETRADE HESPANH	French/Spanish	H.DURANTO	780		749			Ap2'59				*				
"	CONCRECION		J.SICHER	1,219		480			Au16*'59	Ag10*'59	115	57	423				
"	CHARLES MARTEL (Sk)	French	J.C.ATKINS	1,228		900			Se5'59				*				
"	FLORA TEMPLE	American	A.DAVID / JOHNSON	1,594 / 1,722		850			Ag3'59					*			
"	Norwey	American	H.B.MAJOR	2,424		1058			No26'59			130	906				Mutiny, lost parcels.
"	WHIRLWIND	British		978	969				De2*5*'59	Fe11*60	78				969		Mutiny.
"	VILLE DE DIEPPE	American	J.H.MORTON	900 / 946						Jn27*'60	110	25	521				
"	SWALLOW	American		1,443	*	*							*				
"	GOVERNOR MORTON	American		1,323	*								*				
"	THERESA	Spanish	BOLLO	189	*									*			
"	GRAVITHA			426					Fe17*'59								
"	GALILEE	French		502			555				270	82					
"	ADMIRAL BAUDIN	French										24				351	

Table 34

List of Ships Transporting Chinese Laborers to Latin America, 1860

YEAR	NAME OF SHIP	BRITISH	AMERICAN	FRENCH	PERUVIAN	SPANISH	DUTCH	CHILEAN	GERMAN	CAPTAIN	TONNAGE	Canton	HONG KONG	MACAU	SWATOW	DATE OF DEPARTURE	DATE OF ARRIVAL	DAYS ON VOYAGE	DEATHS ON VOYAGE	CUBA	PERU	Br. GUIANA	REMARKS
1860	FANNY KIRCHNER								x		477	550								*			
"	STAGHOUND									BLACK S.B.HUSSEY	1,374								57	342			Mutiny by crew.
"	FLORENCE NIGHTINGALE		x								1,198			400									
"	EMILE FREIRE			x							847			460		Ja20'60				*			
"	WESTWARD HO		x								1,120			670		Fe12'60				*			
"	SOLIDE			x							299			194		Fe25'60				*			
"	KITTY SIMPSON		x							R.CANFIELD	666			356		Fe20'60				*			
"	MESSENGER		x							B.D.MORTON	1,201			373		Fe22'60				*			
"	GUADALUPE			x							903			400		Mr31'60				*			
"	MARIA ELIZABETH						x			JUNKER	825			356		Ap2'60				*			
"	BRAVA LINREE			x							574			301		Ap7'60				*			
"	ALEXANDRIA DELPHIA			x							456			201		Ap8'60				*			
"	SEUTSBERG GEZARD			x							1,013			410		Jn4'60				*			
"	MARIA CLOTILDE						x				517			519		Oc16'60					*		
"	GENERAL WAKEFIELD		x							J.H.YOUNG	1,170			612		Oc28'60				*			
"	TAFOLINIA		x							D.O'WORDY	517			355		No2'60					*		
"	LIVE YANKEE				x					E.A.TIRRNDYE	1,501			728		No3'60					*		
"	LOA				x						407			257		No8'60					*		
"	WESTWARD HO		x								1,120			670		De26'60					*		
"	FRANCIS I (St.)			x							1,585			790		De29'60				*			
"	Mary QUEEN		x							P.G.JORDAN	568			310		De31'60	—			*			
"	REINA DEL OCEANO						x				1,011			294		Ja2'60	Ap4'60	64	4			287	
"	IORA	x									890		351			Fe9'60	My3'60	96	3			307	
"	MINERVA	x									829		310			Mr7'60	Dy23'60	155	14			317	
"	NORWOOD	x									849		331			Ja22'60	Ap6'60	75	3			311	
"	RED RIDING HOOD	x									720	514				Je23'60	Oe9'60	107				255	
"	THOMAS MITCHELL	x									578	252				Fe23'60	Je8'60	95	4			253	
"	SEBASTOPOL	x									988	333				De23'60	Oe28'60	95				323	
"	GREYHOUND							x			294	590					Se14'60		4,553	*			
"	GOVERNOR MORTON		x							J.C.BERRY													
"	CORD				x															117	175		

Table 35

List of Ships Transporting Chinese Laborers to Latin America, 1861

YEAR	NAME OF SHIP	FLAG	CAPTAIN	TONNAGE	PORT OF DEPARTURE	DATE OF DEPARTURE	DATE OF ARRIVAL	DAYS ON VOYAGE	DEATHS ON VOYAGE	DESTINATION (CUBA / PERU / Br. GUIANA)	REMARKS
1861	ENCARNACION	Spanish		567	Macau 808	Jan1/61				Cuba *	Mutiny.
"	GIOVANNA	Spanish		660	Macau 806	Jan22/61				Peru *	
"	MARIA CLOTILDE			547	Macau 258	Feb26/61					
"	FOREST EAGLE	American	PILLSBURG	1,156	Macau 500	Feb19/61					
"	KATE HOOPER	American	E. JOHNSON	1,488	Macau 869	Feb7/61				Cuba *	
"	FIDES	Dutch	ARMAN	880	Macau 398	Apr12/61		128		Peru *	
"	MESSENGER	American	A.D. JORION	1,200	Macau 555	Apr30/61		86	25	Peru *	
"	AGUSTINA	American		407	Macau *	Apr15/61				Cuba *	
"	TEREZA	Chilean	ROLLO		Macau *	May24/61				Peru *	
"	SALADANHA	British	G. DAWSON	1,561	Canton 500	May4/61	Jun14/61	96	9	Br. Guiana 498	
"	MYSTERY	British	H. STAP	1,074	Canton 260	Mar15/61	Jun9/61	97	25	Br. Guiana 337	
"	MONTMORENCY	British	J.J. SLOVBERRY	666	Canton 290	Mar15/61	Mar27/61	105	7	Br. Guiana 283	
"	LANCASHIRE WITCH	British	A.S. MOLLISON	1,386	Canton 461	Mar16/61	May4/61	131	29	Br. Guiana 433	
"	WHIRLWIND	British	L.D. ENGELL	977	Canton 265	Mar19/61	Jun25/61	121	13	Br. Guiana 354	One birth on voyage.
"	EARL OF WINDSOR	British	D. DIEX	784	Canton 325	Mar24/61	Mar17/61	110	24	Br. Guiana 305	2 births on voyage.
"	CLARMONT	British		69?	Canton 282	Mar15/61	Apr27/61	109	1	Br. Guiana 282	One birth on voyage.
"	RED RIDING HOOD	British	NICHOLSON	720	Canton 574	Mar19/61	Jun12/61	84	4	Br. Guiana 300	
"	CHAPMAN	British		732	Canton 305	Mar27/61	Jun9/61	110	15	Br. Guiana 290	
"	SEA PARK	British	KENDALL	895	Canton 299	Mar26/61	Jul7/61	112	20	Br. Guiana 263	
"	AGRA	British	SR. CROIX	724	Canton 287	Mar23/61	Jun16/61	80	1	Br. Guiana 287	
"	FRED A. CROSS	British/American		847	Canton *						One birth on voyage.
"	ALICE THORNDYKE	American									375 sailed from China.
"	MARION	American									
"	FRANCIS P. SAGE	American	T. INGERSOLL	1,306	Macau 550						350 sailed from China.
"	LEONIDAS	American	WOOD	690	289						
"	FRANCIS I (St.)	Spanish		900 *							Mutiny.
"	HENRY G. SUSANNA	American		982				90	199	Cuba *	
"	MAY QUEEN	American		619	*					Cuba *	
"	ULLOA	Spanish		600	*					Cuba *	
"	REINA DEL OCEANA	Spanish			*					Cuba *	
"	PEDRONELLA	Dutch								Cuba *	
"	ALBERS		GREGORY	359	*	Jul18/61					

Table 35 (cont.)

YEAR	NAME OF SHIP	FLAG										CAPTAIN	TONNAGE	PORT OF DEPARTURE				DATE OF DEPARTURE	DATE OF ARRIVAL	DAYS ON VOYAGE	DEATHS ON VOYAGE	DESTINATION			REMARKS
		BRITISH	AMERICAN	FRENCH	SPANISH	DUTCH	AUSTRIAN	GERMAN	CHILEAN	DANISH				CANTON	HONG KONG	MACAU	SWATOW					CUBA	PERU	Br. GUIANA	
1861	INDEPENDENCE		x									THRONE	800		*							*			
"	POMONE			x								SOLARES	851		*								*		
"	NORMA							x				DAPHENZ	355									*			

Table 36

List of Ships Transporting Chinese Laborers to Latin America, 1862

YEAR	NAME OF SHIP	FLAG						CAPTAIN	TONNAGE	PORT OF DEPARTURE				DATE OF DEPARTURE	DATE OF ARRIVAL	DAYS ON VOYAGE	DEATHS ON VOYAGE	DESTINATION				REMARKS
		BRITISH	AMERICAN	FRENCH	PERUVIAN	SPANISH	BELGIAN			AMOY	CANTON	HONG KONG	MACAU					CUBA	PERU	Br. GUIANA	TRINIDAD	
1862	MARION		x					Y.L.GROSS	564				225	Ja26'62					*			
"	GUADALUPE					x		R.MUNEZ	915				936	Mr24'62				*				
"	WESTWARD HO				x			A.deARMDA	1,120				603	Mr17'62					*			
"	EMPREZA				x			CARVACHO	485				299	My29'62					*			
"	CLAIRE			x				L.BORN	498				512	Ap28'62					*			
"	LEOPOLD CADEAUX						x	HICAISE	832				476	Ja5'62		1	475					
"	RED RIDING HOOD	x							720		326					80	3			524		
"	PERSIA		x						1,685			521				72	6			505		
"	SIR GEORGE SEIMOUR	x							730		324					42	35			285		
"	GENGHIS KHAN		x						1,206			572				50	32			480		
"	MAGGIE MILLER	x						JOHNS	1,230			520				80	80				467	
"	LADY ELMA BRUCE		x						920985							97	1				394	

Table 37

List of Ships Transporting Chinese Laborers to Latin America, 1863

YEAR	NAME OF SHIP	FLAG							CAPTAIN	TONNAGE	PORT OF DEPARTURE		DATE OF DEPARTURE	DATE OF ARRIVAL	DAYS ON VOYAGE	DEATHS ON VOYAGE	DESTINATION			REMARKS
		BRITISH	AMERICAN	FRENCH	PERUVIAN	SPANISH	PORTUGUESE	CHILEAN			CANTON	MACAU					CUBA	PERU	Br. GUIANA	
1863	WESTWARD HO				x				A.deARAUJO A	1,120	665		Ja2?63					*		
"	THEREZA							x	J.ROLLO	240		130	Ju12?63					*		
"	ELIZA						x		P.P.dosSANTOS	215		170	Ja29?63					*		
"	MALABAR			x					DUCASSE	512		256	Fe6?63				*			
"	PERSEVERANT			x					DUCIT	242		121	Fe4?63				*			
"	MERCEDES							x	C.A.EL JING	213		373	Ja27?63				*			
"	MARIA							x	J.H.WAGNER	213		132	Ap5?63				*			
"	CEZAR				x				J.VISSER	495		317	Mc1?63					*		
"	LUDEITA				x				J.A.NUNES	685		343						*		
"	D.MARIA de GLORIA						x		E.BAPTISTA	595		296	Oc30?63	De21?63	51A	59 28I		*		
"	CARLOS						x		J.V.MARQUES	836		418	No2?63	De28?63	51B	55 285		*		
"	VASCO da GAMA						x		J.J.daSILVA	1,018		508	Oc12?63	No?63	51A	108 225	287			
"	D.MARIA PIA						x		E.A RODOVALH	774		424	No30?63					*		
"	CAMILO CAVOUR				x				CARAVARRO	1,326		700	De9?63					*		
"	ALPONSO de ALBUQUERQUE						x		C.MARQUES	627		310	De17?63	Mar22?64	102	43 257		*		
"	ARIZONA					x			A.de BALPAREA	597		298	De20?63	Ap25?64	125	19 286		*		
"	WESTWARD HO				x				A. de ARAUCIAI	129		700	De18?63					*		
"	THEREZA				x				J.ROLLO	240		140	De2?63					*		
"	PERSEVERANCIA				x				A.TETENS	648		400	De31?63					*		
"	GANGES	x								899	413		Ap4?63	Ja?63	85	20			396	3 births on voyage.
"	20UAVE									517			De19?63	No28?64	70	10			509	2 births on voyage.
"	PARLIAMENT		x						A.A.McCASLIEI	1,001		*							*	
										1,323	517									

Table 38

List of Ships Transporting Chinese Laborers to Latin America, 1864

YEAR	NAME OF SHIP	FLAG								CAPTAIN	TONNAGE	PORT OF DEPARTURE		PORT OF DEPARTURE	DATE OF DEPARTURE	DATE OF ARRIVAL	DAYS ON VOYAGE	DEATHS ON VOYAGE	DESTINATION				REMARKS
		BRITISH	FRENCH	PERUVIAN	SPANISH	PORTUGUESE	DUTCH	CHILEAN	BELGIAN			CANTON	MACAU						CUBA	PERU	Br. GUIANA	TRINIDAD	
1864	D. FERNANDO			x						J. de SENA	984		492		Ja16a	Ja10a16a	97	21	471				
"	GENERAL PRIM			x						A. de OLANO	294		182		Ja16a	Ja16a				*			
"	CLOTILDE			x						S. BOLLO	357		221		Ja17a	Mar10a	108	2	218				
"	SOL de LIMA			x		x				R. ABARCA	222		110		Ja18a					*			
"	THEREZA					x				M. SICARD	796		500		Ja20a					*			
"	S.V. de PAULA			x						E.P. da SILVA	423		262		Ja25a	Ja25a				*			
"	ROSA CARMEN				x					J. MARISSONI	366		228		Ja30a					*			
"	DINA		x							W. WICH	301		160		Fa1a	Fa1a				*			
"	GASTON		x							LE BAILE	317		200		Fa6a					*			
"	CEZAR			x						J. NISSEN	499		317		Ma2a	Ma2a				*			
"	ONRUST						x			R.J. JENQUER	836		510		Ma29a	Ma2a				*			
"	JULIÃO			x		x				C. de ARUBARRIA	894		500		Mar4a	Mar4a				*			
"	LINA		x							B.J. CASTANEDO	1308		184		Ap7a	Ap7a				*			
"	VITALIA			x						L.P. SAUL	403		260		Ma23a	Ma16a				*			
"	MANDARINA	x								F.S. ROSSI	258		152		Jn8a	Jn8a				*			
"	NAPOLEON CANEVARO		x							R. DENARO	1,275		300		Jn8a					*			
"	Beoclan			x						MENARD	500		308		Jn8a					*			
"	CAMILO CAVOUR		x							J. deLANDABASO	1,326		605		Ja17a	Pa465	226	9	515				
"	CLAIRE		x							L. ROBERT	496		302		Ja17a			10	406				
"	MEDOC		x							DUFEIL	648		324		Oa17a	Pa465							
"	LEOPOLD CATEAUX							x		A. NICAISE	832		416		Oa29a								
"	DAIGORETTE				x					M.S. de URETA	720		360		Oa17a	Nov465	108	45	317				
"	SAINT JOSEPH		x							J. ROUSSEAU	784		366		Nov264a	Nov265	111	5	363				
"	D. MARIA PIA					x				J.F. de SANTOS	778		425		No29a	Nov465	81	25	400				
"	AURORA		x							J. URTI	666		377		Bo12a	Jan465	10a	10	567				
"	ENCARNACION				x					R. VARA	567		283		No29a	Nov465	112	9	274				
"	JOSEPHde ALMIRA			x						V.A. REMEDIOS	1,142		571		No29a	Nov265	99	5	566				
"	ISABEL		x							DECOURC	542		271		Da16a	Nov12a65	95	2	266				
"	CHARLOTTE		x							F. MOREAU	541		270		Da16a			6	264				
"	GUADALUPE			x						F. MUROZ	973		456		Da18a	Ap265	105	5	421				
"	DAVID		x							ROBERT	842		421		Da18a	Ap765	105	8	413				

Table 38 (cont.)

YEAR	NAME OF SHIP	FLAG									CAPTAIN	PORT OF DEPARTURE			DATE OF DEPARTURE	DATE OF ARRIVAL	DAYS ON VOYAGE	DEATHS ON VOYAGE	DESTINATION				REMARKS
		BRITISH	FRENCH	PERUVIAN	SPANISH	PORTUGUESE	DUTCH	CHILEAN	BELGIAN			TONNAGE	CANTON	MACAU					CUBA	PERU	Br.°GUIANA	TRINIDAD	
1864	EMMA					X					C.J.deSEQUEIRA	478		259	Dec20'63	Apr20'64	121	2	1256				
"	THERESA			X							J.SEAFING	240		143	Dec24'64	Apr10'65	107			143			
"	BREECHIN CASTLE	X										527	270		Oct18'64	Jan26'65	100	2			269		
"	MONTROSE	X										750	504		Nov17'64	Feb18'65	93	11				513	2 births on voyage.

Table 39

List of Ships Transporting Chinese Laborers to Latin America, 1865

YEAR	NAME OF SHIP	FLAG									CAPTAIN	TONNAGE	PORT OF DEPARTURE				DATE OF DEPARTURE	DATE OF ARRIVAL	DAYS ON VOYAGE	DEATHS ON VOYAGE	DESTINATION						REMARKS
		BRITISH	FRENCH	PERUVIAN	SPANISH	PORTUGUESE	ITALIAN	NORWEGIAN	GERMAN	CHILEAN			AMOY	CANTON	MACAO	HONG KONG					CUBA	PERU	Br. GUIANA	TRINIDAD	SURINAM	HONDURAS	
1865	TRICOLOR	x															De8/65										Maning.
"	PRIDE of the GANGES	x											620				Fe17/65	An10/65	84	14							5 births on voyage.
"	PARIA	x	x										660				Ja09/65	My17/65	128	1	396		278				
"	PROVIDENZA						x					A.NORGUES	357	395				Ja09/65	My17/65	128	1	177						
"	PORT DURAND		x									DUBOIS	767	176				Ja08/65	Ap22/65	104	2		396					
"	CLOTILDE											J.ROLLO	477	235				Ja14/65	Ap23/65	99	4		278					
"	AUGUST-GUSTAVE											BENASSIT	486	245				Ja17/65	Ap16/65	107	3		340					
"	LOMBARD											BRUSHICHE	350	225				Ja22/65				234						
"	JOANA R. ALCAROS							x				C.PRUDHENICHE	1,086	545				Fe10/65				340						
"	AVON	x										G.FALONE	1,159	594				Fe12/65			24		560					
"	QUEEN of ENGLAND			x								R.FORCUNAES	365	192				Fe16/65			10		182					
"	NOUVELLE PALLAS		x									DUBAN	834	516				No02/65	Ju27/65	125	200		316					
"	JULIE		x									F.L.de PENA	358	164				My4/65					*					
"	EMMANUEL					x						C.deCONDROY	773	495				No16/65	Ja17/65	108	68	427						
"	COLOMBOS						x	x				S.CHIAPPORA	1,215	842				No10/65	Ma23/65	105	20	512						
"	NAPOLEON CANEVARO							x				R.DENGRO	328	200				Mr03/65	Ap06/65	122	77	133						
"	LIMA					x						J.B.CASTHHOLA	636	418				Mr29/65					261					
"	CAMOES											H.C.desGANDS	795	505				My2/65	No02/65	164	344		*					
"	D.JOSE							x				J.GERVANSONI	1,326	520				My2/65					*					
"	CAMILLO CAVOUR						x	x				LANDABASO	299	50				Ju4/65				455						STOP at HAWAII.
"	MATADOR									x		RASMUSSEN	890	505				Fe8/65	So17/65	105	148	256						
"	CHRISTINA			x								J.O.RUAN	499	505				Ju23/65	Oc13/65	112	247	248						
"	PRESTOANOR			x								L.PROFUMO	462	290				My22/65	Oc13/65	90	42		*					
"	CZAR											J.MEISSER	845	240				Ju22/65					*					
"	FALCON			x								SULLIVAN	668	515				Ju30/65					*					
"	LIBUTRA											A.PEZZOLO	794	599				Ae16/65	No18/65	104	10	389						
"	AURORA			x								G.HILL	509	506				Se20/65			344		*					Stop at Tahiti.
"	DEL del MAR									x		A.GIACOMO	459	299				De2/65					*					
"	TIMOIAVE						x					L.BERNARD	491	515				Oc4/65					*					
"	A.N.GERARD			x								B.BOUROH	1,482	210				De29/65					*					
"	NAVIOTE-NASSI DE Compagnia Maritima do Peru			x								L.BELLARD		655				De30/65					*					
"												A.FULLE																

Table 39 (cont.)

YEAR	NAME OF SHIP	BRITISH	FRENCH	PERUVIAN	SPANISH	PORTUGUESE	ITALIAN	NORWEGIAN	GERMAN	CHILEAN	CAPTAIN	TONNAGE	AMOY	CANTON	MACAU	HONG KONG	DATE OF DEPARTURE	DATE OF ARRIVAL	DAYS ON VOYAGE	DEATHS ON VOYAGE	CUBA	PERU	Br. GUIANA	TRINIDAD	SURINAM	HONDURAS	REMARKS
1865	ARIZONA				x						A. de BALPARDA	597			280		No02865				*						
"	ANNE GARDNER		x								C. KNODE	406			290		No26865				*						
"	ADMIRAL PERRONNET		x					x			P. COSTE	495			313		No29865				*						
"	OTILIA						x				C. NISSELL	390			296		De17865				*						
"	VERONA COLLET		x								VIGOUREUX	356			223		De28865				*						
"	ROSINA										PERMANN	487			570		De14865					*					
"	EVA			x							N. CHRISTAFNER	224			120		De16865					*					
"	PROVIDENCIA		x								S. MOTINI	660			413		Ja17865				*						
"	ST. JULIEN						x				NOTE	346			259		Ja17865				*						
"	EMMA + MATILDE	x									H. J. BEHRENS	385			209		De24865										
"	QUEEN of the EAST								x			1,226		490			No15865	Fe28866	106	10			481				One birth on voyage.
"	SEVILLA	x										598		312			No05865	Fe26866	109	8			305				One birth on voyage.
"	ARIMA	x										691		743			No02865	Fe26866	120	32			311				
"	BUCTON CASTLE	x										886		552			No29865	Mr12866	98	30			325				One birth on voyage.
"	LIGHT of the AGE	x											480				Oc23865	De26865	116	6						474	
"	DUDBROOKE	x										571	286				Oc24865	De26865	66	14				572			
"	RED RIDING HOOD	x										720	286				Se27865			2				524			Mutiny.
"	LA COTE d'OR		x											245			Oc12865				*						Mutiny.
"	CAROLINE		x											560							*						
"	LA VILLE ST. LO		x											260			De15865				*						

Table 40

List of Ships Transporting Chinese Laborers to Latin America, 1866

YEAR	NAME OF SHIP	FLAG	CAPTAIN	TONNAGE	PORT OF DEPARTURE	DATE OF DEPARTURE	DATE OF ARRIVAL	DAYS ON VOYAGE	DEATHS ON VOYAGE	DESTINATION	REMARKS
1866	LOUIS	British/French			Canton	Ja1866	Ja1866	26	5	Cuba / Brazil 272 / Surinam 104	Mar.inv.
"	SOBERANA										
"	WANDERER	British	R.HUGHES	668	Hong Kong 400	Jo1866	Jo1866				
"	GOLDEN HORN	British	J.P.RICE	1,114	Hong Kong AUG						
"	KUBA		P.A.ALISON	550	Macau 341						
"	AMERLAND		J.P.HUISMAN	360	Macau 225	Ja1866				Cuba	
"	SOVIERA		W.WILSMAN	572	Macau 317	Ja1866				Cuba	
"	ITALIA	Italian	OKIE	988	Macau 406	Ja1866				Cuba	
"	LOMBARD	Portuguese	PIERS	452	Macau 266	Ja1866				Cuba	
"	EMIGRANTE		D.IRANOYA	722	Macau 359	Ja1866				Cuba	
"	JOSEPHINA-AMATRA		V.REMEDIOS	1,142	Macau 557	Fe1866				Cuba	
"	BARON KILLNER	Russian	J.M.CORUCH	783	Macau 392	Fe1866			23	209 Cuba	
"	CARL		J.BAS	378	Macau 179	Fe1866			3		
"	Compania MARITIMA de PERU II	Peruvian	S.SPEVALO	1,076	Macau 435	Fe1866				Peru 196	
"	ANTOINETTE		CHABANNE	363	Macau 228	Fe1866				Cuba	
"	MOUSSE de NANTES	Norwegian	J. BROSNICHE	265	Macau 291	Ma1866				Cuba	
"	CONSTANTINE		AMUNDSEN	517	Macau 434	Ma1866				Peru	
"	GUADALUPE	Spanish	J.J.AGARDOQUE	912	Macau 495	Ma1866				Cuba	
"	CAFALERA		F.DEMORO	305	Macau 521	Ma1866				Cuba	
"	INDEPENDANT	French	DELIREAU	569	Macau 290	Ma1866				Cuba	
"	BENGALI	French	D.ESTANTE	423	Macau 860	Ap1866				Cuba	
"	NAPOLEON CANEVARO	Spanish	R.DEMORO	1,213	Macau 865	Ap1866				Cuba	
"	ENCARNACION	Spanish	R.VARA	562	Macau 361	Ap1866				Cuba	
"	AUTMGRACIA	Spanish	M.LANDA	480	Macau 829	Ap1866				Cuba	
"	BORDEUS-HAVANA I	Spanish	M.GRANGA	524	Macau 905	Ap1866				Cuba	
"	J. V. A.		M.SOLAURA	522	Macau 284	Ap1866				Cuba	
"	BORDEUS-HAVANA II	Portuguese	J.R.CORCETRA	440	Macau 351	Ma1866				Cuba	
"	D.MARIA PIA		E.A.de SOUZA	778	Macau 422	Ma1866				Cuba	
"	DA VID	Italian	BATRATON	642	Macau 225	Ap1866				Cuba	
"	DENTS	Italian	BARON	568	Macau 225	Ap1866				Cuba / Peru	Mar.inv.
"	UNCOWAH		ORDANO	988	Macau 455	Ap1866				Peru	
"	AMALIA		J.ROLLO	344	Macau 241						

Table 40 (cont.)

YEAR	NAME OF SHIP	FLAG BRITISH	FRENCH	PERUVIAN	SPANISH	PORTUGUESE	ITALIAN	RUSSIAN	GERMAN	CHILEAN	BELGIAN	CAPTAIN	TONNAGE	PORT OF DEPARTURE CANTON	HONG KONG	MACAU	DATE OF DEPARTURE	DATE OF ARRIVAL	DAYS ON VOYAGE	DEATHS ON VOYAGE	DESTINATION CUBA	PERU	Br.·GUIANA	REMARKS
1866	EMMA									x		R.WICH	501			825	Mr22/66	Mr22/66				*		
"	LUIZA CANEYHRO						x					D.A.CAVESSA	1,206			698	Ap10/66	Ap10/66			*			
"	COLOMBO						x					S.CHIAPPARA	775			570	Ap20/66	Ge11/66	144	6		564		
"	JULIÃO					x						J.M.de SOUZA	894			N/A	Au21/66	Au21/66			*			
"	DOLORES UGARTE					x	x					E.P.da SILVI	285			670	My6/66	My6/66			*			
"	CAMILO CAVOUR				x		x					P.deLANDABASO	1,286			634	My9/66	My9/66			*			
"	CATALIÑA (St.)											M.J.VARLO	1,200			477	My2/66	My2/66	65	*				
"	LIMA						x					A.MUNHARDT	328			748	My11/66	Oo2216/66	141	7		141		
"	THEREZA						x					S.ROLLO	1,094			651	Jn2/66	Jn2/66						
"	ASIA						x					TIMOST	820			500	Jn6/66	Jn6/66				*		
"	FRAY BENTOS						x					V.CASTAINHOLA	471			360	Jn20/66	No7/66	142	9		351		
"	PREGOLOMEO											L.FROPUNO	860			455	Jn2/66	Jn2/66						
"	AMALIA				x							J.D.OLDIJAN	449			258	Se23/66	Se23/66				*		
"	SIONNE											W.NORBERG	792			526	Oo4/66	Fe5/67	124	1508				
"	LARICA											R.AURREDONCHA	567			372	Oo4/66	Oo4/66						
"	MEDOC	x										J.ROUX	857			257	Oo4/66					*		Mutiny.
"	EUGENE-ADELLE	x										A.GIRAUD	700			466	Oo7/66					*		
"	JOVEN THOMAZ					x						D.P.CAMPOS	700			400	Oo13/66					*		
"	FALCON				x							W.SULLIVAN	862			246	Oo18/66	Fe9/67	114	2	247			
"	BILBAINA				x							YZAURIETA	673			498	Oo18/66					*		
"	LUISITA					x						R.GORDIA	1,049			555	Oo25/66	Ap4/67	166	4a316				
"	NINA					x						C.J.SEQUEIRA	1,019			549	No2/66	No2/66						
"	AMERICA											EVANS	1,454			602	No10/66	Gua6/67	1773			564		
"	AURELIANA											J.L.BASTERA	482			517	No11/66	Gar10/67	173	1796				
"	GICA					x						J.R.deGANOS	499			288	No15/66	Ma4/67	109	7	881			
"	SAGITAIRE	x										M.GARDONNER	329			165	No15/66					*		
"	DOS HERMANOS											M.TUDON	305			305	No22/66					*		
"	MANILLA BILBAO				x							A.ALCANTENA	426			251	De1/66	No7/67	129	15	236			
"	GLENLEE									x		J.DUAN	635			435	De4/66	De4/66				*		
"	AVON	x								x		E.deVILLOSOLA	1,086			502	De5/66	De5/66	27	N73				
"	NIZAM	x										A.CORIEL	460			262	De11/66	Ma7/67	127	8	65A			
"	AURORA						x					W.C.LINSCOTT	660			272	De24/66	Sa8/67	111	13		259		

Table 40 (cont.)

YEAR	NAME OF SHIP	BRITISH	FRENCH	PERUVIAN	SPANISH	PORTUGUESE	ITALIAN	RUSSIAN	GERMAN	BELGIAN	CAPTAIN	TONNAGE	AMOY	CANTON	MACAU	DATE OF DEPARTURE	DATE OF ARRIVAL	DAYS ON VOYAGE	DEATHS ON VOYAGE	CUBA	PERU	Br.GUIANA	REMARKS
1866	S.VINCENT de PAULO					x					P.P.dosSANTOS	422			596	Dec20'66	Apr9'66	111	9	397			
"	HENRY IV		x								F.ALESAUS	727			456	Dec2'66	Apr6'67	111	9	347			Mutiny.
"	DEMOCRAT-BROWN	x								x	P.FRODDEN	708			367	Dec20'66	Apr9'66	106	6	561		497	
"	LIGHT BRIGADE	x										1,23A 498	460			Jul18'66	Apr66	96	6			=	
"	JEDDO	x									J.WEST	641				Mar18'66	Jun66	161				502	
"	PRIDE of theGANGES	x												300		Mar30'66	Jul16'66	3		*			
"	LIEUTENANT BELLOT		x											250		Jul1'66				*			
"	LA CARMELINE		x											550		Jul22'66				*			Mutiny.
"	HONG KONG		x											560		Jul23'66				*			
"	LA FLORE		x											210		Jul10'66				*			Mutiny.
"	GAULOIS													500		Apr266				*			
"	GRANVILLE													250		Apr366				*			

Table 41

List of Ships Transporting Chinese Laborers to Latin America, 1867

YEAR	NAME OF SHIP	FLAG BRITISH	FRENCH	PERUVIAN	SPANISH	PORTUGUESE	ITALIAN	DUTCH	SALVADORIAN	AUSTRIAN	GERMAN	CAPTAIN	TONNAGE	PORT OF DEPARTURE HONG KONG	MACAO	DATE OF DEPARTURE	DATE OF ARRIVAL	DAYS ON VOYAGE	DEATHS ON VOYAGE	DESTINATION CUBA	PERU	SURINAM	REMARKS
1867	VERITAS	x										CAREY	632	291	304	Mar.6.67				304			
"	HONG KONG				x							YRIBARRI	470		275	Jan.14.67	May 16.67	122		270			
"	DELANGLE		x									DUPONT	362		228	Jan.16.67	May 23.67	16		213			
"	CONFUCIUS										x	M. STENGEL	508		284	Jan.30.67				*			
"	REINA de los ANGELES											V. KUHNELL	506		284	Jan.28.67	Jul.12.67	152		284			
"	NINA				x							J. ACHUTIQUE	1,067		528	Feb.1.67				*			
"	ESPERANZA				x							J.D. OÑATE	400		235	Feb.6.67	Jun.20.67	109	4	229			
"	BANGKOK											E. CHAPPOT	624		410	Feb.9.67	Jun.7.67	116	15	396			
"	NIEMEN		x									BECK WITH	383		295	Feb.10.67				369			Mutiny
"	VICTORIA											S.M. MELANICH	742		525	Feb.17.67	Jun.23.67	105	23	522			
"	JOSEPHINE de ALMEIRA					x						M.P. de SILVEIRA MIRA	705		568	Mar.4.67	Jun.23.67	107	5	565			
"	KRUMPEN							x				ROTIGEN	999		285	Mar.10.67	Jun.23.67	106	6	279			
"	EPHROM											E. BUNCAND	836		447								
"	CHRIST											D. VUESSENBRIEK	729		350	Nov.16.67				*			
"	ALZAGRACIA				x							N. LAIRD	429		290	Nov.20.67				*			
"	JUSTA				x					x		L. AVOCHDA	501		410	Nov.21.67	May 10.67	120	3	415			
"	ALAVESA				x					x		M. DOBARAN	515		520	Dec.2.67	Jun.16.67	204	7	502			
"	J.Jula				x							M. SOLTURA	499		740	Apr.2.67				*			
"	BELLA GALLEGA				x							J.R. de ONAINGE	565		340	Apr.5.67				*			
"	ENCARNACION				x							J.A. GHEOGHE	857		409	Apr.5.67	Aug.16.67	131		409			
"	RUDESIO				x							FENNY	1,025		541	Apr.7.67							
"	CERVANTES											F. EYZAGUIRRE	999		285	May 2.67				*			
"	MARIE LAURE		x									E. AURRI	499		487	Jun.9.67				*			
"	CATALINA (St.)				x							V. ESEANDILLA	200		403	Jun.9.67							
"	R. PRAXOLONGO						x					L. PROFUMO	890		364	Jul.25.67	Nov.6.67	124	18	346			
"	PROVIDENZA						x					MATTINI	660		609	Jul.21.67					*		
"	JOHANNA			x						x		I. NDARASO	1,326		471	Jul.23.67					*		
"	GALILEO						x					SPLIVALO	1,076		499	Jul.25.67					*		
"	DOLORES UGARTE			x					x			A. OLANO	1,283		575	Aug.21.67					*		
"	ASIA						x					CALDERON	1,200		663	Aug.22.67					*		
"	LUIZA CANEVARO			x								R. DEMORO	509		347	Oct.9.67					*		
"	TAMARAVE		x				x					L. BERNARD										*	

Table 41 (cont.)

YEAR	NAME OF SHIP	FLAG										CAPTAIN	TONNAGE	PORT OF DEPARTURE		DATE OF DEPARTURE	DATE OF ARRIVAL	DAYS ON VOYAGE	DEATHS ON VOYAGE	DESTINATION		REMARKS
		BRITISH	FRENCH	PERUVIAN	SPANISH	PORTUGUESE	ITALIAN	DUTCH	SALVADORIAN	AUSTRIAN	GERMAN			HONG KONG	MACAU					CUBA	PERU	
1867	CLAIRE		x									LeROBERT	498		257	Oc25'67	Jc26'68	100	2	*		Via Lisbon.
"	UNKOWAH						x					ROSSLAND	988		848	Oc25'67	Fe16'68			*		Stop at Mauritius.
"	SNYPER		x									LeCAILLET	949		271	Oc29'67				*		
"	MARIA PIA					x						E.A.deSOUZA	671		248	No5'67	Ja24'68	80		555		
"	CARMELINE		x									GALEY	1,285		653	No7'67	Ap17'68				*	
"	BLANCHE		x									BUTOT	533		511	Ja15'67					653	
"	PEDRO I					x						A.FULLE	1,557		560	Ja17'67	Fe11'68	76	27			Mutiny.
"	NELLY		x									J.POILBOUT	848		444	Oc29'67	Ja26'68	13	409			Mutiny.
"	ORCKA		x									GUERARD	927		556	Oc17'67	Ap26'68	13	251			

Table 42

List of Ships Transporting Chinese Laborers to Latin America, 1868

YEAR	NAME OF SHIP	FLAG (French / Peruvian / Spanish / Italian / Dutch / Salvadorian / Russian / German)								CAPTAIN	TONNAGE	PORT OF DEPARTURE (Hong Kong / Macau)		DATE OF DEPARTURE	DATE OF ARRIVAL	DAYS ON VOYAGE	DEATHS ON VOYAGE	DESTINATION (Cuba / Peru / Surinam)			REMARKS
1868	MALABAR	x	x							A.OUDRE	818		500		Jn22'68 Jn29'68	107	1	469			Mutiny.
"	ESPERANZA	x	x							E.RODU	397		500		Jn5'68		217	*			
"	HONG KONG						x			L.DUBERRE	470	516			Jn6'68			*			
"	AURORA	x		x			x			M.GARCIA y GARCIA	668		600		Ja11'68 Ap14'66	93	8		399		
"	AMERICA	x			x					M.L.PERREDROIT	454		610		Se25'68 Ju17'66	III 3	507				Mutiny, returned Macao.
"	THERESA	x								S.ROLLO	1,050	299			Fe3'68			*			
"	ANNA	x								R.ZULUETA	1,086	551			Fe14'66 Jn6'66	III2	557				
"	MYSORE	x	x							L.FAZER	495	294			Fe20'68			*			
"	VILLA de St.LO	x	x							F.DUBOIS	456	280			Fe20'66 Ju27'66	91 6	274				
"	ALTAGRACIA	x		x						N.LANDA	618	362			Fe22'66			*			
"	GUANTANAMO	x								T.YSSARS	248	273			Mr6'68			*			
"	FRAY BENTOS			x						A.ROLLO	560	300			Mr25'68 Jy27'68	III 4		308			
"	EUGENE + ADELE	x								E.NEVERS	655	466			Mr26'68 Jy9'68	III 10	455				
"	ERIC ARRIAGTON					x				J.A.deGARBOODE	437	302			Mr25'68 Jy17'68	98 15	286				
"	ALAVESA	x								M.DOGRAN	669	428			Mr17'68			*			
"	SUOME	x						x		C.V.BORDBERG	942	525			Ap2'68		17	508			Mutiny.
"	CATALINA (Sr.)			x			x			V.ESCANADILLA	1,300	517			Se27'68 Ap4'68	III 15	504				
"	R.PRATOLONGO				x		x			L.PROFUMO	890	464			Mr27'68 Ju26'68	25 21		445			
"	CAMILO CAVOUR				x					A.ASTORQUIA	1,326	555			Jy3'68			*			
"	PROVIDENZA				x					A.RACTINE	660	382			Jy2'68			*			
"	HENRY IV	x								L.MOVELLOT	757	458			Jy1'68 Se20'68	64 14	515				
"	UNCOWAH	x						x		J.ROSSINO	988	499			Ag27'68 Ja1'69	125 21	470				
"	NIAGARA	x								P.MESEC	728	406			Se35'68 Fe14'69	20 396					
"	CONFUCIUS			x				x		H.SEUREL	757	228			Fe18'68 Fe20'69	21 197					
"	DOLARRS UGARTE			x						L.P.SAUL	1,238	602			Se2'68			*			
"	ANTARES	x		x						G.NOLTE	401	263			Mar9'68 Mr26'27	66 197					
"	PACTOLE	x		x						J.OLLIVARD	444	245			Se8'68 Mr9'69	146 25	220				
"	MARIA MORTON	x								B.MORELLO	401	271			No2'68 Mr25'69	57 158					
"	AURORA	x								GARCIA yGARCIA	666	419			No24'68 Mr19'69	39 396					Mutiny.
"	LUCIE	x								D.REGIER	615	360			De28'68 Jn14'69	35 321					
"	ORREST							x		WESSENBRUCK	266	455			De24 Ja3'69 Ja16'69	68 285					
"	MARIE THERESE	x															*				
"	CAVAILT	x								BONNEFOR	502 252				Ap20'68			*			Mutiny.

Table 43

List of Ships Transporting Chinese Laborers to Latin America, 1869

YEAR	NAME OF SHIP	FLAG								CAPTAIN	TONNAGE	PORT OF DEPARTURE		DATES OF DEPARTURE	DATES OF ARRIVAL	DAYS ON VOYAGE	DEATHS ON VOYAGE	DESTINATION			REMARKS
		BRITISH	FRENCH	ITALIAN	PORTUGUESE	SALVADORIAN	RUSSIAN	GERMAN	SPANISH			HONG KONG	MACAO					CUBA	PERU	SURINAM	
1869	VISTULA									W.BURKUT	733		454								
"	NADESTA						x			T.MAUER	600		252								Mutiny.
"	NEVA		x				x			GRAER	1,042		257								
"	ZMARUS	x					x			P.JANNEE	545		300								
"	CHINA+HAVANA									L.ROBERT	926		446								
"	ITALIA			x						ZOLUTA	1,086		520								
"	NELLY		x							POLLROUZ	948		444								
"	MONGOL		x							COURBEE	1,097		466								
"	CAMILO CAVOUR					x				A.ASTORQUIA	1,226		586								Mutiny.
"	CALLAO					x				L.LAVROLLO	1,252		663								
"	FRAY BENTOS					x				R.MOTA	961		592								
"	AMERICA					x				E.PARKS	1,454		669								
"	PROVIDENZA					x				V.VID MURRAZABA	660		396								
"	JOARDAIN									L.ARHARDEAU	840		282								
"	LUISA GANEVARO		x							R.JENORO	1,006		721								
"	DOS HERMANOS					x			x	J.MONASTERIO	402		251								
"	ANGO		x							A.FERRER	622		320								
"	CATALINA (ST.)								x	V.SCOAIADIADIZOO	1,300		528								
"	UNCOWAH				x					J.ROSCIANO	986		576								
"	D.MARIA PIA	x								E.A.deSOUZA	671		370								
"	VERITAS										202										
"	PEROTH AND BRUM							x				296									

Table 44

List of Ships Transporting Chinese Laborers to Latin America, 1870

YEAR	NAME OF SHIP	FLAG								CAPTAIN	TONNAGE	PORT OF DEPARTURE		DATE OF DEPARTURE	DATE OF ARRIVAL	DAYS ON VOYAGE	DEATHS ON VOYAGE	DESTINATION		REMARKS
		FRENCH	PERUVIAN	PORTUGUESE	ITALIAN	SALVADORIAN	RUSSIAN	BELGIAN	COLOMBIAN			HONG KONG	MACAU					CUBA	PERU	
1870	NEVA	x								J.D.OATES	1,182		527				3	574		
"	MANUELA					x				P.BONNET	444		247			99	4		543	
"	CAMILO CAVOUR					x x				A.ASTORQUIA	1,326		662				12	550		
"	FRAY BENTOS					x				RJAOTA	561		555			90	30	523		Shipwreck near Anjer.
"	ITALIA			x						VIDAURRAZAGA	1,086		527							
"	AMERICA									E.FERRIS	1,445		780				26	594		
"	CECELIA		x			x				A.GOMSSOUTTA	592		370				50	520		
"	PROVIDENZA									VIDAURRAZAGA	660		436				4	410		
"	CALLAO					x				L.LAVARELLO	1,555		671				22	549		
"	DOLORES UGARTE					x				J.P.SAIL	1,285		609				80	486		43 sick off at Hawaii.
"	LUISA CANEVARO					x				R.DEMORO	1,026		705				22	585		
"	MARIA GAVTRA					x				GARCIA&GARCIA	289		204				5	199		
"	CLOTILDE					x				GARCIA&GARCIA	1,176		794				44	710		
"	MACAO									S.MORALES	1,076		496				10	486		
"	EPHREM									E.BOUNCAUD	385		285						596	Mutiny.
"	FERDINAND MARIE	x								P.JONQUIER	545		310				14			Mutiny.
"	L.OLIVIER	x								A.AUCAN	395		235					390		
"	JANDRE	x								H.LAYSEAU	475		327				37			
"	D.MARIA PIA			x						E.A.deSOUZA	677		370				55	516		Mutiny, return Macao. Fire on board.
"	NOUVELLE PENELOPE	x								J.LEYGOURECK	490		310							
"	UNCOWAH									R.MOTA	988		577				124			
"	FRAY BENTOS									R.MOTA	561		565				2	562		
"	CAMILO CAVOUR					x				A.ASTORQUIA	1,326		660				9	552		
"	COSMOPOLITE	x								P.DUBREVEIGNE	450		302				3	299		
"	VISUELA									P.GARRIQUE	732		450				17	475		
"	SAINT IVES	x								P.BRETAIN	640		565				9	554		
"	HONG KONG		x							I.YPIREZI	470		517				14	299		
"	PROVIDENZA									VIDAURRAZAGA	660		518				10	406		
"	NELLY	x				x				A.POILBOUGH	895		418				54	410		
"	FREDERIC								x	NICAISE	581		444							
"	COURONNEMENT	x								C.BOURDON	1,294		557				42	515		Mutiny.

Table 44 (cont.)

YEAR	NAME OF SHIP	FLAG								CAPTAIN	TONNAGE	PORT OF DEPARTURE			DATE OF DEPARTURE	DATE OF ARRIVAL	DAYS ON VOYAGE	DEATHS ON VOYAGE	DESTINATION		REMARKS
		FRENCH	PERUVIAN	PORTUGUESE	ITALIAN	SALVADORIAN	RUSSIAN	BELGIAN				HONG KONG	MACAU	BATAVIA					CUBA	PERU	
1870	ESPERANCE																				
"	ORPHEUS				x									*	De '70	Fe '72		107	*	1873	280 left China.
"	HANKOW																	966		1	Nothing,248 left China.

Table 45

List of Ships Transporting Chinese Laborers to Latin America, 1871

YEAR	NAME OF SHIP	FRENCH	PERUVIAN	SPANISH	PORTUGUESE	SALVADORIAN	RUSSIAN	CAPTAIN	TONNAGE	MACAU	DATE OF DEPARTURE	DATE OF ARRIVAL	DAYS ON VOYAGE	DEATHS ON VOYAGE	CUBA	PERU	REMARKS
1871	CALLAO					x		L.LAVARELLO	1,552	650			83	29		664	
"	ALMORACIA			x				J.F.AMAINDE	618	361			30	*	*		
"	PERU					x		A.BASQUITE	690	580			98		350		
"	LUCIE	x			x			D.DIDIER	615	560				*		374	
"	CECELIA				x			J.C.de BASQUITA	555	575			98	1	*		
"	CATALINA (St.)			x				J.ROLDAN	1,300	557					473		
"	LOLA							P.de RIORIETA	890	479			95	4	170		
"	VILLA de GRANADA		x					M.CHANSEL	471	459			85	2	235		
"	CASTI	x	x					P.COULINEAU	295	295			85	47	775		
"	NHA						x	J.M.de San PEDRO	1,652	764							
"	ENCARNACION		x	x				J.A.GANDOQUE	565	827			106	29	700		
"	CLOTHILDE					x		GARCIA y GARCIA	111	729			113	55	195		
"	J.REMU			x		x		A.OSURRIDEO	565	248			111	14	235		
"	Pactole	x						J.CLIVAND	446	276			122		360		
"	FRAY BENTOS		x					R.MOTA	563	372				597	1		Mutiny, ship burned.
"	DON JUAN		x					C GARAY	1,295	655			126	8	725		
"	LUIZA CANEVARO		x					R.RIBEIRO	1,206	725				15	346		
"	ROSALIA		x					GARCIA y GARCIA	835	461			133	8	595		
"	SARA		x					J.R.ANDRACA	708	544			120		18		
"	CONSTANCIA		x					W.JONES	195	18			98	6	598		
"	AMERICA		x					E.PERKS	1,454	644			115	15	423		
"	MACAO	x						M.J.LOUAYTEA	1,067	456			112	11 321	343		
"	BLANCHE	x						A.BUE	555	552			106	39			
"	MILLE JOHNES						x	F.A.SURRABESH	725	492							
"	NAPLES	x						J.SENNE	395	511					*		
"	RENNE							J.PICKBERRY	470	275			111	8	*		
"	HONG KONG							VIDAURRAZAGA	660	504			100	5	506		
"	PROVIDENCIA		x					A.DUBREUNE	475	420			100	26	269		
"	UNIVERS	x						N.SIMON	795	451			128	14	481		
"	CONCEPCION	x	x					A.DUBREUNE	795	495			106	20			
"	SILENCE			x				H.DEPOY	470	217					197		

Table 45 (cont.)

YEAR	NAME OF SHIP	FLAG						CAPTAIN	TONNAGE	PORT OF DEPARTURE		DATE OF DEPARTURE	DATE OF ARRIVAL	DAYS ON VOYAGE	DEATHS ON VOYAGE	DESTINATION		REMARKS
		FRENCH	PERUVIAN	SPANISH	PORTUGUESE	SALVADORIAN	RUSSIAN			MACAU	BATAVIA					CUBA	PERU	
1871	PERU		x					A.BASSAROTTE	690	404		No5ª'71	No22ª'72	98	110		994	
"	D.MARIA PIA				x			E.A.deGUEA	671	329		No9ª'71	Mar2ª'72	112	25	306		Via Lisbon.
"	JULES DUFAURE	x						H.SMITH	482	311		No24'71	No10ª'72	107	5	306		
"	CALLAO	x						A.de ARAUCOA	1,252	629		No28ª'71	No12ª'72	77	19		510	
"	Papillon	x	x					C.LEROUX	496	745		No57'71	No09ª'72	105	3	342		
"	LOLA		x					P.FRIRE	444	260		No17'71	No21'72	124	7	259		
"	CHINA			x				P.de ELIRREZA	990	592		No22ª'71	Ja4ª'72	55	4		588	
"	CAMILO CAVOUR	x						J.M.deS.PEDRO	1,632	762		Ja29ª'71		18	786		-	Storm, returned Macau.
"	BERNICA	x						A.ASSURGUIA	1,326	632	270	No18ª'71	No4ª'71	106	52		220	

Table 46

List of Ships Transporting Chinese Laborers to Latin America, 1872

YEAR	NAME OF SHIP	FLAG	CAPTAIN	TONNAGE	CANTON	MACAO	DATE OF DEPARTURE	DATE OF ARRIVAL	DAYS OF VOYAGE	DEATHS ON VOYAGE	CUBA	PERU	COSTA RICA	REMARKS
1872	FRAY BENTOS	French	A. de MESQUITA	552		271			96	6		265		
"	CECELIA (SP)	Peruvian	C. A. BUCKER	442		380			98	18		262		
"	ALEXANDRE LAVALLEY	French	E. LORGIN	1,515		621			74	18	603			
"	JOHANNA WILLEM	Dutch	C. A. BUCKER	494		260			106	13		242		
"	CLOTHILDE	Peruvian	GARCIA y GARCIA	760		760			74	9		731		
"	LUIZA CANEVARO	Peruvian	P. VINTURINI	1,206		799			82	194		347		
"	EMIGRANTE		J. P. dos SANTOS	892		499			107	107		592		
"	BENGALI	Peruvian	DRETAUX	436		301			83					
"	ROSALIA	Spanish	GARCIA y GARCIA	616		457			99	64		593		
"	ALTAGRACIA		J. B. ONAINDE	616		361					*			
"	AMERICA	Spanish	J. de GREGORY	1,454		690			88	105		565		
"	ANTARES	French	G. NOLTE	401		263			82			131		
"	ROSA de SYRIA		P. VIÑES	645		387					*			
"	MARIA	Peruvian	J. BARCELO	725		413					* *			
"	JACQUES SCEURCH	French	A. NEU	450		300			144	65	255			Mutiny.
"	SARA	Peruvian	I. B. ANDRACA	706		346			23	45		410		
"	ONRUST	Dutch	A. L. KAUFMAN	878		455			100	57		595		
"	CAMILO CAVOUR	Spanish	S. ASTORQUIA	1,226		650			100	39		597		
"	MACAU	Peruvian	A. LABICTVICA	1,075		436			131	39		597		
"	PERU	Peruvian	A. PASSAROIDE	690		406			130	54		552		
"	J. RIGAU	Peruvian	A. VINCURLAGA	364		192			114	7		166		
"	HONG KONG	Peruvian	L. YVLBERI	476		304			112	37		277		
"	CANADIENNE (ST.)	French	G. ESMIN	855		508			112	20		488		Detained by Japan.
"	MARIA LUZ	Peruvian	R. HERREIRA	408		298				10		–		
"	PROVIDENCIA	Peruvian	VIDAUFRAZ RA	660		402			100			412		
"	CALLAO	Spanish	A. de ARAUCA	1,552		694			95	9		665		
"	EMILI	French	P. PLESSIS	455		250			127	20		230		
"	RADAMA	French	F. MAIRUS	520		306			95	4		301		
"	N. ORANGE		W. C. PFAFF	765		395			111	44		252		
"	MANCO CAPAC	Peruvian	L. OLAGUIBEL	1,028		577			111	20		557		
"	LOLA	Peruvian	J. A. BAREÑO	890		597			104	21		576		

Table 46 (cont.)

YEAR	NAME OF SHIP	FLAG							CAPTAIN	TONNAGE	PORT OF DEPARTURE		DATE OF DEPARTURE	DATE OF ARRIVAL	DAYS ON VOYAGE	DEATHS ON VOYAGE	DESTINATION			REMARKS
		FRENCH	PERUVIAN	SPANISH	PORTUGUESE	ITALIAN	DUTCH	AUSTRIAN			CANTON	MACAO					CUBA	PERU	COSTA RICA	
1872	BENGALI	x							R.JICE	799		375	1.12.72	18.5.72	158	179		526		
"	FRAY BENTOS	x							R.MOTA	567		366	24.2.72	20.8.72	172	21		345		Mutiny.
"	PATCHOY (ST.)			x				x	J.PARAJA	1,081		1007	28.6.72	30.8.72	72	95		979		
"	COLOMBIA			x					C.VINCENT	979		500	24.1.72	30.4.72	95	24	935			
"	TRIUNFE BAT (ST.)			x					M.DOLLEGUI	1,494		906	9.5.72	24.8.72	97	167				
"	ANEXIO (ST.)			x					S.ESCURDNASU	1,168		789	24.7.72	1.11.72	85	679				
"	ORACLE			x					A.BROUDGA	1,251		666	1.10.72	1.27.72	85	8	706			
"	BUENAVENTURA (ST.)		x						F.ECHIVARRIA	1,479		864	9.11.72	9.10.72	100	25		644		
"	GLENSERNOCK (ST.)			x					D.CAPELLO	949		668	10.17.72	78	21	84				
"	BLANCHE MARIE	x							C.BALAIS	462		343	10.5.72		35		*			
"	ALAVESA			x		x			S.YZAURIEDE	669		438	24.6.72	9.22.72	106	4.474				
"	CECELIA				x				A.deMENSOUTK	557		378	9.de.4.72	2br.	73	5		573		
"	VELOCE			x					A.ANDRE	425		265	9.1.1.72				*	*		
"	SALVADORA	x									500						*		650	

Table 47

List of Ships Transporting Chinese Laborers to Latin America, 1873

YEAR	NAME OF SHIP	FLAG						CAPTAIN	TONNAGE	PORT OF DEPARTURE			DATE OF DEPARTURE	DATE OF ARRIVAL	DAYS ON VOYAGE	DEATHS ON VOYAGE	DESTINATION				REMARKS
		BRITISH	FRENCH	PERUVIAN	SPANISH	ITALIAN	BELGIAN			CANTON	MACAU	JAVA					CUBA	PERU	Br. GUIANA	SURINAM	
1873	ISABEL			x				P.FUKA	1,311		785		Je9'73	Jy1'73			*				
"	ANDUIZAS				x			J.ROLDAN	696		767		Ja1'73	Ja28'73							
"	AGUSTINA			x				S.BARRIER	947		517		Ja28'73	Feb14'73		18		*			
"	ALEXANDRE LAVALLEY (St.)	x	x					E.LONGUON	1,507		696		Feb14'73								
"	PERU			x				A.BASAQOITE	690		406		Feb28'73					*			
"	HONG KONG				x			D.BORAINCA	470		500		Mar8'73				*				
"	CALLAO			x	x			L.deARANOA	1,552		696		Mar26'73		125	290					
"	ROSITA NENE (St.)				x			E.ALCANTRA	1,256		851		Apr28'73		57			985			
"	PROVIDENCIA			x	x			J.IZAFUEFA	660		422		My9'73					648			
"	SAN JUAN				x			A.URKTRIAGA	1,406		816		My15'73 a Og6'73	116	168			427			
"	EMIGRANTE							P.SOKEO	965		502		Jun4'72		61	75		581			
"	ROSALIA				x			E.DIAZ	615		465		Jy2'73		98	92		571			
"	JUAN (St.)	x			x			L.deGOITRIAGA	1,228		665		Jy20'73				*				
"	GUILLERMO				x			J.B.TABOAGA	328		225		Ag28'73 a '74		52			199			
"	CAMILO CAVOUR				x	x		J.MILBERGI	1,226		685		Ag29'73		22			660			
"	AMBOID (St.)				x			L.MISKETIQUE	1,168		905		Ag29'72				*				
"	GLENTANNOX (St.)	x			x			D.CAPELLO	1,251		720		Se24'73				*				
"	REDIUSCO (St.)						x	F.VanderHEYDEN	1,076		1099		Oc11'73				*				
"	MENECA						x	M.A.LAUCEVIL	1,459		780		No19'73		40		740				
"	MANCO CAPAC				x			L.OLAGUIBEL	1,015		572		De23'73	a De31'73 De24'74	78	58		514			
"	CORONA	x										*				1			988		One birth on voyage.
"	?								1,205988											100	

Table 48

List of Ships Transporting Chinese Laborers to Latin America, 1874

YEAR	NAME OF SHIP	FLAG		CAPTAIN	TONNAGE	PORT OF DEPARTURE	DATE OF DEPARTURE	DATE OF ARRIVAL	DAYS ON VOYAGE	DEATHS ON VOYAGE	DESTINATION	REMARKS
		PERUVIAN				MACAO					PERU	
1874	LUISA CANEVARO	x		P. VENTURINE	1,206	729			85	3	796	
"	NUEVA PROVIDENCIA	x		V.DUARRAZADA	987	524			90	11	513	
"	ISABEL	x		P.FUKA	1,013	713			66	12	701	
"	LOLA	x		J.A.BARRERO	1,180	375			97	6	869	
"	FLORENCIA										22	

Table 49
Indentured Chinese Emigrants to Places Other Than Latin America in the Nineteenth Century

YEAR	NAME OF SHIP	FLAG						PORT OF DEPARTURE						DESTINATION												REMARKS
		BRITISH	AMERICAN	FRENCH	SPANISH	AUSTRIAN	DUTCH	AMOY	CANTON	HONG KONG	SWATOW	SINGAPORE	MACAU	AUSTRALIA	CALIFORNIA	HAWAII	MAURITIUS	MANILA	BORNEO	JAVA	LABUAN	BOMBAY	TAHITI	LOUISIANA	REUNION	
1843	DONNA CARMELITA												*	140												
"	RAMBLER												*	122												
"	EUROPE												*	79												
"	WILLIAM												*	127												
"	WATKINS												*	114											*	
1845	JOSEPH + CLAIRE		x					180																	*	
1846	?		x					200																		
1848	NIMROD	x						*						120												
"	LONDON	x								*				149												
1849	CADET	x						150						138												
"	?					*		500										*								
1850	GAZELLE	x						134								131										
"	DUKE OF ROXBURY	x						272								242										
1851	ARABIA	x						198								179										
"	AMAZON	x						303								290										
"	ONECA		x							*								275								
"	FUTTAH SALAAM							254									-									41 died in storm
"	GENERAL PALMER	x						335								265										
"	MARINER														*	593										
"	STATESMAN	x						180								180										
"	GANGES	x						224								211										
"	DUKE OF ROXBURY	x						240								225										
"	THETIS	x						199									192									
1852	ROBERT BROWNE		x					*								410										MUTINY.
"	ROYAL SAXON	x						227								*										
"	ELEANOR LANCASTER	x						340								230										
"	SPARTAN	x						250								240										
"	THETIS	x						101										101								
"	ELEANOR LANCASTER	x						360								*										
1853	LORD ELGIN	x						152								110										MUTINY.
"	SPARTAN	x						245								*										SHIPWRECKED.
"	UNION					*								300			-									LOST AT SEA.
1854	WHAT CHEER		x								206							-								
"	CLARITA									*					206											
"	ROSE OF SHARON									*					489											
"	BOMBAY											*			219											
1856	LAVANT		x							*					200	*	*									
1858	LORENZA						*						*													SHIPWRECKED.
"	ST.PAUL				x						327						-									
1859	J.BRAGDON									*																
1864	? ?									*													2274			
"	?									*														527		
1865	?									*						527										
"	?									*														598		
"	?									*												62				
1866	SPRAY OF THE OCEAN	x								*													164			
"	GEN. VAN DERBECK									*											426					
"	ANTONIO PETRONELLA								*	*						260										
1870	?									*													70	*		
1872	?									*																

Sources: B.P.P.,A.S.S.,CHINA,Vol.III, 258–259; B.P.P.,CHINA (1868–1869), 144; B.F.O.17/889.

BIBLIOGRAPHY

Reference Works

Baa, Enid M. *Doctoral Dissertations and Selected Theses on Caribbean Topics; Accepted by the Universities of Canada, United States and Europe from 1778-1968.* St. Thomas, Virgin Islands, Bureau of Public Libraries and Museums, Department of Conservation and Cultural Affairs, Government of the Virgin Islands of the U.S., 1969.

Boxer, C. R. and J. M. Braga. *Algumas Notas sobre a bibliografia de Macao.* Macao: 1939.

Britton, Russell S. *The Chinese Periodical Press, 1800-1912.* Shanghai: Kelly and Walsh Limited, 1933.

Catalogue of the Asiatic Library of Dr. G. E. Morrison. Now a part of the Oriental Library, Tokyo, Japan. 2 vols. Tokyo: Oriental Library, 1924.

Catalogue of the Hankow Collection, with Supplements I-V. Hong Kong: Hong Kong University Library, 1922-1928.

Charno, Steven M. *Latin American Newspapers in United States Libraries.* A Union List. Austin: University of Texas Press, 1968.

Comitas, Lambros. *Caribbeana 1900-1965: A Topical Bibliography.* Seattle: University of Washington Press, 1971.

Cordier, Henri. *Bibliotheca Sinica: Dictionnaire Bibliographique des Ouvrages Relatifs a L'Empire Chinois.* 4 vols. Paris: Librarie Orientale et Américaine, 1907-1908.

Fairbank, John K. and Masataka Banno. *Japanese Studies of Modern China: A Bibliographical Guide to Historical and Social Science Research on the Nineteenth and Twentieth Centuries.* Rutland, Vermont: Charles E. Tutle Company, 1955.

General Index to the Published Works of the Diplomatic Correspondence and Foreign Relations of the United States, 1861-1899. Washington, DC: Government Printing Office, 1902.

Great Britain. Public Record Office, London.
    FO 802. Index 28800. China, 1845-1850.
    FO 802. Index 28801. China, 1851-1855.
    FO 802. Index 28802. China, 1854-1858.
    FO 802. Index 28803. China, 1859-1861.
    FO 802. Index 28804. China, 1862-1864.
    FO 802. Index 28815. China, 1865-1881, Coolie Emigration.
    FO 802. Index 28913. France, 1850-1889, Coolie Emigration.
    FO 802. Index 29025. Mexico.
    FO 802. Index 29089. Peru, 1843-1852.
    FO 802. Index 29090. Peru, 1853-1860.
    FO 802. Index 29091. Peru, 1861-1866.
    FO 802. Index 29092. Peru, 1867-1875.
    FO 802. Index 29093. Peru, 1876-1881.
    FO 802. Index 29094. Peru, 1882-1890.
    FO 802. Index 29048. Spain.

Griffin, A. P. C. *Select List of References on Chinese Immigration.* Washington: Government Printing Office, 1904.

Hasse, Adelaide R. *Index to United States Documents Relating to Foreign Affairs, 1828-1861.* Washington, DC: Carnegie Institution of Washington, 1914.

King, Frank H. H. and Prescott Clarke. *A Research Guide to China Coast Newspapers, 1822-1911.* Cambridge: Harvard University Press, 1965.

Lust, John. *Index Sinicus: A Catalogue of Articles Relating to China in Periodicals and Other Collective Publications, 1920-1955.* Cambridge, England: W. Heffer and Sons Limited, 1964.

Möllendorff, P. G. and O. F. von. *Manual of Chinese Bibliography: Being a list of works and essays relating to China.* Shanghai: Kelly and Walsh, 1876.

Taylor, Louise Marion. *Catalog of Books on China in the Essex Institute.* Salem, Massachusetts: The Essex Institute.

Primary Sources

I. Manuscripts

Great Britain. The Colonial Office and Foreign Office Documents, Public Record Office, London.

CO 111/269. West Indies.
CO 275/21. Proceedings of the Legislative Council of the Straits Settlements for 1877.
CO 275/32. Annual Report of the Chinese Protectorate, Straits Settlements, 1886.
CO 295/2. Trinidad.
CO 295/3. Trinidad.
CO 295/6. Trinidad.
CO 295/8. Trinidad.
CO 295/11. Trinidad.
CO 295/13. Trinidad.
CO 295/14. Trinidad.
CO 295/15. Trinidad.
CO 295/16. Trinidad.
CO 295/17. Trinidad.
CO 295/24. Trinidad.
CO 295/33. Trinidad.
CO 318/160. Emigration from China to West Indies.
CO 386/135. India, West Indies, China, 1859-1864.

FO 13/195. Brazil.
FO 13/336. Brazil.
FO 13/474. Brazil.
FO 13/484. Brazil.
FO 13/498. Brazil.

FO 13/539. Brazil.
FO 13/547. Brazil.
FO 13/560. Brazil.
FO 13/563. Brazil.
FO 13/579. Brazil.
FO 13/586. Brazil.
FO 13/587. Brazil.
FO 13/588. Brazil.
FO 13/589. Brazil.
FO 13/591. Brazil.
FO 13/595. Brazil.
FO 17/186. China, Foreign, 1852.
FO 17/190. China, Foreign, 1852.
FO 17/191. China, Foreign, 1852.
FO 17/192. China, Foreign, 1852.
FO 17/193. China, Foreign, 1852.
FO 17/194. China, Foreign, 1852.
FO 17/197. China, Domestic Various, 1852.
FO 17/198. China, Foreign, 1853.
FO 17/199. China, Foreign, 1853.
FO 17/207. China, Domestic Various, 1853.
FO 17/208. China, Domestic Various, 1853.
FO 17/210. China, Foreign, 1854.
FO 17/211. China, Foreign, 1854.
FO 17/214. China, Foreign, 1854.
FO 17/216. China, Foreign, 1854.
FO 17/217. China, Foreign, 1854.
FO 17/218. China, Foreign, 1854.
FO 17/222. China, Domestic Various, 1854.
FO 17/223. China, Domestic Various, 1854.
FO 17/224. China, Foreign, 1855.
FO 17/225. China, Foreign, 1855.
FO 17/228. China, Foreign, 1855.
FO 17/230. China, Foreign, 1855.
FO 17/231. China, Foreign, 1855.
FO 17/232. China, Foreign, 1855.
FO 17/233. China, Foreign, 1855.
FO 17/234. China, Foreign, 1855.
FO 17/235. China, Foreign, 1855.

FO 17/238. China, Domestic Various, 1855.

FO 17/239. China, Domestic Various, 1855.

FO 17/240. China, Domestic Various, 1855.

FO 17/313. China, Foreign, 1859.

FO 17/315. China, Foreign, 1859.

FO 17/873. China, Domestic Various Countries. Coolie Convention and Emigration, 1865-1866.

FO 17/874. China, 1866-1867.

FO 17/875. China, 1868.

FO 17/876. China, 1868.

FO 17/877. China, 1869.

FO 17/878. China, 1870.

FO 17/879. China, 1871.

FO 17/880. China, 1872.

FO 17/881. China, 1872.

FO 17/882. China, 1873.

FO 17/883. China, 1873.

FO 17/884. China, 1873.

FO 17/885. China, 1874.

FO 17/886. China, 1874.

FO 17/887. China, 1875.

FO 17/888. China, 1875.

FO 17/889. China, 1876.

FO 17/890. China, 1878.

FO 17/891. China, 1879.

FO 50/285. Mexico, Domestic, 1855.

FO 50/393. Mexico, Domestic, 1866.

FO 50/394. Mexico, Domestic, 1866.

FO 50/451. Mexico, Emigration from China.

FO 50/546. Mexico, Emigration from China, Korea and India, 1887-1905.

FO 58/125. Kidnapping of South Sea Islanders.

FO 58/126. Kidnapping of South Sea Islanders.

FO 61/133. Peru, 1852.

FO 61/134. Peru, 1852.

FO 61/143. Peru, Domestic Various, 1853.

FO 61/144. Peru, Domestic Various, 1853.

FO 61/147. Peru, Domestic Various, 1854.

FO 61/148. Peru, Domestic Various, 1854.

FO 61/150. Peru, Domestic Various, 1854.

FO 61/152. Peru, Domestic Various, 1854.

FO 61/153. Peru, Domestic Various, 1855.

FO 61/201. Peru, Domestic Various, 1861.

FO 61/204. Peru, Domestic Various, 1862.

FO 61/205. Peru, Domestic Various, 1862.

FO 61/206. Peru, Domestic Various, 1862.

FO 61/207. Peru, Domestic Various, 1862.

FO 61/209. Peru, Domestic Various, 1862.

FO 61/212. Peru, Domestic Various, 1862.

FO 61/213. Peru, Domestic Various, 1863.

FO 61/214. Peru, Diplomatic, 1863.

FO 61/215. Peru, Diplomatic, 1863.

FO 61/217. Peru, Consuls, 1863.

FO 61/218. Peru, Domestic Various, 1863.

FO 61/230. Peru, Diplomatic, 1865.

FO 61/236. Peru, Diplomatic, 1866.

FO 61/240. Peru, Domestic Various, 1866.

FO 61/261. Peru, Foreign, 1870.

FO 61/262. Peru, Foreign, 1870.

FO 61/273. Peru, Commercial, 1872.

FO 61/277. Peru, Foreign, 1873.

FO 61/285. Peru, Foreign, 1874.

FO 61/289. Peru, Foreign, 1875.

FO 61/292. Peru, Domestic Various, 1875.

FO 61/293. Peru, Foreign, 1876.

FO 61/294. Peru, Foreign, 1876.

FO 61/297. Peru, Domestic Various, 1876.

FO 61/299. Peru, Foreign, 1877.

FO 61/305. Peru, Foreign, 1878.

FO 61/318. Peru, Foreign, 1881.

FO 97/101. Coolie Emigration and Chinese Passenger Act, February, 1855 to March 1856.

FO 97/1012A. Coolie Emigration and Chinese Passenger Act, April to December 1856.
FO 97/102B. Coolie Emigration, 1859-1860.

FO 420/1. Correspondence Respecting Guano Islands of Lobos de Tierra and Lobos de Fuera, 1833-1852.
FO 425/37. Correspondence Respecting Coolie Emigration into French Colonies, November 1851 to May 1866.

FO 534/18. Correspondence Respecting the Kidnapping of Natives in the Pacific Islands, February 1868 to October 1869.
FO 541/18. Correspondence Respecting Slavery and the Slave Trade in Foreign Countries and Other Matters, 1871.

Confidential Prints.
FO 881/316. Papers Relating to the Slave Trade and Growth of Sugar in Cuba and Brazil, January 1845 to May 1846.
FO 881/744. Correspondence Respecting Chinese Emigration, 1853-1855.
FO 881/894. Correspondence Respecting Emigration from China, April, 1859 to May, 1860.
FO 881/933. Correspondence Respecting Affairs in China, 1859 to 1861.
FO 881/1590. Slave Trade in the New Hebrides, 1867.
FO 881/1738. Correspondence Respecting the Engagement of Chinese Emigrants by British and French Subjects, 1865-1869.
FO 881/2445. Correspondence Respecting the Macao Coolie Trade, 1873.
FO 881/2594. Correspondence Respecting the Macao Coolie Trade, 1874-1875.
FO 881/2598. Correspondence Respecting Slavery in Cuba and Puerto Rico and the State of the Slave Population and Chinese Coolies in those Islands, 1873-1874.

Foreign Office Library, London.
Confidential Papers. Correspondence Respecting the Engagement of Chinese Emigrants by British and French Subjects, 1865 to 1869. (Same as FO 881/1738)

India Office Library and Records, London.
    G. 34/115. Straits Settlements, Prince of Wales Island, Public
        Consultations, 1826 to 1827.
    G. 34/135. Straits Settlements, 1805 to 1806.
    G. 34/162. Correspondence Relating to General Bonaparte's
        Removal to St. Helena, July 1815 to September 1817.

Portugal

Arquivo Histórico Ultramarino, Lisbon.
    Macau, Maço 29, 1809.
    Macau, Maço 30, 1810.
    Macau, Maço 31, 1811.
    Macau, Maço 33, 1812-1813.
    Macau, Maço 34, 1813-1814.
    Macau, Maço 35, 1815-1816.
    Macau, Maço 36, 1816-1817.
    Macau, Maço 37, 1817.
    Macau, Maço 38, 1818-1820.
    Macau, Maço 39, 1820-1821.
    Macau, Pasta 21, 1864.
    Macau, Pasta 22, 1865-1866.
    Macau, Pasta 24, 1867.
    Macau, Pasta 25, 1868.
    Macau, Pasta 26, 1869.
    Macau, Pasta 27, 1870-1872.
    Macau, Pasta 28, 1873-1874.

United States of America.
United States Department of State, National Archives, Washington.
    Despatches from United States Consuls in Amoy, 1844-1906.
    Despatches from United States Consuls in Canton, 1790-1876.
    Despatches from United States Consuls in Hong Kong, 1844-1906.
    Despatches from United States Consuls in Macao, 1849-1869.
    Despatches from United States Consuls in Shanghai, 1847-1906.
    Despatches from United States Consuls in Swatow, 1860-1881.
    Diplomatic Instructions, China, 1873.

Harvard University, Baker Library, Boston.
Heard Papers: W. M. Robinet and G. M. Robinet, Letterbook (Spanish and English) containing correspondence on the "coolie trade" to the Americas, 1850-1853.

2. Printed Material

Great Britain.

British and Foreign State Papers, Vol. XXVIII, 1839-1840; Vol. LXVI, 1855; Vol. LXVIII, 1857; Vol. XLVII, 1860; Vol. LXXII, 1880-1881.

British Parliamentary Papers, "Mr. Mear's Memorial, April 30, 1790," Vol. LXXVI, 1970.

British Parliamentary Papers, "Report from the Select Committee Appointed to Consider the Practicality and Expediency of Supplying our West Indian Colonies with Free Labourers from the East," Vol. II, 1810-1811.

British Parliamentary Papers, "Correspondence Respecting Emigration: Australian Colonies," Vol. XL, 1838.

British Parliamentary Papers, "Orders in Council or Colonial Ordinances for the Better Regulation and Enforcement of the Relative Duties of Masters and Employers and Articled Servants, Tradesmen and Labourers in the Colonies of British Guiana and Mauritius and of Correspondence Relating thereto," Vol. LII, 1838.

British Parliamentary Papers, "Report of the Committee Appointed by the Supreme Government of India to Inquire into Abuses Alleged to Exist in Exporting from Bengal Hill Coolies; together with an Appendix Containing the Oral and Written Evidence taken by the Committee and the Official Document Laid before them, Calcutta, 1839," Vol. XVI, 1841.

British Parliamentary Papers, "Correspondence Relative to the Introduction of Indian Labourers into the Mauritius," Vol. XXX, 1842.

British Parliamentary Papers, "Return of Immigrants Introduced to Mauritius, January 23 to March 31, 1843," Vol. XXXV, 1844.

British Parliamentary Papers, "Papers Relative to Emigration of Chinese Labourers to the West Indies," Vol. XXXV, 1844.

British Parliamentary Papers, Vols. XVII and XVIII, 1854-1855.

British Parliamentary Papers, "Report of the Select Committee on Consular Service and Appointments; together with the Proceedings of the Committee and Minutes of Evidence," Vol. VIII, 1858.

British Parliamentary Papers, "Correspondence Relative to the Earl of Elgin's Special Missions to China and Japan, 1857-1859," Vol. XXXIII, 1859.

British Parliamentary Papers, "Report of the Commissioners Appointed to Enquire into the Treatment of Immigrants in British Guiana," Vol. XX, 1871.

British Parliamentary Papers, "Mr. Geoghegan's Report on Coolie Emigration from India," Vol. XLVIII, 1874.

British Parliamentary Papers, "Reports Respecting the Condition of Coolies in Surinam," Vol. LXXVIII, 1877.

British Parliamentary Papers, Area Studies Series, China, Vols. III, IV, XXXVIII.

British Parliamentary Papers, China, Vol. III, 1854-1855.

British Parliamentary Papers, Emigration, Vols. IX-XVIII, 1852-1873.

Hansard's Parliamentary Debates, Vol. CCXVII, 1873.

Proceedings of the Legislative Council of the Straits Settlements (with Appendices) for 1876 (British Museum).

Portugal

Corvo, João de Andrade, *Relatorio e Documentos sobre a Abolição da Emigração de Chinas Contratados em Macau Apresentado as Cortes na Sessão Legislativa de 1874*, Lisboa, Imprensa Nacional, 1874.

Negocios Externos: Relatorio e Documentos Apresentados ás Cortes na Sessão Legislativa de 1872 pelo Ministro e Secretario d'Estado dos Negocios Estrangeiros, Vol. II, Lisboa, Imprensa Nacional, 1872.

United States of America

United States Congress, House of Representatives, Executive Document No. 123, 33rd Congress, First Session, 1853.

United States Congress, House of Representatives, Executive Document No. 105, 34th Congress, First Session, 1856.

United States Congress, Senate, Executive Document No. 99, 34th Congress, First Session, 1856.

United States Congress, Senate, Executive Document No. 22, 35th Congress, Second Session, 1858.

United States Congress, Senate, Executive Document No. 30, 36th Congress, First Session, 1860.

United States Congress, House of Representatives, Executive Document No. 88, 36th Congress, First Session, 1860.

United States Congress, House of Representatives, Report No. 443, 36th Congress, First Session, 1860.

United States Congress, House of Representatives, Executive Document No. 16, 37th Congress, Second Session, 1861.

United States Congress, House of Representatives, Executive Document No. 80, 40th Congress, Second Session, 1868.

United States Congress, House of Representatives, Executive Document No. 116, 41st Congress, Second Session, 1870.

United States Congress, House of Representatives, Executive Document No. 207, 42nd Congress, Second Session, 1872.

United States Congress, *The Congressional Globe*, Vol. XXXII: I, 1861-1862.

United States Consular Reports, Vol. III, 1889.

United States Department of State, *Foreign Relations* (some volumes have the title *Diplomatic Correspondence*), 1857-1888.

United States War Department, *Report on the Census of Cuba, 1899*, Washington, Government Printing Office, 1900.

United States Statutes at Large, Boston, Little Brown, Vol. XII.

Secondary Sources

1. Unpublished Works

Baptista, Ilídio Antunes, "A Imigração Chinesa Contratada por Macau, para Cuba e Peru, 1851-1873," Dissertacão para Licenciatura, Universidade Técnica de Lisboa, 1967.

Chang, Chin Chieh, "The Chinese in Latin America: A Preliminary Geographical Survey with Special Reference to Cuba and Jamaica," Dissertation, University of Maryland, 1956.

Conrad, Robert, "Falta de Braços: The Chinese Coolie Controversy in the Brazilian Empire," A short paper, University of Illinois at Chicago Circle, 1973.

Grossman, Jeffrey L., "The Portuguese View of the Chinese Contract Labor Trade: 1851-1874," Seminar paper, Harvard University, May, 1972.

Irick, Robert Lee, "Ch'ing Policy Toward the Coolie Trade, 1847-1878," Dissertation, Harvard University, 1971.

Oades, Rizalindo A., "Chinese Emigration Through Hong Kong to North Borneo since 1880," Master's thesis, University of Hong Kong, 1961.

Powers, Marshall K., "Chinese Coolie Migration to Cuba," Dissertation, University of Florida, 1953.

Wang, Sing-wu, "The Organization of Chinese Emigration 1848-88, with Special Reference to Chinese Emigration to Australia," Master's thesis, Australian National University, 1969.

Zo, Kil Young, "Chinese Emigration into the United States, 1850-1880," Dissertation, Columbia University, 1971.

2. Newspapers

The China Coast

    i.   Hong Kong

China Mail, 1853-1856; 1860-1865; 1867-1875.
Daily Advertiser, 1869-1871.
Daily Advertiser and Shipping Gazette, 1871-1873.
Hong Kong Times, Daily Advertiser and Shipping Gazette, 1873-1876.
   Evening Mail, October 16, 1866.
   Daily Press, 1870-1874.
The *Friend of China* and *Hong Kong Gazette*, 1842-1858; 1860-1861.
Hong Kong Government Gazette, 1853-1890.
Hong Kong Mercury and Shipping Gazette, 1866.
Hong Kong Shipping List, 1855-1857.
Hong Kong Shipping List and Commercial Intelligencer, 1857-1862.
Overland China Mail, 1871.
Overland Friend of China, 1845-1858.

Overland Register and Price Current, 1845-1855; 1858.
O Echo do Povo, 1859-1868; 1869.

ii. Macau

Gazeta de Macau e Timor, 1872-1874.
O Boletim da Provincia de Macau e Timor, 1846-1875. (Various titles:
    *O Boletim da Provincia de Macao, Timor e Solor, O Boletim do
    Governo de Macao, O Boletim do Governo da Provincia de Macao,
    Timor e Solor.*)
O Independente, 1867-1869; 1873-1874.
O Oriente, 1869-1870, 1872.
Ta-Ssi-Yang-Kuo, 1863-1866.

iii. Shanghai

North China Daily News, September 4, 1873.
North China Herald, 1850-1867.
North China Herald and Supreme Court and Consular Gazette,
    1870-1888.

The West

i. Brazil

Anglo Brazilian Times, November 21, 1874.
Diário de Pernambuco, March 16, 1880.
Rio News, October 5, 1879; August 15, 1881.

ii. Great Britain

London Times, 1853-1875.
Pall Mall Gazette, 1866, 1873.

iii. Peru

Callao and Lima Gazette, August 15, 1871.
El Comercio, January 17, 1872.
La Patria, October 14, 1873.
South Pacific Times, 1872-1873.

iv. United States of America

New York Herald, January 31, 1873.
New York Times (*New York Daily Times*), 1852-1875.

3. Books, Pamphlets and Articles

"A Gross Outrage on Coolies in Cuba," *Anti-Slavery Reporter*, Vol. XVIII, No. 3 (October 1, 1872), 75.

"A narrative of the loss of a Chinese Vessel Bound to Batavia with 1600 Persons on Board, of Whom 198 Were Saved by the English Ship *Indiana*, Commanded by Lieutenant Pearl of the Royal Navy," *Chinese Repository*, Vol. VI, No. 3 (July, 1837), 149-153.

"A New Attempt to Send Chinese to Peru," *Anti-Slavery Reporter*, Vol. XXI, No. 1, New Series (February, 1878), 47-50.

"A Sketch of the History of Coolie Missions in British Guiana," *Mission Life*, Vol. VIII, No. 2, New Series (1877), 352-356.

Abbott, John S. C. *South and North; or Impressions Received during a Trip to Cuba and the South*. New York: Negro Universities Press, 1969 (first published in 1860).

Abeel, David. *Journal of a Residence in China and the Neighboring Countries from 1830 to 1833*. London: James Nisbet and Company, 1835.

Abella, Francisco. *Projecto de Emigración Libre China Dirigido a los Sres. Hacendados de la Isla de Cuba*. Habana: Imprenta y Libraria "El Tris," 1874.

Abend, Hallett. *Treaty Ports*. New York: Doubleday, Doran and Company, Inc., 1944.

Adamson, Alan H. *Sugar without Slaves: The Political Economy of British Guiana, 1838-1904*. New Haven: Yale University Press, 1972.

Aimes, Hubert S. *A History of Slavery in Cuba, 1511 to 1868*. New York: G. P. Putnam's Sons, 1907.

Akers, C. E. *The Rubber Industry in Brazil and the Orient.* London: Mathuen and Company Limited, 1914.

Aldus, Don. *Coolie Traffic and Kidnapping.* London: McCorquodale and Company, 1876.

Alley, Rewi, "The Chinese in the Pacific: Fiji to Hawaii," *China Journal of Science and Arts,* Vol. XXVIII, No. 3 (March, 1938), 114-119.

Alley, Rewi and G. T., "The Chinese in New Zealand," *China Journal of Science and Arts,* Vol. XXVIII, No. 2 (February, 1938), 70-79.

Amyot, Jacques, "Chinese Overseas Emigration," *Philippine Studies,* Vol. XI, No. 4 (October, 1963), 593-598.

"An Epidemic in Brazil," *Anti-Slavery Reporter,* Vol. IV, Series 4 (October, 1883).

"Annual Remittances by Chinese Immigrants in Singapore to their Families in China," *Journal of the Indian Archipelago and Eastern Asia,* Vol. I, Series 1 (1847), 34-37.

Arasaratnam, Sinnappah. *Indians in Malaysia and Singapore.* Bombay: Oxford University Press, 1970.

Arona, Juan de (Paz Soldán). *La Inmigración en el Perú.* Lima: Imprenta del Universo de Carlos Prince, 1891.

"Asiatic Free Colonists in Cuba," *De Bow's Review,* Vol. XXIV (May, 1858), 470-471.

Asiegbu, Johnson U. J. *Slavery and the Politics of Liberation, 1787-1861; A Study of Liberated African Emigration and British Anti-Slavery Policy.* London: Longmans, Green and Company Limited, 1969.

Auchincloss, Henry B., "The Chinese in Cuba," *Merchant's Magazine,* Vol. LII (March, 1865), 186-192.

Balestier, J., "View of the State of Agriculture in the British Possessions in the Straits of Malacca," *Journal of the Indian Archipelago and Eastern Asia*, Vol. II, Series 1 (1848), 139-150.

Ball, J. Dyer. *Things Chinese*. Shanghai: Kelly and Walsh, 1925.

Ballou, Maturin M. *Due South or Cuba, Past and Present*. Boston: Houghton, Mifflin and Company, 1898.

——————. *History of Cuba*. Boston: Phillips, Sampson and Company, 1854.

Bancroft, Hubert H. *History of the Northwest Coast*. 2 vols. San Francisco: A. L. Bancroft and Company, 1884.

——————. *The New Pacific*. New York: The Bancroft Company, 1900.

Banton, Michael. *Race Relations*. New York: Basic Books, Inc., 1967.

Barnett, Patricia G., "The Chinese in Southeastern Asia and the Philippines," *Annals of American Academy of Political and Social Science*, Vol. CCXXVI (March, 1943), 32-49.

Barrett, Rev. William Garland. *Immigration to the British West Indies: Is it the Slave-Trade Revived or Not?* London: A. W. Bennett, 1859.

Barth, Gunther. *Bitter Strength: A History of the Chinese in the United States, 1850-1870*. Cambridge, Mass.: Harvard University Press, 1964.

Basto, Fernando L. B. *Síntese da História da Imigração no Brasil*. Rio de Janeiro, 1970.

Bastin, John. *The British in West Sumatra, 1685-1825*. Kuala Lampur: University of Malaya Press, 1965.

——————. *The Native Policies of Sir Stamford Raffles in Java and Sumatra: An Economic Interpretation*. Oxford: The Clarendon Press, 1957.

Bastos, Antonio Joaquim Jr. *O Futuro de Macau ou as Vantagens que Hão de Resultar da Admissão Duma Delegação da Alfandega Chineza em Macau*. Macau: Typographia Mercantil, 1873.

Bateson, Charles. *The Convict Ships, 1787-1868*. Glasgow: Brown, Son and Ferguson, Limited, 1959.

Bauer, Arnold J., "Chilean Rural Labor in the Nineteenth Century," *American Historical Review*, Vol. LXXVI, No. 4 (October, 1971), 1059-1083.

Beaumont, Joseph. *The New Slavery: An Account of the Indian and Chinese Immigrants in British Guiana*. London: W. Ridgway, 1871.

Bedford, O. H., "Chinese Junks," *The China Journal of Science and Arts*, Vol. XXVI, No. 6 (June, 1938), 264-267.

Bell, Kenneth N. and W. P. Morrell. *Select Documents on British Colonial Policy, 1830-1860*. Oxford: The Clarendon Press, 1968.

Bennett, Ira E. *History of the Panama Canal*. Washington, DC: Historical Publishing Company, 1915.

Bethell, Leslie. *The Abolition of the Brazilian Slave Trade; Britain, Brazil and the Slave Trade Question, 1807-1869*. Cambridge, England: University Press, 1970.

Biggerstaff, Knight, "The Establishment of Permanent Chinese Diplomatic Missions Abroad," *Chinese Social and Political Science Review*, Vol. XX, No. 1 (April, 1936), 1-41.

Blue, A. D., "Chinese Emigration and the Deck Passenger Trade," *Journal of the Hong Kong Branch of the Royal Asiatic Society*, Vol. X (1970), 79-93.

_____., "Piracy on the China Coast," *Journal of the Hong Kong Branch of the Royal Asiatic Society*, Vol. V (1965), 69-85.

Blythe, Wilford. *The Impact of Chinese Secret Societies in Malaya*. London: Oxford University Press, 1969.

Blythe, W. L., "Historical Sketch of Chinese Labour in Malaya," *Journal of the Royal Asiatic Society Malaya Branch*, Vol. XX, No. 1 (1947), 64-90.

Bocayuva, Quintino. *A Crise na Lavoura*. Rio de Janeiro, 1869.

Bonilla, Heraclio. *Guano y Burguesía en el Perú*. Lima: Instituto de Estudios Peruanos, 1974.

Boston Board of Trade 1856; Second Annual Report. Boston: Moore and Corsby, 1856.

Boston Board of Trade 1857: Third Annual Report. Boston: George C. Rand and Avery, 1857.

Boxer, Baruch. *Ocean Shipping in the Evolution of Hong Kong*. Chicago: University of Chicago Press, 1961.

Boxer, Charles R., "Notes on Chinese Abroad in the Late Ming and Early Manchu Periods Compiled from Contemporary European Sources (1500-1750)," *Tien Hsia Monthly*, Vol. IX, No. 5 (December, 1939), 447-468.

_____. *The Dutch Seaborne Empire, 1600-1800*. New York: Knopf, 1965.

_____. *The Great Ship from Amacon: Annals of the Macao and the Old Japan Trade, 1555-1640*. Lisbon: Centro de Estudos Históricos Ultramarinos, 1963.

[Braddel, Thomas], "Notices of Pinang," *Journal of the Indian Archipelago and Eastern Asia*, Vol. VI, Series 1 (1852), 143-172.

_____, "Notices of Singapore," *Journal of the Indian Archipelago and Eastern Asia*, Vol. IX, Series 1 (1855), 53-65.

"Breves Considerações sôbre Colonização por A. du Calpe," Rio de Janeiro, 1855, in *Memórias* (Arquivo Nacional), Vol. XVI.

Bridger, J. (Rev.), "The Coolie in British Guiana," *Mission Life*, Vol. V, No. 1, New Series (1874), 233-241.

"British Coolies in Surinam," *Anti-Slavery Reporter*, Vol. XIX, No. 5 (January, 1875), 135.

"British Guiana," *Anti-Slavery Reporter*, Vol. V, New Series (July 1, 1850), 115.

"British Guiana Coolie Mission," *Mission Life*, Vol. VIII, No. 1, New Series (1877), 207-210.

Brito, João Rodrigues de. *A Economia Brasileira: No Alvorecer do Século XIX*. Salvador, Brasil: Livraria Progresso, 1949.

Brüggen, Juan, "Geología de las Guaneras en Chile," *Revista Chilena de Historia y Geographía*, Vol. LXXXV, No. 93 (July-December, 1938), 172-210.

Britton, Russell S. *The Chinese Periodical Press, 1800-1912*. Shanghai, Kelly and Walsh Limited. 1933.

Buckley, Charles B. *An Anecdotal History of Old Times in Singapore*. Kuala Lampur: University of Malaya Press, 1965.

Burns, Islay, Rev. *Memoir of the Reverend William C. Burns, MA, Missionary to China from the English Presbyterian Church*. London: James Nisbet & Co., 1870.

Cameron, John. *Our Tropical Possessions in Malayan India: Being a Descriptive Account of Singapore, Penang, Province Wellesley and Malacca; Their People, Products, Commerce and Government*. London: Smith, Elder and Co., 1865.

Campbell, Persia Crawford. *Chinese Coolie Emigration to Countries within the British Empire*. London: P. S. King and Son, Limited, 1923.

Carrothers, William A. *Emigration from the British Isles, With Special Reference to the Development of Overseas Dominions*. New York: Augustus M. Kelley, 1966.

Cator, William J. *The Economic Position of the Chinese in the Netherlands Indies*. Chicago: University of Chicago Press, 1936.

Cell, John Wesley. *British Colonial Administration in the Mid-Nineteenth Century: The Policy-Making Process*. New Haven: Yale University Press, 1970.

Cesarino, Aprigo. *Conferencia Realisada em São Carlos do Pinhal, Provincia de São Paulo, Sobre a Immigração Chineza, no dia 18 de Março de 1888*. São Paulo: Typographia do Diário Popular, 1888.

Chang, Hsin-pao. *Commissioner Lin and the Opium War*. Cambridge, Mass.: Harvard University Press, 1964.

Chang, T'ien-tse, "China and the Netherlands East Indies," *China Quarterly*, Vol. III, No. 1 (Winter, 1937-38), 45-59.

——————. *Sino-Portuguese Trade from 1514 to 1614; A Synthesis of Portuguese and Chinese Sources*. Leyden: E. J. Brill, 1934.

Chang-Rodríguez, Eugenio, "Chinese Labor Migration into Latin America in the Nineteenth Century," *Revista de Historia de Mexico*, No. 46 (December, 1958), 375-397.

Chao, Yuen Ren, "Languages and Dialects in China," *Geographical Journal*, Vol. CII, No. 2 (August, 1943), 63-66.

Chemin Dupontès, Paul. *Les Petites Antilles*. Paris: Librairie Orientale e Américaine, 1909.

Che'n, Ching-ho. *The Chinese Community in the Sixteenth Century Philippines*. Tokyo: The Center for East Asian Cultural Studies, 1968.

Chen, Chieh, "A Historical Review of China's Treaties," *China Quarterly*, Vol. II (Special Christmas Number, 1936), 29-37.

Chen, Chun-po, "Chinese Overseas," *The Chinese Year Book 1935-36*, 428-455.

Chen, Shao-hsing, "The Migration of Chinese from Fukien to the Philippines under the Spanish Colonization and to Taiwan under the

Dutch Colonization: An Analysis of their Pattern of Development and their Correspondences," *Proceedings of the International Association of Historians of Asia, Second Biennial Conference*, October 6-9, 1962, Taipei, Taiwan, 459-468.

Chesson, F. W., "The Polynesian Labour Question in Relation to the Fiji Islands and Queensland," *Proceedings of the Royal Colonial Institute*, Vol. III, London, Sampson, Low, Marston, Searle and Rivington, 1872, 34-56.

Chin, Siah U., "The Chinese in Singapore: General Sketch of the Numbers, Tribes and Avocations of the Chinese in Singapore," *Journal of the Indian Archipelago and Eastern Asia*, Series 1, Vol. II (1848), 283-290.

"Chinese and Coolie Immigration into Trinidad: Licentious Habits of the Coolies," *Anti-Slavery Reporter*, Vol. VII, No. 74, New Series (February 2, 1852), 31-32.

"Chinese and Irish Immigrants," *Saturday Review*, Vol. XXVIII, No. 20 (1869), 670-671.

"Chinese Christians at Honduras," *Chinese Recorder*, Vol. III, No. 4 (September, 1870), 110-111.

"Chinese Contract Labour in Brazil," *Anti-Slavery Reporter*, Vol. I, No. 8, Series 4 (August, 1881), 140-141.

"Chinese Coolie Trade at Havana," *Merchants' Magazine*, Vol. XXXVII, No. 4 (October, 1857), 518.

"Chinese Coolies in Cuba," *Anti-Slavery Reporter*, Vol. XXI, No. 8, New Series (June, 1879), 177-184.

"Chinese Coolies in Cuba," *Nautical Magazine*, Vol. XLVI, No. 1 (January, 1877), 68-78.

"Chinese Coolies in Cuba," *Saturday Review* (London), Vol. XLIII, No. 1, 108 (January 20, 1877), 77-78.

"Chinese Emigration," *Chamber's Journal*, Vol. XXXVI, No. 392 (July 6, 1861), 9-12.

"Chinese Emigration," *Chinese Recorder*, Vol. XIV, No. 1 (January-February, 1883), 32-38.

"Chinese Emigration to Brazil," *Anti-Slavery Reporter*, Vol. II, Series 4 (January, 1882), 15.

"Chinese Immigration and the Guano Trade," *Anti-Slavery Reporter*, Vol. III, No. 2, New Series (February, 1855), 39-41.

"Chinese Immigration to Brazil," *Anti-Slavery Reporter*, Vol. I, No. 9, Series 4 (September, 1881), 161-162.

"Chinese Immigration to Br. Guiana," *Anti-Slavery Reporter*, Vol. VI, No. 72 (December 1, 1851), 202-204.

"Chinese in Australia," *Quarterly Review*, Vol. CLXVII (1888), 162-185.

"Chinese Labour in Mexico," *Industrial and Labour Information*, Vol. XLVIII, No. 8 (November 20, 1933), 244.

"Chinese on the Canal Zone," *Independent*, Vol. LXI, No. 3021 (October 25, 1906), 1009.

"Chinese Pirates," *Cornhill Magazine*, Vol. II (October, 1860), 432-437.

"Chinese Slavery," *Anti-Slavery Reporter*, Vol. IV, Series 4 (May-June, 1886), 75.

Chuffat Latour, Antonio. *Apunte Histórico de los Chinos en Cuba*. Havana: Molina y Cía, 1927.

Clark, Arthur H. *The Clipper Ship Era: An Epitome of Famous American and British Clipper Ships, their Owners, Builders, Commanders and Crews, 1843-1869*. London: G. P. Putnam's Sons, 1911.

Clark, William J. *Commercial Cuba: A Book for Business Men*. New York: Charles Scribner's Sons, 1898.

Clarke, Henry, "Coolie Immigration to Jamaica," *Anti-Slavery Reporter*, Vol. IV, Series 4 (July, 1884), 161-162.

Clementi, Cecil. *The Chinese in British Guiana*. Guiana: The Argosy Company Limited, 1915.

Clingman, T. L., "Coolies—Cuba and Emancipation," *De Bow's Review*, Vol. XXII (April, 1857), 414-419.

Cochin, Augustin. *The Results of Slavery*. translated by Mary L. Booth. Boston, 1863.

Coffin, Charles Carleton. *Our New Way around the World*. London: Sampson, Low, Son and Marston, 1869.

Coker, Robert E., "Peru's Wealth-Producing Birds," *National Geographic Magazine*, Vol. XXXVII, No. 5 (May, 1920), 537-566.

————————., "Habits and Economic Relations of the Guano Birds of Peru," *Proceedings of the United States National Museum*, Vol. LVI, Washington, Government Printing Office, 1920, 449-511.

"Cold Blooded Murder of Chinese Coolies," *Anti-Slavery Reporter*, Vol. XIX, No. 2 (April 1, 1874), 41-42.

Cole, Fitz-roy. *The Peruvians at Home*. London, 1877.

Colecção das Leis do Imperio do Brasil de 1870, Vol. II. Rio de Janeiro, 1870.

Colwell, James. *A Century in the Pacific*. London: C. H. Kelly, 1914.

Coman, Katherine. *The History of Contract Labour in the Hawaiian Islands*. New York: The Macmillan Company, 1903.

Comber, L. F. *Chinese Secret Societies in Malaya: A Survey of the Triad Society from 1800 to 1900*. Singapore: Donald Moore, 1959.

Congresso Agrícola, Coleção de Documentos. Rio de Janeiro, 1878.

Conrad, Robert. *The Destruction of Brazilian Slavery, 1850-1888.* Berkeley: University of California Press, 1972.

_____, "The Contraband Slave Trade to Brazil, 1831-1845," *Hispanic American Historical Review*, Vol. XLIV, No. 4 (November, 1969), 617-638.

Couturat, M. Léon, "L'Émigration Chinoise," *Bulletin de la Societé Royale de Geógraphie d'Anvers*, Vol. V (1880), 453-482.

Cooke, George Wingrove. *China and Lower Bengal; Being "The Times" Correspondent from China in the Years 1857-58.* London: Routledge, Warne and Routledge, 1861.

"Coolie and Chinese Immigration to the West Indies," *Anti-Slavery Reporter*, Vol. VII, No. 8, New Series (August 1, 1859), 175-179.

"Coolie Emigration to French Colonies," *Saturday Review* (London), Vol. XII, No. 299 (July 20, 1861), 58-69.

"Coolie Immigration," *Anti-Slavery Reporter*, Vol. XXI, No. 1, New Series (February, 1878), 26-29.

"Coolie Immigration," *Anti-Slavery Reporter*, Vol. XVI, No. 1 (January 1, 1868), 15-18.

"Coolie Missions in British Guiana," *Mission Life*, Vol. VIII, No. 2, New Series (1877), 487-497.

"Coolies," *Mission Life*, Vol. IV (September, 1867), 19-21.

"Coolies in the Island of Reunion," *Anti-Slavery Reporter*, Vol. XXII, No. 4 (September 1, 1880), 105-106.

"Coolies in the West Indies," *Saturday Review*, (London), Vol. XXXVI, No. 932 (September 6, 1873), 308-309.

"Cooly Emigration," *Asiatic Journal*, Vol. III, Series 3 (October, 1844), 631-635.

Corbitt, Duvon Clough. *A Study of the Chinese in Cuba, 1847-1947*. Wilmore, Kentucky: Asbury College, 1971.

_____, "Immigration in Cuba," *Hispanic American Historical Review*, Vol. XXII, No. 2 (May, 1942), 280-308.

_____, "Chinese Immigrants in Cuba," *Far Eastern Survey*, Vol. XIII (July 12, 1944), 130-132.

_____, "Los Colonos Yucatecos," *Revista Bimestre Cubana*, Vol. XXXIX (January-February, 1937), 64-99.

Cordier, Henri. *Histoire des Relations de la Chine avec Les Puissances Occidentales 1860-1900*. 3 vols. Paris: Ancienne Librairie Germer Bailliere et Cie, 1901.

"Correspondence Respecting Chinese Slavery Presented to Parliament, March 1882," *Anti-Slavery Reporter*, Vol. II, Series 4 (May, 1882)k 119-122.

Corwin, Arthur F. *Spain and the Abolition of Slavery in Cuba, 1818-1886*. Austin: University of Texas Press, 1967.

"Cost of Coolie Immigration," *Anti-Slavery Reporter*, Vol. XI, No. 7, New Series (July 1, 1863), 165-166.

Costa, Emilia Viotta de. *De Senzala à Colônia*. São Paulo: Difusão Europeia do Livro, 1966.

Costin, W. C. *Great Britain and China, 1833-1860*. Oxford: The Clarendon Press, 1937.

Couling, Samuel. *The Encyclopedia Sinica*. Shanghai: Kelly and Walsh, 1917.

Coulter, John Wesley. *Fiji: Little India of the Pacific*. Chicago: The University of Chicago Press, 1942.

Coupland, Reginald. *The British Anti-Slavery Movement*. 2d ed. London: Frank Cass, 1964.

Courtenay, Philip P. *Plantation Agriculture*. New York: Frederick A. Praeger, 1965.

Cousins, W. M., "Chinese in the Caribbean," *Living Age*, Vol. CCCII, No. 4297 (January 1, 1927), 16-21.

_____, "The Chinese in the Caribbean," *Contemporary Review*, Vol. CXXX (1926), 632-638.

Crawford, John. *History of the Indian Archipelago*. 3 vols. Edinburgh: Archibald Constable and Company, 1820.

_____. *Journal of an Embassy from the Governor-General of India to the Courts of Siam and Cochin China Exhibiting a View of the Actual State of Those Kingdoms*. London: Henry Colburn, 1828.

Croockewit, H., "The Tin Mines of Malacca," *Journal of the Indian Archipelago and Eastern Asia*, Series 1, Vol. VIII (1854), 112-133.

Cumberland, Charles C., "The Sonora Chinese and the Mexican Revolution," *Hispanic American Historical Review*, Vol. XL, No. 2 (May, 1960), 191-211.

Cumpston, I. M. *Indians Overseas in British Territories 1834-1854*. London: Oxford University Press, 1953.

Curtin, Philip D. *The Atlantic Slave Trade: A Census*. Madison: University of Wisconsin Press, 1969.

_____. *The Image of Africa: British Ideas and Action, 1780-1850*. Madison: University of Wisconsin Press, 1964.

Cutler, Carl C. *Greyhounds of the Sea: The Story of the American Clipper Ship*. Annapolis, Maryland: United States Naval Institute, 1961 (originally published in New York in 1930).

Dahl, Victor C., "Alien Labor on the Gulf of Mexico, 1880-1900," *The Americas*, Vol. XVII (July, 1961), 21-35.

Dana, Richard H. *To Cuba and Back: A Vacation Voyage.* Boston: Ticknor and Fields, 1859.

"Danger of Shipping Coolies," *Nautical Magazine and Naval Chronicle,* Vol. XXI (May, 1853), 275.

Davey, Richard. *Cuba, Past and Present.* New York: Charles Scribner's Sons, 1898.

Davidson, G. F., "Plan Proposed for Importing Chinese Mechanics and Laborers from Singapore to New South Wales," *Chinese Repository,* Vol. VI, No. 6 (October, 1837), 299-300.

——————. *Trade and Travel in the Far East; or Recollections of Twenty one Years Passed in Java, Singapore, Australia and China.* London: Madden and Malcolm, 1846.

Davis, David Brion. *The Problem of Slavery in Western Culture.* Ithaca, New York: Cornell University Press, 1966.

Davis, John Francis. *The Chinese: A General Description of China and its Inhabitants.* London: Charles Knight and Company, 1850.

Davis, Sir John Francis. *China During the War and Since the Peace.* 2 vols. London: Longman, Brown, Green and Longmans, 1852.

"De Chinezen in de Verstrooijing," *Vaderlandsche Letter-Oefeningen,* Vol. II (1859), 149-178.

Deerr, Noel. *The History of Sugar.* 2 vols. London: Chapman and Hall Limited, 1949.

Dennett, Tyler. *Americans in Eastern Asia.* New York: The Macmillan Company, 1922.

D'Ewes, J. *China, Australia and the Pacific Islands in the Years 1855-56.* London: Richard Bentley, 1857.

"Die Ausfuhrung der Chinesen durch Europuer eis Kulis nach Westindien und Sudamerica, und ihre Auswanderung nach Californien und Australien," *Das Ausland*, Vol. XXX, No. 37 (September 11, 1857), 886-888.

"Die Auswanderung der Chinesen zur See," *Das Ausland*, Vol. XXX, No. 35 (August 28, 1857), 836-839.

"Die Auswanderung der Chinesen zur See," *Das Ausland*, Vol. XXX, No. 36 (September 4, 1857), 861-864.

Distant, W. L., "Eastern Coolie Labour," *The Journal of the Anthropological Institute of Great Britain and Ireland*, Vol. III (May 6, 1873), 139-145.

Donnelly, Ivon A. *Chinese Junks and Other Native Crafts*. Shanghai: Kelly and Walsh, 1924.

Downing, C. Toogood. *The Fan-Qui in China in 1836-7*. 3 vols. London: Henry Colburn, 1838.

Dubs, Homer H. and Robert S. Smith, "Chinese in Mexico City in 1635," *Far Eastern Review*, Vol. I, No. 4 (August, 1942), 387-389.

Duffield, Alexander J. *Peru in the Guano Age*. London: Richard Bentley and Son, 1877.

Durand, J. P., "The Population Statistics of China, AD 2 to 1953," *Population Studies*, Vol. XIII, No. 2 (1960), 209-256.

Duyvendak, J. L. L., "Chinese in the Dutch East Indies," *Chinese Social and Political Science Review*, Vol. XI (1927), 1-13.

Djang, F. D., "A Historical Summary of Sino-German Relations," *China Quarterly*, Vol. II (Summer, 1937), 489-500.

Earl, George Windsor. *The Eastern Seas, or Voyages and Adventures in the Indian Archipelago in 1832-33-34*. London: William H. Allen and Company, 1837.

Earl and Doctor (G. R. C. Herbert and G. H. Kingsley). *South Sea Bubbles*. London: Richard Bentley and Son, 1872.

Edwards, Bryan. *History, Civil and Commercial of the British Colonies in the West Indies*. 3 vols. London: John Stockdale, 1793.

Eisenberg, Peter L. *The Sugar Industry in Pernambuco: Modernization without Change, 1840-1910*. Berkeley: University of California Press, 1974.

Eitel, E. J. *Europe in China: The History of Hongkong from the Beginning to the Year 1882*. London: Luzac and Company, 1895.

El Obispado de Michoacan en el Siglo XVII. Morelia, Michoacan, Mexico: Finas Publicistas, 1973.

Elkins, Stanley M. *Slavery: A Problem in American Institutional and Intellectual Life*. Chicago: University of Chicago Press, 1959.

Elvin, Mark. *The Pattern of the Chinese Past*. Stanford, California: Stanford University Press, 1973.

"Emigration and the Coolie Trade in China," *Westminster Review*, Vol. C, No. 1 (July, 1873), 75-109.

"Emigration from China," *Anti-Slavery Reporter*, Vol. VIII, No. 10, New Series (October 1, 1860), 259-261.

"Emigration from China to the British West Indies," *Anti-Slavery Reporter*, Vol. XVIII, No. 6 (July 1, 1873), 177.

Encyclopedia Britannica. 13th edition, 1926.

Endacott, G. B. *A History of Kongkong*. London: Oxford University Press, 1958.

Erenchún, Felix. *Anales de la Isla de Cuba: Diccionario Administrativo, Económico, Estadístico y Legislativo*. 4 vols. Havana: Imprenta la Habanera, 1858.

Erickson, Edgar L., "The Introduction of East Indian Coolies into the British West Indies," *The Journal of Modern History*, Vol. VI, No. 2 (June, 1934), 127-146.

Eschwege, W. L. von. *Pluto Brasiliensis*. 2 vols. São Paulo: Campanhia Editora Nacional, 1944.

Fairbank, John King. *Trade and Diplomacy on the China Coast: The Opening of the Treaty Ports, 1842-1854*. Cambridge, Mass.: Harvard University Press, 1964.

Fairmann, John. *Cheap Sugar or Coolie Immigration to the West Indies*. Edinburgh: Paton and Ritchie, 1859.

Falconbridge, Alexander. *An Account of the Slave Trade on the Coast of Africa*. London: J. Phillips, 1788.

Farley, M. Foster, "The Chinese Coolie Trade, 1845-1875," *Journal of Asian and African Studies*, Vol. III, Nos. 1-2 (January-April, 1968), 257-270.

Farquhar, Robert Townsend. *Suggestions Arising from the Abolition of the African Slave Trade for Supplying the Demands of the West India Colonies with Agricultural Labourers*. London: John Stockdale, 1807.

Fauvel, A. A., "La Main-D'Oeuvre Chinoise Dans nos Colonies," *Revue de Géographie* (Août, 1903), 112-127.

Fawcett, Brian, "How China Came to Peru," *Geographical Magazine*, Vol. XXXVII, No. 6 (October, 1964), 423-434.

Fernandes, Bernardino de Sena. *Um Appello ao Publico Imparcial*. Macao: Impresso na Typographia Popular, 1869.

Feyjoo Sotomayor, Urbano. *Isla de Cuba: Inmigración de Trabajadores Españoles. Documentos y Memoria Escrita Sobre Esta Materia*. Havana: Imprenta de J. M. Eleizegui, 1853.

Fischer, C. B. *Personal Narrative of Three Years Service in China*. London: Richard Bentley, 1863.

Fitzgerald, Charles Patrick, "Overseas Chinese in South East Asia," *Australian Journal of Politics and History*, Vol. XIII, No. 1 (May, 1962), 66-67.

_____. *The Third China: The Chinese Communities in Southeast Asia*. London: Angus and Robertson, 1965.

_____. *The Southern Expansion of the Chinese People: "Southern Fields and Southern Ocean."* London: Barrie and Jenkins, 1972.

Fitz-Roy Cole, G. R., "John Chinaman Abroad," *Fraser's Magazine*, Vol. XVIII, No. 106 (October, 1878), 447-457.

Fogel, Robert William and Stanley L. Engerman. *Time on the Cross: The Economics of American Negro Slavery*. Boston: Little, Brown, 1974.

Fong, Ng Bickleen. *The Chinese in New Zealand: A Study in Assimilation*. Hong Kong: Hong Kong University Press, 1959.

Fontpertuis, Ad. F. de, "L'Emigration Chinoise," *Revue Scientifique*, Vol. XXIII, No. 35 (1 Mars, 1879), 829-833.

Fortune, Robert, *A Residence Among the Chinese: Inland on the Coast and at Sea*. London: John Murray, 1857.

Foster, John W. *American Diplomacy in the Orient*. Boston: Houghton, Mifflin and Company, 1903.

Fox, Grace Estelle. *British Admirals and Chinese Pirates, 1832-1869*. London: K. Paul, Trench, Trubner and Company Ltd., 1940.

Fried, Morton H., "Some Observations on the Chinese in British Guiana," *Social and Economic Studies*, Vol. V, No. 1 (March, 1956), 54-73.

Furtado, Celso. *The Economic Growth of Brazil: A Survey from Colonial to Modern Times*, translated by Ricardo W. de Aguiar and Eric Charles Drysdale. Berkeley: University of California Press, 1963.

Galbreath, C. B., "Mongolian Immigration and the British Colonies," *Arena*, Vol. XXXVII, No. 211 (June, 1907), 610-613.

Gale, Essom M., "Far Eastern Trade Routes and Cargoes: A New England Ship Captain's Letters, 1850-1856," *Proceedings of the Pacific Coast Branch of the American Historical Association*, 1930, 119-134.

Gallenga, Antonio. *South America*. London: Chapman and Hall, 1880.

_____. *The Pearl of the Antilles*. London: Chapman and Hall, 1873.

Garcilaso de la Vega, *Royal Commentaries of the Incas and General History of Peru*. 2 vols. Austin: University of Texas Press, 1966.

Gardner, Christopher Thomas, "Amoy Emigration to the Straits," *China Review*, Vol. XXII, No. 4 (1897), 621-626.

Garrison, W. P., "The Coolie," *Nation*, Vol. XIII, No. 321 (August 24, 1871), 131-133.

Gibbes, R. W. *Cuba for Invalids*. New York: W. A. Townsend and Company, 1860.

Gibbs, John Arthur. *The History of Anthony and Dorothea Gibbs and of their Contemporary Relatives Including the History of the Origin and Early Years of the House of Anthony Gibbs and Sons*. London: Saint Catherine Press, 1922.

Gibson-Hill, C. A., "The Steamers Employed in Asian Waters, 1819-39," *Journal of the Malayan Branch of the Royal Asiatic Society*, Vol. XXVII (May, 1954), 120-162.

Gilbreath, Olive, "The Coolie Ship," *Asia*, Vol. XVIII, No. 6 (June, 1918), 459-464.

Gomes, Luis Gonzaga. *Páginas da História de Macau*. Macau: Notícias de Macau, 1966.

Gottwaldt, H. *Die Uberseeische Auswanderung der Chinesen und ihre Einwirkung auf die gelbe und Weisse Rasse*. Bremen, 1903.

Graham, Maria. *Journal of a Voyage to Brazil and Residence There, during Part of the Years 1821, 1822, 1823*. London: Longman, Hurst, Rees, Deme, Brown, Green and J. Murray, 1824.

Graves, R. H. (Rev.), "Some Personal Reminiscences of Thirty Years of Mission Work," *Chinese Recorder*, Vol. XVII, No. 10 (November, 1886), 421-435.

Greenberg, Michael. *British Trade and the Opening of China, 1800-42*. Cambridge: Cambridge University Press, 1951.

Greenidge, C. W. W. *Slavery*. London: George Allein and Unwin Limited, 1958.

Grieve, Averil MacKenzie. *The Last Years of the English Slave Trade: Liverpool 1750-1807*. London: Putnam and Company, 1941.

Griffin, Eldon. *Clippers and Consuls; American Consular and Commercial Relations with Eastern Asia, 1845-1860*. Wilmington, Delaware: Scholarly Resources Inc., 1972.

Groeneveldt, William P. *Notes on the Malay Archipelago and Malacca, Compiled from Chinese Sources*. Batavia: W. Bruining, 1877.

_____. *Notes on the Malay Archipelago and Malacca: Miscellaneous Papers Relating to the Indian Archipelago*. 2 vols. London: 1887.

Guerra y Sánchez, Ramiro. *Sugar and Society in the Caribbean: An Economic History of Cuban Agriculture*. New Haven: Yale University Press, 1964.

Guiral, Paul. *L'Immigration Réglementée aux Antilles Françaises et á la Réunion*. Paris: Jouve et Cie, 1911.

Guiteras, Juan, "La Inmigración China y el Canal de Panamá," *Reforma Social*, Vol. I (April, 1914), 1-6.

Gulick, Edward V. *Peter Parker and the Opening of China*. Cambridge, Mass.: Harvard University Press, 1973.

Gutzlaff, Charles. *A Sketch of Chinese History Ancient and Modern*: *Comprising a Retrospect of the Foreign Intercourse and Trade with China.* 2 vols. London: Smith, Elder and Company, 1834.

—————————. *Journal of Three Voyages Along the Coast of China in 1831, 1832 and 1833*. London: Thomas Ward and Company, 1834.

—————————. *Journal of Three Voyages Along the Coast of China in 1831, 1832 and 1833, with Notices of Siam, Corea, and the Loo-choo Islands, to which is Prefixed an Introductory Essay on the Policy, Religion, etc., of China by the Rev. W. Ellis.* 3d ed. London: Thomas Ward and Company, [1840].

Guyol, Edwin Warren, "Like Slave Days of Old," *Harper's Weekly Magazine*, Vol. LII, No. 2170 (November 28, 1908), 16-17.

Hailly, Ed. Du, "Les Antilles Françaises en 1863," *Revue des Deux Mondes*, Vol. XLVIII (1863), 855-880.

—————————, "Les Chinois Hors de Chez Eux," *Revue de Deux Mondes*, Vol. LXVI (15 November, 1866), 396-420.

Hamberg, Theodore. *The Visions of Hung-siu-tshuen and the Origin of the Kwang-si Insurrection.* Hong Kong; 1854.

Hang Tsen-ming. *The Legal Status of the Chinese Abroad.* Taipei: China Cultural Service, 1954.

Hao, Yen-p'ing. *The Comprador in Nineteenth Century China: Bridge between East and West.* Harvard East Asian Series, 45, 1971.

Haring, C. H. *The Spanish Empire in America.* New York: Harcourt, Brace and World, Inc., 1949.

Harlow, Vincent T. *The Founding of the Second British Empire.* 2 vols. London: Longmans, Green and Company Ltd., 1964.

Harris, John Hobbis. *Coolie Labour in the British Crown Colonies and Protectorates.* London: Edward Hughes and Company, 1910.

Haviland, Edward K. *American Steam Navigation in China 1845-1878.* Salem, Mass.: The American Neptune Incorporated, 1956-1958.

Hazard, Samuel. *Cuba with Pen and Pencil.* Hartford: Hartford Publishing Company, 1871.

Headland, Isaac Taylor. *Home Life in China.* London: Methuen and Company Limited, 1914.

Hertslet, Godfrey E. P. *Treaties, etc., between Great Britain and China, and between China and Foreign Powers, and Orders in Council, Rules, Regulations, Acts of Parliament, Decrees, etc., Affecting British Interests in China, in Force on the 1st January, 1908.* 2 vols. London: Harrison and Sons, 1908.

Higman, B. W., "The Chinese in Trinidad, 1806-1838," *Caribbean Studies*, Vol. XII, No. 3 (October, 1972), 21-44.

Hill, Lawrence (ed.). *Brazil.* Berkeley: University of California Press, 1947.

Hill, Robert J. *Cuba and Porto Rico with the Other Islands of the West Indies.* New York: The Century Company, 1899.

Hillebrand, William. *Report on the Supply of Labor, etc., to the Honorable Board of Immigration of the Hawaiian Islands.* Honolulu: Government Press, 1867.

Hinman, George Warren, "The Oriental Dispersion: An Economic and Missionary Problem," *Chinese Recorder*, Vol. LVI (July, 1925), 448-455.

Hirth, F. *China and the Roman Orient: Researches into Their Ancient and Medieval Relations as Represented in Old Chinese Records*, Shanghai: Kelly and Walsh, 1885.

"Historical Landmarks of Macao," *Chinese Recorder*, Vol. XVIII, No. 5 (May, 1887), 175-182.

"Historical Landmarks of Macao," *Chinese Recorder*, Vol. XVIII, No. 6 (June, 1887), 213-219.

"Historical Landmarks of Macao," *Chinese Recorder*, Vol. XVIII, No. 7 (July, 1887), 264-274.

"Historical Landmarks of Macao," *Chinese Recorder*, Vol. XVIII, No. 10 (October, 1887), 385-394.

"Historical Landmarks of Macao," *Chinese Recorder*, Vol. XVIII, No. 11 (November, 1887), 423-434.

"Historical Landmarks of Macao," *Chinese Recorder*, Vol. XVIII, No. 12 (December, 1887), 474-480.

"Historical Landmarks of Macao," *Chinese Recorder*, Vol. XIX, No. 1 (January, 1888), 74-78.

"Historical Landmarks of Macao," *Chinese Recorder*, Vol. XIX, No. 3 (March, 1888), 121-129.

"Historical Landmarks of Macao," *Chinese Recorder*, Vol. XIX, No. 4 (April, 1888), 168-177.

"Historical Landmarks of Macao," *Chinese Recorder*, Vol. XIX, No. 6 (June, 1888), 317-321.

"Historical Landmarks of Macao," *Chinese Recorder*, Vol. XIX, No. 8 (August, 1888), 371-376.

"Historical Landmarks of Macao," *Chinese Recorder*, Vol. XIX, No. 11 (November, 1888), 522-526.

"Historical Landmarks of Macao," *Chinese Recorder*, Vol. XX, No. 1 (January, 1889), 84-86.

"Historical Landmarks of Macao," *Chinese Recorder*, Vol. XX, No. 4 (April, 1889), 176-181.

Hitchins, Fred H. *The Colonial Land and Emigration Commission.* Philadelphia: University of Pennsylvania Press, 1931.

Ho, Ping-ti. *Studies on the Population of China, 1368-1953*. Cambridge, Mass.: Harvard University Press, 1959.

Ho, S. Dzu-fang. *A Hundred Years of Hong Kong*. Ann Arbor, Mich.: University of Michigan Press, 1952.

Holden, E., "A Chapter on the Coolie Trade," *Harper's New Monthly Magazine*, Vol. XXIX, No. 169 (June, 1864), 1-11.

Holmes, J. H. *Australia, New Zealand, and the Southwest Pacific*. London: Thomas Nelson and Sons, Limited, 1969.

Howe, Julie Ward. *A Trip to Cuba*. Boston: Tricknor and Fields, 1860.

Hsieh, Ting-yu, "Origin and Migrations of the Hakkas," *The Chinese Social and Political Science Review*, Vol. XIII (1929), 202-227.

_____, "The Chinese in Hawaii," *Chinese Social and Political Science Review*, Vol. XIV, No. 1 (January, 1930), 13-40.

Hu, Nai-tsiu, "Internal Chinese Migration," *Agrarian China*, London: Secretariat of the Institute of Pacific Relations, 1939.

Huang, Tsen-ming. *The Legal Status of Chinese Abroad*. Taipei, Waiwan: China Cultural Service, 1954.

Huc, M. *The Chinese Empire: Forming a Sequel to the Work Entitled "Recollections of a Journey Through Tartary and Thibet,"* 2 vols. London: Longman, Brown, Green and Longmans, 1855.

Huck, Arthur. *The Chinese in Australia*. Croydon, Victoria: Longmans Green and Company Limited, 1967.

Huebner, Joseph Alexander von. *A Ramble Around the World, 1871*. London: Macmillan and Company, 1874.

Hulot, Baron Etienne, "Les Chinois Partent (Question de L'Immigration Chinoise)," *Revue du Monde Latin* [Paris], (September-October, 1888), 1-23.

Humboldt, Alexander. *The Island of Cuba*, translated from the Spanish by J. S. Thrasher. New York: Derby and Jackson, 1856.

Hundley, Daniel R., "The Traffic in Coolies," *Merchants' Magazine*, Vol. XXXVI, No. 5 (May, 1857), 570-573.

Hunter, William C. *Bits of Old China*. Shanghai: Kelly and Walsh, Limited, 1911.

_____. *The 'Fan Kwae' at Canton before Treaty Days 1825-1844*. Shanghai: The Oriental Affairs, 1938 (First published in 1882).

Hutchinson, Thomas Joseph. *Two Years in Peru, with Exploration of its Antiquities*. 2 vols. London: S. Low, Marston, Low and Searle, 1873.

"Immigration into the West Indies," *Anti-Slavery Reporter*, Vol. VIII, No. 1, New Series (January 2, 1859), 19-23.

"Indian Coolies in the British Indies," *Anti-Slavery Reporter*, Vol. XVIII, No. 6 (July 1, 1873), 177-178.

Informes sobre la Existencia de Huano en las Islas de Chincha Presentados por la Comisión Nombrada por el Gobierno Peruano. Lima, 1854.

Ireland, Alleyne. *Tropical Colonization*. New York: The Macmillan Company, 1899.

Jackson, James C., "Chinese Agricultural Pioneering in Singapore and Jahore, 1800-1917," *Journal of the Malayasian Branch of the Royal Asiatic Society*, Vol. XXXVIII, No. 207 (July, 1965), 77-105.

Jackson, Robert N. *Immigrant Labour and the Development of Malaya, 1786-1920*. Kuala Lampur: Government Press, 1961.

Jacobs, Alfred, "Les Chinois hors de la Chine," *Revue des Deux Mondes*, Vol. XVIII (1 November, 1858), 121-142.

"Jamaica and Coolie Immigration," *Anti-Slavery Reporter*, Vol. XXI, No. 5, New Series (November, 1878), 108-113.

"Jamaica and Coolie Immigration," *Anti-Slavery Reporter*, Vol. XXII, No. 6 (December 23, 1880), 150-151.

Jen, Yu-wen. *The Taiping Revolutionary Movement*. New Haven: Yale University Press, 1973.

Jenkins, Edward. *The Coolie: His Rights and Wrongs*. New York: George Routledge and Sons, 1871.

Jiménez Pastrama, Juan. *Los Chinos en las Luchas por la Liberación Cubana*. Habana: Instituto de Historia, 1963.

Johnson, R. A., "Coolie Labor at the South," *Nation*, Vol. I, No. 9 (August, 1865), 264-265.

_____., "Coolie Labor and Coolie Immigration," *Cornhill Magazine*, London, Vol. XVI, No. 91 (July, 1867), 74-83.

"Journal of Occurrences," *Chinese Repository*, Vol. VII, No. 2 (June, 1838), 112.

"Journal of Occurrences," *Chinese Repository*, Vol. XVI, No. 4 (April, 1847), 207-208.

"Journal of Occurrences," *Chinese Repository*, Vol. XIX, No. 12 (December, 1850), 680.

Kam-ching Zambrano, Elsa. *Historia de la Colectividad China en Chile*. Santiago de Chile: Universidad de Chile, 1966.

Ken, Wang Lin, "The Trade of Singapore with China, 1819-1869," *Journal of the Malay Branch of the Royal Asiatic Society*, Vol. XXXIII, Part 4 (December, 1960), 5-315.

Kidder, D. P. and J. C. Fletcher. *Brazil and the Brazilians*. Boston: Little, Brown and Company, 1867.

King, James Ferguson, "The Latin American Republics and the Suppression of the Slave Trade," *Hispanic American Historical Review*, Vol. XXIV, No. 3 (August, 1944), 387-411.

Kinsbruner, Jay. *Chile: A Historical Interpretation*. New York: Harper and Row, 1973.

Kirke, Henry. *Twenty Five Years in British Guiana*. London:, Sampson Low, Marston and Company Limited, 1898.

Kirker, James. *Adventures to China: Americans in the Southern Oceans, 1792-1812*. New York: Oxford University Press, 1970.

Kloosterboer, W. *Involuntary Labour since the Abolition of Slavery*. Leiden: E. J. Brill, 1960.

Knapland, Paul. *James Stephen and the British Colonial System, 1813-1847*. Madison, Wisconsin: University of Wisconsin Press, 1953.

Knight, Franklin W. *Slave Society in Cuba During the Nineteenth Century*. Madison: University of Wisconsin Press, 1970.

Knowles, Lilian Charlotte Ann. *The Economic Development of the British Overseas Empire*. 3 vols. London: George Routledge and Sons, Limited, 1928-1936.

Kondapi, C. *Indians Overseas, 1838-1949*. New Delhi: Oxford University Press, 1951.

Kung, S. W. *Chinese in American Life: Some Aspects of Their History Status, Problems and Contributions*. Seattle: University of Washington Press, 1962.

Kuykendall, Ralph S. *The Hawaiian Kingdom*. 2 vols. Honolulu: University of Hawaii Press, 1967.

Laërne, C. F. van Delden. *Brazil and Java: Report on Coffee-Culture*. London: W. H. Allen and Company, 1885.

La Farque, Thomas, "Some Early Chinese Visitors to the United States," *T'ien Hsia Monthly*, Vol. XI, No. 2 (October-November, 1940), 128-139.

"Landverhuizing der Chinezen," *Tijdschrift voor Neerlandsche Indie* (Batavia, 1856), 101-115.

Lane-Poole, Stanley. *Sir Harry Parkes in China*. London: Methuen and Company, 1901.

_____. *The Life of Sir Harry Parkes*. 2 vols. London: Macmillan and Company, 1894.

Lang, Olga. *Chinese Family and Society*. New Haven: Yale University Press, 1946.

Latourette, Kenneth Scott. *A History of Christian Missions to China*. London: Society for Promoting Christian Knowledge, 1929.

_____. *The Chinese: Their History and Culture*. New York: The Macmillan Company, 1941.

_____. *The History of Early Relations between the United States and China, 1784-1844*. New Haven: Yale University Press, 1917.

Layman, (Captain) William. *Outline of a Plan for the Better Cultivation, Security and Defence of the British West Indies, Being the Original Suggestion for Providing an Effectual Substitute for the African Slave Trade and Preventing the Dependence of Those Colonies on America for Supplies*. London: Black, Parry and Kingsbury, 1807.

Lechler, R., "The Hakka Chinese," *Chinese Recorder*, Vol. IX (September-October, 1878), 352-359.

Leclerc, Max, "L'Émigration Chinoise et les Relations Internationales," *Revue des Deux Mondes*, Vol. XCII (1 Mars, 1889), 650-688.

Legge, James. *A Record of Buddhists Kingdoms: Being an Account by the Chinese Monk Fa-hein of his Travels in India and Ceylon (AD 399-414) in Search of the Buddhist Books of Discipline*. Oxford: The Clarendon Press, 1886.

Lemos, Miguel. *Imigração Chinesa. Mensagen do Cento Positivista Brasileiro a S. Ex. O Embaixador do Celeste Imperio junto aos Governos de França e Inglaterra*. Rio de Janeiro, 1881.

Leroy-Beaulieu, Paul. *De la Colonisation Chez Les Pueples Modernes*. Paris: Librairie Guillaumin et Cie, 1886.

Leseur, M. F., "L'Emigration Chinoise," *Bulletin de la Societé de Geographie de Lille*, Vol. IV (1885), 62-82.

Levin, Jonathan V. *The Export Economies: Their Pattern of Development in Historical Perspective*. Cambridge, Mass.: Harvard University Press, 1960.

Levy, Howard S. *Chinese Footbinding: The History of a Curious Erotic Custom*. New York: Walton Rawls, 1966.

"Life in Cuba," *Harper's Magazine*, Vol. XLIII, No. 255 (August, 1871), 350-365.

Lin, Yu, "The Chinese Overseas," *The Chinese Year Book, 1937*, 1245-1261.

Lindsay, William Schaw. *History of Merchant Shipping and Ancient Commerce*. 4 vols. London: Sampson Low, Marston, Low and Searle, 1874-76.

Ling, Pyau, "Causes of Chinese Emigration," *Annals of American Academy of Political and Social Science*, Vol. XXXIX, No. 128 (January, 1912), 74-82.

Lisboa, Henrique C. R. *A China e Os Chins*. Montevideo: Typographia a Vapor de A. Godel-Cerrito, 1888.

Livingstedt, Sir Andrew. *An Historical Sketch of the Portuguese Settlements in China, and of the Roman Catholic Church and Mission in China*. Boston: James Monroe and Company, 1836.

Lobscheid, Rev. William. *Chinese Emigration to the West Indies; A Trip through British Guiana Undertaken for the Purpose of Ascertaining the Condition of the Chinese Who Have Emigrated under Government Contract with Supplementary Papers Relating to Contract Labor and the Slave Trade*. Demarara: "Royal Gazette," 1866.

Loh Fook Seng, Philip. *The Malay States, 1877-1895; Political Change and Social Policy*. London: Oxford University Press, 1969.

Lubbock, Alfred. *The Opium Clippers*. Glasgow: Brown, Son and Ferguson Limited, 1933.

Lubbock, Basil. *Coolie Ships and Oil Sailors*. Glasgow: Brown, Son and Ferguson, Limited, 1955.

——————. *The China Clippers*. Glasgow: James Brown and Son, 1914.

Lucas, Christopher. *Women in China*. Hong Kong: Dragonfly Books, 1965.

Lumsdaine, J., W. R. Jennings and Edward Presgrove, "Report on Population, etc., of the Town and Suburbs of Fort Marlborough 1819-20," in Bastin, John (ed.), *The Journal of Thomas Ortho Travers, 1813-1820*. Singapore; A. G. Banfield, 1960.

Lyman, Stanford, "Overseas Chinese in America and Indonesia," *Pacific Affairs*, Vol. XXXIV, No. 4 (Winter, 1961-62), 380-389.

Macalister, Arthur, "Queensland and Chinese Immigration," *Proceedings of the Royal Colonial Institute*, Vol. IX, London, Sampson Low, Marston, Searle and Rivington, 1878, 43-83.

"Macao and Its Slave Trade," *China Review*, Vol. II, No. 1 (July, 1873), 9-20.

"Macao and the Portuguese Coolie Trade to Peru," *Anti-Slavery Reporter*, Vol. XVIII, No. 4 (January, 1873), 106-107.

McBride, George M., "Features of the Agrarian System in Peru," *Geographical Review*, Vol. XV (January, 1925), 137-139.

MacGowan, "Piracies, Riots and Lynch Law at Ningpo," in *Shanghai Almanac for 1853 and Miscellany*. Shanghai: Herald Office, 1853.

MacGregor, David R. *The Tea Clippers: An Account of the China Tea Trade and of Some of the British Sailing Ships Engaged in it from 1849 to 1869*. London: Percival Marshall and Company, Limited, 1952.

MacNair, Harley, "Chinese Acquisition of Foreign Nationality," *Chinese Social and Political Science Review*, Vol. VII, No. 4 (October, 1923), 1-39.

_____, "Chinese Emigration," *Chinese Social and Political Science Review*, Vol. VII, No. 2 (April, 1923), 55-77.

_____. *The Chinese Abroad*. Shanghai: The Commercial Press Limited, 1924.

MacNair, Harley F., "The Chinese in the British Empire and the New World," *Chinese Social and Political Science Review*, Vol. VII, No. 3 (July, 1823), 1-44.

_____, "The Protection of Alien Chinese Through Chinese Authorities," *Chinese Social and Political Science Review*, Vol. VIII, No. 2 (April, 1924), 48-86.

_____, "The Relation of China to Her Nationals Abroad," *The Chinese Social and Political Science Review*, Vol. VII, No. 1 (January, 1923), 23-43.

_____, "Treaty Rights of Chinese Merchants and Free Laborers Abroad," *Chinese Social and Political Science Review*, Vol. VIII (1924), 136-195.

Marett, Robert. *Peru*. New York: Praeger Publishers, 1969.

Markham, Clements R., "From China to Peru: The Emigration Question," *Geographical Magazine*, Vol. I (December 1, 1874), 367-370.

Markham, Violet R. *The New Era in South Africa, with an Examination of the Chinese Labour Question*. London: Smith, Elder and Company, 1904.

Marsden, William. *The History of Sumatra*. Kuala Lumpur: Oxford University Press, 1966 (first published in London in 1811).

Martin, R. Montgomery. *China: Political, Commercial and Social; in an Official Report to Her Majesty's Government.* 2 vols. London: James Madden, 1847.

_____. *Reports, Minutes and Despatches on the British Position and Prospects in China.* London: Harrison and Company, 1846.

Martin, W. A. P. *A Cycle of Cathay or China, South and North.* Edinburgh: Oliphant, Anderson and Farrier, 1896.

Mathieson, William Law. *British Slave Emancipation, 1838-1849.* New York: Octagon Books, Inc., 1967.

Maude, Wilfred. *Anthony Gibbs and Sons Limited: Merchants and Bankers, 1808-1958.* London: Anthony Gibbs and Sons, 1958.

Maury, M. F. *Explanations and Sailing Directions to Accompany the Winds and Current Charts.* Philadelphia: E. C. and J. Biddle, 1855 (seventh edition).

Mayer, Adrian C. *Indians in Fiji.* London: Oxford University Press, 1963.

Mayer, Brantz. *Captain Canot, or Twenty Years of an African Slaver.* London: George Routledge and Company, 1855.

Mayers, William Frederick. *Treaties Between the Empire of China and Foreign Powers together with Regulations for the Conduct of Foreign Trade, Conventions, Agreements, Regulations, etc.* Shanghai: North-China Herald Limited, 1906.

Mayers, William F., N. B. Dennys and Charles King. *The Treaty Ports of China and Japan.* London: Trubner and Company, 1867.

Meadows, Thomas Taylor. *Desultory Notes on the Government and People of China, and on the Chinese Language.* London: William H. Allen and Company, 1847.

_____, "Land Tenure in China," *Transactions of the China Branch of the Royal Asiatic Society* (1847), 1-13.

Meares, John. *Voyages Made in the Years 1788 and 1789 from China to the Northwest Coast of America*. London: Logographic Press, 1790.

Medhurst, Sir Walter H., "The Chinese as Colonists," *Eclectic Magazine of Foreign Literature*, New Series, Vol. XXIX, No. 1 (January, 1879), 102-109.

_____, "The Chinese as Colonists," *Nineteenth Century*, Vol. IV, No. 19 (September, 1878), 517-527.

"Memorial Showing the Daily Increase of Enervation and Degeneracy in the Province of Kwangtung, and the Urgent Necessity that Exists for Correction and Reform of the Civil Administration and Military Discipline, in Order to Maintain the Native Spirit, and to Improve the Condition of the People, With this View, the Imperial Perusal of the Memorial is Humbly Solicited," *Chinese Repository*, Vol. VII (April, 1838), 592-605.

Mendonça, Salvador de. *Immigração Chineza: Serie de Artigos Publicados no "Cruzeiro" em Resposta ao "Rio News."* Rio de Janeiro: Typographia a vapor no "Cruzeiro," 1881.

_____. *Trabalhadores Asiaticos*. New York: Typographia do "Novo Mundo," 1879.

Meng, L. Kong, Cheok Hong Cheong and Louis Ali Mouy. *The Chinese Question in Australia, 1878-79*. Melbourne: F. F. Bailliere, 1879.

Merivale, Herman. *Lectures on Colonization and Colonies*. London: Oxford University Press, 1928.

Mesnier, P. G., "A Reply to 'Macao and its Slave Trade,'" *China Review*, Vol. II, No. 2 (1873), 112-125.

Michael, Franz. *The Taiping Rebellion: History and Documents*. 3 vols. Seattle: University of Washington Press, 1966.

Michie, Alexander. *The Englishman in China During the Victorian Era as Illustrated in the Career of Sir Rutherford Alcock*. 2 vols. London: William Blackwood and Sons, 1900.

Milet, Henrique Augusto. *Auxilio àLavoura e Crédito Real.* Recife, 1876.

Millones Santagadea, Luis. *Minorias Etnicas en el Perú.* Lima: Pontifica Universidad Catolica de Perú, 1973.

Mills, Lennox A. *British Malaya, 1824-1867.* London: Oxford University Press, 1966.

_____. *British Rule in Eastern Asia: A Study of Contemporary Government and Economic Development in British Malaya and Hong Kong.* London: Oxford University Press, 1942.

Mintz, Sidney W., "Review of *Slavery* by Stanley M. Elkins," *American Anthropologist*, Vol. LXIII (1961), 579-587.

Missão do Visconde de São Januario nas Republicas da America de Sul, 1878 e 1879. Lisboa: Imprensa Nacional, 1880.

Mitchell, Edmund, "The Chinaman Abroad," *Nineteenth Century*, Vol. XXXVI, No. 212 (October, 1894), 612-620.

Mocquet, Jean. *Voyages en Afrique, Asia, Indes Orientales et Occidentales.* Paris: Impr. Aux. Frais du Gouvernement, 1830.

Moges, Marquis de. *Recollections of Baron Gross' Embassy to China and Japan in 1857-58.* London: Richard Griffin and Company, 1860.

Montalto de Jesus, C. A. *Historic Macao.* Hong Kong: Kelly and Walsh, Limited, 1902.

"Monthly Summary," *Anti-Slavery Reporter*, Vol. VIII, No. 1, New Series (January 2, 1860), 2-3.

Mookherji, S. B. *The Indenture System in Mauritius, 1837-1915.* Calcutta: Firma K. L. Mukhopadhyay, 1962.

Morison, Samuel Eliot. *The Maritime History of Massachusetts, 1783-1860.* Cambridge, Mass.: The Riverside Press, 1961.

Morrell, W. P. *Britain in the Pacific Islands.* Oxford: The Clarendon Press, 1960.

_____. *British Colonial Policy in the Age of Peel and Russell.* Oxford: The Clarendon Press, 1930.

Morrell, W. P. *British Victorian Policy in the Mid-Victorian Age: South Africa, New Zealand and the West Indies.* Oxford: The Clarendon Press, 1969.

Morse, Hosea Ballou. *The Trade and Administration of China.* Shanghai: Kelly and Walsh, 1921.

_____. *The Chronicles of the East India Company Trading to China 1635-1834.* 4 vols. Oxford: The Clarendon Press, 1926.

Morse, Hosea B. and H. F. MacNair. *Far Eastern International Relations.* Boston: Houghton Mifflin Company, 1931.

Moule, Arthur Evans. *Half a Century in China: Recollections and Observations.* London: Hadder and Stoughton, 1911.

Moura, Carlos Francisco, "Colonos Chinêses no Brasil no Reinado de D. João VI," *Boletim do Instituto Luis de Camões*, Vol. VII, No. 2 (Summer, 1973), 185-191.

_____. *Macau e o Comércio Português com a China e o Japão nos Séculos XVI e XVII.* Macau: Imprensa Nacional, 1973.

_____, "Relacoẽs entre Macau e o Brasil no Início do Século XIX, segundo as ;Memorias para Servir à História do Reino do Brasil' do Padre Parereca," *Boletim do Instituto Luis de Camoẽs*, Vol. VIII, No. 3 (Autumn, 1973), 261-269.

"Mr. Markham's Happy Coolies in Peru," *Anti-Slavery Reporter*, Vol. XIX, No. 8 (September 1, 1875), 183-186.

Murphy, Robert Cushman. *Oceanic Birds of South America.* 2 vols. New York: The Macmillan Company, 1936.

——————, "The Peruvian Guano Islands Seventy Years Ago," *Natural History*, Vol. XXVII, No. 5 (September-October, 1927), 439-447.

Murray, Henry A. *Lands of the Slave and the Free, or Cuba, the United States and Canada.* 2 vols. London: John W. Parker and Son, 1855.

Nabuco, Joaquim, "Imigração Chinesa (Discurso de 3 de Setembro de 1879)," in *Obras Completas*, Vol. XI, São Paulo: Instituto Progresso Editorial SA, 1949, 59-67.

Neumann, Charles Fried. *History of Pirates Who Infested the China Sea from 1807 to 1810.* London: J. Murray, 1831.

"New Scheme for Importing Contracted Coolies into Cuba," *Anti-Slavery Reporter*, Vol. XXI, No. 6 (New Series, January, 1879), 148.

Newbold, Thomas John. *Political and Statistical Account of the British Settlements in the Straits of Malacca, viz. Pinang, Malacca and Singapore with a History of the Malayan States on the Peninsula of Malacca.* 2 vols. London: John Murray, 1839.

Nieboer, H. J. *Slavery as an Industrial System.* 2d rev. ed. New York: Burt Franklin, 1910.

Norton-Kyshe, James William. *The History of the Laws and Courts of Hongkong.* 2 vols. London and Hong Kong, 1898.

"Notes," *Nation*, Vol. XXV, No. 642 (October 18, 1877), 242-244.

Notes and Queries on China and Japan, Vol. I (June 29, 1867), 77.

"Notes on the Chinese in the Straits," *Journal of the Indian Archipelago and Eastern Asia*, Vol. IX, Series 1 (1855), 109-124.

Nye, Gideon. *The Coolie Question in 1856-1862: A Brief Vindication.* Hong Kong: "China Mail," 1869.

"Official Correspondence Respecting the Slave Trade and the Coolie Traffic," *Anti-Slavery Reporter*, Vol. VIII, No. 10, New Series (October 1, 1860), 250-252.

"Official Inquiry Respecting the Death of Coolies," *The Mercantile Marine Magazine and Nautical Record*, Vol. III, No. 36 (December, 1856), 411-412.

O'Kelly, James J. *The Mambi-Land, or Adventures of a Herald Correspondent in Cuba.* London: Sampson Low, Marston and Company, 1874.

Oliphant, Laurence. *Narrative of the Earl of Elgin's Mission to China and Japan in the Years 1857, '58, '59.* Edinburg: William Blackwood and Sons, 1859.

Oliver, Douglas L. *The Pacific Islands.* New York: Doubleday and Company, Inc., 1961.

Otis, F. N. *Illustrated History of the Panama Railroad.* New York: Harper and Brothers, 1862.

Oxford English Dictionary. Oxford: The Clarendon Press, 1933. Vol. V.

Pachai, Bridglal, "Indentured Chinese Immigrant Labor on the Witwatersrand Goldfields," *India Quarterly*, Vol. XXI, No. 1 (January-March, 1965), 58-82.

Pacific Islands. 3 vols. Geographical Handbook Series, Naval Intelligence Division, 1945.

Palgrave, W. G. *Dutch Guiana.* London: Macmillan and Company, 1876.

_____, "Dutch Guiana," *Fortnightly Review*, Vol. XXV (January, 1876), 194-214.

Parker, E. K. *China: Her History, Diplomacy and Commerce.* London: John Murray, 1901.

Parnaby, Owen W., "The Regulation of Indentured Labour to Fiji, 1864-1888," *Journal of the Polynesian Society*, Vol. LXV, No. 1 (March, 1956), 55-65.

Payne, George E. *An Experiment in Alien Labor.* Chicago: University of Chicago Press, 1912.

Peck, George W. *Melbourne and the Chincha Islands with Sketches of Lima and a Voyage Round the World.* New York: Charles Scribner, 1854.

Pelissier, Roger. *The Awakening of China, 1793-1949.* London: Secker and Warburg, 1963.

Peltzer, J., "Le Coolie Chinois," *Bulletin de la Societé Royale Belge de Géographie*, Vol. VIII (1884), 569-582.

Pérez de la Riva, Juan, "Aspectos Económicos del Tráfico de Culíes Chinos a Cuba, 1853-1874," *Universidad de la Habana*, Vol. CLXXIII (May-June, 1965), 95-115.

_____, "Demografia de los Culíes Chinos en Cuba (1853-74)," *Revista de la Biblioteca Nacional "José Marti"*, Vol. LVII, No. 4 (1966), 3-31.

Perkins, Dwight H. *Agricultural Development in China, 1368-1968.* Chicago: Aldine Publishing Company, 1969.

"Peru and the Coolie System: Dreadful Mortality," *Anti-Slavery Reporter*, Vol. XVIII, No. 3 (October 1, 1872), 69-71.

"Peru: Chinese Bondsmen," *Anti-Slavery Reporter*, Vol. VII, No. 80, New Series (August 2, 1852), 115-116.

Peters, F. J. (comp.). *Clipper Ship Prints, Including Other Merchant Sailing Ships by N. Currier and Currier and Ives.* New York, Antique Bulletin Publishing Company, 1930.

Peters, Richard. *Reports of Cases Argued and Adjudged in the Supreme Court of the United States, January Term 1844.* Vol. XV, Philadelphia: Thomas, Couperthwait and Company, 1841.

Philipps, George, "Early Spanish Trade with Chin Cheo (Chang Chow)," *China Review,* Vol. XIX (1891), 243-255.

"Piracy in the China Seas," *Nautical Magazine and Naval Chronicle,* Vol. XXI (April, 1852), 222-223.

Pitcher, Rev. Philip Wilson. *In and About Amoy.* Shanghai: The American Publishing House in China, 1909.

Plauchet, Edmund, "La Traite des Coulies a Macao," *Revue des Deux Mondes,* Vol. CVI (1 Juillet, 1873), 178-193.

Plumb, J. H. *In the Light of History.* London: Allen Lane, The Penguin Press, 1972.

Pringle, Hall. *The Fall of the Sugar Planters of Jamaica with Remarks on Their Agricultural Management and on the Labour Question in That Island.* London: Trubner and Company, 1868.

"Proposed Immigration of Chinese Coolies into Brazil," *Anti-Slavery Reporter,* Vol. XXI, No. 9 (August, 1879), 226.

"Proposed Scheme for Introducing Chinese into Brazil," *Anti-Slavery Reporter,* Vol. III, No. 7, Series 4 (December, 1883), 300-301.

"Prospectus for the Formation of a Company in Cuba for Coolie Immigration," *Anti-Slavery Reporter,* Vol. XX, No. 11 (September, 1877), 287-289.

Pumpelly, R., "The Chinese Laborers," *Nation,* Vol. VIII, No. 206 (June 10, 1869), 449-450.

Purcell, Victor. *The Chinese in Southeast Asia.* London: Oxford University Press, 1965.

Quesada, Gonzalo de. *Cuba*. Washington: Government Printing Office, 1905.

――――――――. *Los Chinos y la Revolución Cubana*. Havana: Ucar, García y Cía, 1946.

――――――――. *The Chinese and Cuban Independence*. Leipzig: Breitkopf and Hartel, 1925.

Rackham, H. *Pliny's Natural History with an English Translation in Ten Volumes*. London: William Heinemann Limited, 1942.

Radford, Alfred. *Jottings on the West Indies and Panama*. London: William Whiteley, 1886.

Raffles, Sophia. *Memoir of the Life and Public Services of Sir Thomas Stamford Raffles*. 2 vols. London: James Duncan, 1835.

Raffles, Thomas Stamford. *The History of Java*. 2 vols. London: Black, Parbury and Allen, 1817.

Ratzel, Friedrich. *Die Chinesische Auswanderung ein Beitrag zur Cultur-und Handels Geographie*, Breslau: J. U. Fern's Berlag, 1876.

――――――――, "Die Chinesische Auswanderung," *Das Ausland*, Vol. LXIX, No. 2 (October 9, 1876), 801-807.

Reglamento de Emigración China del Puerto de Macao Aprobado por Decreto No. 34 de 28 de Mayo de 1872. Macao: Typographia de J. da Silva, 1872.

Relatorios de Reportição de Estatistica de Macau Acerca da População Chineza da Mesma Colonia. Macau: Typographia de J. de Silva, 1868.

Reports on Trade at the Treaty Ports in China for the Year 1876. Shanghai: Customs Office, 1877.

"Revival of Chinese Coolie Traffic to Peru," *Anti-Slavery Reporter*, Vol. XXI, No. 4 (New Series, October, 1878), 89-90.

Reybaud, Charles. *Le Brésil.* Paris: Guillaumin et Cie, 1856.

Rigg, C. R., "On Coffee Planting in Ceylon," *Journal of the Indian Archipelago and Eastern Asia*, Series 1, Vol. VI (1852), 123-142.

Río, Mario E. Del. *La Inmigración y su Desarrollo en el Perú.* Lima: Sanmarti y Cia, 1929.

Ripley, Eliza Moore. *From Falg to Flag: A Woman's Adventures and Experiences in the South During the War, in Mexico and in Cuba.* New York: D. Appleton and Company, 1889.

Roberts, Stephen H. *Population Problems of the Pacific.* New York: AMS Press, 1969 (first published in 1927).

Robinet, W. M. *Refutation of a Pamphlet Published by the Consul Yglesias and of His Gross Abuse Offered through the Periodicals to W. M. Robinet.* Hong Kong: China Mail, 1856.

Robinson, Tracy. *Panama: A Personal Record of Forty-six Years, 1861-1907.* New York: Star and Herald Company, 1907.

Rodrígues, José Honório, "Brasil e Extremo Oriente," *Politica Externa Independente*, Ano I, No. 2 (August, 1965), 65-69.

——————————. *Brazil and Africa.* Berkeley: University of California Press, 1965.

Rodriguez San Pedro, D. Joaquín. *Legislación Ultramarina.* 16 vols. Madrid: Imprenta de los Señores Viota, 1865-1869.

Romero, Fernando, "The Slave Trade and the Negro in South America," *Hispanic American Historical Review*, Vol. XXIV, No. 3 (August, 1944), 368-386.

Rousset, Léon, "Les Chinois Hors de Chez Eux," *Le Correspondant,* Vol. CXII (10 Juillet, 1878), 92-113.

Rowe, William H. *The Maritime History of Maine: Three Centuries of Shipbuilding and Seafaring.* New York: W. W. Norton and Company, Inc., 1948.

Rugendas, João Maurício. *Viagem Pitoresca através do Brasil* (Tradução de Sérgio Milliet), São Paulo: Livraria Martins Editóra SA, 4ᵉ Edição, 1949.

Rugendas, Maurice. *Voyage Pittoresque dans le Brasil.* Paris: Engelmann et Cⁱᵉ, 1835.

Ruhomon, Peter. *Centenary History of the East Indians in British Guiana, 1838-1938.* Georgetown: "Daily Chronicle," 1939.

Russell, Robert. *North America: Its Agriculture and Climate.* Edinburgh: Adam and Charles Black, 1857.

Saco, José Antonio. *Colección Póstuma de Papeles Científicos, Históricos, Políticos y de Otros Ramos sobre la Isla de Cuba, ya Publicados ya Ineditos.* Habana: Miguel de Villa, 1881.

——————. *Historia de la Esclavitud de la Raza Africana en el Nuevo Mundo y Especial de los Países Americo—Hispanos.* 4 vols. Habana: Cultura S. A., 1938.

——————, "Los Chinos en Cuba," *La America* (Madrid), Vol. VIII, No. 3 (February 12, 1864), 1-3, continued in Vol. VIII, No. 5 (March 12, 1864), 2-3.

Sampaio, Manuel de Castro. *Os Chins de Macao.* Hong Kong: Typographia de Noronha e Filhos, 1867.

Sandhu, Kernial Singh, "Chinese Colonization of Malacca: A Study in Population Change, 1500 to 1957 AD," *Malayan Journal of Tropical Geography*, Vol. XV, 1-26.

——————. *Indians in Malaya: Some Aspects of the Immigration and Settlement, 1786-1951.* Cambridge: The University Press, 1969.

Sargent, A. J. *Anglo Chinese Commerce and Diplomacy*. Oxford: The Clarendon Press, 1907.

Scarth, John. *Twelve Years in China: The People, the Rebels, and the Mandarins*. Edinburgh: Thomas Constable and Company, 1860.

"Scheme for Imparting Chinese Coolies into Brazil," *Anti-Slavery Reporter*, Vol. III, No. 6, Series 4 (November, 1883), 276.

"Scheme for Introducing Indentured Chinese Coolies into Brazil," *Anti-Slavery Reporter*, Vol. III, No. 1, Series 4 (May, 1883), 132-134.

"Scheme for Introducing Indentured Chinese Coolies into Brazil," *Anti-Slavery Reporter*, Vol. III, No. 4, Series 4 (September, 1883), 222-223.

Schlegel, Gustave. *Thian Ti Hwui, The Hung League or Heaven-Earth League: A Secret Society in China and India*. Batavia: Lange and Company, 1866.

Schurz, William L. *The Manila Galleon*. New York: E. P. Dutton and Company, 1959.

Scholefield, Guy Hardy. *The Pacific: Its Past and Future*. London: John Murray, 1919.

Scoble, John. *Hill Coolies: A Brief Exposure of the Deplorable Condition of the Hill Coolies in British Guiana, and Mauritius and of the Nefarious Means by Which They were Induced to Resort to These Colonies*. London: Harvey and Darton, 1840.

Sedano y Cruzat, Carlos. *Cuba Desde 1850 á 1873*. Madrid: Imprenta Nacional, 1873.

Segall, Marcelo, "Esclavitud y Tráfico Culíes en Chile," *Journal of Inter-American Studies*, Vol. X, No. 1 (January, 1968), 117-133.

Seidler, Carl. *Dez Anos No Brasil* (Titulo do Original: *Zehn Jahre in Brasilien Wahrend de Regierung Don Pedro's und nach dessen Entthronung.—Mit besanderer Hinsicht aug das Schicksal der Auslandischen Truppen und der deutschen Colonisten*, Quedlinburg and Leipzig, Druck and Verlag von Gottfr. Basse, 1835). Tradução notas do General Bertoldo Klinger, São Paulo: Livraria Martins, 1835.

Seward, Frederick W. *Reminiscences of a War-Time Statesman and Diplomat, 1830-1915*. New York: G. P. Putnam's Sons, 1916.

Seward, William H. *Travels Around the World*. New York: D. Appleton and Company, 1873.

Sewall, John S. *The Logbook of the Captain's Clerk: Adventures in the China Seas*. Bangor, Maine; 1905.

Sewell, William G. *The Ordeal of Free Labor in the British West Indies*. New York: Harper and Brothers, 1861.

Shang-yu, Yao, "Floods and Droughts in Chinese History," *Far Eastern Quarterly*, Vol. II, No. 4 (August, 1943), 357-78.

Shing, C., "Central America and the Chinese," *Asia*, Vol. XLIII (April, 1943), 209-212.

Silva, José da. *As Fadas de Julho ou A Revolta Fantasiada*. Macao: Typographia de J. da Silva, 1871.

Simkin, C. G. F. *The Traditional Trade of Asia*. London: Oxford University Press, 1968.

Singh, Saint Nehal, "Asiatic Immigration: A World Question," *Living Age*, Vol. CCLXXXII, No. 3658 (August 15, 1914), 387-392.

Sires, Ronald V., "Sir Henry Barkly and the Labor Problem in Jamaica, 1853-1856," *Journal of Negro History*, Vol. XXV, No. 2 (April, 1940), 216-235.

Skinner, William G. *Chinese Society in Thailand: An Analytical History*. New York: Cornell University Press, 1951.

"Slavery in China," *Anti-Slavery Reporter*, Vol. II, No. 3, New Series (March, 1854), 71-72.

"Slavery in China," *De Bow's Review*, Vol. XXI (August, 1856), 151-161.

"Slavery of Chinese in Cuba," *Anti-Slavery Reporter*, Vol. XVIII, No. 1 (March 30, 1872), 5-7.

Smith, George. *A Narrative of an Exploratory Visit to Each of the Consular Cities of China and to the Islands of Hong Kong and Chusan in the Years 1844, 1845, 1846*. London: Seely, Burnside and Seeley, 1857.

Snelleman, J. F., "Chinesche Immigranten in Suriname," *De West-Indische Gids*, Vol. II (1920), 225-248.

Sotomayor, Urbano Feijoo. *Isla de Cuba: Inmigración de Trabajadores Españoles*. Habana: Imprenta de J. M. Eleizegui, 1853.

"South America and Asiatic Labor," *American Review of Reviews*, Vol. XXXVI, No. 5 (November, 1907), 622-623.

Sowerby, Arthur de Carle, "The Junks, Sampans and Inland Waterways of China," *The China Journal of Science and Arts*, Vol. X, No. 5 (May, 1929), 243-248.

_____, "The Overseas Chinese," *China Journal*, Vol. XXIV, No. 3 (March, 1936), 119-123.

Speer, William. *The Oldest and the Newest Empire: China and the United States*. Hartford, Connecticut: S. S. Scranton and Company, 1870.

Squier, Ephraim George. *Peru: Incidents of Travel and Exploration in the Land of the Incas*. London: Macmillan and Company, 1877.

Stanley, E. Lyulph, "The Treatment of Indian Immigrants in Mauritius," *Fortnightly Review*, Vol. XXIII (June 1, 1875), 794-819.

"Statistics on Coolie Emigration," *Anti-Slavery Reporter*, Vol. XVII, No. 8 (December 31, 1871), 223.

Steele, Charles C., "American Trade in Opium to China, Prior to 1820," *Pacific Historical Review*, Vol. IX, No. 4 (December, 1940), 425-444.

Stein, Stanley J. *Vassouras, A Brazilian Coffee Country, 1850-1900.* Cambridge, Mass.: Harvard University Press, 1957.

[Stevens, Edwin], "Clanship among the Chinese: Feuds between Different Clans near Canton; Substitutes for Those who Are Guilty of Murder; Republicanism Among the Clans," *Chinese Repository*, Vol. IV (January, 1836), 411-415.

Stewart C. S. *A Visit to the South Seas in the United States Ship Vicennes During the Years 1829 and 1830, Including Notices of Brazil, Peru, Manilla, the Cape of Good Hope and St. Helena.* 2 vols. New York: John P. Haven, 1833.

Stewart, P. J., "New Zealand and the Pacific Labor Traffic, 1870-1874," *Pacific Historical Review*, Vol. XXX, No. 1 (February, 1961), 47-59.

Stewart, Watt. *Chinese Bondage in Peru: A History of the Chinese Coolie in Peru, 1849-1874.* Durham, North Carolina: Duke University Press, 1951.

_____, "El Trabajador Chileno y los Ferrocarriles del Perú," *Revista Chilena de Historia y Geografía*, Vol. LXXXV, No. 93 (July-December, 1938), 128-171.

_____. *Henry Meiggs, Yankee Pizarro.* Durham, NC: Duke University Press, 1946.

Suarez Argudin, José. *Proyecto de Inmigración Africana para las Islas de Cuba y Puerto Rico y el Imperio del Brasil Presentado a los Respectives Gobiernos.* Habana: Imprenta "La Habanera," 1860.

"Sugar Making in Cuba," *Harper's Magazine*, Vol. XXX (March, 1865), 440-451.

Suzannet, Conde de. *O Brasil em, 1845: Semelhanças e Differenças Apos um Século*, Tradução de Marcia de Moura Castro. Rio de Janeiro: Livraria Editora de Casa do Estudante do Brasil, 1954.

Sullivan, Edward. *Rambles and Scrambles in North and South America.* London: Richard Bentley, 1852.

Swinton, Captain and Mrs. *Journal of a Voyage with Coolie Emigrants from Calcutta to Trinidad.* London: Alred W. Bennett, 1859.

Swisher, Earl. *China's Management of the American Barbarians: A Study of Sino-American Relations, 1841-1861 with Documents.* New Haven: Yale University, Far Eastern Publications, 1951.

Tarling, Nicholas. *British Policy in the Malay Penninsula and Archipelago 1824-1871.* Kuala Lampur: Oxford University Press, 1969.

Tarrant, William. *The Early History of Hong Kong.* Canton: Friend of China Office, 1862.

Teixeira, Manuel, "The So-called Slave Trade at Macao," *Proceedings of the International Association of Historians of Asia, Second Biennial Conference,* October 6-9, 1962. Taipei; Taiwan, 639-646.

Tejeiro, Guillermo. *Historia Ilustrada de la Colonia China en Cuba.* Havana, 1947.

Teng, S. Y. *The Taiping Rebellion and Western Powers: A Comprehensive Study.* Oxford: The Clarendon Press, 1971.

"The Abortive Attempt to Introduce Chinese Coolies into Brazil," *Anti-Slavery Reporter,* Vol. IV, No. 1, Series 4 (January, 1884), 19.

"The Bel Air Coolie Mission," *Mission Life,* Vol. VI, No. 2, New Series (1875), 530-533.

"The China Coolie in Peru," *Anti-Slavery Reporter,* Vol. XVIII, No. 7 (October 1, 1873), 197-200.

"The Chincha Islands," *Nautical Magazine and Naval Chronicle,* Vol. XXV (April, 1856), 181-183.

"The Chinese Coolie Slave Trade," *Anti-Slavery Reporter,* Vol. VIII, No. 4, New Series (April 2, 1860), 94-95.

"The Chinese Coolie Trade," *Anti-Slavery Reporter*, Vol. VII, No. 6, New Series (June 1, 1859), 143-144.

"The Chinese Coolie Trade," *Anti-Slavery Reporter*, Vol. XVII, No. 2, (June 30, 1870), 48-49.

"The Chinese Coolie Trade," *Anti-Slavery Reporter*, Vol. XVIII, No. 1, (March 30, 1872), 22-23.

"The Chinese Coolie Traffic to Cuba and Brazil," *Anti-Slavery Reporter*, Vol. XXI, No. 10 (October, 1879), 263.

"The Chinese in Cuba," *Anti-Slavery Reporter*, Vol. XIX, No. 2 (April 1, 1874), 38-40.

"The Chinese in Cuba," *Anti-Slavery Reporter*, Vol. XIX, No. 4 (October 1, 1874), 107-108.

"The Chinese in Great Britain and British Colonies," *China Journal*, Vol. XXIV, No. 3 (March, 1936), 131-134.

"The Chinese in Peru," *Mission Life*, Vol. V (March, 1868), 249-251.

"The Chinese in the Indo-Malayan and Malayan Region," *China Journal*, Vol. XXIV, No. 3 (March, 1936), 128-131.

"The Chinese Laborers," *Nation*, Vol. VIII (June 10, 1869), 449-450.

"The Chinese on Immigration from China," *Anti-Slavery Reporter*, Vol. XV, No. 6, New Series (June 1, 1867), 135-136.

"The Chinese Passenger Act," *The Mercantile Marine and Nautical Record*, Vol. II, No. 22 (October, 1855), 386-387.

"The Coolie Commission in British Guiana," *Anti-Slavery Reporter*, Vol. XVII, No. 4 (December 31, 1870), 102-104.

"The Coolie Slave Trade," *Merchant's Magazine*, Vol. XLV, No. 3 (October, 1861), 425.

"The Coolie Trade," *De Bow's Review*, Vol. XXIII (July, 1857), 30-35.

"The Coolie Trade in Cuba," *Merchant's Magazine*, Vol. XXXVI, No. 5 (May, 1857), 774.

"The Coolie Traffic," *Anti-Slavery Reporter*, Vol. IV, No. 5 (New Series, May 1, 1856), 113.

"The Coolie Traffic," *Anti-Slavery Reporter*, Vol. VI, No. 4, New Series (April 1, 1858), 84-85.

"The Coolie Traffic," *Merchants' Magazine*, Vol. XLV, No. 2 (August, 1861), 275.

"The Coolies for the Canal," *Independent*, Vol. LXI, No. 3025 (November 22, 1906), 1243-1244.

The Eastern Seas or Voyages and Adventures in the Indian Archipelago in 1832-33-34. London: William H. Allen and Company, 1837.

"The Eighteenth Annual Report," *Anti-Slavery Reporter* (*Supplement*) (July, 1857), 4-5.

"The Emigration Convention of 1866," *China Review*, Vol. I (July, 1872), 63-70; 141-144.

The Export of Coolies from India to Mauritius. London: British and Foreign Anti-Slavery Society, 1842.

"The Guano Islands," *Chamber's Journal*, Vol. XXXV, No. 367 (January 12, 1861), 17-19.

"The Macao Coolie Trade Suppressed," *Anti-Slavery Reporter*, Vol. XIX, No. 2 (April 1, 1874), 37.

"The Pacific Slavers," *Mission Life*, Vol. III, No. 2, New Series (1872), 409.

"The Plight of the Chinese in Mexico," *Literary Digest*, Vol. CXV, No. 25 (June 24, 1933), 11.

"The Polynesian Slave Trade," *Mission Life*, Vol. II, No. 2, New Series (1871), 586-588.

"The Port of Callao, Peru 1873," *Nautical Magazine*, Vol. XLIII (September, 1874), 749-754.

"The Portuguese China Coolie Slave-Trade to Cuba," *Anti-Slavery Reporter*, Vol. XVIII, No. 5 (April 1, 1873), 146-147.

"The Proposed Chinese Coolie Immigration into Brazil," *Anti-Slavery Reporter*, Vol. XXI, No. 11 (December, 1879), 272-278.

"The Sino-Spanish Treaty of Amity, Commerce and Navigation, 1864," *The Chinese Social and Political Science Review*, Public Documents Supplement, 1929, pp. 8-22.

"The Slave Trade and The Coolie Traffic," *Anti-Slavery Reporter*, Vol. VI, No. 6, New Series (June 1, 1858), 138-140.

"The Slave Trade in Chinese," *Anti-Slavery Reporter*, Vol. VII, No. 10, New Series (October 1, 1859), 223-224.

"The Slave-Trade in Chinese," *Anti-Slavery Reporter*, Vol. VIII, No. 5, New Series (May 1, 1860), 115-119.

"The Twin Sister of the Slave Trade," *Anti-Slavery Reporter*, Vol. XVIII, No. 7 (October 1, 1873), 200-202.

Thiersant, P. Dabry de. *L'Emigration Chinois*. Paris: Paul Dupont, 1872.

Thiery, C. de, "The Sons of Han," *Macmillan's Magazine*, Vol. LXXX, No. 475 (1899), 58-66.

Thio, Eunice, "The Singapore Chinese Protectorate: Events and Conditions Leading to its Establishment, 1823-1873," *Journal of the South Seas Society*, Vol. XVI (1960), 40-80.

Thomson, J. D., "Historical Landmarks of Macao," *Chinese Recorder*, Vol. XIX, No. 10 (October, 1888), 451-452.

"Threatened Importation of Coolies into Cuba," *Anti-Slavery Reporter*, Vol. IV, Series 4 (August-September, 1886), 90-91.

T'ien, Ju-k'ang. *The Chinese of Sarawak: A Study of Social Structure.* London: London School of Economics and Political Science, 1950.

Tinker, Hugh. *A New System of Slavery: The Export of Indian Labour Overseas, 1830-1920.* London: Oxford University Press, 1974.

Tirard, Henri, "L'Immigration Chinoise," *Revue Indo-Chinoise*, New Series, Vol. I, No. 11 (Juin 15, 1904), 764-768.

Teng, Te-kong. *United States Diplomacy in China, 1844-1860.* Seattle: University of Washington Press, 1964.

Torr, Dona. *Marx on China 1853-1860: Articles from the New York Daily Tribune.* London: Lawrence and Wishart, 1951.

Torrente, Mariano. *Bosquejo Económico Político de la Isla de Cuba*, Madrid: Imprenta de D. Manuel Pita, 1852.

Tretiak, Daniel, "The Chinese in Latin America," *China Quarterly*, No. 7 (1961), 148-153.

Trollope, Anthony. *South Africa.* 2 vols. London: Dawsons of Pall Mall, 1968 (first published in 1878).

_____. *The West Indies and the Spanish Main.* New York: Harper and Brothers, 1860.

Tronson, J. M. *Personal Narrative of a Voyage to Japan, Kamtschatka, Siberia, Tartary and Various Parts of the Coast of China in HMS Barracouta.* London: Smith, Elder and Company, 1859.

Tschudi, J. J. Von. *Travels in Peru, on the Coast, in the Sierra, Across the Cordilleras and the Andes into the Primeval Forests.* translated from the German by Thomasina Ross. New York: A. S. Barnes and Company, 1854.

Tseng, Marquis, "China: The Sleep and the Awakening," *Asiatic Quarterly Review*, Vol. III (January-April, 1887), 1-10.

Turnbull, David. *Travels in the West, Cuba; with Notices of Porto Rico, and the Slave Trade*. London: Longman, Orme, Brown, Green, and Longmans, 1840.

Ygarte, César Antonio. *Bosquejo de la Historia Económica del Perú*. Lima: Imp. Cabieses, 1926.

Underhill, Edward Bean. *The West Indies: Their Social and Religious Condition*. London: Jackson, Walford and Hodder, 1862.

Unger, Leonard, "The Chinese in Southeast Asia," *Geographical Review*, Vol. XXXIV (April, 1944), 196-217.

Valverde, Antonio L. *Estudios Juridicos e Historicos*. Havana: Imp. "Avisador Comercial," 1918.

_____, "La Trata de Chinos en la Isla de Cuba," *Reforma Social*, Vol. I (July, 1914), 482-497.

[Vaughan, J. D.], "Notes on the Chinese of Pinang," *Journal of the Indian Archipelago and Eastern Asia*, Series 1, Vol. VIII (1854), 1-27.

Vaughan, J. D. *Manners and Customs of the Chinese in the Straits Settlements*. Kuala Lampur: Oxford University Press, 1971 (first published in 1879).

Veness, W. T. (Rev.), "Coolies in British Guiana," *Mission Life*, Vol. V (July, 1868), 464-469.

_____, "A Chinese Church in Br. Guiana," *Mission Life*, Vol. V, No. 2, New Series (1874), 518-527.

Vicuña Mackenna, Benjamín. *El Libro del Cobre y del Carbón de Piedra en Chile*. Santiago de Chile: Imprenta Cervantes, 1883.

_____. *El Libro de la Plata*. Santiago de Chile: Imprenta Cervantes, 1882.

_____. *Historia de la Campaña de Lima, 1880-1881*. Santiago de Chile: Rafael Jover, 1881.

_____. *Paginas de mi Diario Durante Tres Años de Viajes, 1853, 1854, 1855*. Santiago de Chile: Impr. Del Ferrocaril, 1856.

Villanueva, Manuel, "La Emigración de Colonos Chinos," *Revista Contemporanea* [Madrid], Vol. VII (February 15, 1877), 339-376.

Walker, Eric A. *A History of South Africa*. London: Longmans, Green and Company Limited, 1928.

Walrond, Theodore (ed.). *Letters and Journals of James, Eight Earl of Elgin*. London: John Murray, 1872.

Wang, Sing-wu, "The Attitude of the Ch'ing Court Toward Chinese Emigration," *Chinese Culture*, Vol. IX, No. 4 (December, 1968), 62-76.

_____, "Diplomatic Relations Between China and Australia Prior to the Establishment of the Chinese Consulate in Melbourne in 1909," *Chinese Culture*, Vol. X, No. 2 (June, 1969), 31-42.

Warner, Charles Dudley. *My Summer in a Garden*. Boston and New York: Houghton, Mifflin Company, 1898.

Watson, Eugene S., "Chinese Labor and the Panama Canal," *The Independent*, Vol. LXI, No. 3025 (November, 1906), 1201-1206.

Wawn, W. T. *The South Sea Islanders and the Queensland Labor Trade: A Record of Voyages and Experiences in the Western Pacific from 1875 to 1891*. London, 1893.

Whipple, Addison B. C. *Tall Ships and Great Captains: A Narrative of Famous Sailing Ships Through the Ages and the Courageous Men Who*

Sailed Them, Fought or Raced Them across the Sea. New York: Harper and Brothers, 1951.

"White Slaves in Peru," *Anti-Slavery Reporter*, Vol. I, No. 2, New Series (February, 1853). 25.

Whymant, A. Neville J., "The Psychology of the Chinese Coolie," *Asiatic Review*, Vol. XVIII, No. 56 (October, 1922), 645-654.

Wickberg, Edgar, "Early Chinese Economic Influence in the Philippines, 1850-1898," *Pacific Affairs*, Vol. XXXV, No. 3 (Fall, 1962), 275-285.

_____. *The Chinese in Philippine Life, 1850-1898.* New Haven: Yale University Press, 1965.

Wildey, Captain. *A Treatise on Chinese Labourers as Compared with Europeans, the Tribes of Africa, and the Various Castes of Asiatics with a View to Their Introduction into Our West India Colonies as Free Labourers.* London: T. Hurst, 1836.

Williams, Eric E. *Captalism and Slavery.* 2d ed. New York: Russell and Russell, 1961.

Williams, Frederick Wells, "The Chinese Immigrant in Further Asia," *American Historical Review*, Vol. V, No. 3 (April, 1900), 503-517.

Williams, Frederick Wells. *The Life and Letters of Samuel Wells Williams.* New York: G. P. Putnam's Sons, 1889.

_____ (ed.) "The Journal of Samuel Wells Williams," *Journal of the North China Branch of the Royal Asiatic Society*, Vol. XLII (1911), 3-232.

Williams, Lea E., "Indonesia's Chinese Educate Raffles," *Indonesie*, Vol. IX (1956), 369-385.

Williams, Samuel Wells. *The Chinese Commercial Guide.* Hong Kong: A. Shortrede and Company, 1863.

_____. *The Middle Kingdom*. 2 vols. New York: Charles Scribner's Sons, 1913.

Wills, John E. Jr. *Pepper, Guns and Parleys: The Dutch East India Company in China, 1622-1681*. Cambridge, Mass.: Harvard University Press, 1974.

Wingfield, C., "The China Coolie Traffic," *Anti-Slavery Reporter*, Vol. XVIII, No. 6 (July 1, 1873), 165-175.

Winstedt, R. O., "A History of Perak," *Journal of the Malay Branch of the Royal Asiatic Society*, Vol. XII, Part 1 (June, 1934), 78-95.

Wong, Lin Ken, "The Trade of Singapore with China," *Journal of the Malayan Branch of the Royal Asiatic Society*, Vol. XXXIII, Part 4 (December, 1960), 5-315.

Worcester, G. R. G. *Junks and Sampans of the Upper Yangtze*. Shanghai: The Martime Customs, 1940.

_____. *The Junks and Sampans of the Yangtze*. 2 vols. Shanghai: The Marine Customs, 1947-8.

Wray, Leonard. *The Practical Sugar Planter: A Complete Account of the Cultivation and Manufacture of the Sugar-Cane According to the Latest and Most Improved Processes*. London: Smith, Elder and Company, 1848.

"Wretched Condition of Chinese Coolies in Peru," *Anti-Slavery Reporter*, Vol. XIX, No. 2 (April 1, 1874), 41.

Wright, H. R. C. *East-Indian Economic Problems: The Age of Cornwallis and Raffles*. London: Luzac and Company, 1961.

Wright, Stanley F. *Hart and the Chinese Customs*. Belfast: William Mullen and Sons, 1950.

Wright, W. W., "The Coolie Trade," *De Bow's Review*, Vol. XXVIII (September, 1859), 296-321.

Wu, Ching-ch'ao, "Chinese Imigration in the Pacific Area," *Chinese Social and Political Science Review*, Vol. XII, No. 4 (October, 1928), 543-560.

_____, "Chinese Immigration in the Pacific Area," *The Chinese Social and Political Science Review*, Vol. XIII, No. 1 (January, 1929), 50-76.

_____, "Chinese Immigration in the Pacific Area," *Chinese Social and Political Science Review*, Vol. XIII, No. 2 (April, 1929), 161-182.

Wu, Hung-chu, "China's Attitude Towards Foreign Nations and Nationals Historically Considered," *Chinese Social and Political Science Review*, Vol. X (1926), 13-45.

Wu, Paak-shing, "China and Cuba: A Study in Diplomatic History," *China Quarterly*, Vol. III (Autumn, 1938), 389-413.

_____, "China and Peru: A Study in Diplomatic History," *China Quarterly*, Vol. V, No. 2 (Spring, 1940), 275-293.

_____, "China's Diplomatic Relations with Brazil," *China Quarterly*, Vol. V, No. 4 (Supplementary, Winter, 1940), 857-868.

_____, "China's Diplomatic Relations with Mexico," *China Quarterly*, Vol. IV, No. 3 (Summer, 1939), 439-459.

_____, "China's Diplomatic Relations with Panama," *China Quarterly*, Vol. V, No. 1 (Winter, 1939), 129-140.

Wu, T. F., "Overseas Chinese in Australia," *Far Eastern Economic Review*, Vol. XXV (September, 1958), 328-329.

Wurtzburg, C. E. *Raffles of the Eastern Isles*. London: Hodder and Stroughton, 1954.

Wylie, Alexander. *Chinese Researches*. Shanghai: 1897.

Yutang, Lin. *My Country and My People*. New York: John Day, 1935.

Young, Arthur A., "The Progressive Chinese in Trinidad," *China Weekly Review*, Vol. LI, No. 3 (December 21, 1929), 114.

Young, Su-lin C., "The Chinese in the Americas," *China Journal*, Vol. XXIV, No. 3 (March, 1936), 123-128.

Young, Walter, "Chinese Labor Migration to Manchuria," *Chinese Economic Journal*, Vol. I, No. 7 (July, 1927), 613-633.

Zamora y Coronado, José Maria. *Biblioteca de Legislación Ultramarina*. 7 vols. Madrid: Imprenta de Alegría y Charlin, 1844-1849.

Zegarra, Felix Cipriano C. *La Condición Jurídica de los Estranjeros en el Perú*. Santiago: Imprenta de la Liberdad, 1872.

Chinese and Japanese Works

1. Chinese

Chao Ju-k'uo 趙汝廷, Chu Fan Chih 諸蕃志 (On the Chinese and Arab trade in the twelfth and thirteenth centuries), 2 *chüan*, Tokyo, 1914.

Ch'en Ju-ling 陳若霖, *Ta Ch'ing Lü Li Chung Ting Hui T'ung Hsin Ts'uan* 大清律例重訂會通新纂 (Collection ôf laws and statutes of the Ch'ing Dynasty, 1644-1911), 40 *chüan*, 1832.

Ch'en Tse-hsien 陳澤憲, 'Shih Chiu Shih Chi Ch'eng Hsing Ti Ch'i Yüeh Hua Kung Chih' 十九世紀盛行的契約華工制 (The Chinese indentured labour system in the nineteenth century), *Li Shih Yen Chiu* 歷史研究, 一九六三, 第三期 (Historical studies), Vol. LXXIX, No. 1 (1963), 161-179.

Ch'ing-chi wai-chiao shih-liao 清季外交史料 (Historical materials on late Ch'ing foreign relations). 112 ts'e. Peking, 1932-35.

Ch'ing Ju-chi 卿汝楫, *Mei-kuo ch'in Hua shih* 美國侵華史 (History of American aggression against China), 2 vols. Peiping, San-lien shu-tien 三聯書店, 1952.

Ch'ing shih 清史, comp, *Ch'ing shih pien-tsuan wei-yüan-hui* 清史編纂委員會. 8 vols. Taipei, Kuo-fang yen-chiu yüan 國防研究院, 1961.

Ch'ou-pan i-wu shih-mo 籌辦夷務始末 (The complete account of the management of barbarian affairs). Photolithograph of the original ed. Peiping, 1930. Later Tao-kuang period, 80 *chüan*; Hsien-feng period, 80 *chüan*; T'ung-chih period, 100 *chüan*.

Chu Hsiu-hsia 祝秀俠 and others, *Hua Ch'iao Chih—Tsung Chih* 華僑一總志 (Overseas Chinese; a general introduction), Taipei, 1964.

Chu Shih-Chia 朱士嘉, *Mei Kuo P'o Hai Hua Kung Shih Liao* 國迫害華工史料 (Historical sources on restrictions imposed on Chinese labourers by the United States), Shanghai, 1958.

Chu Shih-chia 朱士嘉, comp., *Mei-kuo p'o-hai Hua kung shih-liao* 美國迫害華工史料 (Historical materials on American persecution of Chinese laborers). Peiping, Chung-hua shu-chu 中華書局, 1958.

Chu Shih-chia 朱士嘉, comp., *Shih-chiu shih-chi Mei-kuo ch'in Hua tang-an shih-liao hsuan-chi* 十九世紀美國侵華檔案史料 (Selected archival materials on American aggression in China during the nineteenth century). 2 vols. Shanghai, Chung-hua shu-chu 中華書局, 1959.

Chung-wai t'iao-yüeh hui-pien 中外條約彙編 (Compendium of treaties between China and foreign countries). Taipei reprint ed., Wen-hai ch'u-pan-she 文海出版社, 1963.

Chung-Mei kuan-hsi shih-liao 中美關係史料 (Historical materials on Sino-American relations), comp. and ed. Institute of

Modern History, Academia Sinica. T'ung-chih period, 2 vols. Taipei, Chung-yang yen-chiu yuan Chin-tai shih yen-chiu so 中央研, 1968.

Fei Hsin 究院近代史研究所, comp., *Hsing Ch'a Sheng Lan* 星槎勝覽 (The voyage of Cheng Ho), edited by Feng Ch'eng-chun 馮承鈞, Taipei, 1962.

Feng Ch'eng-chün 馮承鈞, comp. *Chung-Kuo Nan Yang Chiao T'ung Shih* 中國南洋交通史 (A history of China intercourse with Southeast Asia), Taipei, 1962.

H*sien-feng t'iao-yüeh* 咸豊條約 (Treaties of the Hsien-feng period). comp. Ministry of Foreign Affairs. 4 ts'e. Peking.

Hsüeh Fu-ch'eng 薛福成, *Yung-an ch'uan-chi* 庸盦全集 (Collected works of Hsueh Fu-ch'eng), 21 *chüan*. Shanghai, 1897. *Wen-pien* 文編.

Hua ch'iao chih pien-tsuan wei-yuan-hui 華僑志編纂委員會 comp. *Hua ch'iao chih tsung-chih* 華僑志總志 (Overseas Chinese; a general history). Taipei, Hai-wai ch'u-pan-she 海外出版社, 1956.

Li Ch'ang-fu 李長傅, *Chung-kuo chih-min shih* 中國殖民史 (A history of Chinese emigration). Chung-kuo wen-hua ts'ung-shu 中國文化叢書 (Chinese Culture Series). Taipei, Commercial Press, 1966.

Li Hung-chang 李鴻章, *Li Wen-chung-kung ch'uan-chi* 李文忠公 (Collected works of Li Hung-chang). 100 ts'e. Shanghai, 1921. ISKH 全集 (Letters to Tsungli Yamen). *Tsou-kao* 奏稿 (Memorials).

Liu Ta-nien 劉大年, *Mei-kuo ch'in Hua shih* 美國侵華史 (History of American aggression against China). Peiping, Jen-min ch'u-pan-she 人民出版社, 1951.

Ma Huan 馬觀, comp., *Ying Ya Sheng Lan* 瀛涯勝覽 (A narrative of Cheng Ho's expeditions), edited by Feng Ch'eng-chun 馮承鈞. Taipei, 1962.

Shih-erh-ch'ao Tung-hua lu 十二朝東華錄 (Tung-hua records for the twelve reigns). Taipei reprint ed., Wen-hai ch'u-pan-she 文海出版社, 1963. Tao-kuang reign period, 2 vols.; Hsien-feng reign period, 2 vols.; T'ung-chih reign period, 3 vols.; Kuang-hsü reign period, 10 vols.

Ta-Ch'ing li-ch'ao shih-lu 大清歷朝實錄 (Veritable records of successive reigns of the Ch'ing Dynasty). Photolithograph of Tokyo ed. Taipei, Hua-lien ch'u-pan-she 華聯出版社 1964. Tao-kuang reign period, 12 vols.; Hsien-feng reign period, 8 vols.; T'ung-chih reign period, 10 vols.; Kuang-hsü reign period, 8 vols.

Tsung-li ko-kuo shih-wu ya-men ch'ing-tang 總理各國事務衙門清檔 (The Tsungli Yamen Archives; clean files). Deposited at the Institute of Modern History, Academia Sinica, Nankang, Taipei, The Republic of China.

T'ung-chih t'iao-yüeh 同治條約 (Treaties of the T'ung-chih period), comp. Ministry of Foreign Affairs. 10 ts'e. Peking. *Pi-lu* 秘魯 (Peru), *chao-hui* 照會 (Communications); *Pi yüeh* 秘約 (Peruvian Treaty), *tsou-che* 奏摺 (Memorials).

T'ung-shang yüeh-chang lei-tsuan 通商約章類纂 (A classified collection of treaties and regulations with trading powers), comp. Hsu Tsung-liang 徐宗亮. 20 vols. Tientsin, Kuan shu-chü 官書局, 1886.

Wai-chiao pu tang-an tz'u-liao ch'u 外交部檔案資料處 comp., *Chung-kuo chu wai ko kung—ta-shih-kuan li-jen kuan-chang hsien-ming nien-piao* 中國駐外各公大使館歷任館長銜名年表 (A chronology of the chiefs-of-mission and ranks of Chinese legations abroad). Wai-chiao tang-tz'u ts'ung-kan 外交檔資叢刊 (Foreign relations archival materials series). Taipei, Commercial Press, 1969.

Wang Ch'un 王春 , *Mei-kuo ch'in Hua shih* 美國侵華史 (The story of American aggression in China). Peiping, Kung-jen ch'u-pan-she 工人出版社, 1951.

Wang I 汪毅, ed., *Ch'ing Mo Tui Wai Chiao She T'iao Yüeh Chi* 清末對外交涉條約輯 (Treaties between China and other states in the latter part of the Ch'ing Dynasty, 1644-1911), 3 vols., Taipei, 1963.

Yu Neng-mu 于能模 and others, *Chung Wai T'iao Yüeh Hui Pien* 中外條約彙編 (Collection of treaties between China and other states), Shanghai, 1935.

2. Japanese

Fujiwara Sadamu 藤原定, "Shimmatsu ni okeru jinkō kajō no shogenshō to Taihei Tengoku undō" 清末における人口過剰の諸現象と太平天國運動 (Phenomena of overpopulation in the late Ch'ing and the Taiping movement), *Mantetsu chōsa geppō*, Vol. XIX, No. 7 (July 1939), 1-71.

Fukuda Shōzō 福田省三, "Marai ni okeru Kakyō rōdōsha" マライに於ける華僑勞働者 (The overseas Chinese laborers in Malaya), *Tōa-gaku*, Vol. VII (Mar. 1943), 21-56.

Fukuda Shōzō 福田省三, *Kakyō keizai ron* 華僑經濟論 (On the overseas Chinese economy), Ganshōdō Shoten, 1939.

Narita Setsuo 成田節男, *Kakyō shi* 華僑史 (History of the overseas Chinese), Keisetsu Shoin, 1941.

Tabohashi Kiyoshi 田保橋潔, "Meiji gonen no 'Maria Rusu' jiken" 明治五年の「マリア・ルス」事件 (The *Maria Luz* incident of 1872), *Shigaku zasshi*, Vol. XL, No. 2 (Feb. 1929), 230-246; No. 3 (Mar. 1929), 364-375; No. 4 (April 1929), 483-508.

Index

36110197R00283

Printed in Great Britain
by Amazon